# CITIZENS AND KINGS

# CITIZENS AND KINGS

## PORTRAITS IN THE AGE OF REVOLUTION    1760–1830

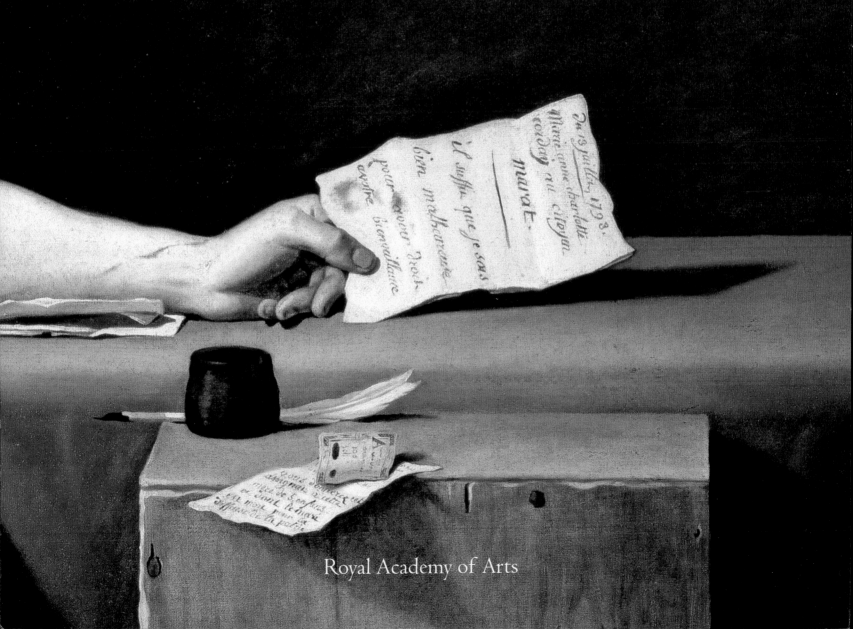

Royal Academy of Arts

This edition first published
on the occasion of the exhibition
'Citizens and Kings: Portraits in the
Age of Revolution, 1760–1830'

Galeries nationales du Grand Palais, Paris
4 October 2006 – 9 January 2007

Royal Academy of Arts, London
3 February – 20 April 2007

Generously supported by
the Benjamin West Patrons Group

This exhibition is organised by the Réunion des
Musées Nationaux and the Musée du Louvre, Paris,
the Royal Academy of Arts, London, and the
Solomon R. Guggenheim Foundation, New York

The Royal Academy of Arts is grateful to
Her Majesty's Government for agreeing to
indemnify this exhibition under the National
Heritage Act 1980, and to Resource, The Council
for Museums, Archives and Libraries, for its help
in arranging the indemnity.

EXHIBITION CURATORS
*Royal Academy of Arts, London*
Norman Rosenthal
MaryAnne Stevens
*with*
Katia Pisvin
Cecilia Treves

*The Solomon R. Guggenheim Museum, New York*
Vivien Greene
Robert Rosenblum

*Musée du Louvre, Paris*
Sébastien Allard
Guilhem Scherf

EXHIBITION ORGANISATION
*Royal Academy of Arts, London*
Idoya Beitia
Cayetana Castillo
Emeline Winston

PHOTOGRAPHIC AND COPYRIGHT CO-ORDINATION
*Royal Academy of Arts, London*
Roberta Stansfield

CATALOGUE: ENGLISH-LANGUAGE EDITION
*Royal Academy Publications*
David Breuer
Harry Burden
Claire Callow
Carola Krueger
Peter Sawbridge
Nick Tite

TRANSLATION FROM THE FRENCH
Caroline Beamish

TRANSLATION FROM THE SPANISH
Translate-A-Book, Oxford

ADDITIONAL COPY-EDITING AND PROOFREADING
Roz Neely

COLOUR ORIGINATION
DawkinsColour

BOOK DESIGN
Isambard Thomas, London

Printed in Italy by Graphicom

FULL-PAGE ILLUSTRATIONS
Pages 2–3: detail of cat. 37; page 6: detail of cat. 14;
page 8–9: detail of cat. 133; page 11: detail of cat. 77;
page 12: detail of cat. 27; page 59: detail of cat. 11;
page 81: detail of cat. 16; page 111: detail of cat. 42;
page 129: detail of cat. 63; page 155: detail of cat. 82;
page 181: detail of cat. 99; page 211: detail of
cat. 120; page 227: detail of cat. 125; page 244:
detail of cat. 136; page 265: detail of cat. 156.

First published as *Portraits publics, portraits privés,
1770–1830*, copyright © 2006, Editions de la
Réunion des musées nationaux, Paris

English edition, redesigned with new material,
copyright © 2007, Royal Academy of Arts,
London

British Library Cataloguing-in-Publication Data
A catalogue record for this book is available
from the British Library

Hardback
ISBN 10: 1-903973-23-6
ISBN 13: 973-1-903973-23-3

Paperback
ISBN 10: 1-903973-85-6
ISBN 13: 978-1-903973-85-1

Distributed outside the United States and
Canada by Thames & Hudson Ltd, London

Distributed in the United States and
Canada by Harry N. Abrams, Inc., New York

This exhibition and its catalogue
are dedicated to the memory of

Robert Rosenblum

1927 – 2006

SCHOLAR, TEACHER, CURATOR AND FRIEND

Foreword    10

Acknowledgements    13


I

Portraiture: Facts versus Fiction    14
ROBERT ROSENBLUM

II

Sculpted Portraits 1770–1830:    25
'Real Presences'
GUILHEM SCHERF

III

Between the Novel and History:    37
French Portraiture towards 1835
SÉBASTIEN ALLARD

IV

The Role of Prints and Printmakers    50
in the Diffusion of Portraiture
TIM CLAYTON


Catalogue plates

1

Portraits of Sovereigns and Heads of State    58
CHRISTOPHER LLOYD

2

The Status Portrait    80
SÉBASTIEN ALLARD

3

The History Portrait    110
GUILHEM SCHERF

4

The Cultural Portrait    128
GUILHEM SCHERF

5

The Place for Experimentation:    154
Artists' Portraits and Self-portraits
VIVIEN GREENE

6

The Family Portrait    180
MARTIN POSTLE

7

The Portrait after the Antique    210
MALCOLM BAKER

8

The Allegorical Portrait    226
GUILHEM SCHERF AND SÉBASTIEN ALLARD

9

Nature and Grace:    244
The Landscape and the Figure
MARYANNE STEVENS

10

Portraiture from 1815 to 1830:    264
Ideal Families and Tormented Geniuses
ROBERT ROSENBLUM


Catalogue entries    289


Endnotes    399

Bibliography    402

Lenders to the Exhibition    420

Photographic Acknowledgements    421

Index    422

# Foreword

THIS REMARKABLE EXHIBITION examines a tumultuous period in the history of Europe and America. Through its panorama of personalities, 'Citizens and Kings: Portraits in the Age of Revolution, 1760–1830' charts the impact on portraiture, both painted and sculpted, of the Enlightenment, the revolutions in America and France, and the rise and fall of Napoleon.

Whereas earlier exhibitions have tended to focus on masters of the genre – among them Reynolds, David, Ingres, Houdon and Thorvaldsen – 'Citizens and Kings' sets out to explore the diversity of portraiture at this time of upheaval by drawing on the work of over ninety artists from many different countries. Its innovative presentation of the dialogue between painting and sculpture, and its concentration on such emerging developments as the allegorical portrait and the representation of children, will permit visitors to appreciate the vital role that artists played in the commemoration and immortalisation of individuals during a moment of great cultural, social, economic and political change.

The exhibition was conceived by the late Robert Rosenblum, Professor at New York University's Institute of Fine Arts and Stephen and Nan Swid Curator of Twentieth-Century Art at The Solomon R. Guggenheim Museum, and MaryAnne Stevens, Acting Secretary and Senior Curator at the Royal Academy of Arts; it was structured and developed with Sébastien Allard, Conservateur in the paintings department at the Musée du Louvre, and Guilhem Scherf, Conservateur en chef in the sculpture department at the same museum, and Vivien Greene, Associate Curator at The Solomon R. Guggenheim Museum, in order to develop the exhibition's many themes during its long gestation.

Robert Rosenblum's first major publication, *Transformations in Late Eighteenth-Century Art*, appeared in 1967. A landmark book which redefined our approach to art from between the Rococo period and Romanticism, it omitted one painting type: the portrait. This exhibition addresses that omission and thus brings Robert's scholarship full circle, establishing an unforeseen but elegant symmetry within his long and distinguished career. 'Citizens and Kings' stands as a tribute to Robert's outstanding achievements as scholar, teacher, writer and critic.

The exhibition is a collaboration between the Réunion des musées nationaux and the Musée du Louvre in Paris,

The Solomon R. Guggenheim Museum in New York, and the Royal Academy of Arts in London. Colleagues in all participating organisations have made exceptional contributions to ensure its realisation. At the Royal Academy, Norman Rosenthal, Cecilia Treves, Idoya Beitia, Cayetana Castillo and Katia Pisvin have ensured the delivery of this ambitious project. Invaluable support and commitment have come from Vincent Pomarède and Geneviève Bresc-Bautier at the Musée du Louvre; from Juliette Armand and Catherine Chagneau at the Réunion des musées nationaux; from Francine Mariani-Ducray at the Direction des Musées de France; and from Lisa Dennison and Thomas Krens at The Solomon R. Guggenheim Museum.

'Citizens and Kings' is a bold undertaking. Although budgetary and logistical constraints prevented our pursuit of loans from more distant locations such as St Petersburg and the west coast of America, our commitment to present the widest possible range of artists and sitters from Europe and North America has meant that we are indebted to some eighty lenders, both public and private. Many of them, such as the Musée du Louvre and Her Majesty The Queen, have been exceptionally generous.

The challenge to find financial resources for the presentation of the exhibition in London has been daunting. We are exceptionally grateful to the Benjamin West Group of Royal Academy Patrons, under their chairman, Lady Judge, for supporting the exhibition, together with other generous Royal Academy Patrons. Such support is a demonstration of their faith in the excellence of the Royal Academy's programme of exhibitions.

With its assembly of personalities depicted by artists of the highest ability, we hope that 'Citizens and Kings', a grandiloquent sweep across the political and cultural landscape of one of history's most turbulent eras, will overturn any lingering preconceptions about portraiture, and reveal instead the richness, variety and inventiveness of a genre which is once again experiencing a renaissance.

Sir Nicholas Grimshaw CBE  *President, Royal Academy of Arts*

Thomas Grenon  *Administrateur général, Réunion des musées nationaux*

Henri Loyrette  *Président-Directeur, Musée du Louvre*

# Acknowledgements

The curators of the exhibition and the publishers of this catalogue would like to thank the following individuals for their invaluable assistance:

Tracey Albainy, Anne Archenoul, Charles Arkwright, Juliette Armand, Amar Arrada, Pierre Arrizoli-Clémentel, Malcolm Baker, Hillary Bauer, Mary Beard, Princesse Minnie de Beauvau-Craon, Rosa Berland, Elena Bianca di Gioia, Bénédicte Boissonas, Marijke Booth, Xavier Bray, Geneviève Bresc-Bautier, Katherine Brinson, Gabriel de Broglie, Maraike Bückling, Else Marie Bukdahl, Manuela Busino, John C. Bute, Marietta Cambareri, Katia Cartacheff, Catherine Chagneau, Françoise Chaserant, Bernard Chevallier, Candida Clark, Michael Clarke, Ron Clarke, Tim Clayton, Meryl Cohen, Ute Collinet, Philip Conisbee, Marguerite Coppens, Françoise Daniel, Susan Davidson, Stephen Deuchar, Christiane Dole, James David Drapper, Gilles Eboli, Martin Ellis, Franca Falletti, Guillaume Faroult, Maria Teresa Fiorio, Margrethe Floryan, Susan Foister, Jean-René Gaborit, Sarah Gallagher, Hubertus Gassner, Derek Gillman, Robin Kaye Goodman, Sabine Grabner, Francesca Grassi, Thomas Grenon, Anne d'Harnoncourt, Anna Harris, Jean-Pierre Hartmann, Steffen Heiberg, Bernard Heitmann, Maria Jesus Herrero Sanz, Rachel Hewitt, Erica Hirshler, James Holloway, Christian von Holst, Jenns Howoldt, Saskia Hüneke, Joel Huthwohl, François Jacob, Dominique Jacquot, Mark Jones, Sophie Jugie, Marion Kahan, Raymond Keaveney, Franklin Kelly, Edward King, Isabelle Klinka, Catherine Koch, Frédéric Lacaille, Alastair Laing,

Sylvain Laveissière, Amaury Lefébure, Patrick Le Nouëne, Jean-Marc Léri, Christophe Léribault, Johanna Lessmann, Christopher Lloyd, Stéphane Loire, Henri Loyrette, Jean-Claude Luche, Jessica Ludwig, Juan J. Luna, Dietmar Lütke, Bernhard Maaz, Simon Macdonald, Linda McLeod, Catherine Marquet, Jonathan Marsden, Manuela Mena Marqués, Olivier Meslay, Christelle Meyer, Stig Miss, Alain Moatti, Kasper Monrad, Edwina Mulvany, Jean Naudin, Hannah Neale, Charles Noble, Antonio Paolucci, Daniela Parenti, Mireille Pastoureau, Gilbert Poinsot, Vincent Pomarède, Martin Postle, Alain Pougetoux, Earl A. Powell III, Cathy Power, Sue Ann Prince, Sylvie Ramond, Francis Ribemont, Christopher Riopelle, Joseph Rishel, Anne Robbins, Sir Hugh Roberts, Duncan Robinson, Thorsten Rodiek, Stephano Roffi, Bertrand Rondot, Francesco Rossi, Geneviève Rudolf, Marianne Saabye, Yves Saint-Laurent and Pierre Berger, Béatrice Salmon, Charles Saumarez Smith, Nick Savage, Uwe Schneede, Klaus Schrenk, Anna Schultz, Cyrille Sciama, George Shackleford, Desmond Shawe-Taylor, Jacob Simon, Claus M. Smidt, Guillermo Solana, Sidsel Maria Søndergaard, Philippe Sorel, Nicola Spinosa, Alexander Sturgis, Aline Sylla, Alain Tapié, D. Dodge Thompson, Gary Tinterow, Simona Tosini Pizzetti, Jacques Toussaint, Wolfgang Trautwein, Letizia Treves, Emmanuelle Trief-Touchard, Marjorie Trusted, Karole Vail, Helen Valentine, Pierre Vallaud, Lluisa Vilalta, D José María Viñuela, Ian Wardropper, Sasha Kalter Wasserman, Bettina Werche, Mr and Mrs C. Whitbread, Paul Williamson, Humphrey Wine, Caroline Worthington, Beatriz Zengotitabengoa.

# I

## Portraiture: Facts versus Fiction

ROBERT ROSENBLUM

IN THE TWENTIETH CENTURY, portraits became an endangered species. The conventional accounts of modern art's evolution told us that the Impressionists were so indifferent to the people who passed before their eyes that they had no hesitation about pulverising their identities into flecks of coloured light. As for Cézanne, it was assumed that when depicting again and again his endlessly patient wife Hortense, he thought of her as nothing more than the inert equivalent of the apples or pitchers he struggled to paint, totally indifferent to her features and personality. The greater revolutions of twentieth-century art pushed the eclipse of portraiture even further. Who would ever have commissioned Mondrian or Rothko to paint a portrait? And even the more earthbound giants of modern art would pose high risks: Matisse might efface a sitter in a pool of colour; Picasso, in a crystalline mountain. Portraiture seemed to recede into long-buried history, a category that evoked vain and wealthy patrons as well as unadventurous artists who chose the path of commercial vice rather than aesthetic virtue.

But, happily, art-historical prejudices keep changing. Against all odds, portraiture, in the hands of contemporary artists, including photographers, has seen an amazing resurrection in the last quarter-century, a revival clearly marked by Andy Warhol's vast anthology of public and private portraits. In an age when countless electronic copies challenge the concept of a unique work and when scientists can consider cloning people as well as sheep and cats, artists and spectators have begun to cling to the miracle of human diversity, or to the singular facts of individual people, themselves included. The list of lively, innovative portraitists and self-portraitists working today is very long. Think only of Lucian Freud, Chuck Close, Gilbert and George, Cindy Sherman, Alex Katz, Francesco Clemente, Thomas Ruff, Yasumasa Morimura. And in tandem with this renewal of interest in real faces and real people, there has been a complementary revival of interest in the portraiture of the past. It is hard to believe that it took until 1996 for an exhibition to be devoted to the now obvious fact that Picasso, throughout his long life, was a major portraitist. For decades, the deformations of Cubism or Surrealism had so obscured the identities of the people who inspired Picasso – lovers, wives, friends – that they disappeared beneath the camouflage of his art. But today, these flesh-and-blood individuals have become visible again, each one a unique human being, with a real biography. And now, when we look at the work of Monet, Cézanne or Matisse and realise that the artists' wives and children keep turning up among their sitters, we may start thinking less about the evolution of modern art than about what complex family relationships might be revealed in these images. This is a sign of our times. Even Renoir's beloved *Luncheon of the Boating Party* (1880–81; Phillips Collection, Washington DC), traditionally perceived as a group of fun-loving, anonymous Parisians dissolved in an Impressionist symphony of coloured light, is being scrutinised as a *roman à clef* in which all but one of the fourteen figures have finally been identified. These people, we learn, have names, and we want to know them. One is Alphonsine Fournaise, the daughter of the man who owns the restaurant; another is Baron Raoul Barbier, the aristocratic son of an ambassador. In short, they are becoming a diverse cast of real men and women who lived in a real time and place.

This welling interest in the people whom artists have chosen to re-create has also altered our view of many portraitists who, because of their distance from mainstream modernism, had temporarily fallen out of fashion. The case of John Singer Sargent is typical. An international success during *la belle époque*, he was commemorated with a major retrospective in 1926, a year after his death; but thereafter, his work was greeted with growingly tepid, at times even hostile responses, as if he were an irrelevant relic from a dead world. But around 1998–99, taste was reversed when another retrospective attracted a new generation of curious spectators who, instead of turning away from a panorama of high society that mirrored a totally different era, looked with fascination at these *tableaux vivants* of a historical past, the equivalent of seeing a Henry James novel come to life or of watching a movie by Merchant and Ivory reconstruct the manners, the clothing, the domestic environment of people who lived in a world different from ours. To move back in time to the chronological territory embraced by this book, there is, for instance, the case of Thomas Gainsborough, who, like Sargent, suddenly became a crowd-pleaser, as was made evident in his retrospective of 2003. This surely had something to do with the seductive appeal of his dazzling brushwork, but what also mattered was the way Gainsborough created a historical fiction, permitting an audience to feel the almost living presence of a time capsule inhabited by real people, with real names, wearing their real clothing, appearing before us as if we had been magically transported to the London or Bath of the reign of King George III.

If the most energetic thrust of the twentieth century was to bury the past and to face a future of fictional Utopias, today's climate is one of nostalgic retrospection, in which history is resurrected and cherished; this phenomenon is conspicuous even among our many contemporary artists who reincarnate the classics of art history, whether by Chardin or Pollock. This book has a similar goal, namely, to focus on a particular period, from 1760 to 1830, and to offer, through the magic of portraiture, a series of images that will transport us to the public and private lives of the people who lived through these years of unprecedented change. And how did artists respond, whether directly or subliminally, to the ongoing upheavals pinpointed in such traumatic events as the American and the

French Revolutions, the rise and fall of the
Napoleonic empire, and the subsequent efforts
to resurrect a world that existed before belief in
monarchy had been threatened and, in good part,
extinguished? In these decades, often described
under such broad rubrics as 'the age of revolution'
or 'the origins of the modern world', everything,
from Christianity to child-rearing, from the artifice
of clothing to the sanctity of the ruler, could be
challenged. And it was a time, too, when new
depths of emotion and imagination were explored,
whether by painters and sculptors scrutinising their
own images as if they were writing a personal diary,
or reinventing the persona of their sitters as literary
fictions or Olympian deities. All of this and much
more is mirrored here in this anthology of real
people, a diverse population that includes military
heroes, celebrity actresses, rabid revolutionaries,
towering geniuses and happy families.

Fig. 1
RICHARD EVANS
*Henri-Christophe, King of Haiti*,
1816. Oil on canvas.
Josefina del Toro Fulladosa Collection,
University of Puerto Rico

This human encyclopaedia embraces, of
course, the most powerful men and women of the
period, namely the sovereigns whose names were
synonymous with the nations they represented,
from Catherine the Great, Empress of Russia, to
Ferdinand VII, King of Spain. Assembled together,
their images tell the story of the ongoing threats
to the concept of absolute monarchy. The aura
of stability and venerable tradition generated by
such state portraits as Callet's of Louis XVI
(cat. 8) or Reynolds's of George III (cat. 2) is
quickly unbalanced by the presence of revolutionary
newcomers who must assume different poses. For
Stuart, George Washington, the first president of
the United States (cat. 5), is a sober, earthbound
legislator, an heir to classical Rome and a political
companion to another revolutionary, Boze's
Mirabeau (cat. 46). For Ingres, Napoleon (cat. 12),
the self-proclaimed emperor of France, is a deity
even more remote and omnipotent than any
Bourbon monarch, a terrifying presence looking
backwards to the Olympian Zeus and forwards
to the extra-terrestrial rulers of science fiction, not
to mention the dictators of the twentieth century.
History keeps casting its shadows on these images.
What happened to these rulers, both legitimate
heirs and usurpers of thrones, by the time that
Napoleon himself had become a closed chapter?
It is fascinating to look at the portraits of post-
Restoration sovereigns, which always seem out
of joint with the images of their pre-Revolutionary
ancestors. Lawrence's spectacular state portrait
of George IV (cat. 13) feels like a wilful revival
of the swagger and luxury associated with an ever
more distant eighteenth-century world, a theatrical
performance that, for a moment, would resurrect
the past. Goya's portrait of Ferdinand VII (cat. 11)
tells a different story, stripping the artist's king of
all panoply and portraying him as nothing more
than an isolated human being posed against an
empty background. We see only a sitter whose
uncommonly ugly face and awkward stance collide

with his inherited royal trappings. Rendered by the painter with old-master virtuosity, these resemble the homeless relics of a buried historical epoch when the mortal flesh of kings and queens was an inseparable part of the splendour of ermine and velvet, crown and sceptre.

Representing royalty remained an ongoing problem that extended to the farthest reaches of Western history. A telling case in point is a portrait of Henri-Christophe, who, born a slave in the Caribbean and fighting for abolition, proclaimed himself King of Haiti in 1811, thereby establishing the first black monarchy, that of a new nation emerging, like France and the United States, from revolutionary ideals of freedom. Looking for an image of authority and finding England sympathetic to his hopes for emancipation, he commissioned Richard Evans, an assistant to Lawrence, to paint his official portrait, which was exhibited at the Royal Academy in 1818 as 'His Majesty Henry Christophe, King of Hayti' (fig. 1).[1] The new king, in breeches and tailcoat, now plays the role of one of Lawrence's royal sitters. Posed at the edge of his palace, Sans-Souci, he stands, sword and hat in hand, against a low tropical horizon and a vast stormy sky, his dramatically lofty silhouette given further weight by the inclusion of his crown as well as the fragments of drapery and architecture that had become routine symbols of aristocratic authority. If Goya metaphorically dethrones his royal sitters, this minor artist makes a heroic effort to persuade us that, from the turmoil of history, an authentic new monarch has been born.

But the contrary impulse, to see heads of state, not to mention other celebrities, as belonging to the earthbound world that we all share, was even more powerful. In the hands of David, who had also painted Napoleon in imperial robes, the emperor could be glimpsed as if paparazzi were revealing to us a flesh-and-blood politician working overtime in his study, with guttering candles and a clock that pinpoints the exact hour, 4.13 am (cat. 24). Even the

most imperious Spanish royalty, whose faces and postures we recognise from Goya's official images, may be rendered in more democratic terms that reunite them with common humanity. So it is with a portrait of King Charles IV by one of Goya's younger contemporaries, José de Madrazo (fig. 2). Rather than the monarch we are tempted to find unworthy of the royal theatre in which Goya so often displayed him, the same king is presented to us close-up with what seems an unedited, sympathetic candour, an accurate record of a weary sexagenarian who, despite the order of the Golden Fleece on his chest and a cushioned crown at his side, looks like any other mortal, whether tradesman or aristocrat. Kings and queens, the portrait tells us, are simply people.

It is a point already made in the 1760s in Zoffany's portrait of Queen Charlotte and her two eldest sons (cat. 87), both born within the first two

Fig. 2
JOSÉ DE MADRAZO
*King Charles IV in Rome*, 1815.
Oil on canvas, 114 × 92 cm.
Palacio Real de Aranjuez, Madrid

years of her marriage to George III. Instead of an official state portrait of the dynastic trio, we have an informal scene of a mother enjoying the company of the infant princes, who appear in fanciful costume. The elder of the two boys, the future George IV, is dressed as Telemachus, the classical paragon of a loyal son; the younger child, Frederick, Duke of York, wears the military uniform of a Turk, adding to the Chinese figurines on the table suggestions of another exotic empire. The royal children's adult obligations to family and state may well be evoked here, just as the queen's profile reflection in the mirror on her dressing table may turn her, for a moment, into a dynastic icon; but, in general, this vignette of domestic life in Buckingham House, with its cheerful garden view, allows the spectator to see that even the British royal family may share ordinary experiences with the commoners.[2] Across the Channel, also in the 1760s, we may observe a similar revelation in Louis-Michel

Fig. 3
LOUIS-MICHEL VAN LOO,
*The Marquis de Marigny and His Wife*, 1769. Oil on canvas, 130 × 98 cm.
Musée du Louvre, Paris

Van Loo's quietly innovative double portrait of the 48-year-old Marquis de Marigny, a major figure in Louis XV's building programme, and his young wife Julie, whom he had married two years earlier, when she was sixteen (fig. 3). They are very much at home, for the marquis has just entered her boudoir; and she, in turn, looks away from her mirror in order to respond. With its insistence on the informal and the momentary, we seem to have a snapshot of an aristocrat's private world, or perhaps of its artificial re-creation in the entrances and exits of a staged play. And at the same Salon, Greuze depicted an equally candid, but far more sentimental glimpse of the domestic life of another blueblood, the Marquis de Laborde, who, returning from the hunt, greets his wife and his abundance of children with outstretched arms. Genre painting and portrait painting, officially separated by academic doctrine, keep merging. There are, of course, major precedents for such a fusion – Velázquez's *Las Meninas* would head the list – but from the mid-eighteenth century on, the intersection of public and private worlds, of portraiture and daily life is a constantly expanding theme.

There are countless examples throughout Europe. In Russia, Dmitri Levitski, a portraitist who had painted both Catherine the Great and Diderot, could also turn his attention to the aristocratic young girls who were students at the Smolny Institute, a boarding school founded by the empress in 1771 after the seventeenth-century model of Mme de Maintenon's St Cyr. In a double portrait of 1773 (fig. 4), Levitski depicts two of the noble *pensionnaires*, Katerina Khrouchtchova and the Princess Katerina Khovanskaia, but, instead of presenting them posed stiffly in a traditional portrait format, he captures them enjoying one of the more pleasurable aspects of their educational programme. The two girls are seen as budding actresses who perform a pastoral play for the empress. The one on the left, in fact, is wearing masculine clothing, in disguise as the wily, smirking suitor of an innocent country girl. The facts of portraiture turn into the artifice of theatre. The same thing happens in a painting of 1784 by Carl Fredrik von Breda, the portrait of another child of the nobility, the Swedish crown prince, Gustav IV Adolf (fig. 5). In a canvas of imposing, life-size dimensions, the equivalent of a theatre curtain at the left is raised to reveal a long-range view of the Chapter Halls in the Royal Palace of Stockholm. There we see, centre stage, the six-year-old prince who, in the hands of his tutor, is mounted on a rearing rocking-horse, a scene of child's play that parallels Zoffany's record of the two infant British princes enjoying a costume party in the royal residence. And here, too, we realise that this genre scene of children's games may have far-reaching public repercussions, in this case, offering an optimistic preview of the leadership appropriate to the future king of Sweden; even though this prophecy was to be ironically belied, as it turned out, by Gustav IV's helplessness against a military coup of 1809 that forced his abdication.

The prose of daily life intruded on every kind of portraiture, including the portraits artists made of themselves. In the case of the Swiss-born Anton Graff, a self-portrait of 1785 offers a double image of the artist seated astride both the world of the paterfamilias and the successful portrait painter (fig. 6). He had painted portraits of many prominent German intellectuals – Moses Mendelssohn, Lessing, Schiller – and here, in the background, he shows himself at work on the oval portrait of Johann Georg Sulzer, the philosopher and aesthetician whose friendship had helped him to secure his position as a successful court painter in Berlin and whose daughter he was to marry. Sulzer, in fact, had died six years earlier, but Graff shows himself re-creating the portrait of his father-in-law, an image that not only hovers over the family as an ancestral figure but as a memory of one of the artist's distinguished sitters. In the foreground, he offers the domestic half of his life, an informal

Fig. 6
ANTON GRAFF
*The Artist's Family in Front
of a Portrait of Johann Georg
Sulzer*, 1785. Oil on canvas,
196 × 148 cm.
Oskar Reinhart Museum, Winterthur

can also be read as a grotesque kind of genre
painting in which the spectator has unexpected
access to the privacy of Marat's frugal dwelling
and his intimate ritual of working for the Republic
while soaking his tormented flesh in bath water.[3]
But far beyond this, the painting also becomes
a portrait of myth-making dimensions, that is,
a propagandistic painting of modern historical
fact whose politically charged message, reiterated
in replicas, was directed to anonymous audiences.
As such, this deification of a modern hero, even
though it documents the gruesome facts of
a violent assassination at home and not on the
patriotic battlefield, enters the timeless realm
familiar to such sculptural projects as Rauch's
plans for a Goethe monument (cats 58–59) or
Thorvaldsen's apotheosis of Napoleon (cat. 120).
Again and again, artists were to elevate the living
memory of illustrious contemporaries to new
versions of Mount Olympus and Valhalla or
to a revolutionary atheist's version of
Christian sainthood.

Throughout these decades, such transports
to mythical heights were, in fact, familiar in both
public and private portraiture; and at least in one
case, Richard Samuel's *The Nine Living Muses of Great
Britain*, first exhibited at the Royal Academy in
1779, the voyage from eighteenth-century earth
to classical heaven was intended to venerate
contemporary women who had contributed
to arts and letters (fig. 7). These modern daughters
of Zeus, swathed in classical drapery and taking
graceful poses in front of the Temple of Apollo,
are the chosen members of a new Hall of Fame.
Their élite sorority includes such famous women
as the painter Angelica Kauffman, the historian
Catherine Macaulay, the singer Elizabeth Ann
Sheridan and the writer Elizabeth Griffith.

But unique as this clubby group may be – with
nine members, the door must now be closed – the
idea of representing a living sitter in mythological
or literary guise is a commonplace in this period.

pyramid of his two sons, his daughter and his
wife who, now also playing the role of a governess,
is fully involved with the education of the three
children; all seem to belong to the new world of
schooling advocated by such *philosophes* as Rousseau
and Pestalozzi. Before our eyes, the children learn
to read, to look at prints and to think while, at the
same time and in the same space, their portraitist-
father advertises his trade and his important
family connections.

Such mixtures of public and private imagery
keep enriching and even confusing the traditional
categories of portraiture, to the point that
a painting as famous as Jacques-Louis David's
image of the murdered Jean-Paul Marat eludes clear
classification (cat. 37). It can be read, of course, as a
portrait, since the sitter's features, however idealised,
are obviously meant to be as recognisable as they are
in David's drawing of Marat's head alone. And it

It is found, for example, in the more staged, theatrical character of Francis Cotes's light-footed depiction of Lady Stanhope and Lady Effingham as Diana and her companions (cat.126); of Reynolds's transformation of the actress Sarah Siddons into the Tragic Muse, watched over by Pity and Terror (cat.130); or of James Barry's haunted fantasy of himself and his friend Edmund Burke as Ulysses and his companions escaping from the lair of Polyphemus (cat.122). But it is even more broadly expanded in the internationally popular form of the sculpted portrait bust that censored contemporary clothing from view, reincarnating modern sitters as companions of the ancients, an illusion fostered by complete nudity or by a minimum of classical drapery. Presumably, these living or recently dead people, whether a philosopher like Kant (cat.111) or a composer like Cimarosa (cat.119), would be completely at home in a Greco-Roman portrait gallery that included Socrates and Marcus Aurelius. But within these conventions, there could be an infinite variety of countenance and emotion. Houdon's portrait of Diderot (cat.53) confronts us with a darting glance from sparkling eyes that mirror his swift intellect. Schadow's portrait of Friedrich Gilly (Akademie der Künste, Berlin), carved a year after the short-lived architect's death, freezes the young genius in time, leaving his eyes fixed but sightless (a misreading of the missing pupils which in antique sculpture would have been supplied by coloured pigment that vanishes over the centuries), and re-creating him in a solemn, commemorative mould whose lucid geometry reflects Gilly's own purist architecture. Sculptors could even create their own images as if they had been metamorphosed into a resident of Mount Olympus, a point made clear in Anne Seymour Damer's marble self-portrait. Having already posed for Ceracchi as the muse of sculpture (fig.61), and having being thoroughly immersed in classical languages, Damer was apparently able to look at her own face and reinvent her hair and features

as if Zeus himself had transformed her into a goddess of flawless perfection, so idealised that she might even have been unrecognisable to her own friends.

Predictably, portraits of artists, whether by themselves or by their artist friends, reflect the character of their art, a point made clear in the portrait that Caroline Bardua painted of Caspar David Friedrich in 1811, the year that the artist had gone on a long excursion into the Harz mountains in order to surround himself fully with the sublimities of landscape (fig.8). Bardua, who belonged to the inner circle of German Romantics and who had also painted Goethe's portrait, depicts Friedrich as a lonely hermit in a wild northern forest, but she also responds to his distinctive features and his awe-inspiring genius. Towering above a mountainous landscape and silhouetted against a vast sky, Friedrich's head, framed like a lion's by his light-red hair and sideburns, radiates the uncommon passion of a visionary who looks far beyond the material world and far above any earthbound spectator who might try to return his fierce gaze. Such images of an artist's or writer's heroic isolation and undaunted ambition could

Fig.7
RICHARD SAMUEL
*The Nine Living Muses of Great Britain: Portraits in the Characters of the Muses in the Temple of Apollo*, 1778.
Oil on canvas, 132 × 155 cm.
National Portrait Gallery, London, NPG 4905

reach unfamiliar heights of intensity. One such example is the almost hallucinatory self-portrait of 1803 (cat. 74), in which James Barry depicts himself as a much younger artist who imagines that he is Timanthes, a classical Greek painter reputed to have had uncommon gifts for depicting emotional drama and fantastic creatures. Moreover, he includes a cropped view of Hercules crushing the serpents of envy, a projection of his own efforts to suppress his personal and professional jealousies. More and more, these portraits reflect the turbulent psyches and exalted goals familiar to the concept of romantic alienation and genius.

Artists' personalities and passions could even be reflected in surrogate form, as in the extraordinary posthumous portrait of Fanny, the beloved dog of the wife of the architect Sir John Soane (fig. 9). Fanny had died at midnight on Christmas Day 1820, and her bereaved master and

mistress wished to commemorate her memory, much as many sitters wanted to express their devotion to dead husbands, wives or children. This point was vividly made in Hugh Douglas Hamilton's portrait of Richard Mansergh St George (cat. 95), who, in a grove of funereal cypress trees, is found grieving eternally, head on hand, at his wife Ann's tomb that bears the inscription 'NON IMMEMOR' (never to be forgotten). Soane turned to James Ward, a specialist in animal painting, for this canine portrait commission. The result, completed in 1822, is almost a portrait of Soane himself, for Fanny is seen reposing in the midst of a vast archaeological site of the kind that had constantly triggered the architect's own variations on classical themes. Mirroring such famous meditations on classical ruins as Tischbein's portrait of Goethe in the Roman Campagna (fig. 49), Fanny is perched on top of a marble fragment decorated with an egg-and-dart pattern. The sweeping view behind her includes a huge Corinthian capital of the kind that her master collected for his eccentric London home and a distant glimpse of the Erechtheum porch of the Acropolis in Athens, with its caryatids. Surrounded by these evocative relics of antiquity, Mrs Soane's dog has herself become part of a dead world that is kept alive by the architect's imagination. He, in fact, buried her remains in his own home, in a funerary monument inscribed 'Alas, Poor Fanny'.

However extreme the fictions of portraiture could become in these decades, the very idea of a portrait demanded the empirical record of the unique facts of each sitter, an individual to be mistaken for no one else. Often, the mixture of classical idealism and contemporary faces familiar to the world of David and Canova might confound identification, just as the artifice of rococo style could be so extravagant that if Madame de Pompadour were to rise from the dead, her portrait by Boucher would hardly provide a clue to her identity. But, from the 1760s on, a strong counter-

Fig. 8
CAROLINE BARDUA
*Caspar David Friedrich*, 1811.
Oil on canvas, 104 × 86 cm.
Museum zur Dresdener Frühromantik, Dresden

22

current of reality kept dispelling these veils of artistic fantasy, focusing on what appears to be the unedited truth of each sitter, the equivalent of a realist rebellion. It was a direction that often came from the artistic provinces, where sitters demanded more empirical prose than abstract poetry in their likenesses. For John Singleton Copley, working in Boston, or for Joseph Wright of Derby, working in the British Midlands, portraits often looked like startling confrontations with very real people. Copley's record of Samuel Adams (cat. 42), a major intellectual force behind the American Revolution, shows him at a critical moment of history, 6 March 1770, when he demanded that the Royal Governor, Thomas Hutchison, remove British troops from Boston. Here, the artifice of portraiture, including the haze of atmosphere and the blur of bravura brushstrokes, is swept away in favour of an ambience of pristine truth and clarity. We are left with the primary facts of a passionately dedicated human being whose wrinkled features and modest, even careless apparel – two buttons of his waistcoat are undone – are as legible as the historical documents, including the Massachusetts charter, to which he points. Similarly, Wright of Derby's portrait of Mrs Sarah Clayton of 1770 (cat. 62) provides the illusion of unmediated obedience to reality, as if we were confronting head-on this energetic middle-aged woman from Liverpool who, in addition to carrying on her father's property business, was knowledgeable about the latest trends in classical archaeology, a fact confirmed by the table display of the ground plan of the Propylaeum in Athens. So real is the physical and psychological presence of a strong-willed individual seated at a desk that the inclusion of a column base and a swag of drapery looks like an anachronism from a moribund world of aristocratic portraiture.

This crystalline vision of material fact, recording with equal precision the sitter's features, clothing and accessories, whether furniture

or documents, kept welling in force as if it represented, in tandem with revolutionary challenges to social hierarchies, an ongoing assault on the traditions of idealisation that had elevated sitters to higher realms of grandeur and power. It is a major current shared by Goya and David, who were both capable of depicting family and friends as well as strangers with such disarming candour that we feel we are on the threshold of photography. David's statement about how his early experience of antique art at Pompeii and Herculaneum was like having cataracts removed from his eyes is directly relevant to his own revolutionary vision of portraiture as well as that of Goya. Their eyes became laser beams of truth that kept cutting through the inherited rhetoric of ideal postures and social grandeur, transforming even kings and countesses into earthbound mortals. Goya's portrait of Ferdinand Guillemardet (cat. 16), the French ambassador to Spain, has the character of a studio set-up in which the sitter, with one hand elegantly poised on his thigh and legs momentarily crossed, poses for the artist as a dashing young representative of a new political order. In 1793, five years before Goya painted him, Guillemardet had voted for the death of the king and now, as a child of the Revolution, he proudly displays the tricolour

of the Republic in his plumes and sashes. And,
like Copley's Samuel Adams, he confronts us
as a human fact, a single, palpable presence that
undermines the artificial fogs of grace and
authority associated with the official portraits
of statesmen. To be sure, he assumes these roles
in his dashing posture and in the splendid
accoutrements of power that range from sword
to quill pen, but the image remains that of an actor
playing a new role.

We may feel a similar assault on conventions in
Jacques-Louis David's full-length portrait of
Juliette de Villeneuve (cat. 143), painted in Brussels
in 1824, a year before the artist's death. The
feminine elegance of the theme, a woman playing a
harp, was a commonplace in the late eighteenth and
early nineteenth century, and could even be
combined, as in the case of Reynolds's allegorical
portraits, with allusions to St Cecilia. In these
almost celestial images, ethereal grace was meant to

reign. But in David's depiction of the 22-year-old
harpist, Juliette stands stiffly, her hands frozen on
the instrument's strings as she faces the artist with
the steady gaze of a sitter who must maintain an
uncomfortable pose. Around her, and recorded with
equally sharp focus, is a clutter of what look like
stage props seen before a performance: a music
stand to which Juliette has temporarily fastened her
flowered bonnet and the back of a chair over which
she has dropped her shawl. And the extraordinary
cropping of the furniture – the legs of both the
chair and the music stand are cut off by the
painting's edges – confirms that the ideal geometry
that weds the harp to the young lady in a frozen
pairing of vertical axes is nothing but staged
artifice. In his late years, in fact, David could paint
portraits whose search for nothing but the truth
reaches extremes that put us on the brink of the
invention of photography. His depiction of Ange-
Pauline-Charlotte Ramel de Nogaret, the wife of
another émigré and regicide in Brussels, seems to
strip portraiture to its bare bones (fig. 10). Here,
in 1820, we already have the equivalent of a
passport photo or a mug shot, an absolutely
factual, presumably impersonal record of a unique
individual whose dour face is recorded with the
same sharp-eyed accuracy as the lace and silk hat
and collar she wears for the moment that will
forever commemorate her. With the hindsight
of history, we are immediately tempted to locate
such a portrait in the world of Louis Daguerre,
just as we tend to perceive Ingres's depiction
of Louis-François Bertin in 1832 (cat. 156) as
a portrait photograph *avant la lettre*. By the 1820s,
even idealists like David and Ingres had achieved
such a firm grasp on visible truths that the
invention of photography seemed to follow their
vision with seamless inevitability. And, as in the
new world of the camera lens, even the fictions that
surrounded the sitters turned into hard facts.
The once unbridgeable gulf between citizens
and kings had been crossed for ever.

# II

## Sculpted Portraits, 1770–1830: 'Real Presences'[1]

GUILHEM SCHERF

Between 1770 and 1830, Europe witnessed considerable development in the art of portraiture.[2] Many of the greatest artists expressed themselves in the genre, which is particularly suited to sculpture. The six decades covered here encompass a chronological span broad enough to include two or three generations of sculptors.[3] The artists can be divided into those who worked under the *ancien régime* and the Revolution, whose shockwaves affected the whole of Europe,[4] those still active under the Empire,[5] and those who practised in Napoleonic Europe and later in the Europe that followed the Congress of Vienna.[6] This period, which in the case of sculpture corresponds to the neoclassical era (the title of a memorable exhibition[7]) and to the antecedents of the romantic movement, witnessed a renewal within society and some important new developments: the scope of commissions broadened, and different types of representation proliferated.

If we examine the great increase in sculpted portraits produced during this period, we shall gain a clearer understanding of the mutations taking place at this moment in European history; the cult of public memory and of moral values went hand in hand with the burgeoning of individuality in public social spaces, and a new emphasis on the intimate. Artistic endeavour was now focused on the problems of resemblance and idealisation: how to transcribe a mental image through reference to antiquity and the use of allegory, to reproduce a sitter's features under the pretence of objectivity, or to translate accurately the image of an interior portrait.

### A Proliferation of Images

One major characteristic of this period is the proliferation of the sculpted portrait. Referential pieces began to fill public spaces like so many *exempla virtutis*. At the same time, however, the private sphere was preferred above all others; here the values celebrating the private qualities of sensibility were expressed. The availability of portraits produced in series for a very diverse clientele demonstrates the way the gradual democratisation of society kept pace with the proliferation of representations.

The portrait constitutes an interface between art and social life: to have one's portrait painted is tantamount to agreeing to appear in public.[8] For a long time this was the prerogative of the patrician class: in its article on the portrait, the *Encyclopédie* quotes the 'Roman noblemen's right to images'. This is particularly true of sculpture, a solemn art employing weighty materials — marble, bronze — in the search for permanence. The formal portrait bust always portrays the subject displaying (below his marble physiognomy) the insignia of power (fig. 11).

The pendant to this right to a portrait, 'a burning topic of theoretical discourse since

Fig. 11
FEDOT IVANOVICH SHUBIN
*Paul I*, 1800. H. 80 cm.
State Russian Museum, St Petersburg

the Renaissance',[9] is the 'right to a monument', not only to celebrate a social élite, but also to commemorate virtue. Memorial spaces, in which the public image is used as an exemplar, were filled with portrait sculptures at a period when nationalisms were becoming more intense and pantheons were growing in popularity.

'History sculpture provides the safest keeping for man's virtues and weaknesses ... [Its] most worthy aim ... from a moral point of view, is to perpetuate the memory of illustrious men and to provide models of virtue.'[10] Portraying great men was the chief enterprise of the period, and it gave sculpture pride of place. The favoured location for statues of great men was the public square. In 1763, Melchior Grimm expressed the desire for the statue of Louis XV in Paris to be surrounded by the eminent personalities of his reign. In 1765, Pierre Patte suggested that statues of illustrious men should be placed on the Pont-Neuf. In 1771, the Baron de Feugères proposed to the States of Languedoc that the equestrian statue of Louis XIV in the Place Royale in Montpellier should be surrounded by groups of the great men who had brought lustre to his reign (this project was only partially realised). In Italy, the Prato di Valle in Padua had housed statues of illustrious Paduans since 1775. In 1786, Antoine Mopinot declared that statues of people with the right to a monument (such as magistrates or inventors) should be placed in public squares, institutional buildings and provincial towns,[11] preparing the way for the 'statue-mania'[12] that was to take hold in the nineteenth century.

It was the pantheon, an enclosed space, however, that was to be the crucible of commemorative sculpture and of the symbolic memory of the nation. The Pantheon in Rome, built by the Emperor Hadrian in the early second century AD and transformed into a church at the beginning of the seventh century, was converted into a mythical memorial dedicated to artists — thanks to the presence of Raphael's tomb. In 1674 a funerary monument was created, with busts of Raphael and of Annibale Carracci. From this moment on, the Pantheon became the main location for memorials to artists who had once lived in Rome; their busts later dispensed with any role as tomb decoration, thenceforward only presenting a commemorative image, with no funerary significance.[13] The heyday was reached in 1782 when portraits of Winckelmann, Mengs and Poussin were installed, paid for by scholars keen to ensure the immortality of their heroes. Canova and his students took possession of the space in 1813, erecting dozens of marble busts until, in 1820, Pope Pius VII, on remarking the absence of any religious motivation behind this intense cult of memory, transferred the busts from the church to the Capitol, where he created a gallery of portrait busts of illustrious men (the present Protomoteca: see cat. 119).

The Church's radical reaction to invasion by the individual, secular memorial coincided with the decision of the First Republic in France, in 1791, to sever the church of Sainte-Geneviève in Paris from the Catholic Church and to devote the building entirely to national glory. Their programme, promulgated for all to see in the inscription 'To our great men, from their grateful country' was entrusted to the former sculptor Quatremère de Quincy. It could be considered the culmination of the celebration of the nation's Great Men which began in France in the early 1770s.[14] The dream of the Comte d'Angiviller, minister to Louis XVI, was to place marble statues representing the great men of France in the Grande Galerie in the Louvre (which was to become a museum) – in other words, great men who had achieved glory during the Bourbon Monarchy – thus creating a glorious pantheon. This remained only a dream, however.[15] It belonged with the contemporary taste for Plutarchism, already illustrated by Voltaire, d'Alembert and Rousseau: the illustrious men named by Thomas, of the Académie Française,

in his *Essai sur les éloges* (1773) could be found a few years later in d'Angiviller's lists.[16] The spirit of d'Angiviller's project was revived during the first decades of the nineteenth century, when art galleries were adorned with busts of artists (see cat. 155), and the Pont de la Concorde suddenly bristled with colossal military figures.[17] For his secular temple, Quatremère relied on statuary; but in the plans which the brevity of the revolutionary period prevented him from implementing, great men were to make way for allegory.[18] However, Alexandre Lenoir's plan was to exhibit exemplary busts in the Petits-Augustins:[19] his Musée des Monuments Français was always designed to be a pantheon, sculpture lending itself quite naturally to the commemoration of illustrious personages.

The British succeeded early in constructing a pantheon inside a religious building, Westminster Abbey, where royalty rubs shoulders with deserving persons of less exalted ancestry. Voltaire was dazzled by Newton's funeral, a national occasion: 'Go into Westminster. It is not the tombs of kings which you admire; it is the monuments erected by a grateful nation to the men who have contributed to her glory; you can see their statues, as one saw the statues of Sophocles and Plato in Athens; and I am convinced that the sight of these glorious monuments alone has stimulated more than one person and formed more than one great man.'[20] The political orientation of such a place was confirmed by the end of the eighteenth century and during the first third of the nineteenth century, when the country wanted to celebrate its military success and the strength of its national art, in a school of British sculpture to rival that of the Italians. Chantrey was the perfect representative for the nation's artistic identity, rivalling (in particular) Canova.[21] Cultural competition with France – the British Museum was erected by the government as a response to the Musée Napoléon – also flourished at the level of public statuary. The great commemorative commissions in Westminster

Abbey and St Paul's Cathedral are contemporary with Denon's heroic versions of the dignitaries and generals of the Empire. The portrait as a statue, eternal hero worship, is the guarantor of posterity. The spectacular installation in 1801 of Flaxman's great marble statue depicting the Earl of Mansfield (1705–1793), in which the imposing Lord Chief Justice sits surrounded by allegories, was the first unattached monument to be erected in this location (fig. 12),[22] one of the culminating moments of an impressive wave of commissions designed to celebrate in Westminster Abbey, as well as in St Paul's around Nelson and Cornwallis, the élite of British leaders and heroes who died for their country.[23]

By the end of our period Germany undoubtedly gave purest expression to the idea of a pantheon for illustrious men, without any religious, funerary or even allegorical overtones. The Walhalla, a colossal

secular temple copied from the Parthenon, was erected near Regensburg on the orders of Ludwig I of Bavaria between 1830 and 1842, having been conceived by him as early as 1807. The building houses a large number of marble sculptures commemorating the German-speaking élite, military as well as cultural. The hundred or so busts are arranged inside in orderly rows, making an ideal 'protomoteca' for this imposing building.[24]

People belonging to the same social or cultural class enjoy contemplating their own reflection. This phenomenon grew more general in the eighteenth century, when opportunities for public socialising became more widespread and began to involve different levels of society. By mid-century, the series of portrait busts used to adorn libraries was intended to glorify the past of these institutions (All Souls College, Oxford; Trinity College, Cambridge), or the high points of universal literature (Trinity College, Dublin). Other institutions followed a less coherent programme, depending on donations received over the years (Sainte-Geneviève, Paris).[25] In the third quarter of the century, foyers of theatres such as the Comédie-Française (see fig. 46) and the Opéra in Paris developed collections connected with their history. In another example, the artist Caffieri specialised in groups of busts, studies in plaster or terracotta, for presentation to academies in Paris (the Académie Française, the Académie des Inscriptions) or in the provinces (Dijon, Rouen)[26] to adorn their lecture halls.

Galleries of portrait busts were often constructed with a more partisan intention. Supporters of the Whig party in Britain trumpeted their political allegiance by having themselves portrayed with their companions: the Duke of Bedford surrounded the bust of Fox with his friends in the Temple of Liberty at Woburn Abbey; and the Marquis of Rockingham did the same in his mausoleum at Wentworth Woodhouse.[27] This diversion of commemorative sculpture to militant

Fig. 12
JOHN FLAXMAN
*Monument to the Earl of Mansfield*,
1795–1801. Marble, H. 366 cm.
Westminster Abbey, London

ends can be compared with Napoleon's motivation in his choice of a programme for his own glorification at the Château des Tuileries: busts of military men (essential props of the regime) in the Salon des Maréchaux; and great men of more international stature in the Galerie des Consuls. The two strands coexisted in a skilful historical evocation in the manner of Plutarch, Napoleon's favourite bedside reading.

The right to an image was not based solely on virtue or setting a good example, nor on a dominant social position. Prominent examples of those fêted in a more open society – from writers to singers – also claimed such recognition. Portraits created to order for private clients began to appear regularly in public exhibitions, even though such works ran the risk of critical rejection: 'What tires and sometimes repels, is to come upon a crowd of busts, of portraits of nameless men, or men who are often employed in slightly antisocial jobs. What do we care for these financiers, physicians, clerks and civil servants; these doleful marchionesses and dreary presidents' wives? ... Their faces seem to say: it was pride that made me pay to be here, on canvas or in marble. When a physiognomy displays nothing that is out of the ordinary, does it merit this distinction? Such a distinction should only be bestowed on people who have earned it by their virtue or their talent, or for service to their country.'[28] Any pedagogical or moral function the Salon may have had was subverted by this display of vanity by the urban élite, whether from the upper or middle classes. By idolising family values, however, the urban élite encouraged the emergence of a new subject – child portraiture, which developed considerably during the period (cat.107).[29] It is in the arena of family portraiture, in fact, that quite modest folk can sometimes be encountered, those neglected by sculpture, with moving faces executed in inexpensive materials such as terracotta (Trippel's aunt: fig.13) or plaster (cat.105).[30] If a poor person is presented, it is only by stealth: Nollekens made

Dr Johnson pose for his portrait, but the doctor's hair was inspired by the hair of a beggar.[31]

A map needs to be made of the private places given over to sculpted portraits. Collections generally bore a direct relationship to a family (dynastic galleries), or portrayed some tutelary figures. A number of places in the house can be identified where busts, or more unusually statues, would be prominently displayed. By the front door, where in the ancient world busts of ancestors would have greeted visitors,[32] the visitor would be welcomed by busts of their host. At the Château de Coppet, between two staircase doors, stood Tieck's statue of Jacques Necker, Louis XVI's finance minister (fig.14).[33] At Woburn Abbey, in the vestibule of the Temple of the Graces, statues of the Duke of Bedford's two daughters could be found, by Chantrey and Thorvaldsen.[34] The gallery allowed taste, whether in sculpture or in political party, to be clearly expressed. After Waterloo, the sixth Duke of Devonshire, an ardent Whig who was fascinated

Fig. 14
CHRISTIAN FRIEDRICH TIECK
*Jacques Necker*, 1816–18. Marble,
H. 179 cm.
Château de Coppet, Switzerland

by Napoleon, made at Chatsworth a collection of remarkable marble portraits by Canova (the statue of Madame Mère, and busts of Madame Mère and Napoleon).[35] A sitting room provides a more intimate space, although open to society, and is well suited to the display of a masterpiece: the Duchesse d'Enville displayed Houdon's marble bust of Condorcet (see cat. 43) prominently on a table. A portrait of a deceased loved one belongs in more discreet surroundings, to which the family withdrew. In Michel Philibert Genod's painting of the Marquise de Marniola and her children (1821; Private collection), the drawing room is dominated by a bust of the dead paterfamilias displayed on a console.[36] It is not surprising to find portrait busts in libraries, a favoured location since ancient times for the display of portraits of role models.[37] Inspiring examples such as these also made their appearance in the study. Celebrated writers would adorn the top shelf of their bookcase or the pediment over the door with a bust of Pope (see cat. 18) or with portraits of leaders to inspire them to action, and to watch over them as they worked. Zacharias Tjernysjev had Catherine II.[38] William Roscoe had Fox.[39]

The glorification of private sensibility is admirably expressed in funerary art, one of sculpture's favourite spheres. The portrait or image of the deceased is there to commemorate a certain person. Sentimental outpourings over the departed were much in vogue at the end of the eighteenth and the beginning of the nineteenth centuries, particularly in Britain. Affecting effigies of dead children, represented as sleeping – whether we think of Banks's *Penelope Boothby* (1793; Ashbourne Church, Derbyshire) or Chantrey's *Robinson Sisters* (1817; Lichfield Cathedral)[40] – always move visitors to churches, as do portrayals of families grouped around a dead figure, which were very popular at the period.[41] The theme of the mother with one or several children, used so frequently in painting, is curiously rare in sculpture. It is possible that

sculpture was seen as too solemn a medium for such a subject to be developed in a warm and intimate register. Leaving aside tomb decorations, groups go beyond the evocation of family happiness, giving hints of something more important. Bartolini's portrait of Elisa Baciocchi (Napoleon I's eldest sister) and her daughter (c.1813; Musée National du Château de Fontainebleau) illustrates the child's affection for her mother, whom she embraces round the neck, but more importantly illustrates the direct line of succession. The small girl is next in line to the King of Rome in the political game of imperial succession. It is no accident that the child is depicted standing above the imperial eagle, nor that she is shown contemplating a medallion showing the profile of her august uncle.[42] Chantrey's marble group depicting Dorothy Jordan and her two children (fig. 15) obviously represents maternal tenderness; however, this secular allegory of Maternity, now discreetly housed in Buckingham Palace, takes on a new significance when we learn that the woman, an actress by profession, was mistress of the future King William IV and bore him ten children before dying in poverty. Seized by remorse, her lover erected this life-size marble monument to her memory six weeks after his accession to the throne. Even more extraordinary was the intended destination of the sculpture – the royal necropolis, Westminster Abbey.[43] In this case, the boundaries between genres have been abolished. The work illustrates an intensely private event, yet it was to be exposed to public gaze in one of the most revered locations in London, a building devoted to the memory of kings and great men of the nation.

The friendship portrait is another type of representation that extols private sensibility; although quite common in painting, it is seldom found in sculpture. We have to look for it via the family, as for example in Schadow's exceptional *Princesses Luise and Frederika of Prussia* (cat. 138), or Bartolini's *Emma and Julia Campbell Dancing* (fig. 69). Funerary monuments sometimes movingly evoke companions in arms who have fallen together in battle, as in Westmacott's handsome group *Major General Packenham and Samuel Gibbs* (1816–19; St Paul's Cathedral, London).[44] The two male figures side by side are forerunners of the ultimate friendship portrait, *Goethe and Schiller* (1849) in an embrace, designed by Rauch for the city of Weimar.[45]

Strong private and public demand encouraged the production of portraits in series, starting what became something of a social phenomenon. This included the spread of engraved portraits (prints after busts by Lemoyne and Houdon) and medals (bearing copies of busts by Chantrey), and the multiplication of small items, such as medallions, made in series, bearing the profiles of celebrated men, terracotta pieces by Nini and Chinard, bronze medals by David d'Angers, that were easy to distribute and sell.[46]

Did a portrait industry exist at this time? A number of the sculptors in this exhibition (Nollekens, Houdon, Dannecker, Bartolini) made a name for themselves through the products of their workshops. Nollekens abused some of his most famous busts, unable to resist the public demand that would make his fortune: at least seventy replicas of his *Pitt* are known, and about fifty of the second version of *Fox* (cat.115).[47] Houdon made multiple versions of his busts of celebrities, in plaster rather than in marble: he was contracted to produce at least thirty replicas of *Sophie Arnould* (cat.128) and sixteen of *John Paul Jones*. He sent every academician a model of his *Voltaire*, and was willing to produce, or have produced, one to two hundred plaster casts of *Washington*.[48] Having gained a reputation as the sculptor of *Voltaire*, which he modelled from life just before the writer's death, he went on to invent various formulae for portrait heads – bareheaded, bewigged and dressed in the French manner, robed in the style of classical antiquity, wearing a headband – in order to satisfy enormous public demand, from foreign courts as well as from provincial drawing schools. Dannecker

exploited the same phenomenon in the wake of his portrait of Schiller: from the same head, modelled during sittings with the poet, in 1794 he distributed a portrait bust superbly draped in the classical manner; two years later he created a new composition cut off at the neck in the antique style; finally, after Schiller's death in 1805, he designed a solemn version as a herm (fig.16). This last version was often repeated, most notably in 1808 for the Walhalla, thereby consigning the writer permanently to the ranks of the immortals.[49] In the realm of political propaganda, the Banca Elisiana in Carrara distributed more than one thousand copies of Chaudet's marble bust of Napoleon all over Europe.[50]

Such serial production need not necessarily devalue the notion of creation: even if reproduced by the dozen in the workshop, the busts of Pitt, Voltaire, Schiller and Napoleon were originally

Fig.15
SIR FRANCIS CHANTREY
*Dorothy Jordan and Her Children*, 1830–34. Marble, H. 137.2 cm.
The Royal Collection, London

Fig. 16
JOHANN HEINRICH
DANNECKER
*Friedrich von Schiller*, 1805–10.
Marble, H. 87 cm.
Staatsgalerie, Stuttgart

sculpted by the artist alone with his model (alive or dead), freely creating his individual interpretation and his own compositional principles. Some copies (those made for particular clients) are more carefully executed than others, however.

*Artistic Challenges*

Any artist undertaking the representation of an individual is faced with a difficult choice between idealisation and likeness. A portrait is a cultural and mental representation. The introduction of nudity in the classical manner, and the role played by allegory in the depiction of the sitter, fuelled an impassioned debate about clothing. Achieving the most accurate likeness possible remained the most important challenge: according to the *Encyclopédie*, 'in every portrait, it cannot be emphasised too strongly, resemblance is the essential perfection'. The use of masks to reproduce facial features, tools for measuring proportions and ingenious methods of catching the sitter's gaze led to a systematic investigation of the body. At the same time, analysis (disguised as science) of the model aimed to identify his or her underlying character and fleeting emotions in an attempt to seek out the inner person and produce, in another way, an ideal portrait.

A portrait guarantees posterity, particularly if it is a statue: 'A monument should not only address the man, it should also address the idea represented by the man.'[51] Napoleon understood this when he allowed effigies of himself to proliferate in the main centres of power; he appears either in the uniform of office or dressed in the toga of classical antiquity.[52] The immortalisation of the trappings of power in marble and the flattering comparison to the Roman emperor all belong in the realm of political propaganda. A problem arose when Napoleon was confronted with Canova's plan to depict him naked, as Mars the Peacemaker:[53] the real hero is the god himself (fig. 59). The statue aroused hostility; it was not exhibited at the Salon

of 1810 and remained hidden behind a partition at the Louvre. Canova made a note of the several conversations he had had with Napoleon in 1810: 'We discussed the custom of clothing statues and I told him that with French dress like his, God himself would be unable to create a beautiful sculpture, that the language of sculpture was the nude, with the drapery appropriate to that art.'[54] The question of dress was an old one. Diderot had already made his position clear: 'It is that flesh is more beautiful than any drapery, however beautiful … Nakedness keeps the world at bay, going back to a more innocent, simpler age … It was the custom of the Greeks, our masters in all the fine arts.'[55] In fact, such aesthetic considerations tended to be thwarted by the self-esteem of the sitters, whether their name was Voltaire, Washington or Napoleon: all were anxious lest their public image become mired in ridicule.[56] Quatremère de Quincy, highly skilled at the *beau idéal* and of the same opinion as Canova on the importance of nudity, nevertheless raised the question of propriety when a living subject was being represented: 'Propriety should have the right to demand certain modifications of appearance or of dress.'[57] This was exactly Cardinal Litta's argument when in 1820 he asked Prince Borghese to conceal from public view Canova's statue of his wife Pauline as Venus.[58]

When the symbolism of a portrait was based on a literal transcription from classical antiquity, it ennobled the contemporary model by transferring to him the merits of the hero in question: Trippel obtained inspiration for his *Goethe* from the head of Apollo in the Giustiniani collection in Rome; Ceracchi and Thorvaldsen transcribed a bust of Trajan (from the Albani collection in the Capitoline) for their portraits of Jean-Baptiste Bernadotte and Ludwig I of Bavaria.[59] The exercise had its limitations, however. Artists who were inspired by the rhetoric of gesture or the hand, taken from classical treatises such as those of Quintilian, risked repeating a formula that was emptied of meaning. Angelini's *Monument to Piranesi* (1779–80; S. Maria del Priorato, Rome) and Chinard's terracotta *Self-portrait* (*c*.1795; Musée de Montargis) borrowed the rhetorical gesture of the concealed hand from the *Eschine* in Naples[60] for no better reason than that it was a posture. The larger-than-life busts by Canova (*First Consul*)[61] or David d'Angers (of Goethe, fig.17),[62] although their size recalls various classical works, such as the impressive pieces to be seen in the park of the Villa Albani in Rome, are primarily the pretext for personal variations on the theme of the colossal. 'A bust should be larger than life-size to convey the impression one receives on seeing a great man. How to render his sublime animation without the illusion of features seen in large scale? It is the soul, the passion of genius that makes these men's features grow larger when they speak so that the head appears colossal.'[63]

Portrait busts and statues of women provide an interesting insight into the debate on the idealisation of dress that was raging during the period. Full-length statues, as we have seen, are suitable for eminent statesmen, whose function is thus immortalised and rendered heroic. Women are often debarred from power; when they are rulers, however, they bear the same insignia as men. The statue of Catherine II by Shubin (1789; Russian National Museum, St Petersburg) is the asexual image of a monarch, weighed down by the accessories connected with her role (ermine cloak, large neck chain, sceptre, open book, horn of plenty).[64] When less exalted women are represented, they wear either contemporary dress, discreetly idealised, or are transformed into classical allegories. The statue of the Margravine Wilhelmine of Bayreuth, sister of Friedrich II, executed by Elias Räntz, was installed ten years after her death in 1773 in the Temple of Friendship in the park of the palace of Sans-Souci in Potsdam, a genuine memorial. Wilhelmine is represented sitting in an armchair with her head resting on her hand,

a small dog on her knee and her feet on a stool.[65] The image, inspired by a painting by Antoine Pesne, is absurd in its earnest concern to reflect daily reality; it illustrates the limitations imposed when contemporary dress is transcribed literally. 'When people dress badly, art should leave their dress alone. What possible use could a sculptor make of your jackets and trousers and your rows of buttons?'[66] Nollekens did not fall into the same trap when he made a statue of Mrs Pelham after 1786 (the date of her death), to be placed in a circular mausoleum. The young woman, seen standing, is the image of virtue; her right hand placed under her chin, she wears a light robe in the classical manner with a veil which, as Nicholas Penny amusingly points out, has the appearance of a seductive scarf.[67] The sculptor has succeeded in portraying her by using a subtle kind of idealisation. The same technique can be found in Thorvaldsen (cat.110) and Bartolini.[68] Canova went even further, favouring allegorical portraits of women,[69] either by exchanging a real person for a deity, or by idealising the subject as a mythical figure (cat.132). Other artists followed him down this road, as if the qualities of the female model could best be expressed under cover of an abstraction or a mythological figure – the pretext for some incomparably elegant pieces: Pajou's *Nathalie de Laborde as Filial Piety* (1792; Private collection), Schadow's *Friederike Unger as Hope* (1801–02; destroyed in Berlin), Rauch's *Adelaïde von Humboldt as Psyche* (model 1810; completed in marble 1826, fig.18)[70] bring radiance to the period with their dainty, refined beauty.

Catching a likeness is a complex operation. Diderot reports: 'The portrait is so difficult that Pigalle told me that he never made one without being tempted to give up. In fact, the face reflects in particular life, character and physiognomy.'[71] The creation of either a portrait bust or a full-length statue poses two different challenges. The bust is essentially a fragment: placed on a pedestal

Fig.17
PIERRE-JEAN DAVID D'ANGERS
*Johann Wolfgang von Goethe*, 1829.
Plaster, H. 83 cm.
Galerie David d'Angers, Angers

Fig. 18
CHRISTIAN DANIEL RAUCH
*Adelaïde von Humboldt as Psyche*,
1810–26. Marble, H. 118 cm.
Schloss Tegel, Berlin

on a plinth, cut off at shoulder level or, more unusually, offering a representation of the arms (cat. 123), it offers itself to the spectator's gaze and can be studied from close up. Catching the likeness is important for the sculptor in this case in order to stimulate engagement between the sitter and the spectator.

Pliny reports that in ancient times busts were made from masks moulded to the face of their subjects, living or dead.[72] Cennini's treatise details the technical operations involved, and a number of sculpted portraits were made from masks in fifteenth-century Florence.[73] During the period under discussion here, which was characterised by the desire to reproduce nature exactly, we know that some sculptors took exact measurements with callipers of the chosen parts of their sitters' bodies,[74] and used masks taken from life (Houdon, Thorvaldsen) or death (Houdon, Nollekens, Banks, Chantrey, Sergel, Schadow, Thorvaldsen). Nollekens was famous for preparing plaster for a cast as soon as he read of the death of a famous man in the newspaper.[75] David d'Angers loathed this practice: 'Moulding from nature never renders the man. It has to be moulded through the brain of the artist.'[76] Houdon was so dependent on the physical presence of his sitters that he asked the Comte d'Angiviller to pose instead of his friend Turgot when Turgot was not available; or Governor Morris to substitute for Washington, whose stoutness he shared, when he had to finish his statue of the American president in Paris[77] (fig. 19). 'For Monsieur Houdon, all that is missing is the means of making his portraits speak; as far as resemblance is concerned, he never misses.'[78] Canova employed a subterfuge to portray the head of Clement XIV, whom he had never known: he used the bust by his colleague Hewetson, which was modelled from life.[79] Some artists, Chantrey for example, used the *camera lucida*, drawing the profile of the model as seen through the machine,[80] then drawing inspiration from it directly. The profile was considered the true vehicle of a likeness: according to Pliny, the origin of a portrait was the figure of a loved one carved in *bas-relief* on a wall;[81] for Lavater, it was the line of the silhouette which gave form and essence to the subject.[82] Some sculptors represented their models from one side, enlivening a portrait by giving a dynamic twist to the head, as in Ceracchi's marble *Reynolds* (Royal Academy of Arts, London) where the sitter looks over his shoulder,[83] or *Alexandrine of Prussia* by Rauch (Schloss Charlottenburg, Berlin).

It is the treatment of the eyes, however, which can bring extraordinary life to a face. We know that in the earliest Roman portraits, during the Republic and in the first century, the eyes were not incised because the iris and pupil were originally painted.[84] At the beginning of the second century, during Hadrian's reign, the contour of the iris began to be incised, breathing life into the face. In the modern period sculptors have oscillated between the two traditions. Bernini made repeated attempts to represent the gaze, using a great variety of techniques: hollowed or engraved irises, or irises ringed in relief, concave or convex pupils, or pupils suggested by a small piece of marble,[85] in an attempt to give immediate vitality. Mathon de la Cour became the champion of marked pupils in the eighteenth century,[86] when they were already the general rule in France and used by Lemoyne, Pajou and Caffieri. Houdon developed a particular technique by hollowing out the iris and detaching the pupil (cat. 53), following Bernini's practice in some of his marble pieces. Blank eyes still had their supporters – among them Canova, Thorvaldsen – who favoured the immaterial representation of the model.

Scientific research into likeness cannot be dissociated from an interest in what lay behind appearance. Although investigation into the expression of the passions revealing the interior man dated from the Renaissance (Della Porta), before it was studied systematically by Le Brun,

Fig. 19
JEAN-ANTOINE HOUDON
*George Washington*, 1785–92.
Marble, H. 188 cm.
Capitol, Richmond, Virginia

it was taken up in greater depth at the end of the eighteenth century. There was an interest in pathognomy – the study of the temporary effects of emotions on the face – and physiognomy – the study of the permanent form of facial features and the cranium as revealing of character – both sciences of bodily form interpreted as expressions of the soul.[87] A portrait made it possible to reveal the truth about the interior man. The writings of Lavater, translated rapidly into several languages and brilliantly illustrated, followed by the writings of Gall, were an inspiration to sculptors: from Messerschmidt, studying the defects of his face in the mirror (cat. 68) to David d'Angers, well versed in phrenology and the study of the cranium, both revealing the soul (cat. 153): 'Phrenology makes it possible to discern on the cranium of the individual the distinctive qualities of which the facial features are the result. The face is the mirror of man's faculties … A statue expresses the almost imperceptible nuances which are like a prism of the passions and infuse the physiognomy with that mysterious quality which only the artist's soul can feel.'[88]

The sculpted portrait developed and diversified considerably between 1770 and 1830. It found a home in large numbers of public and private spaces, and helped to establish new artistic formulae. When a masterpiece seemed to fulfil all the challenges it attained the status of a myth. Crowds jostling in the evening at Palazzo Borghese in Rome, trying to admire by torchlight Canova's beautiful Pauline as Venus Victrix[89] (fig. 20), were seeking a unique experience: the magic of an encounter with a marble statue of a recognisable person, the mystery of a place, the genius of the artist, the alliance of the flesh and the idea, and a tangible and intellectual encounter with beauty.

Fig. 20
ANTONIO CANOVA
*Pauline Borghese as Venus Victrix*, 1805–08.
Marble, H. 200 cm.
Galleria Nazionale della Villa Borghese, Rome

# III
# Between the Novel and History:
# French Portraiture towards 1835

SÉBASTIEN ALLARD

*'The painter's bread and butter'*

AT THE SALON OF 1833, reiterating the long litany of complaints voiced by the critics (beginning with Diderot), Auguste Jal waxed indignant about the growing number of portraits on display. 'What a superfluity of unworthy faces,'[1] he exclaimed. In fact, portraiture, considered as inferior in the academic hierarchy of genres, continued to develop after the end of the eighteenth century: by the beginning of the 1840s, portraits constituted as much as thirty per cent of the works on display. At the Salon of 1841, Louis Peisse counted five hundred portraits in a catalogue of two thousand paintings.[2] By about 1840 the portrait, more than landscape, could claim to be the modern genre *par excellence*. For those who clung to a more traditional view of art, inherited from neoclassical 'regeneration', this state of affairs was the sign of artistic (and possibly also social) decadence. The development of portraiture was proving detrimental to history painting, the *grand genre*, which, by exalting the actions of the illustrious

men of history, or the heroes of modern times, aimed to encourage the public to virtuous acts. Jal, an acute analyst, who was most unlikely to have regretted the Restoration of the monarchy, saw the type of constitutional regime adopted by France after 1830 as one of the causes of the decline of history painting and the rise of the portrait: 'The present form of government is the greatest obstacle to any broad development in the arts; constitutional art is art at a bargain price. It is right to preach economy; one should be frugal, but it is imperative that economy should not impinge on the civilising arts.'[3] In his opinion, by giving up large commissions,[4] the state was transferring the task of encouraging the arts to the private sector, where, in general, individual interest was allowed to take precedence over the general interest. The portrait now gave the ruling bourgeoisie the opportunity to impose its own triumphant image; while enormous history paintings, with their complex iconography, could no longer be accommodated in the modern

Fig. 21
ARY SCHEFFER
*Princess Mathilde*, 1844.
Oil on canvas.
Palazzo Pitti, Florence

home, in which comfort was the main aim. Individualism had succeeded general interest, which art was supposed to serve; the portrait flattered the pretensions of private individuals, even those considered to be historically insignificant. The cult of the great man had been succeeded by the cult of the individual: 'We do not belong with those people who castigate the mania for family paintings ... It is not the passion for portraits which should be attacked (portraits give work to so many artists), it is the pretensions of the people who pose,' fumed Delphine de Girardin in 1837. [5] Very shortly, in fact, the anonymity which had always been the rule in the Salon catalogues – the model in most cases being simply designated by his or her initials – turned into a game of recognition, indicating the importance now given to celebrity in social relations. A number of critics were quick to denounce the discrepancy between the apparent modesty of the biographical information given in the booklet and the ostentatious manner in which society women exhibited themselves at the Salon, covered in jewellery and wearing their smartest clothes like vulgar actresses: 'The Salon is full of women who reveal only a single letter of their name, yet bare their shoulders freely to the gaze of the general public,' remarked Alphonse Karr with some irony in 1840. [6] In Delphine de Girardin's text, the allusion to the family clearly contrasts the private value of the portrait with the public value of art in general. She gives us to understand that, with the great increase in the number of portraits exhibited, the Salon was acting more and more as a shop window for *le Tout Paris*, a kind of 'bazaar', and less and less as a showcase for the glorious national school. Jal argued in similar terms a few years earlier: 'I have seen all these family vanities displayed in handsome frames, one striving to outshine the next.' [7] By mentioning the frames he added a further nuance: the portrait was beginning to be viewed as a luxurious possession. Like a carriage and pair, a private residence or an opulent outfit, the portrait was beginning to be one of the accoutrements of the consumerism now gaining ground among the new ruling classes whose focal range, now no longer affected by the exclusivity of the court, was beginning to grow larger and more complex. Art appeared to be being reduced to a material possession. However critical Jal's comment, it bore witness to a genuine change. From the 1830s on, in fact, portraits began to be matched to ever more inventive frames. Sometimes this was the artist's own choice. Ingres, strongly influenced by Raphael's *Baldassare Castiglione*, designed frames that were both complex and opulent; their aim was to enhance and magnify the sitter whom the artist had treated with great discretion. More often, however, a frame could express a desire for social recognition. Anatole Demidoff thus embellished the austere portrait of his wife, Princess Mathilde (fig. 21), by Ary Scheffer, with a sumptuous border in gilded wood, made by the Pacetti brothers in Florence. His coat of arms, so nobly and advantageously displayed, seems to emphasise his own importance and also the social prestige of his marriage to a princess, celebrated four years earlier amid great pomp and circumstance.

The Salon thus became a place in which to exhibit oneself; here the public could court public notice, manifesting the new thirst for celebrity, now one of the criteria for social inclusion.[8] A more materialistic explanation might be advanced. The portrait, described by Jal as the *pot-au-feu du peintre* (the painter's bread and butter), made life possible for an artist and by its very nature accentuated the connection between art and money – the reverse of the myth of disinterested creation. During his first stay in Rome, Ingres, introduced by Marcotte into the company of rich foreigners (cat. 33), was able to live by painting portraits. It is noticeable that his output of portraits slowed down considerably during the 1830s, once his reputation as a leading light in the art world had been established.

Nevertheless, in his correspondence, he complains continually about the time this activity caused him to waste, preventing him from producing more ambitious works. Let beginners cut their teeth on this inferior genre, he says, they will gain something useful. The critics themselves viewed the portrait as the antechamber to history painting: it gave excellent practice in figure painting as a preparation for more elaborate compositions. No one would complain if painters with little skill specialised in portraits, even if gallery walls became cluttered with the burgeoning number of mediocre images. And great masters might allow themselves the odd portrait, as a way of gaining celebrity. The great painters of the Empire, Gros in particular, gave a good example of this in the first Salons of the Restoration. Deprived of the charismatic figure of Napoleon, Gros's inspiration faltered; for a while he attempted to remedy the matter by taking refuge in portraiture. The critics applauded his output. Nevertheless, that a gifted artist, desirous of fame and fortune, should deliberately sacrifice history painting to this more lucrative occupation seemed quite unacceptable, because the artist was thus placing himself in a position of economic dependency: 'For a man like M. Champmartin, whose history painting was not a success, to retreat to portraiture is absolutely fine; but, having painted *Gustave Wasa*, that he should merrily give up his glory to limit himself to a type of painting that *brings in money*, is what the public can never admit. This explains the lack of interest today in the works of M. Hersent.'[9] Charles Lenormant's remark reveals the contrast between glory, the traditional aim of the artist in the humanist concept of art, and its integration into a more modern network of economic relationships. The discredit attributed to the genre that 'brings in money' was aggravated by the subjection of the artist to the tyranny of a sitter desiring to expose himself (or herself) publicly: 'Is there anything more trying than the endless complaints of a simple woman of the world who is having her portrait painted?'[10] Even Ingres, who, after 1840, was able to choose his sitters, had to endure the remarks of Madame Moitessier: she complained that the artist had painted her eyes too close together and made her arms too fat. Her remark illustrates the submission of the painter to womankind and is more significant than it might seem at first glance. On the one hand, it demonstrates the way in which women were beginning to appear in public, asserting their rank, status and wealth rather than their motherhood (or their position as someone's wife). On the other, it shows that this self-display was experienced as a kind of prostitution, not only by the woman exhibiting herself 'to the gaze of the general public' rather than to select society, as Alphonse Karr pointed out, but also by the painter, whose duty it was to satisfy the whims of the model, to the extent sometimes of having

to abandon his artistic principles. Claude-Marie Dubufe, a society portrait painter *par excellence*, was the target of violent criticism. By posing his female subjects in conventional attitudes inspired by British or Venetian painting he was able to imbue them with wistful charm, deliberately sacrificing resemblance to a slightly stereotyped grace, maliciously described by Gustave Planche as 'marketable beauty'.[11]

The much-discussed tyranny of the sitter requires investigation, however. Although someone commissioning a portrait might with reason want to influence the process of creation, the relationship between the patron and the artist was far from unequivocal. Many painters were able to draw advantage from depicting a prominent personality: it could help to make their name or establish their position. The phenomenon was not new – in the previous century, Elisabeth-Louise Vigée-Lebrun had exploited this kind of publicity (cat. 22) with great skill – but it developed enormously with the rise of the press in the 1820s and the emergence of notoriety as a path to social acceptance. Although Ingres always professed the disdain of the history painter for this inferior genre, he provides a good example: in a letter, he recalls the role played in the building of his reputation by the portraits of Bertin and the Comte Molé: 'Because I painted portraits of Bertin and Molé, everybody now wants one; I've refused or avoided six of them because I cannot abide them.'[12] Worth noting also is that it was thanks to a portrait, *Monsieur Bertin* (cat. 156), that he was awarded the Légion d'honneur.[13] The stakes were much higher, of course, for artists who were just setting out: 'An artist without much reputation needs to exhibit paintings that draw public attention to him, so he has to choose his subjects with care. He approaches prominent people in the world of politics or the arts, or women who have acquired fame through their talent, beauty or some great adventure.'[14] In 1824, Delacroix boosted his reputation with a large

history painting on a contemporary subject: *The Massacre at Chios*. By the 1830s, sign of the times, a simple portrait could achieve the same goal. Interestingly, Jal identifies that the sitters likely to enhance the reputation of a young painter were within a polymorphous élite, removed from the exclusivity of court circles, and including a number of artists themselves. The most striking example of this phenomenon is perhaps the portrait of Father Dominique Lacordaire (fig. 22) by Théodore Chassériau. Chassériau went to Rome in the company of his friend Henri Lehmann. Lehmann told him of his desire to paint a portrait of the Dominican father who was enjoying great prestige with his socially orientated Catholicism. Conscious of what was at stake, Chassériau used his social contacts to gain permission to execute the portrait: 'This is a man about whom, I feel certain, people will go on talking … I needed to execute a fine portrait for the Salon. I'm pleased,' he wrote to his brother in 1840. Even though the painting was greeted with hostility by the critics and did not even have the good fortune to please the priest himself, Chassériau drew advantage from his sitter's aura. Lehmann took his revenge by becoming the favourite portrait painter to women of fashion who were also famous for their intelligence, like Marie d'Agoult (Musée Carnavalet, Paris) or the Princesse de Belgiojoso (whereabouts unknown). A number of artists who benefited at the outset from the prestige of certain sitters became attached to a particular milieu and in a sense became the spokesperson for that milieu. Thus Paul Delaroche came to establish an austere type of portrait, filling the frame to the edge in order to concentrate attention on the figure; these works were particularly suited to the upper bourgeoisie (especially the Protestant bourgeoisie) enjoying political power. The precise, simple composition of these portraits made them straightforward to reproduce by engraving, or even photography. The development of this formula exactly met the expectations of the milieu in which it was evolving. Although Delaroche's portrait of the Comte de Pastoret (1829; Museum of Fine Arts, Boston) still displays a neo-baroque energy and opulence, well adapted to the portrayal of the restored monarchy, the dignified austerity of his portrait of the Comte de Pourtalès-Gorgier (fig. 23) parades the moral principles and gravity of bourgeois society. In the most prestigious cases, the dependence of the painter on his model tended to be readjusted, if not entirely reversed. In the first half of the century, the aura attached to certain artists and the development of their reputation turned a few of them into modern demi-gods, madly sought-after by the great social figures of the day. At the Salon of 1833, Ingres, who was exhibiting *Louis-François Bertin*, was treated like a hero, as Lawrence had been in the past: 'Like Louis-Philippe in politics, M. Ingres this year has been the king of art,'[15]

Fig. 23
PAUL DELAROCHE
*Comte de Pourtalès-Gorgier*, 1846.
Oil on canvas, 123 × 78 cm.
Musée du Louvre, Paris, RF 1998-1

wrote Heinrich Heine. Sometimes the notoriety
of an artist ended by having an effect on the sitter.
After this date, for example, the father of the
*Apotheosis of Homer* became very selective about his
sitters, reversing the dependency of the portrait
painter on his subject. The reversal in this case
took on extreme proportions, in particular when
some who commissioned portraits had to wait
years before they were produced. Madame
Moitessier's first sittings began in 1844, but the
final painting (National Gallery, London) was
not delivered until 1856.

*Form and the Fugitive*
At the beginning of the 1840s there was a growing
tension between the view of portraiture as a genre,
traditionally regarded as inferior and held in
disrepute, and the increasing demand for portraits
from the élite, now reconstituted and enlarged.

In many respects the Revolution, having overturned
the ordered society of the *ancien régime*, had not yet
made its appearance in the fine arts; they were still
dominated by a strict hierarchy of genres. One of
the theoretical obstacles to the rise of the portrait
was the continued importance of the doctrine of
ideal beauty. In 1833, Laviron and Galbaccio
enunciated the problem: 'Our great men make
forms and not thinking heads; thus most people
persistently regard portraits as a secondary genre.'[16]
As the pre-eminent art of imitation, portraiture
was difficult to reconcile with aspiration towards
an ideal which was supposed to drive the arts and
to account for at least part of their nobility. In the
1830s, however, a number of critics attempted a re-
evaluation of the genre; they came to the conclusion
that imitation had been viewed in a manner that was
over-restrictive and superficial, valuing an abstract
idea rather than a way of feeling, a visionary

observation of reality: 'Art does not mean *trompe-l'oeil*, it means reproducing the individual character of each thing.' In their opinion, neoclassical painters preferred classical models to sitters who posed, and thus they often lost the character of the man or woman they were painting; they would make their subject smile in order to lend animation to his or her face and thereby introduce uniformity to the genre. The criteria for evaluating the genres therefore needed to be reassessed, and the hierarchy had to be reconsidered from a less formal point of view. To this end, Laviron summoned history to the rescue: in Venice, Giorgione, Titian and Veronese, 'although they had to paint canvases and murals of all sizes, and although they earned as much money as they could wish, took time to paint portraits, even when it was against their interest ... Viewed thus, and painted so that the intimate truth of every object is revealed, the art of the portrait is possibly the most difficult painting skill to acquire.'[17]

The hierarchy of the genres is no longer viewed exclusively as a formal structure, external to the subject of the painting, but as a manner of feeling. More recently, Thomas Lawrence, the object of a veritable cult among the younger generation, had demonstrated that one could be considered the greatest living painter even while just painting portraits. He exerted a decisive influence on France, not only on portraiture but also on painting in general. Young artists discovered in his paintings the power of colour and of bold drawing. An artist like Sébastien Rouillard managed to combine this influence with a neoclassical manner, reviving and enhancing it with colour. His *Comte Alexandre de Laborde* (fig. 24) reveals Lawrence's direct influence; this allows him to revive the portrait as inspired by David: the sitter cut off at the calf, firmly settled in his armchair and almost facing the spectator, the great curtain in the background, the table, the importance given to accessories and the brilliance of the handling – all suggest on the one hand a prototype directly inspired by Lawrence (fig. 25);

on the other hand the vividness of the face and the candour of the gaze belong to the French tradition. To many painters, Lawrence seemed in some basic way to point towards a reconciliation between a good likeness, the essential attribute of a portrait, and imagination, the essential attribute of the history painter. The full-length portrait in a landscape, inspired by British painting, enjoyed unprecedented success in France at this time. Although a number of artists such as Court or Dubufe managed to produce effects that were picturesque and superficial, others were able to introduce a genuinely heroic dimension. In 1822, Ary Scheffer, in his portrait of the Marquis de La Fayette (fig. 26), succeeded in conveying the aura of the great man with a far-away look and an animated sky. He was much more successful in this than Samuel Morse (1826; City Hall, New York) whose portrait of the same sitter, a few years later,

Fig. 26
ARY SCHEFFER
*Marquis de La Fayette*, *c.*1822.
Oil on canvas.
The Capitol, Washington DC

reused the pose of the *Apollo Belvedere*. Even more impressive, in Jean Gigoux's portrait of Charles Fourier (fig. 27), is the effect of the storm, the inhospitable rock on which the model is seated, and a deliberately restricted range of colours (leaden hues of brown and green). All these convey the strength of mind and the visionary nature of the father of utopian socialism. Henri Decaisne, the Belgian painter then working in Paris, also enlivened the portrait of *La Malibran as Desdemona* (1830; Musée Carnavalet, Paris) with a stormy sky that was well attuned to the melancholy pose of the heroine. The portrait was thus enriched with a narrative dimension which contrasted strongly with the symbolic pretensions of status portraits in which the accessories alone were sufficient to convey the social status of the model. In one sense, as Baudelaire was to emphasise later, the romantic portrait was contemporary with the romantic novel, the literary genre which towered above all others.

Delacroix interpreted the lesson of the great British painter in a more personal fashion. Fascinated by his work, he paid Lawrence a visit in London in 1825. Delacroix's portrait of his friend Schwiter (cat. 148) obviously betrays this influence, although it is adapted to more formal French taste. In June 1829 Delacroix published an article on Lawrence's *Pope Pius VII* (cat. 14) in the *Revue de Paris*. It was intended to be a passionate defence of the portrait.[18] According to Delacroix, the artist's imagination should make it possible for him to capture the sitter's expression, quite apart from any attention paid to his features or to social conventions. The status portrait should be obliterated by the image of the individual. Delacroix was indirectly emphasising the tension between the fugitive nature of this expression and the artificial pose. In his view, therefore, the portrait should be based on movement: 'It is about making him (the man) live, giving him movement and projection on this mute surface.'[19] In almost clandestine fashion, the portrait had abandoned the rhetoric of the eighteenth century and was now concerned with capturing a fleeting expression. At a time when Ingres was questioning finish as one of the principles of creation, since it supplied the distancing effect that was the characteristic of the painter himself, Delacroix was praising a slight fuzziness for the same reason. The light veil covering the artist's youthful portraits was an attempt to render the complex personality of his models. A climax is reached in the portrait of *Madame Simon* (fig. 28). As far as the composition and the concentration on the face are concerned, the painting is inspired by Rubens's portrait of Suzanne Fourment (Louvre, Paris), which Delacroix copied in 1828. However, the candour of Rubens's sister-in-law's gaze is replaced by the melancholy look of Madame Simon, with her tentative half smile. In addition, the original position of the head

Fig. 27
JEAN GIGOUX
*Charles Fourier*, Salon of 1836.
Oil on canvas, 235 × 162 cm.
Musée des Beaux-Arts et
d'Archéologie, Besançon

is here slightly shifted to the right, increasing the impression of mobility and instability. The personalities depicted by Delacroix are difficult to pin down: Baron Schwiter seems to be lurking behind the elegance of his dress; this manner of concealing expression behind a showy appearance was generally reserved for female portraits, but in this case the dandy muddies the borderline of sexual orientation.

Thus in the 1820s, under the triple tutelage of Venice, Flanders and England, the portrait was to benefit from developments encouraged by colourists able to reconcile imitation with imagination; by transcending social and physical appearances, and by abstraction of line, they were able to encapsulate the 'character' of their sitter. While Delacroix presents the instantaneous, the fleeting nature of a personality who is difficult to capture, Géricault uses the portrait as a means of introspection. In his portraits of children he introduces a ground-breaking interpretation of the genre: the notion of 'likeness' is no longer exclusively associated with the accurate reproduction of the subject's physical features. All his children look alike, but they genuinely express the childish psyche. Realism here has its modern psychological meaning. In his portraits of the mentally ill he refuses to give a name to his models and reduces them to the name of their illness, exploiting the tension between their strongly individualised features and a typological perception (fig. 29). The anonymous model is no longer portrayed in a situation that enhances or individualises him or her, but as a type, expressing the subject's battle with madness; the result conveys a feeling of desperate heroism. This new introspection in portraiture sometimes achieved a hallucinatory quality – as in Louis Boulanger's portrait of Achille Dévéria (fig. 30): the unbending frontal pose, the powerful chiaroscuro inspired by Spanish painting, and the emaciated face and large dark eyes produce a violently dramatic image. By presenting us with a painting that is deliberately

Fig. 28
EUGÈNE DELACROIX
*Madame Simon*, 1829.
Oil on canvas, 61 × 51 cm.
Staatliche Kunsthalle, Karlsruhe

confrontational, and by using such psychological hyper-realism, the artist turns the idealisation traditionally attached to the genre upside down. In accepting such a portrait, rather than something more bourgeois, the model confirms his status as a dandy. This is a borderline case, however, one which accentuates the problems associated with the balancing of character with form.

The search for the psychological identity of a model could in fact prove inimical to the integrity of appearances. Laviron and Galbaccio pointed out the danger at the Salon of 1833. When, for example, a great mind is imprisoned in a stunted body, they said: 'it should not be exaggerated so that it becomes an object of disgust, but the reverse: the moral power should be brought out and the physical deformity be subdued to this power.'[20] They viewed the portrait as a noble genre which was still, despite everything, subject to the constraints of the ideal; otherwise there was a danger that it would

Fig. 29
THÉODORE GÉRICAULT
*The Woman with Gambling Mania*,
1819–24. Oil on canvas,
77 × 64 cm.
Musée du Louvre, Paris

Fig. 30
LOUIS BOULANGER
*Achille Dévéria*, Salon of 1837.
Oil on canvas, 165 × 90 cm.
Musée du Louvre, Paris, 20028

be reduced to the level of caricature. They were unable fully to appreciate the bust of Paganini by David d'Angers (cat. 153), any more than could Gustave Planche, who exclaimed: 'He has produced the material version of a caricature.'[21] The inordinately enlarged skull and almond-shaped face testify to David's interest in phrenology and his intention to express the passion that motivated the great musician rather than an idealised, perfect beauty. The bumpy, violent, almost chaotic modelling, the sharp-edged cut below the shoulders and the sharply drawn profile produce a surprising presence; the artist, assisted by the famous bronze-founder Gonon, exploited the potential of bronze to almost grotesque – in the sense that Hugo used the word – effect: the material, hard and cold in reality, throbs with unexpected vitality. The artist has become a demiurge, and has imbued the portrait with the heroic dimension traditionally associated with history painting or monuments.

Delacroix, who was also fascinated by the virtuoso violinist, produced a strange work (fig. 31) in which the boundaries between the portrait and the caricature begin to dissolve, emulating perhaps the expressive exaggeration in which Paganini indulged during his concerts. The musician is represented full-length, playing his violin. Delacroix, like David d'Angers, attempts to capture the heroism of the virtuoso, whose fragile body seems to be lifted into the air by his internal compulsion to play. The posture itself is deliberately awkward, the colours dark, the limbs oversized and the face only sketched in; his enormous hands engulf the violin, which has grown too small. Delacroix translates the spectator's experience of the musician: the painting is jerky, vivid and coarse.

The portraits of Paganini by David d'Angers and Delacroix both reject abstract symbolism in favour of subjective experience – which includes audacities of presentation and form. We can measure the distance that separates these two artists from Ingres. In a drawing made in Rome in 1819, Ingres committed Paganini's features to paper (fig. 32). In his drawing, all trace of effort has disappeared. The virtuoso is depicted in a vigorous but classical pose, and has lost his tortured look. He holds the violin and bow as if they were a metaphor for his art; thus is the portrait joined to history, as in Ingres's allegorical portrait of *Cherubini Accompanied by the Muse* (1842; Louvre, Paris).

*Ingres and the Portrait: The Heroism of Modern Life*
Ingres succeeding in capturing the historical dimension of a portrait (in its modern sense) as no one else could. From the beginning of the 1830s the critics, during whose lifetime History had become a positive science, went to great pains to demonstrate the grandeur of the genre by attaching it to history. Far from being considered a defect, the established connection between a portrait and the

social, cultural, political and economic conditions that engendered it now became a quality. The portrait, in spite of its contingency, began to assert its role as a witness to the customs, habits and organisation of a particular society at a given moment. Many people came to reject the idea that only 'great men' deserved to have their portrait painted. Laviron and Galbaccio went back to the example of Venice again: 'Not a single painting of a courtesan by Giorgione ... omits to inform the spectator of the rank occupied in Venice by these women whom the Senate in its decrees referred to as *le nostre care meretrici*.'[22] A few years before Baudelaire, they grasped the value of modernity, understanding it as 'the transitory, the fleeting, the contingent; that half of art whose other half is the unchanging, the immutable': by portraying the men of the moment, the portrait was its principal vehicle. The eternal, immutable part remained – the half that was art.

Fig. 31
EUGÈNE DELACROIX
*Paganini*, c. 1832.
Oil on canvas, 45.7 × 30.5 cm.
Phillips Collection, Washington DC

Fig. 32
JEAN-AUGUSTE-
DOMINIQUE INGRES
*Paganini*, 1819.
Drawing, 29.8 × 21.8 cm.
Musée du Louvre, Paris, RF 4381 *recto*

The problem lay in marrying the two halves, in fusing the sitter who posed with the classical model who embodied the ideal.

To contemporary critics, the first obstacle was fashion in clothing. On the one hand, current developments in fashion, particularly male fashion, ruled out the picturesque: 'In truth, a great strength of idealisation is needed to create something beautiful and poetic in the midst of all the ugliness and all the poverty of form that we have arrived at,'[23] lamented Théophile Gautier in 1837; 'artists, alarmed by so much ugliness and poverty … have begun to make nude portraits, or portraits of people dressed as Roman emperors.'[24] On the other hand, fashion, by now an essential feature of representation, as Delphine de Girardin reports in her chronicles, was subject to incessant changes in taste. The arguments against modern dress advanced by Roger de Piles in the seventeenth century were reiterated: 'Portraits are deemed ridiculous six years after they have been painted.' Finally, at a more basic level, by constricting the body, modern costume militated against the 'bulging muscles' of the classical ideal, thus rocking the academic edifice to its foundations.

Ingres understood this and confronted these contradictions without flinching. Far from regarding the process of idealisation as transcendent, this supreme realist based his work on the accurate observation of the sitter, whom he regarded as a complete entity, including his expression, his posture and also his clothing. From this observation, rehearsed in drawing after drawing, he would reconstitute an ideal personality. Nothing demonstrates this better than the portrait of Madame Moitessier (1856; National Gallery, London), on which he worked, at first using a life model. In his portraits of women, for example the portrait of Madame Marcotte de Sainte-Marie (cat. 34), he used fashion as the structural framework of the composition, translating the vibrancy of the romantic silhouette into sinuous, abstract lines, exaggeratedly elongated, to emphasise the instability of the woman's character. The body becomes dissociated from form via a linear logic which affirms the graphic handwriting, now gaining autonomy. With the portrait of *Louis-François Bertin* (cat. 156), the alliance between the ephemeral and the eternal, realism and the ideal, reached such heights that the painting gained a historic title: *Monsieur Bertin*, witness to the tension between the individual value that is characteristic of the genre and its dimension as social metaphor. Although bundled into fairly unremarkable clothing, unrelieved by any medals or decorations to mark the status of the sitter, the body possesses an extraordinary presence, the modern version of the bulging muscles of classical antiquity. Ingres has eliminated all the traditional accessories of the status portrait; it is the power of the deliberately inelegant pose which predominates; the man asserts himself irrespective of his function, thus marking the discrepancy between being and representation which constitutes an early expression of modernity. Ingres is sensitive to the body – struggling heroically inside the straitjacket of modern dress (look at the pleats of the waistcoat) – yet he does not forget the character. Like the romantic Delacroix and David d'Angers, he has realised that to make himself heard he has to speak loudly and make use of expressive exaggerations: huge hands, a wart on the sitter's eye and strong contrasts of light and shade on his face. The exaggeration of the detail, on the verge of caricature, allows him to give real substance to a somewhat abstract representation. Unlike in the works of David d'Angers or Delacroix, in Ingres the search for character has no detrimental bearing on form: the drawing is still accurate, the whole is not sacrificed to the parts, nor the detail to the overall effect; the contours are clear and the silhouette stands out clearly against the neutral background. The synthesis of the ephemeral and the eternal has been achieved and the portrait as a genre can now take its place alongside history painting, as its equal. *Monsieur Bertin* was to become the symbol of modern France, dominated by a powerful, self-confident bourgeoisie. A number of contemporary critics drew attention to this. During the exhibition at the Bazar de Bonne-Nouvelle, the columnist of the *Journal des artistes* described the juxtaposition of *Monsieur Bertin* and *Comte Molé* (1834; Private collection, France) as 'an admirable summary of the principles of the revolution of 1789: the new man and the old gentleman, the descendant of Mathieu Molé and the creator of a race that yesterday was unknown'.[25] Was Ingres aware of this? The fact that he designed a frame (fig. 33) inspired by the frame made for Raphael's *Baldassare Castiglione* would seem to prove it. The frame has nothing to do with the sitters' vanity as described by Jal. In this case, it seems to help to emphasise the historic dimension of the portrait, which will one day be summoned to join its illustrious forebear on the walls of the museum. One might question the contempt professed by Ingres for the art of portraiture, and entertain certain doubts about the sincerity of his declarations. Why would he have battled for more than ten years with his portrait of Madame Moitessier, finally delivering an interim version (1851; National Gallery of Art, Washington DC) to his impatient client, in order to achieve a masterpiece, making interminable alterations? Perhaps we should call it irritation rather than contempt: Ingres, the 'pure classicist', may have realised that the traditional notion of the hierarchy of genres was on its way out; the portrait could have been his personal contribution to the advent of the modern subject.

Fig. 33
The frame of Ingres's
*Louis-François Bertin* (1832;
cat. 156) was inspired by that
of Raphael's *Baldassare
Castiglione* (Musée du Louvre,
Paris)

# IV

## The Role of Prints and Printmakers
## in the Diffusion of Portraiture

TIM CLAYTON

'THE PUBLIC ALWAYS STAND much indebted to *Scrapers* and *Engravers*', wrote a reviewer in 1772, 'as 'tis through the channel of this art that the works of the greatest painters are diffused over the world, and people of moderate fortunes enabled to become possessed of all the spirit of those works, otherwise allotted for the cabinets of the curious.'[1] This comment, made in a newspaper review of the prints exhibited by the Society of Artists of Great Britain in 1772, expressed two commonly held notions of the role of the print. Firstly, the translation of a painting onto hundreds of sheets of paper enabled people in distant countries to get a shrewd idea of what it looked like even though they would never see the real thing. The prints made from a painter's work represented him abroad and recorded his works for posterity. Secondly, being multiples and cheaper than fine paintings, prints enabled many (sometimes less affluent) art lovers to enjoy what would otherwise have been the exclusive property of a single individual.

In essence, when a print was made from a painting, that painting was published. As the Abbé Louis Gougenot argued in 1749: 'Engraving is to fine art what printing is to science and literature.'[2] In the case of a portrait, publication drew attention to the artist – chiefly the painter – and also to the sitter. They were published either in order to publicise one or other of these people, or because one or other of them was already so famous that there was an existing demand for images by them or of them. Conflicting motives sometimes caused difficulties. Publishers generally looked for profit, but a publisher might undertake unprofitable portraits as a favour to a painter, trusting that the painter would return the favour later by giving them the rights to a potential bestseller when such a subject came along.

This was an issue raised in 1783 by a prickly correspondence between Sir Joshua Reynolds and Valentine Green about *Mrs Siddons as the Tragic Muse* (see cat. 130).[3] Green was mezzotint engraver to

George III and to the Elector Palatine, an Associate of the Royal Academy, Professor of the Academy at Düsseldorf and a major international print merchant. He had already engraved a large number of prints after Reynolds, including the self-portrait that Reynolds presented to the Royal Academy in 1780 (cat. 73, fig. 34). Reynolds had barely begun his portrait of Mrs Siddons when Green asked permission to publish it. This, he said, was 'almost the only portrait, without the particular support of the party, which an engraver could venture on in the hope of being rewarded for his trouble'. The implication is that the publication of portraits was often subsidised by the sitter. For obvious reasons this was done discreetly and evidence has not usually survived. In this case, however, Green saw potential for a large profit.

He went through what he considered to be the proper channels, asking first the owner, Richard Brinsley Sheridan, then the sitter, Sarah Siddons, and finally the painter for permission to borrow the painting to engrave it. He got sympathetic but non-committal answers until Sir Joshua told him that he had given the portrait to Francis Haward (fig. 35). Reynolds said Siddons wanted it engraved in the fashionable dotted manner (known as stipple). Siddons told Green she thought he was doing it. Green accused Reynolds of lying. He pointed out that he merely wanted to publish the plate, and could have got anybody they wished to engrave it in whatever manner they desired. Finally, Reynolds sent Green a note from Siddons saying that 'the picture should be put into the hands of that person (whose name she cannot at this moment recollect) who has executed the print of the children from the picture by Sir Joshua [The Infant Academy] in so masterly a manner'. The note did not alter Green's conviction that Haward was Reynolds's suggestion, and Green never published another picture by Reynolds. It was natural and probably common for the painter to advise clients on the unfamiliar world of engraving, even though in theory they had the final say.

Fig. 34
After SIR JOSHUA REYNOLDS
*Self-portrait*, 1780.
Mezzotint by Valentine Green,
47.8 × 37.2 cm.
British Museum, London,
BM 1902-10-11-2356

Fig. 35
After SIR JOSHUA REYNOLDS
*Mrs Siddons as the Tragic Muse*,
1787. Dotted manner
by Francis Haward,
63.3 × 45.6 cm.
British Museum, London,
BM 1868-8-22-2128

One motive, therefore, driving the production of portrait prints was the greater glory of the painter. Jean Rouquet wrote in 1755 that, 'Painters of some reputation, as well as those who have none, seek equally to publicise themselves by this method; they get one or several of their portraits engraved in this style [mezzotint], under all sorts of pretexts, but their real motive is to advertise themselves.'[4] The previous year Reynolds himself published the first mezzotint from one of his paintings. Painters continued to use this method of attracting attention. When the American portrait painter Edward Savage came to London he published his own mezzotint of his portrait of George Washington. As a companion he published David Martin's portrait of Benjamin Franklin (cat. 45, fig. 36).

Another motive was simple profit. Printsellers, and engravers turned publisher like Green, were always on the lookout for plates that would make them money. However, in England at least, their access to images was limited by copyright. Between 1735 and 1767 copyright was available to a designer who wished to publish his design, simply by engraving his name and address and the date of publication on the print. This did not cover very many prints and profitable portraits were often copied. So, for instance, Reynolds's portrait of Sir Jeffrey Amherst (cat. 38) was engraved by James Watson and published by the engraver-printseller William Wynne Ryland. Since Amherst had commanded victorious British forces in America in the recent war, his portrait would sell. It was immediately copied in a smaller size for the printseller Robert Sayer (fig. 37).

This practice was outlawed the following year. In 1767 copyright was extended to all kinds of print and vested in the owner of the engraved copper plate, whether or not he was its designer. In *ancien-régime* France and in other parts of Europe copyright could be bought when it was deemed worthwhile. A foreigner could take out a French *privilège* for a print published in his own country, to protect it from French copies, but in general there was no such thing as international copyright. Prints made in one country were freely plagiarised in another if there was a market for copies of them.[5]

Printsellers' catalogues of stock give a clear idea of what they thought would sell. In the popular 14 × 10 inch size, in which he pirated Amherst, Sayer listed 'Royal Personages' followed by 'Statesmen, Land and Sea Officers, Patriots, Judges, &c.' followed by 'Beauties'.[6] The Beauties section contained a number of secondhand plates after Reynolds, together with celebrated courtesans and actresses. The most charismatic celebrities, at that time James Wolfe or Kitty Fisher, were offered in a wide range of styles and sizes from fine to crude and large to small with prices to match. They might be had as fans, as watchpapers (small prints to decorate the lids of watches) or hatmarks (to distinguish hats), or as woodcut sheets for display in cottages. Portraits of Washington, Nelson or Napoleon were available in an astonishing variety of forms.

Sitters who were not sufficiently charismatic to interest the printsellers might choose to subsidise the publication of their own portraits, or even publish them themselves. This might be done for self-publicity: an extreme example is James Gillray's caricature *Metallic Tractors* (fig. 38). It appears that Benjamin Perkins secretly commissioned a caricature of himself using the metallic tractors invented by his father Elisha Perkins of Plainfield, Connecticut, as part of his campaign to sell them in London.[7] A more common pattern was the 'private plate' where the sitter bought the copper plate outright, together with a number of impressions printed from it. These were usually to be given to friends.

Once a decision to publish had been taken the next stage was to choose the medium. The choice depended chiefly on the number of impressions that were required or might be sold. Engraving was

prestigious and an engraved plate would yield thousands of impressions, but the process took considerable time and was expensive in consequence. Scraping a mezzotint took far less time, was relatively cheap and produced beautiful results, but quality deteriorated rapidly as the plate wore with printing. The engraver needed to refresh the plate every fifty impressions or so and the total yield might be only five hundred without major rework. After about 1770 portraits were often executed in the dotted manner. Dotted plates printed larger editions than mezzotints, but took much less time to complete than line-engravings. In the nineteenth century steel plates were employed to extend the print run of mezzotints and small engravings. They produced rather harsh, metallic results. A final option employed from about 1820 onwards was lithography, where the image was drawn on stone. This was cheap and

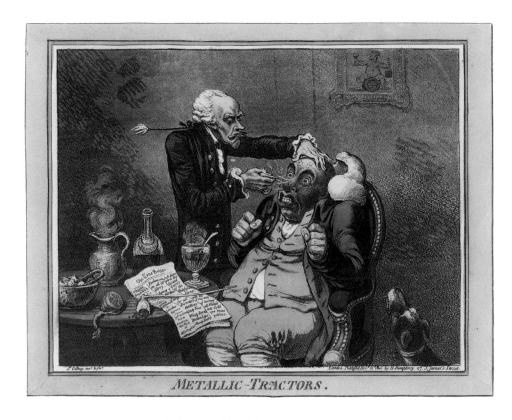

METALLIC·TRACTORS.

Fig. 38
JAMES GILLRAY
*Metallic Tractors*, 1801. Etching with aquatint, 26.7 × 33.3 cm.
National Portrait Gallery, London

the print run almost infinite, but the image lacked the crisp clarity of the traditional processes.

Bringing out a print normally required the agreement of the painter and the sitter as well as the loan of the painting. It was a collaborative process in which the engraver periodically took 'progress proofs' to check his work and invite comments and corrections. In England plates published by the artists were usually sold by subscription. An advertisement would invite those who might be interested to see the original painting and, possibly, proofs of the print at the engraver's studio, before giving him their name and address and, if they wished to subscribe, a deposit of half the final price. Subscription was a device that helped the artists make contact with admirers who might sustain future projects. Some engravers built up a stock of their own copper plates and became small-scale publishers. Others took their profit from the subscribers and then sold the plate to a printseller.

The market for high-quality prints by famous artists or of famous people was international. Traditional producers like Rome, Augsburg and Amsterdam remained important, but were dwarfed by the dominant centres of London and Paris in the period. Publishing houses, often backed by the local prince, were being set up all over Europe. In the United States a number of engravers and printsellers also established businesses modelled on London, but American commissions for sophisticated prints were usually placed in Europe, where the better American-born painters usually elected to work.

In London, Paris and smaller centres advertisements announcing the publication of

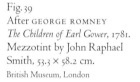

Fig. 39
After GEORGE ROMNEY
*The Children of Earl Gower*, 1781.
Mezzotint by John Raphael
Smith, 53.3 × 58.2 cm.
British Museum, London

prints appeared in newspapers and other journals. Various review journals repeated the news to a wider audience. The most important in the German-speaking world was the *Neue Bibliothek der schönen Wissenschaften und der freyen Künste*, which between 1765 and about 1795 reviewed 2,200 English prints, a similar number from France, and smaller numbers from every other producer in the world. So, for instance, Sir Joshua Reynolds's self-portrait (cat.73), presented to the Royal Academy in 1780, was engraved and published by Valentine Green in December 1780 and reviewed in the *Neue Bibliothek* for the first part of 1781.[8] At that time it was listed as a new print in the stock of C. Bremer of Braunschweig.[9] In 1787 it appeared in a printed list of the stock of Teodoro Viero of Venice.[10] All major European printsellers maintained a significant stock of fine contemporary English and French prints. In Philadelphia in 1786 there was an exhibition of prints after Reynolds imported from Boydell in England.[11] Understandably, there was less of a market abroad for English portraits than for prints with subjects taken from art or literature; if foreigners did not know who the sitter was, they would not be interested unless the engraving or painting was particularly fine in its own right. *The Children of Earl Gower* (fig.39), published in 1781 and reviewed in 1783, was regarded as a masterpiece by John Raphael Smith as well as a fine painting by George Romney (cat.124), and sold on that basis.[12] As they circulated around the globe, prints communicated new ideas and styles. They were instruments of enlightenment, informing people of developments in other parts of the world.

The most dependable consumers for fine prints were collectors. Art lovers constructed albums of works by individual painters or engravers, with prints bound together or pasted in. Print collecting reflected and disseminated the idea of 'Taste'. A discriminating knowledge of the fine arts was held to be an important element in the education of a polite lady or gentleman.

As such notions of politeness spread across cosmopolitan, *ancien-régime* Europe, the market for prints expanded accordingly.

Other, older patterns of collecting portrait prints coexisted with such artistic arrangements. Prints were arranged – again, usually pasted into albums – in order to document history, usually nation by nation. Roger de Piles, whose remarks in his *L'Abrégé de la vie des peintres* (1699) were widely influential, recommended a system invented by the French collector François-Roger de Gaignières:

> Firstly, portraits of sovereigns who have ruled a country, then princes and princesses who descend from them, those who have held some considerable rank in government, in the Church, in the army, at court: those who have distinguished themselves in the professions, and those have who have played some part in historic events.[13]

Variations on this system can be traced in surviving British portrait collections, such as those of Samuel Pepys and George Clarke.[14] In Britain especially, portrait collecting became a passion. Joseph Ames's *Catalogue of English Heads* (1748) listed 2,000 English portrait prints. James Granger's *A Biographical History of England ... adapted to a methodical Catalogue of Engraved British Heads* (1769) further stimulated interest, adding women and notorious characters from low-life to De Piles's categories. It was followed by H. Bromley's *A Catalogue of Engraved British Portraits* (1793).[15]

The enthusiasm for portrait collecting gathered pace throughout the period and sustained the careers of several specialist dealers in the field. One of the most prominent was James Caulfield, who specialised in Granger's twelfth class of 'Persons of both Sexes, chiefly of the lowest order of the People, remarkable from only one Circumstance in their Lives; namely such as lived to a great Age, deformed Persons, Convicts, etc.' These were often the rarest prints. His *Portraits, Memoirs, and Characters of Remarkable Persons* (1790–95) provided modern facsimiles of rare, old prints. He also published a *Catalogue of Portraits of Foreigners who have visited England* (1814) and a *Gallery of British Portraits* (1814). Caulfield edited the fifth enlarged edition of Granger in 1824. It was Caulfield's market that Henry Angelo had in mind when he remarked in 1828 on the fierce competition between collectors who 'contend for a base head-piece to a penny licentious ballad, of the age of Charles the Second, at any price'.[16]

In this field, as in others at this time, Britain led the way, but great collections were also formed abroad. Examples of continental guides are Georg Wolfgang Panzer's *Verzeichniss von Nürnbergischen Portraiten aus allen Staenden* (1790), or P. Lelong's *Bibliothèque historique de la France* (1809). In addition to 27,000 prints arranged by artist, Georg Friedrich Brandes, the official in charge of the University of Göttingen, possessed 15,000 'Portraits de Savans & Personnages distingués dans les lettres' when, having become blind, he offered his collection for sale in 1790.[17] They were pasted onto atlas paper and bound in red leather.

Many prints were bought by collectors, pasted into albums or stored in portfolios and perused at leisure for amusement or instruction. Many others were bought for display. Portrait prints might decorate a wall merely because they were beautiful, but often the choice of portrait was significant and conveyed a message. There were classical precedents, for instance, for displaying the portrait of a patron. Pliny the Elder remarked on 'the rooms and halls of private houses becoming so many public places [as] clients begin to honour their patrons in this way'.[18] Friendships might be celebrated in a similar manner, while a monarch's portrait was very often displayed as a badge of loyalty. Jacques-Louis David's portrait of Napoleon in his study (cat. 24) was frequently engraved, chiefly reduced to head and shoulders. It became a badge of loyalty, not only to Napoleon I while he ruled, but also to his memory among later Bonapartists.

# Catalogue plates

# I

## Portraits of Sovereigns
## and Heads of State

CHRISTOPHER LLOYD

THE MOST IMPORTANT IMAGE OF a head of state in the period 1760–1830 was the portrait made at the time of the assumption of power. Known as the 'state portrait', this combines a convincing likeness with an assertion of authority and an indication of dynastic continuity expressed in a visual language accessible to all. The full-length figure stands resplendent in coronation robes with royal regalia (crown, sceptre, orb, sword of state, orders) clearly evident and is shown in a spacious, timeless setting, usually an interior comprising a column, a furled, embroidered curtain with tassels and pieces of gilt furniture. The state portrait was for public display and was replicated for the widest possible circulation.

The compositional pattern followed precedents established in the seventeenth century by artists such as Rubens, Van Dyck, Velázquez and Rigaud (fig. 40), who were in turn developing ideas originally explored in the Renaissance. The effectiveness of the state portrait depended on the skill with which the constituent elements were manipulated without negating their significance. While Ramsay, Duplessis, Callet (cat. 8) and Lawrence (cats 4, 13, 14) work within the tradition, Eriksen (cat. 7) daringly views Catherine II from below and Goya (cat. 11), after the Bourbon restoration, places Fernando VII isolated against a plain background. These portraits have a theatrical air: the figures are on parade, often frozen in striking poses, with the body hardly discernible through the cascading folds of voluminous robes.

The artist's task was to balance out the specificity of the likeness with the universality of the context. If necessary, poses could be reused. Lawrence's state portrait of George IV (cat. 13), for example, was a bold reworking of the same figure wearing the robes of the Order of the Garter. So ingrained did the compositional formula for the state portrait become that it could be used in different countries and transferred from one political context to another: the gesture indicating the table in Stuart's image of George Washington (cat. 5) also occurs in the portrait of Napoleon as First Consul by Gros (Musée de la Légion d'Honneur, Paris) and later in that of George IV by Lawrence. These portraits should be interpreted as personifications of rulership in which the figure is in addition the incarnation of the country over which that rulership is being exercised. Apart from the need for self-presentation, it was also important that the portraits retained their potency even in the ruler's absence.

The iconography of the sovereign was extended further in official portraits made at intervals during the reign. Such portraits were not necessarily painted by artists with an official position at court, and a greater variety of pose, accessories and formats was expected. Some reference to status is still maintained in the robes or the depiction of a suitable occupation, but this was also an opportunity for making fresh insights into different aspects of sovereignty without recourse to allegory as had been the rule in previous centuries. Less official pursuits and private interests became acceptable subjects. The changing role of sovereigns – indeed, the threat to long-established political systems – opened up many new possibilities for artists. Reynolds, who, even as the first President of the Royal Academy, did not have a happy relationship with its patron George III, chose formal settings for his official portraits of the King and Queen Charlotte (cats 2, 3), but in other pairings of George III and Queen Charlotte by West, Gainsborough and Beechey the exterior settings hint at a narrative to which the figures can be related. At the same time, it was not unusual for the consort to be painted alone with one or more of her children. These images combine dynastic concerns with feelings of sensibility towards children that were being advocated during the second half of the eighteenth century. In this respect Ramsay's portrait of *Queen Charlotte with Her Two Eldest Children* (*c*.1764; Royal Collection, Windsor) is the exact counterpart of Vigée-Lebrun's *Marie-Antoinette and Her Children* (Musée National du Château, Versailles). At the Spanish court Goya was particularly perceptive in his depictions of Charles III and, later, his son Charles IV, in hunting clothes. By offsetting the dignity of the costume and the royal associations of the chase with the informality of the poses and the landscape backgrounds the artist is able to capture a more personable aspect of the monarchs' characters lacking in state portraits. By contrast, equestrian portraits are clearly intended to stress military valour and powers of leadership (cat.1). Even if the ruler in question never set foot on a battlefield, sovereignty included the responsibilities of a Commander-in-Chief.

Although Lawrence was capable of painting George III (cat.4) and Queen Charlotte with the greatest confidence, he belonged to a new generation and so felt greater sympathy with George IV. His portrait of that king, now in the Wallace Collection in London (fig.41), is notable for its relaxed pose and open demeanour: the monarch is seen, as it were, off duty or at home, with the viewer being admitted into his presence almost like a friend. Unlike state portraits, these official images, although frequently included in public exhibitions, were not hung in formal apartments and were more suitable for the private domain. These representations were readily understood and as such they reflect a change in attitudes to monarchy, a move away from traditional concepts based on sanctification and heroism towards what might be termed a gradual process of 'embourgeoisement'.

The most obvious sign of this change is the development of the composition known as the royal conversation piece. Although seventeenth-century precedents exist, it was only during the second half of the eighteenth century that the royal conversation piece became widespread. The purpose was to group members of a royal or princely family together, often incorporating several generations, in a unified space that visually could be interpreted as a continuum of the viewer's own space. A prime exponent of the royal conversation piece in Britain was the German artist Zoffany, whose paintings of George III and Queen Charlotte with their children (cat.87) are uncompromisingly domestic. Usually portrayed in private apartments, absorbed in their own pastimes and surrounded by their own possessions, the sovereigns in such works are seen as part of a family with which others can readily identify. This implication was particularly significant in the case of George III, who regarded

Fig.40
HYACINTHE RIGAUD
*Louis XIV*, 1701.
Oil on canvas, 27.7 × 19.4 cm.
Musée du Louvre, Paris, 7492

the British people as part of an extended family over which he presided. A tension exists in the royal conversation piece, however, as a result of the balance between the appearance of being removed from society and yet part of it; of being privileged and yet ordinary; and of being the personification of an elaborate system of belief and yet at the same time merely human. The informality of these compositions prefigures photography, and to a certain extent there is a shared sense of purpose. More importantly, they illustrate the adjustments that monarchy needed to make in order to retain its credibility in a rapidly changing society.

Ecclesiastical authorities paid as much attention to personal iconography as secular rulers. Indeed, the roll-call of artists who have been involved with the papacy through the centuries is awe-inspiring – Raphael, Titian, Velázquez, Bernini, among others. Pope Pius VII was one of the greatest popes in history, known as much for his sanctity as for the part he played in the downfall of Napoleon. His papacy was a perfect demonstration of a positive alliance between spiritual and temporal power.

Fig. 41
SIR THOMAS LAWRENCE
*George IV*, 1822.
Oil on canvas, 270.5 × 179 cm.
Wallace Collection, London

The success of his policy won universal renown and led to the resurgence of Rome as the religious and cultural capital of Europe. Although Pius VII had been painted by David and Cammuccini and had been sculpted by Canova (cat. 15), George IV commissioned Lawrence to make a portrait of the Supreme Pontiff as part of a series (now in the Waterloo Chamber at Windsor Castle) commemorating those statesmen, commanders and diplomats who had formed the alliance against Napoleon. The circumstances were unusual, as no British artist had previously been asked to make a portrait of a pope, least of all a Protestant painter. Lawrence's experience in painting full-lengths and the sympathetic accord that arose between artist and sitter when they met in Rome resulted in one of the finest formal portraits of the period (cat. 14). To a certain extent Lawrence was helped by the unusually large scale of the portrait which enabled him to choose a dramatic but characteristic pose for the sitter. He shows the seated figure of the Pope seen slightly from below. The capacious papal throne encases the hunched, ageing form of Pius VII who looks away from the viewer out of the composition. The Pope seems alert both in pose and gaze, even if pale and fatigued. The sag of his body belies the sharpness of his mind. Lawrence's eye for detail – the ring, the slippers, the white pileolus (*zucchetto*) – increases the impact of the whole. The Pope is seated in an interior, but Lawrence cleverly suggests the cultural authority of Rome in addition to the spiritual by alluding to the great collection of antique sculpture – much of it recently returned from Paris – which Pius VII was busy installing in the Vatican galleries. Rich in colour, replete with stylistic bravura and redolent with recent history, Lawrence's portrait fulfilled all expectations and was widely admired in Rome before it was sent to Britain.

Sculpture was a discipline in which it was much harder to be innovative. Scale, materials, expense and limitations of form imposed constraints, added to which was the tradition of close adherence to classical prototypes such as the *Marcus Aurelius* in Rome and the *Regisole* in Pavia. Equestrian monuments and free-standing statues amounted to very public displays of monarchical power, more so than painted portraits in so far as sculpture of this type was meant to be seen in open spaces in which people mingled and crowds gathered. The same characteristics apply wherever such sculptures were erected – Britain, France, Germany, Poland, Scandinavia, Spain or Russia. They were particularly evocative demonstrations of power applicable throughout Europe, but especially in France from the reign of Louis XIV onwards. The number of statues in honour of Louis XV was legion. The tendency in all of these was towards greater realism in the design with reduced emphasis on allegorical features. Their visual language was shared and emanated from antiquity. Such monuments – by their sheer scale if nothing else – exuded a sense of domination, but not necessarily domination by force. Armour and trampling hooves gave way to ideas of protection and moral responsibility, expressed by the direction of a glance or a simple gesture such as an extended hand. Significantly, the lively equestrian monument of Peter the Great by Falconet in St Petersburg was commissioned by Catherine II, and in this statue naturalism is married to idealism. The monuments – equestrian or otherwise – commemorating George III, like those created in honour of Louis XV, were inspired by Roman models both in pose and drapery. Carlini (cat.1) stresses military aspects, while Westmacott's use of the *Marcus Aurelius* type (Windsor Great Park) suggests beneficent paternalism. The equestrian sculpture of George IV by Chantrey (Trafalgar Square, London) shows the monarch in contemporary dress, but it lacks any sense of movement, not so much for the perfectly valid reason that George IV was seriously overweight but more because the tradition itself, even in the capable hands of Chantrey, was almost exhausted.

The portrait bust constituted another form of sculpture that was produced in large quantities. The survival of so many examples is partly due to the fact that a successful bust was often widely replicated. Antique sources were again instrumental, but a far greater emphasis was put on individual features and characterisation. The variety of the textures and the liveliness of the techniques that distinguish busts by Nollekens, Bacon, Houdon and Chantrey yield an astonishing array of technical skills which corresponds to the forceful personalities and varied careers of the sitters. Shubin (cat.6) is severely classical and crowns Catherine II with a laurel wreath; Boizot (cat.9) reveals the elegance of Marie-Antoinette, especially in the floral garlands in her hair; and Adán (cat.10) overloads Charles IV with robes which distract from his playful expression.

The portrait bust is a very concentrated art form, but there was, nonetheless, considerable scope in how it was displayed. A bust could be mounted on a base for positioning on a piece of furniture or else supported by a pedestal. If seen stretching in a line down a corridor or in a gallery, or arranged along the top of library bookcases, busts become animated and seem to be in conversation among themselves. Often when they are so grouped the intention is to create a hall of fame or a pantheon of heroes. Busts were frequently commissioned in the late eighteenth century and early nineteenth century for this specific purpose.

Napoleon commissioned artists with the same enthusiasm as he appointed marshals. His personal iconography is one of the most extensive ever created for an individual and is a perfect demonstration of the way in which art could be harnessed to political and military ambition. It is fortunate that the quality of the artists Napoleon chose – David, Ingres, Gros, Canova, Prud'hon – matched the scale of that ambition. The iconography was not limited to the various stages of

Napoleon's ascendancy – General, First Consul, Emperor – but was also retrospective, which widened its terms of reference to include scenes from his childhood. Also incorporated within it were other members of his extended family. Artists were asked to portray Napoleon not only as a brilliant military commander, but also as a magnanimous ruler and statesman, risking his life on the battlefield and toiling long hours in his study on behalf of his subjects (cat. 24). There is a clear indication in the formal portraits that, although Napoleon's power was vested in this world, it was ordained by a higher authority. All these commissions were executed at immense speed as artists endeavoured to keep up with the frantic progression of Napoleon's ascendancy. Furthermore, the outpouring of art in his honour was by no means only commissioned by Napoleon himself. Even after his death his legend continued to grow, giving rise to further image-making.

Napoleon's control over his artists was absolute. No visual art form was neglected – portraiture,

narrative painting, sculpture, prints – and no source was left untouched. The art of the classical, Byzantine, Carolingian, Renaissance and Baroque eras, as well as more recent art, was plundered for propaganda purposes in the task of establishing Napoleon's personal iconography; in the end this proved to be successful and enduring. Although Napoleon preferred realistic representations, artists often resorted to Christian and pagan allegory to heighten the effect. Yet what set out to be dynastic propaganda could, in works by artists of the calibre of David and Ingres, transcend the limitations of its immediate, short-term aim to be numbered among the most authoritative and lasting images in European art.

The portraits of sovereigns and heads of state produced between 1770 and 1830 mark the summation of this particular tradition in painting. Arguably, the skills of the artists and the personalities of their sitters have never been so closely matched. The resulting power of these portraits has never been surpassed.

→ 1    AGOSTINO CARLINI, Model for an equestrian statue of George III.    1768–69. Plaster, 87.6 × 38.1 × 59.7 cm.
Royal Academy of Arts, London, 03/1684

2   SIR JOSHUA REYNOLDS, *George III.*   1779. Oil on canvas, 277.4 × 185.5 cm.
Royal Academy of Arts, London, 03/1303

3   SIR JOSHUA REYNOLDS, *Queen Charlotte*.   1779–80. Oil on canvas, 278.2 × 185.7 cm.

Royal Academy of Arts, London, 03/1304

↗ 4   SIR THOMAS LAWRENCE, *King George III.*  1792. Oil on canvas, 275.6 × 153.7 cm.
The Herbert, Coventry, CH 23

→ 5   GILBERT STUART, *George Washington* (also known as the Munro-Lenox portrait).  *c.*1800. Oil on canvas, 241.3 × 162.6 cm.
Judy and Michael Steinhardt, New York. Courtesy Richard L. Feigen & Co.

← 6    FEDOT IVANOVICH SHUBIN, *Catherine II, Empress of Russia.* 1771. Marble, 80.5 × 33.5 × 30 cm.
         Victoria and Albert Museum, London, A.32-1964

↑ 7    VIGILIUS ERIKSEN, *Catherine II, Empress of Russia.* *c.*1765. Oil on canvas, 275.9 × 202.2 cm.
         Lent by Her Majesty The Queen

← 8   ANTOINE-FRANÇOIS CALLET, *Louis XVI.*  1789. Oil on canvas, 246 × 192 cm.
      Collection du Musée d'Art Roger-Quilliot, Ville de Clermont-Ferrand

↗ 9   LOUIS-SIMON BOIZOT, *Marie-Antoinette, Queen of France.*  1781. Marble, 90.5 × 53.6 × 36 cm.
      Département des Sculptures, Musée du Louvre, Paris, RF 4515

↑ 10    JUAN ADÁN MORLÁN, *Charles IV, King of Spain.*    1797. Marble, 87 × 62 × 40 cm.
Patrimonio Nacional, Palacio Real de Madrid, 10002969

→ 11    FRANCISCO DE GOYA Y LUCIENTES, *Ferdinand VII in Royal Robes.*    c.1815. Oil on canvas, 208 × 142.5 cm.
Museo Nacional del Prado, Madrid, 735

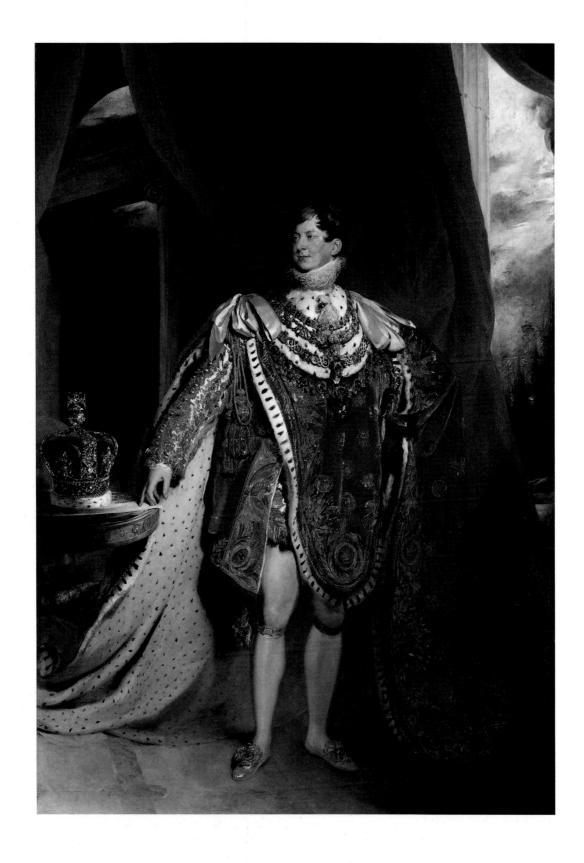

← 12   JEAN-AUGUSTE-DOMINIQUE INGRES, *Napoleon I on the Imperial Throne.*   1806. Oil on canvas, 260 × 163 cm.
Musée de l'Armée, Paris, 5420

↑ 13   SIR THOMAS LAWRENCE, *George IV.*   1822. Oil on canvas, 289.6 × 200.7 cm.
Lent by Her Majesty The Queen, RCIN 405918

↑ 14   SIR THOMAS LAWRENCE, *Pope Pius VII.*  1819. Oil on canvas, 269.4 × 178.3 cm.

Lent by Her Majesty The Queen, RCIN 404946

→ 15   ANTONIO CANOVA, *Pope Pius VII.*  1806. Marble, 69.5 × 70 × 30 cm.

Promoteca Capitolina, Musei Capitolini, Rome, PRO 83

# 2

# The Status Portrait

SÉBASTIEN ALLARD

BETWEEN 1770 AND 1830, portraiture as a genre was struggling to escape from the inferior position to which it had been condemned by academic hierarchies. Critics, theorists and the artists themselves all expressed very clearly the contradictions inherent in the genre: the tension between immutable beauty and ephemeral resemblance; between respect for social and sexual conventions and the expression of an individuality that could not be reduced to a type; and between the private dimension of the genre and its public expression. The increasing numbers of portraits to be found in exhibitions in both France and Britain seemed to be inversely proportionate to the social or historical merit of the sitters. The upshot of this was a certain 'democratisation' of the genre, which went hand in hand with the emergence of a definition of the individual as himself, or herself, without reference to what he or she might represent socially; there was a risk that this might strip the portrait of moral value. A firm line had to be established, therefore, between 'family' portraits, representing ordinary people, and portraits of people whose function, status or destiny singled them out as illustrious; in other words, between the private, memorial function of the genre and its exemplary function.

The exemplary nature of the 'status portrait', to apply to painting a category devised by Diderot in his *Entretiens sur le fils naturel*,[1] brought about a definite levelling of the codes of representation, and allowed the spectator to identify, as well as the sitter, his or her function, and, as well as the individual, his or her social type. This is why the statesman or government minister is generally represented seated with his hand on a table on which documents are displayed, adhering to a convention established during the Renaissance. Copley's portrait of William Murray (cat. 18) is a fine example. The posture of the Minister of Justice is borrowed directly from a history painting, *The Death of the Earl of Chatham* (1779–81;

National Portrait Gallery, London), painted by Copley a few years earlier. Henceforward, the historical dimension of a portrait could be found in attitude or context alone, independent of any narrative purpose or commemorative pretext. The same general characteristics and conventional accessories can be found in the portrait of the minister Calonne, by Vigée-Lebrun (cat. 22), or the portrait of Guillemardet, the French ambassador to Madrid, by Goya (cat. 16). In Goya's portrait, which is dominated by the colours of the Republic, the codes have been turned on their head in the name of expression: although the table and insignia are present, the model's relaxed pose (he has his legs crossed) symbolises the new man, full of determination and not yet civilised by court protocol. However significant a stereotype might be, a portrait was also the outcome of the manner in which it was painted and the price paid for what the painter was commissioned to represent. In addition, there was the problem of balancing respect for iconographic conventions, which translated the permanence of the social 'status' (the type), with the part played by novelty, which conveyed the individuality of the model. The portrait of Calonne confused some visitors to the Salon, who recognised the man but not the minister. The dialectic between the private dimension of the portrait and its public ambition could not have been expressed more clearly. The portrait bust, which was free of any narrative intent, proved perfectly adapted to the status portrait, yet it was afflicted with the same tension. The interest paid by Mérard to the representation of the insignia of the Prince de Conti (cat. 20), the fullness of his figure and his lofty gaze all convey the status of the 'prince of royal blood' in an ordered society; at the same period, in Houdon's more down-to-earth portrait of Benjamin Franklin (cat. 44), the model's highly individual features express the democratic and bourgeois principles of the young American republic. Shortly after this, and particularly in

Britain where national life was more obviously dominated by economic matters, the new bourgeoisie, hungry for social recognition, adopted the conventional codes. Long before Ingres painted Monsieur Bertin (cat.156), Wright of Derby's portrait of Richard Arkwright (fig.42) provides us with a striking example. The sitter, a skilled and wealthy businessman, is portrayed seated beneath an official-looking curtain as if he were a top government official. On the table beside him, the customary pens, papers and letters have been replaced by a machine of his own invention for spinning wool. In spite of the attention paid to proprieties in the portrait, the sitter's somewhat slack pose betrays his background as a well-meaning member of the bourgeoisie, as, later, Monsieur Bertin's posture was to assert the authority of the bourgeoisie who had come to power in France.

Faced with this appropriation by a new bourgeois class of some of the codes of the status portrait, and of the external signs of celebrity, the exercise of a certain discretion (the equivalent of euphemism in literature) came to identify genuine members of the upper classes in the context of the aristocratic portrait. Sometimes it is not so much what is shown as the manner in which it is shown that betokens the dignity and exemplarity of the illustrious man, leaving aside any official function or brilliant feat of arms. David Solkin has demonstrated the way that, by appropriating an antique prototype – the statue of *Tiberius in a Toga* (Louvre, Paris), seen making the gesture of *ad locutio* – Ramsay and then Reynolds managed to enhance the English aristocratic portrait with a public dimension;[2] the sitter, whether the Scotsman Norman MacLeod (1748; Dunvegan Castle, Skye) or Commodore Keppel (1753; National Maritime Museum, London), thus inherited the *gravitas* of the Roman magistrate. The portrait of Omai by Reynolds (1776; Private collection) represents the supreme culmination of this phenomenon:

'a general air of antiquity' transforms the Polynesian, a scientific curiosity, into a distinguished subject. Reference to Van Dyck's 'grand manner' performed a comparable role. Some artists understood this only superficially, and, like Angelica Kauffman, were content simply to dress their models in pseudo-seventeenth-century garb. Borrowing the Flemish master's mode of composition, however, was enough to give distinction to the model. The full-length portrait of a man with his horse, a reinterpretation of Van Dyck's *Charles I* (Musée du Louvre, Paris) became one of the *topoi* of the English aristocratic portrait. Reynolds, with his *John Manners, Marquis of Granby* (1765; Ringling Museum, Sarasota), gives us the

Fig.42
JOSEPH WRIGHT OF DERBY
*Richard Arkwright*, 1789.
Oil on canvas, 244 × 158.5 cm.
Private collection, Great Britain

Fig. 43
SIR JOSHUA REYNOLDS
*Mrs Abington*, 1771.
Oil on canvas, 76.8 × 63.7 cm.
Yale Center for British Art,
New Haven, B1977.14.67

most eloquent and majestic version of this. Raeburn's *Major William Clunes* (cat. 40) bears an even closer resemblance to another portrait by Reynolds, his *Captain Robert Orme* (1756; National Gallery, London). The Scottish artist is not interested in ostentatious military decorations; he favours a fusion of the man with his environment, in a movement in which the individual takes the lead; the pictorial unity, further enhanced by the slightly blurred effect, shifts the spectator's attention from social signs to the model's personality and, last but not least, to the quality of the work of art.

This distinction of attitude took on a different dimension in portraits of women. Here the notion of status is more complex than it seems, to the extent that Diderot himself had difficulty in defining it, since it can be expressed without reference to any social interaction or of any action worthy of being recorded. Upper-class women at this period had no official political role and no profession, so that their domain was essentially private; this did not mean that their likenesses were unworthy of being exhibited in public, however, but that they had to reflect the division of roles and to present a different, more abstract set of attributes. The proof of this can be found in a portrait by Reynolds of the Duchess of Devonshire, who had been accused of mingling too much in public and political affairs; in an attempt to restore her prestige, she is portrayed as a wonderful mother (cat. 90), an image that was widely disseminated as an engraving. At more or less the same moment, Vigée-Lebrun achieved a similar effect with a portrait of Marie-Antoinette and her children (Musée National du Château, Versailles). In less spectacular fashion, the British fashion for portraits of couples, devised as pendants, bears witness to this division of roles. Reynolds's portrait of the Countess of Bute (cat. 25) was probably designed to be hung next to his painting of her husband (National Portrait Gallery, London); the opulence of the costume, the nobility of the pose and the traditional column all demonstrate Lord Bute's status as a public figure. The Countess, like *Lady Alston* by Gainsborough (Louvre, Paris) or the *Montgomery Sisters* (cat.125), is depicted in a landscape (an allusion to land ownership, one of the attributes of aristocracy), and this also underlines the link between female sensibility and the natural world.[3] The 'feminine' status portrait is not exemplary in the true sense, but normative, and it therefore gives rise to a manner of representation that is more general and more abstract. Also worth noting, from Vigée-Lebrun in the 1770s to Ingres, via Goya, are the descriptions of imaginary occupations associated symbolically with women, such as reading, sewing and music. In painting as in sculpture, status is expressed by the deliberate exaltation of beauty to flatter the model: the coquettish pose of *The Comtesse de la Châtre* (who later became Madame de Jaucourt) by Vigée-Lebrun (cat.27) contrasts with the studied carelessness of *The Comtesse de Ségur* (cat.29) by Monot; the sobriety of the dress of Jacques-Louis David's *Marquise d'Orvilliers* (cat.28) contrasts with the extraordinary over-dressed hairstyle of Pigalle's *Comtesse du Cayla* (cat.36). In this ideal context, every variation from the norm becomes meaningful, even provocative. Portraits of actresses exploit this reversal of normal values. *Mrs Abington* (fig.43), sitting astride her chair with one finger in her mouth, arouses the person viewing the painting as it would excite a theatre-goer. In his portrait of the celebrated dancer Giovanna Baccelli (fig.44), Gainsborough parodies the conventions of the aristocratic portrait: the landscape is an opera set, the model, outrageously over made-up, writhes suggestively and the colours burst forth in a symphony of blue and pink.

Reference to classical antiquity in its allegorical dimension allowed portraits of women to possess a 'heroic' value that was comparable to that found in portraits of men.[4] Reynolds's *Montgomery Sisters* (cat.125) bears witness to this. The portrait presents

Fig. 44
THOMAS GAINSBOROUGH
*Giovanna Baccelli*, 1782.
Oil on canvas,
226.7 × 148.6 cm.
Tate, London

much more than a good likeness and idealised beauty: it contains a 'historical' action. The three sisters, dressed in classical costume, are seen covering a statue of Hymen with a garland of flowers; the position of each sister in relation to the statue signifies the relationship of each of them to marriage. The artist, by varying the gestures and expressions, demonstrates to the spectator that he is working in the 'grand genre'. In some cases the allegory had no need to be made so explicit; the allusion was enough on its own. Reynolds's portrait of *The Ladies Waldegrave* (1781; National Gallery of Scotland, Edinburgh) was probably intended to advertise the merits of three young women in search of husbands. For his evocation of the different degrees of female accomplishment, the artist is satisfied with the classical allusion to the Three Graces.

In the 1820s, after the upheaval caused by the Enlightenment and the Revolutions, the dialectic between the individual and his social status, between individuality and type, was reversed. Thanks to the strength of his personality, Monsieur Bertin was able to take his place as a symbol of the triumph of the bourgeoisie. Henceforward the external signs of his social status, including decorations and ceremonial clothing, were no longer necessary; the presence of the man was sufficient on its own to confirm the value of his status.[5]

→ 16  FRANCISCO DE GOYA Y LUCIENTES, *Ferdinand Guillemardet.* 1798. Oil on canvas, 186 × 124 cm.
Département des Peintures, Musée du Louvre, Paris. Bequest of Louis Guillemardet, the sitter's son, 1865

← 17   FRANCISCO DE GOYA Y LUCIENTES, *Don José Moñino y Redondo I, Conde de Floridablanca.*   1783. Oil on canvas. 260 × 166 cm.
Colección Banco de España, Madrid

↑ 18   JOHN SINGLETON COPLEY, *William Murray, 1st Earl of Mansfield.*   1783. Oil on canvas, 227.6 × 149 cm.
National Portrait Gallery, London, NPG 172

↑ 19   ANTOINE VESTIER, *A Knight of Malta Holding the Portrait of Commander Texier d'Hautefeuille.*   1788. Oil on canvas, oval, 102 × 83 cm.
Musée des Beaux-Arts, Dijon, 3496

→ 20   PIERRE MÉRARD, *The Prince de Conti.*   1776. Terracotta, 71.5 × 57 × 37 cm.
Musée des Beaux-Arts, Dijon, D 263

← 21　FRANCISCO DE GOYA Y LUCIENTES, *Don Vicente Joaquín Osorio de Moscoso y Guzmán, XI Conde de Altamira.* 1786. Oil on canvas, 177 × 108 cm.
　　Colección Banco de España, Madrid

↑ 22　ELISABETH-LOUISE VIGÉE-LEBRUN, *Charles-Alexandre de Calonne.* 1784. Oil on canvas, 149 × 128 cm.
　　Lent by Her Majesty The Queen

↑ 23  PIERRE-PAUL PRUD'HON, *Charles-Maurice de Talleyrand-Périgord in the Robes of the Grand Chamberlain.* 1807. Oil on canvas, 212 × 138 cm.
Musée Carnavalet-Histoire de Paris, Paris

→ 24  JACQUES-LOUIS DAVID, *The Emperor Napoleon in His Study at the Tuileries.* 1812. Oil on canvas, 203.9 × 125.1 cm.
National Gallery of Art, Washington DC. Samuel H. Kress Collection, 1961.9.15

↑ 25   SIR JOSHUA REYNOLDS, *Mary, Countess of Bute.*  *c.*1777–79. Oil on canvas, 236 × 145 cm.
Private collection, Mount Stuart

→ 26   ANTON RAPHAEL MENGS, *Isabel Parreño Arce, Ruiz de Alcarón y Valdés, Marquesa de Llano.*  1770. Oil on canvas, 250 × 148 cm.
Museo de la Real Academia de Bellas Artes de San Fernando, Madrid, 705

↑ 27    ELISABETH-LOUISE VIGÉE-LEBRUN, *The Comtesse de la Châtre.*  1789. Oil on canvas, 114.3 × 87.6 cm.
Lent by The Metropolitan Museum of Art, New York. Gift of Jessie Woolworth Donahue, 1954 (54.182)

→ 28    JACQUES-LOUIS DAVID, *Robertine Tourteau, Marquise d'Orvilliers.*  1790. Oil on canvas, 131 × 98 cm.
Départment des Peintures, Musée du Louvre, Paris, RF 2418. Bequest of Comtesse Robert de Fitz-James, 1923

← 29   MARTIN-CLAUDE MONOT, *The Comtesse de Ségur.*   1783. Marble, 68 × 40 × 25 cm.

Musée National des Châteaux de Versailles et de Trianon, MV 5967; RF 1830

↑ 30   ANGELICA KAUFFMAN, *Countess Catherine Skavronska.*   1789. Oil on canvas, 158 × 122 cm.

Germanisches Nationalmuseum, Nuremberg, Gm 1931

↑ 31   FRANÇOIS GÉRARD, *Maria Laetitia Ramolino Bonaparte, 'Madame Mère'.*   *c.*1802–04. Oil on canvas, 210.8 × 129.8 cm.
National Gallery of Scotland, Edinburgh, NGS 2461. Purchased with the aid of the NACF, 1988

→ 32   FRANCISCO DE GOYA Y LUCIENTES, *The Marquesa de Villafranca Painting Her Husband.*   1804. Oil on canvas, 195 × 126 cm.
Museo Nacional del Prado, Madrid

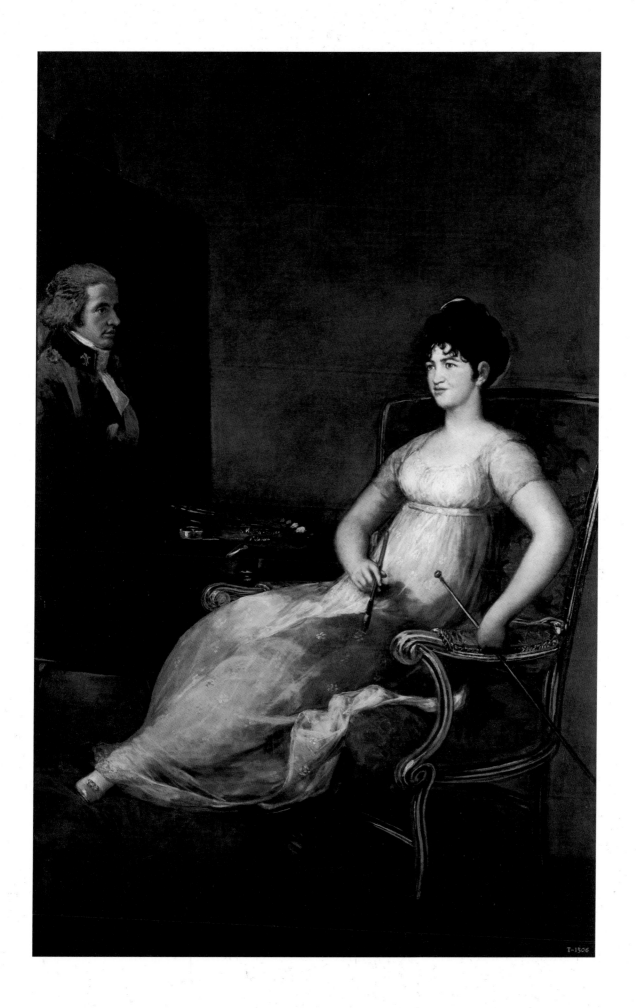

↑ 33   JEAN-AUGUSTE-DOMINIQUE INGRES, *The Comtesse de Tournon.*   1812. Oil on canvas, 92.4 × 73.2 cm.
Philadelphia Museum of Art. The Henry P. McIlhenny Collection in memory of Frances P. McIlhenny, 1986

→ 34   JEAN-AUGUSTE-DOMINIQUE INGRES, *Madame Marcotte de Sainte-Marie.*   1826. Oil on canvas, 93 × 74 cm.
Département des Peintures, Musée du Louvre, Paris, RF 2398

↑ 35   LORENZO BARTOLINI, *Elizabeth Albana Upton, Marchioness of Bristol.*  1815–18. Marble, 71 × 51 × 30 cm.
       The Bristol Collection, Ickworth. Accepted in lieu of tax by HM Treasury in 1956, and transferred to the National Trust

→ 36   JEAN-MARIE PIGALLE, *The Comtesse du Cayla.*  1826. Marble, 77 × 55 × 32 cm.
       Private collection, Château de Craon, Haroué (Meurthe-et-Moselle)

3

# The History Portrait

GUILHEM SCHERF

*I am so fond of contemplating those of my contemporaries who have achieved great things, because I seek to recognise in their facial features some mark of the sublime talent that singles them out ... How I love to feel small, while surrounding myself in my imagination with all those great men, and while enjoying the pleasure of admiring them![1]*

*I should love to see the statue of our good king [Henri IV] surrounded by the generation that has just been born; the children, while remembering their games, would learn early to bless his memory and to recount his virtues to the next generation.[2]*

THE AIM OF A HISTORY PORTRAIT IS to guarantee the immortality and the exemplary status of its subject: 'Statues of illustrious men can arouse in noble souls the desire to imitate them.'[3] Plutarch's words, relayed to us by his eminent sixteenth-century translator Jacques Amyot, opened the way: in his *Vie parallèlles des hommes illustres* he searches for 'signs of the soul, and through them seeks to form a living portrait of the life and habits of everyone, leaving it to historians to describe wars and battles', for 'the highest and most glorious deeds are not always those that best display the vices or the virtue of a man'.[4] Plutarch defines an illustrious man by his moral qualities as well as by the glory of his deeds. Eighteenth-century debate centred around this question. Although Voltaire 'named great men all those who have excelled in the useful or the agreeable; provincial pillagers and looters are only heroes',[5] the Abbé de Saint-Pierre is more precise: a man only becomes great 'by the interior qualities of mind and heart, and by the benefits he procures for society'.[6] A portrait in paint or sculpture allows the spectator to identify himself visually with the memorable man, recognisable by the resemblance of his features and/or the exemplary nature of the chosen composition.

Criteria for the recognition of a history portrait are various. Let us take retrospective portrait busts as an example. When Caffieri designed his bust of

Jean de Rotrou (fig. 46), produced as part of a series of illustrious men connected with the Comédie-Française, he created a raffish figure like a musketeer to evoke the period of Louis XIII, knowing full well that the face of the dramatist was unknown to the public. Houdon, on the other hand, needed to take no pains over the details of the clothing worn by his *Molière* (Comédie-Française, Paris), executed a few years earlier in 1778: the writer was instantly recognisable to all thanks to the portrait by Nicolas Mignard, widely distributed in the form of an engraving. Molière stands soberly dressed with two jacket lapels, a shirt and a knotted cravat. Houdon's task was to breathe life into a famous face rather than to suggest an entire period.[7]

Depiction of a hero in the classical manner guarantees the illustrious subject his place in posterity. Could Chantrey have done other than

Fig. 45
SIR FRANCIS CHANTREY
*Arthur Wellesley, 1st Duke of Wellington*, 1823.
Marble, H. 78.7 cm.
Apsley House, London

depict the victor of Waterloo (fig. 45) with the head of Caesar, with unincised eyes and neck bare under a broad drape? The British sculptor was critical, however, of Canova's model of Washington 'in the warrior costume of a Roman general'[8] when he saw it in the sculptor's studio: his own statue of the American general in Boston, finished in 1826, shows him in contemporary dress enveloped in a cloak.[9] But the image of Wellington, a living legend, deserved the representation it received. In his *Apotheosis of Napoleon I* (cat. 120), Thorvaldsen went as far as he could along the classical route, in its purest archaeological vein: the Emperor rises above his eagle like Titus in Rome on the pediment of his Arch, a sublime and magnificent tribute.

A historical figure is defined by the deeds that bring him glory. The portrait illustrates a 'chosen moment'[10] which fixes the deed in a decisive and expressive manner: Samuel Adams, depicted by Copley (cat. 42), points his finger at the charter and seal granting Massachusetts its privileges, and holds tightly in his hand the petition from the Bostonians requesting the expulsion of the British troops after the massacre of 5 March 1770; Marat, depicted by Jacques-Louis David at the moment of his death, holds the note appealing for compassion which gained his murderess access to his room (cat. 37). Claude-André Deseine – after Houdon, who had had the idea for this very powerful composition – also wished to mark, in the constricted space of a portrait bust, the power of a moment in history, the speech by Mirabeau, the master orator, whose raised arm pointing forward stands as a symbol for his words (cat. 47).

General Lasalle, as painted by Gros (cat. 39), is also seen at a 'specific moment': he holds in his gloved hands the deed of surrender of the city of Stettin, obtained following brilliant feats of arms by the French. His air of melancholy, however, tinges the description of the event – conjured up in the background of the painting by the procession

Fig. 46
JEAN-JACQUES CAFFIERI
*Jean de Rotrou*, 1783.
Marble, H. 92 cm.
Collections de la Comédie Française,
Paris, s. 146

carrying the keys to the city – with a particular intellectual dimension: the general is the incarnation of history beyond life's vicissitudes. This is what Reynolds, a few decades earlier, was able to convey so magnificently in his thrilling portrait of Sir Jeffrey Amherst (cat. 38): the future commandant of the British forces in North America is depicted not as a brilliant military leader, but as a pensive intellectual, with his elbow leaning on his walking stick and his right hand under his chin. This symbol of heroic human virtue, whose qualities of judgement and courage are scarcely even implied by the presence of the map and helmet, is distinguished by his thoughtfulness and meditation.

The modern history portrait, in which the hero is dressed in contemporary costume, records an event of which the work becomes a kind of symbol. Copley's proud representation of Hugh Montgomerie (cat. 41) portrays the Scottish hero in the midst of heroic action, pointing out a target with his extended finger and thus galvanising his troops. The educated public, however, would have recognised behind this figure the victorious image of the *Apollo Belvedere*, and would therefore have imbued the portrait with the heroic glory of classical mythology. When David painted Bonaparte crossing the Alps at the Great St Bernard Pass (fig. 47), combining the uniform worn by the general at Marengo with a vast cape 'definitely from his imagination',[11] the memorable moment is frozen in a grandiose composition in which Napoleon, with the assistance of his painter, builds his own legend. The artist here employs the *ne plus ultra* of heroic composition, the equestrian statue on a rearing horse, lending his hero some glorious antecedents, such as Louis XIV and Peter the Great:[12] 'This is the way Apelles must have

Fig. 47
JACQUES-LOUIS DAVID
*Napoleon Crossing the Alps*,
1800–01. Oil on canvas,
260 × 221 cm.
Musée National des Châteaux de
Malmaison et de Bois-Préau, Rueil-
Malmaison, 4971

GRACE AUX PRISONNIERS !

painted Alexander; and Phidias, Pericles.'[13] The equestrian monument has always been an emblem of military might as well as moral strength.[14]

The Restoration was keen to invent some great men for itself. In June 1816, Louis XVIII commissioned for the Château de Saint-Cloud, formerly a centre for Napoleonic propaganda, a large series of portraits of Vendéen generals. The young Henri de La Rochejacquelein by Guérin (cat. 141) is depicted leading the assault, impassive and determined at the head of his troops, braving the enemy bayonets: 'This portrait is a history painting,' wrote Miel in the margin of the Salon catalogue in 1817.[15] We gain the same impression in front of the Marquis de Bonchamps, who raises himself up from his deathbed to grant a favour to republican prisoners (fig. 48): the funerary monument by David d'Angers, originally placed at the back of the choir, behind the high altar, of the abbey church at Saint-Florent-le-Vieil, gave the dying man the status of a martyr. *Bonchamps* is a striking statue directly inspired by the *Ilissos* on the west pediment of the Parthenon, which David d'Angers had just seen in London. The subject's face[16] was acknowledged to be a good likeness by veterans of the wars of the Vendée. The statue is a brilliant synthesis of classical inspiration[17] with attention to realistic detail and an animated conception.[18] This allegory of mercy, or in other words of national reconciliation, is the quintessence of the history portrait: in comparison, Mahlknecht's statue of Cathelineau, a somewhat run-of-the-mill figure standing near a gigantic cross,[19] although stemming from the same desire to immortalise the Vendéen generals, contains neither the formal boldness nor the energy of the exceptional *Bonchamps*. Mahlknecht's use of contemporary dress serves to render his subject even more commonplace: 'What an unfortunate idea to wish to pass down to posterity a great man wearing the shabby clothes of his period, this costume worn by modern men which bears witness to the infirmities of the poor human race! … I can perfectly understand that the painter should reproduce exactly the accessories that comprise the costume of a great man. It adds up, so to speak, to an inventory using the resources that colour puts at his disposal. Its aim is to give us an idea of reality; but a sculptor who only has materials of uniform colour to work with, for example marble, which renders the colour of death so perfectly, should not and cannot therefore attempt to imitate life. It is the apotheosis of a man that he is commissioned to reproduce, it is his soul, the expression of this soul which was released from the influence of his physical being when he performed the great deeds that have recommended him to the admiration of generations.'[20] This is how David d'Angers represented General Foy, magnificently carved like a classical hero, reserving chronicles of modern times for his narrative *bas-reliefs* (Galerie David d'Angers, Angers).

→ 37   STUDIO OF JACQUES-LOUIS DAVID, *The Death of Marat*.   *c*.1794. Oil on canvas, 162 × 130 cm.
Département des Peintures, Musée du Louvre, Paris, RF 1945-2. Bequest of Baron Jeanin, a descendant of the artist, 1945

116

N'AYANT PU ME CORROMPRE

ILS M'ONT ASSASSINÉ.

↑ 38　SIR JOSHUA REYNOLDS, *Sir Jeffrey Amherst.*　1765. Oil on canvas, 125.7 × 100.3 cm.
Mead Art Museum, Amherst College, Amherst, 1967.85

→ 39　ANTOINE-JEAN GROS, *General Lasalle at the Siege of Stettin.*　1808. Oil on canvas, 248 × 174 cm.
Musée de l'Armée, Paris, 19814/EA 655

↑ 40    SIR HENRY RAEBURN, *Major William Clunes.*   After 1809. Oil on canvas, 236 × 150 cm.
National Gallery of Scotland, Edinburgh, NG 903

→ 41    ATTRIBUTED TO JOHN SINGLETON COPLEY, *Major Hugh Montgomerie.*   c.1780. Oil on canvas, 226.3 × 148.9 cm.
Scottish National Portrait Gallery, Edinburgh, PG 1516

Hugh, 12th Earl of Eglinton.

↑ 42  JOHN SINGLETON COPLEY, *Samuel Adams*.  *c*.1770–72. Oil on canvas, 125.8 × 100 cm.
Museum of Fine Arts, Boston. Deposited by the City of Boston, 30.76c

→ 43  JEAN-ANTOINE HOUDON, *Condorcet*.  1785. Marble, 77.5 × 50.8 cm.
American Philosophical Society, Philadelphia, 58. s. 2

↑ 44    JEAN-ANTOINE HOUDON, *Benjamin Franklin.*  1778. Terracotta, 52.2 × 34.2 × 27.4 cm.

Département des Sculptures, Musée du Louvre, Paris, RF 349

→ 45    DAVID MARTIN, *Benjamin Franklin.*  1767. Oil on canvas, 125.7 × 100.3 cm.

Courtesy of the Pennsylvania Academy of the Fine Arts, Philadelphia, 1943.16.1.
Gift of Maria McKean Allen and Phebe Warren Downes through the bequest of their mother, Elizabeth Wharton McKean

46 JOSEPH BOZE IN COLLABORATION WITH ROBERT LEFEVRE, *Honoré-Gabriel Riqueti, Comte de Mirabeau.* 1789. Oil on canvas, 219.6 × 135 cm.

Musée Granet, Aix-en-Provence

47 CLAUDE-ANDRÉ DESEINE, *Mirabeau.* 1791. Plaster, 80 × 60 × 40 cm.

Musée des Beaux-Arts, Rennes, 877.32.1

# The Cultural Portrait

GUILHEM SCHERF

EIGHTEENTH-CENTURY FRENCH TEXTS such as the *Encyclopédie* or the *Dictionnaire de l'Académie* make no mention of the word 'cultural',[2] thus the so-called cultural portrait is a recent invention. One work which admirably embodies the idea is Tischbein's *Goethe in the Roman Campagna* (fig. 49). In this magisterial portrait the artist manages to convey Goethe's profound sense of being modern while also being the heir to classical tradition. As he poses for the painter in an Italian landscape dotted with classical ruins, Goethe defines himself as a cultural monument.[3] 'We see the poet … with his solemn gaze meditating on the ephemeral nature of things;

he rests on an upturned obelisk which has decayed into a ruinous state … In the distance the Roman Campagna can be seen with its many tombs dispersed along the Appian Way; we assume that these were commemorative monuments erected to transmit to posterity the name of those whose ashes repose beneath … This transformation of Nature and human affairs explains the poet-philosopher's serious gaze; alarming thoughts about the perishable nature of all matter seem to hover over his face.'[4] The physical portrait of the writer is enhanced by the representation of his interior vision: his mental landscape is embodied by the Roman Campagna.

A composition similar to Tischbein's can be found in a painting executed about ten years later by Fabre (cat. 133): the American aesthete Allen Smith contemplates Florence from the banks of the Arno, with a Corinthian capital in the foreground. Like Goethe, he wears a white cloak and, with pensive air, meditates on the passage of time. The portrayal of Anglo-Saxon or German gentlemen completing their Grand Tours in Italy was one of the stereotypes of the social portrait of the well-born traveller. Fabre must have been familiar with Batoni's paintings of art lovers posing in front of famous classical antiquities at the Vatican or the Capitoline. Smith's reverie as he gazes at Florence lingers less on the archaeological past, however, than on the splendour of the contemporary city, which takes up at least half the painting. The persistence of the Italian miracle and the fascinating beauty of the surroundings are also admirably expressed by Catel in his painting of the architect Schinkel literally absorbed by the Gulf of Naples (Nationalgalerie, Berlin). These portraits suggest that their sitters' personalities were transformed by their Italian experience.

The empathy between an environment and the characters within it is subtly analysed by Wright of Derby: the Reverend d'Ewes Coke, an amateur

Fig. 49
WILHELM TISCHBEIN
*Goethe in the Roman Campagna*,
1786–87. Oil on canvas,
164 × 206 cm.
Städelsches Kunstinstitut und
Städtische Galerie, Frankfurt-am-Main

engraver and enthusiastic student of natural history, directs his wife's gaze towards the park he has just inherited as she points at a drawing, part of the plan she is holding in front of her (cat. 136). The actual landscape and the project for its rearrangement are discussed in the presence of a third party, the advocate and parliamentarian Daniel Parker Coke, the clergyman's cousin. Garden design is an aesthetic challenge, a 'liberal art': 'the success of the effects requires a habit of considering proportions and a tact which are closely linked to the ideas of composition in the art of painting, since garden design deals with volume, relationships and contrast … Of the known arts, the one that has the strongest intellectual relationship with the art of the garden is the art of painting.'[5] One must follow one's own ingenuity: 'By getting rid of French monotony, English monotony has become so uniform that we need to make modern gardens even more modern, and imitate nobody.'[6]

Louis-Pierre Deseine's bust of Johann Joachim Winckelmann was produced for the Musée des Monuments Français (cat. 52). It is known that the artist and antiquary Alexandre Lenoir wished to create a gallery in the museum of busts of great men; to include a German scholar, the only foreigner to contribute to this nationalist pantheon, was a heavily loaded gesture: 'Winckelmann has left a number of valuable works for the study of drawing. In his *Histoire de l'art dans l'Antiquité* he mainly developed a chronological history of the arts, with that finesse so characteristic of great erudition and profound practical knowledge. The respect inspired in me by that sublime man and the recognition due to him from artists encouraged me to erect a monument to his memory.'[7] Deseine had the choice of either representing the historian as a classical hero, as Doell had done for the Panthéon,[8] which would have entailed identifying the writer with the subject of his enthusiasm, or following the most popular iconography: the painting by Mengs,

engraved by Copia, which served as a frontispiece to Winckelmann's *Histoire de l'art dans l'Antiquité*, published in Paris in 1794.[9] Deseine preferred Mengs's image, and borrowed from it to depict Winckelmann dressed in an open-necked shirt and a coat. The portrait avoids the sublime, although this would have been appropriate for the subject and its destination, in favour of a more intimate evocation. The results belong within the portrait tradition of eighteenth-century France. In representing Winckelmann as a friend and an intellectual, the sculptor, by artistic conviction, proved himself able to resist the siren song of antiquity.

When Rauch was planning his statue of Goethe (cats 58, 59), whom he wished to represent heroically as a great man, in monumental scale, he also bore in mind the fact that his sitter was imbued with classical civilisation. His portrait had to give due weight to the person of Goethe, represented seated and nobly robed like the illustrious intellectuals of ancient Greece and Rome; Rauch was also concerned that the great poet should be immediately recognisable. In other words, he wished to create a symbol, a notion that was fundamental to Goethe's aesthetic: 'The particular is eternally subject to the universal; the universal must eternally bow before the particular … [Symbolic objects] appear not to exist on their own account, and yet they possess a profoundly significant dimension; this is because an ideal object always possesses a universal dimension.'[10]

It would be a relief to be able to apply Goethe's notion of the symbolic object to Pigalle's *Voltaire Naked* (cat. 54). Under the influence of Diderot, Pigalle planned a work that would combine the sublimity of classical sculpture – for example the nakedness of the dying 'Seneca' – with the reality of an aged body and the flame of the intellect. 'The body is a slave that must obey the soul,'[11] wrote the philosopher in 1754. Accurate representation of Voltaire, without spurious allegory, was at the heart

Fig. 50
AUGUSTIN PAJOU
*Buffon*, 1776.
Marble, H. 290 cm.
Musée National d'Histoire Naturelle, Paris

One work that raised itself to this level, intellectually and physically, is the contemporary statue of Buffon by Pajou (fig. 50), an extraordinary figure commissioned by the French royal household. Although the artist represented the scholar 'in philosopher's dress',[14] his face has a purposeful look: he also wished to identify him with Man, the centre of the universe, at the pinnacle of the scale of being. The statue is a transcription of the marmoreal (and hugely admired) prose of the writer: 'Everything in man, even on the exterior, marks his superiority over all other living beings; he stands straight and tall, his attitude is one of command, his head looks at the sky and presents a noble face on which the character of his dignity is imprinted; the image of the soul is painted there by physiognomy, the excellence of his nature pierces material organs and animates his facial features with divine fire; his majestic gait, his firm and bold approach bespeak his nobility and his rank.'[15] In this sublime portrait, Pajou idealises Buffon, likening him to a classical philosopher as much as to mankind, the object of his studies.

In comparison with these outstanding works by Pigalle and Pajou, the statuettes of Lucas de Montigny representing Voltaire absorbed in a book (cat. 50), Rousseau meditating with a leaf in his hand (cat. 49) and Buffon as the embodiment of sovereign man (cat. 66) seem very modest cultural images. It is interesting, however, that the distribution of such pieces should have attracted the attention of Mirabeau, one of the principal protagonists of the French Revolution: to participate in distributing images of champions of the freedom of thought such as these was to engage in political action.

A cultural portrait is also a portrait of the cultivated man when the representation is influenced by the subject's mental universe. When Houdon made his posthumous portrait of the Marquis de Méjanes (cat. 67), he depicted him neither as a gentleman, nor as a procurator, nor as

of Pigalle's work: nor did he change his mind after his first preparatory sketch was shown at the residence of Madame Necker in April 1770 and was greeted with enthusiasm. Madame Necker understood the artist's basic idea: 'All allegories are weak, and they also distract the mind with a multitude of small ideas; one idea only is needed, a single one.'[12] To the patriarch of the republic of literature, to the humanist of the *Treatise on Tolerance* and of the battle against injustice and prejudice, Pigalle erected a monument to freedom of thought which went well beyond the representation of a man. Voltaire grasped the symbolic message of the statue as soon as work began: 'The union between genuine men of letters has never been so vital. It was solely to erect a monument to this union that people of unusual merit … banded together to employ the chisel of M. Pigalle. I have only been their figurehead.'[13]

a philosopher, but in sober and indeterminate clothing that could be the attire of the Enlightenment *honnête homme*. Similarly, the painting of Joseph Banks by Reynolds (cat. 56), and the engraving made a year after the painting had been exhibited at the Royal Academy,[16] shows the celebrated botanist sitting at his desk with a globe to suggest his trip round the world with Captain Cook. His fist is clenched and his face has a purposeful look: this is the scholar as modern man, devoted to study and action.

Prud'hon's portrait of Sommariva (fig. 51) is imbued with a more contemplative spirit. This wholehearted admirer of contemporary art, and of neoclassical sculpture in particular, is depicted in an idyllic Mediterranean landscape which serves as a casket, like some new Arcadia, for the two statues by Canova that belong to him, *Palamedes* and *Terpsichore* (fig. 52). These are substitutes for the classical ruins painted by Batoni in the background of his portraits of travellers on the Grand Tour. In this case the classical statues 'are replaced by the sculpture of the modern Phidias, who, with his divine art, succeeded in surpassing the ancients. The painting thus assumes the nature of a kind of manifesto for Canova's muse, emphasising the model's intention of being remembered as a patron and friend of the greatest sculptor.'[17]

*John Flaxman Modelling His Bust of William Hayley* by Romney (fig. 53) is both a family portrait and a friendship portrait, enhancing the two arts, painting and sculpture, by presenting an encounter between a carved portrait and a painted portrait within the same painting. Flaxman was a friend of Romney, who depicted himself on the left with his palette; the sculptor, assisted by his young apprentice Thomas, works on the bust of Thomas's father, the poet William Hayley. The painter views the subject face on, while the sculptor works on his profile. The subtle composition of the painting proposes several points of view and provides a fascinating reflection on the act of creation.

It must surely be no accident that the sculpture is larger than life-size: 'since the statue, or the bust of a man, is his apotheosis, the representation of his soul, the sculptor must make a head that is larger than life-size. A model of exact size is only appropriate for the bust of a man of the people.'[18] In similar vein is Flaxman's choice of a profile: 'The profile of the face gives the reality of life, while the face full on gives only a fiction.'[19] Romney's portrait could be used to illustrate the quotation from Edouard Pommier which introduces this text: by encouraging meditation on the arts and on tangible values (friendship, transmission, inspiration, execution), the cultural portrait of a poet, presented in the same painting by a painter and a sculptor, could be the answer to the search for an ideal portrait.

Fig. 53
GEORGE ROMNEY
*John Flaxman Modelling His Bust of William Hayley*, c. 1795–96.
Oil on canvas, 226 × 145 cm.
Yale Center for British Art, New Haven

← 48   ALLAN RAMSAY, *David Hume.*   1766. Oil on canvas, 76.2 × 63.5 cm.
      Scottish National Portrait Gallery, Edinburgh, PG 1057

↑ 49   JEAN-ROBERT NICOLAS LUCAS DE MONTIGNY, *Jean-Jacques Rousseau.*   1790. Terracotta, 44 × 26 × 25 cm.
      Musées Royaux d'Art et d'Histoire, Brussels, 9065

↑ 50   JEAN-ROBERT NICOLAS LUCAS DE MONTIGNY, *Voltaire.*   1781. Plaster, 54 × 23 × 37 cm.
Institut et Musée Voltaire, Geneva, IC 0045

→ 51   JEAN-BAPTISTE GREUZE, *Claude Henri Watelet.*   1765. Oil on canvas, 115 × 88 cm.
Département des Peintures, Musée du Louvre, Paris, RF 1982-66

↑ 52    LOUIS-PIERRE DESEINE, *Johann Joachim Winckelmann.*  1800. Plaster, 72 × 51 × 30 cm.
Musée National des Châteaux de Versailles et de Trianon, Versailles, MV 646; LP 515

↗ 53    JEAN-ANTOINE HOUDON, *Denis Diderot.*  1780. Bronze, 79 × 31 × 30 cm.
Musée d'Art et d'Histoire de Langres, 984-2-1

→ 54    JEAN-BAPTISTE PIGALLE, *Voltaire Naked.*  1776. Marble, 150 × 89 × 77 cm.
Département des Sculptures, Musée du Louvre, Paris (Institut de France deposit), ENT. 1962.1

MONSIEUR DE VOLTAIRE, PAR LES GENS DE LETTRES
COMPATRIOTES, ET SES CONTEMPORAINS. 1770.

← 55   SIR HENRY RAEBURN, *James Hutton.*   *c.*1789–90. Oil on canvas, 125.1 × 104.8 cm.
Scottish National Portrait Gallery, Edinburgh, PG 2686

↑ 56   SIR JOSHUA REYNOLDS, *Joseph Banks.*   1771–73. Oil on canvas, 127 × 101.5 cm.
National Portrait Gallery, London, NPG 5868

↑ 57   POMPEO BATONI, *Wills Hill, Earl of Hillsborough, later 1st Marquis of Downshire.*   1766. Oil on canvas, 227 × 161 cm.
Private collection

→ 58   CHRISTIAN DANIEL RAUCH, *Johann Wolfgang von Goethe.*   1823. Plaster, 42 × 34 × 14 cm.
Staatliche Museen zu Berlin, Nationalgalerie, RM 14

⇒ 59   CHRISTIAN DANIEL RAUCH, *Johann Wolfgang von Goethe.*   1824. Plaster, 46 × 34 × 14 cm.
Staatliche Museen zu Berlin, Nationalgalerie, RM 15

↑ 60    ANGELICA KAUFFMAN, *Joseph Johann, Graf von Fries.*  1787. Oil on canvas, 128.5 × 102.5 cm.
Historisches Museum der Stadt Wien, Vienna, 56.406

→ 61    POMPEO BATONI, *John Staples.*  1773. Oil on canvas, 248.6 × 175 cm.
Museo di Roma, Palazzo Braschi, Rome, MR 1974

↑ 62  JOSEPH WRIGHT OF DERBY, *Mrs Sarah Clayton.*  *c.*1769. Oil on canvas, 127 × 101.6 cm.
Fitchburg Art Museum, Fitchburg, Mass., 1953.1

→ 63  FRANCISCO DE GOYA Y LUCIENTES, *Don José Alvarez de Toledo y Gonzaga, XIII Duque de Alba and XI Marqués de Villafranca.*
1795. Oil on canvas, 195 × 115 cm (with later additions, 195 × 120 cm).
Museo Nacional del Prado, Madrid

↑ 64 MARTIN DROLLING, *Michel Belot.* 1791. Oil on canvas, 72 × 60 cm.
Musée des Beaux-Arts, Orléans, 381

→ 65 JEAN-PIERRE SAINT-OURS, *François Tronchin.* 1796. Oil on canvas, 112.5 × 85 cm.
Société des Arts, Geneva

↑ 66   JEAN-ROBERT NICOLAS LUCAS DE MONTIGNY, *Buffon.*  1791. Plaster, 52 × 21 × 22 cm.
Musée Carnavalet-Histoire de Paris, Paris, s 3635

→ 67   JEAN-ANTOINE HOUDON, *The Marquis de Méjanes (Jean-Baptiste Marie de Piquet).*  1786. Marble, 86 × 65 × 32 cm.
Bibliothèque Méjanes, Aix-en-Provence

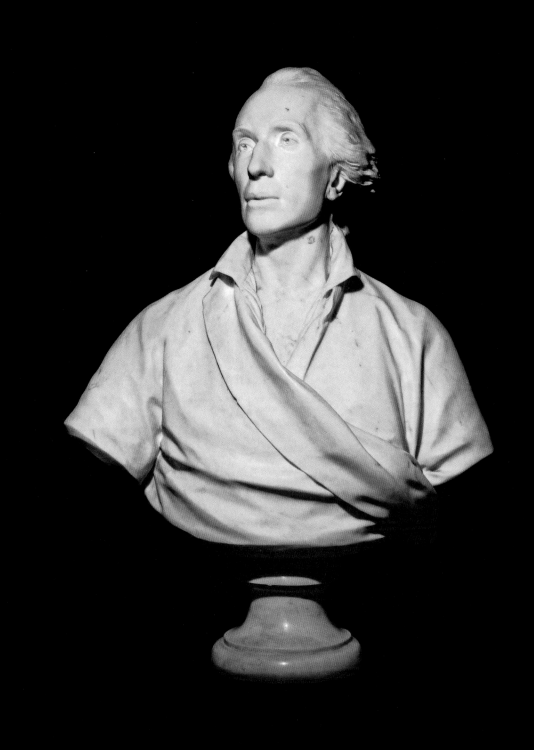

# 5

## The Place for Experimentation: Artists' Portraits and Self-portraits

VIVIEN GREENE

*My purpose is to display to my kind a portrait in every way true to nature, and the man I shall portray will be myself*
JEAN-JACQUES ROUSSEAU [1]

THE LATE EIGHTEENTH CENTURY witnessed the rise of the artist in contemporary society and thought, a phenomenon that was manifest in the portraits they realised of themselves and their peers. More traditional images continued to announce artists' professions as painters or sculptors, showing them with the tools of their trade, often in a studio setting. Formal portraits – in which brushes, easels and chisels are absent – confirm the respectability that artists had attained. Instead, intimate likenesses eschew accoutrements of any kind and, following romantic precepts, focus on the artist's face with the intention of conveying a sense of the sitter's inner persona. Artists also brought themselves into portraiture. They chose not only to represent each other and themselves, either alone or in their studios – which ran the gamut from grandeur to garret – but in group portraits; with their families in informal genre scenes; or even in allegorical narratives. The radical historical changes and philosophical ideas that defined this era were responsible for the increased importance of artists, and led to this expanded breadth of representation in their likenesses.

The shifting position occupied by the artist in eighteenth-century society and thought resulted from a series of interlocking events and the emergence of newly forged attitudes. Revolutionary and Enlightenment ideals, with their emphasis on classical philosophy and the ideologies of republican Rome, propagated notions of civic virtue and democracy which, in turn, saw a loosening of class boundaries. Merit was extolled over birthright. An individual's status was judged by his or her talent and accomplishments rather than bloodline or wealth. Concurrently, the creative

act took on greater meaning in this era. The artist came to be perceived as a figure born with particular powers. The premise of the artist as genius – informed by the philosophies of Immanuel Kant – acquired new currency.[2] These outlooks made space for artists to achieve higher standing. No longer regarded as mere craftsmen, as they had been in previous centuries, painters and sculptors rose in rank. This recasting of their public profile, and the distancing from the association with manual labour, put them on an equal intellectual footing with the producers of culture in other disciplines, from writers to philosophers. They themselves had become subjects worthy of investigation and glorification in paint and marble, and represented their new distinction in the modes of self-portraiture they evolved, as well as in the portrayals of their colleagues.[3]

Nonetheless, artists continued to serve kings, queens, nobles and the recently minted bourgeoisie. However, within a rapidly changing political landscape and, in some cases, a succession of governments, their power to shape opinion became an even more valuable asset. During the momentous historical tumult of the final quarter of the eighteenth century and the first of the nineteenth – from revolutions to restorations – artworks became powerful tools deployed both by patrons and by their makers to further myriad agendas, from the political to the personal. Long-lived monarchies were shored up, new regimes proclaimed, rulers established, and beliefs moulded through visual means. Artists were not only the recognised creators of historical records, but the propagators of images of authority.

In the wake of these events, artists achieved a celebrity status of their own, and earned a place as acknowledged taste-makers.[4] They also became increasingly strategic in their presentation of themselves and in the construction of their role within a larger social framework. Goya negotiated the reigns of radically different Spanish sovereigns as court painter.[5] The neoclassical sculptor Canova was able to choose his clientele and transcend national boundaries, accepting commissions from countries at political odds with his homeland.[6] Jacques-Louis David, despite his allegiance with Robespierre, was powerful enough in France to sidestep execution after the fall of the Jacobins and later become Napoleon's key propagandist. Although few portraits of Goya were executed during his lifetime – that by Vicente López Portaña (Museo del Prado, Madrid) being a rare example – an abundance of portraits of Canova and David attests to the fame and admiration these artists had earned. The Italian was painted by figures as internationally diverse as Thomas Lawrence, Giovanni Battista Lampi and François-Xavier Fabre. These portraits are matched in profusion and variety by those representing David, including the bust by his fellow Bonapartist, the romantic sculptor François Rude (cat.152). Rude met the famed artist when both were in political exile in Brussels. Modelled in 1826, immediately after David's death, Rude's expressive rendition candidly emphasises the deformation of the painter's mouth due to a tumour in his cheek, a disfiguring feature avoided by others who depicted him in profile, and one David himself downplayed in his own psychologically probing self-portraits.[7]

The formalisation of the profession itself through the establishment of official art academies and exhibitions, sanctioned by the ruling monarchies, played a significant part in the elevation of artists' stature.[8] This particular kind of patronage had begun in the previous century with the foundation in 1648 of the Académie Royale des Beaux-Arts in Paris. Nearly half a century later, 1696 saw the birth of the Prussian Academy of Arts in Berlin. This was followed in the eighteenth century by the Real Academia de Bellas Artes de San Fernando in

Fig.54
CHARLES WILLSON PEALE
*Self-portrait with Angelica and Portrait of Rachel*, c.1782–85.
Oil on canvas, 91.8 × 69 cm.
Museum of Fine Arts, Houston.
The Bayou Bend Collection.
Gift of Miss Ima Hogg

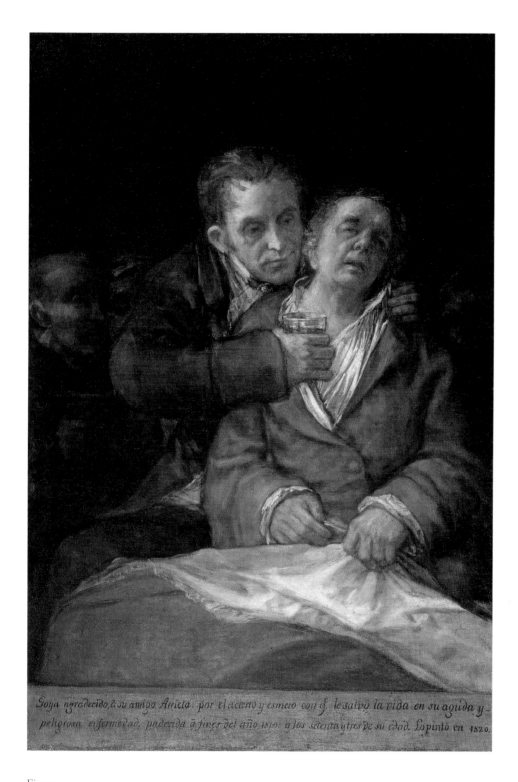

*Goya agradecido, á su amigo Arrieta: por el acierto y esmero con q.<sup>e</sup> le salvó la vida en su aguda y peligrosa enfermedad, padecida á fines del año 1819, á los setenta y tres de su edad. Lo pintó en 1820.*

Madrid (1752), the Royal Danish Academy of Fine Arts in Copenhagen (1754), the Russian Academy of Arts in St Petersburg (1757), the Royal Academy of Arts in London (1768) and the Real Accademia di Belle Arti di Brera in Milan (1776), to name but a few examples. The rarified yet operational atmosphere of these institutions is conveyed in Zoffany's group portrait representing the poised and elegantly clad members of London's Royal Academy (cat. 70), surrounded by classical casts and ostensibly preparing to sketch a nude model. Reynolds, the Royal Academy's first President, articulated the new recognition accorded to artists through the establishment of such official organisations and their exhibitions in the first of his *Discourses*, which he delivered at the inauguration of his prestigious institution:

> There are, at this time, a greater number of excellent artists than were ever known before at one period in this nation; there is a general desire among our Nobility to be distinguished as lovers and judges of the Arts; there is a greater superfluity of wealth among the people to reward the professors; and, above all, we are patronised by a Monarch, who, knowing the value of science and of elegance, thinks every art worthy of his notice, that tends to soften and humanise the mind.[9]

The range of Reynolds's self-portraits – in which the legacy of Rembrandt looms large – maps the artist's increasing freedom to depict himself however he chose. In his early and striking frontal likeness (c. 1747–48; National Portrait Gallery, London), he capitalised on the effects of chiaroscuro. Holding palette and brush in one hand, he shades his eyes with the other, his face illuminated by an unseen light source as he looks straight out of the picture as though at an audience. Over three decades later, he still stares confidently at his viewers (cat. 73), but the tools of his craft are gone. Instead he proclaims his erudition and authority, wearing his doctoral robes and cap, with a bust of Michelangelo behind him.

Fig. 55
FRANCISCO DE GOYA
Y LUCIENTES
*Self-portrait with Dr Arrieta*, 1820.
Oil on canvas, 114.6 × 76.5 cm.
The Minneapolis Institute of Arts.
The Ethel Morrison Van Derlip Fund

Self-portraiture was also a medium through which artists could market their talents. In the United States, where art-making was still a rather new profession and portraiture was the primary genre practised, a self-portrait could serve as a manner of advertisement to a budding clientele. Charles Willson Peale, who opened the first art gallery in America in 1782, understood this. In this same year he began a portrait of himself painting an oval of his wife Rachel; his daughter Angelica stands behind him (fig. 54). Angelica was named after Angelica Kauffman (Peale gave the names of several famous artists, such as Raphaelle, Rembrandt, Rubens, Titian, to his offspring, and several of them went on to be artists in their own right). Angelica poses as the muse of painting, thus enriching this triple family portrait with an allegorical dimension that displays the range of Peale's artistic repertoire in his trademark hard-edged style.[10]

Women artists, who were much fewer in number and presumably had a more difficult time proving themselves, also utilised the self-portrait as a means to showcase themselves and their abilities.[11] The theme of education frequently appears within these images, in part to serve as a reminder that women were formally trained and thus qualified artists, as in Adélaïde Labille-Guiard's *Self-portrait with Two Pupils, Mademoiselle Marie Gabrielle Capet and Mademoiselle Carreaux de Rosemond* (1785; Metropolitan Museum of Art, New York). Others selected different guises to appeal to patrons and public: Angelica Kauffman, bridging the rococo and neoclassical styles, presents herself alternately as a well-dressed young woman, as a dignified painter and, in her preferred genre, in an allegorical composition, choosing between music and art. Elisabeth-Louise Vigée-Lebrun, a favourite painter of Marie-Antoinette, likewise depicts herself in flattering images as an artist and as a lady, but she taps into another archetypal female role, that of mother, portraying herself in

a joyful and sentimental embrace with her daughter. These identities are conflated in Marie-Nicole Dumont's self-portrait *The Artist at Her Occupations* (*c.*1789), in which she represents herself, doubly creative, standing by her baby in a cradle in front of the canvas upon which she works.

Further strains of thought affected images of artists and, in particular, self-portraits. The burgeoning of Romanticism and, with it, the increased significance ascribed to the primacy of the individual and to the centrality of the emotional domain, transformed conceptions of the self. The physiognomic theories of Johann Kaspar Lavater were prevalent and evident in close-up interpretations concentrating on facial features and expressions, most notably in his contemporary Messerschmidt's overly exaggerated, grimacing self-portrait heads, which he began in 1770 (cat. 68). However, explorations of personal identity went beyond the surface of the skin – building upon the writings of thinkers such as David Hume – to delve into notions of inwardness.[12] Artists' portraits and especially self-portraits became vehicles for investigations into inner consciousness. This impulse was, perhaps, most pronounced among Northern European artists: the German painter Runge's penetrating gaze in his three-quarter view of only his face and shoulders (Kunsthalle, Hamburg) can quite literally be seen as a window into these operations, as can the Danish artist Ditlev Blunck's intense scrutiny of his own reflection in a mirror at his studio as captured by his friend Wilhelm Bendz (cat. 82).

It may be that the most influential thinker of this period was Jean-Jacques Rousseau, who called attention to ideas of autobiography as well as the natural state of man in writings that significantly shaped romantic culture. Goya, following kindred lines of thought throughout his *oeuvre*, similarly probed his own image, penetrating the depths of his soul in self-portraits which document his life and span his entire career. The most poignant of these is an 1820 homage to his physician, Eugenio Garcia Arrieta, who cured him from a grave illness (fig. 55). Set in a characteristically shadowy environment that evokes the dark side of reason, Goya shows himself as an elderly invalid leaning back into the gentle embrace of Dr Arrieta, who proffers a glass. Two lines of thanks – 'Goya gives thanks to his friend Arrieta for the expert care with which he saved his life from an acute and dangerous illness which he suffered at the close of the year 1819 when he was seventy-three years old' – run along the bottom of the work, functioning as autobiographical narrative within the painting, which was to be Goya's last self-portrait.

→ 68   FRANZ-XAVER MESSERSCHMIDT, *Character Head: Self-portrait.*   Between 1777 and 1783. Lead, 38.7 × 21 × 21 cm.
Département des Sculptures, Musée du Louvre, Paris, RF 4724

↓ 69   LOUIS-LÉOPOLD BOILLY, *A Reunion of Artists in Isabey's Studio.*   1798. Oil on canvas, 71.5 × 111 cm.
Département des Peintures, Musée du Louvre, Paris, RF 1290 bis

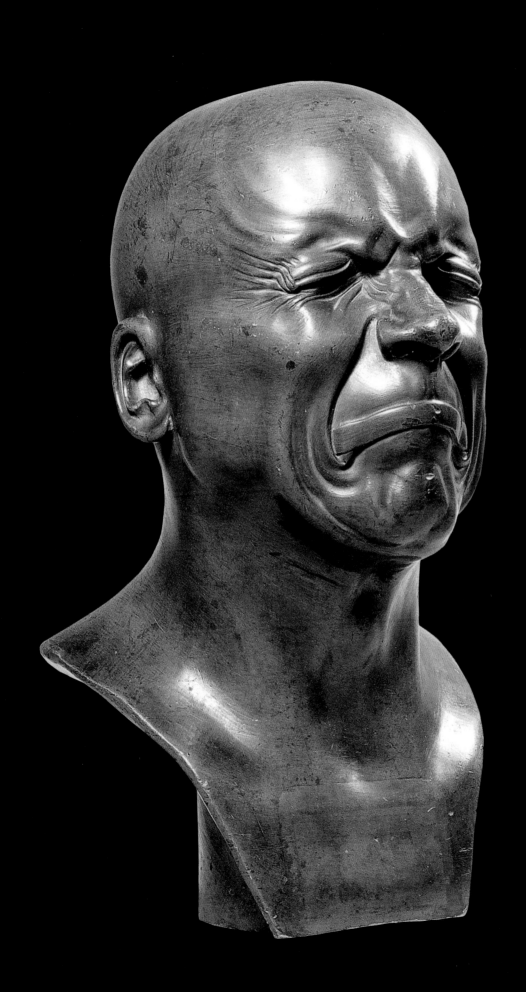

← 70   JOHANN ZOFFANY, *The Academicians of the Royal Academy.*  1771–72. Oil on canvas, 101.1 × 147.5 cm.
Lent by Her Majesty The Queen, RCIN 400747

↑ 71   BENJAMIN WEST, *Self-portrait.*  1792 or 1793. Oil on panel, 101.5 × 132 cm.
Royal Academy of Arts, London, 03/285

→ 72   HENRY SINGLETON, *The Royal Academicians in General Assembly.*  1795 (with portions reworked until 1798).
Oil on canvas, 198.1 × 259 cm.
Royal Academy of Arts, London, 03/1310

← 73   SIR JOSHUA REYNOLDS, *Self-portrait.*   c.1779–80. Oil on panel, 127 × 101 cm.
Royal Academy of Arts, London, 03/1394

↑ 74   JAMES BARRY, *Self-portrait as Timanthes.*   Begun c.1780, completed 1803. Oil on canvas, 76 × 63.5 cm.
National Gallery of Ireland, Dublin, 971

↑ 75  JOHANN HEINRICH DANNECKER, *Self-portrait.*  1796. Plaster, 74.5 × 50 × 30 cm.
Staatsgalerie, Stuttgart, P. 703

→ 76  JEAN-BAPTISTE PIGALLE, *Self-portrait.*  *c.*1776. Plaster, 55 × 27 × 25 cm.
Fondation Saint-Thomas, Strasbourg

77  ADOLPH-ULRICH WERTMÜLLER, *Jean-Jacques Caffieri*.  1784. Oil on canvas, 129 × 96 cm.

Museum of Fine Arts, Boston. Ernest Wadsworth Longfellow Fund

78 JEAN-BAPTISTE DESMARAIS, *Denis-Antoine Chaudet.* 1788. Oil on canvas, 97.5 × 73.5 cm.
M. and Mme Alain Moatti, Paris

← 79   BERTEL THORVALDSEN, *Horace Vernet.*   1832–33. Marble, 50 × 27 × 19.7 cm.
Musée Calvet, Avignon

↑ 80   HORACE VERNET, *Bertel Thorvaldsen.*   1833. Oil on canvas, 99.8 × 75.2 cm.
Thorvaldsens Museum, Copenhagen, B 95

↑ 81   CHRISTEN KØBKE, *Frederik Sødring.*   1832. Oil on canvas, 42.2 × 37.9 cm.
Den Hirschsprungske Samling, Copenhagen, 309

→ 82   WILHELM BENDZ, *A Young Artist (Ditlev Blunck) Examining a Sketch in a Mirror.*   1826. Oil on canvas, 98 × 58 cm.
Statens Museum for Kunst, Copenhagen, 280

← 83   SIR FRANCIS CHANTREY, *John Raphael Smith.*   1825. Marble, 66 × 42 × 30 cm.

Victoria and Albert Museum, London, A.15-1920

↑ 84   HORTENSE HAUDEBOURT-LESCOT, *Self-portrait.*   1825. Oil on canvas, 74 × 60 cm.

Département des Peintres, Musée du Louvre, Paris, MI 719. Gift of Mme Buhner, *née* Maria Dauby, pupil of the artist, 1867

# 6

# The Family Portrait

MARTIN POSTLE

If THERE IS ONE WORD THAT SUMS UP THE changes that affected the family portrait in the eighteenth century it is companionship. When we look at the family portrait in Europe before this period, it is clear that the principal function of the genre is the reinforcement of dynastic ties and bloodlines. In the traditions of courtly portraiture men, women and children inhabit quite distinct and separate spheres, preordained by their position in the family hierarchy. When featured together in family portraits, wives and progeny inevitably take subsidiary roles under the protection of the all-powerful paterfamilias. In an age of high mortality, children counted in number as much as in name, and there was relatively little attempt by portraitists to provide them with individual identities or attributes.

The eighteenth century, it has been argued, witnessed the evolution of the 'permissive' family. The bonds that united family members were regulated by mutual love and respect, rather than through submission and control. In such an atmosphere of give and take, attitudes towards education, play and child-rearing were modified. And as parents allowed greater latitude towards their children, so the family portrait increasingly displayed informal and intimate aspects of this new relationship. In *The Beaumont Family* (fig. 56), the British artist George Romney depicts family members gathered around the portrait of one of the members of the present family group or a relative, possibly a brother who had recently died. This ambitious portrait at once celebrates the kinship of family life, while acknowledging, through the group's focus on the portrait, the vital role of the artist in articulating the sensibility which underlies the familial relationship.

A factor which also contributed to the informality of the family portrait was the Enlightenment cult of sensibility. At its most basic, sensibility was, as Diderot stated, 'a quality peculiar to an animal, which informs it of the relationships between itself and its surroundings'. On a more popular level sensibility was not restricted merely to a capacity for feeling, self-awareness or even the expression of emotion, but to a moral code wherein sensitivity was allied to virtuous behaviour and good works. In this context the family is upheld as a force for moral well-being and model citizenship. As Rousseau asked in his novel *Emile* (1762), was it 'not through one's attachment to the small society of the family that the heart becomes attached to the larger society of one's nation?'.

In this section the growth of a more companionable image of the family is typified by Reynolds's portrait of the Braddyll family of 1789 (cat. 85). Here Wilson Gale Braddyll, soldier, courtier and politician, is confirmed in his position as head of the family, the apex of a compositional triangle formed by himself, his wife and teenage son. At the same time, the group exudes an air of informal relaxation, through the country setting, and even the affection shown towards the family's pet dog, whose ear Mrs Braddyll strokes fondly. Across the Channel, some years later, Claude-Marie Dubufe displays the intimacy of family life in its most extreme aspect as he portrays himself in the bosom of his own family (cat. 99). Here, the family members, through their close physical proximity and gestures of mutual support, are promoted as a single unit – the embodiment of private virtues, notably companionship and affection.

In the promotion of the private virtues intimately connected with family life, the figure of the mother played a central role. In the later eighteenth century, with a rising tide of resentment directed towards the profligacy of courtly life, the bourgeoisie, and certain sections of the aristocracy, increasingly espoused the pleasures of domestic life. Young women were educated primarily to prepare themselves for the role of wife and mother. And while certain theorists, such as Rousseau, preferred to subordinate the female role, others challenged the absolute right of husbands to rule over their wives, and looked towards a truer measure of equality. Women, too, took it into their own hands to promote the concept of permissive motherhood. In Britain Georgiana, Duchess of Devonshire (cat. 90), a fashion icon and political activist, championed the practice of breast-feeding, allying her own maternal instincts to her intellectual fecundity. At the same time the court of George III, through the personal example of the King and Queen (cats 2, 3), offered a paradigm for a marriage of equals, through the promotion of the concept of 'domestic' court life: this was in turn reflected in the family portraits they commissioned, notably those

painted by the German-born court painter Johann Zoffany.

Zoffany's portrait of Queen Charlotte and her two young sons (cat. 87) exemplifies the paradigm of courtly motherhood in the context of domestic family life. Here, the beatific young queen welcomes her offspring, extending her affection towards the family dog, on whose head she rests her hand. While the setting is grand, the masquerade costumes of the young boys, the presence of their toys, and the glimpsed parkland indicate that this portrait is an affirmation of the moral strength of the family, in which the mother plays a central role. Decades later, the French artist François Gérard, in

Fig. 56
GEORGE ROMNEY
*The Beaumont Family*, 1777–79.
Oil on canvas,
204.5 × 271.8 cm.
Tate, London

Fig. 57
PIERRE-PAUL PRUD'HON
*The King of Rome*, 1811.
Oil on canvas, 46 × 56 cm.
Musée du Louvre, Paris, RF 1982-19

his portrait of Hortense de Beauharnais and her son (Musée National du Château, Fontainebleau), produced an image that is in marked contrast to Zoffany's intimate portrait of the British queen and her children. Here, the imperial image of the wife of Napoleon's brother, Louis Bonaparte, is rooted iconographically in the formal traditions of royal portraiture, the relationship between mother and son being designed to reinforce the dynastic and political aspirations of the Bonaparte family, rather than any personal bond.

Today the child is regarded as the *raison d'être* of family life. It is also the norm for parents to celebrate childhood, and to recognise and respect its discrete ludic culture – even in preference to the more formalised rituals that govern adult social behaviour. Many historians have identified the creation of what we might term the 'cult' of the child, and its attendant promotion in visual culture, as an eighteenth-century phenomenon. It was during this period that a 'secularisation' of

childhood occurred in the context of a decline in the moral authority of the Christian church. Children, who had hitherto been perceived as being stained by original sin, and who thus needed to be saved from moral degradation, were increasingly regarded as innocent and free from the corruptions of the adult world. As the British philosopher John Locke argued in his seminal treatise *Some Thoughts Concerning Education* (1693), the mind of the child was a blank sheet, 'white paper, or wax, to be moulded and fashioned as one pleases'. In the Lockean framework, reason supplanted superstition, and the fully rounded education of the child found room for play as well as work. As the world of the child gained social prominence, the child portrait became recognised increasingly as a major genre in its own right.

Henry Walton's portrait of Sir Robert and Lady Buxton with their daughter (cat. 88) exemplifies a particular kind of family portrait that had become fashionable, especially in Britain, by the later 1700s. We see the attentive parents teaching their child to read, as sewing and open books litter the floor and sofa in an atmosphere of controlled disorder. Although the mood is playful, the adults' efforts to educate their daughter add a necessary moral dimension. Indeed, it is a commonplace in child portraiture that the artist should interpose some form of moral or allegorical commentary into the ludic world of the child. This can be seen more forcibly in Goya's portrait of Don Manuel Osorio Manrique de Zuñiga (cat. 102), where the caged birds eyed by the predatory cats create a sinister atmosphere in which the innocent pleasures and attributes of childhood are under immediate threat.

In Western art the allegorical presence of the child was traditionally conveyed through its transformation into various spirit forms, as classical putti or Christian angels. In the eighteenth century, however, a more naturalistic attitude to childhood emerged: it is represented here by Houdon's bust of his infant daughter (cat. 107), one of a number of works by the sculptor which responded to the particular characteristics and expressions of his child subjects. Nonetheless, although naturalism was encouraged in privately commissioned works, the public image of the child continued to be conditioned by more strategic and dynastic impulses. In Prud'hon's painting of Napoleon II (fig. 57), the infant son of Napoleon is presented as a reincarnation of Romulus, as if to underline his future destiny as King of Rome, and his spiritual ancestry. In a more light-hearted manner, neoclassical artists often used the iconography of the ancient world to deify the images of offspring of the gentry and nobility. Thus, the sculptor Chinard frames the face of the young Fanny Perrin (cat. 123) in a classical garland, which, together with the pair of wings attached to her back, transforms her playfully into an infant Psyche.

As the child assumed a dominant role in visual imagery which focused upon the family, so the roles of the parents were redefined. In the case of the mother figure, the shift was one of degree, as bonds of intimacy became more heavily emphasised, and the domestic sphere gained greater prominence at the expense of dynastic concerns. The consequent repositioning of the father within this reformed structure was more problematic, not least because in an age of sensibility the code of masculinity, which underpinned the ethos of the paterfamilias, was challenged by a desire for the male to emote and to be perceived as a sentient being.

One pictorial strategy used to re-evaluate the role of the father figure was to relocate him within a landscape setting, and to demonstrate his affinity with the natural world. Nor was it sufficient to demonstrate that the bond that existed between the male and the landscape was based upon property or ownership; rather it had to communicate a love of nature for its own sake. We can see this strategy in operation in Boilly's portrait of M. d'Aucourt de Saint-Just (fig. 65), in which the subject is not only situated upon his country estate but he performs a task – the cutting of tree branches – more usually associated with a manual labourer. Boilly's portrait presents an image of domestic virility, a man of the world observed in a private environment. At the same time, the archetypal family man was also a man of feeling, who was capable of outward shows of tenderness and affection. In his portrait of Jean-Baptiste Isabey (cat. 89), painted out of gratitude towards his fellow artist, Gérard paid tribute specifically to Isabey's sensibility, by depicting him holding the hand of his young daughter. Behind them, the family dog wags its tail excitedly, indicating perhaps that they are about to take a walk in the garden beyond the doorway in the picture's background.

An awareness of male sensibility could occasionally lead to more eccentric images, notably Joseph Wright of Derby's portrait of the English gentleman Sir Brooke Boothby (cat. 134), reclining in a woodland glade with a volume of the translated writings of Jean-Jacques Rousseau. The most extreme example of male sensibility here, however, is the remarkable portrait of Richard Mansergh St George by the Irish painter Hugh Douglas Hamilton (cat. 95), in which this notoriously romantically inclined gentleman-soldier is observed in an attitude of introspective grief in response to the recent death of his wife. Hamilton's iconography, here deployed in a male portrait, is derived from female figures in mourning, to be found most usually on commemorative monuments and tomb sculpture. Thus, in this portrait, the male subject is at once representative of both the male and female gender. The result is an unsettling image, which, although it acknowledges Mansergh St George's role as a soldier, shows him renouncing his public persona in order to meditate upon his role as husband, the profound nature of the matrimonial bond and its enforced dissolution through death.

← 85    SIR JOSHUA REYNOLDS, *The Braddyll Family*.   1789. Oil on canvas, 238.1 × 147.3 cm.
      Lent by the Syndics of the Fitzwilliam Museum, Cambridge, PD.10-1955. Given by the National Art Collections Fund, 1955

↑ 86    THOMAS GAINSBOROUGH, *George Byam with His Wife Louisa and Their Daughter Selina*.
      *c.*1762, and reworked by 1766. Oil on canvas, 249 × 238.8 cm.
      The Andrew Brownsword Arts Foundation. On long-term loan to the Holburne Museum of Art, Bath

←  87   JOHANN ZOFFANY, *Queen Charlotte with Her Two Eldest Sons.*   *c.*1764–65. Oil on canvas, 112 × 130 cm.
         Lent by Her Majesty the Queen, RCIN 400146

↑  88   HENRY WALTON, *Sir Robert and Lady Buxton with Their Daughter Anne.*   *c.*1786. Oil on canvas, 73.6 × 92.5 cm.
         Norwich Castle Museum and Art Gallery, 1963.268.9

← 89   FRANÇOIS GÉRARD, *Jean-Baptiste Isabey and His Daughter Alexandrine.*  1795. Oil on canvas, 195 × 130 cm.

      Département des Peintures, Musée du Louvre, Paris, RF 4764. Gift of Eugène Isabey, son and brother of the models, 1852

↑ 90   SIR JOSHUA REYNOLDS, *Georgiana, Duchess of Devonshire and Her Daughter, Lady Georgiana Cavendish.*

      1784–86. Oil on canvas, 112.5 × 142.7 cm.

      Chatsworth Settlement Trustees

↑ 91   PHILIPP OTTO RUNGE, *The Artist's Parents*.   1806. Oil on canvas, 196 × 131 cm.
Kunsthalle, Hamburg, 1001

→ 92   UNKNOWN ARTIST, *A Man and His Children* (formerly known as *Michel Gérard, Deputy at the Assemblée
Nationale, and His Children*).   *c.*1810. Oil on canvas, 160 × 127 cm.   Musée de Tessé, Le Mans, 10.288

↑ 93   AUGUSTIN PAJOU, *Charles de Wailly*.   1789. Plaster, 73.5 × 52 × 25 cm.
Palais des Beaux-Arts, Lille, 2001.2.1

→ 94   AUGUSTIN PAJOU, *Madame de Wailly*.   1789. Marble, 76.2 × 50.8 cm.
Lent by The Metropolitan Museum of Art, New York, Fletcher Fund, 1956 (56.105)

← 95   HUGH DOUGLAS HAMILTON, *Lieutenant Richard Mansergh St George.*   *c.*1796. Oil on canvas, 228 × 146.2 cm.
National Gallery of Ireland, Dublin, 4585

↑ 96   DENIS-ANTOINE CHAUDET, *A Woman Holding a Portrait of Her Husband in Her Arms.*   1795. Marble, 87.5 × 36 × 45.8 cm.
Musée des Arts Décoratifs, Paris, 35 302

← 97  POMPEO MARCHESI, *Giulio Mylius.*  1830. Marble, 75 × 65 × 40 cm.

Villa Vigoni, Loveno di Menaggio (Como), s. 51

↑ 98  FRANCESCO HAYEZ, *Luigia Vitali, Mylius's Widow.*  1832. Oil on wood, 131 × 100 cm.

Villa Vigoni, Loveno di Menaggio (Como)

↑ 99   CLAUDE-MARIE DUBUFE, *The Artist's Family.*  1820. Oil on canvas, 64 × 82 cm.

Département des Peintures, Musée du Louvre, Paris, RF 1982-2. Donated to be held in usufruct by M. Edouard Dubufe, great-grandson of the artist, 1982

→ 100   JOSEPH CHINARD, *Madame Chinard.*  1802–03. Terracotta, 65 × 36.5 × 26.3 cm.

Musée des Beaux-Arts, Lyons, B 426

↑ 101   AGUSTÍN ESTEVE Y MARQUÉS, *Don Mariano San Juan y Pinedo, Conde Consorte de La Cimera.* *c.*1810/13. Oil on canvas, 128 × 89 cm.
Museo Nacional del Prado, Madrid, 2876

→ 102   FRANCISCO DE GOYA Y LUCIENTES, *Don Manuel Osorio Manrique de Zuñiga.* 1788. Oil on canvas, 127 × 101.6 cm.
Lent by The Metropolitan Museum of Art, New York. The Jules Bache Collection, 1949 (49.7.41)

EL S.ᴰ MANVEL OSORIO MANRRIQᴢ D. ZVÑIGA

← 103   JOSEPH WRIGHT OF DERBY, *Three Children of Richard Arkwright with a Goat.*   1791. Oil on canvas, 190.5 × 149.9 cm.
Private collection

↑ 104   ANTOINE-JEAN GROS, *Paul-François Des Hours de Calviac.*   1793. Oil on canvas, 73 × 97 cm.
Musée des Beaux-Arts, Rennes

↑ 105    JACQUES-EDME DUMONT, *Madame Dumont, the Artist's Mother*. 1799. Plaster, 53 × 38.5 × 24 cm.
     Département des Sculptures, Musée du Louvre, Paris, RF 657

→ 106    HENRI-JOSEPH RUTXIEHL, *Elfride Clarke de Feltre*. 1813? Marble, 50 × 27 × 20 cm.
     Musée des Beaux-Arts, Nantes, 1844

→ 107    JEAN-ANTOINE HOUDON, *Sabine Houdon Aged Ten Months*. 1788. Marble, 44.5 × 25 × 17 cm.

   Lent by The Metropolitan Museum of Art, New York. Bequest of Mary Stillman Harkness, 1950 (50.145.66)

↑ 108 CONSTANTIN HANSEN, *The Artist's Sisters Signe and Henriette Reading a Book.* 1826. Oil on canvas, 65.5 × 56 cm.
Statens Museum for Kunst, Copenhagen, 3004

→ 109 THÉODORE GÉRICAULT, *Alfred and Elisabeth Dedreux.* 1816–17. Oil on canvas, 99 × 80 cm.
Collection Yves Saint-Laurent and Pierre Bergé

# 7

# The Portrait after the Antique

MALCOLM BAKER

WHETHER IN THE FORM OF THE STATUE or the bust, the sculptural portrait from the Renaissance onwards has always carried associations with the antique.[1] The single standing figure, placed on a plinth, made reference to a genre of sculptural representation established in antiquity, and this connection was still more apparent when the figure, usually male, was shown wearing any generalised dress that recalled the drapery of classical statuary. The authority that the erection of a statue was claiming for the subject represented was in large part that associated with antique sculpture. But it was the bust, even more than the statue, which made this link between the present and the classical past most explicit.

Although the most obvious appropriation of the antique in the Renaissance (and indeed earlier) was the use of the equestrian figure of Marcus Aurelius as the model for equestrian monuments, both freestanding statues and busts from the fifteenth century likewise draw directly on classical precedents in a conscious way. The formulation of the familiar convention of the individual statue may have involved an enlargement of small-scale Etruscan bronze figurines but the transference in the case of the bust was more direct.[2] Even though it drew partly on a medieval tradition of reliquary busts, the portrait bust was primarily based on Roman sculptural portraits, sometimes in a very explicit manner.[3] This was especially the case with images such as Michelangelo's bust of Brutus in which details such as the drapery and the hair, and not simply the form, imitate antique examples.[4] Although the development of the baroque bust made this connection less immediately obvious the association of the bust format with the antique remained in play. The relationship became more explicit once again during the eighteenth century. At this point these two categories of sculptural portrait — the statue and the bust — with inherently classical conventions and connotations begin to be used within a context in which the antique was

being appropriated as the dominant mode for all forms of visual imagery.

By the mid-eighteenth century, the classical was employed, consciously and deliberately, as the model for gardens and dress as well as for painting and sculpture.[5] Such uses of the antique could carry important and varying ideological meanings. In England the landscapes of Richard Wilson were grounded in a discourse of civic humanism in which the authority of the antique was associated with the seemingly natural right of landowners to property and power, while in France the classical could be used by Jacques-Louis David to exemplify revolutionary political ideals.[6] But how were the traditionally classicising genres of sculptural portraiture used during this period?

By the early nineteenth century when, for example, Sir Francis Chantrey's bronze statues of George IV and William Pitt were erected at the intersections of the main streets of the neoclassical New Town in Edinburgh, the neoclassical statue seemed entirely natural and familiar in its mode and format. So did the same sculptor's busts of eminent men of the period, almost all of them clearly variants of the same classicising types, albeit given individuality by Chantrey's distinctive naturalism in representing the physiognomy of his sitters (cats 83, 151). If our view of Regency England and its leading figures (or least leading men) is shaped as much by Chantrey's portrait busts as by Sir Thomas Lawrence's painted portraits of the same sitters, we see these early nineteenth-century personalities through a classicising medium, as if this guise was assumed, a given in the sculptural representation of any person of power and influence. By relying on antique associations and formulae for its authority, portrait sculptures such as these — whether the statue or the bust — can look quite similar to each other. This had not been the case with classicising images early in the eighteenth century.

Around 1730 the bust *all'antica* was becoming steadily more common but the forms which it took were very different. Both Bouchardon's bust of Philipp von Stosch (carved in Rome) and Scheemakers's sculptural portraits of Lord Cobham and his political allies for the Temple of Friendship at Stowe make conscious and explicit reference to Roman portrait sculpture, but these images look very different from each other. By the late eighteenth century, however, the classicising bust had become regularised, and sometimes even standardised, in its format and conventions. Not that there was only one convention for the portrait bust at this date. Canova's bust of Cimarosa (cat. 119) shows the composer bare-chested, as does Chantrey's bust of Johnstone (cat. 151), both imitating Roman busts familiar from the display of sculptural portraits to be seen in the Capitoline from the mid-eighteenth century. Espercieux's marble of the Abbé Raynal (cat. 117) also represents the sitter without drapery but here the format employed for the bust is the herm shape, with straight sides, and cut so that the head emerges from a block of marble. By contrast, Trippel's bust of Goethe (Herzogin Anna Amalia Bibliothek, Weimar) has the bust proper swathed in classicising drapery and the poet wears his hair long, making him resemble Apollo, as the sculptor himself pointed out. But, while the bust *all'antica* around 1800 could take a number of forms, each of these conventions constitutes a familiar and recognisable type that was employed by sculptors working in different countries. For instance, the herm format – perhaps the most ubiquitous type of classicising bust during this period – was employed not only by Espercieux for Raynal but also by Chantrey for his bust of the poet William Wordsworth and by Chaudet for his much-reproduced portrait of Napoleon.

In the main, the portrait bust – especially when representing a male sitter – had a public function. As Byron remarked when sitting for his own, a bust,

Fig. 58
JAMES SAYERS
*The Patriot Exalted*,
published by Thomas Cornell,
15 March 1792.
National Portrait Gallery, London,
NPG D9572

unlike a painted portrait, 'looks like putting up pretensions to permanency – and smacks something of a hankering for *public* fame rather than private remembrance'.[7] The public nature of the bust meant that it was frequently loaded with ideological and political meaning, which was heightened and rendered both more explicit and authoritative through the adoption of an *all'antica* manner. The authority of Napoleon as newly crowned emperor was articulated in Chaudet's bust not only by the laurel wreath but also by the herm form. In this most uncompromisingly classical of images, the political might of the sitter is represented as directly as in any painted portrait by David. It is therefore not surprising that marble replicas of Chaudet's image were produced on a large scale by the workshops at Carrara, under Bartolini's control, and sold by the business established in Paris by Elisa Baciocchi to the large numbers eager to demonstrate their loyalty to the emperor.[8] It was above all the classicising bust – not merely the bust in general – that had these ideological associations. This appears to have been recognised by the English satirical engraver who mocked Catherine II's placement of her bust of Charles James Fox between images of those ancient exemplars of political oratory, Cicero and Demosthenes (fig. 58). (The two classical figures are shown fleeing from their niches as Fox is placed between them.) Although the bust acquired by Catherine II was a version of Nollekens's marble showing Fox in a relatively baroque mode, the engraver instead shows a bust that was far more classical, the more effectively to emphasise (and ridicule) the claim by the politician and his Russian admirer to the authority, wisdom and public virtue of the two ancients.

Another equally telling example of the way different modes of classicising sculptural portrait could carry political meaning in a particular setting is to be found at Apsley House, the Duke of Wellington's house in London. Here, following

Fig. 59
ANTONIO CANOVA
*Napoleon as Mars the Peacemaker*,
1803–06. Marble, H. 340 cm.
Apsley House, London

Fig. 60
VINCENZO FEOLI
*Galleria dei Busti, Museo
Pio-Clementino.*
Engraving, 61 × 73 cm.
Bibliothèque Nationale de France,
Paris

the Duke's victory at Waterloo, Wellington set up
Canova's monumental nude statue of Napoleon
in the central stairwell of the house (fig. 59).
An image initially commissioned to represent
the then emperor in the most boldly antique
manner, like Mars, was recontextualised so that
it was surrounded by busts – likewise *all-antica*
images, albeit ones less open to ridicule – by
Rauch and others, of the leaders and generals on
the winning side.[9] Classicising sculptural images
of different sorts were here being brought into
dialogue to represent a turning-point in
European history.

In these various cases, then, we have a common
European sculptural language, the sharing of which
was no doubt encouraged by the experience of
many, if not most, sculptors of this period of
working for a time in Rome, whether they were
English, Danish, French, Scottish or German.

This language was one that made explicit its
indebtedness to classical precedent and indeed
relied for both its authority and legibility on this
lineage. While neoclassical painting might draw
on the classical tradition for its subject-matter
and its drapery patterns, it was sculpture above all
that could refer most directly to surviving images
from the antique past. These very images were at
this period becoming more easily visible as well
as more clearly ordered and categorised through
both publication and display. Although few of the
influential texts about antique art – most notably
Winckelmann's *Geschichte der Kunst des Altertums*
(*History of Ancient Art*) – discuss classical portrait
busts as a genre, Roman busts were being
increasingly reproduced through engraving. They
figure prominently, for example, in the illustrated
accounts published from the 1760s of the sculpture
collection of the Earl of Pembroke to be seen at

Wilton House.[10] Another index of the attention being given to the antique bust is to be found in the rearrangement of Roman collections, first at the Capitoline and then later in the century in the Museo Pio-Clementino at the Vatican.[11] As part of the new display of the papal collections in the latter, antique busts were arrayed in series on several levels within a room devoted solely to this category of ancient sculpture, the Galleria dei Busti (fig. 60).

Just at the time when these new displays of antique busts were being conceived and set up, contemporary sculptors were producing busts in which modern sitters were being represented in the variety of regular, almost standard formats described above, each of which made direct reference to a classical precedent. Both phenomena, like the wider neoclassical movement of which they are manifestations, suggest that the past – and especially the antique past – was being both understood and used in a new way. Some cultural historians, such as Stephen Bann, have argued that

during this period there emerged a new sense of history – a conception of the past which was qualitatively different and more self-conscious than that of earlier antiquarians.[12] Sometimes, this new notion of history could be registered in a fresh concern with local or national monuments which, in their distinctiveness, could then constitute the material part of a nation's history. But when the same sense of history was applied to the antique past, the artefacts and images of Greek or Roman culture could be ordered in more systematic and coherent manner, as in the displays already mentioned. Viewed in this way, the antique past could, unlike accounts of local or national monuments, be understood as a culture shared by many different national groups in Europe. Correspondingly, the language of the classical portrait bust, with its various familiar and well-defined formats, could be seen as an international one, as well as one that made direct reference to a classical past.

→ 110   BERTEL THORVALDSEN, *Princess Maria Feodorovna Bariatinskaya.*   1818. Plaster, 180 × 57 × 60 cm.
Thorvaldsens Museum, Copenhagen, A 172

↑ III    CARL FRIEDRICH HAGEMANN, *Immanuel Kant.* 1801. Marble, 51.5 × 23 × 26.5 cm.
Kunsthalle, Hamburg, 1939/82

↗ II2    GIUSEPPE CERACCHI, *George Washington.* 1795. Marble, 73.3 × 55.9 × 33 cm.
Lent by The Metropolitan Museum of Art, New York. Bequest of John L. Cadwalader, 1914 (14.58.235)

→ II3    IL VOLPATO (GIOVANNI TREVISAN), *José Nicolas de Azara and Anton Raphael Mengs.*
*c.*1785. Porcelain, 28.1 × 17 × 14 cm.
Accademia Carrara, Bergamo, sc. 167

Live to speak the Patriot
Heart, embracing all M...
Fortitude, unbroke by T...
...rofound and Eloqu...
...al to save a Venal...
...one be lost in Politic...
...expiring F...
acquires ...

...ds, Humanity's neglected Cause
...from After Ages sure Applause

← 114   JOSEPH NOLLEKENS, *Charles James Fox.* 1791. Marble, 69 × 54 × 26 cm.
     Private collection

↑ 115   JOSEPH NOLLEKENS, *Charles James Fox.* *c.*1802 (but possibly after 1823). Marble, 72 × 52 × 34 cm.
     Victoria and Albert Museum, London, A.1-1945

↗ 116   JOSEPH NOLLEKENS, *Charles James Fox.* 1805 (but possibly after 1823). Marble, 67 × 42 × 25 cm.
     National Portrait Gallery, London

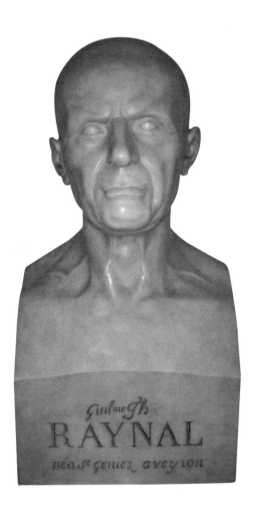

↑ 117   JEAN-JOSEPH ESPERCIEUX, *The Abbé Raynal.*   Executed in 1837, from a model made in 1790. Marble, 56 × 28 × 25 cm.
Mairie, Saint-Geniez-d'Olt

↗ 118   THOMAS BANKS, *Dr Thomas Addington.*   1790. Marble, 76 × 48 × 25.5 cm.
Victoria and Albert Museum, London, A.2-1955

→ 119   ANTONIO CANOVA, *Domenico Cimarosa.*   1808. Marble, 75 × 60 × 28 cm.
Promoteca Capitolina, Musei Capitolini, Rome, PRO 24

120  BERTEL THORVALDSEN, *Apotheosis of Napoleon I.*  *c.*1830. Marble, 105 × 67 × 46 cm.
Thorvaldsens Museum, Copenhagen, A 867

# 8

# The Allegorical Portrait

SÉBASTIEN ALLARD AND GUILHEM SCHERF

AFTER THE 1760S, THE ALLEGORICAL or mythological portrait enjoyed an unprecedented vogue, particularly in Britain where the influence of Van Dyck was very strong. This portrait type had had its origins mainly in court portraiture and portraits of royalty.[1] The revitalised genre, promoted most strongly by Reynolds in painting and Canova in sculpture, demonstrates the growing proximity of portraiture and history painting, and the alliance of a new 'realism', in the representation of features and the nude, with drapery from classical antiquity. The artist who transfigured reality in this way was asserting the idealising dimension of the genre. Portraits of women and, to a lesser extent, children were one of the favoured areas. In sculpture, although Thorvaldsen and Bartolini made full-length figures that were not allegorical (see cat. 110 and fig. 69), the genre followed the same general trend. In both painting and sculpture it presented an opportunity to portray 'heroic' women, thus asserting its status as a kind of female pendant to the 'history portrait'. In most cases, anyway, the historical or mythological disguise was more than just fancy dress or a mask: it was a means of ennobling the sitter by expressing the eternal value of one particular characteristic or, in a more general way, her social status. In 1753, Madame de Pompadour had herself portrayed by Pigalle as Friendship (Louvre, Paris) to welcome the king to Bellevue; her allegorical transformation should in this case be seen as a political ruse aimed at consolidating her position at court. In Great Britain, well-born young women had themselves portrayed as Hebe, the handmaiden of the gods, an allusion to their duties as wives or daughters. In the case of Reynolds's *Mrs Muster* (1782; Iveagh Bequest, Kenwood), this has its ironical aspect. The exaltation of beauty, the most important female quality, is expressed on more than one occasion by the obvious allusion to Venus, reaching a climax in Canova's *Pauline Borghese as Venus Victrix*

(fig. 20). In this particular case, the subject's nakedness illustrates the way in which in the early nineteenth century the personality of a woman was projected through her whole body.[2] Canova made a speciality of this, in this masterpiece as well as in *Elisa as Polyhymnia* and *Marie-Louise as Concord*; some critics viewed this as a form of political disengagement.[3] By employing a classical reference to plump putti, Romney ennobled the pedigree of the children of Lord Leveson-Gower (cat. 124). The eldest girl is depicted as a bacchante with a tambourine; sexual connotations are ignored here in favour of music, celebrated as the union of the soul and the body. The identification of women with music can be found in numerous portraits of women as St Cecilia (Reynolds, *Mrs Billington*, 1789; Beaverbrook Art Gallery, New Brunswick). In the case of *Mrs Hale as Euphrosyne* by Reynolds (1762; Harewood House), the prototype for a number of images of this type, the allusion to music is justified by the fact that the painting was probably meant to hang in the music room at Harewood House. In similar fashion, under Canova's chisel, Alexandrine de Bleschamp (fig. 52), an occasional poet, ended up as the muse of lyric poetry.

Allegorical or mythological disguise was not of advantage to aristocratic women alone. In fact, it could give dignity to models who either lacked it or were trying to acquire it, independently of their social status. This is why the sculptress Anne Seymour Damer (fig. 61) had herself depicted in the guise of the muse of sculpture. Elisabeth-Louise Vigée-Lebrun gave Madame de Staël the facial features of her most celebrated heroine, Corinne (cat. 131). A few years later, Gérard's posthumous portrait of Necker's daughter (radically enhanced) became a genuine history painting in *Corinne at Cape Misenum* (fig. 62). It was the actresses, however, who benefited most from this, illustrating the importance now attached to celebrity as a route to social recognition. The most striking example of this is, of course, Reynolds's *Mrs Siddons* (cat.130). In a composition recalling Michelangelo's *Prophets* in the Sistine Chapel, Mrs Siddons, a hugely admired actress, becomes a kind of eternal deity; the portrait represents more of a transfiguration than a disguise. In his portrait of *Garrick between Tragedy and Comedy* (1761; Private collection), Reynolds abandons the grandiose abstraction of his *Mrs Siddons* in favour of realism; the actor is presented playing a part, rather than being turned into an icon. Thus the allegorical portrait begins to flirt with the status portrait. Courtesans, who, like Kitty Fisher, enjoyed enormous popularity in English society, enhanced their social standing by remembering the precedent set by Cleopatra. On Reynolds's easel, inspired by a poem by Dryden, the beautiful Emily Pott took on the attributes of Thaïs (1781; Waddesdon Manor). Clearly, the torch she is holding set more than just Persepolis alight! The most famous hetaera of all, Emma Hart, the future Lady Hamilton, posed as Ariadne for Vigée-Lebrun (1790; Private collection). The opportunity was beneficial to Vigée-Lebrun's ambitions as a portrait painter, while also displaying to advantage Emma Hart's dazzling flesh and long dark hair. In this case, the mythological portrait was an allusion to the model's taste for mime shows, in which she would appear on stage striking 'attitudes' in the guise of a literary, historical or mythological character. This type of portrait therefore also fits into the context of society games and amusements.

Although allegory bore all the signs of a renewed, or confirmed, respectability, it could be a redoubtable weapon to those who wished to deride. It was infrequently used to satirical ends in sculpture, as the work takes so long to create, and even more infrequently in an expensive material such as marble. One patron, however, had a bright idea: Frederick Hervey (1730–1803), fourth Earl of Bristol and Bishop of Derry, was one of the most eccentric figures of the century.[4] He was an admirer

Fig. 61
GIUSEPPE CERACCHI
*Anne Seymour Damer as the Muse of Sculpture*, c.1777.
Marble, H. 174 cm.
British Museum, London

of Pitt, and in Rome in 1796 commissioned a colossal group representing Hercules as a child strangling two serpents. The Italian sculptor was Pietro Perantoni Sposino. Hervey asked the artist to give Hercules the head of Pitt and the serpents the heads of his political enemies, Fox and North. The idea for the composition came from a caricature by Rowlandson published twelve years before.[5] The result is, aesthetically, a monstrosity, and in fact none of the protagonists emerges unscathed. Marble congeals satire, which requires a livelier material, one that can slip through the fingers like clay.[6] Anne-Louis Girodet wished to take his revenge on Mademoiselle Lange for failing to admire an earlier portrait he had done of her. A few days after the rebuff he depicted her as a modern Danaë (fig. 63). The painting caused an uproar. The actress is portrayed naked, under a shower of gold coins, some of which fall onto her private parts. The animals and accessories around her reveal the names of her numerous lovers, while her husband wears the features of a ridiculous turkey. A dove, wearing a necklace bearing the motto 'Fidelitas', lies dying, shot through the heart by a gold coin. The frame completes the satire. The violence of this allegory was enormously

Fig. 62
FRANÇOIS GÉRARD
*Corinne at Cape Misenum*,
Salon of 1822. Oil on canvas,
266 × 277 cm.
Musée des Beaux-Arts, Lyons

increased by its public character; it was exhibited at the Salon of 1799, with the 'historical' title of Danaë, daughter of Acrisius. None of the visitors to the exhibition was in any doubt about the subject's identity.

Although the allegorical or mythological portrait had a strong public dimension, particularly the female portrait, more personal and intimate connotations could sometimes be found, in self-portraits above all. In his *Self-portrait with Burke as Ulysses and a Companion Fleeing from Polyphemus* (cat.122) the Irish painter James Barry produced a metaphor for his own position as a misunderstood artist, pursued by unwarranted dislike. In even more personal and esoteric terms, Jean-Baptiste Régnault created a Masonic allegory (cat.121) which was to remain a family secret 'until circumstances permit it to be made known and turned to good account'. The allegorical portrait sets out as a profession of faith in which the model – the artist himself – is a utopian visionary prophesying the arrival of a new society. The tension between the private nature of the representation and its public value is here brought to a climax by the demonstrative gesture of the man. During the 1820s, the public value of these substitute identities began to be diluted by the gradual decline of the status portrait and the search for the 'character' of the model.[7] It remained present in private images, as is evident in Delacroix's precocious *Self-portrait as Ravenswood* (Louvre, Paris). Classical antiquity and mythology were no longer used to project an image; the literature of Modern Times and the fascination of the younger generation in France for things English had begun to take over.

Fig.63
ANNE-LOUIS GIRODET,
known as GIRODET-TRIOSON
*Mademoiselle Lange as Danaë*,
Salon of 1799. Oil on canvas,
65 × 54 cm.
The Minneapolis Institute of Art

← 121   JEAN-BAPTISTE RÉGNAULT, *The Physical Man, the Moral Man and the Intellectual Man.*   *c.*1810. Oil on canvas, 159 × 131 cm.
Musée des Beaux-Arts, Brest, 72.5-1

↑ 122   JAMES BARRY, *Burke and Barry in the Characters of Ulysses and a Companion Fleeing from the Cave of Polyphemus.*
*c.*1776. Oil on canvas, 127 × 102 cm.
Crawford Art Gallery, Cork, 418-P

← 123   JOSEPH CHINARD, *Fanny Perrin, with the Attributes of Psyche, Playing with a Wreath of Flowers.*
        1808. Marble, 54 × 31 × 25 cm.
        Collection du Musée d'Art Roger-Quilliot, Ville de Clermont-Ferrand, 894-325-1

↑ 124   GEORGE ROMNEY, *The Leveson-Gower Children.*   *c.*1776–77. Oil on canvas, 202 × 232 cm.
        Abbot Hall Art Gallery, Kendal, AH 1185/74

↑ 125   SIR JOSHUA REYNOLDS, *The Montgomery Sisters: 'Three Ladies Adorning a Term of Hymen'.*  1773. Oil on canvas, 233.7 × 290.8 cm.
Tate, London, N00079. Bequeathed by the Earl of Blessington, 1837

→ 126   FRANCIS COTES, *The Hon. Lady Stanhope and the Countess of Effingham as Diana and Her Companion.*  1765. Oil on canvas, 240 × 152.5 cm.
York Museums Trust (York Art Gallery), YORAG: 1414. Purchased with the aid of grants and donations from the National Heritage Memorial Fund, the Museums and Galleries Commission
through the Victoria and Albert Museum, the National Art Collections Fund, the Pilgrim Trust, the J. Paul Getty Jr Charitable Trust, the Friends of York Art Gallery, York Civic Trust,
York Georgian Society, Anthony Boynton Wood Esq. and John Miller Esq.

↑ 127　CHRISTIAN DANIEL RAUCH, *Queen Luise of Prussia as the Ludovisi Juno.* 1805–06. Marble, 77 × 42 × 40 cm.
Skulpturensammlung, Stiftung Preussische Schlösser und Gärten Berlin-Brandenburg, 1015, GK III, 4821

→ 128　JEAN-ANTOINE HOUDON, *Sophie Arnould in the Title Role of Gluck's 'Iphigenia in Aulis'.* 1775. Marble, 81 × 51 × 29.5 cm.
Département des Sculptures, Musée du Louvre, Paris, RF 2596

↑ 129    SIR THOMAS LAWRENCE, *John Philip Kemble as Coriolanus.*   1798. Oil on canvas, 287.2 × 179.7 cm.
Guildhall Art Gallery, City of London, 844

→ 130    SIR JOSHUA REYNOLDS AND STUDIO, *Mrs Siddons as the Tragic Muse.*   1789. Oil on canvas, 239.7 × 147.6 cm.
By permission of the Trustees of Dulwich Picture Gallery, London, DPG 318

↑ 131   ELISABETH-LOUISE VIGÉE-LEBRUN, *Madame de Staël as Corinne.*  1809. Oil on canvas, 140 × 118 cm.

Collection des Musées d'Art et d'Histoire de la Ville de Genève, Geneva

→ 132   ANTONIO CANOVA, *Ideal Head: Juliette Récamier as Beatrice.*  1819–22. Marble, 58.4 × 27.9 × 25.4 cm.

Museum of Fine Arts, Boston, 2002.318. William Frances Warden Fund, Edward J. and Mary S. Holmes Fund, John Lowell Gardner Fund, Russell B. and Andrée Beauchamp Stearns Fund, Helen B. Sweeney Fund, Frank B. Bemis Fund, Seth K. Sweetser Fund, H. E. Bolles Fund, Arthur Mason Knapp Fund, and Benjamin Pierce Cheney Donation

9

# Nature and Grace:
# The Landscape and the Figure

MARYANNE STEVENS

THE HISTORIAN ROY PORTER DECLARED: 'The key enlightenment concept was Nature.'[1] However, to give a single, clear definition of the term as it was applied during the eighteenth and early nineteenth centuries is problematic. Not only did its meaning vary and shift during the course of the eighteenth century but it also took on different guises across national boundaries, most notably between Britain and continental Europe, which brought with them different modes of representation. Thus, although Nature was identified as an objective moral force at the beginning of the eighteenth century, by its close it could be seen as the source of individual emotional experience and creative inspiration. Likewise, while a figure in a relaxed pose and wearing modest dress could be seen in France as 'natural' and hence synonymous with Nature, in England, Nature was more commonly referenced by placement of the figure within the context of a setting deemed to be 'natural'.

The Enlightenment's engagement with Nature brought with it a repositioning of the subject of the portrait – the sitter – in respect of the external world. It also entailed a radical reassessment of the moral, psychological and aesthetic qualities of Man that, in themselves, became subjects appropriate to be communicated through portraiture. Whereas in Renaissance, baroque and rococo portraits the sitter was often posed beyond the confines of palace or home, his or her relationship to that external location is one of disconnection. The landscape acts as a backdrop which could fulfil a number of functions: a demonstration of the source, quality or symbolism of the light; a contribution through imagery to an understanding of the status and significance of the sitter; or a demonstration of the need to control and limit an external world which was deemed to be hostile. The absence of any interaction between the sitter and external nature is reinforced by costume. Despite being set within a landscape, sheltered only by a large rock,

the elderly anonymous female sitter in Van Dyck's portrait of 1634 (Kunsthistorisches Museum, Gemäldegalerie, Vienna) wears a shimmering black silk dress which seems inappropriate to the wild setting. It stands in sharp contrast to the simple, post-revolutionary shift and straw bonnet in which Louis-Léopold Boilly portrays Madame d'Aucourt de Saint-Just (fig. 64) as she stands within a landscape that seems to respond to the contemporary aesthetic principles defining an appreciation of the range and variety of Nature: the sublimity of a towering cliff and the beauty of the sunlit landscape beyond.

The transformation of attitudes towards Nature and the natural world played a fundamental part in the re-evaluation of their role and the meaning of the 'natural' in eighteenth-century portraiture. From an English perspective, this was facilitated by the impact of the Glorious Revolution of 1688, which accomplished the removal of the Catholic king, James II, his replacement by the Protestant William of Orange (William III) and his consort Queen Mary, daughter of Charles II, and the establishment of a constitutional monarchy. A new spirit of optimism replaced the pessimistic view of both Man and Nature that had prevailed throughout much of the seventeenth century. In theological terms, this held that Man inhabited a world after the Fall, whose condition represented punishment for Original Sin. Nature, in its natural condition, was thus antipathetic and deformed, incapable of representing perfection or truth. Indeed, truth or beauty could only find visual expression through the idealised landscapes of Claude and Poussin and the rigorous organisation and control of Renaissance and seventeenth-century formal gardens.

The optimism ushered in with the events of 1688 had an impact on attitudes to Nature and the world, and portraits evoked and reflected its philosophical, intellectual and aesthetic implications. In the wake of Isaac Newton and the rapid expansion of 'natural philosophy', scientists and philosophers came to view the world around them less as a mirror for theological reflections on the Creation and Heaven and Hell, and more as a subject for careful scrutiny whose method and conclusions would extend the possibility of redefining 'Nature' as the ultimate manifestation of divine artistry in this world, the vehicle by which Man could contemplate the majesty of God. This reconfiguration of Man's relationship to Nature was captured in the almost breathless catalogue of the constituents of the natural world that Edward Young gives in his nature poem 'The Complaint' (better known as 'Night Thoughts on Life, Death and Immortality'), first published in 1746:

*Seas, rivers, mountains, forests, deserts, rocks,*
*The promontory's height, the depth profound*
*Of subterranean, excavated grots,*
*Back-brow'd, and vaulted high, and yawning wide,*
*From Nature's structures, or the scoop of time.*

Such a reassessment of Nature permitted her to be contemplated not in an improved or idealised form but in a condition which clearly recognised and celebrated her many manifestations in the external world. This provided a basis for the development of Nature poetry, the school of British landscape painting and the taste for portraits set within landscapes. Within this latter genre, dominated by British painters such as Reynolds, Gainsborough and Wright of Derby, the subject either moved through an idealised or generalised landscape – as in Gainsborough's portraits of Countess Howe (1762; Iveagh Bequest, Kenwood) and Mrs Sheridan (cat. 135), and in Reynolds's representation of Mary, Countess of Bute (cat. 25) – or inhabited a scene that hinted at greater specificity of location, as in Gainsborough's portrait of Mr and Mrs Andrews (c. 1750; National Gallery, London) and Romney's portrait of Mrs Penelope Lee Acton (1791; The Huntington Library, Collections and Botanical Gardens, San

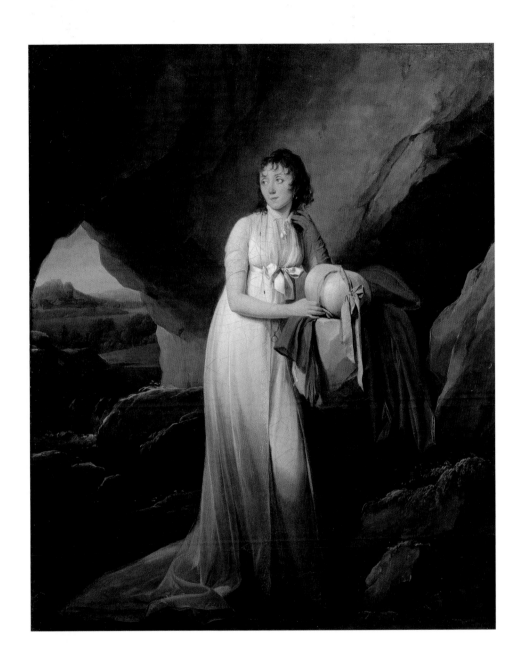

Fig. 64
LOUIS-LÉOPOLD BOILLY
*Madame d'Aucourt de Saint-Just,*
*c.* 1800. Oil on canvas,
56 × 64 cm.
Musée des Beaux-Arts, Lille

critic of *The Morning Chronicle* (31 May 1792) rightly admired the work as an exercise in the play of light across sitter and setting, light also fulfils an expanded aesthetic role. By casting the sitters in semi-shadow, and allowing shafts of sunlight to bring into focus such details of the landscape as the river and the distant hills, Raeburn allows light to become the mechanism whereby the spectator notes the prospect towards which he is guided by the outstretched arm of Sir John Clerk and the admiring gaze of Lady Clerk. The two protagonists convey the fact that, by surveying and responding to the landscape, they are at one with Nature. Despite the relative shift in scale demanded of a portrait, the pose adopted by Sir John and his wife echoes the admirers of landscape prospects who were positioned as staffage in contemporaneous topographical landscape paintings by Richard Wilson and others, in order to mediate the connoisseur's appreciation of the visual journey which must be taken from foreground to distant horizon. This was recorded in nature poetry of the period, such as 'The Seasons' by James Thomson:

> *Heavens! what a goodly prospect spreads around,*
> *Of hills, and dales, and woods, and lawns, and spires,*
> *And glittering towns, and gilded streams, till all*
> *The stretching landskip into smoke decays!*[2]

The representation of Sir John and Lady Clerk of Penicuik within a landscape can also be seen to contain further messages that reflect the eighteenth century's new perception of Nature and the natural. By extending his arm as if to embrace 'the full extensive view' of his estate, Sir John would also be able to make reference to another manifestation of Nature as God's divine work, namely, that nature was beneficent and placed at the service and enjoyment of Man. Nature was thus not only a source of passive contemplation but also the subject of physical improvement, as Oliver Goldsmith noted in 1774:

Marino). Equally, conversation between identified sitters could be conducted within a seemingly 'natural' landscape setting no longer circumscribed by formal terraces and regularised grounds, as in Wright of Derby's portrayal of the Revd Thomas Gisburne and his wife Mary (1786; Yale Center for British Art, New Haven), and Wheatley's portrait of George and Mary Browne and their children (*c.*1773–74; Yale Center for British Art, New Haven). In all instances, the presentation of the sitter in a landscape setting introduced a new set of conventions for the portrait that reflected changing attitudes to the understanding and appreciation of Nature.

Raeburn's portrait of Sir John and Lady Clerk of Penicuik (fig. 66) places the subjects in sober dress within a landscape setting. Although the

*This habitation [the Estate], though provided*
*with all the conveniences of air, pasturage, and water,*
*is but a desert place without human cultivation.*
*A world thus furnished with advantages on the one side*
*and inconveniences on the other is the proper abode of*
*reason, is the fittest to exercise the industry of a free and*
*a thinking creature.*[3]

Consideration of improvement of Nature for the benefit of mankind and to the glory of God would also appear, in part, to inform the representation of the Revd d'Ewes Coke, his wife Hannah and his distant cousin Daniel Parker Coke MP in the triple portrait by Wright of Derby (cat.136), and of Boilly's presentation of M. d'Aucourt de Saint-Just (fig.65). We cannot be certain precisely what the three sitters in Wright of Derby's portrait might be engaged in as they are positioned outdoors, in rapt contemplation, a green umbrella or parasol resting on a rustic wooden table, directing their gaze out across a landscape prospect which lies beyond the left-hand edge of the canvas. It has been suggested that they might be considering the landscaping of the Revd d'Ewes

Coke's estate, in the manner of 'Capability' Brown, whose improvements to the grounds surrounding country houses sought to convey the impression of Nature in her natural condition rather than in one constrained by artifice. Indeed, the Revd d'Ewes Coke might well have been responding to the admonitions of the anonymous author of *The Rise and Progress of the Present Taste in Planting Parks, Pleasure Grounds, Gardens, Etc.*, published in 1767:

*O study Nature! And with thought profound,*
*Previous to laying out with taste your ground:*
*O mark her beauties as they striking rise,*
*Bid all her shining, all her shadowy grace,*
*And to conceal them every blemish trace:*
*Yet there's a happiness that baffles Art,*
*In showing Nature great in every part,*
*Which chiefly flows from mingled lights and shades,*
*In lawns, and woods, hills, rivers, rocks and glades;*
*For only happy's that assemblage made,*
*Where force of light contends with force of shade.*
*But when too busy Art destroys each grace,*
*And shades with ornaments her lovely face,*
*We abdicated beauty eye with pain,*
*And Art presides, where Nature ought to reign . . .*[4]

Fig. 66
SIR HENRY RAEBURN
*Sir John Clerk and Lady Clerk of Penicuik*, 1791. Oil on canvas, 144.8 × 204.5 cm.
National Gallery of Ireland, Dublin, 4530

Alternatively, it has been suggested that the three sitters are engaged in a walk through the landscape, guided by art. They are armed with a drawing, held by Daniel Parker Coke MP, to which Hannah d'Ewes Coke is pointing, and their appreciation of the view is guided by the Revd d'Ewes Coke himself, possibly the author of the drawing, since he holds a drawing tool in his left hand. In this regard, the three sitters demonstrate that they are persons of taste and sensibility, fully cognisant of the new 'Picturesque' aesthetic as promulgated by the Revd William Gilpin most notably in his *Observations on the River Wye, and Several Parts of South Wales Etc. relative Chiefly to Picturesque Beauty* (1782), which widened the appreciation of the natural landscape through painterly conventions, and was later gently satirised by Jane Austen in her early novel *Northanger Abbey* (published posthumously in 1818).

Whether or not the Revd d'Ewes Coke was indeed considering landscaping improvements on his estate, it is certain that M. d'Aucourt de Saint-Just wished the spectator to understand that he was doing just that in his portrait commissioned from Boilly (fig. 65) around 1800. Set against a landscape of studied informality, denoted by the winding path that moves towards the brow of the hill, the sitter is actively, if somewhat cautiously, engaged in fashioning a rustic bridge out of roughly cut, untrimmed branches with the help of his carpentry tools which lie on and beside a green country-style chair.

Boilly's country-style chair and rustic bridge hold within them a further extension to the meaning of Nature, namely that it is synonymous with simplicity and therefore the antithesis of artifice. This proposition, cast within a moral framework, had already been enunciated at the beginning of the century by Lord Shaftesbury, and subsequently advocated by, among others, Hutcheson, Hume and Adam Smith, who held that social virtue based upon a redefinition of

Nature was the key to notions of benevolence, compassion, sympathy and fellow feeling which 'formed the basis of the social ethic that informed British philosophical and moral discourse for the whole of the eighteenth century'.[5]

An alternative position regarding the opposition of Nature and artifice, the natural and the civilised, was enunciated by Jean-Jacques Rousseau, and had a profound impact on portraiture beyond superficial references to rustic bridges and country-style chairs. Arguing that man was good when in his natural state, but corrupted once he became part of civilised society, Rousseau not only provided a rationale for the celebration of the 'noble savage' – as in Reynolds's portrait of the Tahitian Omai (1776; Private collection, on loan to the National Gallery of Ireland, Dublin) and Romney's depiction of the Canadian Native American chief Joseph Brant (Thayendanegea) (1776; National Gallery of Canada, Ottawa) – but also privileged the natural over the sophisticated. As a friend of the philosopher, and editor of a posthumous edition of his writings, Brooke Boothby could claim the right, in his portrait by Wright of Derby (cat. 134), to be represented clutching a book whose spine bears Rousseau's name. However, pose, setting and costume also serve to underscore the degree to which this portrait purports to be a manifesto for Rousseau's definition of Nature and the natural. Brooke Boothby lies recumbent upon the rough ground, near a stream, surrounded by an apparently unimproved (and thus natural) wooded landscape. His dress is simple, with a sense of the casual introduced by the unbuttoned waistcoat. While such attributes summarise Rousseau's position on the superiority of the natural over the cultured or civilised, the reclining pose – possibly derived from the seventeenth-century Jacobite miniaturist Isaac Oliver's portrayal of the melancholic Edward Herbert (Private collection) – extends the reading to make reference to the sitter's psychological state. No longer engaged with the contemplation of external nature, Brooke Boothby is absorbed in his own feelings, thus echoing Rousseau's advocacy of the self as enunciated in his *Confessions* (1770; published 1782). With the use of the natural setting and pose to express an emotional state, it was a simple progression to employ landscape and natural conditions as the source of artistic inspiration: Chateaubriand, in his portrait by Girodet (1808; Musée d'Histoire et d'Ethnographie, St-Malo), stands within a windswept landscape, his hair ruffled by the wind, his features troubled; Granet is presented by Ingres against a thunderous sky (1805; Musée Granet, Aix-en-Provence); and Walter Scott perches beside a ruined building on a stormy Scottish moorland in the monumental portrait made by Raeburn in 1808 (Private collection).

Brooke Boothby's intention to present himself as a Rousseaesque natural man, despite his somewhat modish dress, also informs French representations of feminine beauty at the turn of the eighteenth century. In Gérard's portraits of Mme Juliette Récamier (1805; Musée Carnavalet, Paris) and Mme Tallien (Thérésia Cabarrus, Comtesse de Caraman; cat. 140), Nature elides with the natural and the graceful. Both women sport simple Empire-style white dresses, and are shown caught between exterior and interior, Mme Récamier seated within a loggia, Mme Tallien entering from a breezy landscape. Yet, despite their unpretentious poses and, in the case of Mme Récamier, her bare feet, both reveal a somewhat circumspect attitude to the natural. Mme Tallien, draped in a luxurious Kashmir shawl, trips lightly into a grand interior which could easily afford her protection from external, untamed nature, while Mme Récamier is protected from any danger of cold feet by the presence of a hypocaust system which puffs steam through small apertures in the loggia's marble floor.

More unconditional manifestations of Rousseau's doctrine can, however, be found in other

Fig. 67
JOSEPH CHINARD
*Juliette Récamier*, c. 1805–06 from a terracotta version made between 1801 and 1802. Marble, on integrated marble pedestal, 80 × 42 × 30 cm.
Musée des Beaux-Arts, Lyons, B 871

Continental works. Chinard's portrait bust of Mme Récamier (cat. 67) strips away any of the references to the Antique which underscored David's portrait of the same sitter (fig. 68), and presents her with demure simplicity, her ringlets bound by a plain ribbon, and her shoulders informally draped with a modest shawl. On a more ambitious scale, the two sculpture groups by Schadow and Bartolini representing, respectively, the Prussian Princesses Luise and Frederika (cat. 138) and Emma and Julia Campbell (fig. 69) are both equally committed to conveying a sense of the natural. Both pairs of sisters wear simple shifts derived from the antique. However, rather than prompting an allegorical reading (see pp. 226–43), the Prussian princesses' pose presents no reference to their royal status but instead to sisterly affection, while the two Campbell sisters dance with a grace and freedom that

expresses their innocence and youth. As if to underscore the association between pose and Nature, Schadow's initial depiction of the two princesses included the elder Louisa holding a basket of flowers in her right hand, an immediate reference to the association between the child and Nature, the human being responsive to the natural world.

Schick's portrait of Wilhelmine von Cotta (cat. 139), Prud'hon's presentation of the Empress Josephine (1805–09; Louvre, Paris) and Delacroix's grandiloquent portrait of Baron Schwiter (cat. 148) retain a Continental caution about the degree to which the figure is fully integrated into the natural environment. The wooded landscape and rough rocks which surround Josephine are tempered by the elegant urn that sits to her left, while the dandy Baron

Fig. 68
JACQUES-LOUIS DAVID
*Madame Récamier*, 1800.
Oil on canvas, 244 × 74 cm.
Musée du Louvre, Paris

Schwiter prefers the security of a well-designed terrace to the rougher terrain beyond. However, the preference of British artists for the natural setting, as found in the portraits of Lawrence, such as that of David Lyon (cat. 147), is enthusiastically adopted by Waldmüller in his representation of the Eltz family (cat. 146), set against a backdrop of the Alps and sporting bourgeois dress and national costume: Nature and the natural here seem comfortably at ease.

*Grace and Naturalness: Some Definitions*
GUILHEM SCHERF

The notions of grace and naturalness, which occupy a central place in Renaissance works such as *The Courtesan* by Baldassare Castiglione (1528), were debated at great length during the second half of the eighteenth century, and were subject to further development in, for example, the *Encyclopédie* – with two successive articles devoted to grace by Voltaire and Watelet – and its *Supplément* published by Panckoucke. In addition, the concept of grace is central to the work of Winckelmann: he devoted a whole treatise to it in 1759 and returned to it thereafter on many occasions.[1]

Grace, 'in persons or in works of art, does not mean simply what pleases; it means what pleases with charm. This is why the ancients imagined that the goddess of beauty should never appear without the Graces. Beauty never displeases, but it may be devoid of the secret charm that invites one to look at it, which attracts, which fills the soul with sweet feelings. In their form, their bearing, their action and their speech, the Graces depend on this virtue that attracts … Grace in painting or in sculpture is found in the softness of the contours, in a gentle expression … [in] the combination of the parts, the union of figures who enliven one another, and who obtain pleasure by their attitudes and their looks.'[2]

Watelet defines this 'charm' described by Voltaire, the charm that leads to empathy: 'The word grace is used very frequently in the arts. It appears, however, that the meaning it carries has always contained something vague and mysterious, and that by general agreement people have been happy to understand more or less what it means without any explanation … The grace of figures depicted to look like living creatures consists principally in the perfect structure of the limbs, in their exact proportion, and in the accuracy with which the whole is put together. It is in the

Fig. 69
LORENZO BARTOLINI
*Emma and Julia Campbell Dancing*,
1820–21. Plaster, H. 167 cm.
Galleria dell'Accademia, Florence, 1183

movements and attitudes of a man or a woman that this grace that charms the eyes is to be found.'[3] The dance of the Campbell sisters, so reminiscent of the classical *Graces*, depicts a moment of harmony in which beauty and elegance mingle naturally: 'Grace in style can be found in the ease, suppleness and variety of movements, and the natural and straightforward passage from one to the other.'[4]

The tender manner in which Luise and Frederika of Prussia are intertwined, the familiarity of Lady Clerk's head on her husband's shoulder, the artless tapping of Joséphine's fingers on her temple, the artful pose of the intellectual Brooke Boothby, recumbent in the undergrowth as if he were in his study, Juliette Récamier's gesture of modesty, Thérésia Tallien's suspended progress or the startled attention of Wilhelmine von Cotta all apply (with exquisite sophistication) the notion of naturalness as defined by Sulzer: 'Natural, adjective by which artificial objects are designated when they are presented to us as if art had nothing to do with them, as if they were the product of nature … Sometimes used also to indicate in a particular manner anything which is unconstrained; something represented in a flowing manner – since in fact everything directly produced by nature bears this characteristic. This is what makes it acceptable to

apply the word "natural" to an object which may not have been sourced in nature by the artist, but which he has invented by the strength of his imagination, provided he is capable of lending it the stamp of nature.'[5]

This pose captured by the artist, which flows from the source because it originates from a natural, true-to-life attitude, seems to have been a social grace which the *tableaux vivants* organised by Elisabeth-Louise Vigée-Lebrun, Emma Hamilton and Ida Brun could handle with great skill: 'Between nonchalant ease and distinguished unself-consciousness, what [Baldassare Castiglione] names *sprezzatura*, is the social form of grace … a kind of elegance which is the reverse of application.'[6]

This high-society view of grace, meaning in fact carefully controlled skill in the art of self-display, was obviously not Winckelmann's view. The writer's deeply held vision was of something altogether superior: 'the perfect correspondence between the contemplation which the soul attains when it moves beyond passion and suffering, desire and pain; and the plastic form which, beyond the accidental and the particular, leads on towards the indeterminate state which is the harbinger of ideal beauty.'[7]

Did Canova not bring Winckelmann's vision into being with his *Ideal Heads* (cat. 132)?

FRANÇOIS-XAVIER FABRE, *Allen Smith Before a View of Florence.* 1797. Oil on canvas, 70.9 × 90.5 cm.

Lent by the Syndics of the Fitzwilliam Museum, Cambridge. Given by the Friends of the Fitzwilliam Museum in celebration of their 75th anniversary, with the aid of the directors of Hazlitt, Gooden & Fox and contributions from the National Art Collections Fund and the Cunliffe, Percival and Purchase Funds

JOSEPH WRIGHT OF DERBY, *Sir Brooke Boothby.* 1781. Oil on canvas, 149 × 207 cm.

Tate, London. N04132. Bequeathed by Miss Agnes Ann Best, 1925

← 135   THOMAS GAINSBOROUGH, *Mrs Sheridan.* 1785–87. Oil on canvas, 220 × 154 cm.
National Gallery of Art, Washington. Andrew W. Mellon Collection, 1937.1.92

↑ 136   JOSEPH WRIGHT OF DERBY, *The Reverend d'Ewes Coke with His Wife Hannah and Daniel Parker Coke MP.* *c.*1780–82. Oil on canvas, 152.4 × 177.8 cm.
Derby Museums and Art Gallery, 676-1965

↑ 137 JEAN-ANTOINE HOUDON, *Madame Houdon.* 1786. Plaster, 61.5 × 39.5 × 26.7 cm.
Département des Sculptures, Musée du Louvre, Paris, RF 1391

→ 138 JOHANN GOTTFRIED SCHADOW, *Princesses Luise and Frederika of Prussia.*
*c.*1796–97 (from a model of 1796). Porcelain, 55 × 30 × 19.5 cm.
Museum für Kunst und Gewerbe, Hamburg, 1906.272

GOTTLIEB SCHICK, *Wilhelmine von Cotta.*   1802. Oil on canvas, 132 × 140 cm.

Staatsgalerie, Stuttgart, GVL 87

→ 140   FRANÇOIS GÉRARD, *Thérésia Cabarrus, Comtesse de Caraman.*   *c.*1805. Oil on canvas, 212 × 127 cm.

Musée Carnavalet-Histoire de Paris, Paris, P. 2738

# IO

## Portraiture from 1815 to 1830:
## Ideal Families and
## Tormented Geniuses

ROBERT ROSENBLUM

ANY SIGNIFICANT MOMENT OF HISTORICAL change looks both backwards and forwards, but few periods have so complicated a mixture of retrospection and innovation as the years that followed the collapse of Napoleon's dreams of imperial expansion. In 1815, the Western world had to be reconstructed. The liberating legacies of the American and the French Revolutions, which promised ever greater social mobility and which had undermined the authority of both the Church and the monarchy, had become deeply ingrained; but the Congress of Vienna was determined to resurrect the venerable dynastic tables interrupted by Napoleon's conquests, and nowhere more conspicuously than in France, where Louis XVIII, the brother of the king who had been guillotined 22 years earlier, was restored. Yet, by 1830, the new French king, Louis-Philippe, was to be called not 'le Roi de France', but 'le Roi des Français', making clear that the pre-Revolutionary concept of absolute monarchy had been adjusted to accommodate the realities of a people who had had more than a taste of republican freedom.

We may sense this seesawing balance between inherited ideals and contemporary facts in Jacques-Louis David's portrait of a prominent, endlessly honoured general, Etienne-Maurice Gérard (cat. 142). It was painted in 1816, in Brussels, where, as a regicide, David was living out his life in exile, befriending and often receiving commissions from his refugee compatriots who were also forced to cross French borders after the political turnabout of 1815. Like David, Gérard, then 43 years old, had been at the cutting edge of history, fighting first in the Revolutionary campaigns and then going on to distinguish himself in one Napoleonic battle after another, from Germany to Spain to Russia. But in 1816, Gérard, like David, was deposed from his central role in the drama of history, suddenly homeless and temporarily unemployed, although, in fact, he was soon to return to France, where, with chameleon politics, he gained new honours in each

of the changing regimes, from Louis XVIII to Napoleon III. The staging of this full-length portrait could not be more traditional: its stance of masculine authority silhouetted against a balustrade and an animated sweep of luxurious red brocade lifted above a column base immediately echoes a genealogical table that runs back from Reynolds to Van Dyck and Rubens. But the even, flattening light, not to mention the sharp-focus detail that permits us to read the writing on the envelope the general holds, transform the traditional rhetoric of aristocratic and military portraiture into commonplace fact. We might almost be looking at a mannequin in a uniform, topped by a portrait bust of such physiognomic precision, including the small cleft in the sitter's chin, that it almost seems detached from its stiffly posed body. As in many royal portraits of the Restoration period, we feel that this is an ordinary mortal who is playing an old-fashioned role on a modern stage, the equivalent of a photograph of an actor in the costume of a military hero whose plumed bicorn and abundance of decorations have just been borrowed from a theatrical wardrobe. It is an effect of translating what was once poetry into documentary prose that is closely paralleled in David's later portrait of Juliette de Villeneuve at her harp (cat. 143), discussed on p. 24.

In a world of ever-increasing social mobility, portrait traditions were subject to surprising reinterpretations, among them the memorable depiction of a Philadelphian, Pat Lyon, as a blacksmith (fig. 70). By the mid-1820s, Lyon was wealthy enough to commission John Neagle, a disciple of Gilbert Stuart and Thomas Sully, to paint his full-length portrait. But, proud of his humble roots, he told the artist he did not wish to be represented as what he was not, that is, a gentleman. Lyon was born in poverty in London and, after emigrating to the United States, first made his living as a blacksmith. It was in this early role as a manual labourer that he wished to be commemorated, standing regally in his apron in front of a glowing, smoking forge. Behind him, an apprentice is seen, a youth who may follow his employer's successful tracks; and through the window, we catch a glimpse of the cupola of the Walnut Street prison, where Lyon had been jailed for three months after being unjustly suspected of a major bank robbery. In short, the sitter has insisted that the artist provide a documentary biography of his lower-class roots. But the greater irony is that this image of a wealthy, self-made business man is not only painted with the brushy, bravura swagger familiar to Baroque traditions of aristocratic portraiture, but that Lyon's very pose usurps that of Louis XIV and his Bourbon successors as first defined by Rigaud's state portrait of 1701 (fig. 40).[1] What was once the king's sceptre has now become a hammer on an anvil.

In this mixture of modern facts and inherited fictions, Lyon also becomes something of a hero, an extraordinary individual who, by dint of his own will and courage, has distinguished himself from the masses. Such a concept, often defined in the later eighteenth century, whether through images of political martyrs like David's *Marat* (cat. 37) or alienated artistic geniuses like Barry's *Self-portrait* (cat. 74), continued to loom large in the years after 1815. It could be presented, for example, in official propagandistic terms, as was the case with Guérin's reconstruction of the death of General Henri de La Rochejaquelein in the civil wars of 1794 (cat. 141). Exhibited in 1817, at the first Salon of the Bourbon Restoration, this painting was part of a commissioned series honouring those Royalists in the Vendée who had dared to oppose Republican military forces. La Rochejaquelein, only twenty-one years old, is seen at his last, heroic moment when, silhouetted against the white Royalist flag with its inscription, 'Vive le Roi!', he has climbed to the top of a hill, his right arm in a sling, his left arm holding a bayonet, to confront the forces of the enemy, who remain invisible, except for the pointed

Fig. 70
JOHN NEAGLE
*Pat Lyon at the Forge*, 1829.
Oil on canvas, 93 × 68 cm.
Museum of Fine Arts, Boston

blades of their weapons. According to legend, La Rochejacquelein wanted to spare the lives of the Republican soldiers his troop had just discovered in the bushes, but despite his plea for mercy, one of them shot him dead, creating an instant martyr in the sainthood of monarchy. Twenty-three years after the fact, La Rochejacquelein's courageous sacrifice was resurrected for Parisian audiences who were again the subjects of a Bourbon king. As depicted by Guérin, the scene is played out as a highly staged melodrama in which the hero strikes an uncommonly graceful pose of a courageous body and spirit ascending to lofty heights; but, at the same time, the acute sense of crystal-clear, documentary truth, whether in the life-size dimensions, the tattered flag, the meticulously accurate uniform, or the startlingly abrupt croppings, makes us feel that we are looking at a still from a historical movie.

Such rhetoric, venerating sitters who transcend ordinary mortals, was especially apparent in portraits of creative geniuses, sitters who soared far above the familiar spheres of professional or domestic life. An extreme case in point is Walenty Wankowicz's almost mythical vision of Poland's most famous romantic poet, Adam Mickiewicz, painted in St Petersburg between 1827 and 1828, when both artist and sitter were still in their late twenties (fig. 71). Then a political exile in Russia, Mickiewicz, in his life as in his poetry, easily inspired an image of exalted but tragic alienation, the private mirror of his country's own search for national identity. Prompted by one of the poet's *Crimean Sonnets*, published in 1826, his compatriot depicted him on 'the cliff of Judah', a romantic pinnacle of remoteness from an almost invisible terrestrial world below. One hand on his heart, the other supporting his head, the meditative poet, wrapped in a Circassian cloak, is alone amidst the full spectrum of nature's power, from rugged cliffs high above the waters to a threatening storm that may resolve into sunlit serenity. It is an extravagant

image instantly defined by the word 'Byronic', a word coined in 1823 even before the English poet's death and one appropriate to many portraits of the 1820s. But it also has such precedents as Vigée-Lebrun's 1808 portrait of another literary genius, Madame de Staël (cat. 131), in the sibylline role of Corinne, who, alone and with eyes turned towards the heavens, also finds inspiration high above a wild landscape setting, in this case, Cape Misenum.

The same fire of genius spread to many portrait busts of the period, igniting even Rude's posthumous portrait of David, the artist who presumably symbolised classical reason and order (cat. 152). In this marble, the tradition of depicting great sitters as timeless, passionless antiquities is shattered by what seems an explosion of fierce energy. It is not only a question of the actual disfiguration of David's left cheek that bursts the bonds of physiognomic decorum; but, even more so, the hair, whose wild agitations extend even to the artist's eyebrows and sideburns. And the neoclassical convention of imitating the sightless eyes, bereft of pupils, found in antique portrait busts whose painted surfaces had vanished – a convention that usually produces an illusion of eternal emotional blankness – has the opposite effect here: David seems like a blind genius bursting with rage.

It was the kind of furore that by 1830 reached its summit in David d'Angers's bronze of the demonic violinist and composer Niccolò Paganini (cat. 153). This Italian virtuoso was a perfect candidate for a vision of almost supernatural genius, touring European capitals as a solo performer and exuding the charisma of a frenzied rock star. Rumour had it that he had acquired his breathtaking technical abilities by selling his soul to the devil. Be that as it may, his performances, with eyes rolled back and angular body swaying, captivated audiences, moving them to gasps of awe and terror. But even if the sitter's identity were unknown to us, we would still sense in David d'Angers's bust the presence of a fiercely tormented spirit, whose face crackles with muscular and psychological stress and whose hair and sideburns envelop his head like the fiery aura of a soul in hell.

In the annals of romantic portrait sculpture, this image of turbulent genius has few if any rivals, although its prevailing mood of mystery can often be discerned in other busts of the 1820s. A case in point is Roman's posthumous portrait of Girodet

(cat. 155). Begun in 1827, at about the same time that Rude was working on the posthumous bust of Girodet's master, David, this was completed in time to be shown at the Salon of 1827, three years after the painter's death – a Salon in which a younger generation of artists, who followed the creed of the romantics, at last seemed to prevail over the Establishment. Roman's homage to Girodet, despite its references to the traditional portrait bust *all'antica*

Fig. 71
WALENTY WANKOWICZ
*Adam Mickiewicz on the Cliff of Judah*, 1827–28. Oil on canvas.
Muzeum v Narodowe Warszawie, Warsaw

Fig. 72
ANTOINE-MARIE,
known as ANTONIN MOINE
*Queen Marie-Amélie*, 1833.
Marble, 96 × 68 cm.
Musée Carnavalet-Histoire de Paris,
Paris, s. 1697

in the fixed pose, the whiteness of the marble and the generalised draperies, clearly registered the darker, more imaginative side of the painter who was famous for rebelling against his master's classical rules. Shadowy pockets punctuate Girodet's features, especially the deep eye sockets, and the hair and sideburns, like the drapery folds, have an unexpected animation that radiates a passionate temperament only partly restrained by this classical format.

In the years after 1815, such explorations of the mysterious inner life of sitters whose genius distinguished them from the multitudes were constantly balanced by an ever-expanding acceptance of more commonplace realities, especially those of a domestic kind. Even artists could be represented as law-abiding residents in spotless, orderly households, as was the case, for example, in Danish portraits, such as Købke's of the painter Sødring (cat. 81). This was a phenomenon best pinpointed by the French term 'embourgoisement', a word difficult to translate gracefully into English, but one that means adaptation to middle-class values, something more easily emulated than towering genius. Family portraits, which in the age of Reynolds often reflected a pre-Revolutionary grandeur and aristocracy, mirrored this gradual change to a cosy, prosaic domesticity, depicting what in German-speaking nations, by the late nineteenth century, was often referred to as 'Biedermeier' culture, in reference to the pseudonym of a poet of the 1850s whose satirical verses, with their simple-minded veneration of ordinary, upright people and things, became a huge popular success. There are many eighteenth-century previews of what often seem to be illustrations to Tolstoy's famous first words of *Anna Karenina*, 'Happy families are all happy in the same way...', but this pleasant sanctification of what in the late twentieth century were to be more piously and militantly called 'family values' reached its climax after 1815.

At times, artists offer agreeable vignettes of their own family lives, as in Hansen's informal glimpse of his two younger sisters, Henriette and Signe, poring over a book (cat. 108); but equally characteristic is the full-scale portrait of father and mother and happy offspring in their living room or in a landscape (see, for example, cat. 144).

Of these celebrations of attainable happiness, a painting by Waldmüller of the family of a lawyer, Dr Josef Eltz, says it all (cat. 146). Not at home, in Vienna, but in their country retreat at Bad Ischl, a spa near Salzburg, Eltz, his wife, and their eight children (ranging from infant to teenage daughter) are clearly enjoying the salubrious Alpine landscape, whose mountainous heights, once so daunting and mystical to the lonely travellers of an earlier romantic generation, seem to have been domesticated for the consumption of well-heeled tourists. In fact, behind the family group, we have a glimpse of the summer resort where Eltz had just built a private villa that was later rented by Metternich. The paterfamilias seems to have just arrived, since his wife and children (the baby excepted) turn to greet him with a communal wave of joy as he completes this image of an ideal family in an ideal landscape, both rugged in the distance and comfortable in the foreground. In contemporary terms, Eltz looks like the father who has been working in the city, but is about to join his wife and children for a well-earned sojourn at their country house. But for all this informality, the courtly gestures and the sense of paternal hierarchy aspire to the myths of aristocracy, as if we were glimpsing an official photograph of a Habsburg emperor on holiday. By the 1830s, it had become ever more difficult to tell the difference between the once opposing worlds of nobility and commoners. Consider Moine's marble bust of the new Queen of France, Marie-Amélie, who had both Bourbon and Habsburg blood in her veins (fig. 72). Presented to the public at the Salon of 1833, the portrait shows us a rather homely woman (famous, in fact, for her large nose), who, with plumed hat and every ringlet in place, is dressed for a fancy occasion. But history has severed her ties to Marie-Antoinette. She now looks as if, with a quick change of clothing, she could join the Eltz family for an informal weekend in the country.

↑ 141   PIERRE-NARCISSE GUÉRIN, *Henri de La Rochejacquelein*.   1817. Oil on canvas, 217 × 142 cm.
Dépôt de l'Etat au Musée d'Art et d'Histoire de Cholet (on loan from the Musée du Louvre, Paris, 5187)

→ 142   JACQUES-LOUIS DAVID, *General Etienne-Maurice Gérard, Marshal of France*.   1816. Oil on canvas, 197.2 × 136.2 cm.
Lent by The Metropolitan Museum of Art, New York. Purchase, Rogers and Fletcher Funds, and Mary Wetmore Shively Bequest,
in memory of her husband, Henry L. Shively MD, 1965 (65.14.5)

273

← 143   JACQUES-LOUIS DAVID, *Juliette de Villeneuve.* 1824. Oil on canvas, 197 × 123 cm.

      Département des Peintures, Musée du Louvre, Paris, RF 1997-5. Gift of the Amis du Louvre, 1997, on the occasion of their centenary and in memory of Président F. Puaux, with a contribution from the Fonds du Patrimoine and with the participation of a group of the Amis du Louvre and the Société LVMH

↑ 144   FRANÇOIS-JOSEPH NAVEZ, *The De Hemptinne Family.* 1816. Oil on canvas, 150 × 127 cm.

      Musées Royaux des Beaux-Arts de Belgique, Brussels

← 145   JOHANN VALENTIN SONNENSCHEIN, *Charlotte Wyttenbach.* 1807. Terracotta, 35 × 32.5 × 28 cm.
            Bernisches Historisches Museum, Berne, 18473

↑ 146   FERDINAND GEORG WALDMÜLLER, *The Eltz Family.* 1835. Oil on canvas, 124 × 110 cm.
            Österreichische Galerie Belvedere, Vienna, 2567

277

↑ 147 SIR THOMAS LAWRENCE, *David Lyon.*  *c.*1825. Oil on canvas, 219.5 × 134 cm.
Museo Thyssen-Bornemisza, Madrid, 217 (1981.55)

→ 148 EUGÈNE DELACROIX, *Louis-Auguste Schwiter.*  1826–30. Oil on canvas, 217.8 × 143.5 cm.
The National Gallery, London. Bought, 1918

149   FRANCISCO DE GOYA Y LUCIENTES, *Joaquín María Ferrer y Cafranga.*   1824. Oil on canvas, 73 × 59 cm.
Private collection, Switzerland

150 FRANCISCO DE GOYA Y LUCIENTES, *Manuela Alvarez Coiñas Thomas de Ferrer.* 1824. Oil on canvas, 73 × 60 cm.
Private collection, Switzerland

↑ 151   SIR FRANCIS CHANTREY, *Edward Johnstone.* 1819. Marble, 61 × 45 × 26 cm.
Birmingham Museums and Art Gallery

→ 152   FRANÇOIS RUDE, *Jacques-Louis David.* 1831 (after a model of 1826). Marble, 57.5 × 26 × 21 cm.
Département des Sculptures, Musée du Louvre, Paris, RF 419

↑ 153    PIERRE-JEAN DAVID D'ANGERS, *Niccolò Paganini.*   1830–33. Bronze, 61 × 40 × 32 cm.
         Musées d'Angers, MBA, 836.3

→ 154    FRIEDRICH VON AMERLING, *Amalie Klein, née von Henikstein.*   1834. Oil on canvas, 127 × 103.5 cm.
         Österreichische Galerie Belvedere, Vienna, 3832

↑ 155    JEAN-BAPTISTE LOUIS ROMAN, *Girodet*.  1827. Marble, 78 × 67 × 44 cm.

Département des Sculptures, Musée du Louvre, Paris, CC 182

→ 156    JEAN-AUGUSTE-DOMINIQUE INGRES, *Louis-François Bertin*.  1832. Oil on canvas, 160 × 95 cm.

Département des Peintures, Musée du Louvre, Paris, RF 1071

J. INGRES PINXIT.
1832.

L.E. BERTIN.

287

# Catalogue entries

EDITORS' NOTE

The catalogue entries are arranged
in alphabetical order, by artist; when
several works by an artist are included,
they are ordered chronologically.

Dimensions are given in centimetres,
height before width (before depth,
in the case of works of sculpture).
The dimensions of all works of
sculpture include pedestals and plinths
unless otherwise stated.

Bibliographic references to books and
articles are abbreviated by combining
the author's surname with the date of
publication. Bibliographic references
to exhibition catalogues are abbreviated
by combining the name of the city in
which the exhibition opened with the
date of its opening. Letters are used
to distinguish bibliographic references
when more than one appeared in a year.
Full listings of bibliographic sources
are given on pages 402–19.

CONTRIBUTORS' INITIALS

| | |
|---|---|
| SA | Sébastien Allard |
| AA | Amar Arrada |
| MB | Malcolm Baker |
| KB | Katherine Brinson |
| CC | Candida Clark |
| VG | Vivien Greene |
| JJL | Juan J. Luna |
| BM | Bernhard Maaz |
| SM | Simon Macdonald |
| MMM | Manuela Mena Marques |
| GS | Guilhem Scherf |
| AS | Anna Schultz |

# Juan Adán Morlán

TARAZONA, ARAGON, 1741 – MADRID, 1816

**10**

*Charles IV, King of Spain*

1797
Marble, 87 × 62 × 40 cm
Inscription: *Adan f. en M. 1797*
Patrimonio Nacional, Palacio Real de Madrid, 10002969

PROVENANCE: commissioned by Manuel Godoy,
the 'Prince of Peace', and exhibited in the gallery of his
palace in Madrid; later in the Spanish royal collection
EXHIBITED: London, 1972, no.290
LITERATURE: Pardo Canalís 1958, p.17, pl.10; Pardo Canalís
1979, p.309, repr.; Bottineau 1986, p.359

Juan Adán Morlán, a pupil of the painter
Ramírez in Saragossa, went to Italy at his own
expense in 1765. Three years later he was granted
an allowance by the Real Academia de Bellas Artes
de San Fernando, Madrid, and won the title of
academician in 1774. The Accademia di San Luca
in Rome also honoured him for his work in 1775.
He returned to Spain in 1776, where he worked
on the new cathedral in Lerida. He then produced
some religious sculpture in Andalucia before
settling in Madrid in 1786. On 20 May 1793 he
became Sculptor of the Chamber, an honorific title
that came into force on 2 March 1795. The bust of
Charles IV in the Patrimonio Nacional, dated 1797,
is the official representation of the sovereign and
was always exhibited in the reception rooms of
the royal palace in Madrid.

Charles IV (1748–1819) ascended to the
throne of Spain in 1789 (remaining king until
1808). In 1765 he married his cousin, Maria Luisa
of Parma. The couple commissioned a great many
portraits (Pardo Canalís 1960, p.335), although
posterity has remembered only those by Goya. The
great Spanish artist executed two groups of royal
portraits. The first series dates from 1789, the year
of the coronation (Prado, Madrid: other versions
were mainly painted in the studio). The second was
executed from 1799, immediately after Goya was
appointed First Painter to the Court, to celebrate
ten years on the throne. The portraits of this
period are some of the painter's most celebrated
works, the climax coming with *The Family of Charles
IV* (1800–01; Prado, Madrid).

Having completed the bust of the King in
1797, Adán only knew Goya's first groups, probably
when he saw them in the royal palace of Aranjuez
(Angelis 1976, no.237, repr.). Goya painted Charles
IV standing (there are also some half-length
versions), wearing a wig with a single row of curls
and the ribbons of two different orders across his
chest. Adán used a similar format but made it even
more sumptuous. The King sports a similar wig,
a large decoration and the insignia of three orders:
the Golden Fleece, the Order of Charles III (Spain)
and the Neapolitan Order of St Januarius. The
portrait bust is very large in scale and is cut off
at waist level. The shape of the arms is skilfully
hinted at under the jacket, on the right, and under
the ermine-lined cloak on the left; the cloak makes
a diagonal bar across the composition and ends
sumptuously in a generous swell of fabric. The
pedestal is unusual: it is in the form of a fortified
castle with battlements and cannons, and a lion
on a globe in the centre, an allusion to the Spanish
royal coat of arms. A marble replica of this bust
exists in the Real Academia de Bellas Artes de San
Fernando, signed but not dated, commissioned by
the Academia in 1794 and presented to it in 1797
(Azcue Brea 1994, pp.241–46, repr.). Adán also
executed a bust of Queen Maria Luisa on a similar
pedestal (undated; Palacio Real, Madrid; Pardo
Canalís 1958, pl.11).

Even in the context of an official portrait,
in the manner of Goya, Adán was unable to avoid
reproducing the sovereign's unattractive features,
his large empty eyes and his foolish smile. He
compensated for these faults by exaggerating
the clothing and adding insignia; appropriate
packaging for this royal puppet.

Adán's two royal portraits are mentioned in
the gallery of Manuel Godoy, the Prime Minister,
'Prince of Peace' and lover of the queen, in the
description of a visit made to his residence on
12 November 1800 (Pardo Canalís 1979, p.300).
They were installed near a bust of the master of
the house, executed by Adán in 1794 and now in
the Real Academia de Bellas Artes de San Fernando
(Azcue Brea 1994, pp.238–41, repr.) In contrast
to the bust of Charles IV, the bust of his Prime
Minister is represented in the classical style with
short hair, blank eyes with no pupil, a military
breastplate and a cloak pinned to his left shoulder;
the ram of the Golden Fleece hangs casually over
his chest. The sharing of the roles was perfectly
illustrated: on one hand the monarchy is evoked in
the ceremonial garb of its symbolic power, on the
other the genuine source of power is presented
under the aegis of classical antiquity. GS

# Friedrich von Amerling

VIENNA, 1803 – VIENNA, 1887

**154**

*Amalie Klein, née von Henikstein*

1834
Oil on canvas, 127 × 103.5 cm
Signed and dated at the lower left: *FrAmerling 1834*
Osterreichische Galerie Belvedere, Vienna, 3832

PROVENANCE: acquired 1941
EXHIBITED: Vienna, 2003, no.21 (Sabine Grabner)
LITERATURE: Probszt 1927, no.300

For a large part of the nineteenth century Friedrich
von Amerling was regarded as Austria's finest
portrait painter. His output included a number
of likenesses of the imperial family. His impressive
*Kaiser Franz I of Austria in Imperial Robes* (1832;
Schatzkammer, Kunsthistorisches Museum,
Vienna), with its view of the sitter from the front,
as in Ingres's *Napoleon I on the Imperial Throne* (1806;
cat.12), and its romantic pathos, introduces a new
kind of royal portrait. Amerling moved easily in
Viennese society and his work was in great demand
among the aristocracy and upper middle classes,
particularly the banking fraternity, as this portrait
of Amalie Klein (1806–1871) shows. Amalie was
the daughter of a rich businessman, Josef Ritter
von Henikstein, a friend of Mozart and director
of the National Bank of Austria. In 1824 she
married the banker Carl Ferdinand Klein and
from then on divided her time between Vienna
and St Petersburg, where he had business.

Wearing an opulent gown of garnet velvet,
Amalie Klein is seen sitting at a slight angle in an
armchair over which her dark-green velvet cape
is draped. This painting is an excellent example
of the way the conventions of female portraiture,
as reinterpreted by Sir Thomas Lawrence, spread
throughout Europe, playing an important part
in the development of the romantic portrait.
Amerling came under the influence of British art
when he visited London during the summer of
1827, possibly with the sole intention of meeting
the great English painter – as Delacroix had done
in 1825 (cat.148). Lawrence was well known in
Vienna, having been there from 1818 to 1819 to
paint a portrait of the Prince of Schwarzenberg
for the gallery of Napoleon's conquerors in the
Waterloo Chamber in Windsor Castle.

After his visit to London, Amerling attempted
to adapt the formula of the full-length portrait
in a landscape, but, owing to his lack of interest
in landscape painting, the results (see *Franz I in the
Uniform of a Prussian General*; Belvedere, Vienna)
were uneven; his portraits of children were much
more successful (for instance, *Bertha von Neuhaus*;
1830; Private collection). In the portrait of
Amalie Klein, however, Amerling substitutes the
extravagant colour schemes of the later Lawrence
with a more measured palette, based on a series
of subtle colour combinations. Particularly
noticeable in this work is the juxtaposition of
garnet red, green and orangey-yellow, somewhat
reminiscent of certain contemporary French
portraits, including those of Ingres (such as
*Madame Marcotte de Sainte-Marie*; 1826; cat.34).

The subtlety of the colour scheme is echoed
by the layout of the restrained composition:
Amerling plays with the broad curves of the sleeves
and the cape, softening what might otherwise have
been an over-rigid pose in the upper body. The way
the head tilts slightly to the left also introduces
movement and gives life to the portrait. The
delicately flushed face, brought to life by a slight
smile, stands out against a neutral background
enhanced by dramatic effects of shade. To fill
the space left by the figure, shifted slightly to the
right of the composition, the artist has added

a Biedermeier table, sketchily painted, on which there lies a beautifully executed glove. This exceptional painting makes it plain why the artist enjoyed such success as a society painter. His way with colour, his taste, sense of detail and also his ability to capture the expression of the subject of the portrait allow him to achieve a subtle balance between creating a likeness, the impression of the physical presence of the sitter, and the idealisation required by the genre.

With his consummate art and elegance, Amerling can paint a portrait that flatters without fawning. A comparison of this portrait with the portrait of *Madame Marcotte de Sainte-Marie* by Ingres, painted slightly earlier in 1826, reveals the different manner in which each artist viewed pictorial representation and his relationship with the sitter. The paintings by Ingres and Amerling have a number of features in common: the attention paid to fashion and the romantic hairstyle, the restrained style of a portrait standing out against a plain but subtly shaded wall, the gaze directed at the spectator, plus closer details such as the hands and astonishingly subtle juxtapositions of colour. However, whereas Amerling remains mindful of the expectations of his clients and respectful of his sitter, aiming at achieving a good likeness, Ingres subjects everything to his artistic imagination, paying most attention to the painted surface. SA

# Thomas Banks
LONDON, 1735 – LONDON, 1805

## 118
### *Dr Thomas Addington*

1790
Marble, 76 × 48 × 25.5 cm
Unsigned and undated
Victoria and Albert Museum, London, A.2-1955

PROVENANCE: commissioned by the sitter's son, Speaker Addington, later Lord Sidmouth; sold by his descendants at the sale of Up Ottery Manor, 22 July 1954; purchased by Piers Raymond; purchased from Raymond by Dr W. L. Hildburgh; donated by him as a New Year gift to the museum, 1955

This portrait of a celebrated physician who treated George III is perhaps the finest of the busts executed by Thomas Banks, the first British sculptor to work in a fully neoclassical style. Banks's originality was recognised in his own lifetime. His role in introducing poetic subjects taken from Greek mythology was praised by John Flaxman in his address, *On the Death of Thomas Banks*, composed for the Royal Academy's Council in 1805. Banks is best known for his reliefs, some of which are closely linked in style to the compositions of the painter Henry Fuseli, but he also produced some notable busts, although for a relatively limited circle

of friends and acquaintances. Most of them are lost and known only through engravings.

Banks was evidently working on a portrait of Addington in 1790, as he mentions it in one of his letters. A year later a 'Bust of the late Dr Addington of Reading' was shown at the Royal Collection. Julius Bryant has suggested, however, that it was not this version that was exhibited then but a more finished marble version now in a private collection in the USA. In 1798 the present bust was seen by Joseph Farington in the house of Addington's son, the Speaker of the House of Commons. According to the entry in Joseph Farington's diary for 3 January 1798, 'the Speaker showed us his house … a Bust of his father by Banks, from cast taken after his death – but so like that Mr Pitt said "it was the only bust he could ever talk to".'

Despite Banks's role as a pioneering exponent of Neoclassicism in sculpture, his busts do not conform closely to any obvious or standard classical model; instead they have a distinctive individuality in both their format and execution. None of the few surviving examples illustrates this better than the bust of Addington. The sitter's physiognomy has a delicacy – almost a fragility – that may be explained only in part by its dependence on a death mask. It gives the appearance of being slightly smaller than most busts and, when viewed from the side, is seen to be quite shallow. This, together with the way in which the edges of the drapery on the sitter's right side is, in places, extended and flattened, have a hint of the relief rather than of a bust conceived in the round. The drapery worn by Addington is unusual and even, at points, confused. It would be difficult to find in other busts such a detail as the running scroll decoration around the edge of the sitter's right sleeve – carved to suggest that it has been embroidered – and it is unclear how the two layers of drapery connect with each other. Yet, although the bust of Addington does not correspond to a distinctive type, its delicacy, alertness and obviously carefully considered format – qualities that bear out the rather later claim of Allan Cunningham that 'England had no sculptor of mind until Thomas Banks' – single this portrait out from the busts of such earlier sculptors as John Michael Rysbrack, Peter Scheemakers and Louis-François Roubiliac. MB

# James Barry
CORK, 1741 – LONDON, 1806

## 122
### *Burke and Barry in the Characters of Ulysses and a Companion Fleeing from the Cave of Polyphemus*

c.1776
Signed, not dated

Inscribed on ram's horn: *Jaᵗ. Barry Pinxᵗ.*
Oil on canvas, 127 × 102 cm
Crawford Art Gallery, Cork, 418-P

PROVENANCE: R. H. Solly by 1848; sold Ann-Phillips, Son and Neale, 26 July 1955, lot 187; Jack Gold, 1955; sold Sotheby's, London, 8 February 1956, lot 118; bought Leggatt Bros.; presented by the Friends of the National Collections of Ireland to the Crawford Art Gallery, 1956
EXHIBITED: Royal Academy, 1776, no.18; for later exhibition history see Pressly 1981, p.239
LITERATURE: see Pressly 1981, p.239

This double portrait was exhibited at the Royal Academy in 1776 under the title 'Portraits in the character of Ulysses and his companions escaping from the cave of Polypheme. Homer's Odyssey'. The painter, the Irishman James Barry, depicts himself as a companion of the Irish politician and writer Edmund Burke (1729–1797), whom he shows as Ulysses. The narrative moment depicted is when Ulysses cautions his men to be silent while they escape from the cave of the Cyclops – whom they have already blinded – by holding on to the undersides of his sheep as he puts them out to pasture at dawn. The resulting picture has been described as 'one of the most bizarre and original constructions of the eighteenth century' (Pressly 2005, p.64).

Barry first met Burke in 1763 in Dublin; Burke and his family provided the young artist with uncommon extended patronage, including financial support for travel, first to London and, later, for several years of sojourn in France and Italy so as to complete his education as a painter. Through Burke, Barry had attracted the favourable notice of Sir Joshua Reynolds; having settled in London on his return from the Continent in 1771, he was made an Associate of the Royal Academy the following year, and became a full Academician in 1773. He never, however, translated his talents into commercial success; indeed, his rejection by, and independence of, patrons became 'what gave his work currency' (Myrone 2005, pp.77, 94).

The painting of this 1776 image was not the first occasion that Barry had depicted Burke. It seems in fact that Burke did not pose to Barry in 1776: his portrait was apparently based on an earlier portrayal by the artist made around 1771. When painting Burke on another occasion in 1774, the artist nearly contrived to fall out with his sitter. Ostensibly resenting Burke's arrival unannounced at his studio – the busy statesman found it difficult to arrange sittings in advance – Barry's deeper animus appears to have been in regard to Reynolds. Barry was by this point alienated from Reynolds, but the latter was admired by Burke (indeed, Reynolds was painting his portrait at the time) (Pressly 1981, pp.71–72, 76).

Although on this occasion Burke had gone out of his way to patch up their relationship, the two men argued again and became estranged around 1774–75, and this seems to be the context of Barry's double portrait. Accordingly, the representation of Burke as Ulysses may not be flattering. It has recently been argued that the painting operates as an allegorical denunciation by Barry of his former sponsor: just as the leadership of Ulysses was open to question during the events portrayed, so the implication might be that 'Burke had led Barry into danger by financing his entry into English culture' (Myrone 2005, p.92). In this reading, the painting is a self-dramatisation of the Irish Catholic Barry's confrontation with the English Establishment, personified in the man-eating and – perhaps significantly for a frustrated artist – sightless Cyclops. (Among the wider possible contemporary reference points for the allegorical conflict being played out on Barry's canvas were the war being waged against the revolting American colonies – to which both Burke and Barry were sympathetic – and British misrule of Ireland [Pressly 2005, p.67].) This encounter is one for which the artist, unlike Burke, is visibly ill-equipped. The painting, indeed, is a rarity among eighteenth-century portraits in that it shows 'the effects of fear' (Myrone 2005, p.94). Thus the only precedents that have been found for the depiction of perspiration on Barry's brow are pictures of Christ in scenes of the Passion (and this reference too may have been part of Barry's heroic self-projection) (London 1983, pp.33–34).

Through such discordant realist touches, forcefully suggesting pain, danger and self-preservation, the image may evoke the concept of sublime terror discussed in Burke's writing on aesthetics. Moreover, in making the figures of Burke and of himself contrast with the rest of the painting, Barry drew attention to irreconcilable tensions between genres of portraiture and history painting in a way which may have been an implicit critique of Reynolds, much of whose career success was built upon conflating the two genres (Pressly 1981, pp.73–74). For the upper half of his scene, the artist used a history-painting source: Giovanni Lanfranco's Orco, Norandino e Lucina (Galleria Borghese, Rome), an illustration from Ludovico Ariosto's Orlando Furioso (Pressly 2005, p.67, repr.).

Barry showed the completed painting at the Royal Academy in 1776; he never exhibited there again. Horace Walpole took note of the picture with praise: 'Good colouring, in the style of the old masters' (Graves 1905–06, vol.1, p.132). Some press reports, however, were deeply unfavourable. The Morning Post's critique of Barry's works began with the declaration that: 'We have avoided speaking of this artist as long as possible, because it is unpleasant to censure, even tho' we find no room whatever for commendation.' This 'historical piece' it deemed 'an object for censure; the drawing and colouring of no one figure are either correct or pleasing, from the manner in which the artist has treated the subject, allowing that he has read the passage in Homer, we cannot believe that he ever entered into the spirit of it' (Morning Post, 1 May 1776).

Given that the artist had undertaken so personal, complex and ambiguous an image, such reactions were nigh inescapable. As one scholar has recently concluded, the artist was alienated from his audience, deliberately concealing his full intentions (Pressly 2005, p.67). SM

## 74
### Self-portrait as Timanthes

Begun c.1780, completed 1803
Oil on canvas, 76 × 63.5 cm
National Gallery of Ireland, Dublin, 971

PROVENANCE: Christie's, the artist's sale, 10–11 April 1807, lot 98, bought Mrs Bulkley; Frank W. Collings (a London art merchant, who found it in Devon); R. Langton Douglas, from whom it was purchased by the National Gallery of Ireland, 1934
EXHIBITED: see Figgis and Rooney 2001, pp.78, 80
LITERATURE: see Figgis and Rooney 2001, p.80

The Irishman James Barry was one of the few artists in eighteenth-century Britain who worked in the highest but usually the least remunerative of genres in the visual arts: history painting. Yet arguably his self-portraits – 'a painted autobiography' extending across his career – form 'his greatest artistic legacy' (Pressly 1983, p.150). They demonstrate 'a continuing engagement with what it means to be an artist in a commercial society with little interest in promoting the grand style. His self-portrayals are far more rivetingly intense and hauntingly personal than the more public masks worn by his colleagues' (Pressly 2004, p.138). Completed in 1803, three years before his death, this image is Barry's final public self-representation, effectively his 'last will and testament' (Pressly 2005, p.72). Iconographically, it constitutes a kind of 'triumphant affirmation at the end of his life of those precepts and aspirations which had governed his whole career' (Wark 1954, p.154).

Barry had in fact begun work on the canvas around 1780 – when he completed the head – in order to create a final preparatory study for part of the much larger Crowning the Victors at Olympia (1777–84). The latter was the third of a series of six murals painted to adorn the Great Room of the Society of Arts in London, a spectacular endeavour in history painting which has few equivalents in Britain (Pressly 2004, pp.136, 139). The relevant detail from the mural and the Self-portrait as Timanthes largely correspond; the chief difference between the two works is that in the later image the artist portrayed himself in modern dress.

Barry wrote in his account of the murals that 'as there is no portrait of Timanthus remaining (from a vanity not uncommon amongst artists) I shall take the liberty to supply him with my own' (Barry 1783, p.57). Timanthes was a classical painter, recorded by Pliny as 'the only artist in whose works more is always implied than is depicted, and whose execution, though consummate, is always surpassed by his genius'. In Timanthes' works – and by

extension in Barry's – 'the underlying concept is that invention or the idea underlying a work is of greater importance than the execution'. That in both images Barry/Timanthes holds a porte-crayon, the instrument 'with which one lays down the outline or idea', emphasises this (Pressly 2005, p.70).

The painting Barry holds within the Self-portrait is his own re-creation (from Pliny's description) of Timanthes' celebrated image of a sleeping Cyclops, approached by cautious satyrs seeking to take the measure of his awesome dimensions (Pressly 2005, p.70). These two figures, moreover, relate to another earlier work by Barry, Ulysses and a Companion (cat. 122), in which Barry and his friend the politician Edmund Burke appear as the protagonists. Thus the image completed in 1803 encompasses a synthesis of scenes reflecting the artist's whole oeuvre (Pressly 1983, p.150).

In his first self-portrayal as Timanthes in the Society of Arts mural, Barry was shown seated on the base of a statue of Hercules treading upon the serpent of Envy. In the 'highly condensed 1803 rendering, the radical juxtaposition turns the fanged serpent's head into a terrifying presence directly adjacent to his right ear' (Pressly 2005, p.72). As Barry had written in his account of his murals: 'it is no doubt a good and a wise distribution, that envy should continually haunt and persecute the greatest characters; though for the time, it may give them uneasiness, yet it tends, on the one hand, to make them more perfect, by obliging them to weed out whatever may be faulty, and occasions them, on the other, to keep their good qualities in that state of continued unrelaxed exertion, from which the world derives greater benefit, and themselves in the end, still greater glory' (Barry 1783, p.57). Thus Barry arguably 'sees himself as continually harassed by his jealous colleagues and benighted critics, but listening to the serpent's hiss will only make him stronger' (Pressly 2005, p.72).

In Horace's account, cited by Barry as his source for the theme of Hercules trampling Envy, this last labour 'cost his life before it could be effected' (Barry 1783, p.57). Just as Hercules ultimately triumphed by dying himself – since only then did others stop begrudging his superiority – so too Barry's greatness puts him at risk: 'ironically only death can rescue him from his contemporaries' venom'. The self-portrait also contains references to Christ, as 'the supreme example of a virtuous and superior man who was martyred at the hands of a sinful world' (Pressly 2005, pp.75–76).

Yet, for all the heroicisation of the self-image, it has been argued that in the final analysis this work may be an ambiguous one: 'Barry is an artist of heroic stature, whose porte-crayon can almost stand being measured against the crozier-like staff of the Cyclops, which projects from between his thighs. Only Envy will deny this; and Envy will be crushed. And if this is the statement the picture seeks to make, it also negates it, of course, as soon as we ask why the artist should choose or need to make such a representation of himself' (Barrell 1992, p.208). SM

# Lorenzo Bartolini

SAVIGNANO, 1777 – FLORENCE, 1850

**35**
*Elizabeth Albana Upton, Marchioness of Bristol*

1815–18
Unsigned
Marble, 71 × 51 × 30 cm
The Bristol Collection, Ickworth. Accepted in lieu of tax by HM Treasury in 1956, and transferred to the National Trust

PROVENANCE: presumably commissioned by the sitter or her husband, Frederick William, First Marquis of Bristol; at the family seat, Ickworth House, Suffolk; acquired with the house by the National Trust, 1956
LITERATURE: Kenworthy-Browne 1978, p.338; Prato 1978, p.71

Although unsigned, this lively marble portrait may be firmly attributed to Bartolini because the plaster model for it is preserved among the sculptor's models in the former convent of San Salvi in Florence. If we are to judge from the proportion of women represented among these surviving models, Bartolini was evidently a sculptor who was preferred by patrons for female portraits. The format employed in this example, with the bust's truncation taking the form of a low curve of drapery, is one of two patterns he employed, the other being a waist-length bust, with arms folded across the chest. But, although his formats were somewhat formulaic, Bartolini rejected any idealisation of facial features in favour of an acutely observed representation of individual physiognomies. In his busts of women Bartolini made much of the details of elaborate coiffure, which were contrasted with the more generalised features of dress. As well as giving his busts a contemporary appearance, this trait means that Bartolini's busts often recall painted portraits by David and his followers, notably Ingres. This is unsurprising since Bartolini – a passionate admirer of the Revolution – spent some years in Paris and was well acquainted with both painters, becoming a good friend of Ingres. Perhaps as a result, no other sculptor's portraits from this period are so closely allied to those of contemporary painters.

After his return to Florence in 1815 Bartolini, a former supporter of Napoleon, had to work hard to re-establish his reputation and clientele. He managed to secure some commissions for 'ideal' works – statues of mythological figures – but the majority of his work took the form of portrait busts, always the most commercially viable part of a sculptor's practice. This was recognised by the English visitor, Mary Berry, who commented

in 1817: 'He makes very good likenesses in his busts; but he works to sell, and not to immortalise his name.' As was the case earlier with Canova, Bartolini was frequently commissioned by British patrons. The most ambitious of such commissions was the group representing the two granddaughters of the Duke of Argyll as dancers (National Gallery of Scotland, Edinburgh) but, with its alert turn of the head, the bust of Lady Bristol is a fine example of Bartolini's more modest female portraits. MB

# Pompeo Batoni

LUCCA, 1708 – ROME, 1787

**57**
*Wills Hill, Earl of Hillsborough, later 1st Marquis of Downshire*

1766
Oil on canvas, 227 × 161 cm
Signed and dated on base of altar at left:
*POMPEIUS BATONI PINXIT / ROMÆ ANNO 1766.*
Inscribed by a later hand on the sarcophagus,
*…insano juvat indulgere dolori, / …njux. non hac sine numine Divum / Eveniunt;* and below, *WILLS. HILL. EARL OF HILLSBOROUGH. / MARGARETTA Cᵃ OF HILLSBOROUGH.*
Private collection

PROVENANCE: by descent in the collection of the Marquises of Downshire, Hillsborough Castle, Co. Down, and East Hampstead Park; sale, property of the Marchioness of Downshire, Sotheby's, London, 9 July 1975, lot 10; bought Legatt Brothers, from whom it was acquired by the present owner; on indefinite loan to the Ulster Museum, Belfast
EXHIBITED: Dublin, Industrial Exhibition Palace; Belfast Free Library, 1888, no.47; *James Stewart of Killymoon: An Irishman on the Grand Tour 1766–1768*, Ulster Museum, Belfast, 1999, no.21; *Il Settecento a Roma*, Palazzo Venezia, Rome, 2005–06, no.67
LITERATURE: Steegman 1946, p.60; Clark 1985, p.304; Belfast 1999, no.21; Rome 2005, p.186

Pompeo Batoni's fame was firmly established among British travellers to Italy by the time this portrait of Wills Hill, Earl of Hillsborough (1718–1793), was made. Notable recent sitters to the artist had included George III's brother Edward Augustus, Duke of York, and the actor David Garrick (both sat in 1764). The circumstances of Hillsborough's portrait, however, made the work quite different in character to the more typical Batoni image of the British or Irish gentleman in Rome (see for example cat.61).

Hillsborough sat to the artist in March or April 1766, shortly after the death of his first wife, Lady Margaretta Fitzgerald (1729–1766). Wearing a blue coat braided in gold over a black waistcoat and breeches, he is pictured alongside the winged figure of Hymen, Greek god of marriage. Hymen, wrapped in orange and yellow drapery, rests an oval portrait of Hillsborough's late wife on top of a sarcophagus, and extinguishes a flaming torch at the base of her portrait. The widower, his head bowed in grief, surveys the image of his departed

spouse (her likeness is presumably based on an earlier portrait or miniature) (Rome 2005, p.186). A brown whippet lying by his feet, Hillsborough leans against a sacrificial altar, embellished with a winged sphinx surmounted by a ram's head, which has been identified with a type not uncommon in the first century AD (Clark 1985, p.304).

Nothing is known of Hillsborough's education and upbringing, but it seems that, unlike most of Batoni's sitters, he did not make a Grand Tour in his youth; his trip to Italy from 1765 to 1766 appears to have been his only visit to the country (Ingamells 1997, p.499). Born into a powerful Anglo-Irish family with major landholdings in Co. Down, he sat as MP for Warwick from 1741 until 1756. In 1742 he succeeded his father as 2nd Viscount Hillingdon; he was himself created Viscount Kilwarlin and Earl of Hillsborough in 1751. Further to these titles in the Irish peerage, he obtained the British title of Baron Harwich in 1756 (he continued to be known as Hillsborough). Ever ambitious for advancement, he gained additional promotions in rank in later years; he ended life as Marquis of Downshire.

His marriage to Lady Margaretta Fitzgerald, daughter of the 19th Earl of Kildare, took place in 1748. The union brought Hillsborough a substantial dowry and reinforced his political connections. Husband and wife were pictured, along with two of their children, in a conversation piece by Arthur Devis dating from the mid-1750s (Preston 1983, pp.62–63, 115, repr.). The couple's journey to Italy took place during a year-long hiatus in Hillsborough's tenure of the presidency of the Board of Trade. (He lost his post in July 1765 following a change in ministry.) It may be that his wife was ill prior to their excursion, and that the Hillsboroughs travelled in the hope of restoring her health (Rome 2005, p.186). They had arrived in Naples by early December 1765. Late that month, Lady Hillsborough's decline was described in a letter written by William Hamilton to Sir Horace Mann: 'Poor Lady Hillsborough that arrived here about 3 weeks ago, grows weaker every day, and will not, I fear, live many weeks' (Ingamells 1997, p.499). She died in Naples on 25 January 1766. Around six weeks later Hillsborough travelled to Rome; Batoni's portrait was begun at some point between then and Hillsborough's arrival in Florence at the end of April. The artist normally needed two or three sittings to take a likeness, and his portraits were nearly always completed only after the sitter had left Rome (Clark 1985, p.38). Hillsborough was back in England by the beginning of August, when he was restored to his former post at the Board of Trade.

The painting has recently been restored and found to be in excellent condition following cleaning. A number of pentimenti are now visible: these can be detected in the area surrounding Hillsborough's head (possibly indicating that Batoni at first planned to include a hat), in the area around his feet and the dog's head, and about the fingers of Hymen's right hand. Given the dimensions of the canvas, these adjustments would appear to be comparatively minor, suggesting that Batoni – as was his normal practice – may have made preliminary compositional studies (Rome 2005, p.186).

Like the majority of his contemporaries, Batoni seems to have found the basis of his design for Hymen in a lost antique statue by Praxiteles, the *Apollo Sauroctonos* (Clark 1985, p.304). Copies of this were available in the Borghese and Albani collections in Rome, and had been discussed by Winckelmann two years prior to Batoni's painting (Haskell and Penny 1981, p.152). It has been observed that representations of the figure of Hymen gained currency in the late eighteenth century, along with 'a new, enlightened interest in conjugal love' (Clark 1985, p.304).

The inscription on the sarcophagus is a later addition to the image, undertaken not by Batoni himself but by another hand at around the same period (Rome 2005, p.186). The words, taken from Virgil's *Aeneid* (2, lines 776–78), are those spoken to Aeneas by the ghost of Creusa after her death: 'What's to be gained by giving way to grief / So madly, my sweet husband? Nothing here / Has come to pass except as heaven willed.' SM

## 61
### John Staples

1773
Signed and dated on the pedestal base lower right:
*P. BATONI PINXIT ROMÆ / ANNO 1773*
Oil on canvas, 248.6 × 175 cm
Museo di Roma, Palazzo Braschi, Rome, MR 1974

PROVENANCE: by descent in the family of the sitter's wife at Castletown, Co. Kildare; sale, property of the Rt Hon. Lord Carew, Castletown, Sotheby's, London, 26 June 1957, lot 32; bought Sestieri; with M. & C. Sestieri, Rome, 1957–62, from whom the Museo di Roma acquired it, 1962
EXHIBITED: see Clark 1985, p.329
LITERATURE: Steegman 1946, p.63; Pietrangeli 1971, p.137; Bella Barsali 1985, pp.126–27; Clark 1985, p.329; Johns 2004, p.385

John Staples (1734–1820) was born into the Anglo-Irish landed gentry. His father, the Revd Thomas Staples of Lyssan, the younger son of a baronet, was Rector of Derryloran, Co. Tyrone; his mother, Grace Stewart, was the daughter of John Houston of Castle Stewart, Co. Tyrone. Their eldest son, John Staples was educated at Trinity College, Dublin (1753–57); he succeeded his father in 1762. He may have been the 'Mr Staples' who purchased his portrait from Sir Joshua Reynolds around 1762–63 (Mannings and Postle 2000, vol.1, p.434). In 1764 Staples married Harriet Conolly; her brother, Thomas Conolly of Castletown, Co. Kildare, was a prominent politician and landowner, 'the richest man in Ireland' (Stephens 2004, p.986). Through Conolly's influence, Staples was brought into the Irish House of Commons in 1765, as MP for Newtown Limavady (1765–68), and then

Clogher (1768–76). A consistent government supporter, by 1772 he had been made a Commissioner of Customs, with an income of £1,000 a year (Johnston-Liik 2002, vol.6, pp.322–23).

A year after his wife's early death in 1771, Staples travelled to Italy, where he followed a characteristic Grand Tour itinerary. In late 1772 he was in Florence, where he commissioned some alabaster vases; he travelled to Naples in December. By February 1773 he was in Rome; the following month he arrived at Venice (Ingamells 1997, p.890). At around the same date as Batoni's portrait, Staples was also depicted in two conversation pieces attributed to Philip Wickstead; in both he is shown with James Byres, a *cicerone* (or guide) resident in Rome, along with different groups of fellow British visitors (Ford 1974B, pp.450–51, repr.). Byres introduced Batoni to many potential clients (Clark 1985, p.47). Of the nine *milordi* depicted with Byres in the conversation pieces attributed to Wickstead, Staples and five others were also painted by Batoni in 1773 (Ford 1974B, p.454).

Batoni's studio offered a cosmopolitan 'fashionable outpost' as much as a workroom (West 2004, p.40). He was 'perhaps the most famous living artist in Europe', and a portrait by him constituted 'an internationally recognised signifier of social status, wealth and cultural ambition' (Johns 2004, p.384). In the 1760s Batoni charged the equivalent of £25 for a full-length, while Reynolds's price was £150: 'For the British customer especially, Batoni's portraits clearly had the added advantage of being cheap' (Clark 1985, p.41). Of the artist's approximately 265 surviving portraits, three-quarters depict British and Irish sitters, for whom being painted by Batoni was something of a Grand Tour rite of passage. The average age of his British patrons was twenty-two: most of these sitters had undertaken Grand Tours so as to consummate their education after leaving university; at nearly forty, Staples was therefore untypical (Clark 1985, pp.42–44).

Nevertheless, his portrait is exemplary of the genre. Staples is depicted in spruce civilian apparel, his hat and walking stick to hand and his canine companion beside him, producing an image of 'the insouciant elegance of the travelling gentleman' (Johns 2004, p.385). The dog appears to be a cocker spaniel – a hunting dog, and thus a further status attribute: 'only landed men of a certain income could hunt or participate in the Grand Tour' (West 2004, p.31). In the foreground lie a broken portion of frieze surmounted by a griffin, and a Corinthian capital; these were part of Batoni's studio equipment, used in more than a dozen portraits (Clark 1985, p.50). Staples's foot rests on a plinth in a pose that Batoni had earlier used in *Thomas Dundas* (1764); this kind of stance usually portrayed the subject 'lost in reverie or absorbed in the grandeur of the past' (Johns 2004, p.385).

Upon the plinth rests the Ludovisi Mars, in a formula Batoni applied in several other full-length

portraits around this period, for instance that of *John Chetwynd Talbot* (1773) (Clark 1985, p.329). Such emblematic use of antiquities demonstrated both a sitter's presence in Rome and their 'status as a learned, cultivated, yet leisured aristocrat' (Philadelphia 2000, p.306). This particular classical statue was acquired by the Ludovisi family in 1622 and displayed at their villa on the Pincio in Rome from at least 1633; it retained its high reputation in the eighteenth century, 'despite the limited access to the Villa Ludovisi, and the rarity of casts or full-scale copies' (Haskell and Penny 1981, pp.260–62, repr.). It was 'particularly praised by Winckelmann, and it is probably a reflection of the authority of his opinion that Batoni employed the statue as an accessory' in several full-length portraits painted in the period from 1773 to 1782 (Clark 1985, p.330).

While Batoni was not the originator of the Grand Tour portrait – indeed, 'nearly all the features that we associate with his portraiture were anticipated by the leading portrait painters of the previous generation' – he nevertheless brought a 'precision of draughtsmanship' to the genre; few contemporary painters 'could match his ability to produce an accurate likeness' (Clark 1985, p.30). Following his death and the decline of his reputation, 'Romans could no longer claim that they were providing the indigenous talent to set the standards of artistic achievement in Europe' (Craske 1997, p.250). When this portrait was acquired by the Museo di Roma in 1962, it became the only Grand Tour portrait by Batoni to have returned to the city (Johns 2004, p.407). SM

## Wilhelm Bendz
ODENSE, 1804 – VICENZA, 1832

## 82
### A Young Artist (Ditlev Blunck) Examining a Sketch in a Mirror

1826
Oil on canvas, 98 × 58 cm
Signed: *VF BENDZ 18 28/3 26*
Statens Museum for Kunst, Copenhagen, 280

PROVENANCE: acquired 1826
EXHIBITED: see Copenhagen 1996B, p.89, no.26
LITERATURE: see Copenhagen 1996B, p.89, no.26; Larsen 1997; Mortensen 2000; Mortensen 2001; Copenhagen 2001, p.76, fig.3; Copenhagen 2002, p.44

Wilhelm Bendz's complex portrait depicting his friend at work in this cluttered room is the best-known example of Danish Golden Age painting focusing on the theme of the artist in the studio. Bendz painted the image in 1826 and showed it that same year in the annual exhibition of the Academy at Charlottenburg, where it simultaneously received harsh criticism for its overt romantic symbolism and acclaim for the quality of its execution (Los Angeles 1993, pp.55–58). Despite the negative press, the portrait was purchased by the Danish royal collection. This elevated endorsement was well deserved: Bendz's picture displays intricate compositional strategies and multiple layers of significance which, in part, recall the Dutch seventeenth-century painting that served as a touchstone for nineteenth-century Danish artists. Visually rich, the work is suffused with warm tonalities and textures. A golden light fills the interior and brings to life the variegated browns of the many wooden surfaces; it falls upon the lush areas of red in Blunck's cap and the rumpled fabric draped over the edge of the table. Within this complicated pictorial space the artist also integrated *trompe l'œil* and still-life elements. Among the latter, the human skull introduces a prescient *memento mori* motif, as Bendz was to die of an illness while travelling in Italy at the age of 28 (Johansson 1996, p.19).

Ditlev Blunck (1798–1854), shown as an intense young man smoking a pipe as he scrutinises a small painting, was both a genre and a history painter (Los Angeles 1993, p.66). In this likeness, Blunck himself was working on a portrait of a fellow artist, the engraver Carl Edvard Sonne (1804–1878) (Los Angeles 1993, p.68). We see Blunck looking at the oil sketch for his work in the mirror, a practice which artists employed at that time to determine their progress on a composition (Copenhagen 1996B, p.89). Blunck's final, finished oil portrait of Sonne was also hung at the 1826 annual exhibition where it too was acquired by the Danish royal collection, testament to the official support that contemporary portraiture and everyday themes received in Denmark during this period (Los Angeles 1993, p.68).

Bendz utilised the essentially mundane subject-matter of genre painting to highly allusive and metaphorical effect. His painting is filled with parallel images from the 'real' space within the studio and the illusory space of the mirror, but each pairing gives us slightly different views of the same thing. We see one side of the easel in the studio, and the reflection of the top half in the mirror. Bendz incorporated another optical twist with the realistic inclusion of a crack across the upper section of the glass, which causes the easel's reflection to distort (the statue of *The Discus Thrower*, which is present in the composition only by way of reflection in the mirror, is similarly offset (Copenhagen 1996B, p.90). The skull again plays with the artifice of parallel images, appearing once as itself, showing the hollowed opening into the cranium, and again in a drawing on a page in the sketchbook upon which it sits, where Blunck has drawn its intact profile.

The doubling of images persists with the subject(s) of this portrait within a portrait. A partially cropped, albeit highly finished, drawing of a face, which is visible in its entirety in the mirror,

is pinned to the easel. Moreover, this is a drawing of Sonne, who is also the subject of the oil sketch which Blunck is examining. Like the skull, the preparatory oil also is shown from two different sides: the back of the canvas and the stretcher frame exist in the physical space of the studio, while the painted surface may only be seen in the reflected space. Finally, two different images of Blunck appear in the picture, that of his actual profile and that of his full face in the mirror. The use of this convoluted series of quasi-duplicate images in tandem with the mirror (many are a result of the mirror), which adds another pictorial dimension to the painting, allowed Bendz to investigate the potential instabilities of vision and painting, surpassing mere genre or portraiture to question ideas regarding representation and artistic creation. VG

# Louis-Léopold Boilly

LA BASSÉE (NORD), 1761 – PARIS, 1845

## 69
### *A Reunion of Artists in Isabey's Studio*

1798
Signed at bottom right: *L. Boilly*
Oil on canvas, 71.5 × 111 cm
Département des Peintures, Musée du Louvre, Paris, RF 1290 bis

PROVENANCE: Biesta-Monrival bequest to the Louvre, 1901; entered the Louvre, 1911
EXHIBITED: Paris, Salon of 1798, no.39; for later exhibition history see Lille 1988, p.78
LITERATURE: see Lille 1988, p.78

This work, the most ambitious portrait piece ever undertaken by Boilly, shows 31 figures professionally involved in the arts. The ostensible narrative incident around which the gathering is orientated is the inspection of a picture placed on an easel at the left of the scene, and invisible to the viewer. This was almost certainly *Isabey and His Family*, a drawing by Jean-Baptiste Isabey which was exhibited at the Salon of 1798 as a pioneering step on the part of its creator, who was known as a miniaturist. Boilly's picture, likewise, went beyond his specialist field of genre painting. Both works were exhibited at the 1798 Salon to popular acclaim – although art critics were divided on the merits of Boilly's image – and both 'celebrated and contributed to the cult of the modern artist' (Siegfried 1995, pp.97–98).

Although the majority of the men shown were painters (eighteen in total), the balance of the group extended Boilly's cultural net to embrace more widely both the visual arts and other artistic professions: along with three sculptors, three architects and two engravers can be seen a pair of actors, a composer, a dramatic critic and a singer. Isabey himself stands immediately to the right of the easel, with the history painter Gérard sitting by

his side; another history painter, Prud'hon, can be seen in the background immediately to the left of the easel. The two standing figures at the centre of the image are the history painter Lethière and the battle painter Vernet; to their right sits the actor Baptiste. At the right of the image, the history painter Girodet sits to the left of a guitar, and to the right of the instrument is the sculptor Chaudet. Boilly himself – his head is the ninth from the right-hand edge of the image – looks out at the viewer from the background.

The setting in which the sitters are depicted – which reflected the very latest style in interior decoration in 1798 – was nominally the studio of Isabey, but was actually imaginary. This fantasy served the purpose of associating the modern artist with sophistication and cultural education. The roundels showing great artists of the past which adorn the top of the studio wall – and, below them, an image of Minerva, flanked by allegories of the arts – offer both a concession to the importance of the art of the past, and a claim that the living models shown have the cultural currency to appreciate the tradition in which they figure (Siegfried 1995, pp.96–97).

The preparation of the image is well documented. Twenty-four sketches of individuals survive at the Musée des Beaux-Arts, Lille. There are also three preliminary works for the composite picture which indicate that the composition became progressively more ambitious – there were initially eleven sitters (Lille 1988, pp.62–77, repr.). Although this process may have brought an element of chance to the final placement of figures, it has been proposed that a general pattern can nevertheless be observed: history painters – those at the top of the academic hierarchy – tend to appear in the foreground of the image, while artists specialising in 'lower' genres (including Boilly) are placed further back. Indeed, Boilly's painting may also serve as a protest against this ranking system (Lille 1988, p.61).

The work both fed off the fame of the artists depicted and offered a further fillip to their celebrity. In offering the public a fictive intimacy with the artistic talents displayed, Boilly performed a valuable service in publicising their likenesses at a period when patterns of patronage were unsettled: he was aiming perhaps less at posterity and more at the newly rich beneficiaries of social change catalysed by the French Revolution (Lille 1988, pp.61–62). Thus, in posing his sitters he paid close attention to their distinctive features, even to the point of caricature; his painting had an 'explicitly promotional function in acquainting an ignorant public with a new generation of artists' (Siegfried 1995, p.100). It is notable that Boilly generally did not include in his tableaux artists for whom promotion was superfluous, most especially Jacques-Louis David; nor did he risk portraying artists associated with extreme Jacobinism, then politically unfashionable (Lille 1988, p.61).

If the work was in part intended to attract patrons, it also constituted a 'declaration of independence for French artists' (Siegfried 1995, p.96). Although visual statements of this nature had precursors in England – among them such images as Zoffany's *The Academicians of the Royal Academy* (cat.70) – the type was new to Paris. Representations of artists and their studios were an established and recurring theme in Boilly's work, but one which changed markedly in the years following the French Revolution, shifting from 'intimate, playful erotic scenes to ones involving the public recognition of their professional status and their work' (Siegfried 1995, pp.95–96). Given the conspicuous absence of women artists, it has been suggested that *A Reunion of Artists in Isabey's Studio* also helped to mould 'a thoroughly gendered myth of the modern artistic persona as essentially male' (Lajer-Burcharth 1997, p.729).

Not least among artists in search of patronage was Boilly himself. Recourse to such an experimental and large-scale work was one route available to artists when faced with the competitive environment of the Salons of the Directoire period. National art competitions offered a further means of gaining publicity, and were embraced by Boilly, who indeed won a *prix d'encouragement* for the painting in 1799. Although its early provenance is disputed, one likely outcome of Boilly's appeal to the public eye was that the painting was purchased by Armand Séguin, an art patron who had recently become affluent (Siegfried 1995, pp.53, 101). SM

# Louis-Simon Boizot

PARIS, 1743 – PARIS, 1809

## 9
*Marie-Antoinette, Queen of France*

1781
Marble, 90.5 × 53.6 × 36 cm
Département des Sculptures, Musée du Louvre, Paris, RF 4515

PROVENANCE: Ministry of Foreign Affairs, Versailles, 1781; documented in the same place, 1787; all trace lost until it entered the collection of Alphonse de Rothschild; then passed to his descendants Edouard and Guy de Rothschild; sold at Sotheby's, Monaco, 1 July 1995, no.289; acquired at that sale by the French Government
EXHIBITED: Paris, Salon of 1781, no.205; Versailles, 2001–02, no.14
LITERATURE: Picquenard 1996; Musée du Louvre 1998, vol.1, p.104, repr.

The exhibition at the Salon of 1781 of the bust of Marie-Antoinette (1755–1793), Queen of France since 1774, passed almost unnoticed. A few printed reports, nevertheless, made haste to describe the portrait as 'a very good likeness' (Jean-Baptiste Radet, *Réflexions joyeuses; Lettre d'Artiomphile; Journal encyclopédique*: McWilliam 1991, nos 318, 321, 334),

but this was probably a discreet homage to the Queen rather than an aesthetic point of view. The critic of the *Mémoires secrets*, influential papers that circulated clandestinely before being published as fiction in London, made no mention of it. Only Diderot, that independent spirit whose opinion of the works in the Salon was not published, proclaimed his lukewarm appreciation loudly and clearly: 'This bust is mean in form, the eyes are fashioned without wit. Only a few details to praise' (Diderot 1995, p.359).

The bust is noted in the Salon booklet as being 'executed for the Department of Foreign Affairs'; it was made at the request of the Secretary of State for Foreign Affairs, the Comte de Vergennes and commissioned from the specialist in sculpture portraits of the queen, Louis-Simon Boizot. The date 1781 is significant: this was the year when the queen's second pregnancy made the birth of a longed-for heir to the throne seem possible (he was born on 22 October, after the Salon closed). The personal status of Marie-Antoinette was considerably boosted by the birth.

Boizot's previous portrait, done the year the Queen came to the throne in 1774, was distributed in biscuit-ware by the Sèvres Porcelain Factory and was available in two sizes (see Versailles 2001, no.10): the young woman with draped shoulders and a bare neck looks towards the right, in the same position that the sculptor used again in the bust of 1781, but with greater fullness. The composition of the present work consists of an idealised representation of the Queen; it was also distributed in a biscuit-ware version – Boizot was head of the sculpture workshop at Sèvres from 1773 – and as an engraving. With her chest bared in order to show off her neck, which was greatly admired, Marie-Antoinette wears a gown edged with lace and adorned with jewels (braided with pearls joined by a jewel on her bust). The sumptuous cloak of fleur-de-lis, edged with ermine, is held by a cord according to the tradition of the royal portrait bust; the same convention can be found in Augustin Pajou's *Madame du Barry* (1773; Louvre, Paris) and Jean-Antoine Houdon's *Princesse de Mecklembourg-Schwerin* (1782; Staatliches Museum Schwerin): this allows the heavy fabric to stand away from the skin and to spread in broad folds around the pedestal, giving fullness and also a sense of extravagance to the bust.

The bared chest is discreetly full, indicating the sitter's happy state of prospective motherhood. The Queen's hair is opulently dressed and says much about the enormous interest she took in her personal appearance. Her head is held high; a large plait pinned from the nape of the neck to the top of the head is surrounded by curls that caress her skin; her hair is well pulled back from her forehead; the gauze veil, studded with roses and adorned with a tiara with a fleur-de-lis, is artfully crumpled: it falls splendidly behind and produces a particularly elegant back view. Marie-Antoinette's face is easily

recognisable: 'Her features were not regular; she inherited from her family that long, straight oval face that is particularly Austrian. Her eyes were not big; their colour was almost blue, her gaze was lively and gentle, her nose fine and pretty and her mouth was not too big, although the lips were a little thick' (Vigée-Lebrun 1984, p.64).

This magnificent composition, obviously designed with the utmost care, is the representation of a queen, clearly identifiable by her attributes – the fleurs-de-lis, the tiara – who also bears the attributes of a woman in full bloom, a wife and mother. The destination of the bust was significant: it was commissioned by the department of Foreign Affairs and should have been sent to a court abroad (it is mentioned in the register of gifts to be given by the King in 1781); for some unknown reason it remained in the ministry in Versailles and was still there in 1787. Perhaps Vergennes liked the marble bust too much, or was he paying court to the Queen by keeping her portrait beside him? Whatever the reason, the portrait had everything it took to please, and in particular to please the assiduous Maria Theresa of Austria, who, in 1775, received a copy of the previous portrait in biscuit-ware and could possibly have been the intended recipient of the marble bust.

This ceremonial portrait belongs to the tradition of female portraiture that Jean-Baptiste II Lemoyne (1704–1778) had made his speciality. Boizot must certainly have seen in the Salon of 1771 his bust of Marie-Antoinette, then wife of the Dauphin, which was sent to Vienna to her mother by Louis XV (Réau 1927, pl.XXXIV). Boizot borrowed the idea of the drapery enveloping the shoulders and completely encircling the bust, a device that Lemoyne had used on several occasions, giving a sumptuous air to the composition, as he did in *Madame Adélaïde* (1768; Louvre, Paris). He does not make his drapery as full as Lemoyne (was he constricted by proportions of his block of marble?), which provoked Diderot's accusation (certainly unwarranted, it must be said): 'The bust is mean in form'.

The writer's following remark – 'the eyes are fashioned without wit' – deserves attention. It was inconceivable to represent the Queen with blank eyes, even if the archaeologist and man of letters the Comte de Caylus thought that there was 'more art and advantage to let the spectator imagine the action of the eyes' (Caylus 1752, vol.1, p.155). The great portraitists – Lemoyne, Pajou, Jean-Antoine Houdon – always chose to mark the pupil in order to give 'expression and life to the eyes' (Mathon de la Cour, commentary on a bust of Louis XV in the Salon of 1763: McWilliam 1991, no.153). Different artists used different techniques, however, simply engraving the outline of the iris (Pajou), incising the pupil (Lemoyne) or hollowing out the iris quite deeply (Houdon). Was Diderot comparing, to Boizot's disadvantage, the treatment of his eyes with that of Houdon, which he admired (see cat. 53)? In fact, Boizot, although using Houdon's technique of hollowing out the iris and leaving a fragment of material in the cavity to simulate the pupil, avoided digging too deep. The effect is much less frank than the effect achieved by Houdon, who succeeds in making his models full of vivacity and wit: 'M. Houdon is possibly the first sculptor who has known how to fashion eyes' (Grimm 1880, p.103).

Boizot's bust is particularly interesting even outside the historical context of the sovereign on display; it is the discovery of a moment of feminine seduction, within a supremely artificial arrangement: Marie-Antoinette was also the queen of fashion. This is a constant in all her iconography, and was admirably served by Elisabeth-Louise Vigée-Lebrun, whose paintings 'are society portraits rather than symbolic representations of the French monarchy, and Marie-Antoinette's primary wish was to be represented as an arbiter of taste' (Baillio 1981, p.38). She far surpassed any previous queen of France in this respect.

She also triumphed over Louis XV's two famous mistresses, whose strategies were inevitably different: Madame de Pompadour had herself depicted at work and Madame du Barry as an object of desire. Marie-Antoinette was placed immediately above them in rank, as royal consort and arbiter of taste: her supremacy was unquestionable. 'In relation to the king, she adopts a personal strategy of domination in which fashion becomes her field of action and power' (Sapori 2003, p.70). Madame Du Barry had set the process in motion.

It was perfected by the Queen and her accomplice, the fashion dealer Rose Bertin, eight years her senior. Rose Bertin had an appointment with the Queen twice a week at a fixed time in her small apartment, an unheard-of favour, one seldom accorded even to the ladies of the court. 'The art of the saleswoman, received in the house despite the custom that barred all persons of her class without exception, helped provide her with the means of wearing a new fashion of some sort every day. Until then the Queen had developed very simple tastes in dress; now she began to make it her main occupation; she was of course imitated by everyone' (Campan 1988, p.73). In 1781, when Mademoiselle Bertin was her main dealer by a long way (Sapori 2003, p.78), the fashion was for a large number of accessories and a high, layered hairstyle that Boizot has reproduced faithfully: he has engraved in marble, for eternity, the memory of a fashion that, by its nature, was ephemeral. The image of Marie-Antoinette is preserved in all the finery of her official portrait, but at this time it also reveals the frivolity of her mind. GS

# Joseph Boze
LES MARTIGUES, BOUCHES DE RHONE, 1745 – PARIS, 1826

*in collaboration with*

# Robert Lefevre
BAYEUX, 1755 – PARIS, 1830

## 46
### *Honoré-Gabriel Riqueti, Comte de Mirabeau*

1789
Oil on canvas, 219.6 × 135 cm
Not signed
Musée Granet, Aix-en-Provence

PROVENANCE: bought by Gabriel Lucas de Montigny, from Boze's widow in February 1826 for 2,000 francs; by descent to Charles-François-Gabriel de Montigny; bequeathed to the Musée Granet, 25 March 1912
EXHIBITED: Paris, 1900; Marseilles, 1906; Aix-en-Provence, 1961; Paris, Detroit and New York, 1974–75; Aix-en-Provence, 1977; Marseilles, 1989; Versailles, 1989
LITERATURE: *Gazette nationale ou le Moniteur universel*, 22 October 1790, no.295; *L'Art à l'Exposition coloniale*, 1906, p.145, no.482; André Paul-Lesmoine, *Les Arts*, no.167, Paris, 1918, p.12, repr.; Aude 1912, p.55; Antoine Schnapper, in Paris 1974A, pp.333–34, no.13, pl.55; Badet 1989, p.82, repr. p.24; Lemoine 1989, p.145, repr. p.111; Martigues 2004, no.53, p.172

This imposing work portrays one of the key personalities of the French Revolution: Honoré-Gabriel Riqueti, Comte de Mirabeau (1749–1791). The large-scale format was atypical for Joseph Boze, who excelled in bust-length or miniature portraits executed in delicate pastel. He had mastered this medium as a student of the great pastel specialist Maurice-Quentin de la Tour, and had subsequently built up a busy little practice catering to the constant demand for likenesses in court circles. Boze was not an Academician, so he did not show at the Salon, and this lack of formal academic training put him at a distinct disadvantage when working in oils on a more ambitious scale. Therefore, when he wished to expand a bust-length pastel of Mirabeau that he had drawn from life earlier in 1789, he enlisted the services of Robert Lefevre, a talented young artist known for his skill in portraying textiles. This was not the first time the two artists had collaborated: Boze's surviving account book, which covers the period between 1783 and 1788, details numerous transactions involving Lefevre, including a payment of 2,400 livres for work on a 1786 portrait of Louis XVI. It was a widely established practice for a successful portraitist to delegate less individualised pictorial elements to other hands, but this particular partnership was to become the source of a bitter dispute later in the artists' careers. In 1801, a large painting by Robert Lefevre and Carle Vernet, depicting Napoleon and General Berthier at the Battle of Marengo (untraced), was publicly exhibited by Boze in Amsterdam and London as one of his own works. Lefevre, who by this point was enjoying significant favour at the Imperial court, was incensed, and published a stinging condemnation of Boze's deceit, claiming that the artist was incapable of producing a full-length figure of any quality. After an unconvincing public

response from Mme Boze, Lefevre followed with the claim that he was solely responsible for other well-known works that Boze had passed off as his own, including this portrait of Mirabeau. Although Boze was certainly guilty of misleading the public with the Battle of Marengo canvas, it seems highly unlikely that Lefevre's accusation regarding this portrait is accurate. Boze must have at least painted the head, basing it directly on his existing pastel of Mirabeau – a conjecture supported by the fact that this section is executed in a different technique to the rest of the portrait, 'painted very freely in hatchings like a pastel' (Schnapper, in Paris 1974A, p.334). Although it is difficult to ascertain which artist had the greater influence on the overall creative conception of the painting, it can reasonably be assumed that both Boze and Lefevre made significant contributions.

This division of artistic labour certainly did not reduce the powerful impact of the finished portrait, which imparts a vivid impression of the subject's commanding persona. Mirabeau was a colossal presence, in terms of both his towering physique and his mesmeric personal charisma. He was celebrated for a sort of monumental ugliness, marked by his heavy-set features and ravaged complexion – the legacy of a virulent attack of smallpox at the age of three. This idiosyncratic appearance, heightened by eccentric piles of shaggy powdered hair, seemed rather to attract than repel, and was certainly no handicap to Mirabeau in his legendary romantic adventures. He was notorious for his debauched and debt-ridden lifestyle, and was imprisoned and exiled repeatedly in his younger years, often at the instigation of his own father. But he was also possessed of considerable learning and ability, and the calling of the Estates General in 1789 provided him with an ideal platform to secure the political power to which he had long aspired. Elected by the people of Aix as a delegate to the Third Estate, having been rejected by his own noble class, Mirabeau quickly emerged as a natural leader and took centre stage as the crisis at Versailles escalated. Framing himself as the voice of the people, Mirabeau assumed a pivotal role in the drafting of the Tennis Court Oath, in which the delegates of the Third Estate pledged to continue meeting until a national constitution had been established.

Above all, Mirabeau is remembered for a dazzling eloquence that allowed him to win over any audience to his cause, and galvanise them into action. Here he assumes a declamatory stance appropriate to a renowned orator, with the texts of an address laid beside him on the floor, as if he were taking a few moments to gather his thoughts before delivering one of his trademark thundering speeches. He is depicted in an austere classical interior, watched over by statues of France and Liberty. The painting's rigorous formal geometry and restrained, near-monochrome palette announce a decisive stylistic departure from the decorative charm of Boze's court portraiture. The luminaries of the Revolution required a different aesthetic register, and this portrait succeeds admirably in constructing a new heroic ideal for the transformed social structure that was emerging from the dramatic events of 1789. The *bas-relief* running across the centre of the painting depicts Minerva dictating the Rights of Man to the legislators, and Truth delivering the victims of despotism from their dungeons – allegorical scenes that make explicit the political ideology of the portrait. When an engraving of the painting was offered for sale by subscription in an announcement in the *Gazette nationale ou le Moniteur universel* in 1790, it was suggested that all good citizens would want to possess a picture of the famous deputy as an *exemplum* of patriotic devotion. Less than a year later, this iconic image was to assume a commemorative function, when Mirabeau's premature death at the height of his influence and popularity was met with unprecedented scenes of public mourning on the streets of Paris. KB

# Antoine-François Callet
PARIS, 1741 – PARIS, 1823

## 8
### *Louis XVI*

1789
Oil on canvas, 246 × 192 cm
Collection du Musée d'Art Roger-Quilliot,
Ville de Clermont-Ferrand

PROVENANCE: commissioned by the directors of Buildings to the King; entered the national collections at the time of the Revolution; deposited at the Musée Bargoin, 1872
EXHIBITED: probably the painting exhibited in the Salon of 1789 as no.69; Paris, 1974–75, no.17 (catalogue entry by G. Lacambre)
LITERATURE: Engerand 1901, pp.180–83; Heim, Béraud and Heim 1989, pp.36, 157; Lang, Stoll and Becker 1997, p.17

Even as the French Revolution approached, royal portraits continued to offer versions of the prototype, Hyacinthe Rigaud's *Louis XIV* (Louvre, Paris), although this was beginning to cause some comment. Callet's portrait of Louis XVI, exhibited at the Salon of 1789, is a case in point. The monarch stares out at the spectator, standing slightly turned to one side, in front of a huge drape that forms a dais. He wears the royal cloak covered in fleurs-de-lis and the insignia of the Order of the Holy Spirit; in his hand he holds the sceptre, the incarnation of the power and authority conferred on him by God's grace. The crown is placed on a stool at his side. A large column, the traditional symbol of power since the Renaissance, supports the composition on the left. On the sovereign's right, the figure of Justice is carved on a *bas-relief* behind the throne, echoing the hand of justice

placed beside the crown. The most important of all royal functions, the administration of justice was the justification for the existence of royalty and the king's coronation, the power of justice lying solely in the means of its implementation.

Callet's portrait of Louis XVI was designed to be widely distributed via numerous copies, under the strict control of the Director of Buildings (in this case the Comte d'Angiviller) to King Louis XVI; the copies were executed in a studio under the aegis of a painter from the Académie whose job was to guarantee the quality of the work. Many versions of the painting exist, at Versailles, in the Prado, in the Musée de Grenoble, the Musée de Saumur, Valenciennes, Vienna, in the town hall of Geneva (the gift of Louis XVI); the high-quality version in Clermont-Ferrand seems to a large extent to have been painted by Callet himself.

There was no scope for Callet to display originality in the composition of this painting; he does not stray from the standard French royal portrait type which was considered to be the perfect expression of the king's double nature, the man of flesh and blood and also the incarnation of power. Although a historical figure, the monarch represented in this way transcended the relativity of history in favour of the expression of essential values that were of their nature eternal and immutable. Modernity has no meaning in the context of the official portrait; hence, during the reign of Louis XVI, modernity found its expression mainly in the official portrait of the Queen, who herself could possess no authority. The portrait of Marie-Antoinette and her children by Elisabeth-Louise Vigée-Lebrun (Salon of 1787; Musée National du Château, Versailles) was designed to respond to a set of very precise historical conditions; in this case, the pose was heavily inspired by English examples.

In its uniqueness, the portrait of the King could not be used by the artist to display his abilities; unable to express these out of a sense of decorum, he had to deploy his talents in his rendering of the monarch's features. The official portrait could thus occupy its role as a substitute for the King's presence (for example, no one was allowed to turn their back on the portrait). The problem of resemblance met obstacles, nevertheless, over the manner in which the artist was authorised to depict the king's features, and therefore over the number of sittings he obtained. The authorities often paid more attention to the resemblance of the regalia rather than that of the face. For one portrait, commissioned in 1778, Callet arranged for the coronation robes and regalia to be lent to him by the prior of the Basilica of Saint-Denis, where they were housed. He probably used the studies he made at that time for the painting under discussion here. Artists tended to paint the rest of the canvas, leaving the face sketched in, before finishing it or advancing it as soon as possible after they had spent a few moments with the monarch. In 1779,

commissioned to produce an image for the Ministry of Foreign Affairs, Callet was able to catch a few moments with his sitter during the King's luncheon (Engerand 1901, p.183). It is very unlikely that the present canvas was based on any further studies from life.

It is pleasantly ironic that when the portrait of Louis XVI was presented at the Salon of 1789 it was hung near to Antoine Vestier's portrait of Latude (Musée Carnavalet-Histoire de Paris, Paris), a bitter attack on the arbitrary nature of royal power. Callet's painting arrived late at the exhibition, and in a very unfavourable political climate (the Salon opened on 25 August, the day of the King's birthday); it elicited no reviews, possibly because the public was bored by such repetitive portrayals of their ruler. In the 1770s, critical opinion had pinpointed the need to modernise the formula and to free images of the sovereign from weighty symbolism. Some advised that more care should be taken over achieving a likeness, demonstrating the new importance of mankind in the order of things, and recalling the demands of portraiture. Other, more radical commentators spoke of the necessity of situating the art of portraiture in its historical context. It has to be said that, despite the slightly anachronistic nature of the French royal portrait, the Empire remained loyal to its traditions, tempering the genre with a slightly increased attention to physical resemblance. SA

# Antonio Canova
(POSSAGNO, 1757 – VENICE, 1822)

## 15
### *Pope Pius VII*

1806
Marble, 69.5 × 70 × 30 cm
Inscription, on a small rectangular block of marble placed between the sculpture and the pedestal: *A. CANOVA. FECIT*; on the front of the pedestal: *PIO VII*
Promoteca Capitolina, Musei Capitolini, Rome, PRO 83

PROVENANCE: presented by Canova to Pius VII in 1807; given by Pius VII to the Protomoteca Capitolina on the occasion of its opening, 1820
EXHIBITED: Venice, 1992, no.136; Bassano del Grappa and Possagno, 2003–04, no.IV–17
LITERATURE: Martinelli and Pietrangeli 1955, pp.40–44, p.78, no.63, pl.XI; Sass 1963–65, vol.3, pp.48 and 199, repr.; Pavanello 1976, no.158, repr.; Olson 1986, p.90, repr.

Between July and September 1803, Antonio Canova executed a portrait of Gregorio Luigi Barnaba Chiaramonti (1742–1823), elected Pope with the name of Pius VII in 1800. The plaster model (Gipsoteca, Possagno) was used for the creation of three marble busts: the first was given to Napoleon I in 1804, through the offices of Cardinal Fesch, on the occasion of his coronation, the sculptor receiving a gratuity (Versailles, Château;

damaged in the Tuileries in 1830, nose and mouth repaired); the second, carved in 1806, was presented by the artist to the Pope in the following year (this is the version here); the third was executed between 1820 and 1822, largely by the studio, for the Braccio Nuovo of the Museo Chiaramonti in the Vatican (in situ). There are a number of other unsigned replicas.

This portrait bust was made at a pivotal moment in the Pope's political life. In 1801 he had signed a concordat with France to restore the Catholic religion in France. However, the articles drawn up by Bonaparte and Talleyrand, added at the time of the concordat's publication, undermined the situation of the head of the Church by restraining his influence. This caused some tensions, which were not allayed by the pontiff's trip to Paris in 1804 to crown Napoleon and were to continue to grow thereafter.

Having finished the model in September 1803, Canova wrote to Quatremère de Quincy to tell him that he had found the Pope serene and gentle, despite the political difficulties he was enduring. He attempted to express this moment of inner peace by rendering the spirituality of the sitter in a restrained manner. The Pope was a Benedictine monk by the age of sixteen. He climbed the career ladder of the Church (abbot, then bishop) before being appointed cardinal in 1785. Jacques-Louis David, who painted his portrait from February to March 1805 (Louvre, Paris), exclaimed after his series of visits: 'This good old man, what a venerable figure! How simple he is … and what a fine head he has! A truly Italian head; the large eyes set so well, very pronounced!… He's a true Pope, that one! Poor, humble; he's only a priest' (Delécluze [1855], 1983, p.248). David had met Canova in Rome and when he painted the Pope he must certainly have seen the Italian bust (Honour 1972, p.315).

Pius VII is represented by Canova in a sober way, with the insignia of his office: the skullcap on his head, a broad stole over his buttoned cape, which is lined with ermine; the double knot of the cord makes a handsome loop in the front, adding a decorative note to a magnificently sacerdotal figure. The representation does not stray far from customary papal portraits, however, and from this point of view does not depart from, for example, the busts of Clement XIV by Christopher Hewetson or Pius VI by Giuseppe Ceracchi.

The presentation of such an image to Napoleon was not without an ulterior motive: it was intended to confirm the sitter's sovereignty, which was neither temporal nor limited, but universal. The Pope was second to no man (not even an emperor). In this respect, the way the stole is decorated is significant: it is embroidered with a series of crosses and stars (the Chiaramonti emblem) with the Benedictine motto PAX (which does not appear in David's painting, in which the stole is purely ornamental). This motto, repeated under each cross, identifies Pius VII and refers to his role as a peacemaker (Olson 1986, p.90).

In order to convey the Pope's interior life, and to do away with any trace of anecdote, Canova has avoided incising the eyes: Pius VII has no gaze, he cannot look at anyone – another feature that is different from David's painting – his eyes are perfectly smooth with no pupils. However, in order to tone down the coldness of the mask, the sculptor has left the lips slightly parted. Perhaps the slight smile of the patient diplomat (the Pope) can be glimpsed. The marble head in the Capitoline is extraordinarily beautiful: the face is energetic but does not show any signs of tension; the soft, extremely fine way in which the sculpture has been modelled contrasts with the brilliant, almost Bernini-esque carving of the hair. The curls escape freely from beneath the skullcap, giving the sculptor the excuse to develop his work with the chisel. The more mechanical treatment of the clothing suggests that this part of the sculpture might have been left to an assistant in the studio, under the watchful eye of the artist, of course. Stendhal found that the portrait had 'too much ideal grace' (quoted in Sass 1963–65, vol.3, p.53). Bertel Thorvaldsen's bust, made in 1824 from a death mask, possibly catches the Pope's likeness a little better (Sass 1963–65, vol.3, p.54).

The bust presented by Canova to Pius VII symbolises their personal relationship. The sovereign pontiff made much of the artist: decorated, appointed inspector general of antiquities and arts of the Papal States, of the Academy of St Luke, the Vatican Museums and the Capitoline; he enjoyed enormous intellectual and administrative power. His talent was also symbolically celebrated when his Perseus was acquired by the Pope and placed in the courtyard of the Belvedere in place of some antiquities that were taken to Paris, in particular the Apollo. This strong link between Canova and Pius VII was revived in 1815 when the sculptor supervised the return of the antiquities to Rome (see cat.14). The gift by Pius VII of his bust at the time of the inauguration of the Protomoteca in 1820 preceded the installation, also in the Protomoteca, of the monument by Giuseppe De Fabris dedicated to Canova (Martinelli and Pietrangeli 1955, p.88, no.93, pl.XXIV): the Pope and the sculptor, dead within a year of each other, are thus symbolically reunited in the shrine to Italian memory (see also cat.119). GS

## 119
### Domenico Cimarosa

1808
Marble, 75 × 60 × 28 cm
Inscription on the cut, right:
ANTONIO CANOVA SCOLPI. ROMA MDCCCVIII;
on the pedestal, twice: DOMENICO CIMAROSA
Promoteca Capitolina, Musei Capitolini, Rome, PRO 24

PROVENANCE: commissioned by Cardinal Ercole Consalvi; deposited in the Panthéon 1816; transferred to the Protomoteca [sic] Capitolina, 1820
EXHIBITED: Venice, 1992, no.139; Milan, 2002, no.VII.28; Bassano del Grappa and Possagno, 2003–04, no.IV.20
LITERATURE: Martinelli and Pietrangeli 1955, p.65, no.20, pl.XIII; Pavanello 1976, p.111, no.161, pl.XXXV; Pasquali 2004, p.47

This bust of Domenico Cimarosa (1749–1801), the celebrated composer of such comic operas as Il Matrimonio Segreto (1792), was commissioned in 1808 by Cardinal Ercole Consalvi, former secretary of state to Pius VII (he was forced by the French to resign in 1806). Without a doubt it is Canova's most astonishing portrait. The sculptor knew Cimarosa well, and was able to breathe unforgettable character into his posthumous portrait. Uncompromising realism in the transcription of his features – the bull neck, the heavy chin, the fleshy skin, the broad forehead and curly hair – which can be found in painted portraits of the composer, such as the one by Francesco Saverio Candido (1785; Museo di San Martino, Naples) is combined with an imposing composition in the classical style.

The musician is represented with eyes almost blank – a fine incision encircles the iris – and naked. The bust is cut low, in the middle of the torso. It includes the shoulders and beginning of the arms, plus the chest. The chest is broad but flaccid, very far removed from the compact musculature of the heroes of antiquity. Canova rejected systematic idealisation, preferring to depict poorly toned flesh as it really was. He may have been influenced by examples of Roman funerary art showing a comparable type of person, for example the stele of the cobbler Julius Helius (end of first century AD; Centrale Montemartini, Capitoline Museums, Rome).

Cardinal Consalvi was a close friend of Cimarosa and considered his genius to be comparable to that of Raphael (Antonello Cesareo in Bassano del Grappa 2003, p.390). He was chosen by the musician to take care of his manuscripts while he went to Russia, intervened on his behalf when he was arrested in Naples after the return to power of Ferdinand IV (he had composed a revolutionary hymn), and, in 1801, celebrated a mass in his memory at which the composer's Requiem was performed.

The marble bust was destined for the Pantheon, Rome, where funerary monuments and commemorative sculptures were housed. There it was in the company of busts of Raphael and Annibale Carracci, Nicolas Poussin, Anton Raphael Mengs and Johann Joachim Winckelmann, and also the busts of two musicians: Arcangelo Corelli by Angelo de Rossi (1713, transferred to the Panthéon in 1725; Martinelli and Pietrangeli 1955, p.66, no.23, pl.V) and Antonio Sacchini by Francesco Carradori (1786: Martinelli and Pietrangeli 1955, p.81, no.73, pl.XII). Domenico Cimarosa was installed in 1816, a year before the bust of his rival, Giovanni Paisiello, who had just died, by Pietro Perantoni (1817; Martinelli and Pietrangeli 1955, p.76, no.55). Overcrowding in the church reached crisis point from 1813 to 1818 with the dozens of busts produced in Canova's studio; this hastened the removal in 1820 of all the commemorative sculpture to a secular environment, the Protomoteca in the Palazzo dei Conservatori on the Capitoline Hill.

An epitaph, now lost, below the bust in the Pantheon testified to the tribute paid: *Domenico Cimarosa / n.to MDCCXLVIII morto MDCCCI / Ercole Card. Consalvi / p. / MDCCCXVI / Antonio Canova scolpi* (Martinelli and Pietrangeli 1955, p.65). The monument erected to Cimarosa by Cardinal Consalvi was situated among those realised by the friends of other great men: the painter Carlo Maratta to the memory of Raphael and Annibale Carracci (1674), Cardinal Ottoboni to the memory of Corelli (1725), Ambassador Azara to the memory of the German painter Mengs (1782), the scholar Johann Friedrich Reiffenstein to the memory of Winckelmann (1782), the historian Jean-Baptiste-Louis-George Séroux d'Agincourt to the memory of Poussin (1782), the music-loving Dannery to the memory of Sacchini (1786), Cardinal Riminaldi to the memory of Metastasio (1787), and so on. Cimarosa's entrance to the Panthéon can be seen as evidence of the friendship and respect for a loved teacher felt by Cardinal Consalvi, and to a great musician, and also as the desire to leave something personal in a very large series of celebrations to national heroes. To crown the affair, he was perspicacious enough to enlist the services of one of the greatest living sculptors. GS

## 132
### Ideal Head: Juliette Récamier as Beatrice

1819–22
Marble, 58.4 × 27.9 × 25.4 cm
Museum of Fine Arts, Boston, 2002.318. William Frances Warden Fund, Edward J. and Mary S. Holmes Fund, John Lowell Gardner Fund, Russell B. and Andrée Beauchamp Stearns Fund, Helen B. Sweeney Fund, Frank B. Bemis Fund, Seth K. Sweetser Fund, H. E. Bolles Fund, Arthur Mason Knapp Fund, and Benjamin Pierce Cheney Donation

PROVENANCE: supposed to be Bensi family, Genoa, 1930s; sold by Bensi to a private collection, Italy, by 1954; by descent within the family, until 2002; sold to a private collector, 2002; sold then to the Museum of Fine Arts, Boston, 2002

Antonio Canova met Juliette Récamier (1777–1849) (fig.67) in Albano, near Rome, in 1813. She had been exiled from Paris by Napoleon, who disapproved of her friendship with Madame de Staël and other opponents of the regime. The sculptor was bowled over, and planned a portrait that became an idealised portrait of Beatrice, Dante's muse. The story is told by François-René de Chateaubriand, a close friend of Madame Récamier, who reports what was said by their mutual friend, the writer Pierre-Simon Ballanche,

fervently though platonically in love with the beautiful Juliette: 'An artist of great renown ... a sculptor who has lately brought brilliance to Dante's illustrious homeland, and whose classical masterpieces have so frequently exalted the graceful imagination, one day, for the first time, caught sight of a woman who was, for him, like a living apparition of Beatrice. Full of that religious feeling that genius supplies, he at once required the marble, obedient as ever to his chisel, to express the sudden inspiration of that moment; and Dante's Beatrice passed from the vague domain of poetry into the physical domain of the arts ... Canova carved three busts of his admirable Beatrice, made in the image of Madame Récamier: including one for his model, a portrait taken from life, wearing a laurel wreath' (Chateaubriand 1998, vol.4: 'Fragments retranchés', p.623).

The artist made two clay portraits of Juliette, one with a veil and the other with hair (Mellini 1999, p.139). Only the first produced a plaster cast (Gipsoteca di Possagno: Pavanello 1976, no.250): the arrangement of the curls and, in all likelihood also the veil, remind us of the model posing for the artist, or spotted furtively in Albano. By contrast, the incised, uplifted eyes already suggest a process of idealisation: sublimated, Juliette becomes Beatrice. Melchior Missirini, one of Canova's earliest biographers, tells us in the second edition of his book published in 1825 that the sculptor made three marble versions: by exchanging the incised eyes for blank eyes with no pupil, however, he disembodied the portrait for ever.

After Canova's death, a marble version was sent to Juliette by her half-brother, Giambattista Sartori. Now in the Musée des Beaux-Arts, Lyons (Rocher-Jauneau 1957), and of disappointing workmanship, it is judged to be a studio piece (Pavanello 1976, no.249; Fernando Mazzocca in Venice 1992, no.146; Mellini 1999, p.140). There is an olive branch on the veiled head (an allusion to Dante's lines: Beatrice appeared to him wearing an olive wreath) and a tunic on the body. These two accessories are absent from the plaster cast in Possagno, which represents the character with a veil on her head but wearing no other garment, just as in the marble version sent by the artist to his friend Leopoldo Cicognara in June 1819 (known from an old photograph that was in the Giovanelli collection in Venice before 1911: Pavanello 1976, no.289; Mellini 1999, repr. p.274). The plaster cast in Possagno has a curved cut below the shoulders, whereas the Cicognara marble version is quadrangular. The more distant provenance of the Boston version is unknown, but the workmanship is of good quality. Between the socle and the bust, there is a vertical marble inset – the plinth of the back reinforcement – which can also easily be seen under the Cicognara marble version, the Lyons version and the Possagno plaster cast, but appears to be absent from other known copies (Stefani 1999, fig.192; Mellini 1999, p.274).

This bust typifies an important aspect of Canova's personality and his portraiture: his ambiguous attitude to the reproduction of the sitter's features and his tendency towards idealisation. As a sculptor, Canova is certainly no realist, eager to transcribe nature as it is. His bust of *Pope Pius VII* (cat.15) seeks to some extent to convey the physiological likeness of the Pope, but does not manage to do so because of the blank eyes with no pupils. The absence of any eye contact with the spectator gives the portrait an unreal feeling. The same detachment can be found in the busts of *Napoleon, Domenico Cimarosa* (cat.119), *Cicognara* and *Sartori* (see Venice 1992, nos 138–41): the eyes are barely incised – only the contour of the iris is engraved – and the geometry of the cut below the shoulders is not softened by any clothing. The general prevails over the particular. This means that a large part of Canova's activity was devoted to allegorical portraits, and his most important masterpieces fall within this genre, in statuary, and also in his busts. From 1811 he invented the concept of *Ideal Heads*. One of the first of these is *Helen* (signed and dated 1811; Private collection: see Venice 1992, no.142), given to the writer Isabella Teotochi Albrizzi as an ideal portrait; her image thus joins the image of the fabulous Helen of Troy. The process is similar with Juliette Récamier, who became the mythical and inaccessible Beatrice.

Canova made a complete series of similar heads, dreamy faces above a bold cut below the shoulders, with no drapery: they correspond entirely to his ideal of grace and feminine beauty – regular features, perfect oval face, straight nose, fleshy lips, curls and blank eyes with no pupil – impeccable but detached. These images of Calliope, Helen, Sappho, Beatrice, Laura, Eleonora d'Este, or unidentified people – the *Ideal Heads* made for English collectors (see Oxford 1997, pp.66–67) – are made with geometric precision and great delicacy; they enjoyed a huge commercial success and were repeated several times by the artist, with more or less intervention by the studio hands.

Canova wrote to Cicognara on 18 April 1818 to tell him that he had executed his head of Beatrice with passion. He considered it more innovatory than his other *Ideal Heads*, different from the classical heads and different even from his own heads. His friend expressed enthusiasm for the prototype of beauty that Canova had thus created, a synthesis of Greek art, art of the Italian Renaissance and of the purity of his own genius. GS

# Agostino Carlini

GENOA, c.1718 – LONDON, 1790

## I
## Model for an equestrian statue of George III

1768–69
Inscribed on the plinth: *Carlini*
Plaster, 87.6 × 38.1 × 59.7 cm
Royal Academy of Arts, London, 03/1684

PROVENANCE: given to the Royal Academy by the sculptor
by 1781
EXHIBITED: Royal Academy, London, 1769, no.9
LITERATURE: Radcliffe 1969, pp.44–46; Trusted 1992–93,
pp.781–83 (1992); p.190 (1993)

One of three sculptors who became founder
members of the Royal Academy in 1768, Agostino
Carlini showed his model of George III on
horseback at the Academy's first exhibition the
following year. It is unclear whether there was any
plan to execute the work on a larger scale for a
public setting and certainly no full-scale version
was erected. However, Carlini himself produced
plaster versions of his model that were already
featuring in the *Public Advertiser* in April 1768 and
three of them, together with the clay model and the
moulds, later appeared in the sale that took place
on 13 January 1791 after Carlini's death.

As well as being replicated in these multiple
versions, the model was reproduced as an engraving
by Francesco Bartolozzi, another Italian founder
member of the Academy. Bartolozzi's print, the
plate for which appeared in Carlini's 1791 sale,
shows the full-scale equestrian figure in a landscape
and on rollers, as if the completed work were
being taken to its intended site. It appears that
the sculptor had presented the model to the
Academy by 1781. In 1775 this representation of the
King was described as 'the best that has appeared'.
By this date, visitors to the Academy would also
have seen the marble bust of George III, shown by
Carlini in 1773.

Carlini's composition was no doubt conceived
with an awareness of several earlier equestrian
statues that had attracted much attention. The
most celebrated and widely discussed of these
statues were the images of William III produced
by Michael Rysbrack and Peter Scheemakers for
Bristol and Hull respectively. With their classical
armour and short hair, these images of a Protestant
king were strikingly different from another
celebrated equestrian – Le Sueur's baroque image of
Charles I, placed at the head of Whitehall. Carlini's
figure, by contrast, is noticeably less classicising
and, by showing the King with a wig, recalls the
earlier tradition used on the Continent for the
representation of absolute monarchs.

Often such images – François Girardon's Louis
XIV, for example – were made available as small-
scale bronzes and it is possible that Carlini had
such reductions in mind when he designed his
equestrian figure. Details such as the form of the
base and the shield lying below the horse are indeed
more familiar on bronzes of this type rather than

on full-scale statues. Carlini's production and
marketing of multiple plaster versions and the
absence of any evidence for a full-scale statue
suggest that the figure was from the start conceived
as a small-scale figure. It could thus serve both
as a sculptural commemoration of the newly
established Academy's first royal patron, for display
in its own rooms and as a composition that might
be profitably replicated. While later equestrian
statues, by Chantrey among others, consciously
reworked a classical formula already followed by
Rysbrack and Scheemakers, Carlini's figure of
George III still seems to refer back to a late baroque
tradition of equestrian figures of the sort that
would have been familiar to the Genoese-born
sculptor. MB

# Giuseppe Ceracchi

ROME, 1751 – PARIS, 1801

## II2
## George Washington

1795
Marble, 73 × 55.9 × 33 cm
Inscription on the reverse: *CERACCHI FACIEBAT /
PHILADELPHIA / 1795*
Lent by The Metropolitan Museum of Art, New York.
Bequest of John L. Cadwalader, 1914 (14.58.235)

PROVENANCE: acquired from the artist by Joseph de Jaudenes
y Nebot, Cadiz, c.1795–1812; Richard Meade, Philadelphia,
c.1812–28; his wife, 1828–52; acquired by Governor Kemble,
Cold Spring, New York, 1852–75; his heirs 1875–1904; acquired
by John L. Cadwalader, 1904–14; bequeathed by Cadwalader,
1914
EXHIBITED: Rome, 1989, no.12; Philadelphia and Houston,
2000, no.123
LITERATURE: Eisen 1932, pp.841–46, pl.CCXIII; Ten Eyck
Gardner 1948, *passim*, repr.; Desportes 1963, pp.160, 162, 166–68,
figs 7–8

Armed with a letter of introduction from
Thomas Jefferson, Giuseppe Ceracchi travelled
to Philadelphia during the winter of 1790–91
(Desportes 1963, p.145) in the hope of winning the
commission for the equestrian monument to
George Washington (1732–1799), planned by the
American Congress in 1783. While his project was
under discussion – he exhibited his full-size model
at the end of 1791 – he made portrait busts of
various influential figures; his reputation was high
because he had made busts of prominent people in
Europe, including Pius VI, Friedrich II, Joseph II
and Joshua Reynolds, President of the Royal
Academy. He appears to have been granted several
sittings with Washington when he was working on
his features. He returned to Europe in 1792 with a
model in terracotta (which he showed successfully
in Amsterdam). A letter from the sculptor to
Jefferson, written on 27 March 1794, reports that a
marble version of the portrait, with those of other

Americans, had been produced (Desportes 1963,
p.160).

Ceracchi returned to Philadelphia at the end
of summer 1794, hoping to obtain a commission
for another monument, this time dedicated to
Liberty. In order to curry favour with Washington,
he requested more sittings to correct the marble
version that had been produced in Italy. He
offered the finished bust to Washington, who
turned it down, agreeing only that it should
adorn the presidential residence in Philadelphia.
Disappointed by the failure of the subscription
for the new monument, he asked an exorbitant
price for the bust, which he had previously
offered for nothing. Washington replied that he
would agree to pay him a sum established by an
independent expert. Finally, the sculptor sold his
work to the Spanish chargé d'affaires, Josef de
Jaudenes y Nebot, who hoped to present it to his
sovereign (letter from Jefferson, 22 January 1816:
Fehl 1968, p.529). The bust was shipped to Spain,
but appears to have remained in a crate in Cadiz
(Ten Eyck Gardner 1949, p.192). It was sold by the
widow of the chargé d'affaires to an American
agent in Cadiz, an important collector, Richard
Meade, who took it back to the United States.
It finally found a home in the Metropolitan
Museum of Art in that country.

There are several marble versions of this
portrait, executed from moulds taken from a plaster
cast left by Ceracchi in Bordeaux in 1795. According
to Ulysse Desportes, the plaster cast in Bordeaux
may have been taken from the bust in terracotta
acquired by the diplomat François Cacault from the
sculptor's widow; it is noticeably different from the
marble in New York (Musée des Beaux-Arts,
Nantes, held to be the very large model made for
the equestrian monument: Desportes 1963, fig.1).
The terracotta in Nantes must also be the original
of the unsigned marble versions to be found in
various American collections (Desportes 1963,
pp.168–69).

Only Houdon and Ceracchi produced models
of Washington during his lifetime. Nevertheless,
people held very different opinions on the way in
which the model's facial features were portrayed.
The portrait by Houdon – 'the premier sculptor
of the world' according to Jefferson – executed at
Mount Vernon in 1785 from a mask taken from life
(see Versailles 2004, no.49) became the canonical
image of the general, and was widely distributed
via the medal struck by Duvivier in 1789, and also
especially by the huge popularity of the statue
erected in the Capitol in Richmond in 1796.

Nevertheless, Ceracchi's version of the face
was considered a better likeness by a number of
Washington's friends (see James Harper in
Philadelphia and Houston 2000, p.246). Jefferson
himself, who had a plaster cast by Houdon on show
in his *Tea Room* in Monticello, preferred Ceracchi's
portrait to the portrait by Houdon (Desportes
1963, p.171). Having retired to his house in Virginia,

he probably was not aware of the marble bust that was finished by Ceracchi during his second visit to the United States, but only knew the model in terracotta made during his first visit. When Canova executed the head of the statue commissioned by the town of Raleigh (destroyed by fire in 1831), he modelled it from a copy of Ceracchi's bust (Pavanello 1976, no. 301, repr.). Yet it was Houdon who provided the model for Henry Kirke Brown's equestrian statue (1835–56).

These differences of opinion over the likeness of portraits done from life show that in the end the challenge lies elsewhere. The portrait of Washington cannot be reduced to the reproduction of his features, but to the interpretation given by the artist. Houdon's image of the general is, as usual, more composite than realistic. The combed back hair is treated as a mass, the face is geometrical and the sculptor does not linger over the details. The idea is to express the general's imperious presence, and his dynamism. By contrast, Ceracchi's head presents the hair in neat curls; the wide mouth has well-defined thin lips, which were particularly admired. The character seems more intimate, caught in a moment of inner reverie.

The composition of the two busts is also very different. Houdon, whose plaster casts left behind in the United States (and notably in Franklin) were taken from the terracotta in Mount Vernon, projects a heroic, unclothed Washington, with an abstract, naked cut (see Versailles 2004, p. 275, fig. 2). By contrast, Ceracchi, faithful to his Italian roots and to the aesthetic of the majority of portraits he executed in Europe, shows Washington as a Roman statesman, with short hair, incised eyes and a powerful broad body amply draped in the costume of a Hadrian or a Marcus Aurelius. This imperial vision might surprise us in an artist with known Jacobite sympathies – he was expelled from Rome in 1792 and died on the guillotine following a failed conspiracy against Bonaparte. Yet his bust of Washington, as has been seen, was supposed to be the gateway to a much larger project. Did Ceracchi realise that his sitter, a modern Cincinnatus, who chose to withdraw from power, detested the idea of being represented in classical garb? GS

# Sir Francis Chantrey

NORTON, NEAR SHEFFIELD, 1781 – LONDON, 1841

## 151
### Edward Johnstone

1819
Signed: *Edwd. Johnstone Esq. CHANTREY Sculptor 1819*
Marble, 61 × 45 × 26 cm
Birmingham Museum and Art Gallery

PROVENANCE: commissioned by Richard Colley Wellesley, brother of the Duke of Wellington, 1818; delivered to Johnstone,

c. 1826; acquired by Birmingham Museum and Art Gallery, 1962
EXHIBITED: Royal Academy, London, 1819, no. 1204; National Portrait Gallery, London, 1981, no. 23
LITERATURE: Potts 1981A, p. 29; Whinney 1988; Yarrington et al. 1994, p. 93

Edward Johnstone was the illegitimate son of Richard Colley, Marquis Wellesley, the brother of the Duke of Wellington. Despite being illegitimate, Johnstone was highly regarded by his father, who made him his private secretary when he became Lord Lieutenant of Ireland in 1822. Wellesley commissioned the bust in 1818 and it was shown at the Royal Academy the following year. However, the entry in Chantrey's ledger records that Johnstone did not pay the sum of £105 until 1826, still leaving £21 unpaid.

The handsome young Johnstone is shown with a contemporary hairstyle, including long sideburns, but the format of his bust is more obviously classical than most other portraits by Chantrey. By showing the upper body nude and truncated low on the chest, Chantrey and his patron were adopting a convention used for some Roman imperial portraits and then, in the mid-eighteenth century, by sculptors such as Edmé Bouchardon. In Chantrey's adaptation of the convention, antique and the modern are combined. Though unusual for Chantrey in its format, the bust is supported on a turned socle that was standard on busts from his studio. The same type of socle was also used for earlier busts by various sculptors at Windsor when Chantrey was involved in the re-ordering of the sculpture in the Royal Collection for George IV. MB

## 83
### John Raphael Smith

1825
Signed: *CHANTREY, SC./1825*
Marble, 66 × 42 × 30 cm
Victoria and Albert Museum, London, A.15-1920

PROVENANCE: commissioned by Sir Simon Clarke, 1824; still in Chantrey's possession, 1835; given to the museum by Mrs O. Stuart Andreae and Miss South, 1920
LITERATURE: Holland 1851, p. 43; Whinney 1971, p. 148; Potts 1981A, p. 18; Whinney 1988, p. 422; Yarrington et al. 1994, p. 200; Bilbey and Trusted 2002, pp. 235–36

Chantrey, the leading portrait sculptor of Regency Britain, executed busts and statues of almost all the celebrated figures of the period. Many of these people – such as the writer, Sir Walter Scott – are known to us from Chantrey's images, which were often reproduced in plaster replicas. Before achieving success (and amassing a fortune) in London, Chantrey was apprenticed to a Sheffield frame maker and was said to have received instruction from the engraver John Raphael Smith. As engraver to the Prince of Wales (later George IV), Smith may well have been responsible for introducing the young sculptor to a figure who was later to become one of his most important patrons.

A plaster model for Smith's bust was shown in the Royal Academy in 1811 but this particular

marble was commissioned by Sir Simon Clarke in 1824. Chantrey's meticulously kept ledger reveals, however, that the bust was still in the sculptor's possession in 1835 and apparently remained with him until his death in 1841. It is possible that Chantrey kept the bust because of his continuing affection for an early supporter and friend, as well as his affinity with another successful artist.

In its format the bust of Smith combines the conventions of the neoclassical sculptural portrait – the bare chest and drapery in a general classical style – with the carefully observed and brilliantly executed features of the sitter's rugged face. Chantrey was particularly good at carving marble so that the surfaces vividly suggested the qualities of ageing flesh. Any neoclassical, ideal elements were always balanced, if not dominated, by this concern with the particular features of the subject. Chantrey was a great admirer of Louis-François Roubiliac, who worked in the mid-eighteenth century, and the two sculptors share an essentially empirical approach, as well as an acute awareness of what could be achieved through the surface finish of sculpture.

There may even have been a more particular and explicit reference in Smith's bust. It is most unusual to find a soft cap such as the one Smith wears in sculpture of this period. However, this feature had frequently been employed in the eighteenth century for images of writers or artists and Chantrey may be drawing on this tradition. It is indeed possible that the bust of Smith, the engraver, was intended to recall Roubiliac's portrait of Hogarth – another engraver – who was also shown in a soft cap. The specific nature of Smith's bust is also heightened by what early commentators recognised as Chantrey's response to the sitter's deafness. John Holland observed that 'the peculiarity of listening is conveyed with unmistakable precision'. Apparently in response to another animating feature of the bust – the slightly open lips – Chantrey himself explained to visitors to his studio how 'the expression of deafness was conveyed principally by the mouth, "If you observe a deaf man's mouth, you will always find the lips unclosed when he is attending to you" '. It is not surprising that many, including the sculptor John Flaxman, considered the bust of Smith one of Chantrey's best works. MB

# Denis-Antoine Chaudet

PARIS, 1763 – PARIS, 1810

## 96
### A Woman Holding a Portrait of Her Husband in Her Arms

1795
Marble, 87.5 × 36 × 45.8 cm
Inscription on the plinth (on the right): *Chaudet S. 1795*
Musée des Arts Décoratifs, Paris, 35 302

PROVENANCE: sold in Paris, 24 April 1856, no.23; 'A fine group
in white marble, by Chaudet, representing Prudon and his
mistress'; acquired by the expert Théret; sold by Gleizes, the
dealer in curiosities, in Paris, 16–19 January 1860, no.184:
'A very fine group in marble executed by Chaudet and signed.
It represents the bust of the painter Prud'hon, with a weeping
woman nearby'; bequeathed to the museum by Madame
Delicourt, 1945
EXHIBITED: Paris, Salon of 1795, no.1015; Amsterdam, 1957,
no.114
LITERATURE: Leroy-Jay Lemaistre 1998, p.330

Chaudet exhibited a work described as follows
in the Salon of 1795: 'A woman holding in her
arms the portrait of her husband. Both heads are
portraits.' Although the material is not mentioned,
this description must refer to the marble sculpture
now in the Musée des Arts Décoratifs, signed and
dated 1795. A plaster cast signed 'Chaudet' at the
base of the monument was in a Parisian collection
in 1931: if we believe the evidence of an old
photograph now in the Department of Sculpture,
the variations between the plaster cast and the
marble sculpture are infinitesimal (the hair on the
marble bust is neatly cut with scissors, the base of
the pilaster is moulded). We do not know why the
male portrait has been identified as the painter
Prud'hon (sales catalogue, 1856, repeated in 1860),
who died in 1823, thirteen years after the death of
the sculptor.

In 1795, Chaudet was still at the beginning of
his brief career (he died at the age of forty-seven).
He was a pupil of Jean-Baptiste Stouf and Etienne
Pierre Adrien Gois. In 1784 he won the first prize
for sculpture at the Académie Royale in Paris. He
was a scholar at the French Academy in Rome from
1784 to 1788. Having been accepted as 'agrée' by the
Académie Royale in 1789, he exhibited a marble
sculpture with a delightfully sentimental subject at
the Salon that year, *Sensitivity*: 'She is examining a
sensitive plant that she has just touched. On the
plinth are engravings of four different historical
subjects depicting the various effects of sensibility'
(Salon booklet, no.310; the marble piece was
acquired by Sommariva and featured in the sale of
his collection in 1839; the plaster is now in the
Villa Carlotta, Tremezzo).

He continued in this vein in the Salon of 1791,
when he showed a terracotta statuette, *Friendship
Enchaining Love* (Musée Jacquemart-André, Paris:
Froissart 1999, figs 5–8), and in the Salon of 1793,
when he presented a wax model of one of his most
famous works in this amatory genre, *Cyparissus
Weeping for His Stag* (the marble statue was later
acquired by the Empress Joséphine). In 1795 he
worked on a touching scene of *Paul and Virginie in the
Cradle* (plaster, whereabouts unknown). Chaudet's
extreme sensitivity, powerfully conveyed in his
intense portraits (such as the portrait by Desmarais:
cat.78, and the pastel by Augustin du Louvre,
dating from 1804: Froissart 1999, fig.4), is also

evident in his moralising subjects such as *Belisarius*
(terracotta in the Salon of 1791; plaster: Musée
du Louvre 1998, vol.1, p.139, repr.): the afflicted
adolescent at the feet of the hero is the brother
of the weeping widow in the monument of 1795.

This marble group belongs to a genre, the
small commemorative monument or indoor
cenotaph, which was in favour during the third
quarter of the eighteenth century, in particular
with Jean-Jacques Caffieri in his *Monument to Madame
Favart* (marble; 1774; Musée du Louvre 1998, vol.1,
p.126, repr.). On full-sized tombs of the period the
figure of mourning was represented by a weeping
woman rather than a representation of the deceased
(see examples by Louis-Claude Vassé and Ignace
Broche). These examples of neoclassical art had
been completely assimilated by the time Chaudet
was practising sculpture.

For his 1795 piece he chose the reduced size of
an indoor cenotaph and the funerary vocabulary of
the weeping woman, making it a double memorial:
the portraits of a couple separated by death. The
figure of the woman appears to be an allegory
of Marital Fidelity or Friendship (the widow
resembles a drawing exhibited in the Salon of 1796
and engraved, *Friendship in Tears at the Gates of a Prison*:
Froissart 1999, fig.15), with her gown in the classical
style and her bare feet, tenderly embracing the base
of the herm, which is surmounted by the bust of
her husband. The choice of a herm may have a
symbolic significance. 'The ancients used to place
a kind of statue [surmounted by the head of
Mercury] at crossroads on trunk roads, because
Mercury was the messenger of Jupiter, and was
regarded as the god responsible for roads'
(Lacombe de Prezel 1779, vol.1, p.280), in other
words, for destinies.

The two figures represented by Chaudet in
his moving family portrait are clearly individualised.
The wife is dressed in a high-waisted dress with a
belt, in the fashion of the day. Her hairstyle, with
the hair held back by a broad headband, is refined,
although slightly tousled as she expresses her
sorrow. Her husband, who died in his prime, has
strong, virile features, with closed lips and a fixed
gaze. Contemporary fashion – curled hair swept
back, thick sideburns on his cheeks – contrasts
with the unincised eyes and the severe presentation
of the bust as a classical herm. The sincerity of
the affection expressed by the monument, and the
simple effectiveness of its design, preserve it from
demonstrative pathos and the display of feeling
to which many comparable works were prone.

The plaster cast made by Sophie de Sermézy,
a few years later, *To the Memory of the Best of Fathers*
(undated; Musée Marmottan, Paris; Hubert 1976,
fig.6), in which a mother in a bonnet points out
with raised arm to her daughter the bust of her
side-whiskered father, depicted naked on a
pedestal placed on an apartment column, is an
irresistibly bourgeois piece already displaying
Biedermeier charm; it contrasts strongly with

Chaudet's noble, straightforward vision, filled with
the passion of the heroines of Richardson and
Goethe, and moving because of its restrained
tenderness. GS

# Joseph Chinard
LYONS, 1756 – LYONS, 1813

## 100
## *Madame Chinard*

1802–03
Terracotta, 65 × 36.5 × 26.3 cm
Inscription, on front of plinth: *Chinard statuaire à Lyon l'an XI*;
on front of pedestal: *Tu vivras toujours dans / la pensée de ton époux*;
below, traces of a worn inscription, or one scratched and
subsequently disguised
Musée des Beaux-Arts, Lyons, B 426

PROVENANCE: acquired 1887
EXHIBITED: Paris, 1909–10, no.52; Lyons, 1989–90, no.36
LITERATURE: Cantinelli 1905, p.148, repr.; Desvernay 1915,
p.124; Rocher-Jauneau 1978B, pp.61–63, repr.

Chinard married the embroideress Antoinette
Perret (1752–1794) on 16 January 1788 in Lyons.
She was the daughter of a master carpenter and had
been his companion for a long time. She remained
in Lyons while the sculptor went to study in Rome
(from 1784 to 1787). Their marriage took place on
his return. A few years earlier, in 1786, Chinard had
won a prestigious prize at the Accademia di San
Luca in Rome for his *Perseus Rescuing Andromeda*
(1786; Accademia di San Luca, Rome). He was in
Rome again when, in 1792, he experienced serious
problems with the pontifical police and was
incarcerated in the Castel Sant'Angelo; it was his
wife who got in touch with the French authorities
to demand his release (La Chapelle 1896–97, p.93).
She died on 4 September 1794.

Eight years later, the artist began modelling a
portrait bust of her, adding the following moving
epitaph: 'You will live for ever in the thoughts of
your husband.' In fact, he had been living since 1794
with Marie Berthaud, whom he had met at the
beginning of the year when he was in prison in
Lyons, and whom he married in 1811. Why did he
feel the need to make a portrait bust of his first
wife between 1802 and 1803 – in two versions?
A second version of the bust, also in terracotta and
dated Year XI, is now in the Walters Art Museum
in Baltimore. It is almost identical to the bust in the
Musée de Lyons, except for a longer inscription on
the pedestal: *Tu seras toujours présente à / ma pensée /
Le souvenir de tes vertus me / servira de guide / et me consolera
jusqu'au moment / qui doit nous réunir.* (You will always
be present in / my thoughts / The memory of your
virtues / will serve as my guide / and will console
me until the time when / we shall be reunited.)
Does this bear witness to his deep sadness when
he thought about his youthful companion during

the difficult period of the Revolution? Yet Chinard's career was approaching its peak: he was a member of the Académie de Lyon, a correspondent of the Institut and official sculptor to his home town. He was shortly (in 1804) to be summoned to Carrara to carve portraits of the Napoleon clan. Perhaps his tremendous professional success could never mask the reality of his inner pain.

Chinard used the memory of his first wife to represent her as beautiful and full of energy, although somewhat distant, as if to suggest the distance of death. He produced a detailed image of an elegant woman, using all his skills as a sculptor. Antoinette Perret is wearing a high-waisted dress, with a belt under her bust and a large shawl covering her shoulders. She wears an extraordinary feathered hat, with a broad strap under the chin – a feathered bonnet – a popular style at the time (Leloir 1951, p.89, no.8). In his terracotta busts of women, such as the one of Jeanne de l'Orme de l'Isle in the Musée des Beaux-Arts in Lyons executed at the same period (see Lyons 1989, no.37), Chinard liked to reproduce pleated silks and soft fabrics; he may have been recalling his father's trade – he was a master craftsman in cloth of gold and silver, and silk – and the fabrics he saw at home. Antoinette Perret was herself an embroideress. This posthumous portrait pays homage to the memory of a sincere and capable companion at times of trouble, a stylish and fashionable wife and an unforgettable personality. GS

## 123
### Fanny Perrin, with the Attributes of Psyche, Playing with a Wreath of Flowers

1808
Marble, 54 × 31 × 25 cm
Collection du Musée d'Art Roger-Quilliot, Ville de Clermont-Ferrand, 894-325-1

PROVENANCE: in the collection of the sitter, second wife of General Baron Louis-Jean Desaix de Veygoux (1790–1845); sold by his son, Nicolas-Louis-Arthur, Comte Desaix, at Le Havre, 19 December 1883; bought at the sale by Marie-Alexandrine de Girardin, separated wife of Comte Desaix; bequeathed to the city of Clermont-Ferrand, 1884
EXHIBITED: Paris, Salon of 1808, no.60; Paris, 1909–10, no.72; London, 1972, no.345; Clermont-Ferrand, 1983, no.9; Paris, 1986, no.182; Paris, 1999–2000, no.428

This bust was exhibited at the Salon of 1808 with the title 'Mlle Fanni P***' with the attributes of Psyche, playing with a wreath of flowers'. The sitter was Fanny Perrin (1801–1854), who in 1828 married Louis-Jean Desaix de Veygoux, nephew of the famous general killed at the Battle of Marengo in 1800.

The circumstances surrounding the execution of this portrait are not known. Although details of the relationship between the Perrin and Desaix de Veygoux families remain uncertain, their presumed closeness has given rise to the hypothesis that Chinard was able to make the bust during a

possible stay in Clermont-Ferrand, when the monument to General Desaix was being planned (Isabelle Leroy-Jay Lemaistre in Paris 1999, no.428).

The portrait of little Fanny is unusual in both composition and in its allegorical theme. Chinard showed two other busts of women at the Salon of 1808, both with the same identifying feature as this bust: they are cut off at waist level and they have arms; one of the two represents Madame de Verninac, wife of the Prefect of the Rhône, as Diana (Musée du Louvre 1998, vol.1, p.146, repr.), the other, Madame Ab., mistress of Albert de Permont, superintendent of police in Marseilles, as Sappho playing the lyre (Rougier sale, Galerie Georges Petit, Paris, 3–4 May 1904, no.158, repr.). Chinard had already carved Juliette Récamier with her two arms raised to her bosom (see fig.67), and exhibited at the Salon of 1810 a bust of Madame Gauldrée-Boilleau holding an image of her deceased son (Musée des Arts Décoratifs, Paris; Moreau-Nélaton 1909, repr.). The waist-level bust with arms was not Chinard's own creation: it existed in Italy at the end of the fifteenth century (Verrocchio) and was fairly widespread in the seventeenth century (Algardi, Artus I Quellin), although it was not used in France. Chinard made the fuller composition, descending to the waist and including all the upper limbs, popular in France at the beginning of the nineteenth century. The liberation of the hands was responsible for enlarging the portrait bust, now essentially a statue cut in half: compositions of this type had greater freedom to express a dynamic scene, with accessories. Chinard would add an allegorical interpretation, illustrated by an attribute of some kind held in the subject's hands, a device that allowed the sculptor unprecedented freedom. Juliette Récamier lifts her veil to her breast with a mixture of coquetry and modesty; Madame de Verninac as Diana brandishes an arrow whose tip she tests; Madame Ab. as Sappho is seen playing the lyre; Madame Gauldrée-Boilleau supports the head of her son, who appears to her as a seraphim. Fanny Perrin uses both hands to hold up a garland of flowers in front of her, a charming halo that echoes the oval of her face. Two little butterfly wings attached to her back reveal the identity of her disguise in terms of classical iconography: she is Psyche, the soul in Greek and the heroine of Apuleus' tale, in which she aspires to rise up to meet the divinities. The reasons for the Perrin family's request that their daughter should be thus represented are not clear; perhaps they wished to follow fashion: Neoclassicism under the Empire, in its most elegiac vein, produced many evocations of this gentle heroine, although she was usually represented as an adolescent (see Schneider 1912). Did the idea come from the sculptor, charmed by the young girl's grace and candour, worthy of the ancient myths? He dressed her in an unmistakably classical tunic,

with pretty pleats as untidy as are the locks of her hair.

The mixture of allegorical representation (the reference to antiquity is further emphasised by Fanny's blank eyes, with no pupil) and the realism of the face (the wild, curly ringlets, the attractive pout outlined by her parted lips, the round cheeks and plump chin), plus the chubby arms and hands, make this a highly unusual portrait and demonstrate the originality of the artist. GS

# John Singleton Copley
BOSTON, MASS., 1738 – LONDON, 1815

## 42
### Samuel Adams

c.1770–72
Oil on canvas, 125.8 × 100 cm
Museum of Fine Arts, Boston. Deposited by the City of Boston, 30.76c

PROVENANCE: John Hancock; gift to the City of Boston by Hancock's heirs, 1836; deposited at the Museum of Fine Arts, Boston, 1876
EXHIBITED: Boston 1983, no.5; Boston 1995, no.62
LITERATURE: Parker and Wheeler 1938, pp.17–19, pl.114; Prown 1966, pp.83–84; Boston 1983, p.199; Boston 1995, pp.275–78

Thought to be a commission by Adams's friend and fellow patriot John Hancock, this image of the individual dubbed the father of American Independence marks an important shift in the iconographic dimensions of Copley's portraiture (Troyen in Boston 1995, p.277). By the 1770s, the American-trained Copley had ceased to rely upon the British prints he had formerly used as source material for his sitters' poses, accessories and even clothing (Staiti in Boston 1995, p.33). Adams is shown without many of the details that would usually inform the background of such a portrait. Rather, Copley chose to focus on his sitter's character. Adams dominates the pictorial space of the canvas and is set against a plain background. The portrait represents Adams's confrontation with Governor Thomas Hutchinson the day after the Boston Massacre of 5 March 1770, in defence of the rights of the colonists (Troyen 1995, p.277). As such, Samuel Adams crosses over into the realm of history painting in its subtle adherence to the narrative conventions of this genre.

There is some irony in the fact that Copley painted Adams's portrait as, a year later, Adams was to call for the Boston Tea Party, an act of rebellion by American colonists against the taxation of this comestible by the British. The tea dumped in Boston Harbor belonged to Copley's in-laws. In fact, Copley's acceptance of this commission calls attention to his somewhat ambiguous position vis-à-vis American politics (Staiti 1995, pp.43–47 and Troyen 1995, p.277). Married to Susanna Farnham Clarke, who came from a family of staunch Loyalists – supporters of the British monarch, King George III – Copley hardly championed the independence of the colonies. However, neither did he endorse all the governing decisions made by the British for America, including taxation. Adams, who was later to become a key figure in the American Revolution, belonged to the Sons of Liberty, a colonial group formed in response to the heavy taxation imposed by King George III on printed matter via the Stamp Act in 1765.

The subject of this image, Copley's most pointedly political portrait, is specifically anti-royalist. Adams faces Hutchinson, the representative of the British crown, to demand the removal of British troops from Boston following the deaths of some colonists at the hands of British soldiers in the Boston Massacre. Copley included documents specific to this instance. On the table Adams points magisterially to the seal of Massachusetts and an impressive roll of parchment on which 'Charter of Willm & Ma[ry] to Massachusetts' can be made out, reminding us of the privileges granted to that state by British monarchs in the seventeenth century (Parker and Wheeler 1938, p.18). Rolled up in his hand is a petition signed by Bostonians protesting against the Massacre; on this formal complaint can be seen the words 'Instructions of … Town Boston'. Adams later wrote of Hutchinson: 'It was then, if fancy deceive me not, I observ'd his knees to tremble. I thought I saw his face grow pale (and I enjoyd the sight) at the Appearance of the determined citizens peremptorily demanding the Redress of Grievances' (Samuel Adams to James Warren, Boston, 25 March 1771, *Warren–Adams Letters*, p.382).

Copley's image of this highly charged moment is sober in conception. The only visible backdrop to the figure of Adams is a monumental set of columns which dissolve into the darkened recesses of the work. Albeit rather stocky, Adams is nonetheless upright and determined in his stance, his jaw firmly set, his gaze direct. He is plainly clad in a russet suit set off by the white cuffs and collar of his shirt. These bright accents of white highlight the focal points of the image, his face and hands (which, in turn, bring our attention to the documents that supply textual narrative). Adams is positioned almost frontally, his face turning slightly and his body angled towards the viewer, so that the strong, raking light strikes his features to heighten the drama of the portrait. Copley conveys the importance of the scene while presenting an everyman's hero: Adams is middle class in appearance, honest in character and quintessentially American, a stalwart and unyielding leader making a stand on behalf of the people of Massachusetts. VG

18
*William Murray, First Earl of Mansfield*

1783
Signed at bottom right: *J.S. Copley pinx*
Oil on canvas, 227.6 × 149 cm
National Portrait Gallery, London, NPG 172

PROVENANCE: the artist's son, Lord Lyndhurst; his sale, Christie's, 5 March 1864, lot 81; bought for the National Portrait Gallery
EXHIBITED: Royal Academy, 1783, no.5; for later exhibition history see Ingamells 2004, p.329
LITERATURE: Prown 1966, vol.2, pp.285, 297–98, 426–27; Pressly 1995, pp.50–52, 70; Ingamells 2004, pp.329–30

William Murray (1705–1793) was born into the Scottish aristocracy and became a leading British judge and politician. Created Baron of Mansfield in 1756 and Earl of Mansfield in 1776, he served as Lord Chief Justice for thirty-two years. Shortly before this portrait by the American-born painter John Singleton Copley was exhibited at the Royal Academy in 1783, one newspaper punningly observed: 'if a *jury* of painters were impannelled, it must be their opinion that the noble Earl had even *justice* in his picture!' (*Morning Herald*, 23 April 1783). Copley's portrait indeed refers closely to Mansfield's legal and political careers. He is shown wearing a legal wig and perusing manuscripts, while over his black suit he wears an earl's parliamentary robes. The bust above the door may probably be identified with one in Mansfield's possession at Kenwood House, his home near London, portraying his friend the poet Alexander Pope (Ingamells 2004, pp.329–30).

Most commentators on the 1783 exhibition concurred that the portrait was a good likeness. Horace Walpole described it as 'very like, rather hard' (Graves 1905–06, vol.2, p.159). Press coverage was generally favourable. Even the highly critical reviewer in the *Public Advertiser* on 1 May allowed that *Mansfield* 'cannot be dismissed without congratulating the Noble Lord, who is the subject of it, on the apparent Melioration of his Taste' in terms of portraitist. A 'Vogue of Copley' was underway, albeit one which this critic dismissed as 'accidental' and arising 'more from a lucky Selection of Subject, than from any ascendant Skill in the Manner of treating it'.

The portrayal of Mansfield was in fact based on *The Death of the Earl of Chatham* (1779–81), an earlier image by Copley that had helped to establish him in 'vogue'. This showed the dramatic scene in the House of Lords when the former Prime Minister collapsed while arguing against recognising American independence. In order to depict this scene, Copley made sketches of members of the House of Lords. The survival of a scaled drawing of Mansfield's head would seem to indicate that he did sit to Copley on this occasion (Prown 1966, vol.2, p.285, fig.406). The later portrayals of Mansfield and of two other sitters (the Earl of Bessborough and Viscount Dudley and Ward) were all based on *The Death of Chatham*. This approach allowed Copley to save

time, 'allowing the initial sittings to do double duty and obviating the need to repeat them', and added another facet to the completed individual portraits by linking them to the historic scene in *The Death of Chatham* (Neff 1995, p.70).

A number of compositional drawings which Copley undertook for *Mansfield* survive (Prown 1966, vol.2, figs 430–35). In these, although the position of the head remains constant, the artist experimented with how to arrange the rest of the body, which suggests that Mansfield did not sit to Copley again. The portrait's ultimate design remained closely related to Mansfield's depiction in the earlier picture. It is unlikely, however, that Mansfield himself would have solicited revisiting such a representation. For it has been noted that the task of painting *The Death of Chatham* 'was surrounded by political booby traps, and in the case of the representation of the Earl of Mansfield Copley may have tripped one' (Prown 1966, vol.2, p.285). Mansfield was a long-standing opponent of Chatham, and, as one press review of the painting had described, 'Lord Mansfield is distinguished from the Rest by being drawn sitting, while the sympathetick Alarm had brought up all the Members of the House. This has a fine Effect on those who know that Lord Mansfield must have felt some secret Satisfaction at the probable Exit of a Man who had ever been his Scourge and his Terrour' (*St James's Chronicle*, 9–12 June 1781). Whether or not it was the artist's intention, *The Death of Chatham* drew adverse attention to Mansfield, who could 'hardly have been pleased by Copley's dramatisation of his indifference, and it is almost inconceivable that he would subsequently commission a portrait by Copley' (Prown 1966, vol.2, p.285).

Indeed, if one newspaper report is to be credited, the 1783 portrait was not commissioned by the sitter but 'was painted for Mr. Justice Buller. Various other Portraits of his Lordship are, we understand, at this time bespoke by different gentlemen of the law, either on the Bench, or high at the bar' (*Morning Chronicle*, 30 April 1783). Certainly, Francis Buller had ample motive for glorifying Mansfield, who had fostered his rising career, enabling his appointment to the chief justice's court at the precocious age of thirty-two (Pressly 1995, p.52). Although *Mansfield* eventually passed to Copley's son, it is possible that Buller, who died in 1800, had possession of the work prior to this (Ingamells 2004, p.329).

In any case, Copley too may have welcomed the opportunity to make pictorial amends by giving Mansfield a more flattering portrayal. Although the pose of the 1783 portrait was founded on the artist's earlier image of the sitter, the end results were thoroughly different in tone: the 'passive figure in *The Death of the Earl of Chatham* now forcefully eyes the viewer, while firmly gripping a rolled legal document as a commander would his staff' (Pressly 1995, p.52). SM

## Attributed to
# John Singleton Copley

**41**
*Major Hugh Montgomerie*

c.1780
Inscribed bottom right: *"Hugh", 12th Earl of Eglinton.*
Oil on canvas, 226.3 × 148.9 cm
Scottish National Portrait Gallery, Edinburgh, PG 1516

PROVENANCE: sold among lots which 'were from the Property of the Rt Hon. The Earl of Eglinton and Winton, and have been removed from Eglinton Castle, Irvine, Ayrshire', Christie's, London, 14 July 1922 (no.20) [as by David Martin]; bought Col. M. A. W. Swinfen Broun; sold by order of his executors, Christie's, London, 10 December 1948 (no.104) [as by David Martin]; bought Marshall Spink; from whom purchased [as by David Martin] by the Scottish National Portrait Gallery, 1949
EXHIBITED: original version exhibited at the Royal Academy, 1780 (no.172); exhibitions of the version shown here: *Scottish Exhibition*, Palace of History, Glasgow, 1911 (no.204) [as by Henry Raeburn]; *Tartan*, Fashion Institute of Technology, New York, 1988–89
LITERATURE: see Houston 1995, pp.114–15

Copley's only exhibit at the Royal Academy in 1780 was a painting of Major Hugh Montgomerie (1739–1819). Later that year the sitter became an MP; his portrait may have been a mark of his parliamentary ambitions. He proved a silent member, as Robert Burns noted in a 1785 poem (Namier and Brooke 1964, vol.3, p.159), calling him 'sodger [soldier] Hugh':

> I ken if that your sword were wanted,
> Ye'd lend a hand;
> But when there's aught to say anent it,
> Ye're at a stand.

As Burns hinted, Montgomerie was chiefly famed for his military career. When Copley's portrait was exhibited, a press review described the subject as 'A Highland officer, so like, that [it] is unnecessary to name him' (*Morning Chronicle*, 22 May 1780). During the Seven Years' War (1756–63), he had served initially with the regiment raised and led by his cousin Archibald Montgomerie, whom he succeeded in 1796 as Earl of Eglinton. A portrait of this cousin formed part of Copley's *The Death of Chatham* (1779–81), and may have led the artist into contact with Hugh Montgomerie (Houston 1995, p.114).

An exhibition guide entitled *A Candid Review* described Copley's painting as showing 'Major *Montgomery*, who signalised himself in the destruction of the *Cherokee* Settlements last war', and highlighted 'the burning of the town' in the background (Candid Review 1780, p.26). This guide was apparently produced as part of the Academy's publicity apparatus (Hallett 2001, p.72). Therefore, it is likely that it reflects Copley's own account of his image. Thus, this text would seem to confirm that the scene relates to a specific series of events in which Montgomerie had taken part as a subaltern during the 1760 campaign against the Cherokees on the South Carolinan frontier: the attacking and razing of several villages known

together as the 'Lower Towns', and of one further settlement, Etchoe, among the 'Middle Towns' (Mante 1772, p.293; Annand 1961, pp.39–40).

This British assault was led by Archibald Montgomerie, fielding detachments of his own and of another regiment, together with some American colonial forces and a party of Catawba Indian allies. In the initial encounters over a hundred Cherokees were killed or captured and, as one of the British commanders recorded, 'every house and town in the Lower Nation' was destroyed: 'I could not help pitying them a little: their villages were agreeably situated, their houses neatly built' (*Gentleman's Magazine*, 30 [July 1760], p.306).

But, when the British moved further into Cherokee territory, towards the Middle Towns, they were so harried by the Indians as to be forced to break off their campaign. Overall, the venture achieved little of military value (necessitating a second expedition in 1761, which seems not to have involved Hugh Montgomerie) (Anderson 2000, pp.462–63; McCulloch 2006, vol.2, p.93). The decision, then, to evoke in the portrait an incomplete series of attacks which was in fact a prelude to withdrawal – and which dated to long before the time of painting – might appear rather odd. A number of factors, though, may have resulted in this focus on the past. Six months before the exhibition of Copley's painting, Montgomerie's current regiment, the Western Fencibles, had suffered unfavourable publicity on account of a mutiny (Annual Register 1780, pp.230–31). Moreover, a commemoration of Montgomerie's involvement in an action from the Seven Years' War, a conflict which had ended in British mastery of North America, conspicuously avoided direct reference to Britain's wider military malaise in 1780, a period when the American colonies which had helped win that previous war were successfully revolting against the mother country.

Representing a past victory in a distant land also served to elevate a portrait by giving it something of the complexion of history painting. Similarly aggrandising was Montgomerie's pose, whose ultimate source may have been the *Apollo Belvedere* (a reference clearer in Copley's preparatory sketches for the painting [Houston 1995, p.114; ill. Prown 1966, vol.2, nos 390, 390a]). Through this allusion to a famed classical statue, Montgomerie – unlike his opponents and the troops he leads – visibly transcends the historical moment depicted (Tobin 1999, pp.205, 222). From an elevated prospect he makes a gesture with his left hand which seems at once to direct his troops' onslaught and to point to the successful enactment of his commands.

The image was not without ironies. It celebrated the Highlanders' military vigour, but this had ceased to be suspect only during the Seven Years' War, when it was directed against the King's enemies, rather than against the monarch, as it had

been during the Jacobite rebellion. The rebellious Cherokees proved loyal to the British crown in the American War of Independence. The artist himself was American-born, but had consummated his career in the imperial capital; here he painted an image for Montgomerie which suggested oblique warnings to Americans of the costs of rebellion and to Britons of their decline from a previous generation's exemplary manliness. Copley's painting exposed some of the difficulties of alluding in art on public show to the divisive contemporary conflict in America (Hoock 2003, pp.150–64).

A version of the image signed and dated 1780 by Copley is in the collection of the Los Angeles County Museum of Art. The canvas displayed here has been described by one Copley scholar as an 'early copy' (Prown 1966, vol.2, p.276). SM

# Francis Cotes
LONDON, 1726 – RICHMOND, 1770

**126**
*The Hon. Lady Stanhope and the Countess of Effingham as Diana and Her Companion*

1765
Signed and dated at centre right: *F Cotes* [the 'FC' in monogram] *px'. 1765*; inscribed with the names of the sitters on the ground beneath the feet of each figure: *The Hon^le Lady Stanhope* and *Kath:. Count': of Effingham*
Oil on canvas, 240 × 152.5 cm
York Museums Trust (York Art Gallery), YORAG: 1414. Purchased with the aid of grants and donations from the National Heritage Memorial Fund, the Museums and Galleries Commission through the Victoria and Albert Museum, the National Art Collections Fund, the Pilgrim Trust, the J. Paul Getty Jr Charitable Trust, the Friends of York Art Gallery, York Civic Trust, York Georgian Society, Anthony Boynton Wood Esq. and John Miller Esq.

PROVENANCE: passed from Lady Stanhope to her sister Sarah, Countess of Mexborough; thence by descent to John, Eighth Earl of Mexborough; purchased by York City Art Gallery, 1987
EXHIBITED: *The Picture of the Month: Treasures from Yorkshire Houses*, Leeds City Art Gallery, 1951, no.45; *Pictures from Yorkshire Houses*, Temple Newsam House, Leeds, 1958, no.9; *The Portrait in British Art*, National Portrait Gallery, London, 1991, no.33
LITERATURE: see London 1991B, p.102

This double portrait shows Lady Stanhope in the guise of the classical goddess Diana, the huntress, who is identifiable by the crescent moon over her brow. She holds a spear in one hand and gestures with the other towards a distant stag; her companion, Lady Effingham, posed as one of Diana's nymphs, prepares to unleash a pair of hounds in pursuit.

The artist's signature and the date 1765 can be seen between Lady Effingham's left elbow and the frame. This period was one of success for Francis Cotes. Indeed, this work is 'arguably his master-piece', and only his early death at the age of forty-four 'prevented his becoming a serious rival to his more famous contemporaries' (Green 1988, p.106).

In undertaking such an ambitious portrait with an allegorical theme, Cotes's obvious rival was Sir Joshua Reynolds, the artist most associated with fashionable portraiture mythologising aristocratic female subjects (Pointon 1993, p.35). In this image, it has been suggested that Cotes 'clearly had in mind' Reynolds's *Lady Sarah Bunbury Sacrificing to the Graces* (1765), which also showed two women, a principal sitter with an acolyte (Green 1988, p.107). A feature common to both images is the use of 'timeless' classical garments (Postle 2004A, p.567). Those worn by Ladies Stanhope and Effingham are 'artistic invention and could never have existed in reality' (Green 1988, p.107; Ribeiro 1995, p.213). But although Reynolds sought 'to progress from the particular to the general' – the notion that the friendship between the women he depicted 'mirrors the universal ideal of perfect friendship' – Cotes conversely 'wanted to stay with particular appearances' (Johnson 1976, pp.30–31). His interest in emulating Reynolds's grand-manner portraiture was 'superficial, undertaken principally to appeal to current fashion rather than from any inner conviction' (Postle 2004A, p.567).

Reynolds also completed a portrait of Lady Stanhope in 1765, and that she sat for Cotes too is an indication of the alternative which he offered for fashionable society. Indeed, in 1764 the *Public Advertiser* had favoured him over Reynolds, declaring that 'he generally preserves a beautiful Correctness in his Pictures, which the latter Master too often neglects' (Postle 2004A, p.567). Cotes also charged less than Reynolds. In this image, Cotes arguably offered 'a seductive essay in the classicising manner being popularised by Reynolds', but without 'the vapidity and excessive theatricality which mar many of Reynolds's own attempts in this vein' (Green 1988, p.106).

Little is known about Lady Effingham (1746–1791), *née* Catherine Proctor. A daughter of Metcalfe Proctor of Thorpe, near Leeds, and his wife Martha Disney, she married Thomas Howard (1747–1791), 3rd Earl of Effingham, in 1765. Much more is known about the main sitter, Lady Stanhope (1737–1812), born Anne Hussey Delaval. She married Sir William Stanhope (1702–1772) in 1759. Her husband was thirty-five years her senior, and his two previous wives had predeceased him. The couple travelled to Italy together in 1761, and returned to London in 1763 where they split immediately (Ingamells 1997, p.888). Horace Walpole recorded Sir William's parting comment to his wife: 'Madam, I hope I shall never see your face again'. She replied, 'I shall take all care I can that you never shall' (Walpole 1937–82, vol.22, p.164). Sir William's brother, the famous Lord Chesterfield, negotiated their separation. He criticised the lack of reflection that had led his brother to marry at such an age, with his 'crazy, battered constitution', and 'deaf into the bargain', to 'a young girl, just turned of twenty, full of health, and consequently of desires' (Stanhope 1932, vol.6, p.2544).

Lady Stanhope's 'life of relative independence' arguably gave her depiction as a classical figure a degree of depth: while such images were 'on one level, conceits – elaborate forms of visual flattery', they also 'invite the viewer to contemplate contemporary womanhood liberated from social constraint, free to enjoy a pastoral life remote from household accounts, difficult servants and even more difficult husbands' (Pointon 1993, p.35).

A puzzling aspect of this work which remains unresolved is the ornate carved and gilded frame. It is adorned with martial motifs: at the sides are halberds, swords and plumed helmets; at the bottom are a pistol, sword and cannon barrel. At the top centre, surmounted on trumpets, is an armillary sphere, a symbol of the universe. The pattern of waves and seashells along the edges suggests a maritime theme. Five other frames were made according to this pattern and used for a variety of images, so the possible bearing of these emblems on any of the works they contained must remain largely hypothetical (Green 1988, pp.107–09). It has been argued that the frame connects the women in a way that is 'unlikely to have been accidental' to their families' histories of war heroism: the Effinghams' most illustrious ancestor had led the defeat of the Spanish Armada, and Lady Stanhope's brother was knighted after participating in a raid on St Malo in 1758. Thus the frame promoted family glory while subsuming the female subjects 'into a frame-work of natural and masculine signifiers. The one plays off the other: military distinction acquires lustre from association with the fleet-footed goddess of the hunt, and the women of the family are assimilated into a martial discourse. The arts of war and the arts of peace, the naval offensive and the stag hunt, are to be seen as complementary' (Pointon 1993, p.36). SM

# Johann Heinrich Dannecker

STUTTGART, 1758 – STUTTGART, 1841

## 75
*Self-portrait*

1796
Plaster, 74.5 × 50 × 30 cm
Staatsgalerie, Stuttgart, P.703

PROVENANCE: bequeathed to the Staatsgalerie, Stuttgart, by Dannecker's widow, 1868
EXHIBITED: Stuttgart, 1987, no.72

Johann Heinrich Dannecker, who lived into his eighties, was sculptor to the court of Stuttgart. He left only one self-portrait in sculpture, made when he was thirty-eight; it shows him in full possession of his faculties. Unlike other portrait artists working around 1800, such as Anton Graff, who made around seventy self-portraits, Dannecker

portrayed himself only once. He has no hesitation in producing his own portrait, and, when he had made it, was evidently so pleased with the bust that he deemed it unnecessary to make any subsequent alterations, large or small, or even another version.

The portrait or even another version shows a man filled with youthful energy and longing for fame and success. The artist's father was a coachman and groom in the service of the Duke of Württemberg. The son went first to the military academy in Stuttgart, and then began to climb up the social ladder. Although at eighteen he signed a contract binding him to a lifetime's service at court, this portrait bears witness to the fact that he was able to retain his personal liberty.

The nobility of the carriage of the head is what first strikes you about this bust; the young artist is draped in a manner that owes nothing to his period, and everything to aesthetic considerations and the calculated search for elegance. The hollow folds fall dramatically from one shoulder and rise to the other, while the vertical folds, narrower and more static, follow the slope of the left shoulder: calm and movement are related in dialectical opposition.

The broad pedestal, with its heavy cushion, becomes smaller as it disappears beneath the tunic; the distribution of the weight passes almost unnoticed – to such an extent that, despite its amazing breadth, the bust seems to have minimal material presence. Unlike Johann Gottfried Schadow in his bust of Friedrich Gilly (1801; Akademie der Künste, Berlin), Dannecker minimises the physical weight in favour of an airy and spiritual nobility. Intellectual and emotional expressions are concentrated, as they should be, in the facial features. His broad forehead quivers with sensitivity: the seat of the intellect lights up the whole face. He has wide open eyes, with large pupils, and carefully drawn, powerful eyebrows: the seat of sensory perception is of crucial importance, particularly for an artist. His mouth is slightly open, and he seems to be breathing very lightly: the artist's speech is silent in contrast to his vision. This all makes Dannecker appear to be not only a brilliant thinker, fully conscious of his power, but also a sensitive and watchful observer.

Dannecker's hair is cut short at the front and falls in abundant loose curls and locks over the nape of the neck at the back, producing a lively effect. It serves to remind us that the plait had had its day, as had neatly curled wigs and tidy hairstyles; and also that Joseph Anton Koch, another Stuttgart artist and former student with Dannecker, had cut off his own plait a few years earlier, a bravado gesture designed to make it abundantly clear that he refused to serve at court any longer. Koch, rebellious and rude, even sent his severed plait to Strasbourg, in 1791, to the studio where he had received his training in his home town, to make his refusal to serve more explicit and irreversible. As a sculptor, Dannecker would not have been able to risk such provocative behaviour; in exile, he would not have been able to find an upper middle class to supply enough commissions to enable him to make a living.

In the intellectual context of this portrait bust, another name comes to mind. Just as Alexander Trippel's portrait bust of Goethe (1790; Herzogin Anna Amalia Bibliothek, Weimar) would be unthinkable without a close link between the sculptor and the person represented, it would be difficult to image Dannecker's self-portrait without Friedrich Schiller. Schiller went to the same military academy as Dannecker and Koch, the Hohe Carlsschule. While there, Schiller showed himself to be as inventive as he was intractable: he also fled, after his play *Die Räuber* caused conflict between him and the prince.

We are familiar with Schiller's career (he became the German national poet), but we know less about his friendship with Dannecker. The latter made a portrait of Schiller that conveys the image of a perfectly independent character. The hair in both portraits is similar; and this similarity could be interpreted as proof of close friendship and admiration. Schiller's portrait, an icon of German classicism, was soon widely distributed and was reproduced long after Dannecker's death. By contrast, Dannecker's self-portrait, similar in inspiration, was in the possession of his widow for a long time, before entering the Staatsgalerie, Stuttgart, in 1868.

Dannecker created a self-portrait for private use that was an ideal vision; it represented a young court artist, at the height of his success, who nevertheless retained his intellectual independence, and was proud of having done all that was in his power, as a self-made man, to achieve the social status that he enjoyed. Yet he dared not present this portrait, which represented his innermost thoughts, to the public.

Dannecker's self-portrait was coated in a patina of polished bronze, as if to imitate the smooth softness of his young skin. In appearance, however, the material looks more like fired clay than bronze. Clay was popular for modelling at the end of the eighteenth century. Dannecker, at any rate, wished to give the impression of a smooth, vibrant skin, and of genuine 'warmth'. BM

# Jacques-Louis David
PARIS, 1748 – BRUSSELS, 1825

**28**
*Robertine Tourteau, Marquise d'Orvilliers*

1790
Oil on canvas, 131 × 98 cm

Signed at the lower left and dated: *L. David 1790*
Département des Peintures, Musée du Louvre, Paris, RF 2418.
Bequest of Comtesse Robert de Fitz-James, 1923

PROVENANCE: remained in the sitter's family, with her daughter the Comtesse de La Tour-du-Pin, then with her great-grandson; sold to Comtesse Robert de Fitz-James, 1914; bequeathed by her to the Louvre, Paris, 1923
EXHIBITED: Munich, 1964–65, no.71; Paris and Versailles, 1989–90, no.95 (A. Schnapper)
LITERATURE: Brookner 1980, pp.94–95; Schnapper 1980, p.122

Robertine Tourteau, Marquise d'Orvilliers (1772–1862) was the daughter of Jacques Rilliet, a rich Protestant banker from Geneva. In 1789 she married the son of the Collector General of Taxes (*Receveur général des finances*), Jean-Louis Tourteau d'Orvilliers. During the early years of the Revolution, David remained loyal to his clientele of bankers and financiers, and, in 1790, painted this portrait and the portrait of the sitter's elder sister, Anne-Marie-Louise Thélusson, Comtesse de Sorcy (Neue Pinakotek, Munich). Although the circumstances surrounding the commissioning of the latter portrait are well known (see A. Schnapper in Paris 1999), those surrounding the commissioning of the portrait of the Marquise d'Orvilliers remain unknown. The two paintings share the same format and the same date, but it is highly improbable that they would have been commissioned together. On the one hand, the date of this painting and the modest attitude of the Marquise d'Orvilliers suggest a wedding portrait. On the other hand, David may have devised them as artistic pendants, permitting him to try out a new, more austere and monumental style.

Although the artist here reinterprets the composition favoured by Vigée-Lebrun, with the model seated and cut off at ankle level, he avoids the manner in which his rival frequently placed the figure in a stage-set, as if caught unawares or surprised reading a book (cat. 27). David distances his women from any activity that might situate them socially – apart from the fact of having their portrait painted – and also any activity that might express (symbolically) their female condition (reading, sewing, writing, music). In both portraits the seated model stands out against a neutral background – in subtle shades – that is not intended to describe the space. David thus eschews the traditional link between woman and the idea of intimacy; like Madame Thélusson, the Marquise d'Orvilliers is seated on an armchair of no particular distinction, which could be a piece of studio furniture, in contrast to the comfortable sofas in Vigée-Lebrun's work. Painted in the early days of the Revolution, these portraits seem imbued with a spirit of republicanism that (in an illusory way) rejects the coded artifice of the aristocratic portraits of the *ancien régime*. From this time on the emphasis was on the individual.

David willingly assumes the artificiality of the pose, lending it classical severity and purity. In spite of their shared spirit and layout, the two portraits

are subtly different, and this emphasises their experimental character. Madame Thélusson is portrayed in a majestic way, sitting up straight, facing the spectator in the centre of the canvas. Her full white dress and shawl, which is wrapped round her, soften the geometrical precision of the composition, which is also given a warm glow by the soft red of the belt and the armchair. The Marquise d'Orvilliers wears the same red belt, with a matching red hair band. The sober way in which she is dressed, appropriate for the austere fashions of the late 1780s, is emphasised by her mainly black gown. Some time later, David returned to these formal experiments with black and white in the portrait of Madame Louise de Pastoret and her son (1791–92; The Art Institute, Chicago) and the contemporary portrait of Madame Louise Trudaine, the wife of Charles-Louis Trudaine (1791–92; Louvre, Paris). By thus endorsing the value of fashion, David rejects the neutrality of the pseudo-classical gown, made of draped fabric, thereby also rejecting convention in favour of the 'truth' of the portrait.

In comparison with her sister, the Marquise d'Orvilliers seems more relaxed: for the first time, David tries out a composition in which the seated model supports her elbow on the curved chair-back, possibly a distant memory of the antique *Agrippina* in the Vatican; he used this pose in more monumental, more imperious fashion in *Madame Raymond de Verninac* (1798–99; Louvre, Paris). The highly original idea of the entwined fingers demonstrates his search for naturalness. In addition, unlike the portrait of Madame Thélusson, the portrait of the Marquise d'Orvilliers is one of the few by David in which the sitter does not look towards the spectator. In *Madame Charles-Pierre Pécoul* (1784; Louvre, Paris) this artifice was justified by the sitter turning towards the image of her husband. In our painting, the evasive glance introduces a hint of melancholy, which, allied to the sitter's slight smile, lends a tenderness that is most unusual in David's work. As was normal at this period, the artist favours psychological analysis over social representation, the individual over his or her status. Finally, the indefinable quality and the apparent modesty of the young woman are reinforced by the subtle shifting of the figure from the centre downwards to the left. Far from filling the space with the assurance of her sister, the Marquise d'Orvilliers seems almost overwhelmed by it.

This austere view of the portrait, in which the modern notion of introspection makes its appearance, is served by a brush that rejects the Rubensesque seductions of a Vigée-Lebrun (particularly when she was painting on the more vibrant surface of wood). The range of colours is muted and restrained, the tints placed accurately, but also economically: the light, dry material suits this formal purity, with its breath of republicanism. SA

## 24
### The Emperor Napoleon in His Study at the Tuileries

1812
Oil on canvas, 203.9 × 125.1 cm
Signed and dated at the lower left: *LVD.ci DAVID OPUS/1812*
National Gallery of Art, Washington DC. Samuel H. Kress
Collection, 1961.9.15

PROVENANCE: commissioned in September 1811 by Alexander,
Marquis of Douglas (later the 10th Duke of Hamilton),
completed in March 1812 and forwarded to Hamilton Castle
in Scotland that November; the painting hung in the dining
room; by inheritance to his son, the 11th Duke of Hamilton;
by descent to his son, the 12th Duke of Hamilton, who sold it
at Christie's, London, 8 July 1882; in the collection of Archibald
Philip Primrose, 5th Earl of Rosebery; by descent to his son,
the 6th Earl of Rosebery; sold by him to Wildenstein and Co,
London, 1951; acquired by the Samuel H. Kress Foundation,
New York, 1954; gift to the National Gallery of Art,
Washington DC, 1961
EXHIBITED: David's studio, April–May 1812; London and
Manchester, 1948–49, no.23; Paris, 1955, no.17; Paris, 1969,
no.158 (N. Hubert); Paris, Detroit and New York, 1974–75,
no.36 (A. Schnapper); Edinburgh, 1985, no.49; Paris and
Versailles, 1989–90, no.206 (A.Schnapper); Los Angeles
and Williamstown, 2005, no.12 (P. Bordes)
LITERATURE: Eisler 1977, pp.352–58; Schnapper 1980,
pp.260–62; Brookner 1980, pp.168–69; Bordes and
Pougetoux, 1983, pp.26–27; Eitner 2000, pp.196–208;
Prat and Rosenberg 2002, vol.1, p.292

The intimate yet posed nature of *The Emperor Napoleon in His Study at the Tuileries* introduced an unusually modern dimension into the iconography of portraits of sovereigns. The painting probably represented the basis of portraits of French heads of state from the July Monarchy to the Fifth Republic. It was not commissioned by the Emperor, however, but by a powerful Scot, the Marquis of Douglas, the future 10th Duke of Hamilton (1767–1852), who was infatuated by French art and was a fervent admirer of Napoleon. Douglas wanted a portrait of the Emperor, because he was fascinated by the Great Man and because he wanted to resuscitate the old alliance between France and Scotland. In fact, he commissioned other 'royal portraits' to adorn his castle and, in the British tradition, to symbolise his pretensions to the throne (Haskell 1975). His letter was sent to David via the painter and dealer Ferréol Bonnemaison in August 1811. The artist, who had never been happy with his official portraits of the Emperor, all rejected, accepted immediately; he must also have felt flattered that his reputation had gone beyond the boundaries of the Empire. He delivered the canvas the following year.

The requirements of the Marquis were very precise. David should 'commit to the canvas the features of the Great Man and represent him during one of those events that have made his name immortal' (letter from David to Douglas, 20 September 1811). The term 'Great Man' qualifies Douglas's intentions: he did not want a ceremonial portrait, he wanted a history portrait in the tradition of *Napoleon Crossing the Alps*. In the painting delivered by David, the Emperor, wearing the blue uniform of a colonel in the Foot Grenadiers of the Imperial Guards, is standing in front of his desk, beside a ceremonial chair designed by David and located in the Grand Cabinet in the Tuileries, rather than in Napoleon's study. On the back wall, the hands of the clock stand at 4.13 am; the candles are almost burnt out, giving us to understand that the Emperor has been working all night. He is preparing to don the sword that is lying on the chair and to review his troops. It seems that David did not meet the expectations of the Marquis fully; Douglas was probably hoping for the depiction of an exceptional *action*, which would serve to identify the 'Great Man'.

In the painting, the artist discards the exceptional in favour of the habitual, the exterior in favour of a carefully staged intimacy: 'I have represented him pursuing the activity that is most habitual to him, work,' wrote David to the Scottish aristocrat on 8 May 1812. During the process in which the incarnation of the 'Great Man' takes over from his apotheosis, David emphasises (at first glance) the realism of the portrait. On the one hand, the accessories (desk, sword, uniform) are all painted from life, and, on the other, the artist has depicted Napoleon's features with painstaking accuracy, striving for a good likeness: the dishevelled hair, the rings under the eyes and the paunch, emphasised by the whiteness of the breeches. Alexandre Lenoir praised the portrait for being 'the best likeness that has ever been done of the Emperor'.

A preparatory drawing, now in the Musée des Beaux-Arts et d'Archéologie, Besançon, gives an idea of David's efforts at realism and the way he has handled the realistic effects. In his study, David lays great emphasis on the sitter's heavy figure and his dumpy appearance. In the painting for Douglas, he straightens and trims the Emperor, and gives him a gentler look. Compared with the drawing in Besançon, David has subtly enlarged his subject within the frame, enhancing the impact of the portrait by concentrating attention on the figure. All the elements in the picture relate directly to the figure; the realism of the image gives it a symbolic dimension, made explicit by the 'real' details without recourse to artifice – as the busts of the great men of antiquity do in Garnier's portrait. Napoleon is sufficient in himself.

However, the pose, artificial and contrived as it is, shatters the illusion of a 'realist' portrait. Although the folds of the carpet under the Emperor's feet introduce a note of dynamism and emphasise the energy of the character, David reinterprets, in a more natural way than François Gérard does in *Napoleon I in Coronation Robes*, the conventions of the ceremonial portrait: the head is given a slight three-quarter turn, the gaze is directed at the spectator, the left leg is lightly *contrapposto*, which in this case lightens the silhouette. The only gesture appropriate to an emperor is the right hand tucked into the waistcoat. David also discards the ostentatious official dress in favour of the more simple clothes that the Emperor preferred to wear, particularly on Sundays and when he was receiving visitors. The range of colours provides a subtle reminder of the national dimension of this image. The composition is structured around the great patch of white in the centre of the painting; around this are, on the left, the blue of the uniform, the wall-hanging and the carpet protecting the desk and, on the right, the red of the decorations, the cuffs, the cloak and the velvet stamped with imperial bees on the ceremonial chair.

David, who used accessories sparingly in his portraits, introduces a lot of them here, painted with great accuracy, for example, the candlestick. They require close attention because, surrounding the figure as they do, they bear the weight of the symbolic narration requested by the Marquis; they would have been omitted from a run-of-the-mill portrait. The allusion to the great men of antiquity is not provided by busts, but by a book: Plutarch's *Lives of the Noble Greeks and Romans* on the footing of the desk. The uniform, the sword placed on the chair, the map on which David has placed his signature all betray the man of action, the general-in-chief in the classical tradition, the hero in its revolutionary sense. The lion, which acts as the foot of the bureau, painted in a highly realistic way from the front, is like an echo of the figure. Should we interpret this as an allusion to the Emperor's sign of the zodiac (he was born on 15 August), or as a puzzle connected with Napoleon's own name? Whatever the intention behind the lion, it adds an element of determination to the figure of the 'Great Man'.

On the desk, the pen and papers inform us that Napoleon has spent the night drafting legislation. David has reproduced the iconography of which Bonaparte approved: the statesman peacemaker, a model introduced by Gros in 1802 in his portrait of Bonaparte First Consul (Musée National de la Légion d'honneur et des Ordres Chevalerie, Paris). Only the word 'Code' can be read on the roll of parchment. In his description of the painting, David identifies this detail as the Civil Code of the French, published in 1804 and renamed the Napoleonic Code in 1807. In fact, the absence of a qualifying adjective in the painting could be designed to draw attention to the whole legislative apparatus of the Empire: in addition to the Civil Code, there was the Code of Civil Procedure (1806), the Commercial Code (1807), the Code of Criminal Instruction (1808) and the Penal Code (1810). With this falsely realistic allusion, David was reiterating one aspect of imperial propaganda, by promoting the fiction of the Emperor's personal contribution in drawing up the various Codes. Although the Revolution extolled law as the expression of the common will, which produced an essentially allegorical iconography, from 1805 the Empire moved on to a radical personalisation of the figure of the legislator in which Napoleon identified himself with the common will. In 1805 Chaudet made a sculpture of Napoleon as legislator in the tradition of classical antiquity.

David's genius lay in the way he modernised this reference, moving it on from the classical tradition developed during the Enlightenment. In this painting, it is Napoleon's own hard work (while his people sleep) on which his legitimacy as legislator is based, and not on any divine or supernatural inspiration.

David started restoring the sovereign's image with this exceptional painting. Unencumbered by the traditional attributes of power or the ostentation connected with it, Napoleon is portrayed as a modern statesman; the sources of his greatness and the justification of his power are to be found within him. In some ways, David rejects transcendence in favour of immanence; the man is placed at the heart of the representation and the expressive value proper to a portrait is reaffirmed. David proves that the realism inherent in the genre can convey the idea it embodies, and that the tension between truth and decorum, between the myth and its incarnation, at work in the portrait of a ruler, can be resolved without forgoing appearances. In 1812, however, *The Emperor Napoleon in His Study at the Tuileries* had not yet achieved the status of an official image.

François Gérard, who was naturally pragmatic and very sensitive to current trends, was stimulated into action by David's composition. At the request of Louis XVIII, he painted a large portrait of the King for Madame du Cayla's *château* at Saint-Ouen (Château d'Haroué; replica at Versailles). Seated because of his infirmity, Louis XVIII is portrayed writing the Charter of 1814 at a small pine desk that accompanied him on his British exile. The painting was presented at the Salon of 1824 and enjoyed considerable success; it was widely known through an engraving. The image of the modern statesman invented by David was beginning to replace the portrait of the ruler dressed in coronation robes, but again this was for a 'private' commission. The public would have to wait until the replica, painted in 1812 by David (Louvre, Paris, on permanent loan) and exhibited, after 1860, in the Salon des Maréchaux in the Tuileries, would be used as a model for the portrait of *Napoleon III* by Hippolyte Flandrin; only then did this type of representation win permanent acceptance. SA

## 142
### General Etienne-Maurice Gérard, Marshal of France

1816
Oil on canvas, 197.2 × 136.2 cm
Signed and dated on the base of the column:
*L. David 1816 / BRUX.*
Inscription on the envelope: *A son Excellence / L[e] Gé[néral] Gérard / Com[mandant en] Chef*
Lent by The Metropolitan Museum of Art, New York. Purchase, Rogers and Fletcher Funds, and Mary Wetmore Shively Bequest, in memory of her husband, Henry L. Shively MD, 1965 (65.14.5)

PROVENANCE: collection of General Gérard in Brussels and, from 1817, in the Château de Villers Saint-Paul; remained in the family until 1959; sold to the firm of Wildenstein and Co. in New York, 1959; acquired by The Metropolitan Museum of Art, New York, 1965

EXHIBITED: London, 1972, no.70; Los Angeles and Williamstown, 2005, no.50 (P. Bordes)
LITERATURE: Schnapper 1980, pp.282–84; Brookner 1980, p.178; Schnapper in Paris 1989E; Prat and Rosenberg 2002, vol.2, p.1161

David cast his vote in favour of the death of Louis XVI and was sentenced to exile when the Bourbons returned permanently to the throne in 1815. After considering Italy, he took refuge in Brussels, where he spent the rest of his life. In the Belgian capital he continued to devote himself to portraits, especially in the first year, in order to pay the expenses of moving. The portrait of General Gérard is probably one of the first paintings he did in Brussels, in the spring of 1816. Although we have no detailed information about the conditions of the commission, the model is well known.

Etienne-Maurice Gérard (1773–1852), one of Napoleon's leading generals, was made a baron in 1809 and a count in 1813. He therefore belonged to the new aristocracy founded under the Empire on the battlefields. Having distinguished himself in the Russian campaign, he acknowledged Napoleon's abdication in 1814, but rallied to him immediately on his return from Elba in 1815, and participated in the Belgian campaign. During the second Restoration he was also forced into exile in Brussels. David was probably chosen to paint his portrait out of a sense of solidarity that bound together former loyal supporters of the Empire. Most of the portraits that the master painted at the end of his life are either of members of the Bonaparte family, for example Joseph Bonaparte's daughters Zénaïde and Charlotte (1821; The J. Paul Getty Museum, Los Angeles), or of people close to the Emperor, for example Comte Henri Amédée de Turenne (1816; portrait bust in the Sterling and Francine Clark Institute, Williamstown; seated portrait in the Ny Carlsberg Glyptotek in Copenhagen).

In his portrait of General Gérard, David portrayed his subject in a different way from most of his previous paintings – in full-length pose – as he had previously done in his portrait of *The Emperor Napoleon in His Study at the Tuileries* (cat.24), completed in 1812. It is possible that the sitter was responsible for this choice of pose, as he may have wished to own an image of himself in a style that was normally used to depict the Empire's aristocracy. The painting, in which the general appears in ceremonial dress covered in decorations, also bears witness to the exile's nostalgic attachment to a world that has gone for ever. Apart from his failed official portraits of the Emperor, David never painted such images; it was his pupil François Gérard who excelled in this sphere. In 1816 he proclaimed his allegiance to Louis XVIII in his *Entry of Henri IV into Paris* (Musée National du Château, Versailles). It is possible that, forced to express himself in this genre, David sought to rival Gérard, who, in fact, had popularised a formula inspired by Van Dyck amongst the aristocracy of the Empire.

In Brussels, David could enjoy direct contact with the work of the Flemish masters of the Golden Age, thus returning to the roots of the genre; his understanding of their forms and the vigour of his composition are unrivalled. In his portrait of *General Gérard* he exploits all the conventions of the ceremonial portrait: the pose, with its slight *contrapposto*, is a variation on the pose of *The Emperor Napoleon in His Study at the Tuileries*. A wide red curtain occupies the left-hand side of the composition, falling over a column; on the right, beyond the balustrade, there is a blue-tinted landscape of Italian inspiration, similar to the one painted by David in *Cupid and Psyche* (1817; Cleveland Museum of Art).

The artist has produced a composition that reconciles opposing elements. The portrait's conventional aspects contrast with a feeling of realism in the sitter's features that is typical of the late David. As usual, the painter reproduces the artificiality of the pose, but for the first time here he stages it in a particularly theatrical fashion. The skilfully heightened painting of the background contrasts with the more austere, detailed rendering of the costume and the face: the figure seems to be standing in front of a stage-set. The relatively spacious composition and the absence of the usual accessories (table, armchair etc) increase this impression. In comparison with the refined elegance of Gérard's official portraits, David reproduces the grandiloquent opulence of a neo-baroque ceremonial portrait.

In search of a new style, David allows himself to be seduced by colour, and this persists throughout much of his Brussels work (see the portraits of the *Comte de Turenne* and the *Comtesse Vilain XIII and Her Daughter*; National Gallery, London). The vibrant red of the vast curtain is echoed by the red ribbon of the Légion d'honneur, the sword and the seal on the letter; just as vibrant is the marble floor with its tiles in yellow, green and brown. This well-controlled excess of colour betrays the experimental nature of the work; is there not perhaps a note of irony, or of psychological insight, in the artist's relationship to his sitter, the fallen hero who is nevertheless still called 'Excellency' and 'Commander-in-Chief' on the letter in his hand? We can interpret the tension between convention and naturalism as a search, similar to the one carried out by David in his history painting, for a new equilibrium between realism and the ideal. SA

## 143
### Juliette de Villeneuve

1824
Oil on canvas, 197 × 123 cm
Signed and dated on the base of the chair, lower right:
*L.DAVID. BRUX. / 1824*
Département des Peintures, Musée du Louvre, Paris, RF 1997-5. Gift of the Amis du Louvre, 1997, on the occasion of their centenary and in memory of Président F. Puaux, with a contribution from the Fonds du Patrimoine and with the

participation of a group of the Amis du Louvre and the Société LVMH

PROVENANCE: in the collection of Honorine Clary, the sitter's mother; remained in the sitter's family until 1997; presented to the Louvre by the Amis du Louvre, 1997
EXHIBITED: Paris, 1997C, pp.179–181; Los Angeles and Williamstown, 2005 (P. Bordes)
LITERATURE: Schnapper 1980, p.288; Schnapper in Paris 1989E, pp.631–32; Cuzin 1997; Cuzin and Allard 2002, p.141 (J.-P. Cuzin)

We know when this imposing portrait was painted thanks to a letter dated 4 June 1824, written by David to Michel Stapleaux, a young painter who worked with him in Brussels. The artist mentions a 'sketch for the portrait of Mlle de Villeneuve'. On 26 October 1824 the artist wrote a letter to the sitter's mother to confirm the receipt of 6,000 francs in payment for the portrait. *Juliette de Villeneuve* is therefore David's last original painting; before his death in December 1825 he only otherwise painted a replica of his *Anger of Achilles* (1825; Private collection) for the printer and typographer Firmin Didot.

The sitter for this portrait belonged to the group of Napoleonic exiles in Brussels – a characteristic in fact of all David's last clients. Juliette de Villeneuve (1802–1840) was the daughter of M. Blait de Villeneuve and Honorine Clary, sister of Julie Clary, wife of Joseph Bonaparte and former Queen of Spain, and of Désirée Clary, wife of Marshal Bernadotte and Queen of Sweden and Norway. After Waterloo, Julie, whose husband had taken up residence in the United States, chose to live in exile in Brussels, where she presided over a busy salon. David was a regular visitor.

Far from allowing his genius to wither away in the repetition of well-tried formulae during his exile in Brussels, David decided to experiment and to search for a balance between the idealisation appropriate for a society portrait and the fundamental realism of his work. The outcome, after a few years, was a versatility of style that is well represented by this austere image, far removed from the neo-baroque extravagance of his portrait of *General Etienne-Maurice Gérard* (cat.142), painted only eight years earlier. As he approached death, the artist returned to the full-length portrait, which seemed to preoccupy him during his later years. Hitherto he had very seldom succumbed to the temptation to animate any portrait with an activity in order to justify the pose, as in the portrait of *Alexandre Lenoir*, who was depicted writing (1817; Louvre, Paris). With its psychological insight, the portrait was sufficient in itself. In some respects David, confident of his own genius, held the genre in greater esteem than his colleagues, who felt the need to dramatise each representation in order to raise it above its status.

The reverse is true here: Juliette de Villeneuve is painted in the act of tuning a superb harp. By the end of the eighteenth century, the association of women with the harp had become a commonplace. It allowed the artist to depict a standing pose naturally and emphasised the role played by music in the education of a woman of superior standing, as in Rose Ducreux's *Self-portrait with Harp* (c.1790; Metropolitan Museum of Art, New York) or in Jean Antoine Theodore Giroust's *Mademoiselle d'Orléans Taking a Harp Lesson* (1791). As P. Bordes notes (Los Angeles 2005), the harp was the modern version of the lyre of classical antiquity, and was highly esteemed as an instrument by Juliette's aunt. By reverting to this model from the past, David was seeking to evoke his sitter as exactly as possible. Similarly, the reference to Van Dyck, exaggerated here for effect, conveyed the lost dignity of the former general of the Empire. The modernity of David's Brussels period probably lies in his 'pre-historicist' attitude; he gives a contemporary twist to conventions that were thought to have died out.

Although after the first decade of the nineteenth century he began to take more freedom with the brush and to use a softer, more coalescent touch, the portrait of *Juliette de Villeneuve* shows development in the other direction, giving full rein to description. With the exception of *Emperor Napoleon in His Study at the Tuileries* (cat.24) – and, of course, his early portraits, for example, *Antoine-Laurent Lavoisier and His Wife* (1788; Metropolitan Museum of Art, New York) – David had always been sparing with accessories. In the portrait of *Juliette de Villeneuve*, however, he accumulates them, taking evident pleasure in their description and adding the shawl on the armchair, the hat and the music stand, the harp and the magnificent stole, in a manner recalling Ingres. Where Ingres mingled the accessories playfully, David places them authoritatively in a composition that is rigorously organised around the large triangle formed by Juliette's dark silhouette and the harp, and in which one plane follows the next very abruptly. The austere, authoritative composition is toned down by a bold colour scheme in which the dark red of the carpet and the deep black of the dress are set off by the various shades of white, the yellow of the hat, and the blue and gold of the stole. Having reached this threshold of formal perfection, and pushed the neoclassical ideal to its limits by applying it to everyday objects, David enlivens his painting by rendering his sitter's plain face with uncompromising realism. SA

# Studio of Jacques-Louis David

## 37
### *The Death of Marat*

c.1794
Oil on canvas, 162 × 130 cm

Inscription on the block in the foreground:
*N'AYANT PU ME CORROMPRE / ILS M'ONT ASSASSINE*
Inscription on the note held by Marat:
*Du 13 juillet 1793 / Marie anne charlotte / Corday au citoyen / marat. / . il suffit que je sois / bien malheureuse / pour avoir droit / à votre bienveillance*
Inscription on the note on the block:
*vous donnerez cet / assignat à cette / mère de 5 enfants / et dont le mari / est mort pour la / défense de la patrie*
Département des Peintures, Musée du Louvre, Paris, RF 1945-2. Bequest of Baron Jeanin, a descendant of the artist, 1945

PROVENANCE: replica executed in David's studio, to be transferred to tapestry, of the painting presented by him to the Convention on 14 November 1793, now in the Musées Royaux des Beaux-Arts, Brussels; it was in the painter's studio when he died, with the original and another replica, now at Versailles; after the second sale of David's effects, 1 March 1835, when the original had been bought by Baroness Meunier and Eugène David, the painting in the Louvre was given to Baroness Jeanin and the Versailles painting similarly given to J. David; bequeathed by Baron Jeanin, a descendant of David, to the Louvre, 1945
EXHIBITED (the replica): Paris, 1989E, no.807 (J. Benoît); Tokyo and Kyoto, 1997, no.63 (S. Allard); Yokohama and Kyoto, 2005, no.16 (S. Allard)
LITERATURE (the replica): David 1867, pp.12, 14–17,19; Schnapper in Paris 1989E, p.282; Malvano 1989–90, p.370

On 14 November 1793, David presented to the Convention a painting depicting *The Death of Marat* (Musées Royaux des Beaux-Arts, Brussels). The painting was intended as a pendant to another one he had presented a few months earlier: *Le Pelletier de Saint-Fargeau on His Deathbed* (whereabouts unknown). The two pictures belong in the highly charged political context of the weeks following the execution of Louis XVI on 21 January 1793. Aware of the trauma caused by the death of the King, and worried that he might appear as a martyr, the Convention redoubled its efforts to establish a civic religion, capable of federating the nation while emphasising the dangers of counter-Revolution. The assassination by a fanatic of Michel Le Pelletier de Saint-Fargeau, a young nobleman who voted in favour of the King's death, only three days after Louis XVI died on the scaffold, was skilfully used as propaganda to revive the cult of martyrs. *Le Pelletier de Saint-Fargeau on His Deathbed* was the first stone laid in this propaganda campaign.

The assassination of Marat by Charlotte Corday, a Girondist sympathiser, on 13 July, increased the public's fear of enemies of the Revolution. At the time of his death, Jean-Paul Marat (1743–1793) enjoyed a level of fame that Le Pelletier de Saint-Fargeau did not. He was an aggressive publicist who, in his newspaper *L'Ami du peuple*, called for the murder of all lukewarm patriots and counter-revolutionaries. Having been accused of treason by the Girondists, he was acquitted by the Revolutionary Tribunal in April, following a trial that turned him into a kind of hero; he took an active part in plotting the downfall of the Girondists and obtained an order banning them in 1793.

David was at the time president of the Jacobin cell to which Marat belonged and was given the task of organising a highly dramatic funeral at night for him. At the funeral, the objects accompanying the journalist in his last moments were paraded like the instruments of the Passion: the bath in which he was soothing his sore skin, his blood-soaked shirt and the knife with which the young woman had pierced his side. Fully aware of the political power of images, and also probably motivated by personal ambition, David decided to present an idealised vision of this controversial figure – just as the authorities were deliberating over whether his remains deserved to be deposited in the Panthéon.

Marat played the most important role of all the revolutionary heroes (especially in Year II of the French Republican Calendar) as the process of substituting images of martyrs of the Revolution for images of saints progressed. As Lise Andries has pointed out, Marat's cult, developed largely through prints, was mainly based on portraits rather than on representations of his death. David's painting is part of this trend, but transcends it. Marat, with a cloth wound round his head, is seated in his bath; in his right hand he holds a quill pen, a symbol of his work as a journalist and the cause of his death; in his left hand is the letter that gained Charlotte Corday her audience. A knife with mother-of-pearl handle, the instrument of his death, lies on the ground. As in David's contemporary (unfinished) portraits of Madame Trudaine, Madame de Pastoret and Monsieur Joubert, the figure stands out against a plain background, scumbled and predominantly empty.

In the context of *The Death of Marat*, however, the emptiness of the composition has important connotations: David removes all physical accessories that could turn the picture into the representation of a sensational news item. Paradoxically, the historical dimension of the picture stems from the complete absence of narrative elements, although the symbolic connotations of the accessories make up for this. Whereas in *Le Pelletier de Saint-Fargeau on His Deathbed*, David (in more classical vein) exploits the *topos* of the deathbed, much in vogue in the 1780s, in *The Death of Marat* he takes his inspiration from Caravaggio's *Deposition from the Cross* (*c.*1600–04; Pinacoteca, Vatican), transforming Marat into a Christ-like figure.

With his apparent realism, David confuses the levels at which the painting can be read. In *Le Pelletier de Saint-Fargeau on His Deathbed*, the allegorical character of the painting is manifest: the sword hanging in abstract fashion above the corpse translates as the Sword of Damocles, threatening the Revolution. There is nothing like that in *The Death of Marat*. The reconstruction, featuring the bath, the knife and the letters, looks plausible. Nevertheless, doubts are soon raised: Marat, without his shirt, is depicted in heroic nudity. All trace of violence has gone – indeed, he seems to be slightly smiling. David reinterprets the codes of religious representation to give his painting metaphysical stature. In fact, he was adept at this. At the centre of *The Death of Socrates* (1787;

Metropolitan Museum of Art, New York), the philosopher's hand stretching out to take the cup of poison is a symbolic reiteration of the celebration of the Eucharist. In *Marat*, as Jorg Traeger has shown, the bath becomes a kind of altar and the blood flowing from the journalist's wound is an allusion to this. The cloth wound round his head evokes the holy shroud. The letter placed on the block underscores Marat's exemplary generosity, ready to give his last *assignat* to support the widow and her orphans. At the same time, the allusion to a father dead in defence of his country evokes the man himself.

The letter from Charlotte Corday has various levels of meaning: on one level it expresses the goodwill of the journalist who was willing to receive her; on another it very clearly addresses the spectator: the murderess draws attention to the benevolence of the sacrificial victim. The association of Marat with Christ was certainly not made after the event: it was deliberately planned at the outset to provide propaganda. In order to sway public opinion, an eminently modern concept, the Revolution took the most universal language, the language of religion, and stood it on its head. When Marat's ashes were transferred to the Panthéon on 21 September 1794, the following litanies could be heard: 'Marat, friend of the people, Marat, consoler of the afflicted, Marat, father of the unfortunate, have pity on us!' (Traeger).

Thanks to this metaphysical dimension, therefore, *The Death of Marat* transcends the canons of historical representation, as it becomes more than a straightforward portrait. In the same way that he rewrites history, David also proceeds to re-create the facial features of the 'Friend of the People', effacing all trace of his legendary ugliness, although not completely altering his looks by idealising them. His almond-shaped eyes and high cheekbones can be found in the wax mask taken by the future Madame Tussaud on the day after the assassination. In addition, as in the pen-and-ink drawing probably done the day after the funeral (Musée National du Château, Versailles), David makes much of the cadaver's swollen eyelids. This detail emphasises the tension between the apparently realistic nature of the representation, closer to portraiture, and the idealised composition created by David, the history painter.

On 17 November the Convention gave orders for an engraving to be made of the painting, in order to ensure its wide distribution, particularly to political cells and provincial assemblies. Shortly afterwards, Jacques-Louis Copia engraved a drawing of Marat's face, which became popular in its own right; these engravings took over from the pictures of saints that had previously loomed so large as objects of devotion. In May 1794 the Assembly, acting on a report, decreed that the two paintings should be turned into tapestries by the Gobelins factory. The idea was not only to ensure

wider circulation of the images to the public, but also to provide work for the Gobelins factory, which had been dramatically affected by the loss of royal commissions.

David was asked to make two copies for this purpose. The painting exhibited here remained in David's studio until his death, then in his family; the second is in Versailles. It is of very high quality, and it was certainly painted under the direction of David, possibly by his pupil G. G. Serangeli, as Jules David suggests. In comparison with the original, the painting in the Louvre (which is identical in every other respect) has one important modification: the inscription on the block. In the Brussels painting, David made do with '*A Marat / David / l'an deux*'. In this replica, the inscription in the style of an ex-voto in the original is replaced by '*N'ayant pu me corrompre, ils m'ont assassiné*' (unable to corrupt me, they assassinated me), inspired by Tacitus. The inscription in the Brussels painting is commemorative, the one in the painting in the Louvre clearly didactic, as befits an image that is to be used for propaganda. SA

# Pierre-Jean David d'Angers

ANGERS, 1788 – PARIS, 1856

## 153
*Niccolò Paganini*

1830–33
Bronze, 61 × 40 × 32 cm
Inscription, front: *Nicolo Paganini*; left: *P. J. David / D'Angers / 1830*; right: *FONDU PAR / HONORE GONON / ET SES DEUX FILS / 1833*
Musées d'Angers, MBA, 836.3

PROVENANCE: gift of the artist, 1836
EXHIBITED: Paris, Salon of 1834, no. 2006; London, 1932, no. 412; Paris, 1986, no. 195; Angers, 1994–95, no. 25
LITERATURE: Jouin 1878, vol. 1, p. 258; vol. 2, p. 477; Benoist 1928, new edition, 1994, pp. 182–86, fig. 113; Chesneau and Metzger 1934, no. 267; Holderbaum 1980, pp. 40–41, fig. 25; Huchard 1984, p. 84, repr.; Caso 1988, p. 186, fig. 124; Baridon and Guédron 1999, p. 149, pl. X, fig. 30; Maaz 2004, pp. 66–67, fig. 22

David d'Angers met Niccolò Paganini (1782–1840) when he was in Paris during a triumphant tour of Europe. Paganini, a violin virtuoso, made remarkable use of his skill in his own compositions, revealing the full potential of the instrument. He gave his first concert at the Paris Opéra on 9 March 1831. With his almost supernatural ability, he was the archetype of the romantic musician, with a life shrouded in mystery – it was rumoured that he had made a Mephistophelean pact with the devil. Liszt, Chopin, Berlioz and Schumann all fell under his spell. 'His long hair, his gaze, his pallor, his blue frock coat with its fur collar and little high-heeled shoes were all very strange. He was like Crespel, Hoffmann's character … His awkward air when he came in with his violin under his arm, his eagle eye, pale face – it is all perfectly extraordinary' (Fontaney 1832, quoted in Paris 2002B, p.242).

It is not surprising that such a character should fascinate David, nor that the sculptor should desire to make his portrait. In a review of the Salon of 1831, Gustave Planche announced that a marble bust was shortly to be made of Paganini (Holderbaum 1980, p.41), similar to the ones made recently of Goethe and Chateaubriand. David's meeting with the admirable bronze caster Honoré Gonon, a specialist in the lost-wax technique of casting and principal protagonist in the rekindling of interest in this age-old technique, must have convinced the sculptor to abandon marble, and it is possible that he altered his first model. The double signature on the bust indicates the vital role played by Gonon in its realisation. Bronze was the romantic sculptors' material *par excellence*, and Gonon's dexterity made it a particularly sensitive means of expression in portraiture.

The bust was given lukewarm reviews when it was exhibited at the Salon of 1834, with Planche leading the way: 'The head of Paganini, like that of Goethe, is neither simple nor harmonious; there is something febrile and frenzied in the exaltation of this face, greatly weakened by exaggeration … Anyone who has seen Paganini will not be astonished when they see the bust … but it would have been better to simplify the sitter's peculiarities during the design phase. Although I do not deny any of the features of the face, nor do I dismiss any of the emphasis on the powerful head, it would have been a good idea to make the whole conform to the harmonious rules of statuary … its qualities would have been even more striking if the bust, reduced in scale, had been more simply fashioned' (quoted in Barbillon 2004, p.238).

In fact, David had an ambition to do much more than merely portraying facial features in a conventional way. He was interested in the theories of Johann Kaspar Lavater, whom he mentions in his notebooks, and in particular, from the mid-1820s, in the work of Franz Joseph Gall; he became a member of the society of phrenology in 1832. 'Beyond physiognomy and facial expression, phrenology deals with the cranium, in as far as it moulds the brain, to borrow Gall's expression … [His] anatomical work allowed him to reveal the existence of different parts of the brain. From this time on, protuberances on the surface of the cranium were linked with the development of certain faculties' (Baridon and Guédron 1999, pp.141–42).

As phrenology argued that qualities evident in facial features could be discerned on the cranium of the individual, the forehead became of utmost importance. In making a portrait of the inner Paganini (the only feature of interest to the sculptor), the forehead – 'centre of his sublime genius' (Bruel 1958, vol.1, p.198) – is crucial. This lumpy, wrinkled brow, a monstrous excrescence

framed by bushy tufts of hair, devours half of the face but is really the heart of the face. The blank, un-incised eyes (the musician's gaze is focused inwards) and the closed mouth echo the intensity of the oversized forehead, whose weight makes the whole head tilt. 'It appears that the soul exercises a tyrannical power over this feeble body – he never laughs, he has too much genius … When I told him that I wanted to ask him to move his head forward and to the side, like a man playing a violin (in the bust), he said to me: "Yes, because I draw upon my inner self for my outer self"' (Bruel 1958, vol.1, pp.198–99). The whole portrait creates an imposing impression, which is emphasised by its huge scale: the dimensions are larger than life-size, and the exaggerated style was the focus of most of the reviews in 1834. 'The colossal proportions raise the spirits and make the hero look bigger' (Bruel 1958, vol.1, p.87): David d'Anger's *Paganini* personifies genius.

There is one striking feature in the sculptor's composition: he did not use a regular cut or pedestal. Whereas the sublime *Goethe* in the Weimar library is presented on a base that supports a regular, circular cut section (marble, 1831; Maaz 2004, fig.10), and while *Lamartine* is mounted on a pedestal (marble, 1830; Musée du Louvre 1998, vol.1, p.204, repr.), *Paganini* finishes at the lower edge in asymmetrical fashion, without embellishment, and is intended simply to be placed on a surface. 'Cut off like a workshop study, [the bust reveals] the work as if it were a fragment from a portrait … like a striking evocation of artistic creation at the time and place it was accomplished' (Caso 1988, p.186). GS

# Eugène Delacroix

SAINT-MAURICE, 1798 – PARIS, 1863

## 148
*Louis-Auguste Schwiter*

1826–30
Oil on canvas, 217.8 × 143.5 cm
Signed lower left: *Eug. Delacroix*
The National Gallery, London. Bought, 1918

PROVENANCE: Schwiter collection; his sale in Paris, 28 March 1890, lot 4; collection of Edgar Degas; his sale, 26 March 1918, lot 24; bought by the National Gallery, London
EXHIBITED: Paris, 1963, no.75 (catalogue entry by M. Sérullaz); New York, 1997–98; London, 2002A, pp.125–27 (catalogue entry by A. Hollander); London, Minneapolis and New York, 2003–04, no.52 (catalogue entry by P. Noon)
LITERATURE: Robaut 1885, no.190; Johnson 1981, no.82; Maltese 1965, pp.33, 124, 148; Jobert 1998, p.98; Athanassoglou-Kallmyer 2005

A few days after the National Gallery in London acquired this portrait at the sale of the collection of Edgar Degas in March 1918, a journalist on *Le Temps* voiced indignation that the museums of France

should have been unable to raise the funds to ensure that the painting went to the Louvre. Indeed, France had just lost the largest and most handsome of Delacroix's portraits. However, the fact that the work's new home was to be London could be justified in some respects, because the painting demonstrates so strongly the British influence which, thanks to the calming of international relations in the 1820s, had come to pervade French art. In general, Delacroix's inspiration was more imaginative than imitative and he was not much drawn to portraiture. It is no accident therefore that most of his portraits, at least his best ones, date from the 1820s and early 1830s, a period when he felt the British influence most. This influence was especially strong in two genres that were generally regarded as inferior: landscape via Constable, who exhibited *The Hay Wain* and the *View of the Stour* at the Salon of 1824; and the portrait via the example of Thomas Lawrence, revered by the younger generation who came to Paris to paint great statesmen, the Duchesse de Berry or the Duc de Richelieu. In 1825, young French people flocked to London to see the paintings that Lawrence was showing that year: *Lord Lambton* (Lambton Estate), *The Duke of Wellington* and *Lady Peel* (Frick Collection, New York). Delacroix was among them; he met Lawrence in his studio and was able to admire his portrait of *Pope Pius VII* (cat.14), publishing an article on the subject in *La Revue de Paris* in June 1829. The article, which begins with a defence of portraiture as a genre, is proof of the association of the British influence with the re-evaluation of the portrait.

Probably begun in 1826, a few months after his return from London, the present portrait admirably expresses the personal (and very French) manner in which Delacroix reinterpreted the aristocratic English portrait. The origin of the commission is not known. Delacroix and Louis-Auguste Schwiter (1805–1889), son of an Empire marshal who was created baron in 1808, met at the house of Jean-Baptiste Pierret, a close friend of Delacroix, and remained closely connected all their lives. Schwiter, who dressed as an English dandy, lived in luxury in Paris, collecting works of art and making frequent visits to London where he kept a mistress, a certain Sophia, who is mentioned by Delacroix in his correspondence. In addition to paying tribute to Lawrence, the choice of a portrait 'in the English style' was supposed to represent the character of the sitter. Delacroix depicts him in a tailcoat, standing on a terrace with a landscape and the setting sun in the background. Ever since his first attempts at portrait painting, the artist had been at pains to fuse the figure with the landscape, as is demonstrated in his early and informal portrait of his elder brother, *General Charles Delacroix at Louroux* (1822; Private collection, France). However, in contrast to the relaxed pose of his brother, Delacroix here favours a majestic full-length and life-size portrait (the only one he ever painted), clearly reminiscent of English aristocratic portraits, those produced by Reynolds in particular. The influence of Lawrence is especially obvious in the importance given to the landscape and to the spirited manner in which it is painted. Dense clumps of trees loom above a large lawn, suggestive of an English park; this opens out onto blue-tinged mountains in the background with the setting sun behind them. Moreau notes that 'the landscape background was partly painted by M. Paul Huet'. Huet, connected (as was Delacroix) with the Fielding brothers, played a crucial role in the diffusion of British art in France. The background to the portrait of Schwiter might remind us of his technique, with dusky colours that dissolve shapes into the atmosphere and a lazy way of drawing trees. Delacroix also appreciated these effects, however, although it is impossible to trace the intervention of a second pair of hands. Huet may have helped his friend in the placing of a few details.

By fusing his sitter and his environment quite naturally, Lawrence managed to renew the formula of the aristocratic portrait and to free it from the rigidity of too stuffy a pose. A comparison of Lawrence's portrait of David Lyon (cat.147) with Delacroix's portrait of Schwiter reveals the manner in which Delacroix reinterpreted his source: he rejects the faked relaxation of Lawrence's sitter in favour of a formality that seems to return to the roots of the genre. The rigid frontality of Schwiter's pose betrays an assumed character brought in to reinforce the *topos* of the terrace with the balustrade; the layout has more of Gainsborough to it than of the Lawrence of the 1820s. Delacroix also rejects the stylised poses inspired by classical statuary; he avoids *contrapposto* and over-expressive gesture, favouring a slightly self-conscious attitude, full of characteristically French grace, a mixture of the natural and the artificial, which is particularly sought after in portraits of women. Like the Mannerists, he toys with the expressive distortion of a very slender body with arms that are too long: he concentrates on expressing the idea of refined and aristocratic elegance rather than his friend's psychological makeup. In addition, the sitter's attire is smart beyond affectation: with his long, black, waisted coat, long trousers (recently invented by Beau Brummel), carefully tied white cravat, leather gloves and patent leather pumps, Schwiter looks dressed for a ball rather than a day in the country. Like Ingres, but in a different spirit, Delacroix proved that fashion, far from diminishing the significance of a portrait because of its ephemeral nature, could constitute its formative principle.

Delacroix's debt to Lawrence is revealed in all its ambiguity in this portrait. Through the exaggerated formality of the pose and the accessories, the artist reveals the inherent contradictions found in the British aristocratic portrait. Nina Athanassoglou-Kallmyer discerns a mild irony behind the very obvious anglophilia of the image, expressing Delacroix's ambiguous feelings towards the British – 'This Frenchman posing in British finery ... is he not slightly, or perhaps more, bordering on masquerade?' (Athanassoglou-Kallmyer 2005, p.167) – and making a derisive statement about Schwiter. His dandyism is thereby denounced as a borrowed identity; his aristocratic pretensions are betrayed as phoney. In some ways, the most British of French portraits would be unable to depart from its congenital national rigour, and the rigidity of the pose would thus express the permanence of the status portrait, transcended by the artist's virtuoso use of colour. Seldom has any portrait, in fact, achieved such intensity of colour, surpassing even the instinctive, seething brilliance of the latest Lawrence. Here the composition is structured by the use of colour, with its subtle echoes. The blue distances, like the distances in Venetian paintings, respond to the unexpected yet sublime blue pottery planter placed at Schwiter's feet. The very up-to-date blackness of his tailcoat contrasts with the white of the cravat, the gloves, handkerchief and gaiters; the flowers growing in the planter echo this whiteness. Finally, the entire painting is warmed by the intense red of the hat held by the future baron. With this masterpiece, influenced by British art, Delacroix laid the foundations of the great 'natural' French portrait which was to find its great exponent in Edouard Manet. SA

# Claude-André Deseine

PARIS, 1740 – PETIT-GENTILLY, 1823

## 47
*Mirabeau*

1791
Plaster, 80 × 60 × 40 cm
Inscription on cut surface of right arm: *fait par Deseine sourd muet 1791 / riquetti [sic] Mirabeau / mort le 2 avril / 1791*
Musée des Beaux-Arts, Rennes, 877.32.1

PROVENANCE: first prize in the competition organised by the Société des Jacobins, 1791; collection of the sculptor Jean-Baptiste Barré (1804–1877); acquired from Barré's heirs, 1877
EXHIBITED: possibly Paris, Salon of 1791, no.594; Paris, 1989A, no.569
LITERATURE: Le Chatelier 1903, pp.13–15, 17; Bordes 1976, *passim*

When Honoré Gabriel Riqueti, Comte de Mirabeau (1749–1791) died on 2 April he was at the peak of his popularity, despite having been through various ups and downs since 1789. On 6 April the Assemblée Nationale decreed that the church of Sainte-Geneviève should become the French Panthéon, and that Mirabeau should be the first person to be interred there. The 'pantheonisation' of the hero took place the same evening. The Abbé d'Espagnac, who had asked Houdon to make a mould of the face of the deceased the day after his death, proposed to the assembly of the Club des Jacobins that the sculptor should also make a bust of Mirabeau. The commission, which had automatically passed to the famous Houdon, was then cancelled, as the Jacobins preferred to organise a more egalitarian competition, just as the Assembly had done in February for the monument to Jean-Jacques Rousseau (see cat.49). The competition to create a marble bust to be placed 'in perpetuity' in the meeting room of the club (the Société des Amis de la Constitution) was opened on 23 May.

Four sculptors were able to make funeral masks of Mirabeau on 3 April: Jean-Antoine Houdon, Jacques-Philippe Dumont, Tessier and Claude-André Deseine. There was fierce competition between these artists. Jean-Robert Nicolas Lucas de Montigny, who had had the privilege of making a portrait of Mirabeau during his lifetime, also took part; each presented a plaster model to the Assemblée Nationale during the months of April and May (Bordes 1976, p.62), and in September they were all back at the Salon (apart from Tessier). Houdon refused to take part in the competition, arguing that he had been chosen first. It was a mistake on his part, and his arrogant attitude drew strong criticism.

Judging took place on 7 September: preference was given to the bust by Deseine. The artist was far from unknown: he was the elder brother of the Sculptor to the King, Louis-Pierre Deseine. Claude-André was deaf and dumb from birth, was a pupil of Pajou but not a member of the academy, and was employed by the Duc d'Orléans in about 1787, lodging in the Hôtel des Ecuries in Orléans. His links with that seditious environment seem to have made him receptive to revolutionary ideas. He had made a number of busts of influential personalities of the day (the French writer and politican Jérôme Pétion de Villeneuve; Maximilien de Robespierre, one of the main leaders in the French Revolution: terracotta; Musée de la Révolution Française in Vizille), and, from 1793 to 1794, of the martyrs Louis Michel Le Peletier de Saint-Fargeau (plaster; Musée Lallemant, Bourges), Jean-Paul Marat (see cat.37) and Joseph Chalier, as well as the wife of Georges Jacques Danton (a plaster version in the Musée des Beaux-Arts, Troyes). It is likely that Deseine's political sympathies worked in his favour (it also seems that the intervention of Pétion was of crucial importance in the competition of 1791: Bordes 1976, p.62). Whatever the truth of the matter, the Jacobins' judgement was rewarded with a handsome work, one of the unquestionable successes of the sculptor's short career (he made nothing more after the Directoire in 1799 and died forgotten).

In an advertisement published in the *Journal général de la France* on 6 May 1791, Deseine paid ribute to the celebrated painting by Joseph Boze (1790; Musée Granet, Aix-en-Provence) that represented Mirabeau haranguing Dreux-Brézé, who had just ordered the members of the Assemblée Nationale to disperse. This recalled the Jacobins' wish to inscribe on the base of the bust the famous sentence: 'Go and tell those who send you that we are here by the will of the people and that we shall not leave without the force of bayonets' (Bordes 1976, p.61).

Rather than being compared to Boze's iconic painting, Mirabeau's bust should be compared to the portraits executed by his two principal rivals, Lucas de Montigny and Houdon. Lucas was a friend of Mirabeau, whom he had met in 1781. In spite of the count's relationship with his wife – which produced a child – the sculptor had no strong feelings of rancour towards the rakish, flamboyant political luminary. He made three busts of him: one in 1781 (Marcel 1901, p.279, repr.), another in 1790 (sold at Drouot, Paris, 10 June 1980, no.87, repr.) and the third for the competition of 1791 (executed in marble; Musée Paul Arbaud, Aix-en-Provence, replica in the Louvre: Musée du Louvre 1998, vol.2, p.476, repr.). The two earlier busts were similar in composition; they show a bewigged aristocrat with his buttons undone and his shirt open to display a broad chest; he wears a triumphant smile on his lips. The bust of 1791 – known to us through a version presented as a herm, cut at right angles at the shoulders – is more sober: the gaze is preoccupied, and only the twisted cravat suggests the ardour of the tribune.

Houdon's work is completely different. It is known to us through a marble bust whose present whereabouts are unknown (Scherf 2006, under no.19; repr.) and a version in plaster at the Musée des Beaux-Arts, Angers (see Angers 1994, no.20, repr.). It was put on public display in April 1791 (the clay version from 13 April, the original plaster from 18 to 30), and had a decisive influence on Deseine, who presented his plaster version to the Assemblée on 14 May (Bordes 1976, p.62). Houdon wanted, above all, to express the power of the personality: wearing a suit in the French style, with a wig and cravat tucked into his waistcoat, Mirabeau is depicted in the act of making a speech, pointing his right arm with great emphasis. To give greater strength to the composition, the artist cut off the orator's arm, transforming it into a stump pointing forward: 'Whereas under the *ancien régime* busts were enveloped in drapery, the brutally amputated arm evokes the potency of the famous orator's words' (Sauerländer 2005, p.58).

Deseine kept the stump, making it even more spectacular by cutting it vertically – Houdon's cut is oblique – further knitting the sitter's brows and completing the figure's ferocious aspect by making the cravat hang loose outside the waistcoat. Deseine's emphatic rendering could be considered to have gone too far, exaggerated as it is by the politician's pockmarked face, disfigured by smallpox in childhood. Deseine clearly wanted to display even more expression than Houdon. In fact, he far outstripped all his competitors (Bordes 1976, figs 5, 6 and 7).

In September 1791, Deseine's plaster bust was placed in the council chamber of the Jacobins, and three thousand *livres* were granted to the sculptor to execute the piece in marble. The discovery in the Tuileries, in December 1792, of compromising letters between the royal family and the venal Mirabeau caused the collapse of the latter's reputation (he was ejected from the Panthéon and his remains were thrown into a common grave). Deseine, of course, never produced the marble bust. The composition, engraved by Bréa, was retrieved by the porcelain manufacturer Jean Baverstock, heir to the factory of the Duc d'Orléans (one version in biscuit-ware is now in the Museum of Fine Arts, Boston: see MFA 1999, p.236, repr.), but the production of a series of busts was halted by the unexpected downfall of the sitter. GS

# Louis-Pierre Deseine
PARIS, 1749 – PARIS, 1822

## 52
### *Johann Joachim Winckelmann*

1800
Plaster, 72 × 51 × 30 cm
Musée National des Châteaux de Versailles et de Trianon, Versailles, MV 646; LP 515

PROVENANCE: commissioned and executed for the Musée des Monuments français, Paris, 1800; entered the Musée historique du Château de Versailles, 21 March 1834
EXHIBITED: Paris, Salon of 1800, no.421 (described erroneously as marble); Paris, 1989A, no.239
LITERATURE: Le Chatelier 1906, pp.97, 110; Schulz 1953, p.63, fig.31; Pommier 1989, p.15, fig.2; Hoog 1993, p.375, no.1759, repr.; Gröschel 1994, p.21

Alexandre Lenoir, who commissioned this bust for the Musée des Monuments français, wrote in 1796: 'Winckelmann has left a number of valuable books for the study of drawing. In his *Histoire de l'art dans l'Antiquité* [*Geschichte der Kunst des Alterthums* of 1764; *History of Ancient Art Among the Greeks*], he mainly developed a chronological history of the arts, with that finesse so characteristic of great erudition and profound practical knowledge. The respect inspired in me by that sublime man and the recognition due to him from artists, encouraged me to erect a monument to his memory. I have placed in the pedestal that bears his portrait bust one of the Etruscan bas-reliefs that he published in his books. Michallon is the author of this bust' (Lenoir 1797, p.209, no.401). This entry figured in the museum catalogue until the end of the century, with the number 401. The material was not specified.

The bust mentioned was undoubtedly the plaster model, or a cast. It seems that Lenoir asked Louis-Pierre Deseine to finish the marble bust after the accidental death of the sculptor Claude Michallon in August 1799. Deseine, however, preferred to make a new model and on 25 June sent a plaster bust to Lenoir (AMMF 1886, vol.2, p.360). This was presented at the Salon of 1800, then exhibited in the Musée des Monuments français, Paris, where it began to be catalogued under the name of Deseine from 1802, still as no.401 (Lenoir 1802, p.317; described as 'terracotta' in Lenoir 1815, p.128, no.401). This is probably the version that is in Versailles today. Deseine finished the marble version much later, under the Restoration (signed and dated 1818, Musée des Augustins, Toulouse: AMMF 1897, vol.3, pp.254–55; see Toulouse 2002, no.31, repr.).

The reputation of Johann Joachim Winckelmann (1717–1768) in enlightened circles in France was established by the end of the eighteenth century; his first written works were translated from 1755 to 1756, the monumental *History of Ancient Art Among the Greeks* in 1766, then again in 1781; his main texts were widely discussed, particularly during the Revolution, when his defence of liberty in Greece found many echoes (see Pommier 1989, *passim*).

The most symbolic sign of the German scholar's influence in France was his association with Alexandre Lenoir, creator of the Musée des Monuments français, at one and the same time an illustration and a defence of the history of the art of the country. Lenoir's commissioning of a portrait of Winckelmann, the only foreigner in this nationalist pantheon, had tremendous implications: 'Lenoir paid homage to the historian, perhaps because he owed his revelation of what he calls "the scale of the centuries" to reading his works; homage also to the theorist, whose teaching remained indispensable to artists; homage finally to the sublime man, whose life became an example to citizens … By placing the bust of Winckelmann in the cloister of the Petits Augustins, Lenoir paid tribute to him as the inspiration behind his wish to give to "French monuments", saved by him from destruction or dispersal, the dignity of a history, on the same model of history as Winckelmann had sketched out for Greek art' (Pommier 1989, p.15).

The iconography of Winckelmann is based on two aspects of the man, seen in his daily life or empathising with the main subject of his preoccupations, classical antiquity. The two images of the learned man executed from life, by Angelica Kauffman (1764; Kunsthaus Zurich; Pommier 2003, fig.4) and by Anton von Maron (1768; Schlossmuseum, Weimar: Pommier 2003, fig.1) show him in contemporary dress, wearing a dressing gown, and writing. The marble bust by Friedrich W. Doell, installed in the Panthéon in 1782 (Martinelli and Pietrangeli 1955, no.89, pl.X) is re-created after classical models with short hair, eyes with no pupil and drapery with regular pleats;

Anton Raphael Mengs apparently advised his compatriot to work from the plaster cast of a portrait of Cicero in the Uffizi, Florence, because it looked like Winckelmann (Pommier 2003, text below fig. 9).

Deseine's interpretation is nothing like either of these two types. In fact, it derives from the most celebrated portrait of the writer, the one painted by his friend Mengs, whose painting (Metropolitan Museum of Art, New York; see Washington 1976, no. 155, repr.), possibly begun in 1777, was engraved by Jacques-Louis Copia and served as a frontispiece to the *History of Ancient Art*, published in Paris by H. Jansen in 1794 (Pommier 2003, fig. 12). The great man is shown with short hair, looking straight ahead – in Mengs's portrait he is interrupted reading the *Iliad* – wearing an open-necked shirt and a coat. Apart from this connection with Mengs's image, the bust belongs to the eighteenth-century French portrait tradition – in this case the representation of a friend and an intellectual – to which Deseine, by artistic conviction, was far more susceptible than he was to the siren call of antiquity. GS

# Jean-Baptiste Desmarais

PARIS, 1756 – CARRARA, 1813

## 78
*Denis-Antoine Chaudet*

1788
Oil on canvas, 97.5 × 73.5 cm
M. and Mme Alain Moatti, Paris

LITERATURE: Bailey 2002, p. 184, fig. 167; Scherf in Paris 2003A, p. 31, fig. 12

At the end of the eighteenth century, the process of creation itself became a major subject in portraits of artists and self-portraits. This portrait of the sculptor Denis-Antoine Chaudet (1763–1810) by Desmarais embodies the theme. Chaudet, a pupil of Jean-Baptiste Stouf and Etienne-Pierre-Adrien Gois, became one of the most important sculptors of the Revolution and the Empire: he created a large relief for the peristyle of the Panthéon, *Patriotic Duty* (1793; *in situ*), then various images of Napoleon, including a famous bust designed for distribution, the statue at the top of the Vendôme Column (1808; destroyed) and *Napoleon the Legislator* (1805; Hermitage Museum, St Petersburg). In addition to this official output, he was one of the best representatives of the anacreontic vein in sculpture, fond of Hellenistic subjects handled with elegance, grace and a concern for formal purity (cat. 96). When Desmarais painted him, the sculptor, then aged twenty-five, was spending his final year as a scholar at the French Academy in Rome; the following year he was accepted into the Académie Royale de Peinture et de Sculpture, Paris.

Wearing an elegant frock coat with large buttons and a luxurious white cravat around his neck, Chaudet looks as if he wants to be regarded as a man of fashion; this was the current iconography attached to the artist that reached its peak in Louis-Léopold Boilly's *Meeting of Artists in Isabey's Studio* (1798; Louvre, Paris; cat. 69). This manner of representing the artist was very different from the studied pomp usually attached to the academician (Chaudet was not one yet), or the idea of referring to a great master (cat. 73) or any of the more informal representations.

In a melancholy pose, the sculptor leans with his elbow on a worktable and holds a modelling tool. He looks dreamily at a small version of the group *Friendship Enslaving Love* that he had finished in Rome (letter from Ménageot to d'Angiviller, 6 August 1788) and exhibited at the Salon of 1791 (terracotta; Musée Jacquemart-André, Paris: Froissart 1999, pp. 178–79). The presence of a sponge ready to moisten the clay indicates that the work is in progress. The sculptor is portrayed at an intimate moment, in a very different manner from the lofty way in which Robert Lefevre represents Pierre Guérin.

While Guérin jealously guards the secret of creation, identified only by the painting tools he is holding in his hands, Chaudet exposes it here for all to see. Whereas in her contemporary portrait of *Hubert Robert* (1788; Louvre, Paris) Vigée-Lebrun represents inspiration as a sort of inner necessity, a violent and passionate enthusiasm, difficult to control, Chaudet depicts it as something altogether more thoughtful. Both the painter and his sitter probably wished to emphasise the manual aspect of the sculptor's art, as well as its intellectual dimension. Chaudet, in the pose of a thinker, holds the modelling tool as if it were a pen: he could just as well have been a writer. AA

# Martin Drolling

OBERBERGHEIM, NEAR COLMAR, 1752 – PARIS, 1817

## 64
*Michel Belot*

1791
Oil on canvas, 72 × 60 cm
Signed: *M. DROLING PINXIT 1791*
Musée des Beaux-Arts, Orléans, 381

PROVENANCE: the artist's family; bequeathed to the Musée de Peinture et de Sculpture, Orléans, 1872, with portrait of the artist's sister-in-law, Mademoiselle Belot, by Auguste-Lazare Belot, son of Michel Belot; entered the museum's permanent collection, 1878
EXHIBITED: Misme Museum Shipment, 1925, repr.; Musée de l'Orangerie, Paris, 1931, no. 11; Musée des Beaux-Arts, Orléans, 1953, no. 6
LITERATURE: Vitry 1922, p. 43; Vitry 1931, p. 66; *L'Illustration*, 15 October 1932, p. 222, repr.; Brière 1931, p. 198, no. 11; Nicolle 1931, p. 127; Paris 1974A, p. 399; O'Neill 1977, no. 42, p. 55

The Alsatian painter Martin Drolling was renowned for his highly descriptive interior genre scenes. His candid portraiture constitutes only a small proportion of his output and mainly depicts his family. Michel Belot was his father-in-law, and this work is one of Drolling's finest portraits. Belot is depicted between a three-quarter profile and a frontal view, in a classic, formal half-length pose.

Largely self-taught, Drolling was initially influenced by Jean-Baptiste Greuze (1725–1805), but his study and absorption of seventeenth-century Flemish and Dutch Old Masters at the Louvre and the Luxembourg Palace were instrumental in the development of his style, which is characterised by a high, porcelain finish, a subdued colour scheme, a meticulous rendering of detail and a great facility with the contrasts and play of light. Thus, stylistically, he is comparable to Louis-Léopold Boilly and, in his thematic focus on bourgeois life, to such German and Scandinavian artists as Caspar David Friedrich or Wilhelm Bendz. However, Drolling was a singular figure within his genre niche, abjuring any dominant narrative or emblematic content that might subordinate his subject's individuality, or even that of an inanimate object; the discrete hairs of a sweeping brush, the crumbs on a rough-hewn peasant's table, or the dull sheen of a copper pot are as intimately, realistically and lovingly rendered as a face. In his *Annales* of 1817 Charles Paul Landon praised him, together with Greuze, for 'ennobling' the genre, yet Drolling had less of the older artist's propensity for drama. Conversely, he delighted in the mundane and in striking verisimilitude. Popular lithographers and engravers, such as Leroy, P. L. Debucourt, Noel and Muller, reproduced his genre subjects, enhancing his reputation.

Drolling's first wife Madeleine Welker died childless in 1781. He married Louise-Elisabeth Belot in 1785, and engendered a family of painters. His son, Michel-Martin Drolling (1786–1851), a pupil of David from 1806, was predisposed to mythological and history painting, as well as to portraiture, while his daughter, Louise-Adéone (1797–1831) – known as Mme Joubert – was a prize-winning painter. Their grandfather Michel Belot was himself a painter, founding a business in paint colours, as is implied in an inscription on the back of Drolling's portrait, which reads 'le fondateur d'une maison de commerce en couleurs fines, 3, rue de L'Arbre-Sec à Paris'. The critic Auguste Jal mentions that Belot was also an art dealer.

Abandoning the English manner of utilising a landscape background, which Drolling favoured in his own, notably patrician self-portrait (*c.* 1791; Musée des Beaux-Arts d'Orléans), the portrait of Belot has a plain, shadowy backdrop. Nor does the artist employ an architectural device, such as a window, as a frame for his subject, as he had in *Portrait of the Artist's Son* (1800; Los Angeles County Museum of Art), which is replete with *trompe-l'oeil* details. The tenebrous, austere background of Belot's portrait throws his face and upper torso into relief. Turning his head to the left, Belot glances out to the side at the viewer, his eyes heavy-lidded and earnest, with the dark lashes and liquid, dilated pupils favoured by Drolling. Given his fluency in producing appealing genre images of children and families, the forbidding, grave aspect of the sitter is arresting. Belot's wide mouth is tightly set. The naturalistic and modelled flesh, conveyed in rich impasto, contrasts with the high finish of the thinly applied paint of the wide-collared velvet jacket. Belot's brightly lit forehead – emphasising his learning – is framed by a smart, powdered, heart-shaped wig. Drolling captures an air of erudition and severity in his sitter, pointedly excluding any reference to his profession or the business of painting. Instead, Belot holds a pamphlet, whose cover reads 'PROJET.../AU FRAN … MIR (?)'. This title may refer to a speech given by Mirabeau at the Assemblée Nationale on 14 January 1791, the year the painting was executed, and three months before Mirabeau's death. Belot is represented as a serious, politically aware bourgeois citizen, a 'Friend of the Constitution'. This presentation corresponds with Drolling's own self-portrait, which, conspicuously, contains neither references to art nor to his profession.

It is not known why Drolling would wish to de-emphasise his own or his father-in-law's association with painting. He did not do this in the case of his children's portraits, for example, in which he appears proud to include all the accoutrements of the profession. Drolling was a somewhat inscrutable figure, and the chronology and character of his life are fragmentary. He was baptised as an infant in 1752, in Alsace, and received preliminary training from a minor painter at Sélestat before arriving in Paris in around 1780. There he took classes at the Ecole des Beaux-Arts without becoming a member of the Academy. Unconstrained by the hierarchies and competitions of the Academy, he flourished as an artist and, at his death, left a thriving studio, which included many female students. Drolling exhibited at the Salon de la Correspondance in 1781, 1782 and again in 1789. After this pivotal year, the elitist institutions of the *ancien régime* were deregulated and, from 1793, he was free to exhibit his work at the Salon du Louvre, hence heightening his profile within a newly empowered consumer society. Settling into life in Paris during the tense, pre-Revolution years of the 1780s, Drolling might appear to have chosen a bipartisan, apolitical stance in his steady concentration on genre scenes and occasional portraits, and yet the subtext of his choice of subject-matter is often critical of the wretched state in which the vast majority of the population lived; his scenes of bourgeois life are a quiet celebration and sanctification of the ordinary citizen. CC

# Claude-Marie Dubufe
PARIS, 1790 – LA CELLE-SAINT-CLOUD, 1864

## 99
### *The Artist's Family*

1820
Oil on canvas, 64 × 82 cm
Département des Peintures, Musée du Louvre, Paris, RF 1982-2. Donated to be held in usufruct by M. Edouard Dubufe, great-grandson of the artist, 1982

PROVENANCE: remained in the artist's family; presented to the Louvre, to be held in usufruct, by Edouard Dubufe (1883–1984), great-grandson of the painter, 1982; entered the Louvre 1984
EXHIBITED: Paris, 1983, pp.60–61 (S. Laveissière); Tokyo, 1991, no.123 (J. Foucart); Paris, 2000, no.208
LITERATURE: Bréon 1984, p.119

Claude-Marie Dubufe was descended from a long line of painters and was one of the most active painters in France in the first half of the nineteenth century. Having studied in the studio of David, he became a sought-after society painter under the Restoration and the July Monarchy, to the extent that he was known as the 'Van Dyck of pretty women'. This painting shows the artist in intimate mood. He portrays himself in profile on the far right, with his wife. In the foreground to their left, his son Edouard, born in 1819, who also became a painter, and his mother gaze out at us. A young woman reading can be seen beside them. She could be a relative of Dubufe whom he had already portrayed reading a book: Mademoiselle Duménillet. At the back of the picture stand the artist's sister, Joséphine-Anne, and her husband, Arnoux-Philibert de Pincepré.

This sort of family gathering, reduced to a collection of juxtaposed heads, is relatively rare in French art. Although this type of work was unusual in France, it was relatively common in Germany, particularly in the work of Friedrich Wilhelm Schadow and Peter von Cornelius; it may have derived ultimately from portrait medallions. It is worth noting the portrait by Merry-Joseph Blondel, painted in 1813, in the Kunsthalle Bremen; the family of the artist is depicted in a similar composition that also includes a figure in profile with a far-away look in her eye. The deliberate simplicity and the somewhat abrupt juxtapositions (reminiscent of collage) betray the primitivism that may have influenced the artist during his apprenticeship in David's studio, and which his contemporary painting *Apollo and Cyparissa* (1821; Musée Calvet, Avignon) serves to illustrate.

For whom would this painting have been intended? We have no way of knowing, apart from the presence of the baby in the centre of the composition, the apparent focus of interest. Was the portrait painted to celebrate the child's birthday? Or was it a celebration of family values, as the strict separation of the couples and the prominent display of Madame Dubufe's wedding ring might lead us to believe? The young woman reading on the left, whose face (unlike the others) is in the shade, is the only unmarried person in the painting.

This touchingly intimate portrait may at the outset have been nothing more than an exercise in style, with the painter attempting to render a variety of different expressions, rather in the style of Louis-Léopold Boilly's characters, but without the element of caricature. The artist was to reuse the poses in separate portraits. In fact, Claude-Marie Dubufe seems to have been particularly fond of close-up portraits of his sitters, cut off at chest level. The idea of the girl reading can be found in other paintings including *Reading* (whereabouts unknown). The melancholy gaze of the artist's sister brings to mind the *Young Woman in Pain* (Louvre, Paris), and the mother's wide-eyed gaze has an expression similar to that of the artist's wife in his portrait of her (1818; Louvre, Paris).

The impression of depth is skilfully produced by the manipulation of light and shade, particularly on the girl reading and the child, and the brother-in-law's face turned slightly to the right. In this painting the artist displays an elegant, refined style and a subtle range of colours; his brushstrokes are smooth, giving a porcelain-like finish, which adds to the charm of this family gathering. AA

# Jacques-Edme Dumont
PARIS, 1761 – PARIS, 1844

## 105
### *Madame Dumont, the Artist's Mother*

1799
Plaster, 53 × 38.5 × 24 cm
Département des Sculptures, Musée du Louvre, Paris, RF 657

PROVENANCE: gift of Madame Augustin Dumont, widow of the artist's son, who was also a sculptor, 1884
EXHIBITED: Paris, Salon of 1799, no.419; Paris, 1989C, no.202
LITERATURE: Vattier 1890, pp.88 and 235; Musée du Louvre 1998, vol.1, p.355, repr.

This portrait bust is of the sculptor's mother, née Marie-Françoise Bertault (1727–1800). Her son portrayed her towards the end of her life, when she was seventy-two years old.

Jacques-Edme Dumont, the son of a sculptor, was a pupil of Augustin Pajou. Having won first prize at the Académie, Paris, in 1788, he was entitled to a period of study at the French Academy in Rome. He returned to France in 1793 and was plunged into the aftermath of the Revolution; however, his career did not really take off until the Empire.

Although he usually showed delicate terracotta pieces at the Salon, he broke with this tradition in 1799 with this portrait of his mother, having produced very few portraits before this date. Jacques-Edme had a very close relationship with his mother. Marie-Françoise Bertault was the wife of the royal sculptor, Edme Dumont, who died in 1775, leaving her a widow with four children. The eldest, Jacques-Edme, then only just fourteen, thus had to support his family from a very young age. This is why he soon joined the studio of the sculptor Pajou, an old friend of his father (the two artists occupied neighbouring studios at the Louvre). Pajou evidently took on the role of father. However, he was sometimes rather heavy-handed, as the following letter written by the young Jacques-Edme to his mother in Rome in 1788 indicates: 'I continually admire the zeal and constancy with which M. Pajou assists us. I should prefer it if he were as gentle in the manner in which he gives advice to his students as he is obliging' (quoted in Vattier 1890, p.49).

Apart from what it tells us about Jacques-Edme's filial devotion, the bust of Madame Dumont is interesting as a portrait of an older person belonging to a relatively modest social class, quite a rarity in sculpture. In this respect, it can be compared with the terracotta bust of the sculptor Trippel's aunt, the pride of the Museum zu Allerheiligen, Schaffhausen (fig.13). Marie-Françoise Bertault is portrayed in everyday clothing, without ostentation or pomp. On her head she wears a morning bonnet of the type known in French as a *baigneuse* or sometimes *pierrot*, worn by women in the home since the mid-eighteenth century (see Paris 1989c). A simple neckerchief is knotted loosely around her neck. She could be one of those steadfastly bourgeois women painted by Chardin. Her ageing features, the half smile on her closed lips and her inwardly turned gaze all betray an unspoken melancholy. This modest bust bears admirable witness to an age of sensibility in which it was acceptable to pay tribute in public to a son's love for his mother. GS

# Vigilius Eriksen
COPENHAGEN, 1722 – COPENHAGEN, 1783

## 7
*Catherine II, Empress of Russia*

*c.*1765
Oil on canvas, 275.9 × 202.2 cm
Lent by Her Majesty The Queen

PROVENANCE: first recorded in the archives of the British Royal Collection, 30 November 1813; previously attributed to Johann Baptist Lampi, and Dmitri Grigorievitch Levitski
EXHIBITED: *Great Britain, USSR*, 1967, Victoria and Albert Museum, London (organised by the Arts Council of Great Britain)
LITERATURE: Colding 1970, p.2; London 1967, p.17; Stockholm 1999, p.100; Andersen 1965, pp.57–58; Andersen 1970, no.74; Montreal 2005, p.150

Vigilius Eriksen painted this full-length portrait of Catherine II (1729–1796) in her coronation robes during his fifteen-year residency in Russia in the service of the Imperial court. He had left his native Copenhagen in 1757, having failed to win the gold medal at the Royal Academy of Art, and after some initial difficulties had established himself as one of St Petersburg's leading portraitists. Eriksen found particular favour with the charismatic wife of the Grand Duke Peter, and by the time she seized power from her husband in 1762, he was ideally positioned to assume a central role in fashioning the public image of the woman who was to become known as Catherine the Great. Throughout the 1760s, Eriksen produced a remarkable series of portraits that were said by the connoisseur Jakob von Stahlin to be 'the most lifelike and accomplished portraits of Her Majesty' (Stockholm 1999, p.101).

Catherine's coronation was celebrated with a lavish series of festivities on 22 September 1762. Eriksen is known to have been in Moscow at the time, and it is probable that he was granted a number of sittings with the Empress to produce a state portrait. Catherine was pleased with the result, and in the subsequent decade the artist was commissioned to produce duplicates for official dissemination throughout Europe. Versions were sent to the courts of Prussia and Denmark, and this example must have been presented as a diplomatic gift to George III. There is no evidence that Eriksen supported a large studio in Russia, and these copies most likely to have been produced by the artist himself rather than by assistants – particularly in view of the fact that Catherine instigated a strict system of quality control over her portraits, even insisting that the version bound for the Christiansborg Castle in Copenhagen make the lengthy diversion from St Petersburg to Moscow so that she could personally ensure that the canvas met her exacting standards (Andersen 1965, p.57).

Such assiduous concern stemmed less from Catherine's vanity than her shrewd use of her portraits as political tools. As a woman with almost no Russian blood and a decidedly shaky claim to the throne, she was faced with an urgent need to legitimise her royal standing. Although her aptitude and strength of character had won her widespread admiration among the Russian élite, her rise to power was received less warmly in Europe, where she was frequently dismissed as a licentious regicide ruling over an uncivilised hinterland. In another monumental portrait dating from this period, Eriksen portrays Catherine on the day of her coup d'état, astride her horse in a man's military uniform, brandishing a sword (after 1762; State Hermitage Museum, St Petersburg). This audacious work presented her as a bold leader, channelling the spirit of her professed model, Peter the Great, but it also played into the hands of some of her critics. The coronation offered an opportunity to project a different image, emphasising Catherine's feminine decorum and the splendour of the Russian court. The official visual record of the event was to serve as a strategic centrepiece in a carefully orchestrated campaign to present her as an enlightened and modern monarch, inaugurating her lifelong programme of infusing European culture into Russia.

Accordingly, this work is conceived in the most elevated register of European court portraiture. Eriksen trained in the studio of Johann Salomon Wahl, where he would have been exposed to Wahl's portraits of the Danish royal family painted in the French grand manner. In St Petersburg he would have absorbed the lessons of Louis Tocqué's majestic full-length portrait of the Empress Elizabeth Petronova (1758; State Hermitage Museum, St Petersburg), which imported the elegance of Versailles to the Russian court. In his portrait of Catherine, Eriksen deploys a lucid style and a simple pyramidal composition, conveying the necessary sense of grandeur while eschewing any excessive baroque flourishes. In keeping with the commemorative function of the portrait, the coronation regalia is delineated with careful precision. Catherine wears the imperial crown, ornamented with over five thousand diamonds and surmounted by a four hundred carat ruby, which was created for the event by the court jeweller Jeremiah Posier. She holds the sceptre and orb, the attributes of her new authority, and wears a blue silk sash fastened at the hip with the badge of the order of St Andrew, Russia's highest order of chivalry, with which she invested herself on the day of her coup. Catherine wanted to amplify her respect for Russian tradition in addition to her international sophistication, and particular prominence is given to the crowned double-headed eagle, the symbol of Russia, which is picked out in gold embroidery on her dress, formed in diamonds on her necklace, and wrought in gold on the backdrop above her right shoulder. As she steps forward on the dais, Catherine radiates majestic authority, but even in this most formal of contexts, something of her singular character shines through in her alert and benevolent countenance. This balance of the personal with the public was to find its most complex expression in Eriksen's *Portrait of Catherine II in Front of a Mirror* (1762–64; State Hermitage Museum, St Petersburg), in which a sensitive portrait of Catherine caught in a moment of quiet thought is juxtaposed with her reflection in the adjacent mirror, which distils the impassive profile of the ruler used on coins and cameos. Eriksen's brush served Catherine faithfully in her pivotal first years as Empress. The coronation portrait presents a vision of regal dignity that presages the achievements of her long and glorious reign, deftly proving the artist's assertion that 'a portrait painter is just as important at Court as a painter of historical events' (Andersen 1965, p.52). KB

# Jean-Joseph Espercieux
MARSEILLES, 1757 – PARIS, 1840

## 117
## The Abbé Raynal

Executed in 1837, from a model made in 1790
Marble, 56 × 28 × 25 cm
Inscription, front: *Guilme Th / RAYNAL / né a St Geniez aveyron*;
left: *fait d'après nature à marseille / en 1790 par son ami Espercieux*;
on the reverse, note in pencil: *marbre des pyrénées / 2631*
Mairie, Saint-Geniez-d'Olt

PROVENANCE: bought from the artist by the state, 13 April 1837;
deposited at Saint-Geniez-d'Olt, 13 May 1839 (A.N. F21 0005,
dossier 31, artists)
EXHIBITED: Rodez, 1996, no.87
LITERATURE: Caso 1996, p.554, note 4, p.618, fig.252; Lafont
2003; Bosséno 2003, pp.141–43, repr.; Paris 2005C, p.328, fig.222

The bust of Raynal became famous when Girodet
included it in his painting of Jean-Baptiste Belley
(1797; Château de Versailles). The comparison
between the sculpture in the painting and
Espercieux's bust exhibited in the Salon of 1796
had been made several times (see London 1972,
no.106; Scherf 1988, pp.15–16; Weston 1994, p.84,
note 1), but was finally accepted when this marble
bust in Saint-Geniez-d'Olt came to light. Today the
piece is appreciated for two different reasons –
firstly for its contribution to the iconography of
Abbé Raynal and secondly for its relationship to
Girodet's masterpiece.

Jean-Joseph Espercieux studied at the
Académie in Marseilles, then in Paris with Charles-
Antoine Bridan; he was not a member of the
Académie Royale, but participated in the Salon as
soon as it was opened to all artists in 1791. He was
politically active during the Revolution, becoming
one of the presidents of the Société populaire et
républicaine des arts. Espercieux knew Raynal
(1713–1796) in Marseilles, where the writer spent
the years from 1786 to 1791. A letter from Raynal
dated 17 January 1791 notes: 'M. Espercieux ... a
hardworking and honest artist. He has made here
(in Marseilles) a bust of me and some other very
successful works' (Feugère 1922, p.93). The bust
was exhibited at the Salon of 1796 (no.614), the
year of Raynal's death. At that time the writer's
anti-revolutionary stance, expressed in the
Assemblée in 1791 and heavily criticised, was viewed
very favourably. His election to the Institute in 1795
affected his permanent rehabilitation as a historic
figure of the Enlightenment.

The material from which the bust is made
was not indicated in the leaflet: is it the terracotta
version modelled in the presence of the writer in
1790? Or the plaster copy presented by the artist
after the exhibition closed to the Musée des
Monuments français, on 24 October 1796
(disappeared; Lenoir 1797, no.416; AMMF 1886,
vol.2, 1886, p.398)? The white colour of the bust in
the painting might confirm this last hypothesis.
The inscription transcribed by the painter – *G. T.
RAYNAL* – is simpler and more direct than the one
on the marble bust in Saint-Geniez-d'Olt (Bosséno
2003, figs 20 and 21). In fact, the marble bust, as

Espercieux's letter to the Minister of the Interior
on 20 March 1837 makes clear, was carved at this
date, after the terracotta model of 1790: 'Minister,
in 1790 I made in Marseilles a bust of Abbé
Raynal, I possess the terracotta model of it which
dates from that period ... I have just made it in
marble and suggest that it should be placed in
spacious surroundings such as a public library.
I think it my duty, Minister, to pray you to acquire
it' (A.N. F²¹ 0005, dossier 31); the minister acquired
it one month later. It is clear that the local and
explanatory character of the inscriptions result
from the marble version being made much later.
It is not known whether the medallions adorning
the two sides – on the left, a caduceus consisting
of two snakes coiled round a wand, the symbol
of eloquence; on the right a flare and a trumpet,
symbols of renown – were designed in 1790 or
only in 1837.

The portrait by Espercieux is astonishingly
austere, very different from the jovial bust made
by Jean Pierre Antoine Tassaert (and dated 1784),
when the writer was in Berlin (Académie, Lyons;
Scherf 1988, repr.) Raynal liked Tassaert's piece very
much, because he was grateful to the sculptor for
having made 'a very good likeness, full of life and
almost handsome' (quoted in Feugère 1922, p.93).
Tassaert chose a classical composition in a patrician
version: the subject, raised on a circular pedestal, is
dressed in becoming drapery in the antique style;
the draped garment crosses his chest in the front
and is attached by a button on the left shoulder.
His eyes have deeply incised pupils and look to the
right, full of life, the lips are parted as if in speech.
Tassaert's creation was admired and a number of
plaster casts were in circulation (there is a copy
in the Wittum palace in Weimar).

Espercieux created something radically
different: a bust as a herm, impassive, with sharp
lines unsoftened by drapery; Raynal's eyes are
blank, his mouth closed and his mouth fixed in a
severe grimace. The form chosen is reminiscent of
classical antiquity at its most austere, during the
heroic days of Brutus or Scipio. Tassaert's *Raynal*
represents an Enlightenment writer who has just
left a Parisian salon, a cosmopolitan and easy-going
man, having an aura of glory from being a well-
known author. The *Raynal* of Espercieux is a grim,
determined person, full of the fervour of the
convert, the dogged defender of difficult ideas. It is
easy to imagine the shock wave that this powerful
image of strong will must have sent through the
Salon of 1796.

The Abbé Raynal's fame was based on a
book that created a great stir: this was the *Histoire
philosophique et politique des établissements et du commerce des
Européens dans les deux Indes* (1770). The third edition,
published in 1780, signed with his name, was
condemned by Parliament, causing the Abbé
to flee from France into exile. The book, written
in collaboration with Diderot, concentrated in
particular on the living conditions of indigenous

populations, and contributed, with Condorcet's
*Réflexions sur l'esclavage des nègres* (1781) and the
activities of the Société des Amis des Noirs
(founded in 1788) to bring about the abolition
of slavery by the Convention in 1794.

Girodet's painting of Jean-Baptiste Belley
in the costume of a representative of the people
in the Convention (he was the deputy for Saint-
Domingue) was painted in the days after the Salon
of 1796, to no specific commission. The painter
represents the head of the black man on the same
level as the white bust, thus giving material
presence to the similarities of the two men's
fight for equality (Weston 1994, p.88). When
the painting was shown at the exhibition in the
Elysée in October 1797, the figure of Belley was
not identified in the leaflet, unlike the 'bust of
the celebrated Raynal, philosopher and historian,
a tribute to the gratitude owed by the people of
colour to the first advocate of liberty for French
Americans' (quoted by Sylvain Bellenger in Paris
2005C, p.330). Girodet's work was more of a tribute
to Raynal than a political portrait. The painter
modified the title of the work when it was
exhibited at the Salon in the following year: the
*Portrait of a Negro* became a portrait of Citizen *Belley,
ex-representative of the Colonies*. The significance of
the painting was perceptibly altered. GS

# Agustín Esteve y Marqués
VALENCIA, 1753 – VALENCIA?, AFTER 1820

## 101
## Mariano San Juan y Pinedo,
## Conde Consorte de La Cimera

*c.*1810/13
Oil on canvas, 128 × 89 cm
Museo Nacional del Prado, Madrid, 2876

PROVENANCE: Condesa de Goyeneche, Madrid; the sitter's
family; bequeathed to the Museo Nacional del Prado by the
Conde de La Cimera, 1944
EXHIBITED: Madrid, 1913, no.136; London, 1920, no.131;
Madrid, 1983, no.28; Tokyo, 1987, no.45
LITERATURE: see Soria 1957, p.140, no.160; Mena Marqués 2000,
p.128

This exquisite work is a paradigm of the infant
portrait during a period rich in aesthetic
transformations. Its painter is not as well known
as he deserves to be, given his interesting creations.
Although he has been the subject of group and
partial studies, he awaits a full-scale monograph
to gather, classify and analyse his sizeable *oeuvre*.

Probably the son of the sculptor Agustín
Esteve, and a disciple of the Real Academia de
Bellas Artes de San Carlos in his native city,
Agustín Esteve y Marqués entered the competitions
of the Real Academia de Bellas Artes de San
Fernando in Madrid in 1772 and 1778. He was

highly favoured as a painter by the Dukes of Osuna, and also worked as Goya's assistant. He seems to have been overshadowed by Goya's enormous personality, which perhaps resulted in a certain obscurity for his own work. During the reign of Charles IV, he was protected by the all-powerful royal favourite, Manuel de Godoy, Príncipe de la Paz, and he also continued to collaborate with the great Aragonese master in making replicas and copies of portraits. They influenced him when he later came to produce his own works. In 1800 he received the prestigious appointment of Pintor de Camára at the Madrid court. Until at least 1808 he continued his work as a portrait painter for members of the ducal house of Osuna, who were excellent clients, well known for their love of the arts. Under King José Bonaparte, a monarch imposed on the Kingdom of Spain by Napoleon, Esteve's excellent position at court was weakened. Things became worse still from 1815, when Ferdinand VII, the legitimate King, was restored and began to persecute those who had fraternised with the French. Esteve became ill and short of money and retired to Valencia, where he was still living in 1820. He produced a large number of works, mainly portraits. Some are wrongly attributed to Goya, and such errors will need to be corrected by future research so as to define the fundamental characteristics of Esteve's own distinctive art.

The sitter was born on 17 January; he married Doña María Salomé Mendinueta y Muzquiz, Condesa de La Cimera, a title created by Charles IV in 1795 for the bride's father, who had been a member of the Treasury Council. The portrait seems to have been painted using a delicate technique, almost miniaturist, that shows the tiniest details, a stylistic feature redolent of a training dating from the last third of the eighteenth century.

The graceful figure of the boy, who is dressed in his uniform as a naval cadet, is shown against sketched-in parkland whose tonalities are harmonised and dominated by a subtle range of greys. The child's intense, profound gaze already shows intelligence and sharpness. His calm, simple figure makes a pleasant, fresh impression. He is relaxed and points with a gesture that is not imperious, another positive note in this favourable image. As he appears to be between eight and ten years old, the work should be set in the contemporary context of the War of Independence (1808–13) and closer to the first years of the century's second decade.

Although it is not signed, the portrait's attribution to Esteve has always been accepted unanimously; indeed, it is considered one of his best works. His habitual tendency towards elegant stiffness and a certain severity in his compositions is corrected here by an emphasis on the human aspects, which in the present case involve a happy capturing of the amiable and candid spirit of the child-sitter, coupled with close observation of his character and personal particularities. The evocation of Goya, so frequent in Esteve's paintings, seems to disappear into an atmosphere prefiguring German romanticism. Any idea of fragility is absent and the softness of Esteve's other paintings has been transformed into a conscious firmness and the affirmation of very distinct pictorial principles.

The painting was first attributed to Esteve by Elías Tormo (Tormo 1916, p.315), an opinion that has been followed by all art historians, especially by Martín Soria, who collected many of the artist's works (Soria 1957, p.140). The work was carefully studied prior to its exhibition in Japan (see Tokyo 1987, pp.150, 151). The sketch for the head is in the private collection of distant relatives of the sitter who are descended from another branch of the family and who are the present holders of the title. JJL

# François-Xavier Fabre
MONTPELLIER, 1766 – MONTPELLIER, 1837

## 133
### Allen Smith Before a View of Florence

1797
Oil on canvas, 70.9 × 90.5 cm
Signed and dated: *F. X. Fabre Florentiae 1797*
Lent by the Syndics of the Fitzwilliam Museum, Cambridge. Given by the Friends of the Fitzwilliam Museum in celebration of their 75th anniversary, with the aid of the directors of Hazlitt, Gooden & Fox and contributions from the National Art Collections Fund and the Cunliffe, Percival and Purchase Funds

PROVENANCE: commissioned in 1797 by Allen Smith; entered the Fitzwilliam Museum, 1984
EXHIBITED: London, 1998, no.331 (D. Shawe-Taylor)
LITERATURE: Pellicer 2000, p.27; Hilaire 2000, p.56

When the French Revolution broke out, François-Xavier Fabre, a pupil of David, was in Rome nearing the end of his time as a scholar at the French Academy. In 1793, following violent anti-French riots in the Eternal City, Fabre, who enjoyed the protection of the Duchess of Albany and her companion, the poet Vittorio Alfieri, escaped to Florence. Finding himself without money in the Tuscan capital, he took up the lucrative art of portrait painting, taking advantage of the large cosmopolitan society to be found there. It was in this international context that in 1797 he received a commission for two portraits of Allen Smith, one small and one large – 'life-size amidst the ruins of Ancient Rome'. A sketch now in the Musée Fabre in Montpellier gives some idea of what this work, probably never executed, might have been like (Montpellier 1979, no.29, entry by Laure Pellicer). The drawing was a pastiche of Tischbein's great painting, *Goethe in the Roman Campagna* (1786; Städelsches Kunstinstitut, Frankfurt), of which Fabre possessed a drawing (Musée Fabre, Montpellier, inv. 837-I-991): the artist reuses the recumbent pose adopted by the great German poet, with classical fragments and landscape in the background. The idea of echoing this evocation of the celebrated 'tourist' seems to have reached the ears of the patron, who may have seen Tischbein's work in Naples, as a letter from the painter to his protector in Holland suggests: 'The honour of the composition belongs entirely to him; mine is at best the merit of its execution' (Montpellier 1979, no.29).

A journey to Italy had by now become an essential part of the education of an English gentleman (and to a lesser extent of a Russian or French gentleman); the Grand Tour portrait, hung ostentatiously in an English residence, often in the hall, carried something of a social message. Pompeo Batoni established the norms in the 1760s: the young aristocrat, full length, often opulently dressed and life-size, posed amidst well-known antiquities or near ruins. Tischbein's portrait exploited these same ideas, but adapted them for the depiction of a great writer, the expression of social status in this case being less important than the painting's cultural content and the symbolic value of the ruins. *Allen Smith Before a View of Florence* embodies both of these meanings. The sitter was a great traveller and collector, and probably wished to make his social status manifest in such a work. At the same time the reference to Goethe, which he seems expressly to have desired, reveals his wish to transcend the conventions of the genre by adding an intellectual dimension to the work. The painting's format, relatively modest by comparison with the portraits of Batoni or Tischbein, emphasises the way this type of portrait was to develop – ostentatious dimensions were becoming less popular. In fact, although the composition owes much to Tischbein's masterpiece, the result is closer to the formula popularised by Louis Gauffier, for those who wanted to remember their journey to Italy without being overburdened. Gauffier, who was closely connected to Fabre, promoted a type of portrait that could be qualified as the 'souvenir portrait'. Much less formal, it gave freer expression to the psychology and state of mind of the sitter, employing delicate symbolism and using the landscape as a space for mental projection.

Enveloped in his travelling cape, Allen Smith sits in front of a view of Florence in which can be identified the Ponte Santa Trinità and the Ponte Vecchio; further back, against a backdrop of hills, the church of San Miniato al Monte can be glimpsed. Fabre's perfectly composed view of Florence reveals his experience as a painter of historical landscape. His work is close to the graphic abstraction of Jacob Philippe Hackert and lacks the naturalism of Gauffier, whose eye is more sensitive to the effects of light and shade; Gauffier constructs his image around a succession of levels in which highly organised areas of shade and light alternate. It is interesting to note the tension between the genuine observation of architectural elements (bridges, palaces, churches) and their idealised re-composition. Fabre is unwilling to depart from a certain formality, favouring the descriptive value of the portrait over any intimacy. The representation of Smith in such severe profile, as on a classical medallion, seems to place him in eternity, removed from any specific time, while rejecting any psychological enquiry. He is seen leaning against a relief adorned with Egyptian hieroglyphics, meditating on the passage of time from antiquity, which stretches back to ancient Egypt, to the Middle Ages, as represented by Florence, whose landscape occupies almost half the composition. The severity of the sitter's perfectly outlined profile is softened by the elegance of the pose and the tender expression on the faintly pink face; the slightly open mouth seems to breathe life into this abstract image. Although in this portrait Fabre seeks no psychological introspection, and nor does he succeed in characterising his sitter with a single trait (as does Gauffier), he nevertheless succeeds in creating an atmosphere, bringing the spectator right to the threshold of Smith's meditation. SA

# Thomas Gainsborough

SUDBURY, 1727 – LONDON, 1788

## 86
### George Byam with His Wife Louisa and Their Daughter Selina

c.1762, and reworked by 1766
Oil on canvas, 249 × 238.8 cm
The Andrew Brownsword Arts Foundation. On long-term loan to the Holburne Museum of Art, Bath

PROVENANCE:  by descent to Selina Byam, who married the Revd William Hony of Liskeard, Cornwall;  their son, Archdeacon William Hony;  by descent to his grandson, Henry C. Hony;  presented by him to Marlborough College, 1955;  Marlborough College sale, Christie's, London, 10 June 1999, lot 9;  sold by private treaty to The Andrew Brownsword Arts Foundation
EXHIBITED:  see Bath 2001, p.45
LITERATURE:  see Bath 2001, p.45

This image shows George Byam (1734–1779) with his wife Louisa (died 1779) and their daughter Selina (1760–1846). Byam was a member of a family long established in Antigua; in the early 1760s they were among the wealthiest sugar plantation owners on that island, their 366 acres worked by 132 slaves. Byam himself spent almost all his adult life in Antigua, where he was born and died; and it has been observed that Gainsborough's image is in effect 'a portrait of a plantation owner on holiday' (Bath 2001, p.6). He appears to have

come to Britain shortly before the outbreak of war with France in 1758 and to have married Louisa Bathurst soon after his arrival. She was the eighth daughter of Peter Bathurst (1687–1748) by his second wife, Lady Selina Shirley. Her father had been a long-serving MP in the interest of his brother, Lord Bathurst. Byam married into a family of consequence (Bath 2001, p.18).

His new wife had family connections in Bath, where local papers reported the presence of a 'Mrs Byam' in October 1758. Gainsborough, too, had arrived there earlier that month to assess what business prospects the fashionable resort-town held for him; encouraged by what he found, the following October he transferred his painting practice there full-time. There are several press references to 'Mr and Mrs Byam' visiting Bath during the 1760s, and it seems that the Byams' portrait must have been undertaken in the course of these sojourns (Sloman 2002, p.233, note 53). They may have come to the artist via Louisa Byam's uncle, Benjamin Bathurst, who commissioned a portrait of two of his children from Gainsborough around 1759–60 (Bath 2001, p.18).

Byam is shown leading his wife with his left arm, gesturing towards the landscape with his right. He holds his hat in his right hand, in adherence with prevailing contemporary social etiquette. His left hand lies inside his waistcoat, in a pose derived from classical sculpture which was well established in painting by Gainsborough's time, especially in England, where it was tantamount to a patriotic gesture (despite primarily being imported through French art) (Meyer 1995).

Technical examination of the Byams' portrait indicates that it did not originally include their daughter Selina, and that the couple's clothing was initially different: for instance, she wore a pink-red dress and a fabric hat, while he had a blue waistcoat and suit. So, in its first incarnation, the image would have been an example of the sub-genre of portraiture which represented promenading couples. This type of imagery was often used in celebrating marriage; indeed, the style of the fashion in which the Byams were presented suggests a date early in the 1760s.

Ozias Humphry, a fellow-artist who was in Bath from 1760 to 1764, described Gainsborough's practice during this period in his reminiscences (written several decades later): 'altho' his pictures were exactly like, and to the parties for whom they were painted and their Families highly satisfactory at the time, whilst the prevailing modes were daily seen, and the Friends approved and beloved in them; yet the satisfaction arising from this fixed Resemblance was lessening daily, as the fleeting Fashions varied and were changing from time to time' (Sloman 2002, p.57).

In the Byams' case, indeed, the later reworking of their picture was apparently an intervention aimed at updating the couple's costumes to accommodate developments in style, such as that

the colour blue had superseded red in women's dress trends. (Gainsborough, moreover, effectively incorporated the earlier colour-scheme into underlayers which complemented the new overpainting.) Additionally, Gainsborough introduced the Byams' child Selina into the group. She was the eldest of their four daughters; the other girls did not survive (the couple also had a son, George, who died prematurely in 1774) (Bath 2001, pp.20–21, 23–24).

The internal dimensions of Gainsborough's early 1760s studio in Bath are known, and at times over its lengthy gestation this sizeable image might have occupied a conspicuous position on the artist's walls (Bath 2002, p.55). In a letter of April 1766 the Revd John Penrose described a visit to 'the Pictures', singling out 'a fine portrait of a father, mother and child'. Since Penrose's family were staying very close to Gainsborough's studio, it seems very likely that this comment refers to his paintings, and in particular to the (revised) Byam Family, thus giving an approximate date by when the image's reconfiguration was completed (Sloman 2002, p.85). According to Penrose, the cost of painting the two adult figures alone was £120 (Bath 2001, p.21). The studio spectacle of Gainsborough's success in the difficult task of transforming the Byams' image without undermining the final product may well have constituted an advantageous advertisement to potential clients of the painter's prowess. SM

## 135
### Mrs Sheridan

1785–87
Oil on canvas, 220 × 154 cm
National Gallery of Art, Washington. Andrew W. Mellon Collection, 1937.1.92

PROVENANCE:  Mrs Edward Bouverie, a friend of the sitter, Delapré Abbey, Northampton;  by descent to General Everard Bouverie;  Baron Lionel de Rothschild, Gunnersbury, Middlesex, by 1873;  by descent to Victor, 3rd Baron Rothschild; sold by him to Duveen Brothers, London, c.1936–37; from their New York branch purchased by The A. W. Mellon Educational and Charitable Trust, Pittsburgh, 1937
EXHIBITED:  Gainsborough's studio, Schomberg House, Pall Mall, London, 1786;  for later exhibition history see Hayes 1992, pp.103–04
LITERATURE:  see Hayes 1992, p.106

This portrait has been identified with one described in 1785 by a friend of the artist, the journalist Henry Bate Dudley: 'Mr. Gainsborough is engaged on a portrait of Mrs. Sheridan; it is a full length. She is painted under the umbrage of a romantic tree, and the accompanying objects are descriptive of retirement. The likeness is powerful, and is enforced by a characteristic expression, which equals the animation of nature' (Morning Herald, 30 March 1785). Although there are no 'accompanying objects' in the final picture, Gainsborough is known to have made significant changes to the work. He included the piece in his 1786 exhibition at his studio at Schomberg House, Pall Mall, when Bate

Dudley wrote that 'Mrs. *Sheridan*'s portrait, is to assume an air more pastoral than at present it possesses, by the introduction of some lambs' (*Morning Herald*, 30 December 1786); they are now visible in the background. The sitter's sister-in-law Betsy, who also visited the painting at Gainsborough's 1786 show, noted: 'I am not delighted with that of Mrs Sheridan tho' he has alter'd the idea of making her a Peasant, which to me never appear'd judicious' (Sheridan 1960, p.80). The artist had also exhibited a full-length portrait of Mrs Sheridan at the Royal Academy in 1783, but this is thought to have been a distinct (now lost) work (London 1988, pp.76–77).

Gainsborough had known his sitter, Elizabeth Sheridan, *née* Linley (1754–1792), since her childhood, and painted her a number of times (as did his great rival Sir Joshua Reynolds). An object of much contemporary fascination on account of her singing talents and beauty, Miss Linley was described by one bishop as 'the connecting link between woman and angel' (Highfill et al. 1991, p.331). When she sang in London in 1773, Horace Walpole reported that the King 'ogles her as much as he dares to do in so holy a place as an oratorio' (Walpole 1937–82, vol.32, p.106).

She eventually married Richard Brinsley Sheridan in 1773, after they had eloped the year before. At that time, Gainsborough had noted: 'Miss Linley is walkd off sure enough with young Sheridan', just when 'I was just finishing her Picture for the Exhibition' (a reference to *The Linley Sisters*, portraying Elizabeth and her sister Mary, shown at the Royal Academy in 1772) (Hayes 2001, p.96). Sheridan soon put a stop to her professional career, writing to her father that 'your daughter's marriage' constituted 'quite as natural a period to your rights over her as her death' (Sheridan 1966, vol.1, p.80). Samuel Johnson approved Sheridan's stance, asking: 'Would not a gentleman be disgraced by having his wife singing publickly for hire? No, Sir, there can be no doubt here. I know not if I should not *prepare* myself for a publick singer, as readily as let my wife be one' (Boswell 1970, p.630). Nevertheless, Sheridan profited from his wife's talents in other ways: she was advertised to sing at 'private' subscription concerts, assisted in his stage productions, and later helped him to forge a political career (Aspden 2004, p.924). It has been remarked that 'between them they were irresistible to anyone who wanted to be regarded as fashionable' (O'Toole 1997, p.133). She was prominent among the leading Whig ladies who canvassed for Charles James Fox in the Westminster election in 1784. When Mrs Sheridan complained of feeling unwell in June 1785, her sister-in-law reflected: 'Indeed the life she leads would kill a horse, but she says one must do as other people do' (Sheridan 1960, p.49).

It has been observed that, although his sitter's life was 'at its most socially active' around the time of painting, Gainsborough chose, 'with his wild woodland setting, to express the other side of Elizabeth's character – the woman who wrote "God knows London has no charms for me" and who begged Sheridan "to let me have a little quiet home"' (London 1988, p.77). Indeed, she is pictured as 'so entirely in tune with nature that she seems almost to be absorbed by it' (London 2002B, p.268). Her costume 'has a transitory quality: it is a mere surface of natural colour and texture, insubstantial and mobile, which serves to extend her body into the landscape. The sitter is conceived of it in terms of incorporeal surfaces to an extent that suggests the picture's central theme is transience' (Asfour and Williamson 1999, p.220).

One transient element in the sitter's life was her husband's fidelity. Frances Burney wrote in 1779 that 'the *elegance* of Mrs. Sheridan's Beauty is unequaled by any I ever *saw* except Mrs. Crewes' (Burney 1988–2003, vol.3, p.226). Indeed, it was with the latter, a Whig hostess, that Sheridan conducted his first notable affair between the mid-1770s and the middle or late 1780s. By 1790 the Sheridans had all but separated. She also took a lover, Lord Edward Fitzgerald, bore his child in 1792, and died from tuberculosis soon after.  SM

# François Gérard

ROME, 1770 – PARIS, 1837

## 89
*Jean-Baptiste Isabey and His Daughter Alexandrine*

1795
Oil on canvas, 195 × 130 cm
Signed and dated lower left: *F. Gérard/1795*
Département des Peintures, Musée du Louvre, Paris, RF 4764.
Gift of Eugène Isabey, son and brother of the sitters, 1852

PROVENANCE: painted in return for Isabey's commission of Gérard's 1795 Salon entry, *Belisarius*; given to the Louvre by Eugène Isabey, son and brother of the sitters, 1852
EXHIBITED: Paris, Salon, 1796, no.194; Paris, 1849; Paris, 1913; Nancy, 1955, no.1; Paris, 1957–58, no.30; Montauban, 1967, no.251; Hamburg, 1977–78, no.292; Paris, 1989B; Montargis, 2005; Nancy and Malmaison/Bois-Préau, 2006, no.35
LITERATURE: Lenormant 1846–47, pp.30ff. and 35; Gérard 1852–57; Gérard 1867 (1886), p.2; Gérard Letters 1880; Paris, 1913, no.125, p.40; Osmond 1947; Taigny 1859, p.51; Latreille 1973; Sterling and Adhémar 1958–61, vol.2, p.34; Crow 1995, p.224, fig.149; Halliday 1998

Exhibited at the Salon of 1796, Gérard's portrait of his friend and fellow artist Jean-Baptiste Isabey (1767–1855), a virtuoso miniaturist, graphic artist, lithographer and watercolour painter, was greeted with immediate critical and public approbation. This was to prove a pivotal point in Gérard's career and defined him as the portrait artist of choice for decades to come, through Thermidor, the Directoire, Napoleon's reign and the Restoration. Gérard and Isabey were both part of an exclusive intellectual and social milieu, in the orbit of Madame de Staël, Chateaubriand and Madame Récamier. A charming and lively individual, Isabey hosted many sophisticated and cultured gatherings; one was recorded for posterity in Boilly's *A Reunion of Artists in Isabey's Studio* (cat.69).

Gérard's life-size portrait follows the seventeenth-century Netherlandish tradition of Van Dyck in its realistic depiction, sharp contours, and sober palette. Isabey and his young daughter Alexandrine (1791–1871) are seen in their apartments at the Louvre. Although private commissions were on the increase for Isabey, he still resided in relatively modest, simple lodgings. Entering the stone vestibule from the staircase behind, father and daughter are about to descend to the sunlit gardens glimpsed through the arch on the right. Isabey looks out to an unidentified point at the left, allowing a frontal view of his face. A great admirer of Sir Thomas Lawrence, Gérard conveys a degree of Anglophilia in the treatment of his subject. Debonair, svelte, with pleasing features, dark eyes and Byronic curls, the artist is elegantly dressed in a smart, dark short-coat. His elaborately arranged, high white cravat and his well-polished tasselled riding boots give the impression of a gentleman of leisure, and this is reinforced by the presence of a gun dog in the background, affectionately looking up at his master.

This highly personal image of a father and daughter – not a common pairing in family portraiture – emphasises the more central position of the child within the family unit in post-Enlightenment society. In 1790, at the height of the Reign of Terror, Isabey married Laurice de Saliennes, from Meudon. One of their three children, Alexandrine – who was to become Mme Cicéri – is shown in a fashionable, high-waisted full-length dress, wearing a delicate lace bonnet, her soft hair framing her round face. She shyly meets the gaze of the viewer, her fingers curled around her father's hand, which wraps around hers, denoting the close bond between parent and child.

Significantly, Gérard does not include the familiar emblems of Isabey's profession in this portrait, instead representing the artist as an English gentleman, 'defined, like an aristocrat, by progeny and sport rather than the tools of the trade' (Crow 1995, p. 224). The representation of the artist as a self-reliant citizen, cultured and politically aware, rather than as an artisan was a phenomenon of the post-revolutionary and nascent Directoire period (see also Drolling's *Michel Belot*, cat.64). The veritable deregulation of *ancien-régime* structures engendered a more commercially oriented, meritocratic artistic society, and a new clique of society portrait painters came to the fore. Simultaneously, as class barriers gave way, there were new means and a desire for privately commissioned portraits, preferably small or domestically scaled and inexpensive. Isabey's work was enormously successful in this new, egalitarian society, unhindered by the dogma of size, format and technique as dictated by the Académie Royale. Though generally still reliant on commissions for a living, artists – no longer codicillary dependants on a single patron's largesse, or the whim of a fickle court – were growing accustomed to being regarded as arbiters of taste and culture.

Isabey was born in Nancy (Lorraine) where he trained with Jean Girardet (died 1778), then the master miniaturist Jean-Baptiste Charles Claudot (1733–1805). Although a member of David's atelier after his arrival in Paris in 1785, scarcely any oil paintings appear in Isabey's output (see Basily-Calliminski 1909, p.27), and he did not exhibit any at the Salons. Like Gérard, Isabey avoided the expensive indentures of training in the traditional academic fashion. He capitalised on his prodigious talents in miniature painting and drawing, creating and satisfying the demand that grew for drawings *à la manière noire*, which lent themselves readily to engraving, and hence the thriving market for prints. Following his arrival in Paris, he was patronised by the Duc de Berry and his circle, an association which, during the zenith of revolutionary fervour, earned him the epithet 'the little court painter', and contemptuous remarks from David, such as: 'Tu n'es pas patriote' (Osmond 1947, pp.49, 59). However, a propitious meeting with the publisher of the biographies of the members of the Convention resulted in a commission to paint 228 portraits of Deputies and so, metamorphosing into Citoyen Isabey, the painter survived this perilous time. Then, fortuitously, through his pupil Hortense de Beauharnais, Isabey was introduced to Napoleonic patronage. From 1793, he exhibited regularly at the Salon, both miniatures and drawings, and, in 1794, his *manière noire*, first described as *manière anglaise* (Halliday 1998, note 3), captured the public's imagination. This style of drawing, effectively simulating the appearance of a mezzotint engraving, but worked from light to dark, using Conté's crayons (or 'crayons d'Isabey', as they came to be known), belonged more to the thriving, cross-Channel Anglo-French market for prints and engravings.

Gérard's smoothly naturalistic and engaging portrait of Isabey and his daughter was both a gesture of appreciation for Isabey's timely commission of Gérard's 1795 Salon entry, *Belisarius*, and a brilliant showcase of his talent for portraiture. Just as Isabey, with his democratic, Anglophile associations, transcended the internecine squabbles of the *ci-devant* Academicians, Gérard's success through three violent political regime changes attests to his own versatility, independence and identification with his friend Isabey as a self-made, modern citizen. cc

**31**
*Maria Laetitia Ramolino Bonaparte, 'Madame Mère'*

*c.*1802–04
Oil on canvas, 210.8 × 129.8 cm

Signed lower left: *fco Gerard*
National Gallery of Scotland, Edinburgh, NGS 2461.
Purchased with the aid of the NACF, 1988

PROVENANCE: collection of Jérôme, King of Westphalia, Kassel; received by Anatole Demidoff, possibly as part of the dowry of Jérôme's daughter, Mathilde, whom he married, 1840; Paul Demidoff's sale, San Donato, Florence, 15 March ff. 1880, no.960; Mme Asselin, Paris; Eugène Schneider, 1900, and thence by descent; Nouveau Drouot, Paris, 17 December 1983, lot 12; bought Herner/Aaron; Heim Gallery, London, from whom purchased by the National Galleries of Scotland, with the aid of the National Art Collections Fund, 1988
EXHIBITED: Museo San Martino, Elba, 1870; Paris, 1895, no.520; Paris, 1900, no.315 (lent Schneider); Paris, 1945, no.49; Houston, 1986, no.24; Tokyo, Miyazaki and Yokohama, 1993, no.19; New Orleans, 2003, no.109
LITERATURE: Lenormant 1846–47, p.182; Gérard 1852–57, vol.1; Gérard 1867, p.2; Gérard Letters 1880; Latreille 1973; Paris 1974A, pp.431–39; Clarke 1989, pp.139–41; New York 1992

In 1802, during the early Consular period, Napoleon required aggrandising representations of himself and his family to consolidate and legitimise his rapid ascendancy. François Gérard produced six versions of *Madame Mère*, and this portrait was triumphantly successful as a propagandistic image – a narrative of sovereign rule – which sitter, patron and artist colluded to convey. *Maria Laetitia Ramolino Bonaparte, 'Madame Mère'* is depicted in a traditional aristocratic pose, based on the fourth-century Roman *Seated Agrippina* (Capitoline Museum, Rome). Smiling at the viewer, she is posed in a highly structured, geometric composition; yet Gérard combines a fresh naturalism, complex tonalities and sympathetic characterisation to enliven an otherwise staged, rhetorical format. The bust of her son, Napoleon, in his military Consular uniform, is loosely based on the widely reproduced sculpture by Louis-Simon Boizot. His face is youthful, the shoulders and torso vital, but the 'blind' eyes – in the sculptural 'ideal' manner – imply timelessness and the weight of history, lending the figure gravitas beyond his years. *Madame Mère* is a superlative example of Gérard's portraiture, and Laetitia herself has an air of ease that transcends the stock 'court portrait.'

Gérard was born in Rome, where his parents were in domestic service to Cardinal de Bernis, French Ambassador to the Papal States and a confidante of Madame de Pompadour. Gérard and his family moved back to France in 1782. After studying with David, the young painter established his reputation at the Salon of 1796 with a portrait of Jean-Baptiste Isabey which was acclaimed for its elegant veracity and exquisite finish. By 1800, Gérard had become the most celebrated portrait painter in Paris. He was charming and intellectually gifted, and his atelier came to be a glittering and select nexus for eminent intellectuals, scientists and notable society figures of the day, such as Juliette Récamier, Chateaubriand, and the Prussian naturalist Alexander von Humboldt. A courtier of the calibre of Talleyrand, Gérard adapted to the vicissitudes of turn-of-the-century political life with circumspection and aplomb, and progressed

smoothly from being a leading painter of Napoleonic contemporary history to the position of First Painter to the King after the Bourbon Restoration in 1814.

The portrait's sitter, Maria Laetitia (1770–1837), *née* Ramolino, was born in Ajaccio, Corsica, to an Italian family of minor nobility. She married Carlo Buonaparte in 1764. At the end of the Seven Years War, in 1769 (the year Corsica was annexed following the insurrection against her prior oppressor Genoa), Laetitia's second son, Napoleon, was born. A firm and ambitious matriarch of the large *casa Buonaparte*, she enlisted the aid of the French governor of Corsica, the Comte de Marbeuf – with whom she was rumoured to have had an affair – to obtain a scholarship for Napoleon to attend the aristocratic military school at Brienne, in which he excelled.

In this quasi-double portrait, Gérard employs familiar tropes to suggest venerable lineage in a royal portrait: an opulent setting, majestic architectural elements, and appropriate physiognomic and iconographic references. Situated in a luxurious interior, Madame Mère wears a white satin gown, with a rich, forest-green velvet pelisse. Her gold-embossed gossamer veil, held on by a jewelled diadem, expands the pale light which centralises the focus on her torso and face. Her countenance and bearing is one of gentle imperiousness, as she slightly inclines her head to the viewer in a regal manner. However, Gérard offsets any aloofness or arrogance which might alienate the public, capturing maternal benevolence in her demeanour. The pristine, gloved hands resting on her lap hold a handkerchief, suggesting recent tears from reading the letter she has just laid down on the table, perhaps having learnt of her son's heroic exploits far away on his nascent Imperial campaigns.

Madame Mère sits on a fashionable Directoire chair with a heavily tasselled dark-gold silk taffeta curtain cascading behind her. The burnished colour is echoed in the stars on the gauze veil, the earrings, the intricate brocade edging of the pelisse, and the hem of her dress. The monochrome shades of the grey tablecloth, interspersed with the warmer shot-marble of the pedestal and the cool stone hue of the bust above, are balanced by the lushness of the green velvet, the creamy white dress and the opulence of the red velvet. Gérard's colour scheme softens the strict planar arrangement of the composition, creating rich visual depth.

Outside the window, in waning light, a small picturesque landscape forms in the architecture of the Tuileries. However, this recalls tensions in the relationship between mother and son. The apartments in the Tuileries, formerly the residence of Marie-Antoinette and Louis XVI, were occupied by Napoleon and some of his family. But Laetitia preferred to live with her eldest son Joseph and his wife Julie in the Rue du Rocher. Though splendidly attired here, she had habitually worn black, as a dowager Queen, since her husband's death. She was so dissatisfied with the title that Napoleon had conferred upon her – 'Son Altesse Impériale, Madame la Mère de l'Empereur' – that she did not attend his coronation. When speaking she favoured her native Corsican-Italian to French, and retained her provincial accent. Memories of financial struggle after Napoleon's father's death never left her and, even though she could enjoy her son's largesse – her jewellery collection was renowned – she was far from a sophisticate, remaining financially prudent to the point of parsimony; all of this embarrassed Napoleon. Furthermore, she was well known to be barely literate, a fact belied by Gérard's inclusion of an open letter on the table beside her. Though pragmatic in many ways, she displayed the ego of her progeny, inciting the Hundred Days when, on Elba, she said to Napoleon: 'Fulfil your destiny … you were not meant to die on this island.' After his defeat at the Battle of Waterloo, she retired to Rome under the protection of the Pope, with her half-brother Cardinal Fesch. It is likely that her grandchild Mathilde brought the portrait as part of her dowry when she married Anatole Demidoff, a mining heir from the Urals, in 1840 and moved to his villa, San Donato, in Florence. cc

## 140
### Thérésia Cabarrus, Comtesse de Caraman

c.1805
Oil on canvas, 212 × 127 cm
Musée Carnavalet-Histoire de Paris, Paris, P.2738

PROVENANCE: in the ownership of the sitter's descendants at the Château de Chimay; bought by the Musée Carnavalet, 2001
EXHIBITED: Paris, 2005A, no.84
LITERATURE: Lenormant 1846–47

Thérésia Cabarrus (1773–1835), better known as Madame Tallien, was (with Joséphine de Beauharnais and Juliette Récamier) one of the three most celebrated merveilleuses – women who, thanks to their wit, beauty and elegance, came to symbolise the period of moral freedom that followed the Terror. The daughter of a wealthy banker, she married in 1794 her second husband Jean-Lambert Tallien, the Commissary of the National Convention, who had played a decisive role in the fall of Maximilien Robespierre in the same year. Madame Tallien, nicknamed the 'Queen of Paris', reigned over the most brilliant salon in the French capital after 9 Thermidor (27 July 1794, the revolt against the excesses of the Reign of Terror) and struck up a friendship with Joséphine. She was the mistress of the politician Paul Barras, then of the rich financier Gabriel Ouvrard; having divorced Tallien in 1802, she married in 1805 François-Joseph-Philippe de Riquet, Comte de Caraman, soon to become Prince de Chimay.

Although we have no information about when this painting was commissioned, the wedding ring worn ostentatiously by Thérésia suggests that it might have been painted soon after her marriage, perhaps even to celebrate it. François Gérard, who had recently painted his famous portrait of Madame Récamier (1802–05; Musée Carnavalet-Histoire de Paris, Paris), preferred by the beautiful Juliette to the painting left unfinished by David (Louvre, Paris), was then at the peak of his celebrity. The portrait of Thérésia Cabarrus differs in spirit from the portrait of the other merveilleuse, Madame Récamier, demonstrating the skill with which Gérard could adapt his style to the personality of his sitter. In the latter portrait he uses a very precise line, neoclassical décor and a serpentine pose to convey Juliette's pure and indefinable beauty; in the present portrait he depicts Thérésia Cabarrus climbing the stairs leading to a French window – like the 'femme d'action' she was. With this movement he also clears the air of any whiff of scandal that might linger around the name of the former Madame Tallien in favour of the image of a married woman, the new Comtesse de Caraman.

Gérard is returning here to the prototype that gave him such success at the Salon of 1796: Isabey and His Daughter (Louvre, Paris). Post-revolutionary society developed in such a way as to democratise the full-length, full-sized portrait, which had traditionally been reserved for the royal family in particular. The emergence of the new formula under the Directoire and the Consulate, when it became associated with striking female personalities such as Joséphine, Madame Tallien and Madame Récamier, was probably stimulated by the cultural eminence achieved by women during this period. By wearing décolleté gowns, as here, and white, sometimes transparent dresses, they asserted the importance of their bodies as part of their identity. A portrait bust was no longer adequate for the depiction of a merveilleuse.

Gérard was quick to understand this and soon became the specialist in the genre; he was strongly influenced by Van Dyck. In the case of Thérésia Cabarrus, Comtesse de Caraman, this northern reference is obviously coupled with an English influence (also attributable to Flemish painting). The portrait is an action, rather than a posed, portrait. The sitter is depicted as if she were returning from a walk in the gardens of her country property. Walking was the aristocratic activity par excellence, linked to the idea of leisure and land ownership; Reynolds had contrived to make it a recurrent theme in English female portraiture (cat. 25).

Gérard reinterprets the formula in a very original manner, however, by presenting a front view of his sitter. Rather than distancing the spectator with the idea of the 'passing model', he proposes a direct confrontation. The symbolic and social value of the code gives way to the evocation of the sitter's personality. In addition, the traditional accessories of the ceremonial portrait are reinterpreted in a very natural way: the large curtain has a genuine function and the column has become the jamb of the French doors.

Gérard was to reuse the same layout of the accessories in his portrait of Queen Hortense and Her Son, the Prince Royal (Château de Fontainebleau). In order to enhance the intimate dimension of this portrait, Gérard has turned the basic principles of the aristocratic portrait upside down. The relationship between the exterior and the interior, frequently only hinted at by a balustrade, generally moves from inside out; in this portrait, however, Thérésia Cabarrus is moving towards the interior of the house, where the hypothetical visitor awaits her, thus dramatising the visitor's presence. Painted for private display, the portrait of Thérésia Cabarrus is intended to convey the impression that the mistress of the house is bursting in at the back door.

This impression is increased by the artist's fondness for back lighting, which here adds dynamism and an impression of naturalness to the painting. At the beginning, Gérard considered reusing the idea he had developed in the portrait of Madame Barbier-Walbonne (1798; Louvre, Paris), in which the figure stands out against a back-lit curtain, placed behind the upper part of her body. A wash drawing with some handwritten notes gives an idea of the original composition (sold at Sotheby's, London, on 27 November 1986 in the 'Nineteenth-Century European Drawings' sale, no.64): we see that the artist deliberately uses light and shade to provoke an effect of surprise, emphasising his painterly skill. In the final painting, however, Gérard has reversed these elements in a highly original manner. The dark foreground has the light behind it, and the figure is seen against a marvellous blue sky rather than against a dark background. The light seems to illuminate Thérésia Cabarrus, who is seen in the middle ground wearing a sumptuous and diaphanous white dress. The way the light is arranged lends the figure the appearance of an apparition. The mild distortion of the sitter's body, slightly too tall in relation to her head, enhances her physical presence. The range of colours used ensures the unity of the whole: it is based on contrasting white (gown, walls, flowers) with orange-red (curtain, shawl, flowers). Madame de Caraman wears a garland of anemones on her head, a detail that is repeated in the portrait painted by Chassériau of her granddaughter forty-three years later (Mademoiselle Cabarrus, 1848; Musée des Beaux-Arts, Quimper).

Although the portrait of Thérésia Cabarrus may lack the formal purity and extravagant elegance of the much more posed portrait of Madame Récamier, it nevertheless stands out as one of the most ambitious examples of the new portraiture of women that began to develop around 1800. This new portraiture was based on an innovatory combination of a large format with an intimate dimension, often (as in Prud'hon's portrait of Joséphine) marked by a touch of melancholy. The originality of Thérésia Cabarru, Comtesse de Caraman lies in the absence of melancholy, replaced here in favour of a dynamic that plays on the illusionism of the genre. SA

# Théodore Géricault

ROUEN, 1791 – PARIS, 1824

## 109
*Alfred and Elisabeth Dedreux*

1816–17
Oil on canvas, 99 × 80 cm
Collection of Yves Saint-Laurent and Pierre Bergé

PROVENANCE: exhibited in *Portraits du siècle (1783–1883)*,
Ecole des Beaux-Arts, Paris, in 1883; acquired by Mme Becq de
Fouquières under the title *Alfred de Dreux and His Sister*; by descent
to Becq de Fouquières; sold Hôtel Drouais, Paris, 8 May 1925;
bought M. Brame (62,000 francs); sold Gallery Georges Petit,
Paris, 11–12 May 1931, no.17 (118,000 francs) to 'Baron de X'
(Baron de Forest); at exhibition *Gros, Géricault and Delacroix*, 1954,
mentioned as being in 'Collection Becq de Fouqui Fouquières
and Vicomte Beuret'; collection of Pierre Bergé and Yves Saint-
Laurent, Paris
EXHIBITED: Ecole des Beaux-Arts, Paris, 1883, no.105; Galerie
Charpentier, Paris, 1923, no.210; Paris, 1924, no.249; Galerie
Bernheim-Jeune, Paris, 1954, no.31; Galerie Schmit, Paris, 1974,
no.25, col. repr.; Musée des Beaux-Arts de Lyon, 2006
LITERATURE: Dimier 1914, p.57; Flament 1921, p.158, repr.;
'Revue des ventes de mai', in *Le Figaro artistique*, 4 June 1925, p.539;
'Le Carnet d'un curieux', in *La Renaissance de l'Art français*, July 1925,
p.331; 'A propos d'Alfred de Dreux', in *Beaux-Arts*, 15 June 1929,
p.24; Eitner 1959, p.124, note 7; Eitner 1960, p.32; Lem 1963,
p.87, no.13 bis, pl.V; Los Angeles 1971, no.23; Grunchec 1978,
p.105, no.116; Rome 1979, p.226; Bazin 1987, vol.5 (1992), p.238,
no.1723; Paris 1991, p.110, repr., no.363, cited in no.126;
Lyons 2006, pp.114–18

Commissioned portraits are rare in Théodore
Géricault's *oeuvre* and those identified are
predominantly of Géricault's family and personal
confidants. Alfred and Elisabeth Dedreux were the
children of the architect Pierre-Anne Dedreux-
Dorcy, brother of the Parisian artist Pierre-Joseph
Dedreux-Dorcy (1789–1874), who was Géricault's
closest friend during his short and turbulent life.
There is some uncertainty about the date of this
unsigned and undated double portrait, but it is
thought to have been painted some time around
Géricault's seminal 1817 trip to Italy. It is similar
to *Alfred Dedreux Seated in a Landscape* (1818;
Metropolitan Museum of Art, New York),
and the recently discovered full-length *Elisabeth
Dedreux Standing in a Landscape* (1817–18; Private
collection, Paris), which exemplify the robust,
heavily contoured and highly artificial 'antique
manner' that Géricault developed during his self-
imposed study of the Old Masters at the Louvre
from around 1811 to 1815. Then, inspired by
Michelangelo – before whose works he 'trembled'
in Rome – and events such as the riderless Barbari
horse-race on the Corso in that city, he rejoiced in
the expressive power of the nude and returned to
Paris in the autumn 1817 with a greater, if still not
fully developed, mastery of the human form.
Indicative of this period, *Alfred and Elisabeth Dedreux*,
with their glossy hair and knowing eyes, contains
passages of compelling, haunting realism alongside
a weakness in underlying anatomy.

As a student of first Carle Vernet, then Pierre
Guérin – who marvelled at his non-conformist and
erstwhile pupil having 'the stuff of three or four
painters in him' – Géricault resisted an academic
education. A privileged only child, he was fortunate
to have an independent income from 1808.
As a result, he was not obliged to standardise
his style to the academic norm, nor submit to
courting portrait commissions, state patronage
or the illustrative work on which other painters
had to rely in order to earn their living. Impulsive
and restive, he lasted barely six months in the
structured, rigorous atelier of Guérin, which was
based on that of David. However, setting up his
easel in the Louvre before paintings by Rembrandt,
Van Dyck, Rubens, Pier Francesco Mola, Titian
and Salvator Rosa crystallised his precocious talents
and he determined to master the classical style,
developing a singular 'antique manner'
characterised by sharp contrasts and
voluminous forms.

The subjects of this portrait are set in a
barren, crepuscular landscape, and there are few
topographical features to distract the viewer.
Elisabeth is centralised in the composition, but
her elder brother Alfred (who was born two years
earlier than his sibling, in 1810) dominates. He
rests his left hand on the rock to support his
weight, appearing to proffer his sister, as if he were
introducing her formally. Géricault ensures that the
entire focus is on the physiognomy of the children.
The realistic detail of Elisabeth's face contrasts
with her cursorily finished hem, pantaloons and
barely sketched left foot. The Dedreux children's
pale, alabaster skin radiates from the canvas to
relieve the darkness of the twilight hour, as does
the thick milky-white colour of Elisabeth's simple
Empire-style dress, which is picked up in Alfred's
shirt-collar, and, further down the canvas, in his
stockings. With entwined arms, the children gaze
out of the composition, but remain a hermetically
sealed unit, oblivious to the viewer. They are near-
replicas of each other, their indivisibility reinforced
by their overlapping bodies. Their legs and feet
form an X-shape, further emphasising their
intimate, almost symbiotic relationship in a likeness
that gives a precocious, alien quality to both
subjects in their mutual self-absorption.

Géricault's 'antique manner' consists of a
geometric approach to anatomy which, rather than
being linear, relies upon cylindrical forms, such as
the rounded contours of Alfred's head and arms.
Nonetheless, he painted the boy's body in a strange,
foreshortened position, and his feet appear small
and boneless in relation to his larger, detailed head.
There is little sense of the child's physicality, of
bone and tissue. The existence of a preparatory
sketch for the double portrait, *D'Alfred et Elise
Dedreux* (Louvre, Paris) suggests that Géricault did
attempt to capture anatomical form. However, in
this too Alfred's outstretched left leg is shapeless
and oddly proportioned. In the small pencil
drawing, the composition is pyramidal, with
Elisabeth also seated on the rock, turning her
head to face her brother. Alfred's beige jacket has
a defined row of military-style gilt buttons, but
the treatment of the rocks and the shading of the
figures and background are all realised in quick,
expressive, painterly lines and subtle gradations of
shade. The finished oil portrait is less spontaneous,
yet the sensuous, textural quality of the folds and
creases of Alfred's coat and the orb of Elisabeth's
sleeve are evidence of Géricault's prodigious talents
for another technique: modelling in clay. Despite
the sometimes problematic rendering of volume,
the children have a sculptural quality and a feeling
of monumentality which presages the powerful,
heroic eloquence of *The Raft of the Medusa* (1819;
Louvre, Paris), which the artist was soon to begin.

In *Alfred and Elisabeth Dedreux*, Géricault applied
a unique and particular 'child-portrait' strategy,
which reappears in his portrait of Louise, the
eight-year old daughter of his friend, Horace
Vernet (1822; Louvre, Paris). In this later image
Géricault 'reverted' to stocky, Uccello-like forms
in which colour, texture and body mass diminish
in significance. This same year he was producing
the technically brilliant and penetrating portraits
of the monomanias manifested in the anonymous
patients of the innovative psychiatrist J.-E.-D.
Esquirol (see fig.29). A mercurial, exploratory
virtuoso, Géricault was not motivated to create
a signature manner. His multifarious style is
unsurprising for an autodidactic artist who
strenuously continues to defy categorisation. CC

# Francisco de Goya y Lucientes

FUENDETODOS, SARAGOSSA, 1746 – BORDEAUX, 1828

## 17
*Don José Moñino y Redondo I, Conde de Floridablanca*

1783
Oil on canvas, 260 × 166 cm
Signed lower left, on the piece of paper at the artist's feet:
*Señor / Frant° Goya*
Colección Banco de España, Madrid

PROVENANCE: by descent to the Marquesa de Martorell y
Pontejos; later passed to the Conde de Miraflores y Marqués
de Villanueva de Valdueza; acquired by the Banco Urquijo,
Madrid; passed to the Banco Central Hispano, Madrid;
later sold to the Banco de España, Madrid
EXHIBITED: Madrid, 1900, no.93; Madrid, 1928, no.4;
Madrid, 1946, no.45; Granada, 1955, no.87; Madrid, 1961,
no.XXIV; Madrid, 1983, no.3; Brussels, 1985, no.3; Madrid,
1988, no.4; Gijón, 1998, p.146; Washington, 1998, unnumbered;
Frankfurt, 1999, no.99; Saragossa, 2002, unnumbered
LITERATURE: Pérez Sánchez 1988; Tomlinson 1989, pp.74, 75;
Morales y Marín 1994, pp.173, 174, no.120

This portrait of the powerful statesman Don José
Moñino y Redondo I (1728–1808), whom Charles
III appointed to various high offices during his
reign, has a key place in Goya's production, and is
undoubtedly one of the artist's first portraits to be
both spectacular in its conception and deliberately

complex in its composition. Goya was confident that his subject's political importance and influence at court would open doors for him and enable him to establish himself as an artist in official circles in Madrid. He alluded to these hopes in a letter to his friend Zapater on 26 April 1783.

Goya represents himself in the portrait, in a respectful pose, offering Floridablanca a painting which, it has been suggested, is a sketch for a canvas commissioned at precisely this period by Floridablanca for the church of San Francisco el Grande. However, it is now thought that this cannot be the case, since the two outlines are not the same.

The subject of Goya's portrait was an important figure in Spanish political life in the reign of Charles III and one of the most influential forces in Spanish Enlightenment thought. Born in Murcia, he studied law and was appointed public prosecutor for the Council of Castile from 1756. He was responsible for a number of important reports and in 1766 was nominated Procurator of Castile. He served as Spanish ambassador in Rome in 1773, and was Charles III's Prime Minister from 1777, maintaining all his influence in the final years of the king's reign. During the reign of Charles IV he continued to be a powerful political figure, first as Minister of State and then Prime Minister between 1788 and 1792, in which position he had to confront the difficult situation created by the French Revolution, to which he was violently opposed. The outright enmity between Manuel de Godoy, the royal favourite, and Queen María Luisa caused Floridablanca's downfall in 1792 and his exile to Pamplona. He was tried, acquitted, but remained in retirement on his Murcia estates, until the French invasion in 1808 caused him to re-enter public life. He was nominated Chief of the Central Junta, with the title of Royal Highness and honours of Infante of Spain, in the face of the invaders. He was not to exercise this office for long, as he died a few months later.

The title Conde de Floridablanca was granted to him by Charles III in 1773 as a result of his important role in the negotiations that led to the expulsion of the Society of Jesus from the vast territories of the Spanish empire. Floridablanca was a key figure in the years during which the Enlightenment spirit held most sway in Spain. Deeply concerned with the economic regeneration of the country, the development of industry and trade, and with the protection of the arts, he especially distinguished himself in matters of agriculture and irrigation, tackling important hydraulic works involving marshes and canals.

Goya's painting can be considered an allegory of good government, within an iconographic tradition that was prevalent in his own time and had been in vogue since the end of the Middle Ages. The portrait of Charles III, hanging at the top of Goya's composition, presides over those portrayed and gives the King the role of

protagonist. Thus the Conde de Floridablanca, who is surrounded by a series of props alluding to his functions, is portrayed as the intelligent instrument of royal rule.

Apart from the monumental clock (a symbol of the sovereign or ruler), the plans on the table, one of which has fallen onto the floor, have an equally important symbolic significance. The plan on the floor has the clear inscription 'Plano del Canal de Aragón / Al Excmo. Señor Floridablanca, año 1783' ('Plan of the Aragon Canal / for the Most Excellent Señor Floridablanca, 1783'). Indeed, at the time the portrait was painted, Floridablanca, by royal command, had taken over the expenses of this project, on behalf of the Secretariat of State. This vitally important work aroused much admiration at the time, so it is not surprising that it should have such a significant place in the portrait.

It has been suggested that the other figure, in the background, is either Francisco Sabatini or Ventura Rodríguez; both architects were involved in Floridablanca's initiatives. However, it may be someone more directly linked to the Aragon Canal, or perhaps the architect Julián Sánchez Bort, a military engineer who directed the canal's final works programme and assumed control of it from 1776, a post he occupied when the portrait was painted.

The protection that Floridablanca gave to the arts is also expressed by the presence of the *Práctica de la Pintura* (*The Practice of Painting*) by the painter and writer Palomino; its title is clearly visible on one of the books scattered on the floor.

Various workshop replicas and copies of the portrait exist, showing the isolated figure of Floridablanca in the sacristy of the church of San Isidro, Madrid; the Enseñanza Media de Murcia; and, in the Prado Museum, on deposit in the Presidency of the Government. A lithograph of the whole composition was made by F. Bellay. JJL

## 21

*Don Vicente Joaquín Osorio de Moscoso y Guzmán, XI Conde de Altamira*

1786
Oil on canvas, 177 × 108 cm
Colección Banco de España, Madrid

PROVENANCE: acquired by the Banco de San Carlos (former name of the Banco de España), Madrid, from the painter, 1787, as the result of a commission
EXHIBITED: Madrid, 1900, no.24; Granada, 1955, no.95; Munich, 1958, no.73; Madrid, 1961, no.24; London, 1963, no.63; Madrid, 1982, no.11; Madrid, 1983, no.7; Brussels, 1985, no.7; Madrid, 1988, no.374; Stockholm, 1994, no.11; Madrid, 1996, no.69
LITERATURE: Pérez Sánchez 1988; Morales y Marín 1994; Madrid 1996; Glendinning and Medrano 2005

The title Conde de Altamira, one of the oldest in the kingdom of Castile, was granted by King Henry IV in 1475 to Señor de Altamira y Moscoso. His descendant, the eleventh count, was fifteen

times Grandee of Spain and a Knight of the Order of Charles III, whose badge and sash he wears in this portrait. He came from one of the most aristocratic families of Galicia. Beside him on the table a costly silver writing set with two quill pens and various documents attest to his administrative functions.

The work belongs to the group of paintings made by Goya from April 1785 for the Banco de San Carlos, today the Banco de España; it has remained in the bank's collection ever since. Also in the series are portraits of Charles III, José de Toro y Zambrano, Francisco Javier de Larrumbe, the Marqués de Tolosa and the Conde de Cabarrús (Pérez Sánchez 1988). In the portrait under discussion, a balance between the aesthetic tendencies of Mengs and the traditional formulations of Velázquez (Glendinning and Medrano 2005) is in evidence.

One of the first directors of the bank, who belonged to it as a representative of the nobility, Don Vicente Joaquín Osorio de Moscoso y Guzmán (1756–1816) held many titles: XVI Marqués de Astorga; XVII Conde de Cabra; VIII Duque de Sanlúcar la Mayor; VI de Medina de las Torres; VI de Atrisco; XIV de Sessa; XII de Terranova, XII de Santangelo, among others. He was Alférez Mayor (a position similar to Lord Lieutenant) of Castile and of the City of Madrid, a member of the Real Academia de Bellas Artes de San Fernando from 1796 and a councillor of the Academia in 1815. He was one of the most wealthy men of his day. Although popular rumour has it that the palatial mansion in Madrid which he commissioned from Ventura Rodríguez – a part survives in the Calle de la Flor Alta – was never finished because King Charles III forced him to moderate his plans, fearing that the building would surpass the royal palace in its dimensions and splendour, this is hard to maintain in the light of the known historical facts and the architectural remains visible today.

The count's art collection was very important and he possessed one of the most extensive galleries, full of first-rate paintings, in all Spain. Only the royal collection itself could compare with it. He went on to commission various other portraits from Goya: his wife María Ignacia Álvarez de Toledo with their daughter María Antonia in her arms (Lehman Collection, Metropolitan Museum of Art, New York); his son Vicente, his heir (Private collection, New York); and his son Manuel, Señor de Ginés (Metropolitan Museum of Art, New York). Of exceptional quality, these are among the artist's best portraits, especially the last, particularly for their portrayal of children (see New York 1995).

Curiously, although it has many positive features, the present portrait does not have the charm of those mentioned above. They were intended for an everyday, private environment, whereas the work under discussion was designed for an official public centre. The composition is unfortunate because of the placement of the sitter by a table that is too high for him (the count was not tall). Nevertheless, Goya showed the model as he was: a short man who looked even shorter against the furniture around him, together with the awkward positioning of his arms and legs and the stiff way in which his coat-tails fall. Lady Holland remarked rather maliciously that the count was 'noted for his short stature' and Lord Holland added that he was 'the smallest man I have ever seen in society and tinier than any of the dwarfs that people pay to see'.

It is probable that the idea for the composition was suggested by the portrait of the young Ferdinand IV of Naples by Mengs (Prado Museum, Madrid), which then belonged to the royal collection. Or it may have been inspired by other portraits of children, including some by Goya himself, in which he emphasises their small stature by putting them beside furniture or other paraphernalia of daily life. However, the image of the count, with his tiny, perhaps deformed figure, or simply short stature, cannot have offended the sitter, since in the following year he commissioned Goya to paint the portraits of his family listed above.

Colour is used with great refinement, the objects on the writing desk are depicted with fine precision, and the minutiae of the fabrics and embroidery show the artist's mastery of detail. Goya was paid on 29 January 1787, at the same time as he received payment for his portraits of Charles III and the Marqués de Tolosa, mentioned above, which also still belong to the collection of the Banco de España. According to the archives, the artist received 10,000 reales, a considerable sum which indicated the high value placed on the work and the esteem in which Goya was held. JJL

## 102
### Don Manuel Osorio Manrique de Zuñiga

1788
Oil on canvas, 127 × 101.6 cm
Signed on the card held in the magpie's beak: *Dn Franco Goya*
Inscription: *EL Sr. Dn. MANVEL MANRRIQUE DE ZUNIGA Sr DE GINES NACIO EN ABR A II DE 1784*
Lent by The Metropolitan Museum of Art, New York. The Jules Bache Collection, 1949 (49.7.41)

PROVENANCE: Altamira collection, Madrid; Private collection, until 1878; sold in Paris, 30 March 1878, no.17; M. and Mme Henri Bernstein, Paris, by 1903–25; E. Jonas collection, Paris [not mentioned by Met]; Duveen Brothers, New York, 1925–27; Jules Bache Collection, New York, until his death in 1944; given to The Metropolitan Museum of Art, New York, 1949
EXHIBITED: New York, 1995, p.67; Lille and Philadelphia, 1998–99, no.19 (J.-L. Augé)
LITERATURE: Baticle 1992, p.132; Tomlinson 1994, pp.64–65; Baticle 1995, p.91; Augé 1996, pp.44–45

Goya often painted children. The portrait of Don Manuel Osorio is one of his most successful works in this genre, not only because of its formal qualities but also because of the complex iconography of the painting, which still has to reveal all of its secrets. When he painted the picture, Goya was at the peak of his career. He was appointed deputy director of painting at the Real Academia de Bellas Artes de San Fernando in 1785, and painter to the King in 1786. The choice of sitter for this painting shows that he was by this time well integrated at court; he was the favourite artist of the Marquis de Jovellanos and of the Osuna family. Don Manuel Osorio Manrique de Zuñiga belonged to one of the most prestigious families in Spain: the Counts of Altamira. He was the son of Don Vicente de Moscoso Alvarez de Toledo, lieutenant general of the province of Castille and the city of Madrid, and of Maria Ignacia Alvarez de Toledo, both already painted by Goya, as his elder brother, Don Osorio de Moscoso, had been.

The originality of this painting in the Metropolitan Museum of Art, New York, can be ascribed to its allegorical dimension, which transforms the portrait into a kind of puzzle. Don Manuel Osorio is portrayed upright, wearing an extravagant red outfit that stands out against a grey-green background. As he usually does, the artist heightens the impact of his colour scheme with luminous greys (the belt) and whites (the lace collar). He uses the powerful chromatic effects of the period, adding his own love of luxurious detail to the painting of the lace collar and the subtle movement of the waistband.

The child is holding on to a magpie that carries in its beak the painter's calling card with his signature. Behind the bird, three cats with wide eyes stand guard, watching it closely; on the right a green cage holds some other birds. The apparent simplicity of the conventional mixture of children and animals takes on a strange dimension here, hinting at various layers of meaning.

The critic Jean-Louis Augé has suggested that the painting contains Christian symbolism. In his view, the cats represent cunning and freedom, but also the forces of evil – as their predatory attitude might suggest. The object of their interest, the magpie, is generally associated with premature death. The cage contains goldfinches, symbols since the Renaissance of the Christ Child. This allusion would transform the young Don Manuel Osorio into a new Emmanuel. A simpler interpretation could be that the birds and cats allude to freedom, the lead and cage to servitude, the birds to life and the magpie to death; this could be an evocation of the narrow path between good and evil that the child must follow during his lifetime.

As a secondary theme, finally, should the calling card bearing the signature not be read as an allusion to the status of the artist himself, held captive by his patrons and closely watched by malevolent critics? In spite of appearances, therefore, the painting could be an expression of Goya's natural pessimism. AA

## 63
### Don José Alvarez de Toledo y Gonzaga, XIII Duque de Alba and XI Marqués de Villafranca

1795
Oil on canvas, 195 × 115 cm (with later additions, 195 × 120 cm)
Museo Nacional del Prado, Madrid

PROVENANCE: the dukes of Alba; the marquises of Villafranca, Madrid, c.1801; Condesa de Niebla, Madrid, 1917; bequeathed to the Museo Nacional del Prado by Alonso Álvarez de Toledo, Conde de Niebla and Marqués de los Vélez, 1926
EXHIBITED: Geneva, 1939, no.5; Barcelona, 1977, no.24; Bordeaux, Madrid and Paris, 1979, no.26 (French edition) and no.22 (Spanish edition); Eisenstadt, 1982, no.414; Madrid, 1996, no.84; Berlin and Vienna, 2005
LITERATURE: Gassier and Wilson 1970

Born in 1758, Don José Alvarez de Toledo y Gonzaga belonged to the two most illustrious families of the Spanish aristocracy. He was the eldest son of the Marqués de Villafranca and, at his marriage in 1775, to the only heiress of the dukedom of Alba, María Teresa Pilar Cayetana de Silva, he undertook to adopt his wife's title in first place, the highest ranking after the King. Because of the importance of his family, the duke was Gentleman of the Bedchamber to Charles IV, while the latter was still Príncipe de Asturias, and in 1789 he became Grand Chancellor and Registrador Mayor (Chief Registrar) of the Indies, with a voice and a vote on the Council. In 1798 he received the Order of Charles III and in 1791 the Golden Fleece. As well as these royal honours, Alba had others of a different nature: he was Counsellor of the Real Academia de Bellas Artes de San Fernando, Madrid, Chief Equerry of the Maestranza of Córdoba, and Chief Brother of the Cofradía de la Santa y Real Hermandad del Refugio y Piedad, Madrid. Alba exemplified the Spanish nobleman of the Enlightenment and was a member of various enlightened societies: of the Reales Sociedades Económicas de Amigos del País, of the Vascongada Society, the first to be set up in Spain, from March 1777, and of the Seville Society from January 1778.

Alba's reputation and his contacts with the most advanced politicians of his time, such as Gaspar Melchor de Jovellanos, together with his high aristocratic position, were probably what made Alejandro Malaspina, the famous navigator who sailed round the world in charge of the scientific and botanical expedition that bore his name, propose Alba as Prime Minister instead of the King's favourite, Manuel Godoy, who did not belong to the high nobility. Malaspina's plot was discovered in November 1795 and rigorously repressed. Although Alba may not have known about the navigator's plans, it is probable that he fell into disgrace; he retired to his Andalusian estates, where he died at his palace in Seville, in his wife's arms, on 12 June 1796.

Alba loved riding. His skilled horsemanship led the King to invite him to take part in the challenging equestrian exercises known as the Parejas Reales, which took place periodically in Aranjuez. He was also a great lover of music.

In his collection, which became known through the inventory made at his death, there were numerous musical instruments: an 'English clavichord', a 'feather clavichord', three fortepianos, one of them also English, a violin and three violas, one Stradivarius violin, one Jacob Steiner violin, and a six-string guitar. The duke was an excellent viola player, and he used to play with the Infante Don Gabriel, the king's brother and an excellent harpsichordist, and probably also with Charles IV himself, who favoured the violin. From the 1780s, Alba was in contact with Haydn, through his agents in Vienna, and ordered many musical scores from him. It was from this composer that he obtained the score that included, according to Goya's careful inscription, 'Cuatro Canc.ˢ, / con Aconp.ᵗᵒ de Fortep.ᵒ / del Sʳ Haydn' ('Four songs, / with Fortep. Accomp. / by Mr Haydn'). Although it is difficult to identify the songs, they were most probably recent works by Haydn, such as 'VI Lieder beim Klavier zu Singen. Die Musik ist von Herrn Joseph Haydn', published by the Viennese firm Artaria (Hob. XXVIa 13–24) in 1784 (although they were reissued in 1794), or perhaps the 'VI English Canzonettas' (Hob. XXVIa 25–30) of 1794 on poems by Anne Hunter, wife of the surgeon John Hunter, a London patron of Haydn. The reference to 'Mr Haydn', 'Herrn Haydn', in Goya's score only existed in editions from Artaria.

The titles of Haydn's songs from his English period – among them 'Piercing Eyes', 'Fidelity', 'Despair', 'Pleasing Pain', 'She Never Told Her Love', 'O Tuneful Voice' – give an idea of their poetic content, which is characterised by a deep pathos in their descriptions of love, linking them with the pre-romantic *Sturm und Drang* movement. Thus the duke showed himself to be a person of sensibility, as the term was used in his time, a cultivated music-lover, and an *aficionado* of music by the composer then considered the greatest in Europe. Goya's portrait of Alba in his private chamber, holding a musical score, stands out among Spanish portraits, many of them anodyne in their conventionality, or those by other artists on the same level as Goya in France or England. The appearance of the elegantly relaxed duke reflects contemporary descriptions of him, as does his serene mood, while his face, with its lively and intelligent expression, looks out at the viewer with sympathy and friendliness. He wears elegant riding clothes in the French fashion, and leans on a cabinet table, not on a fortepiano, as the literature has kept repeating since he was thus described by Charles Yriarte in the first study published on the life and art of Goya. 'Brownish face, medium stature, courteously affable', as he was described by Baron Maldá in 1784, Alba appears here in private, but he is also shown as an expert horseman and an experienced musician, capable of mastering his horses or interpreting Haydn's challenging scores, thus giving the portrait a symbolic character. In this way Goya described the intelligence and harmony of Alba's personality, which was stressed by all contemporary sources, and his management skills as administrator of his estates. Yriarte referred to the portrait as one of Goya's 'plus remarquables'. Indeed, the artist united naturalness in the representation of his subject with the grand environment of elegance and sophistication in which he lived in his palace on the Calle del Barquillo in Madrid, a building which had won the praises of the learned Antonio Ponz.

In 1795, when the portrait was painted, the duke and his wife had taken up Goya and become his new patrons. He had already painted other members of the Villahermosa family, such as Alba's mother, or the various portraits of the Conde and Condesa de Altamira and their children. Perhaps Alba had given him a studio in their palace, and appointed him their painter.

The original width of the portrait (115 cm), which has been recently revealed by radiography and confirmed by the cleaning of the painting, goes against the idea traditionally maintained in the literature that Alba's portrait was the pendant of the famous portrait of the duchess dressed in white (Palacio de Liria, Madrid), whose dimensions are 194 × 130 cm. Although it has the same date, the latter work must have been intended for a different destination. MMM

16

*Ferdinand Guillemardet*

1798
Oil on canvas, 186 × 124 cm
Département des Peintures, Musée du Louvre, Paris.
Bequest of Louis Guillemardet, the sitter's son, 1865

PROVENANCE: collection of Ferdinand Guillemardet; bequest of Louis Guillemardet, Ferdinand's son, to the Louvre, 1865
EXHIBITED: Real Academia de Bellas Artes de San Fernando in Madrid, 1799; The Hague and Paris, 1970, no. 21 (J. Batîcle); Madrid, New York and Boston, 1988–89, no. 31 (M. Moreno de los Heras); Madrid, 1992–93, no. 45; Lille and Philadelphia, 1998–99, no. 31
LITERATURE: Desparmet Fitz-Gerald 1928–50, vol. 2, no. 380; Angelis 1976, no. 365; Morales y Marín 1997, no. 292; Gerard Powell and Ressort 2002, pp. 289–91 (J. Batîcle); Wilson-Bareau in Paris 2003B, pp. 108–09, 138, 155

During his long career as a portrait painter, Goya painted many more half-length portraits than he did large full-length ones of men. However, the three full-length portraits he painted in 1798 are amongst his greatest masterpieces; it is as if he were experimenting with the possibilities of this form. They are the portraits of the Minister of Finance, Don Francisco de Saavedra (Courtauld Institute Galleries, London), the Minister of Justice, Gaspar Melchor de Jovellanos (Prado, Madrid) and this painting. The two Spaniards were liberals, closely linked to the *ilustrados*, the circle responsible for the spread of the Enlightenment in Spain, and the Frenchman was at the time the representative of the French Republic in Madrid.

Ferdinand Guillement (1765–1809) was born near Autun (which explains his connection with the French diplomat Charles Maurice de Talleyrand-Périgord, who was at one time Bishop of Autun); after extended medical studies in Montpellier, Guillement was elected to the Convention in 1792. In Paris he was a frequent guest of Charles Delacroix, the father of Eugène Delacroix, who was himself a good friend of Guillement's son Félix. It was through Guillement that Delacroix became familiar at an early stage with Goya's *Caprices*.

In 1798, Talleyrand, then Minister of Foreign Affairs, appointed him French ambassador to Madrid. In the Spanish capital, Ferdinand soon became acquainted with Mariano de Urquiijo, Goya's protector and director of the Real Academia de Bellas Artes de San Fernando. Appointed First Painter to the court in 1799, Goya was then at the peak of his official career. It was therefore not surprising that the ambassador appealed to him when he had just arrived in the capital. The details of the commission are not known, but it is likely that the links between the painter and his sitter were even closer. Guillemardet may, in fact, have participated in publishing *The Caprices*, placing an attic in the French Embassy at Goya's disposal (Batîcle 1972, pp. 253–54). Was the painting executed partly as a tribute?

Goya follows the tradition of the portrait of a minister or a statesman, depicting Guillemardet seated at a table, on which can be seen papers and an inkwell. However, the artist turns the conventions of the genre upside down. At the very least the ambassador's pose (he is represented full-length) pushes the norms of the official portrait to their limit. The manner in which his legs are crossed was considered vulgar under the *ancien régime* but began to become more acceptable by the 1780s: it indicated naturalness and a certain relaxed mood. Vigée-Lebrun's portrait of Charles-Alexandre de Calonne (cat. 22) bears witness to this.

In Goya's painting it is further emphasised in a highly original manner, however, by the casual way in which the sitter uses the chair and the unnatural position of the left arm. The slight awkwardness with which the arm is attached to the body and is presented to the spectator conveys the experimental character of the portrait. In it, as in the portrait of Jovellanos, Goya is trying to move beyond the social conventions of the genre in order to capture the psychological depth of the sitter. In both cases, this attention to the interior life of the sitter expresses itself in 'deviation' from the traditional norms. The position of the minister, with his head on his left hand, conveys his melancholy nature, whereas the cavalier posture of the French ambassador betrays the impetuous character of the man of action – with a hint of vulgarity.

Citizen Guillemardet displays the symbols of the young French Republic in a very ostentatious way. The official portrait has reappeared. Goya knows exactly how to exploit the tricolour cockade and scarf. All the finest colourists could make something good of the combination of blue, white and red. A few years before Goya, Gros made similar use of the colours in his *Bonaparte at the Pont d'Arcole* (1796; Musée National du Château, Versailles). In the portrait of *Ferdinand Guillemardet*, the picturesque effect of the three colours is enhanced by lavish use of gold on the chair, the fringes of the table covering and, especially, on the embroidery of the scarf, a virtuoso display. The colours of the new France dominate the harmony of the whole and their sparkle reinforces the energy of the pose.

According to the critic Laurent Matheron, Goya considered this masterpiece to be one of his greatest successes. He had managed to make Guillemardet, an obscure doctor who became ambassador of the young, victorious Republic, a symbol of the new man – full of determination and not yet civilised by the customs of the court. No more beautiful, contrasted pendant could be imagined than this for the melancholic, utopian portrait of Jovellanos. AA

## 32
### *The Marquesa de Villafranca Painting Her Husband*

1804
Oil on canvas, 195 × 126 cm
Inscribed on the arm of the armchair *Goya 1804* and on the palette *Dña. María Tomasa de Palafox*
Museo Nacional del Prado, Madrid

PROVENANCE: by direct descent in the sitter's family; bequeathed to the Prado by the Conde de Niebla, 1926
EXHIBITED: Madrid, 1805; London, 1972, no.115; Madrid, 1992, no.28; Madrid, 1996, no.120; Saragossa, 1996, no.48; Rome, 2000, no.24; Madrid and Washington, 2001–02, no.68; Berlin and Vienna, 2005–06, no.82; Tokyo and Osaka, 2006
LITERATURE: Yriarte 1867, p.134; Gassier and Wilson 1970, no.810; Madrid 1992, pp.122–25

In 1798 María Tomasa Palafox y Portocarrero, XII Marquesa de Villafranca and Duquesa de Medina-Sidonia, married Francisco de Borja Alvarez de Toledo y Gonzaga, who had inherited his family's titles on the death of his brother the Duke of Alba in 1796 (cat.63). María Tomasa was born in Madrid in 1780, daughter of one of the most extraordinary aristocratic families at court, that of the counts of Montijo. The Condesa de Montijo, who had Jansenist ideas, gave her six children, including her four daughters, an enlightened education. She moved in intellectual court circles, where she was the friend of important figures such as the writer and politician Gaspar Melchor de Jovellanos, Francisco de Cabarrús, Bernardo de Iriarte, the poet Meléndez Valdés and the historian and academic José de Vargas Ponce, all of whom were painted by Goya. Lady Elisabeth Holland, who visited Spain between 1802 and 1805 and from 1808 to 1809, remarked on both mother and daughter in her *Spanish Journals* (British Library, London), saying that the young woman closely resembled her mother both 'physically and morally', and that the mother herself was 'gifted with unusual wit and talent'.

The young María Tomasa had already been painted on two occasions by Agustín Esteve, an assistant of Goya, always in family groups, with her mother and sisters or with her husband and son, which were intended to highlight the family's aristocratic lineage. However, Goya's portrait focuses on the lady's tastes, a common theme in the iconography of female portraits in the eighteenth century. In this case, what gives the composition its special character is the fact that Doña Tomasa was an artist, or at least an amateur painter, and Goya shows her in the act of painting her husband's portrait. The palette and brushes, as well as the canvas on the right, establish a parallel with the figure of Velázquez in *Las Meninas*. Doña Tomasa did not earn her living by painting, as Angelica Kauffman or Elisabeth-Louise Vigée-Lebrun had done in other European countries, and no works identified as being painted by her have come down to us. Nevertheless, she was nominated as an academician, with merit, of the Academia de Bellas Artes de San Fernando in 1805, when Goya's portrait was exhibited there. Her academic recognition, like that of her brother, the Conde de Teba, who was an honorary member of the painting branch of the Academia, was an example of the institutional honours paid to members of the high aristocracy.

At any rate, Goya's portrait is an extraordinary work, in whose composition he changes the usual style of his feminine portraits, in which the figure stands or sits in front of a landscape; this was the formula he used for his previous portraits of members of the nobility, such as the Marquesa de la Solana, the Duchess of Alba, Queen María Luisa, the Condesa de Fernán-Núñez, and even his portrait of an actress, 'La Tirana'. Now, with the beginning of a new century, he seems to be seeking new attitudes and presentations for these ladies with intellectual concerns, like the Marquesa de Santa Cruz, whom he represented as a muse with her guitar-lute, or the Marquesa de Villafranca, whom he portrayed as an artist. Goya does not make her the embodiment of the traditional figure for the allegory of painting described by Cesare Ripa in his well-known *Iconologia*, although perhaps he used the beauty and nobility of the young woman's attitude as a reflection of the same qualities in the Art of Painting. Her black hair, which is too loose and untidy for the hairstyle then in vogue, also symbolises the agitated thoughts of the artist.

In fact, Goya has painted a high-born young woman with a liking for painting. Her gauze dress in the Parisian fashion, her fine satin shoes and her gilded armchair upholstered in red silk all highlight her beauty and the wealth that surrounded her, a member of one of Spain's most important noble families. Her artistic efforts are secondary here, since Goya stresses her indolent position, as she lies back in her armchair, resting her feet on a soft cushion. Her expression does not have the analytic

sharpness that appears in his self-portraits or his portraits of other artists. Goya defines with psychological precision the young woman's loving look at her husband, who is not present in person. He appears here, by the visual trick of the painted portrait, returning his wife's loving gaze. Francisco de Borja Alvarez de Toledo, an illustrious aristocrat and a career soldier, had been a brigadier in the Royal Regiment and, from 1802, was an officer in the Line Infantry. Lady Holland noted the love of husband and wife for one another in her diaries, and perhaps Goya used the poetic resource of his painting to represent their affection visually.

From the technical point of view, the portrait shows Goya's development in the new century. He has left behind the delicacy, fineness and colouring of the eighteenth century, and now his brushstrokes are energetic, sure and clearly visible. The silk brocade and the arm and foot of the armchair are painted in this new way, and they have a key role in the whole scene with an intensity that could be described as surreal. In this image, Goya is working within the genre of the aristocratic portrait of the time. Nevertheless, the impact and freshness of the image, very different from other portraits of women painters of the period, anticipates the portraits of this genre later in the nineteenth century. In the context of Goya's image, the most interesting are the portraits of women artists by Manet: *Eva Gonzalès in Her Studio* (Dublin City Gallery The Hugh Lane, Dublin) and *Repose*, a portrait of Berthe Morisot (Museum of Art, Rhode Island School of Design, Providence). Even though the young woman does not appear as a painter in the latter, the work has an interesting parallel with Goya's painting, with the sitter dressed in white gauze, reclining lazily and pensively in a red silk armchair. MMM

## 11
### *Ferdinand VII in Royal Robes*

c.1815
Oil on canvas, 208 × 142.5 cm
Museo Nacional del Prado, Madrid, 735

PROVENANCE: belonged to the Ministerio de la Gubernación, Madrid; sent to the Museo de la Trinidad, Madrid, 1871; entered the Prado Museum after 1872
EXHIBITED: Barcelona, 1977; Madrid, 1996, no.145 (M. Moreno de las Heras)
LITERATURE: Gassier and Wilson 1970, no.1540; Batîcle 1992, p.407; Tomlinson 1992, p.199; Morales y Marín 1994, no.447

When the monarchy was restored to the throne of Spain in 1814, Goya's position became very difficult. There was an inquiry to assess the degree to which personnel in the royal household had collaborated with the Napoleonic Empire. After a lengthy investigation, Goya was exonerated: although First Painter to the royal chamber, he had refused to draw his salary during the war. He had also denounced the horrors of war. Later, he painted a number of portraits of Ferdinand VII, none of them apparently commissioned by the Crown.

The King probably disliked the artist, or, more likely, was suspicious of him. In spite of their manifest differences, all these portraits have one thing in common: the monarch has the same head, facing the same way and wearing the same expression. Only the context changes: the King is presented in royal robes (this painting), standing in a military encampment (Prado Museum, Madrid) or in uniform seated with his elbows on a table, on which can be seen the regalia and an allegory of Justice (Museo de Bellas Artes, Santander).

The different versions of the painting clearly illustrate the manner in which the portrait of the King was constructed; an artist was only allowed a few hours, or even a few minutes, with the subject sitting, often during the King's meals, so he would have to return repeatedly to a single prototype. It seems highly probable that Goya used a study from life made in 1808, which he had already employed for an equestrian portrait, painted soon after the King's accession to the throne (Real Academia de Bellas Artes de San Fernando, Madrid). Although this manner of proceeding often led to a stereotyped rendering of the royal features (cat. 8), in which the symbolic value of the image was favoured over physical resemblance, the portrait exhibited here shows that this was not Goya's practice. The artist made every effort to make his sitter live, and we are only aware of the template (in its real sense) if we are familiar with the other versions.

Seen without his court wig, Ferdinand VII is depicted with his characteristic plain looks: a strongly protruding chin and large ears and nose. Goya had been official portrait painter to the court since the reign of Charles IV and had never sought to flatter his sitters; this realism overturned all the existing conventions of royal portrait painting. A number of authors have detected a certain irony behind his manner, or an implied criticism; this interpretation might seem particularly suited to Ferdinand VII, for whom the artist felt no sympathy at all. In fact, the image of the ruling monarch was extremely strictly controlled and it seems highly unlikely that this type of portrait would or could contain any satire.

By contrast, Goya deliberately plays here on the discrepancy between the accurate rendering of the facial features and the flair with which the traditional insignia of power are handled: the crimson, gold and ermine cloak, the staff of office and the sword. The discrepancy is further emphasised by the total absence of background (the figure stands against a neutral wall – absolutely unheard of in a royal portrait), and, as so often, slight irregularities in the proportions. Never has an official portrait expressed the double nature of the King so clearly – the ambivalence between the abstract symbols of monarchy and their embodiment in a man of flesh and blood, treated like a genuine portrait. In spite of everything, Goya's insistence on the man himself (which gives

the portrait a slight air of fancy dress) clearly refers to the historical upheaval caused by post-revolutionary events, and to the insecure and ambiguous nature of this restoration of the monarchy.

In formal terms, few royal portraits have ever been handled with such flair, particularly in the rendering of the accessories. The composition is given structure by the colour scheme and character by the artist's touch, which, in places, emphasises the material substance of the paint. The cloak constitutes a large expanse of red, standing out against the grey background and contrasting with the green of the breeches; the green adds a touch of brilliance to the portrait. The gold embroidery is not depicted in any detail; it is simply suggested by small, thick flecks of yellow, black and white paint, painstakingly placed side by side. Goya does not use local colour but rather a more evocative slight blur. The material effects are observed from the real world. The net result is an uncertainty with regard to planes, but this helps convey the ambivalence of the figure and the insignia of power. Goya seems to be delivering an image of disenchantment rather than satirical comment. AA

## 149
### Joaquín María Ferrer y Cafranga

1824
Oil on canvas, 73 × 59 cm
Signed and dated on the right: *Goya Paris 1824*
Private collection, Switzerland

PROVENANCE: Joaquín Maria Ferrer, Paris, 1824; by inheritance, Marqués de Baroja, Madrid; Marquesa de la Gándara, Rome; private collection, Switzerland
EXHIBITED: Madrid, 1900, no.113; Bordeaux, 1951, no.57; Berlin, 2005, no.139 (not exhibited in Vienna); New York, 2006, no.8
LITERATURE: Beruete y Moret 1916, vol.1, pp.146–47; Gassier and Wilson 1970, no.1659; Rull Sabater 1991, vols 19–20, document 16, p.168; Crónica 1994, vol.2, pp.1020–23 (I am grateful to the owners of the work for kindly supplying some of these bibliographical details)

On 8 July 1824, the playwright Leandro Fernández de Moratín wrote to the Abbé Melón from Bordeaux that Goya, a friend of them both, was in Paris. The police register records his presence in the city on 30 June. Moratín had recommended the artist to another Spanish emigrant, Vicente González Arnao, a lawyer and later a translator, who had undertaken 'to look after you and advise you as far as he can'. He had found Goya lodgings with some of his relations in the Hôtel Favart, 5 rue Marivaux, opposite the Théâtre des Italiens. The police registers show that Goya was being watched – 'He looks older than he really is and is completely deaf' – and record that he did not go out except to visit monuments and walk in the public parks. According to Moratín, Arnao 'is proposing to continue his good offices on behalf of the young traveller, and has agreed to send him here in the month of September'. Goya returned to Bordeaux in the middle of that month. Perhaps at the end of August he visited the Paris Salon, which was

unusually controversial in 1824 because of tensions between traditional and modern artists. There he might have seen portraits by Elisabeth-Louise Vigée-Lebrun together with the *Massacre of Chios* by the young Delacroix or *The Vow of Louis XIII* by Ingres and Constable's *Hay Wain*, which won the gold medal that year, shared with Richard Parkes Bonington and Anthony Copley Fielding.

Perhaps it was Arnao who introduced Goya to the political exile Joaquín María Ferrer y Cafranga, who is described in the police registers as a 'fearsome revolutionary'. Ferrer was born in Pasajes (Guipúzcoa) on 7 December 1777. He died in Santa Agueda, a fashionable Guipúzcoa spa, in 1861. His elder brother José Joaquín had lived in Peru as a merchant, but on his return to Spain as a rich man, he devoted himself to astronomy. In 1801 he was invited by the American Philosophical Society of Philadelphia to expound his discoveries, and he later he made some studies at the Greenwich Observatory in London. In his youth Joaquín María followed in his illustrious brother's footsteps, as well as those of another brother, Francisco Javier, who traded in Cadiz and the American colonies. Although the information available is not very precise, it seems that Ferrer travelled to Argentina and Peru, settling in Lima, where he figures as Captain of the Regimiento de Voluntarios Distinguidos de la Concordia, and also acted as a diplomat in the period of the emancipation of the American colonies. It is thought that he returned to Spain in 1820 (although some sources state that he returned five years earlier) as a member of the Sociedad de Amantes del Orden Constitucional. During the Liberal Triennium (1821–23), in which King Ferdinand VII ratified the progressive constitution of 1812, Ferrer was assembly member for Guipúzcoa and Vizcaya, sat on the board of the Banco de San Carlos and the Compañía de Filipinas. With the entry into Spain on 7 April 1823 of the 'Hundred Thousand Sons of St Louis' and the King's absolutist reaction, Ferrer, like many other liberal compatriots, was condemned to death. He fled first to London and later to Paris, where he settled.

In 1824 Ferrer was living in Paris with his wife, at 15 Rue Bleue, in the district of Grande-Batelière, where most Spanish political emigrants lived. He led a comfortable life, dedicated to finance, and was in contact with the Delessert and Mallet Frères banks, as well as with numerous Spanish exiles, among whom were Arnao, the Marqués de Pontejos and the Duque de San Carlos, whom Goya had painted in 1816. From 1826, Ferrer was also a publisher of illustrated books, dedicated to Golden Age literature: *Obras escogidas de Miguel de Cervantes* (1826), *Aventuras de Gil Blas de Santillana* (1827), *Vida del Lazarillo de Tormes* (1827), *La Diana enamorada* by Gaspar Gil Polo (1827), *El Diablo cojuelo* (1828), *Historia de la monja Alférez* (1829), with translations into French and German, and a famous miniature edition of *Don Quixote* (1827). Goya kept in contact with Ferrer from Bordeaux, trying to get him to sell some of his new works, such as the lithographs of the *Bordeaux Bulls*. Goya wrote to him about this a few times and also to recommend Rosarito Weiss, the daughter of Leocadia Zorrilla, with whom Goya lived in his final years, hoping that she might be able to pursue her painting studies in Paris. Ferrer did not sell Goya's works or help Rosarito, but he did suggest a new edition of the *Caprichos*, which were already admired in France. Goya was not interested in this – 'I now have better ideas' he wrote to Ferrer – perhaps because he no longer had the copper plates, which he gave to the King in 1804. Ferrer was pardoned in 1829 and returned to Spain in 1833. He continued his brilliant political career, as assembly member for Guipúzcoa and Vizcaya, alderman of Guernica and president of the Cortes constituyentes. He took part in the drawing up of the 1837 Constitution, and between 1840 and 1841, as a member of the Progressive Party, he was briefly Minister of State and Minister of the Treasury. In 1842 he negotiated the trade agreement between Spain and England. He owned many iron foundries and coal mines in his native land, where he lived as a senator for life when he retired from politics.

Ferrer's portrait, which is a pair with that of his wife (cat. 150), was painted between 30 June and mid-September 1824. It is a half-length, slightly smaller than life size. The artist only painted portraits in this format in his late Bordeaux period. The figure is set against a neutral background, with no particular spatial or decorative reference. The result is a very modern work in the simplicity of its composition and in the direct and powerful expressiveness of the sitter. In his final years in Spain Goya had already begun to make this type of portrait, severe and direct in black, such as that of Tiburcio Pérez Cuervo (Metropolitan Museum of Art, New York), which anticipated his late development and the advance towards modernity of such artists as Manet, Degas and others. Ferrer holds a beautiful little book, bound in red, the only note of bright colour in the entire painting. It stands out further because of the precise and intentional touch of light that Goya allows to fall on the sitter's hand. Perhaps the book was an allusion to Ferrer's work as a publisher, although no publications are known to have been issued before 1826. If we take into account the sitter's political leanings, the book may allude to the famous 1812 constitution, whose 1820 edition propounded similar measures, and for whose defence he had been condemned to death.

Ferrer's fine, sharp features, betraying his Basque origins, are also known to us from an engraved, anonymous portrait most probably executed in Paris, given its closeness to the style of Ingres. The cold, assured, official character of the person in the engraving contrasts with the tense and rather melancholic inner life reflected in Goya's work. The artist has ruffled his sitter's hair,

accentuating this with his firm brushstrokes and intermingled with touches of light, giving Ferrer a thoroughly romantic air, with his meditative, concentrated and idealistic expression, without covering up the hardness and determination of a man of action. MMM

## 150
### *Manuela Alvarez Coiñas Thomas de Ferrer*

1824
Oil on canvas, 73 × 60 cm
Signed at the bottom right: *Goya 1824*
Private collection, Switzerland

PROVENANCE: Joaquín María Ferrer, Paris, 1824; by inheritance, Marqués de Baroja, Madrid; Marquesa de la Gándara, Rome; private collection, Switzerland
EXHIBITED: Madrid, 1900, no.118; Bordeaux, 1951, no.58; Berlin, 2005, no.140 (not exhibited in Vienna); New York, 2006, no.9
LITERATURE: Beruete y Moret 1916, vol.1, p.146; Barriga 1941–48, vol.3, pp.354 and 357; Gassier and Wilson 1970, no.1660; Fauqué Villanueva Etcheverría 1982, pp.550–51, 554–55, 560–62; Bâticle 1992, pp.462 and 467; Bâticle 1998, p.84 (I am grateful to the owners of the work for kindly supplying some of these bibliographical details)

The portrait of Manuela Alvarez Coiñas Thomas forms a pair with that of Joaquín María Ferrer, her husband (cat. 149). These two works complete the series of paired portraits that Goya painted throughout his life, beginning in 1784 with those of his first patrons, the Infante Don Luis de Borbón and his wife, Doña María Teresa de Vallabriga. The portraits of the Infante and his wife, bust-length and in profile, had a strong neoclassical influence, inspired by the emperor profiles found on Roman coins. The paintings of Ferrer and his wife portray a new social class in Spain, that of rich merchants who had worked in banking, industry and politics, and who had also advanced liberal ideas. We do not have as much biographical information about Doña Manuela as for her husband, and we do not even know the date or place of her birth and death. However, some information given by descendants of the two sitters permits us to trace Doña Manuela's family background.

Like Joaquín María Ferrer she belonged to a Spanish family which, like many others, was based in the American colonies for political, military and commercial reasons at the end of the eighteenth century, during the difficult rise of the colonies' movements towards independence. Doña Manuela's father was the Spanish brigadier Antonio Alvarez y Ximénez, and her mother Doña Isabel Thomas y Ramzé, who was born in Barcelona. Her father was the second governor of the province of Arequipa from 1786 to 1792, in the south of the enormous Viceroyalty of Peru. Arequipa was the city with the largest number of Spanish inhabitants in Peru, although after the 1784 earthquake and the independence uprisings the Spanish population began to decline. Alvarez left a *Memoria*, telling of his activities and visits in the region, and in 1794 the *Plano Escenográfico* of Arequipa and its provinces (British Museum, London, Add. MS 15, 740) was

published a project commissioned during his time in office and carried out by the mathematician Francisco Vélez Rodríguez.

One of the couple's children, Major Colonel Ignacio Alvarez Thomas, who was among the first liberators of Argentina, was born in 1787 in Arequipa. The other two, José, born about 1796, and Manuela, must have been born in Buenos Aires, where the family lived for a number of years. Their father followed his official career and returned to Spain in 1797, leaving his family in Argentina because of the danger of crossing the Atlantic during the war between Spain and England. But he returned to Buenos Aires in 1803, to collect his family on his way to his new posting in the extreme south of Chile, in the Chiloé Islands, as political and military governor. His son Ignacio remained in Argentina and, thanks to his *Recuerdos personales*, written in 1839, we have some further news of his family, whom he never saw again. It appears that they moved to Lima at an unknown date, and finally returned to Spain: 'My work for the cause of liberty was regarded with great displeasure by my family. They were wholly dedicated to the defence of the Crown, and were very distressed that one of their sons should join the "insurgents", as they were called at that time. My mother, who loved me dearly, made great efforts to tear me away from the Revolution, offering me advantages in the royal army, if I were to go to Lima. But because I resisted, she cut off all communication. After many years and when she was back in Spain, she re-established contact with the same affection as before, and so did my brothers and sisters. My father was already dead...' Perhaps it was on their return to Spain that the family added the surname Coiñas to that of Alvarez, thus detaching themselves from one of the Argentinian 'insurgents'.

Doña Manuela, Ferrer's future wife, was younger than him, as the portrait shows, perhaps by almost twenty years; she must have been born in about 1797 or even after 1803. She may have met her husband in America, as both of them lived in Lima and Buenos Aires, or after her return to Spain. In 1824, when Goya painted her, she had followed her husband to France, by way of Cadiz and London, in the company of her brother José, then aged 27. She was expecting her first child, Flora, who was born on 20 February 1825. Goya congratulated the couple in his letter of 6 December that year: 'I heard with great pleasure of your good health and that of Señora Doña Manuela and the beautiful daughter that heaven has given you: I congratulate you.' The couple, who from 1826 lived in the elegant Parisian suburb of Montmorency, had two more daughters, Aurora and Isabel.

Goya brilliantly captured Doña Manuela's serene personality, which was very different from that of her melancholic husband. She was both haughty and determined, and directs her attentive and pleasant gaze at the spectator. Doña Manuela holds a closed fan in her right hand, as if pointing to their expected child, a subtle indication that Goya also used in his portrait of the Condesa de Chinchón, who does not have a fan but whose gesture makes the same point. Doña Manuela is dressed and her hair is arranged in the latest French fashion. Her elegant black costume, like that of her husband, is highlighted by the transparent white of her gauze collar, her belt buckle and her thick gold watch chain. Goya focuses on this for its size and the strong light falling on it, and indeed it seems to have the same importance for Doña Manuela as the small red book has for her husband. Although no doubt a fashionable object in the dress of the period, the watch chain's central and highlighted position shows its importance within the painting. Perhaps this should be related to traditional symbolism, of Time, for a woman expecting her first child, or for husband and wife, living in exile and longing to return home to Spain. Goya's calculated presentation of his sitters in this double portrait, with each facing the other in the traditional way, gives the husband, who was taller than his wife, a more imposing presence than her; she appears more peaceful and luminous. MMM

# Jean-Baptiste Greuze

TOURNUS, 1725 – PARIS, 1805

## 51
*Claude Henri Watelet*

1765
Oil on canvas, 115 × 88 cm
Département des Peintures, Musée du Louvre, Paris, RF 1982-66.

PROVENANCE: mentioned in the Salon documents of 1763, the portrait was completed upon Watelet's return from Italy and exhibited for the first time at the Salon of 1765 (no.116); not included in the posthumous sale of Watelet's effects, 12 June 1786, in Paris, it was probably given by Watelet to his mistress, the artist Marguerite Lecomte; perhaps sold to M. Loliée, Paris, 4–5 March 1816 (no.3), although the dimensions do not match exactly; at an unknown date, the portrait passed to the Collection Béguin-Bilcoq, at the Château de Valbreuil, Aupst, near Aix-en-Provence; acquired by the Louvre, 8 July 1982

EXHIBITED: Paris, Salon of 1763, no.131 (but only exhibited at Mathon de la Cour, as unfinished); Paris, Salon of 1765, no.116; Paris, 1983, pp.50–53; Paris, 1984B, no.64, pp.241–44
LITERATURE: Watelet 1786; Goncourt 1880, pp.340–41; Martin and Masson 1906, no.174, pp.1258–60; Hautecoeur 1913; Brookner 1972, pp.64–65, 101–15; Hartford 1976; Laveissière 1980; Haskell and Penny 1981, p.326 (on the *Medici Venus*); 'Les Recentes Acquistions des musées nationaux', in *Revue du Louvre*, nos 5–6, 1982, p.389; *Nouvelles Acquisitions du Département des Peintures (1980–82)*, *Musée du Louvre*, Paris, 1983–84, pp.50–53; Barker 2005, p.9

Exhibited at the Salon of 1765, this painting was one of nearly twenty works submitted by Greuze that year, including the genre scenes for which he is best known. Among them were the sentimental *A Girl Weeping over Her Dead Bird* (1765; National Gallery of Scotland, Edinburgh), portraits, *têtes d'expression*, pastels and drawings. His third portrait submission that year was a portrait of the financier, connoisseur and dilettante Claude Henri Watelet (1718–1786), whose affluence afforded him the opportunity to pursue his cultural interests as an art critic, playwright, poet, engraver, author and a theoretician on landscape architecture.

Greuze's ready skills at portraiture are displayed to great effect in this painting. His portrait of Watelet, a patron of his, shows the sitter at his desk. A bronze reproduction of the *Medici Venus* is positioned directly in front of him. Watelet gazes at the statue, holding a compass to measure her proportions. It has been suggested that the portrait may depict Watelet as he wrote his poem 'Art de peindre' (1760). Greuze, who excelled in the rendering of rich details, fully exploits his gifts on the representation of the elaborately furnished interior and Watelet's sumptuous clothing, from the ornately carved, Louis XIV gilded desk and the chair upholstered in an opulent red damask cloth, to Watelet's resplendent, dove-grey silk-taffeta pantaloons, matching coat and waistcoat. These visually seductive fabrics and textures are all marvellously painted. The sitter's face and hands, pale and soft, are delicately modelled, and, lost in thought, his expression is passive. The shadowy background, against which the highlighted figure stands out, owes much to Dutch antecedents, although the generally bright, lustrous colour scheme is a dominant characteristic of Greuze's style.

Watelet is remembered today for his *Essai sur les jardins*, published in 1774. Several editions are illustrated with drawings and etchings by Watelet himself and, among others, Hubert Robert. Watelet was an early proponent of the picturesque in garden design and much of the book is dedicated to Moulin Joli, his own garden and estate, in the environs of Paris. The book illustrates the shift in taste to a more natural, relatively 'uncultivated' style of landscape design, in contrast to the more formal landscape design that had predominated earlier in the century. Presaging Rousseau's tenets, Watelet proposed the establishment of an ideal country estate and community, which would incorporate the utilitarian and the aesthetically pleasurable. His innovative treatise planned for a working farm, stables, a dairy, a medical laboratory and a clinic, within a horticultural paradise of flowerbeds, vistas, paths and lawns, enhanced with decorative sculptures and topiary. Watelet also wrote as a critic on the arts, contributing entries to the *Dictionnaire des Arts de Peintures, Sculpture et Gravure*, published in 1786.

Greuze was best known for his moralising genre scenes which, by the late 1760s, had given way to sentimental, idealised views of family life and often suggestive representations of women. He underwent only partial formal training, his early work displaying the influence of the seventeenth-century Dutch masters and Chardin. Greuze travelled to Italy in 1755, returning two years later to Paris, where he was to remain until his death. Capitalising on the thriving market for engravings, Greuze attained financial success through the dissemination of prints, such as *The Marriage Contract*, which was enormously popular when it was exhibited at the Salon of 1761. Greuze went on to seek approbation and recognition as a *peintre d'histoire*, with his submission in 1769 of *The Emperor Severus Reprimanding His Son Caracalla*, a *morceau de réception* in the Poussinesque deathbed tradition, which came fourteen years after he had been named an 'agrée' in 1755 (a work was usually expected within six months). Much to his dismay, it was rejected and the Académie categorised him as a genre painter. His bristly character ensured that he did not show at the Salon again for thirty years. Nonetheless, he successfully exhibited at his own, private studio, and shrewdly expanded his clientele through the medium of engravings and prints of his work, not by his own hand, but initially through the influential print-maker Jean Georges Wille. He was popular among Russians and counted the Youssoupov family among his patrons. Denis Diderot championed him in his early forays at the Salon, although he lambasted the portrait of Watelet for its overabundance of 'grey satin' and the sitter's 'gloomy' aspect. The prominent critic's writings in Melchior Grimm's *Correspondance littéraire* chart much of Greuze's lengthy, rather turbulent and erratic career.

For many years Greuze was praised as a moral educator, and his paintings were considered subjects of visual edification. Although he attempted to engage with the revolutionary politics and ideology that were sweeping the country in the 1780s, joining the Commune des Arts in 1793, Greuze remained within the eighteenth-century tradition of Boucher and the decorative effects of the rococo. His ambitions – to uplift and elevate morality – were not translated through his paintings as they were to be by the new generation of artists, led by David, who had successfully marshalled the profound ideological power of classicism in his work, imbuing it with urgent political significance. Greuze's history paintings continued to be poorly received, as did his moral allegories. However, his talents as a brilliant draughtsman were uncontested, and within his prodigious output he executed many distinguished portraits, counting among his sitters such luminaries as Condorcet, Franklin, Napoleon, Fabre d'Eglantine, his early patron the Abbé de Chezal-Benôit and even such Revolutionary figures as Robespierre. CC/VG

# Antoine-Jean Gros

PARIS, 1770 – MEUDON, 1835

## 104
### *Paul-François Des Hours de Calviac*

1793
Oil on canvas, 73 × 97 cm
Signed lower right: *GROS 1793*; inscription identifying
the sitter on the verso
Musée des Beaux-Arts, Rennes

PROVENANCE: by descent to Mme Léon Schulz;
sold by Galerie Marcus, 1970; entered Musée des Beaux-Arts
de Rennes, 1970
EXHIBITED: Tokyo, 1986; Nancy, 1989; Autun, 1991
LITERATURE: Tripier-Lefranc 1880, p.83; Escholier 1936, p.46,
no.10; Bergot 1973, p.56; Rosenblum 1989, p.33; Chevalier 1994

Although his fame rests primarily on his brilliant
accomplishments as a history painter in the service
of Napoleon, Gros relied almost exclusively on
portraiture as a means of making a living in his
formative years. This portrait dates from a key
transitional period in his career, when he had been
liberated from the strictures of Jacques-Louis
David's studio and was attempting to forge an
independent artistic identity. As one of his master's
favoured protégés, Gros would have expected to
pass smoothly through the academic hierarchies
and system of state patronage, but by the year this
portrait was painted his expectations had been
shattered. The chaotic instability of post-
revolutionary society, coupled with the death of
his father and the subsequent bankruptcy of his
family, left him in a precarious position. Eager to
leave Paris, and still smarting from his failure to
win the Prix de Rome the previous year, Gros
decided to undertake an extended visit to Italy –
an indispensable rite of passage for any aspiring
history painter. David used his political influence
to secure a passport and letters of recommendation
for his former student, and in February 1793 Gros
set out for Florence, having been forced to abandon
his dream of visiting Rome due to the ferment
of anti-French feeling in the city.

Problems with his official papers forced him
to delay his voyage, and he settled temporarily in
Montpellier as he awaited permission to travel.
There he had the good fortune to encounter the
sculptor Augustin Pajou, an old acquaintance from
his youthful connection to the studio of Elisabeth-
Louise Vigée-Lebrun. Pajou immediately offered
assistance to Gros, whose financial situation was
becoming increasingly desperate, by introducing
him to the local artistic community and securing
him commissions from his own patrons. Gros's
earliest biographer, J. B. Delestre, notes that he
painted two portraits at Montpellier, one of which
– a full-length of a child, for which he was paid
480 francs (Delestre 1845, p.19) – must be the work
under discussion. Paul-François Des Hours de
Calviac (1788–1878), better known as Paulin des
Hours-Farel, was five or six years old at the time
he sat to Gros. He belonged to a prominent
Montpellier family, and was later to become

the mayor of the city. The painting was
commissioned by his bachelor uncle, the wealthy
manufacturer François Farel, who had adopted the
child as his heir. Gros received the commission in
late March 1793, and soon afterwards received the
validation of his passport he had been waiting for.
His letters prove that he was already in Italy by
May, after a lengthy voyage, so this painting must
have been executed with great rapidity; this may
account for its fresh and vigorous execution.

Paulin is depicted in an attitude of childish
triumph as he snatches up a goldfinch that he has
trapped in his capacious hat. It was a popular
conceit to portray children holding birds: in a 1740
portrait by Allan Ramsay (Private collection,
Scotland) a young boy draws a squawking finch
from a group of hatchlings in his hat, while Vigée-
Lebrun depicted the Dauphin squeezing a small
bird in his hand in her portrait of Louis-Joseph-
Xavier-François de France and Marie-Thérèse
Charlotte de France (1784; Musée National du
Château, Versailles; as referenced in Chevalier 1994).
However, Gros's audacious decision to capture the
child in a moment of boisterous play stands in
marked contrast to the demure sentimentality that
characterised conventional French portraits of
children. Rather than imposing an adult bearing
on his subject, Gros 'forces the spectator to move
down to the eye-level of a five-year-old boy' and
allows us to engage directly with 'the mysterious
world of a child's scale, psychology, and
physiological closeness to the vital energies of
nature' (Rosenblum 1989, p.33). This convincing
naturalism is indicative of the marked shift in
attitudes towards children and childhood that took
place in the second half of the eighteenth century.
Paulin could be Rousseau's Emile, the 'natural'
child who is allowed to develop his identity
through a joyful engagement with nature, shielded
from the restrictive conventions of corrupt adult
society. It should be noted, however, that this
sense of innocent freedom is counterbalanced
by a pointed reference to the child's dynastic
duty and social destiny. Gros depicts his subject
playing in the fields surrounding his uncle's estate
of Lavalette, on the banks of the River Lez, with
the grand castle that he is to inherit looming in
the background.

The close integration of the figure with the
pastoral setting was a hallmark of the British
portrait tradition, in which sitters of all ages
and stations were depicted in harmony with
their natural surroundings to denote an exquisite
sensibility. It is difficult to ascertain the extent to
which Gros had been exposed to British portraiture,
but there was certainly a healthy culture of cross-
Channel exchange throughout the period. Works
such as Gainsborough's unfinished portrait of
his young daughters chasing a butterfly (*c.*1756;
National Gallery, London) or Reynolds's *Miss
Bowles* (*c.*1775; Wallace Collection, London)
celebrate a spontaneous communion of their

infant subjects with nature and animals. Reynolds,
in particular, made this mode of portraiture
something of a speciality. His *Master Hare* (1788;
Louvre, Paris) – which was engraved by R. Thew
and published under the title *Infancy* in 1790 –
'quickly became something of a prototype for
the child of nature' (Steward 1995, p.92). The
diagonal composition and shallow picture plane
provide a close echo to the portrait of Paulin;
indeed, in one version in a private collection
(Mannings and Postle 2000, no.838) a small bird
is perched on Master Hare's outstretched hand.
Gros also recalls Reynolds in his ability to convey
a sense of windswept movement, and his lively
brushwork. This stylistic vitality is enhanced by
a warm, rich palette, aligning the painting more
with the energy of Romanticism than the flawless
neoclassical modelling promoted in the studio of
David. It has frequently been proposed that Gros
absorbed both the lessons of British portraiture
and the colourism of Rubens during his stay in
Italy; this painting amply demonstrates that these
elements were characteristics of the artist's style
before he left French soil. KB

## 39
### *General Lasalle at the Siege of Stettin*

1808
Oil on canvas, 248 × 174 cm
Signed and dated at the lower left: *Gros 1808*
Musée de l'Armée, Paris, 19814/EA 655

PROVENANCE: in the sitter's family; presented to the Musée
de l'Armée by the Comtesse Raymond de Noblet, a descendant
of the sitter, 1967
EXHIBITED: Paris, Salon of 1808, no.274; Paris, Salon of 1814,
no.478; Paris, 1999–2000, no.397 (A. Pougetoux)
LITERATURE: Tripier-Lefranc 1880, pp.264–65; Schommer
1968

Gros was at the pinnacle of his career when he
exhibited this portrait at the Salon of 1808. The
success of *Napoleon Bonaparte Visiting the Plague-Stricken
in Jaffa* (1804; Louvre, Paris) and of the *Battle of
Aboukir* (1806; Musée National du Château,
Versailles), *Napoleon on the Battlefield of Eylau* (1808;
Louvre, Paris) confirmed him finally as one of the
finest living history painters, a close runner-up to
his teacher Jacques-Louis David. Having put his
brush at the Emperor's disposal, he received the
Légion d'honneur from him at the close of the
Salon – as did Anne-Louis Girodet de Roussy-
Trioson, Horace Vernet and Pierre-Paul Prud'hon.
Gros immediately began to paint a large picture
(which he never finished) to commemorate the
event (begun in 1808; Musée National du Château,
Versailles): Napoleon, who had always been
depicted in the role of conqueror, was now
presented as the patron of the arts.

While engaged on this task, he continued
to work as a portrait painter, a lucrative activity
for which Gros professed the scorn that could be
expected from a history painter. In spite of the
conventional views of the critics, Gros understood

the modernity of the genre, its historical dimension, and the powerful contribution it could make to the creation of an image, based on military exploits. *General Lasalle at the Siege of Stettin* was the first of a series of monumental representations of great soldiers; it was followed by the portrait of General Fournier-Sarlovèze (1812; Louvre, Paris) and culminated in the equestrian portrait of *Joachim Murat, King of Naples* (1812; Louvre, Paris), in which the sovereign is identified with the soldier.

Antoine-Louis-Charles Lasalle (1775–1809), who was born in Metz, belonged to the minor nobility. He was the hero of the Battle of Rivoli in 1797, Napoleon's companion during the Egyptian campaign, which took place from 1798 to 1801, was famed for his intrepid nature and his fiery outbursts and became, in 1805, one of the principal military leaders of the Empire. He headed a celebrated brigade of hussars, nicknamed 'the infernal brigade', which won victory after victory, notably in Prussia and Spain, contributing thus to the outward expansion of the Empire. He was killed by a bullet to the head at the Battle of Wagram in 1809.

This monumental work illustrates the development during the Empire of the full-length portrait, popular in England but until this time quite rare in France, or very carefully controlled. The English influence manifests itself mainly in the pose and in the way the figure is placed in the landscape. In a pose inspired by classical antiquity and commonly adopted in large English portraits such as Pompeo Batoni's *Colonel William Gordon* (1765–66; Fyvie Castle, Aberdeenshire), the general leans on his sabre, looking into the distance and turning slightly to one side. It is unlikely that Gros had seen this painting, but he was evidently aware of British painting in general, possibly through the travellers he could have met in Florence in the 1790s, or, more probably, through engravings. The *Portrait of Second Lieutenant Charles Legrand* (c.1810; Los Angeles County Museum of Art) demonstrates this even more clearly. Wearing the traditional uniform of the hussars, with his cocked hat at his feet, plus an extravagant meerschaum pipe at his feet and a tobacco pouch, General Lasalle is seen enjoying the full glory of his status, exalting the status portrait on a very grand scale.

As a history painter, however, it was Gros's intention to transcend the inferior genre in which he was operating, as he had already done in 1796 with *Bonaparte at the Ponte d'Arcole* (Musée National du Château, Versailles). The artificiality of the pose is justified by the history taking place before the spectator's eyes; the expression of the sitter's status is transcended by the commemorative value of the portrait. In the present painting, the artist shows General Lasalle receiving the keys of the town of Stettin, one of his most glorious exploits. Although he had only 700 mounted soldiers at his disposal, he succeeded in forcing the surrender of the Prussian stronghold, guarded by 5,500 men and

a powerful artillery, by a ruse: in the background, Prussian dignitaries can be seen carrying the keys of the town on a tray and the general holds the deed of surrender in his right hand. The clenched right fist, with its white glove, introduces some of the energy of the man of action into this elegant, conventional pose, emphasising the ambivalence of the representation – somewhere between a status portrait and a history portrait. Gros was thus following the trail blazed by David's *Napoleon Crossing the Alps* (fig.47), but, whereas David skilfully merges the conventions of portraiture (equestrian and circumstantial) with the heroism appropriate to the history painter, Gros emphasises the need for choice but fails to come down on one side or the other.

His depiction of the general has grandeur, but is static; Gros did not recapture the enthusiasm of his *Bonaparte at the Ponte d'Arcole*. Although fully aware of the communicative value of the portrait in the constitution of the new aristocracy, he seems constrained by the need for representation in this genre. Even in his exuberant, half wheeling equestrian portrait of *Joachim Murat, King of Naples*, the action seems frozen by the weighty display of the insignia of victory: medals, plumes, breastplates, sabres, the horse's ostentatious harness. Could Lasalle's melancholy pose not be interpreted as his victorious exhaustion after the trials of battle? It is not surprising that the most attractive of Gros's 'military' portraits is posthumous, the portrait of a young man who died before enjoying the laurels of victory; in the *Portrait of Second Lieutenant Charles Legrand*, Gros takes up the conventions of the Anglo-Flemish aristocratic portrait in an assured and tender way.

Nevertheless, despite the evident manner in which Gros hesitates, *General Lasalle at the Siege of Stettin* marks an important stage in the development of French art. From a formal point of view, it illustrates the contribution made by Gros in the use of more intense colour in painting around 1810. The artist was a great admirer of Flemish painting, Rubens in particular, and here he uses warm colours, yellows with large splashes of red (the general's trousers, the decorations, the tobacco pouch), to contrast with the grey-blue of the sky and the hussar's jacket.

As in *Bonaparte at the Ponte Arcole*, but on a larger scale, Gros plays with the effects of fragmentation. Although the description focuses on the figure of the hero of Stettin, who commissioned the work, the overall composition of the painting implies that the portrait should be understood symbolically as a part of a much greater whole (the surrender of the town) and returns us to the notion of Gros as a history painter. The positioning of the figure in the landscape reinterprets the conventions of battle painting: the general stands on a hill from which he can keep an eye on operations.

In addition, Gros repeats a procedure he had followed in *Napoleon Distributing Swords of Honour to the Grenadiers of the Consular Guard after the Battle of Marengo*

(1803; Musée National du Château, Malmaison), adding the picturesque figure of a hussar on the right, wearing his Légion d'honneur and standing to attention as he holds Lasalle's horse. This was the general's way of paying tribute to the courage of his men, and emphasising the collective effort of the victory. A few years later, in the *Wounded Cavalryman Leaving the Firing Line* (1814; Louvre, Paris) Géricault managed to cross the line between portrait and action by freeing his sitter, an anonymous soldier, from any social identity. Unlike Gros, Géricault does not focus on the hero, the general-in-chief, he concentrates on a simple soldier – like this anonymous hussar. Times had changed, and the glory of victory was replaced by the despair of defeat. SA

# Pierre-Narcisse Guérin

PARIS, 1774 – ROME, 1833

## 141
### Henri de La Rochejacquelein

1817
Oil on canvas, 217 × 142 cm
Dépôt de l'Etat au Musée d'Art et d'Histoire de Cholet (on loan from the Musée du Louvre, Paris, 5187)

PROVENANCE: commissioned in 1816 by the Minister of the King's Household for the Salle des Gardes in the Palais de Saint-Cloud; after 1830, in the reserves of the Musée du Louvre; lent to the Musée d'Art et d'Histoire de Cholet, 1914
EXHIBITED: Paris, Salon of 1817, no.400; Paris, 1974–75, no.95 (catalogue entry by J. Villain)
LITERATURE: Bottineau 1975; Nantes 1995, p.96; Chaudonneret 1999, pp.166–67

In June 1816, the Comte de Pradel, Minister of the King's Household, suggested to Louis XVIII (now restored permanently to the throne) that a group of full-length portraits should be commissioned depicting the generals who had fought and died for the King in the Vendée between 1793 and 1795. A few days later, Louis XVIII accepted this proposal. On the advice of Prosper de Barante, Pradel then commissioned paintings from some of the most prominent artists of the day: Girodet painted Cathelineau and Bonchamps; Paulin Guérin, Charette; François Gérard, Moreau; Steuben, Pichegru; Robert Lefèvre, Lescure; Mauzaisse, Suzannet; Delaval, Louis de La Rochejacquelein; and Pierre-Narcisse Guérin, Henri de La Rochejacquelein. The commission of course fell within the dynamic of the Empire, which used the portrait as a means of celebrating a new aristocracy whose merit was partly founded on heroism on the battlefield. The Salon des Maréchaux in the Tuileries embodied this trend. The new series was designed to form a gallery, a kind of pantheon to royalist glories, and was intended above all as a token of reassurance to the ultra-royalists. It was undertaken as a response to pressure from the victims' families (Chaudonneret 1999), particularly the Marquise de La Rochejacquelein, who, during the uprising in the Vendée, lost her first husband, Lescure, her second husband, Louis de La Rochejacquelein, and also his brother Henri (1772–1794). Louis XVIII's canny policy was to balance the maintenance of certain principles gained under the Revolution with the support of counter-revolutionary values; he was suspicious of any ostentatious signs of reaction, since they might revive discord between the people of France. As a result, the portraits were not to be displayed in the official apartments at the Tuileries but, more discreetly, in the Salle des Gardes at the Palais de Saint-Cloud instead.

Because they were posthumous portraits, the families had to supply all the information necessary for the production of a good likeness; for the most part the artists had never known the generals. Because of the retrospective character of the portrait and its commemorative status, the reverse phenomenon can be seen here from that which fuelled Jacques-Louis David's portrait of *Napoleon Crossing the Alps* (fig. 47), in which any close resemblance had to give way to a more generalised idea of the great man. The Marquise de La Rochejacquelein therefore sent Pradel a miniature and some very detailed handwritten notes, and it was from these that Guérin composed his painting, reconstituting the face of the young general, who died at the age of twenty-two at the hands of a republican soldier. The idealisation so often found in history painting was here exaggerated by the absence of the sitter: Guérin built his composition around the idea of headstrong youth cut down in the prime of life. On the one hand, the young man's face, with his eyes trained on enemy lines, has the abstract purity of a classical statue. On the other hand, his energetic stance at the foot of a small mound, with his left hand aiming his pistol and his right arm in a sling, recalls the efforts made by modern monumental masons to enhance the communicative content of public monuments. In the same Salon in 1817, David d'Angers was exhibiting the plaster model of his *Grand Condé* made for the Pont de la Concorde (Galerie David d'Angers, Angers). Guérin playfully juxtaposes the gentleness of La Rochejacquelein's features with the fervour of his fighting spirit. Girodet, in his portraits of Bonchamps and, in particular, Cathelineau (Salon of 1824) adopted a more modern stance, expressing the retrospective character of the portrait in a melancholic, almost absent fashion. Guérin favoured action, inserting this representation into the same historical family as David's *Napoleon Crossing the Alps*; he exalted historical illusion and, by using the idea of a slice of life, transcended the genre in which he was commissioned to express himself: 'This portrait is a history painting' remarked Miel, the critic, in his review of the Salon (*Journal des débats*, 31 July 1817).

Guérin was one of the official artists of the Empire and a past master in the representation of battle. Dressed in bourgeois apparel, whose cleanliness and elegance betray the idealisation espoused by the painter, La Rochejacquelein wears the Sacred Heart of the Vendéens on his chest, with the corresponding white cockade of the royalists on his hat; the large white flag is adorned with the words 'Vive le Roi'. The notion of a modern hero standing out against a flag to emphasise the national scope of the representation is a reinterpretation of the portrait of *Bonaparte at the Ponte d'Arcole* by Gros (1796; Musée National du Château, Versailles). The young man's gesture was probably inspired by David's *Napoleon Crossing the Alps*. However, whereas David played on the ambiguity of the representation and the meaning it should be given, Guérin deals with it more prosaically. The idea of the bayonets in the background and the soldiers depicted almost without colour in order to set off to best advantage the ideal beauty of the main figure is derived from the same source. In David's case it was merely the means of evoking a historical event that was transcended by the aura of the great man; here, the details acquire a particular political significance. They make it possible for the artist to avoid representing the enemy, which would have risked reviving memories of the civil war: 'We see the end of the republican bayonets, but we do not see the French fighting the French' (Miel, *Journal des débats*, 31 July 1817).

After 1819 a number of versions of the painting were executed at the expense of the crown for the families involved. The series was immediately engraved and lithographed, which meant that it could be distributed as propaganda for the ultra-royalists, particularly via reinterpretations in popular prints. SA

# Carl Friedrich Hagemann
BERLIN, 1773 – BERLIN, 1806

**III**
*Immanuel Kant*

1801
Marble, 51.5 × 23 × 26.5 cm
Inscription on the back: *F. Hagemann / fecit*; on the left shoulder: *EMANUEL / KANT. / 1801*
Kunsthalle, Hamburg, 1939/82

PROVENANCE: gift of Thusnelda von Hess, Hamburg, 1866
EXHIBITED: Hamburg, 1995
LITERATURE: Friedländer 1890, p.63; Eckardt 1987, pp.64, 78, 454, 492, ill. 116; Grolle in Hamburg 1995, *passim*

The mark left by Immanuel Kant (1724–1804) on the thought of his period was greater than that made by any other German philosopher. He spent his life in Northern Germany and remained in his home town, Königsberg (now Kaliningrad) in East Prussia; he never left the region, and almost never went out of his house except to take regular walks outside the walls. For him, the world of the intellect took the place of *Lebensraum*, giving him a feeling of complete freedom; his daily routine was unchanging: the microcosm of his home town represented the macrocosm of the whole world to him. He avoided travelling long distances, and his philosophical ideas were disseminated thanks to the development of printing and also to the students who attended his exceptional lectures. In 1798 the Berlin sculptor Emmanuel Bardou (1744–1818) made a portrait of Kant in the shape of a herm, a precursor to Hagemann's portrait bust: he represented the thinker in the traditional classical form given to Greek philosophers, a herm, with classical drapery and non-incised eyes.

Hagemann was Johann Gottfried Schadow's favourite pupil in the early 1800s. If he had not died so young, at the age of thirty-three, he could have been one Schadow's most important disciples, along with Friedrich Tieck, the Wichmann brothers and Christian Daniel Rauch; his few remaining works make this abundantly clear. Evidence of his precocious talent can be found in the marble statuette of a naiad, half life-size, which King Friedrich-Wilhelm III of Prussia bought at the exhibition held by the Berlin Academy in 1802 and placed in his palace in Unter den Linden. The fact that it was put on such prominent display gives an idea of the esteem in which the young artist was already held. This *Naiad* was taken to Paris by Vivant Denon for the Musée Napoléon, revealing the exceptional reputation enjoyed by Hagemann, abroad as well as in Germany. Vivant Denon took very few contemporary works back to Paris.

In addition to the *Naiad*, this portrait of Kant was also exhibited for the first time at the exhibition held by the Berlin Academy in 1802. The size of the small bust, almost reduced to just a head, suggests that the physical presence of the old man has been minimised in order to concentrate the spectator's gaze on the facial features; the slenderness of the herm emphasises the philosopher's fragility and imminent demise. The bust's pedestal is original and painstakingly carved; its two ornamental volutes and trapezoid shape accentuate even further the spirituality and immateriality of the piece. Hagemann has succeeded, paradoxically, in combining the weight of the marble – which he chose in order to produce a monument in the classical style – with a light, insubstantial composition.

The features of the emaciated face, lined by years, seem almost asexual. Only the fleshy mouth, from which the thinker's words issue, and the vigilant eyes, tools for reading, are emphasised. The virtual lack of hair does not, however, correspond to the official view of Kant, who, in public, wore a wig, as his contemporaries did – as can be verified in portraits, painted and drawn. The choice of natural hair for this bust reveals a preference, and reminds us that the sculptor Jean-Antoine Houdon also, when representing Voltaire and Rousseau, gave alternative versions, with and without a wig. Hagemann's choice of short hair should be seen as an unconventional pledge of sincerity (at the same moment, portraits by Schadow and other sculptors were usually adorned with completely official, conventional hairstyles and wigs). It is also possible to interpret this choice as a clear reference to the classical portraits of philosophers.

Hagemann did not start making the bust on his own initiative; the commission was born out of a fortunate chain of external events – Kant's admirers, grouped around Jonas Ludwig von Hess in Hamburg, wished to erect a monument to the philosopher. They turned to Schadow who, keen to encourage his pupil, then in his late twenties, passed the commission on to him. The story goes that Hagemann encountered Kant in 1801 and asked him 'if he wished to be represented completely faithfully?' (he was ready to deliver either a strongly realistic bust, or something more classical and idealised). Kant is said to have replied: 'You must not make me as old and ugly as I am' (Hamburg 1995, p.25). Evidently the philosopher was hoping for a subtly enhanced portrait.

Hagemann did his best: he smoothed and softened the philosopher's face. The result is an elderly, slightly asexual, man; above all, the sculptor produced a very typical portrait of an introverted thinker, fragile and intense. Even though the realism of the features – the scrawny neck and hollow cheeks – recalls the realistic portraits of republican Rome, the presentation of them is highly personal. Kant was slightly hunched in posture, and this is conveyed in the portrait by the head, which is slightly tilted towards the front.

The first version of the bust is lost and is only known by a plaster cast now in the Staatsbibliothek, Berlin; it adorned Kant's tomb in Königsberg for a time, and bore the inscription: 'Immanuel Kant. *Sapienti amicorum pietas*' (The wise enjoy the loyalty of their friends), reminding us of the veneration in which the elderly sage was held by his circle of friends. Only the second version, which differs in a few details, was found in Hamburg. BM

# Hugh Douglas Hamilton
DUBLIN, *c*.1739 – DUBLIN, 1808

## 95
*Lieutenant Richard Mansergh St George*

*c*.1796
Not signed or dated
Inscribed on tomb: *NON · IMMEMOR* (not forgotten)
Oil on canvas, 228 × 146.2 cm
National Gallery of Ireland, Dublin, 4585

PROVENANCE: commissioned by the sitter from 1795 to 1796; by descent to Frances Jane Edith Mansergh St George, later Mrs Edmund John Winn; by descent to Sophie Winn; Sotheby's, London, 18 November 1992, lot 52; bought in; subsequently purchased by the National Gallery of Ireland by private treaty, 1992
EXHIBITED: Society of Artists of Ireland, Dublin, 1801, no.56
LITERATURE: see Figgis and Rooney 2001, vol.1, p.178

Hamilton's portrait was occasioned by the death of the sitter's wife. It shows the bereaved husband in cavalry uniform, leaning against his late spouse's tomb, inscribed 'NON IMMEMOR' ('not forgotten'); his head rests on his hand, his helmet lies on the ground. Cypress trees – symbols of death and mourning – surround the scene; through them, a distant stretch of water and what might be an island may be glimpsed.

Richard St George Mansergh St George (1751/52–1798) was a scion of Anglo-Irish landed gentry. Educated at Westminster School, the Middle Temple and Trinity College, Cambridge, he added the final 'St George' to his name in 1774 on inheriting property from his mother's family.

His portrait must have been begun after 26 April 1796, the date when he was promoted to lieutenant in the 18th Regiment of (Light) Dragoons, in whose uniform he is depicted (Figgis and Rooney 2001, vol.1, p.179). First shown in Dublin in 1801, it was 'a picture highly esteemed', as one diarist who visited the exhibition noted (Cullen 2000, p.240). This diarist also observed: 'I had several years ago seen and admired it' at Hamilton's house, which suggests that the artist must have brought the image to a more or less complete state fairly rapidly.

The sitter's grieving pose had been used before by Hamilton in a pastel commemorating Jonas Brooke (Figgis and Rooney 2001, vol.1, p.179). Similar stances had also been used by Romney in 1781 (*The Hon. William Courtenay*) and Wright of Derby in 1786 (*Dorothy Gell of Hopton*). Tomb sculpture by Hamilton's friend Canova also prefigured the posture (Cullen 1983, p.418; Cullen 1997, p.107).

Artist and subject were perhaps long acquainted: in 1786, at Rome, fellow Irishman abroad Henry Quin recorded the presence there of both Hamilton and an unspecified (almost certainly Mansergh) 'St George' (Ingamells 1997, pp.451, 836). Mansergh St George had a lifelong interest in the arts. He was an amateur artist himself, and several of his caricature designs were published in the early 1770s. He joined the army in 1776; a Gainsborough portrait commemorates his departure for the American War of Independence (Myrone 2005, pp.237–39). A pair of battle paintings by Xavier Della Gatta shows the encounters that ended in his being grievously injured at the battle of Germantown in 1777, when a musket-ball was lodged in the back of his skull and he was trepanned. Invalided, he married Anne Stepney by 1788. Sons were born

in 1789 and in 1791, and a portrait of mother and eldest son was painted by George Romney in the summer of 1791, shortly after doctors had warned of Anne's 'fatal symptoms' (Cullen 2000, p.50). She died, it appears, on 22 August 1792 (Monthly Register 1792–93, vol.2, p.39).

This portrayal of Mansergh St George with his hand on his head not only symbolically suggests the melancholic associations of the tomb on which he leans, but also the ongoing physical pain of the sitter's war wound, inflicted two decades earlier. His friend Anna Seward, when she addressed a poetic epistle to him in 1783, described him as having 'a considerable part of his head shot away', 'feeble, emaciated, and in almost constant pain' (Seward 1810, vol.2, p.216). It was noted in 1788 that his wound had never healed, having 'baffled the skill of the most eminent' European doctors (Hamwood Papers, 1930, p.74). Hamilton himself made two other images of the sitter (Cullen 1984, p.199). One of these is extant and shows the cap that he used to cover his damaged skull (repr. in Crookshank and Glin 2002, p.112).

Mental instability was the long-term effect of his head wound. A fellow officer in America described him as 'quite military mad', declaring that 'I often thought that St George wished to be wounded' (Hunter 1894, pp.21–22). Even before his injury, his conduct was 'of an eccentric cast'. His wife's death appears to have further unhinged him; his grief was described as 'boundless and almost unexampled' (Gentleman's Magazine 1798, p.98). Not without reason did his friend Sir Brooke Boothby (see cat.134), himself mourning the loss of his daughter, address a 1796 sonnet thus:

> *Dear Mansergh! of the few this breast who share,*
> *And share in pitying sympathy its woe,*
> *You best my vast excess of passion know.*

Shortly after Anne's death, her distraught widower drafted a letter to his acquaintance, the artist Henry Fuseli. He outlined his extraordinary grief: 'convulsive attacks … nightly hallucinations and dreadful visions … sudden delirium'. He then suggested an equally extraordinary catharsis: the creation by Fuseli of an image that would reflect the horrible power of his anguish. Thereby, 'having as it were transferred the Image to you, it will cease to haunt me'. In a further gothic twist, the picture was to be locked away in a room for his sons to discover after his death (Cullen 2000, pp.50, 48).

The letter was apparently neither finished nor sent, and Hamilton's eventual portrait was of an altogether less extreme order. But taken together, it has been argued, they constitute a compelling instance of a particular Anglo-Irish cultural condition: 'The portrait and letter are cries for the continuation of a class' (Cullen 1997, p.114).

Brutally killed while venturing in person to quash growing resistance in a remote area of his estates, the circumstances of the sitter's death further attest to his reckless courage, but perhaps also to his latent mental imbalance. As the diarist who attended the 1801 exhibition noted, Hamilton's melancholic portrayal took on added poignancy after his death, given 'the recollection of the late shocking termination of his existence by the hands of assassins' (Cullen 2000, p.240). sm

# Constantin Hansen
ROME, 1804 – FREDERIKSBERG, 1880

## 108
*The Artist's Sisters Signe and Henriette Reading a Book*

1826
Oil on canvas, 65.5 × 56 cm
Statens Museum for Kunst, Copenhagen, 3004

PROVENANCE: purchased 1910
EXHIBITED: see Copenhagen, 1991, p.144, no.12
LITERATURE: Hannover 1901, pp.22–24; Copenhagen 1983, p.102, no.134; London 1984, pp.172–73, no.74; Monrad 1989, p.117, fig.97; Copenhagen 1991, p.144, no.12; Monrad 1994, pp.108–09, no.31; Brøns 2002, p.163

One of Denmark's 'Golden Age' painters of the nineteenth century, Hansen was still an art student when he executed this portrait of two of his sisters reading. At this time, the young man had only recently switched from architecture to painting at the Royal Danish Academy of Fine Arts in Copenhagen (London 1984, p.172). There, in 1829, he began his study with one of Denmark's most famous artists, Christoffer Wilhelm Eckersberg, who, in his turn, had been a student of David's in Paris. Under Eckersberg's tutelage, Hansen began to work along more rigorous classical lines. This painting, created in 1826, before he had met Eckersberg, displays Hansen's inherent skills as a colourist, his nuanced handling of tonalities, his modelled forms and his sensitivity in representing his sitters' mood. It also reveals knowledge of Dutch seventeenth-century genre painting, a stylistic and thematic source Hansen would further explore in his later work.

The birth of the Danish Golden Age coincided with a rise in interest in seventeenth-century Dutch art. Parallels have often been drawn between the Dutch Golden Age and the Danish Golden Age (Rønberg 2001, p.74). The presence of a strong bourgeoisie in both countries, as well as the affinity between the Protestant ethics and values these nationalities upheld, is evident in the art of both countries. Not only were examples of Dutch painting available to Danish artists in Denmark's royal collections, but artists such as Hansen travelled through Holland on their way to Italy

(Copenhagen 2001, pp.8–9). Thus, seventeenth-century Dutch genre representations of middle-class life and everyday scenes – among these depictions of the nuclear family or women in interiors – were a source of inspiration for Hansen and his contemporaries. The combination of genre and portraiture also has roots in the work of the Dutch, although in Danish painting the sitter is always identifiable, whereas in many Dutch examples the subject is often anonymous. Hansen's representations of women hark back to the work of his Dutch predecessors in their tranquil stillness and the ways in which he made use of the light peculiar to northern Europe within these interiors.

Hansen frequently painted his sisters, who were readily available as models, engaged in various activities around the family home (Los Angeles 1993, p.118). This portrait demonstrates Hansen's masterly treatment of colour in the warm red and olive tones of the girls' matching dresses and the soft light cast upon their faces as they bend over a book. The overall geometry of the composition provides evidence of his earlier training in architecture and his awareness of spatial relationships. The spareness of the furniture in this image – a settle upon which they sit – focuses attention on the sisters, as does Hansen's close framing of their forms in the frontal plane of the composition. The comfortable familiarity between the girls, manifest in their physical proximity and in the easy way in which Henriette clasps Signe's shoulder, reveals the bond between the two siblings and distinguishes this work from straightforward genre painting – which traditionally addresses the anecdotal – moving it into the domain of intimate portraiture. In this tender informality the work differs from the scripted scenes characteristic of commissioned nineteenth-century Danish family portraits (Rønberg 2001, p.80).

The subject of this painting – two girls reading – underscores the northern European, bourgeois emphasis on a well-ordered home life, proper upbringing and education (Rønberg 2001, p.81). Moral rectitude and good behaviour began in the home. It was here that parents inculcated children with the appropriate values and customs to prepare them for the future, especially the daughters, who would instil these mores into the next generation when they established their own households and families. The themes of literacy and education are also implicit and point to the level of learning young middle-class women received in Denmark. All of these qualities come through in Hansen's perceptive depiction of his sisters absorbed in the act of reading. vg

# Hortense Haudebourt-Lescot
PARIS, 1784 – PARIS, 1845

## 84
*Self-portrait*

1825
Oil on canvas, 74 × 60 cm
Signed on the lower left: *Haudebourt Lescot / 1825*.
Département des Peintures, Musée du Louvre, Paris, MI 719.
Gift of Mme Buhner, *née* Maria Dauby, pupil of the artist, 1867

PROVENANCE: given to the Musée du Louvre by Mme Buhner, *née* Maria Dauby, pupil of the artist, 1867, MI 719
EXHIBITED: Castres, 1973; Paris, Detroit and New York, 1974; Los Angeles, 1976
LITERATURE: Both de Tauzia, in Paris 1878, no.783; Lafenestre 1888, no.41, p.27; Brière 1924, p.128; Escholier 1941–43, p.102; Sterling and Adhémar 1958–61, vol.3, 1053, ill.379, p.1; Robertson and Julia 1974, pp.486–87; Nochlin 1976, pp.218–19

Just over forty years old when she painted this self-portrait, Hortense Haudebourt-Lescot was at the height of her success as a portrait and genre painter. As the child of well-to-do Parisian parents, she displayed a precocious talent for drawing, and at the age of seven she entered the studio of Guillaume Guillon, known as Lethière, a family friend and notable history painter, who was appointed Director of the French Academy in Rome in 1807. The young Mlle Lescot – also an accomplished dancer – followed her mentor to Italy the next year, and lived there until 1816, studying the Old Masters and absorbing the vivacity of Italian life. Her experiences inspired her quotidian scenes, which are replete with charm and realistic detail. A member of the Accademia di San Luca, she sent paintings to Paris be exhibited at the Salon; over 110 of her works were shown between 1810 and 1840, winning her several awards, including, ultimately, the first-class medal in 1827 and the distinction of being chosen to work on Charles X's series of eminent historical figures for Versailles in 1830. Quite exceptional for a woman artist at the beginning of the nineteenth century, her student experience abroad was instrumental in her success in the niche of picturesque, Italianate genre scenes, prefiguring J.-V. Schnetz and Léopold Robert, who were to become veterans of genre painting. Haudebourt-Lescot was also a lithographer and teacher, and one of her pupils, Mme Buhner (*née* Maria Dauby), owned the 1825 self-portrait until she gave it to the Louvre in 1867.

Haudebourt-Lescot sat to Ingres, although his portrait of her is now lost (a drawing dating from 1814 exists in the San Francisco Museum of Fine Arts), and the delicacy and lapidary quality of her drawings and watercolours show the influence of this artist, who lived in Rome from 1806 to 1824. In his small, engaging drawing she is dressed in an elaborate, rustic Italian peasant costume and Ingres captured the features she was sedulously to render herself eleven years later: the same long nose, wide upper lip and slightly prominent chin. In her self-portrait, she holds her head in a similar position, the curls of her dark, shining hair escaping from a heavy, black velvet beret which forms an inky halo around her head, deepening the overall chiaroscuro of the work. Her face and neck brightly contrast with the shadows of the plain background. Emphasising the importance of her right hand, in which she holds the artist's brush, Haudebourt-Lescot supports and cradles it in her left. The brush she holds is a symbol of the arts of painting and writing, hence, of learning and wisdom.

Typically, the women in Haudebourt-Lescot's signature genre style are fashionably attired with luminous eyes, arched brows, aquiline features, exaggerated waists and attenuated feet, such as those in *Le Choix d'un chapeau* (c.1818; Edouard Rahir Collection, Paris), in which two society matrons, flanked by their serving maids, with a rapt suitor on the left, debate the merits of various hats. In contrast, the 1825 self-portrait is particularly distinguished: Haudebourt-Lescot omits any extraneous details in the simple, intense focus of the composition. The rich, shadowy *sfumato* of the background is reminiscent of Rembrandt's portraits, as is the supple fluidity in the handling of oils and the depth of characterisation. Though she excelled in depicting domestic scenes with highly descriptive interiors, Haudebourt-Lescot emphatically eschewed any ornamentation or embellishment, adopting a relatively severe and stark male idiom. She wears the traditional artist's beret, with the accoutrements of the brush and gold chain, in the typical guise of a male artist – unusual, if not unprecedented, dress for a female artist.

With heavy-lidded eyes, a pink blush on her cheekbones and nose, and a high, thin brow, Haudebourt-Lescot did not idealise her features to make them conform with the attractive standard that she employed for the women in her genre repertoire. She wears a pensive expression and gazes down into space. Given her relatively confident, if not audacious, decision to cast herself in the traditional garb of the male artist, it is curious that she does not meet the spectator's eye, in confrontation, choosing instead to remain contemplative and remote. Her lips are slightly parted, evoking a sense of anticipation, as if she is about to speak or, perhaps roused from her reverie, return to her work. Overall, the influence of seventeenth-century Flemish painting is strong in the Eyckian sheen of the portrait's highly polished finish, the presence of distinct iconographical elements, the plain, sombre dress, the gleaming pearl ear-rings, and the balance of the composition. Yet symbolism and any potential narrative are kept to the barest minimum. Haudebourt-Lescot did not admit any distractions to the portrait and presents a pure, unadulterated definition of herself as a working artist.

Notably, from 1827 to 1828, she only exhibited portraits at the Salon. In her later work, portraits and royal commissions came to replace the sentimental, moralising or literary genre themes

that were so widely reproduced in engravings and lithographs. Haudebourt-Lescot's private, portrait commissions are of a high calibre, even impressing the notoriously truculent art critic Auguste Jal, who commented on the 'remarkable' quality of her entries to that pivotal Salon of 1827–28. This self-portrait suggests Haudebourt-Lescot's determined effort to distance herself from the relatively lowly categorisation of a 'charming' genre painter. Unequivocally, her self-image rests on her role as a professional artist and – through the calculated de-emphasis of genre elements – her identity as a portraitist specifically. At this period, as disillusionment with the vicissitudes of political life set in, Parisian society no longer looked to the state or the monarchy for edifying role models. Portraiture had come to be considered the last bastion for the display of a person's integrity or a code of ethics. Although Haudebourt-Lescot had exploited the public's appetite for moralising, religious or literary subtexts in her genre scenes, she presented an image of herself as a serious, working painter, intelligent and worthy of as much respect and recognition as her male peers. CC

# Francesco Hayez

VENICE, 1791 – MILAN, 1882

## 98
*Luigia Vitali, Mylius's Widow*

1832
Oil on wood, 131 × 100 cm
Villa Vigoni, Loveno di Menaggio (Como)

PROVENANCE: through descent in the family to current collection, which was a bequest from Don Ignazio Vigoni to Germany, 1983
EXHIBITED: see Mazzocca 1994, p.224, no.175; Milan, 1999, p.72, no.4
LITERATURE: Mazzocca 1994, p.224, no.175; Milan 1999, p.72, no.4

Following the death of his son, Giulio, Enrico Mylius commissioned Francesco Hayez to paint a portrait of the young man's mourning wife, Luigia Vitali (Mazzocca 1994, p.224). Mylius was a wealthy German banker who, in 1792, relocated from Frankfurt to Milan, where he soon became an important patron of the arts and literature (Rebora 1999, p.33). His intellectual circle included the writers Wolfgang Goethe and Alessandro Manzoni, he championed painters Hayez and Pelagio Palagi and sculptors Pompeo Marchesi and Bertel Thorvaldsen, and he endowed a prize for painting in his name at the Real Accademia di Belle Arti di Brera in Milan. Hayez – a leading proponent of historical Romanticism – was one of the artists Mylius most fervently supported and had already executed a portrait of his wife, Friederike Schnauss, in 1828 (Mazzocca 1994, p.190).

Giulio was only thirty when he died. Shaken by the tragedy of his son's early death, Mylius had him immortalised by several of his favourite artists. He commissioned Marchesi to realise a marble bust, which represents Giulio in antique garb (cat.97), as well as an allegorical neoclassical *bas-relief* depicting the moment of his death. Later, he asked Thorvaldsen to create two more *bas-reliefs*, *Nido degli amori* (*The Cupids' Nest*) and *Nemesi* (*Nemesis*). These works, along with Marchesi's, now decorate a cenotaph located in a memorial *tempietto* on the grounds of the family's villa (Rebora 1999, p.33). Mylius was also deeply attached to his daughter-in-law. Luigia had married Giulio for love, even though her family had attempted to stop the wedding going ahead because Giulio was foreign, Protestant and not of noble blood. Despite the onset of a sudden and terminal illness, he and Luigia wed (Milan 1999, p.72). Mylius's commission to commemorate Luigia's suffering was not only a gesture of love towards her and his son, but one in recognition of his daughter-in-law's dedication to Giulio and the Mylius family.

Hayez's painting is in fact a double portrait of both the seated widow and Giulio, represented in the Marchesi bust. The placement of a grieving woman next to the sculpted effigy of the deceased loosely follows funerary iconography. However, Hayez based his composition upon that of an earlier portrait with a very different mood, *Cristina di Belgioioso* (1830–31), which depicts a well-known young Milanese noblewoman in a smiling, slightly enticing guise, next to a bust of her mother (Mazzocca 1994, p.215). Despite this earlier work, Hayez realistically represented Luigia in a state of sorrow: her face is a little pinched, she has visible circles under her slightly reddened eyes, and she gazes at the viewer, deep in thought. She is simply dressed in black widow's attire, adorned only with a fur trim and lace cuffs on her dress. The artist makes a visible contrast between Marchesi's sculpture, which is turned to look into the dark part of the painting, and his wife, who faces in the opposite direction to the sculpture and looks out at an unseen light source. Luigia's pale face and white sloping neck emerge from the dark cloth of her dress as she takes on the semblance of a bust and makes a visual parallel with her husband's marble form. This portrait was greeted with acclaim by the critics when it was exhibited at the annual Salon at the Brera in 1832 (Mazzocca 1994, p.224).

Hayez was best known for his historical and medievalising subjects, which were often inspired by significant events from Italy's past, especially at moments when Italians expelled foreign rulers (Italy was not unified until the spring of 1861). Implicit in many of these nineteenth-century portrayals of earlier glory were subversive political statements about foreign domination in modern Italy. Sometimes these statements were more overt and specific to current events, as with his *Count Colonel Francesco Teodoro Arese Lucini in Jail* (1828), a nobleman who supported the overthrow of the Austrians who governed Lombardy (Mazzocca 1994, p.187). In 1832, when Hayez completed Luigia Vitali's portrait, the region was still under Habsburg control. Giuseppe Mazzini formed the *Risorgimento* (resurgence) group, *La Giovane Italia* (Young Italy) and the writer Silvio Pellico, a member of the *carbonari*, published *Le mie prigioni*, an account of his incarceration in the Speilberg prison at the hands of the Austrians. Mylius himself supported the liberal Italian cause in moderate form, later trying to act as a bridge between Italian and Austrian relations in Milan (Milan 1999, pp.26–27). Yet, at the time of this portrait's execution, these political inferences did not enter into play, and the overriding personal tragedy of the Mylius family took centre stage. vg

# Jean-Antoine Houdon

VERSAILLES, 1741 – PARIS, 1828

## 128

*Sophie Arnould in the Title Role of Gluck's 'Iphigenia in Aulis'*

1775
Marble, 81 × 51 × 29.5 cm
Inscription on the reverse, on the edge of the bust:
*SOPHIE ARNOULD, Houdon F. 1775*
Département des Sculptures, Musée du Louvre, Paris, RF 2596

PROVENANCE: commissioned by Sophie Arnould by contract, 5 April 1775; in the collection of the sitter, at least until the Revolution; then appears to have been sold during her lifetime; sale of the Véron collection, 22–23 March 1858, no.64; acquired by the 4th Marquis of Hertford (1800–1870); bequeathed by him to his natural son Sir Richard Wallace (1818–1890); then to his wife, Lady Wallace; after her death in 1897, in the collection of her husband's secretary (and her adviser) Sir John Murray Scott (1843–1912); bequeathed to Victoria, Lady Sackville (1862–1936); she sold the bust to Edgard Stern before 1925; presented by Madame Edgard Stern and her children, 1947
EXHIBITED: Paris, Salon of 1775, no.257; Washington and Los Angeles, 2003–04, no.8, repr.; Versailles, 2004, no.8, repr.; Fontainebleau, 2005–06, no.70, repr.
LITERATURE: Réau 1964, vol.1, pp.376–78, vol.2, no.81, p.25, pl.XXXVII; Arnason 1976, pp.37–38 and note 73, p.115, fig.79 and pl.25; Musée du Louvre 1998, vol.2, p.430, repr.; Sauerländer 2005, pp.28–30, fig.10; Scherf 2006, no.2, repr.

Jean-Antoine Houdon represents the singer Sophie Arnould (1740–1802) in the role she created in Paris in 1774, Iphigenia in Christoph Willibald von Gluck's *Iphigenia in Aulis*. Before her triumph in this part, Sophie Arnould had excelled in traditional French repertory, particularly in the works by the composer Jean-Philippe Rameau. Her extraordinary musicality, despite a light voice, her elegance and her talent for expression were unanimously praised. It is well known that Gluck's arrival in Paris in 1773 was important. During the battle against the supporters of Niccolò Piccini that ensued after the première of *Iphigenia in Aulis*, Gluck was supported by his former student in Vienna, Marie-Antoinette.

The Dauphine was present at the opening of *Iphigenia* on 19 April 1774, and led an enthusiastic *claque*. Sophie Arnould had been more moving than ever. The composer is said to have declared: 'Without the charm of the voice and the declamatory style of Mlle Arnould, my Iphigenia would never have been accepted in France.' The singer's career declined from then on: she was earmarked to create the role of Alcestis in France in 1776, but had to make way for Rosalie Levasseur, a protégée of the Comte de Mercy-Argenteau, the powerful ambassador to the court of Vienna. She ceased to belong to the Académie Royale de Musique on 1 January 1779.

Houdon executed the portrait of Sophie Arnould at the same time as the portrait of Gluck: the two busts were exhibited together at the Salon of 1775. The sculptor worked very rapidly: the contract with the singer dates from 5 April, and the marble bust had to be ready for the opening of the Salon on the following 25 August. She had included in her contract the distribution of at least thirty plaster casts to her admirers, to be retouched by the sculptor and delivered in time for the Salon of 1775. Houdon was also willing to sell her some supplementary casts, although no more than twenty. We know the whereabouts of only one of these plaster casts today (Goethes Wohnhaus und Goethe-Nationalmuseum, Weimar).

Houdon has produced a strong image of a heroine, depicted at a moment of crisis: as she sacrifices her life. In the manner of the 'expression' heads that all ambitious students at the Académie wanted to produce, the head of Iphigenia expresses an elevated sentiment – the acceptance of pain. Sophie Arnould excelled in tragic roles: 'I have never before seen, in the person of a single actress, so much grace, truth, sentiment, nobility of expression, profound study, intelligence and warmth; I have never seen more admirable pain; her whole facial features display it, depict all its horror, without her face losing any of its beauty' (Collé 1868, vol.2, p.147). Houdon's bust is the personification of Tragedy.

With her high hairstyle held in place by a veil, from which sprigs of roses and rows of pearls emerge, her languishing eyes raised to heaven, her naked breast quivering, this carved Iphigenia is led forth to sacrifice in an imagined draped costume that bears no relation to the theatrical costume of the time. The costume has a whiff of the classical about it, with a diagonal cross belt adorned with alternating crescent moons and stars that allude to the cult of Diana; it is purely imaginary and resembles nothing that the public might have seen in 1774. Sophie Arnould should in fact be dressed in a long-sleeved dress, wrapped in a veil and holding a handkerchief in her hand, as she is depicted in the watercolours of Louis-René Boquet (Kerhoas 2005). According to Willibald Sauerländer, Sophie's bare left breast, over her heart, evokes the iconography of *Friendship*, as codified in

particular by Cesare Ripa: while preparing herself for sacrifice and taking leave of her betrothed, Achilles, she thus demonstrates her fidelity to her heart's choice. gs

## 44
*Benjamin Franklin*

1778
Terracotta, 52.2 × 34.2 × 27.4 cm
Inscription, on the cut edge of the right shoulder: *Houdon f. 1778*; on the cut on the reverse: *franklin*; on the reverse, fragments of the studio's red wax seal: *ACADEM / ROYALE / DE PEINTURE / ET SCULPT / HOUDON SC*
Département des Sculptures, Musée du Louvre, Paris, RF 349

PROVENANCE: sale of works from Houdon's studio, 8 October 1795, no.98, unsold (?); estate sale of the sculptor, Paris, 15–17 December 1828, no.27; collection of François-Hippolyte Walferdin (1795–1880); presented by his heirs in his name, 23 March 1880
EXHIBITED: Paris, Salon of 1779, no.221; La Rochelle and Blérancourt, 1989, no.95, repr.
LITERATURE: Sellers 1962, pp.304–06, pl.18; Réau 1964, vol.1, p.402, vol.2, p.31, no.121; Arnason 1976, p.58; Musée du Louvre 1998, vol.2, p.423, repr.; Washington 2003, pp.248–9, fig.2; Versailles 2004, pp.257–59, fig.2; Sauerländer 2005, p.34, fig.13; Scherf 2006, no.17, repr.

Benjamin Franklin (1706–1790), the illustrious scientist – he invented the Franklin stove and the lightning rod – and one of the Founding Fathers of the United States, already knew Paris and had had his books translated into French when he arrived in France in December 1776 as commissioner for the United States, sent to negotiate an alliance with the French. This was only a few months after the Declaration of Independence of the United States. The alliance came into force after the insurgent victory at Saratoga, in October 1777. On 6 February 1778 the treaty of friendship and trade between the two countries was signed, initialled by Franklin, who had become official minister plenipotentiary of the young republic, now recognised by Louis XVI. Franklin returned to the United States in 1785, two years after peace had been concluded with England.

During the nine years of his stay in Paris, Franklin became extremely well known in French society. He went out of his way to be different in the salons of Paris, leaving his hair as it was, dressing plainly, being affable; he projected the image of an un-powdered Quaker, a simple and virtuous man. The following vivid description is by Elisabeth-Louise Vigée-Lebrun: '[Franklin at Versailles] came with the embassies to visit the court; I was struck by his extreme simplicity: he was clothed in a plain grey suit, his straight, unpowdered hair hung to his shoulders and if it had not been for his noble face I should have taken him for a fat farmer; he made such a contrast with the other diplomats, who were all powdered, gorgeously dressed and bedecked with gold and decorations. No one in Paris was more fashionable, no one more sought-after than Doctor Franklin: the crowd followed him when he went out walking or in town; hats, walking sticks, tobacco pouches –

all were *à la Franklin* and it was considered the greatest stroke of luck to be invited to a dinner party where this celebrated character was to be found' (Vigée-Lebrun 1986, vol. 2, pp. 255–6). The writer and economist André Morellet adds more: 'He was the pleasantest of men: absolutely affable, simple in manner, with a directness of mind that could be felt in the smallest of transactions; he was extremely tolerant and, above all, had a gentle serenity that easily turned to cheerfulness' (Morellet 1988, pp. 244–45).

Franklin soon became fashionable and was much in demand with portrait artists. Jean-Jacques Caffieri made contact with him in the early weeks of 1777 in order to sculpt his portrait from life (the last sitting was before 26 March) and to exhibit the terracotta in the Salon that same year (Bibliothèque Mazarine, Paris). The sculptor represented the old diplomat wearing a jacket, a knotted scarf that hid the buttons of his waistcoat, with his hair pulled back and hanging around his neck. He has a tense expression with a closed mouth and a preoccupied gaze. He is the non-picturesque vision of a public figure.

The following year Houdon presented a more realistic portrait of Franklin with this terracotta version, now in the Louvre: the old man bears the signs of ageing, his flesh is flabby and his eyelids heavy; the subtle, almost malicious gaze is enhanced by the bust's naturalistic treatment. The portrait was executed before 14 November 1778, according to François Métra's *Correspondance secrète*: he reports the interest that visitors to the sculptor's studio took in the bust on that date. Two marble versions survive, executed from the model in the Louvre: the superb, serious bust in the Metropolitan Museum of Art, New York, is dated 1778 (like the terracotta) and the marble bust in the Philadelphia Museum of Art, with its slightly more laboured effects, dates from 1779.

The Salon booklet of 1779 makes no reference to the type of material used for the bust of Houdon. However, the 'Lettre d'un Italien sur le Sallon', published in the *Mercure de France* on 18 September, clearly indicates that it was in terracotta. The work is almost unanimously identified with the one now in the Louvre. The impression of life in the bust of Houdon has led commentators to wonder if Franklin sat for the sculptor, as he had for Caffieri. There is no documentary evidence at present that would answer the question, but if we consider, on the one hand, Houdon's concern for anatomical accuracy, and, on the other, Franklin's strategy of leaving no stone unturned in his search for influence during these critical years, when public opinion had to be swayed in favour of the American cause, the answer surely has to be positive. Franklin also used to say: 'I have, at the request of my friends, posed for so long and so frequently for painters and sculptors that it has literally made me ill' (quoted in Réau 1964, vol. 1, p. 401).

Houdon's position as the most brilliant portrait sculptor of the moment was confirmed at the Salon of 1777, when he had already captured the features of four members of the royal family and one minister, and had received commissions from various foreign personalities. He probably met Franklin, the hero of the hour, at the Loge des Neufs Soeurs, one of the leading Masonic lodges in Paris, to which both were affiliated in 1778. We know that Houdon executed the bust without a commission, as did Caffieri (Ingersoll-Smouse 1913, p. 214, no. XVI and pp. 216–17, no. XIX), because he was perfectly well aware that it would help his reputation. His ambitions and those of the ambassador were the same.  GS

## 53
### *Denis Diderot*

1780
Bronze, 79 × 31 × 30 cm
Musée d'Art et d'Histoire de Langres, 984-2-1

PROVENANCE:  sent by Diderot to the town council in Langres, 1780
EXHIBITED:  Washington and Los Angeles, 2003–04, no. 21; Versailles, 2004, no. 21
LITERATURE:  Réau 1964, vol. 1, pp. 78–79, 353, vol. 2, p. 30, no. 115;  Arnason 1976, pp. 24–25, pl. 12b;  Scherf 2006, under numbers 8–9, repr.

On 29 August 1780, the town council of Langres, the birthplace of Denis Diderot (1713–1784), declared that 'it would be satisfactory and glorious for all citizens to see his portrait [Diderot's] in one of the chambers of the town hall, where he was born. He was stopped immediately in his tracks by cheering; the council should write to Monsieur Diderot to beg him to agree that the town of Langres should have his portrait made' (decision quoted in Tourneux 1913, pp. 186–87). The mayor and four deputies wrote to the philosopher at once. Diderot 'sent them his bust in bronze executed by M. Houdon. It is placed in a chamber of the town hall, on a small cupboard containing the *Encyclopédie* and his written works. The day it was installed, an official dinner was held, the bust was placed above the table and its health was drunk. These details given by the mayor to my father gave him some happy moments. The town sent some trifle to M. Houdon, who replied by sending to these gentlemen plaster casts of the busts whose version in bronze they had been celebrating' (Vandeul 1830, p. 60).

Houdon had made a first bust of Diderot, exhibited at the Salon of 1771 (undoubtedly the terracotta in the Louvre: Scherf 2006, no. 8, repr.). A few years later, and probably as a direct result of the wishes expressed by the town councillors of Langres, he took his model back and modified it slightly (particularly the hair), while remaining faithful to the initial choice of composition. The first one pleased Diderot, who wrote in his review of the Salon two short but vital words: 'good likeness' (Diderot 1995, p. 242). Even if

there is no proof, it is likely that the writer would have posed for the sculptor. He had already sat for Etienne-Maurice Falconet, Marie-Anne Collot and Jean-Baptiste Lemoyne.

Houdon got back from Italy at the end of 1768, was accepted 'agrée' by the Académie Royale in 1769, and presented his work at the Salon that year; his work had received a favourable reaction from the art-loving public. Houdon's skill lies in having produced a vision of Diderot that suited the taste and sensibility of the subject, and matched his ideal. In fact, the composition that Houdon chose, a discreet evocation of classical antiquity, was bound to satisfy the philosopher, who had been brought up on the classics. With his head turned to his right, short hair and no clothing, the rounded base cut shows off his 'medallion head' to great advantage (critic of the *Mémoires secrets*, Fort 1999, p. 97). Houdon is experimenting with the kind of sober, effective composition that he later used with Voltaire, Jean-Jacques Rousseau, the Comte de Buffon, George Washington and Jean le Rond d'Alembert. Diderot is, in fact, the only great Enlightenment intellectual in the sculptor's gallery to have been represented solely in this manner.

Portrayed in the style of Cicero or Menander, Diderot has avoided any more literal, gloomy transferral into antiquity. Houdon opens the mouth of this indefatigable talker, makes his lips move and manages to animate his eyes by hollowing out the iris very deeply, suggesting the pupil by emptying out the bottom, and simulating the vivacity of the gaze by means of a small piece of matter left on the lid, which catches the light and shade. The portrait of Diderot is thus a double likeness: it reproduces the features of his face, as recognised by all the reviewers, and remains faithful to the mental image the philosopher had of himself.

We know that the writer had rejected the painting by Louis-Michel Van Loo (now in the Louvre, Paris), exhibited in the Salon of 1767, in which he is wrapped in a luxurious dressing gown and wears a smirk. By contrast, he liked his representation by Madame Therbouche, in which he is shown with a naked chest engraved; see Versailles 2004, p. 147, fig. 4): 'I was naked, but completely naked. She painted me, we chatted with a simplicity and innocence worthy of the earliest centuries' (Diderot, *Salon of 1767*, 1995, p. 375). According to the *Encyclopédie*, the portrait should promote 'the respect of the individual, the natural, the true; there should be wariness of accessories … and attributes … and poses that run counter to the sitter's character'. This is exactly what Houdon understood. The clearest proof of its success is Diderot's desire to send the bust to commemorate him, in his home town.  GS

## 43
### Condorcet

Marble, 77.5 × 50.8 cm
Inscription, on the cut end of the left shoulder:
*houdon / fecit / 1785*
American Philosophical Society, Philadelphia, 58. s. 2

PROVENANCE: appears to have been commissioned by
Marie Louise Elisabeth Nicole de la Rochefoucauld, Duchesse
d'Enville, who kept it until her death in 1798; after her death
given by her granddaughter Alexandrine Charlotte Sophie de
Rohan-Chabot, Duchesse de La Rochefoucauld, to an old family
friend, William Short, former secretary to Thomas Jefferson at
the American Legation in Paris; the bust remained in the port
of Cherbourg from 1812 to 1819; sent on to Philadelphia and
deposited immediately at the American Philosophical Society,
Philadelphia; formally given to the American Philosophical
Society, 1830
EXHIBITED: Worcester, 1964, pp.78–80
LITERATURE: Réau 1964, vol.1, pp.82, 367, vol.2, p.30, no.110,
pl.LIII; Arnason 1976, pp.76–77, pl.92; Hecht 1997, *passim*,
repr.; Scherf 2006, under no.16, repr.

Marie Jean Antoine Nicolas Caritat, Marquis
de Condorcet (1743–1794), was born into an old
family that was part of the provincial nobility;
he showed early promise as a mathematician.
He became acquainted with the mathematician
and philosopher Jean le Rond d'Alembert, who
introduced him to the economist and statesman
Turgot; it was thanks to d'Alembert that he became
a member of the Académie des Sciences (becoming
permanent secretary in 1776). He graced the
best salons in Paris (including those of Julie de
Lespinasse and the Duchesse d'Enville, friends of
d'Alembert and Turgot respectively, and also the
salon of Madame Helvétius, where he met
Benjamin Franklin and the philosopher Morellet).
He also led a double career as a scientist
(he wrote the volumes on mathematics for the
*Encyclopédie méthodique*, published between 1784 and
1786) and as an Enlightenment intellectual,
campaigning for equality between men, and
between the sexes, and for the legal rights of the
accused before the law. In 1782 he was elected to
the Académie française. His various writings show
a man convinced of the perfectibility of human
nature and of the need for reform. He was a member
of the Société des Amis des Noirs with Duc Louis
Alexandre de la Rochefoucauld and shared the
latter's advanced political thinking; he admired the
American Revolution, as did La Fayette, who was
the leading witness at his marriage in 1786. He was
elected deputy in the Legislative Assembly, and then
to the Convention. His responsibility was public
education, a subject that was particularly dear to
his heart. Politically, he sided with the Girondists
and was forced into hiding for eight months after
their downfall; during this period he wrote his
masterpiece, *Esquisse d'un tableau historique des progrès
de l'esprit humain*. He was subsequently arrested and
committed suicide in prison.
The bust of Condorcet, which never appeared
in the Salon, seems to have been commissioned
by Marie Louise Elisabeth Nicole de la
Rochefoucauld, Duchesse d'Enville. She was closely

attached to him, considering him in fact as a second
son. Documents published by Johanna Hecht
demonstrate the loyal devotion of the duchess
to Condorcet, and her attempts to understand
him despite his revolutionary opinions; she only
resolved to shut her door to him in July 1791,
after he had adopted an openly republican stance.
William Short, Jefferson's secretary at the
American Legation, often saw this bust in the
La Rochefoucauld residence, displayed on a
marble table in the drawing room; this was before
the grandchildren of the old duchess banished
it to a storeroom. Its installation in the reception
rooms of the American Philosophical Society in
Philadelphia (of which Condorcet, proposed by
Franklin, was one of the first members in 1788),
where it stands beside the busts of Turgot and
Jefferson, also by Houdon, re-creates some of the
magic of the literary gatherings held before the
dark hours of the Revolution, when humanist ideas
were exchanged in a serene and civilised atmosphere.
Condorcet was already famous when
Houdon made his portrait. He is represented rather
severely, with an unadorned suit in the French style.
A perfectly tied cravat encircles his neck, with a
narrow jabot hanging over the waistcoat; the curl
around his wig is carefully ordered, with the locks
at the back gathered into a voluminous bow. His
lips are closed, his gaze incisive, turned left as if
looking towards a fixed point. It is an austere and
upright image, but magnificent, subtly indicating
the sitter's social standing, as well as his intellectual
prowess. Other busts by Houdon, depicting men
engaged in intellectual and social life, such as
Jefferson (marble; 1789; the Museum of Fine
Arts, Boston), give the same impression of
perfect integrity and resoluteness.
Condorcet's huge head with its lightly
pockmarked skin – he apparently caught smallpox
in 1775 (Badinter 1990, p.39, note 3), and his face
continued to bear the scars – his broad sloping
forehead, his deep-set eyes can be found in other
portraits, as for example the profile engraved by
Augustin de Saint-Aubin, noted as 'a good likeness'
in the *Mercure de France* in November 1786. The
philosopher's slightly sulky expression could result
from the shyness manifested by Condorcet in public,
which was sometimes misunderstood: 'His face,
without being remarkably handsome, bore a striking
expression. His forehead was huge and domed, his
gaze searching … his nose aquiline and very
pronounced; his smile was calm, but easily became
satirical. It bespoke an intimacy which was not
conveyed by the slightly mocking expression that
lifted the corners of his mouth when the thought
it accompanied became too strongly felt' (Duchesse
d'Abrantès, quoted in Badinter 1990, p.240).
The marble bust is meticulously detailed,
including the reverse. It is easy to imagine it as
an image reflected in the looking glass in the salon
of the Duchesse d'Enville, a handsome ornament
for one of the last meeting-places of the

Enlightenment at the end of the *ancien régime*.
Houdon distributed versions of his piece, but only
a small number: the scholar and political economist
did not have the same allure as Denis Diderot,
Voltaire or Jean-Jacques Rousseau, whose portrait
busts had been produced in large numbers in the
sculptor's studio. An excellent version in terracotta,
moulded but retouched by the artist, can be found
in the Louvre. A plaster cast used to be in the
collection of Prince Heinrich of Prussia, in his
castle at Rheinsberg (damaged in 1945): the brother
of King Friedrich II was in fact acquainted with the
Duchesse d'Enville and always attended her salon
when he was in France. GS

## 137
### Madame Houdon

Plaster, 61.5 × 39.5 × 26.7 cm
Département des Sculptures, Musée du Louvre, Paris, RF 1391

PROVENANCE: probably executed before 1 July 1786, the date
of Houdon's marriage to the sitter; probably exhibited at
the Salon of 1787, no.258 (*Head of a Girl*); remained with the
sculptor; then with his daughter Claudine (1790–1878), wife
of Désiré Raoul-Rochette; her daughter Joséphine, wife of
Luigi Calamatta; her daughter Marcelline, wife of Maurice
Sand; their daughters Aurore Lauth-Sand and Gabrielle Palazzi;
acquired by the Louvre, 1905
EXHIBITED: Paris, Salon of 1787, no.258? (*Head of a Girl. In
Plaster*); Washington and Los Angeles, 2003–04, no.17,
pp.133–36, repr.; Versailles, 2004, no.17, pp.133–36, repr.
LITERATURE: Réau 1964, vol.1, pp.417–18, vol.2, p.33, no.135,
pl.LXV, 135B; Arnason 1976, p.89, fig.172, pl.111; Musée du
Louvre 1998, p.425, repr.; Sauerländer 2005, pp.50–53, fig.24;
Scherf 2006, no.30, repr.

Houdon exhibited a *Head of a Girl. In Plaster* at
the Salon of 1787. In 1905 this was identified
as the bust in the Louvre, which came directly
from the sculptor's family, and was recognised
as representing Marie-Ange-Cécile Langlois
(1765–1823), Houdon's young wife.
The piece was reviewed by one of the Salon
critics (*Tarare au Sallon de peinture*; McWilliam 1991,
p.444): 'His head of a girl rivals the most graceful
work of classical antiquity. Proportions in the
features; soft, fluid contours; elasticity of the flesh;
a lively, gentle, innocent face – all attract the
admiration of the connoisseurs and even astound
the ignorant. Stunning whiteness, grace, sensuality,
ease in the muscles; this is what is noticeable in the
neck and head: the remainder, however, is not above
reproach. How irritating that the artist, tired out by
the masterpiece that is the head, has placed the
nipples a little too low … Perhaps it is the sitter's
fault.' This physiological detail, not in fact invented
by our scrupulously naturalistic artist, plus the
private character of the portrait, in which the young
woman presents herself, with her dazzling smile
and laughing eyes, implies such intimacy between
the sculptor and his sitter that the identification
would be hard to contest. In addition, it is
endorsed by comparison with a miniature
representing Mme Houdon painted around 1792
by Louis Lié Périn-Salbreux (Louvre, Paris: Scherf

HOUDON 341

2006, p.166, fig.84); we recognise the abundant locks, the slightly pronounced chin and large, laughing eyes.

Marie-Ange-Cécile Langlois was born in Paris, the daughter of 'an employee in the King's business' (her mother died a month after her birth). She married Houdon on 1 July 1786. She was an Anglophile: her adoptive mother, the Comtesse de Villegagnon, married Thomas Walpole (Horace Walpole's cousin and her second husband) in 1787. She also had a minor career as a translator (she translated *Belmour* by Mme Dymmer in 1804). She dealt with her husband's correspondence and accounts on a regular basis, promoting his interests as best she could.

Marie-Ange-Cécile Langlois is depicted with a light, tousled hairstyle in a imaginative piece (the reverse side in particular). Her hair is drawn up by a fillet into a chignon from which ringlets (with strings of pearls) escape. As was his usual practice, Houdon incises some stray locks of hair on his sitter's temples and forehead. She is smiling broadly, clearly displaying her teeth. The iris is hollowed out, with a pupil. The cleavage and undulation of the upper part of the breasts add to the irresistible charm of the figure, one of the artist's masterpieces. The bust is an original plaster cast, in other words it was poured into a sunk mould taken from the clay model (the model and the mould being destroyed by the process of unmoulding). This gives the bust unusual immediacy, because it exactly reflects the clay model. There is no inscription: we really are in the artist's private domain. GS

## 67
### The Marquis de Méjanes
### (Jean-Baptiste Marie de Piquet)

1786
Marble, 86 × 65 × 32 cm
Bibliothèque Méjanes, Aix-en-Provence

PROVENANCE: commissioned in 1786 by Mgr de Boisgelin, Archbishop of Aix, following the bequest of the Marquis's library to the Etats de Provence
EXHIBITED: Aix-en-Provence, 1986, no.62
LITERATURE: Aude 1933, p.43, pl.XVII; Réau 1964, vol.1, p.317, vol.2, p.37, no.160, pl.LXXVIII; Arnason 1976, pp.86–87, fig.165; Lavagne 1988, *passim* repr.

One of the most noted bibliophiles of his century, Jean-Baptiste Marie de Piquet, last Marquis de Méjanes (1729–1786), belonged to the minor nobility of Arles. He studied with the Jesuits in Paris, subsequently obtaining a diploma in law. He returned to Arles after the death of his father in 1747 and devoted the remainder of his life to local administration. Having served twice as Consul in Arles (in 1761 and 1774), he became First Consul in Aix (1777–78). This was an important position: Méjanes became public prosecutor of the province, in other words 'permanent delegate to the assembly of communities, with responsibility for administration', wielding extensive powers in respect of the exchequer, highways and public

health. He was in fact the chief administrator of the province, working alongside the President of the States of Provence, Mgr de Boisgelin, Archbishop of Aix. He lived in Paris from 1783 until his death in 1786; he had been sent on a deputation by the town of Arles in order to defend his privileges at court. Interested in agriculture and agronomy, a disciple of the physiocrats, much taken up with public campaigning, Méjanes was a man of the Enlightenment, full of curiosity and highly observant (interestingly, his library included Montesquieu's *Esprit des Lois* and Voltaire's *Zadig*). His passion for books and manuscripts was all-consuming: he chose to live modestly, but bought books and related items with compulsion, in salerooms and bookshops. His wife declared: 'He deprives me of everything in order to buy books; I am even unable to take candles to church!' (quoted in Aude 1933, p.38).

When Méjanes bequeathed his library to the Etats de Provence in his will of 26 May 1786, his inspiration may have been the example of Mgr d'Inguimbert (1683–1757), Bishop of Carpentras (the bishop opened a public library there in 1747), and he was certainly encouraged by Mgr de Boisgelin; a condition of his bequest was that a public library, with no lending rights, should be established in Aix. While awaiting the construction of a new building to house the donation, the books – almost 300,000 bibliographical items (Lavagne 1988, p.257) – were lodged in the town hall; this was where the library was opened to the public in 1810.

Despite Méjanes's request that no homage be paid to him, Mgr de Boisgelin decided to commemorate the bibliophile's generosity by commissioning a portrait bust: 'I believed I was anticipating the wishes of the province when I requested Houdon to make a mask of the deceased. The celebrated sculptor will make a bust to be placed in the library. It will cost one thousand *écus* [or three thousand *livres*], payable half in advance and half on delivery' (quoted in Aude 1933, p.43).

Houdon did not know Méjanes, but, because his subject died in Paris, he went to make a mould of his face. The bust of the marquis is thus a posthumous portrait. Houdon created relatively few of these under the *ancien régime*, preferring to work from life. The use of the death mask by sculptors in the eighteenth century has been little studied and would repay more detailed scrutiny. The practice was a commonplace in Roman times, and may have been more widespread than we realise in the eighteenth and early nineteenth centuries (see Paris 2002A); Nollekens made a speciality of it in London. Examples also exist by Banks, Schadow and Sergel. In France it was practised by Houdon, but few examples are known (not all the posthumous busts by Houdon were made from moulds). He made masks of the faces of the deceased Rousseau (1778), Mirabeau (1791), of the Marquise de Créqui (1803), and of the poet Collin

d'Harleville (1806). The mask of Méjanes was thus made eight years after the celebrated moulding of Rousseau's face a few hours after his death.

Houdon's bust of Méjanes represents an eminent figure of the Enlightenment. Although the thin features and hollow cheeks testify to the illness that accompanied the last moments in the life of the marquis, the lively gaze and half-open mouth, giving the illusion that he is in the middle of a conversation, bear witness to the sculptor's desire to depict Méjanes in the process of communicating: openness to others and a passion for communication were apparently dominant features of his personality. The sculptor chose not to represent him in French dress, which would have made him look like any other notable figure; nor in classical dress, which would have glorified him too blatantly, against his wishes. He decided instead to create a familiar image, without unnecessary pomp. The hair is natural, brushed back, rather like that of Washington (Houdon had just returned from America, where he had portrayed Washington after taking a mould of his face from life). The fine shirt of the marquis is open-necked, as had become the custom in France in portraits of artists and intellectuals since the time of Desjardins and Coysevox. The coat is unique in Houdon's production: the figure wears it on his shoulders and arms – the bust is large and cut quite low, almost like a half figure, and the tops of the arms are visible – and it is fastened at the front with a large diagonal lapel. When Houdon made a posthumous marble bust of Condorcet's great friend, President Dupaty of the parliament of Bordeaux (1744–1788), he designed quite a different over-garment to ennoble this important Enlightenment figure, a cape with multiple pleats at the back (Private collection; Réau 1964, vol.2, no.117, pl.LVI). In his plaster bust of the astronomer Lalande (in the Observatoire de Paris in 1801; Réau 1964, vol.2, no.235, pl.CXXIII), he designed something similar to the costume seen in the bust under discussion, with an open-collared shirt. However, the drapery over the astronomer's torso refers more closely to classical antiquity, with regular, oblique pleats in parallel rows. The bibliophile's coat is a compromise between an ordinary overcoat, immediately recognisable as such, and something more heroic. Its sober grandeur gives the portrait an impressive solidity, adding emphasis to the fatigue in the face, the dimming energy of the eyes, the final wish to speak of this admirable man of letters, who was so committed to plans for his town. 'The man presented to us in this bust by Houdon is almost a poet' (Arnason 1976, p.86). GS

## 107
### Sabine Houdon Aged Ten Months

1788
Marble, 44.5 × 25 × 17 cm

Inscription on the reverse: *Sabinet Houdon / 1788*
Lent by The Metropolitan Museum of Art, New York. Bequest of Mary Stillman Harkness, 1950 (50.145.66)

PROVENANCE: the sitter's descendants, until after *c.*1905; collection of Jacques Antoine Doucet by 1906; sold at Galerie Georges Petit, Paris, 6 June 1912, no.113, repr.; acquired by Duveen Bros., London and New York, 1912; collection of Judge Elbert H. Gary, New York, by 1914; sold at Plaza Hotel, New York, 19–21 April 1928, no.251; acquired at the sale by Mrs Edward Stillman Harkness, New York; bequeathed by Mary Stillman Harkness to the Metropolitan Museum of Art, New York, 1950
EXHIBITED: Paris, Salon of 1789, no.246: *Head of a Child Aged Ten Months*, amongst the 'Small-sized marble heads'
LITERATURE: Réau 1964, vol.1, p.418, vol.2, p.34, no.136, pl.LXVI; Arnason 1976, p.90, fig.177; Scherf 2006, under no.31, repr.

Houdon exhibited a *Head of a Child Aged Ten Months* (no.246) in the Salon of 1789. The child can be convincingly identified with the sculptor's eldest daughter, Sabine (1787–1836), born on 25 February. The marble bust, signed and dated 1788, bears the nickname 'Sabinet' on the reverse; this inscription is absent from the model, the original plaster version now in the Louvre, Paris.

It is easy to understand why Houdon wished to exhibit the portrait of his child anonymously. It was to protect his private life (unlike Elisabeth-Louise Vigée-Lebrun, who exhibited paintings of her daughter, named, alone or with her mother, a number of times during the 1780s). It was unusual in the eighteenth century to exhibit portrait busts of identified children: the children by Pigalle, Saly and Vassé, in the middle of the century, are anonymous. Augustin Pajou showed the children of the Comte de Voyer d'Argenson at the Salon of 1767 (missing). He was followed by Houdon in 1777 with his terracotta portraits of Louise and Alexandre Brongniart (Louvre, Paris); then, in 1781, with the marble bust of Anne Audéoud (Private collection) and, in 1783, with the daughter of Hubert Robert (missing). Anonymity was the general rule, however, and it helped blur the boundaries between the portrait and the expression figure or study head.

Sabine was the eldest child. With the bust of his daughter aged ten months, Houdon created an image that was very rare in the eighteenth century, particularly in sculpture.

Two statuettes made before this bust can be held up as examples: the *Child with a Cage* by Jean-Baptiste Pigalle, made in marble and exhibited at the Salon of 1750 (Louvre, Paris), which is known to represent the son of the financier Pâris de Montmartel, aged one; and Martin-Claude Monot's *Child Playing with His Feet*, shown in the Salon of 1779 and indicated as being a portrait (unfortunately unidentified) in the booklet (plaster; Louvre, Paris). Houdon's interest in very young children manifested itself even before the birth of his own daughter, in a bust of a new-born baby, thought to be son of an architect, Auguste-Romain de Bourge, born 4 March 1786 (various versions are known: see Scherf 2005A, vol.2, pp.95–97, repr.). This portrait anticipates the detailed and

individualised description of children's faces that Houdon developed when portraying the features of his three daughters.

In his portrait of his daughter Sabine aged ten months, Houdon opts to cut the figure under the arms with a curved cut extending to just above the nipples, an arrangement he had already adopted for the figure of his mother (1787; original plaster in the Louvre). The same cut occurs in the bust of Sabine aged four years (1791; original plaster in the Louvre) and in the bust of the younger daughter, Anne-Ange (1791, original plaster in the Louvre; marble in a Private collection). The artist also used a draped version of the same cut for the marble bust of Sabine aged four years (1791; Private collection) and for the bust of the youngest, Claudine (1793; marble; Worcester Art Museum, MA; see Versailles 2004, no.18; and Scherf 2005A, pp.96–98, repr.).

Because he designed all these busts at almost the same time, particularly between 1791 and 1793, the sculptor was strongly influenced by his emotions – he was the doting father. However, he was also following his commercial instincts: the revolutionary period was difficult for everyone in France – Houdon had to sell part of the capital tied up in his studio in 1795 – and public taste for figures of children swelled that particular market, which had been around for several decades already. Bearing this in mind, it is interesting to note that the busts of his children were presented anonymously by Houdon in the Salon (except in the first booklet of 1791, rapidly pulped after a reorganisation of the exhibition), and are only described allusively in the sales catalogue of 1795, as 'heads of children with hairstyles'. The designation 'family portrait' had to be erased in favour of the more generic quality, 'head of a child'. A number of plaster or terracotta casts of the portrait of Sabine aged four years are known (the unclothed version), and of Anne-Ange and Claudine; they were easy to make in the studio because of their small size. Known versions of the first bust, of Sabine at ten months, are much rarer.

In the marble bust in the Metropolitan Museum of Art, New York, Houdon analyses the child's facial features in great detail, the full cheeks, the fine triangular mouth, the dimples below the eyes and the sparse hair. The head is completely natural; a faint smile hovers over the lips and the child's searching gaze is turned slightly to her right. The expression is that of a tomboy, which could perhaps account for the nickname 'Sabinet'? The child looks serious. In fact, the image is somewhat severe; no attempt has been made to sentimentalise it. There are no curls or flirtatious looks. The child represented here is an individual, despite her young age, captured truthfully and not designed simply to please. The later figures of Anne-Ange and Claudine were made to look more winsome. GS

# Jean-Auguste-Dominique Ingres

MONTAUBAN, 1780 – PARIS, 1867

## 12
*Napoleon I on the Imperial Throne*

1806
Oil on canvas, 260 × 163 cm
Signed at lower left: *Ingres pxit*
Dated at lower right: *Anno 1806*
Musée de l'Armée, Paris, 5420

PROVENANCE: probably commissioned by the Ministry of the Interior; entered the Corps Législatif (Palais-Bourbon), 26 August 1806; transferred to the Louvre when the Empire fell, inventoried as MR 2069; deposited at the Hôtel des Invalides, 1832; now in the Musée de l'Armée, Paris
EXHIBITED: Paris, Salon of 1806, no.202; Paris, Detroit and New York, 1974–75, no.104 (J. Foucart); London, New York and Washington, 1999–2000, no.10 (P. Conisbee); Paris, 2005D (S. Laveissière); Paris, 2006, no.34 (V. Pomarède)
LITERATURE: Lapauze 1911, pp.64–66; Bessis 1969; Siegfried 1980; Connolly 1980; Toussaint 1985, pp.32–41; Vigne 1995, pp.58–61; Allard and Chaudonneret 2006, pp.86–94

Until the Salon of 1806, Ingres had only exhibited a portrait of an unidentified woman at the Salon of 1802; in 1806 he attracted critical notice with three portraits: the portrait of Caroline Rivière (Louvre, Paris), the portrait of Madame Rivière (Louvre, Paris), and the one that drew the most attention, *Napoleon I on the Imperial Throne*. The history of the commission remains unclear. On 26 August 1806, the Corps Législatif offered to buy the painting for the sum of 3,000 francs, whereas Ingres was only asking 2,400 francs. Some commentators have suggested that the artist, in order to make his name, may have painted this uncompromisingly official portrait on his own initiative, and then tried to sell it. It seems highly improbable, however, that the young penniless painter should have acquired such a large canvas and stretcher without any certainty that he would be paid back; also that he would have been able to show it at the Salon.

In addition, on 24 August 1806, the painter Léonor Mérimée mentioned the work in a minute to the Minister of the Interior (*Archives de l'Art français*, 1969, pp.89–90), which could be taken as proof of the existence of an official commission issued by this particular ministry (Allard and Chaudonneret 2006, p.147, note 1). Finally, the iconography suggests that the painting was executed for a specific destination, unless it was simply an allusion to the coronation of Napoleon as King of Italy the previous year. In fact, to the right of the throne, Ingres has depicted an escutcheon that is difficult to decipher now, but on which can be distinguished the arms of the Papal States. A preparatory drawing (Private collection; Toussaint 1985, VI) makes things clearer. J. Conolly has deciphered the coats of arms of the d'Este family, the Papal States, of Lombardy, Venice and Savoy, surmounted by the crown of Italy. Was the painting not commissioned for an Italian institution, via the minister responsible for that type of commission, the Minister of the Interior? Possibly refused on account of its iconography, the painting could have finally been acquired by the Corps Législatif to adorn the president's reception room.

*Napoleon I on the Imperial Throne* belongs in a very particular context. After the coronation ceremony in 1804, it was important to find the best way of representing this new type of French monarch and of circulating his image throughout the Empire. In 1805, François Gérard, who was the first to be given the task of painting Napoleon as Emperor in a portrait for the Ministry of Foreign Affairs, with great pragmatism rearranged the traditional royal portrait that had been produced in France since Hyacinthe Rigaud's *Louis XIV* (Louvre, Paris): Napoleon in 'ceremonial dress' and holding the regalia stands in front of the throne designed by Percier and Fontaine. At the Salon of 1806, Robert Lefèvre, whom the critics compared to Ingres, attempted to give new life to this model by adding a gallery containing busts of Charlemagne, Alexander, Caesar and Scipio, thus symbolising Bonaparte's progress from the status of Great Man to the status of Emperor. The formula for the ceremonial portrait, inspired by Hyacinthe Rigaud, offered a balance between the inherent symbolism of this type of image and physical resemblance; this meant that the sovereign was not reduced to a simple expression of his mythical function, but was presented as a flesh-and-blood individual.

Ingres, who 'avoided anything that might recall the portraits of our modern sovereigns' (Léonor Mérimée), was on the whole trying to break with this type of representation, emphasising instead the abstract value of this kind of emblematic portrait. Like some kind of Olympian Jupiter, Napoleon sits on the imperial throne looking exactly like Charlemagne as he is depicted on the tip of the sceptre. By putting such weight on this reference, Ingres was complying with imperial propaganda that, after 1804, attached particular value to the medieval emperor.

However, as was his habit, he envisaged his subject from a historicising perspective, including the style; Léonor Mérimée noticed immediately: 'The author, by using the type found in images of Charlemagne, has also even adopted the decorative style of the period.' The most strikingly archaic feature is the way the Emperor Napoleon is portrayed in a rigid pose from the front, which, because of its hieratic overtones and the overwhelming distance it creates between the subject and spectator, had not been employed in royal portraiture since the Middle Ages. Ingres took his inspiration for the pose from Byzantine ivories, from a Jupiter reproduced in Caylus's *Antiquities* and probably from God the Father painted at the top of Jan van Eyck's Ghent altarpiece *The Adoration of the Mystic Lamb*; the central part of the polyptych was exhibited from 1797 in the Grande Galerie of the Louvre, Paris.

By trying to renew this link with the past, Ingres produced an overwhelming image that was bound to shock his contemporaries. The painter removed any positive value from the actions that had allowed Bonaparte, who had become Napoleon, to build up his power and his myth, so well conveyed by Jacques-Louis David. 'Why paint the portrait of the Emperor from the front?' Chaussard exclaimed, 'It is the most difficult thing to render. The character of a great man, this heroic face … are these not already difficult enough to capture?' (Chaussard 1808, p.179).

By 1806, the hero had had his day; the Revolution was in the past, even though the title of emperor was intended to mask the 'monarchical' tendencies of the regime. Ingres, younger than Gérard or David and less political, perceived the authoritarian basis of this new power and translated it with great lucidity. He was not constructing a myth, he was producing an effigy that undermined the foundations of the portrait. Seen from the front, Napoleon has lost all his human aspects: he has become the implacable symbol of power. Resemblance, the constituent element of the genre, has paid the price. All the critics agreed in finding the likeness to the Emperor very poor: 'As for the head, it is too big, not a good likeness at all, and a fake colour, too pale' (Chaussard 1808, p.180). Worse, it did not even look real; one observer wondered if it was made of wax or plaster (*Lorgnette du Salon de 1806 par un amateur*, Paris, 1806, p.7). By doing away with the naturalism expected of him, Ingres deliberately sacrificed the human element required in a ceremonial portrait, exalting only the symbolic aspect and thereby elevating the genre, even when no action was taking place, to the status of a history painting. From that time on everything in his painting becomes symbolic in order to justify the stylistic regression he is proposing.

Chaussard ends his review by noting that Napoleon's head 'does not come out of the canvas'. He wished to point out that the face is painted on the same plane and with the same precision as the accessories: the laurel wreath, the costume, the armchair in whose gold the signs of the zodiac on the carpet are reflected, the chain of the Légion d'honneur, the regalia, the throne adorned with seven stars (probably a Masonic reference, as are the ivory bowls). The hierarchical divide between the human figure and the details, always strictly observed in modern portraits since the Renaissance, is here taken up again with archaic photographic realism, influenced by the Flemish primitives. To Ingres's contemporaries, *Napoleon I on the Imperial Throne* looked like a monstrous illumination, in which the effigy of the sovereign disappeared behind the panoply of his attributes. In reality, Ingres made a break with illusionism based on chiaroscuro in order to emphasise the symbolic dimension of the portrait of the ruler, a political allegory.

With his liking for optical effects and reflective surfaces, and his microscopic detail and realism, Ingres drew attention to his own professional skill, forcing the spectator to admire the stunning virtuosity of his brushwork, which should transcend the immediate understanding of the subject. By affirming the value of the 'delicate finish' with such authority (to quote Chaussard), Ingres emphasised, to his own advantage, the ambivalence of the subject and of his handling of it. Reviewers were disconcerted: 'How, with so much talent … has Ingres managed to paint a bad painting?' he wondered. 'It is because he wanted to make something singular, extraordinary' he replied to himself. Revealing the originality of his artistic vision, this work by Ingres shocked his contemporaries as it went against the principles of the 'beau idéal' in painting. *Napoleon I on the Imperial Throne*, too abstract and too original in its provocative archaic style, stood in complete contrast to the Emperor's more dramatic tastes, which favoured images that were more royal than imperial. SA

## 33
### *The Comtesse de Tournon*

1812
Oil on canvas, 92.4 × 73.2 cm
Signed and dated at the lower right: *Ingres, Rome. 1812*
Philadelphia Museum of Art. The Henry P. McIlhenny Collection in memory of Frances P. McIlhenny, 1986

PROVENANCE: commissioned by the sitter's son, Comte Camille de Tournon (1778–1833); Comte Jean de Chabannes-la-Palice by 1911; sold to Paul Rosenberg, Paris, 1935; purchased by Henry P. McIlhenny, 1935; bequest to the Philadelphia Museum of Art, 1986
EXHIBITED: Philadelphia, 1987–88 (J. Rishel); London, New York and Washington, 1999–2000, no.33 (K. Jones)
LITERATURE: Alazard 1950, pp.49–50; Wildenstein [1954–56], no.84; Rosenblum 1968, p.92; Ternois and Camesasca 1968, no.68; Ternois 1980; Vigne 1995, p.82

Ingres met Charles Marcotte (1773–1864), Inspector-General of Forests in Rome, in 1810 when his stay at the French Academy in the Villa Medici was drawing to a close. Marcotte was looking for an artist to paint his portrait (National Gallery of Art, Washington DC). The two became friends, and Marcotte obtained a number of commissions for Ingres from senior French officials in posts in Rome, including Charles Cordier (Louvre, Paris), Monsieur de Norvins (National Gallery, London) and Hippolyte Devillers (Foundation E. G. Bührle Collection, Zurich). Painting portraits made it possible for hard-up artists to survive, and also to make their name in circles in which they might be able to sell history paintings. The Comtesse de Tournon, mother of the Prefect of Rome, Camille de Tournon, belonged to these glittering circles. It was through Marcotte, therefore, that the Prefect commissioned the portrait of his mother, delivered in 1812.

The portrait of the Comtesse de Tournon is one of the rare paintings in which Ingres depicts an older woman. Since 1806, Ingres had been producing a style of female portrait in which he strove for pure beauty rather than psychological insight: surface effects were favoured, often to the detriment of the sitter's physical presence. In this respect, Ingres was at odds with his teacher Jacques-Louis David, who was moving towards greater realism. The portrait of Sabine Rivière (Salon of 1806; Louvre, Paris), for example, constitutes a masterpiece of formal abstraction. The artist's inspiration does not seem to come from painstaking observation of his sitter's features, but from the creative act itself, from the faculty of idealisation, in what he commits to canvas. Ingres's reservations about portraiture as a genre can be understood: 'The history painter renders the species in general, whereas the portrait painter only represents the individual in particular, and as a consequence often paints a model who is ordinary and full of faults' he wrote in his famous notebook IX.

The representation of a mature, far from good-looking woman posed a challenge, therefore, a challenge that Ingres took up readily. Instead of disguising her faults, he compensated for the Comtesse's lack of conventional beauty by paying closer attention to her psychological makeup, making this truly remarkable portrait one of his most empathetic works. In one sense, Ingres painted the Comtesse de Tournon as, in the 1810s, he painted men. Firmly seated in her chair, the Comtesse almost fills the whole canvas, in a similar way to the contemporary portrait of *Monsieur de Norvins*, or the focus used at the same period by David, such as that in the portrait of *Comtesse Daru* (1810; Frick Collection, New York). For this reason the monumental and physical presence of the figure is emphasised by the accumulation of *beaux morceaux*. Ingres reintroduces the accessories that contributed to the success of his portrait of Sabine Rivière: the cream-coloured shawl with the cashmere pattern, the wood of the chair, the bare arm, the stiff curls and the veil on her head. Instead of concentrating on continuing and developing the lines, he pays most attention to the contrasting materials: the velvet of the dress contrasting with the fine wool of the shawl and with the shiny surface of the mahogany.

Instead of the flowing lines that were the attraction of the 1806 painting, he substitutes density. The tender colour scheme of the portrait of Sabine Rivière gives way to more opulent, dense colours, for example the dark green of the dress seen against the leaden blue of the cushion. The quest for a dark or dazzling colour scheme, linked to the effects of fabrics and materials, can also be found in the portrait of *Monsieur de Norvins*, close in feeling to that of the *Comtesse de Tournon*. Even the veil, naturally light and airy, falls as if weighed down; it is painted with exceptional skill, as is the ruff worn to disguise the Comtesse's double chin. The astonishingly creamy right arm

introduces a note of freshness. Where David would have used soft, sticky paint to reproduce material effects, Ingres prefers to render them in delicate detail (the pattern on the shawl, the small bow on the dress, the embroidery on the veil); he breathes an air of coquetry into his portrait that is like a response to the Comtesse's ironical smile.

The effect of the mass of detail is to set off the expression on the face, placed quite high in the centre of the canvas, and this introduces a subtle distancing effect. The armchair is not set at a perpendicular to the plane of the canvas, as so often in David's work – such as *The Comtesse Vilain XIII and Her Daughter* (1816; National Gallery, London), or slightly at an angle in *Madame Pierre Sériziat and Her Son* (Salon of 1795; Louvre, Paris) – but is almost parallel. It fulfils the function of the parapets of former times, setting the Comtesse in her own space.

This method of establishing a distance between the sitter and the spectator allows the artist to create a likeness that is at once intimate and noble. Like David, Ingres takes on the pose in all its artificiality. The pose is sufficient in itself to express the social standing of the sitter. The Comtesse de Tournon gazes directly at the spectator, with wide eyes firmly outlined by Ingres. The artist pays particular attention to painting the Comtesse's ugly nose, a little as David was to do with his own wife's nose the following year in *Madame David* (1813; National Gallery of Art, Washington DC), or as he himself did in the portrait of *Monsieur de Norvins*. In fact, it is the nose that breathes character into this unattractive face. Like the Chief of Police in Rome, the mother of the Prefect of Rome has a tight-lipped smile that denotes a lively and intelligent mind. The portrait of the *Comtesse de Tournon* is like a female double to the portrait of *Monsieur de Norvins*. The artist has experimented with different ways in which to capture her personality, as he had previously done in his pencil portraits. Having celebrated the range of the paintbrush, and sought to liberate painting from the tyranny of the model, in this portrait of an old woman Ingres has restored a feeling of the physical presence of the sitter – something his teacher David was so skilled at conveying. SA

## 34
## *Madame Marcotte de Sainte-Marie*

1826
Oil on canvas, 93 × 74 cm
Signed and dated at middle left: *Ingres 1826*
Département des Peintures, Musée du Louvre, Paris, RF 2398

PROVENANCE: collection of the sitter until her death, 1862; collection of Henri Marcotte de Sainte-Marie, her son; bequeathed by him to his children, 1916; acquired by the Louvre, with the collaboration of David David-Weill, 1923
EXHIBITED: Paris, Salon of 1827, no.576; Montauban, 1967, no.101; Paris, 1967, no.139; Montauban, 1980, no.50; London, New York and Washington, 1999–2000, no.97 (A. C. Shelton); Paris, 2006, no.104 (V. Pomarède)

LITERATURE: Lapauze 1911, pp.277–78; Wildenstein [1954–56], no.166; Ternois and Camesasca 1968, no.118; Toussaint 1985, pp.68–69; Vigne 1995, p.183; Ribeiro 1999, pp.26, 34, 137–42; Ternois 2001, p.145

In 1826, two years after his return to Paris, Ingres painted the portrait of the sister-in-law of his friend and protector in Rome, Charles Marcotte d'Argenteuil. Suzanne-Clarisse de Salvaing de Boissieu (1803–1862) had married in 1823 the younger brother of Marcotte d'Argenteuil, Marcotte de Sainte-Marie (1783–1859), twenty years her senior. Ingres at the time was at the peak of his reputation and apparently on the verge of becoming the new *chef d'école*: the Comte de Forbin, director of museums, and Charles Thévenin, director of the Villa Medici, had done all they could to obtain prestigious commissions for him (Allard and Chaudonneret 2006, Chapter 2). Busily immersed in this work, between 1824 and 1827, he slowed down his production of portraits, painting only two: the portrait of the *Comte de Pastoret* (1826; Art Institute, Chicago) and this one. Ingres was in the habit of exhibiting a choice of portraits, some of them several years old, alongside his history paintings; he knew that they would attract clients and, despite his better feelings, consolidate his reputation. In the Salon of 1827, although celebrated already, he exhibited only these two new portraits.

Even though the figure in the portrait of the *Comte de Pastoret* stands out against a vividly coloured background in a similar way to the figure of *Monsieur de Norvins* (1811–12; National Gallery, London), the portrait of Madame Marcotte de Sainte-Marie provides a simpler, more composite interpretation of the prototype, *Sabine Rivière* (1806; Louvre, Paris), further developed in the portrait of *Madame de Sennones* (1814; Musée des Beaux-Arts, Nantes). As in his history paintings, Ingres, who found inspiration through a process of crystallising his ideas, here also enjoys revisiting compositional elements and details, varying them ad infinitum.

In this case, he is assisted by developments in fashion. Like Madame de Sennones, Madame Marcotte de Sainte-Marie is seated on a yellow satin sofa whose iridescence contrasts with the brown fabric of her gown, recalling the juxtaposition of yellow and green in one of Vigée Lebrun's self-portraits with her daughter (Louvre, Paris). To the subtle sensuality of the décolleté and the red velvet of Madame de Sennones's Empire dress, however, Ingres responds with the exceptionally voluminous leg-of-mutton sleeves that were in fashion at the beginning of the 1830s, a broad belt pulled in tight around the waist and a small gauze collar. The shawl, at the time beginning to go out of fashion, is relegated to the far left of the composition. Variations in fashion were traditionally regarded as detracting over time from the significance of a portrait; this was one of the arguments advanced for refusing to give the genre a more noble status. Portrait painters such as Vigée-Lebrun and, to a lesser extent, David, preferred to dress their sitters in dark, sober clothes, drapery and timeless shawls. Ingres broke with this tradition.

His 'realism' made him aware of developments in taste and clothing and, far from shunning them, he confronted them squarely in order to transcend them. He may also have considered them to be an important part of the historical dimension of a portrait. Anyway, he did not treat them in a picturesque or superficial manner; on the contrary, in this painting particularly, fashion is an integral part of the composition. Although the Empire style encouraged elongation and generous curves and ovals, the strong contrasts of the female romantic silhouette gave him the chance to play with the effects of dilation and retraction, based on a complex network of sinuous lines developed in an exaggerated manner: the wavy outline of the collar, echoed by the rolls of the extraordinary hairstyle and the pleats of the bodice.

The result is an overall impression of instability, emphasised by the vibrations of the brush in the painting of the natural folds of the fabrics. Madame Marcotte's body, which appears to have slipped in amongst the cushions, describes an arc from shoulder to leg. The effect of the curve, the overriding principle of the image, is consciously sought here. A preparatory drawing now in the Musée Ingres in Montauban endorses this view. The study shows that Ingres first planned a more upright pose, possibly inspired (for the hands) by Raphael's portrait of *Maddalena Doni* (1506; Palazzo Pitti, Florence). The curve also brings the sitter's face to life: Madame Marcotte gazes at the spectator with great round eyes; her mouth, on the small side, has lips whose outline echoes the curves of the hair. *Madame Marcotte de Sainte-Marie* is a good example of the 'immanent' manner in which Ingres planned his portraits, and the tension between realistic observation and invention. The artist departs from the study of what he can see (fashion, the clothes) in order to develop his own interpretation, here partly geometrical, to which resemblance is added, and the independence of the painting material is celebrated.

The carefully staged feeling of instability can be explained by the woman's pose. For the first time Ingres employs a trick that Elisabeth-Louise Vigée-Lebrun (cat.27) and, closer in time to Ingres, François Gérard both used frequently: Madame Marcotte de Sainte-Marie seems to have been interrupted as she reads; the spectator is plunged into an artificial intimacy, suitable for the romantic spirit that animates the portrait. Lapauze recounts a story about the picture, probably based on the unusual pose. Madame Marcotte de Sainte-Marie, it appears, was so active by temperament that she could not bear to sit still as she posed for the painter. The artist had achieved his goal: art had become reality. SA

## 156
*Louis-François Bertin*

1832
Oil on canvas, 160 × 95 cm
Signed at the upper left: *J. INGRES PINXIT. / 1832*
Inscription at lower right: *L. F. Bertin*
Département des Peintures, Musée du Louvre, Paris, RF 1071

PROVENANCE: in the collection of the sitter; bequeathed by him to his daughter Louise Bertin; she bequeathed it to her niece, Madame Jules Bapst; Madame Bapst bequeathed it to Madame Georges Patinot; the Louvre bought it from Madame Patinot, 1897
EXHIBITED: Paris, Salon of 1833, no.1279; Bazar de Bonne-Nouvelle exhibition, Paris, 1846, no.47; Paris, 1855, Exposition Universelle, no.3372; J. A. D. Ingres exhibition, Paris, 1867; Paris, 1967, no.156; London, New York and Washington, 1999–2000, no.99 (A. C. Shelton); Paris 2006, no.106 (V. Pomarède)
LITERATURE: Lapauze 1911, pp.290–98; Toussaint 1985, no.XIII; Amaury-Duval 1993, pp.236–39; Ockmann 1995, pp.97–98, 108–09; Vigne 1995, pp.160, 170, 186–89, 196, 250, 254; Ternois 1998; Ternois 2001, pp.53–54; Goetz 2005, pp.28–30; Shelton 2005, *passim*; Allard and Chaudonneret 2006, pp.80, 136–37

By the time Ingres presented *Louis-François Bertin* at the Salon of 1833 (he had been designated *chef d'école* at the exhibitions of 1824 and 1827) his production of portraits had considerably slowed down (see cat.34). He had won recognition as a history painter and no longer felt the same need, either for financial reasons or for his reputation, to devote himself to a genre for which he had always professed a certain disdain. Nevertheless, the few portraits that he painted at this period show new ambition. None, however, achieved such a historic dimension as *Monsieur Bertin*, the outcome of a long period of gestation. Perhaps the artist was beginning to feel that, faced with the rise and rise of a bourgeoisie eager for portraits of themselves, the portrait painted by a genuine history painter could become the modern genre *par excellence*?

His contemporaries certainly wondered if this were so. At the end of the Salon, in which he had only exhibited two portraits, this one and the portrait of *Madame Devauçay* (1807; Musée Condé, Chantilly), the artist received the Légion d'honneur on the recommendation of the Comte de Forbin, director of museums at the time. The decoration was normally reserved for artists who had shown history paintings (Allard and Chaudonneret 2006, p.80). The historical dimension of the portrait of Louis-François Bertin, made the painting qualify as a 'major work' in the view of the critics Annet and Trianon (*Examen critique du Salon de 1833*, p.88). The impression was confirmed when the painting was shown again at the exhibition in the Bazar de Bonne-Nouvelle in 1846. Here it was hung next to the portrait of *Comte Molé* (1834; Private collection, France). The chronicler of the *Journal des artistes* saw in this juxtaposition 'an admirable summary of the principles of the revolution of 1789: the new man and the old gentleman, the descendant of Mathieu Molé and the creator of a race that yesterday was unknown' (*Journal des artistes*, 22 February 1846, p.62). The portrait of M. Bertin encapsulates the historical situation of France in the 1830s.

Louis-François Bertin, known as Bertin the Elder (1766–1841), was at this time the powerful editor of the *Journal des débats*, which he had founded with his brother, Bertin de Veaux, after the 18th Brumaire, when Napoleon Bonaparte overthrew the Directoire government. As the two men opposed the Empire, their periodical was confiscated in 1811, an act that caused their downfall. When they had recovered their property, however, after the return to power of Louis XVIII, the *Journal des débats* became the principal organ of the liberal middle class. The Bertin brothers disagreed with the drift to the right of the governments of Charles X and supported the accession to the throne of Louis-Philippe, whose politics corresponded with their own views.

When Ingres painted this portrait, Bertin the Elder was at the height of his power and fame. The *Journal des débats* gave a reasonable amount of space to art criticism. Ingres had been lampooned on more than one occasion by Jean-Baptiste Boutard, Bertin's father-in-law, in particular when Ingres's *Napoleon I on the Imperial Throne* (cat.12) was exhibited; Boutard's replacement, however, Jean-Etienne Delécluze, was favourable towards him. Ingres was often a guest at Les Roches, the estate where Bertin entertained all the most prominent personalities from the world of the arts, literature and politics, and this is probably where he received this commission.

Ingres, who was struggling to finish *The Martyrdom of St Symphorien* (Salon of 1834, St-Lazare Cathedral, Autun), worked on the portrait of Louis-François Bertin for a long time, an indication of the importance he attached to it. He had the greatest difficulty in finding a pose that would express the sitter's character. To him, a likeness was more than just the realistic painting of the features; it required a comprehensive rendering of the subject's physique, worked on separately.

A drawing now in the Musée Ingres in Montauban reveals his first idea: Bertin is shown standing, with his elbows on a sort of small column, in a pose that could have been influenced by Titian's *Man with a Glove* (Louvre, Paris). The artist changed his mind, however, and decided to portray the journalist sitting down. Bertin's pose has been likened to various portraits by Raphael, in particular to *Pope Leo X and His Nephews* (Uffizi Gallery, Florence) and to *Tommaso Inghirami* (Galleria Palatina, Palazzo Pitti, Florence); in my opinion, Ingres's debt to Titian is just as great. The way in which *Louis-François Bertin* fills the whole canvas is reminiscent not only of Titian's portrait of *Pietro Aretino* (Galleria Palatina, Palazzo Pitti, Florence), but also, and above all, of his late *Self-portrait* (Gemäldegalerie, Berlin). The position of Bertin's right hand and arm is identical to that of the left arm of the Venetian artist. The bulky quality in the portrait of Bertin could also be compared to the portrait of the painter *Etienne Jeaurat* by Greuze (Salon of 1769, Louvre, Paris), which entered the royal collections in 1824; the facial expressions are similar, and the pleats of the jacket rendered in the same way.

Whatever the painter and critic Etienne-Jean Delécluze may have had to say about it, the composition of the painting owes something to a system of classical references, adapted by Ingres to make it look natural – so natural that his contemporaries felt bewildered. In 1848, the artist P. N. Bergeret wrote indignantly: 'As for the pose of the person represented, it calls to mind certain natural functions that are best forgotten' (*Lettre d'un artiste sur l'état des arts en France, considérés sous les rapports politiques, artistiques, commerciaux et industriels*, Paris, 1848, p.66), a tricky comparison that was also made by Théophile Silvestre in 1856: 'This personage is seated on his chair as if it were a commode' (*Les Artistes vivants*, vol. 2, Paris, 1926, p.34).

Ingres had broken with the conventions regarding the pose, in other words with the subtle equilibrium between the sitter and the details that had hitherto characterised the status portrait. Louis-François Bertin occupies all the available space, leaving no room for the traditional accessories (a table, papers, an inkwell) that would have identified him as the editor of the *Journal des débats*. Nor does Bertin sport any decorations, for example the Légion d'honneur, which would have signalled that he belonged to the ruling class. From this time on, posture becomes more important than the symbols of status, the man more important than the traditional expression of his function. For the first time, a portrait emphasises the discrepancy, so characteristic of modernity, between the person and his or her social representation. In the way that the subject is presented front on, *Monsieur Bertin* is closely related to *Napoleon I on the Imperial Throne* (cat.12), but (a sign of the times) he expresses the exact opposite: the triumph of the individual.

With precise brushstrokes, the artist seeks to reproduce the sitter's features even when they are imperfect or unsightly – the spot over the right eye and the tousled hair. The studied naturalness of the pose is matched by an intensity of description that probably owes much to Holbein and the primitives. In one sense, *Louis-François Bertin*, in its obsession with accurate likeness, is as 'gothic' as *Napoleon I on the Imperial Throne*. The glimpse of the studio in which the journalist is posing bears witness to this. Bertin appears to be before us, alive; yet close scrutiny confirms that this is only an illusion. Most critics denounced the size of his hands, and Annet and Trianon remarked that: 'You only have to have seen M. Bertin's head to know that that is not the colour of his flesh' (*Les Artistes vivants*, vol. 2, Paris, 1926, p.34). The tension between history and the portrait is evident. The obvious photographic realism does not represent a desire to reproduce the sitter's physique with perfect accuracy, but a wish to idealise it.

Ingres seeks to bypass vulgar physical resemblance, as this classifies portraiture as an inferior genre and the portrait painter as a skilled copyist; he seeks rather to capture the expression.

The relationship between the body and the costume is, in this respect, very significant. In his portrait of Bertin, Ingres does not seek, as he does in the portrait of *Madame Marcotte-de-Sainte-Marie* (cat.34), to transcend the ephemeral nature of fashion by using the more abstract lines of the romantic costume, to the extent of causing the body to disappear. Here he does the reverse, exalting the presence of his sitter's body, as has already been confirmed by the pose: thanks to Bertin's size, buttons, pleats and seams all appear to be at bursting point. Ingres refutes the attacks mounted by many of the critics, Théophile Gautier in particular, against contemporary dress, especially male dress, which has the reputation of being sinister, unattractive and inexpressive. In *Louis-François Bertin*, the pleats are exaggerated and given a vertical movement that defies the laws of physics. The heroism of the painting, its driving force, derives partly from this struggle between the body and modern clothing; it hints at the individual's battle with the constraints of fashion.

Overdone realism, a mark of the history painter who wants to deliver the hidden meaning of objects, is achieved by exaggeration, almost by caricature. Aware of what is at stake, and of the manner in which pictorial representation can distort, Ingres exaggerates in order to be understood, as an actor speaks loudly in the theatre in order to be heard. The work is portrayed with exaggeration rather than with realism; caricature allows the artist to achieve the degree of idealisation that befits a history painting. This way of idealising a portrait allowed the representation to be detached from its sitter, *Louis-François Bertin* the painting from Louis-François Bertin the man. The portrait, viewed as the ideal reconstruction of a particular individual, could attain supreme dignity. Realistic though a portrait might seem, it is no substitute for a person; it is the person's reflection, idealised in order to acquire meaning. At the exhibition in the Bazar de Bonne-Nouvelle, the critics missed no opportunity to emphasise this in relation to the portrait of *Louis-François Bertin*. The artist, conscious of the emblematic value of his painting, designed a frame recalling Raphael's *Baldassare Castiglione* (Louvre, Paris). Just as *Baldassare Castiglione* became the emblem of Renaissance humanism, so *Louis-François Bertin* was destined to become the symbol of nineteenth-century modernity. SA

# Angelica Kauffman
CHUR, SWITZERLAND, 1741 – ROME, 1807

## 60
### *Joseph Johann, Graf von Fries*

1787
Oil on canvas, 128.5 × 102.5 cm
Historisches Museum der Stadt Wien, Vienna, 56.406

PROVENANCE: Fogdor bequest, 1935
EXHIBITED: see Milan 2002, p.517 no.XV.9

When Johann Wolfgang von Goethe visited Rome on his famous Italian journey, he spent much time with Angelica Kauffman. She had settled there permanently with her husband Antonio Zucchi in 1772. Kauffman shared Goethe's passion for art and antiquities and gladly showed him around. He was full of admiration not just for the art he saw, but also for Angelica, as a diary entry of 22 July attests: 'It is a great pleasure to look at paintings with Angelica, for she has a trained eye and knows a great deal about the technical side of painting. Moreover, she is sensitive to all that is true and beautiful, and incredibly modest.' Goethe also became acquainted with the most active art collector in Rome at the time, the young Austrian Count Joseph Johann Fries (1765–1788), the elder of the two sons of, and the heir to, the immensely wealthy merchant and financier Johann Reichsgraf von Fries (1719–1785).

The count's field of collecting ranged from paintings to prints and drawings, and extended to cameos and antique sculpture; he was undeterred by hugely inflated prices. Goethe reported on 17 July 1787 that 'Count Fries buys a great deal, including a Madonna by Andrea del Sarto [now at Ascott House, Buckinghamshire] for 600 zecchini … Last March Angelica had already offered 450 for it and would have given the entire sum, had her vigilant husband not objected. Now they both regret it.' Count Fries was also a passionate admirer of Kauffman, both as an artist and on a personal level. His dressing room was entirely decorated with stipple engravings after her works.

It is not surprising that Fries, patron to many painters, and himself an amateur artist, wished to be painted by Kauffman. The diary of her confidant Goethe records: '[She was] not as happy as she would deserve to be considering her great talent and fortune … and tired of commissions, but her old husband rather likes that much money comes in as the result of easy labour.' Having become an internationally celebrated artist, Kauffman was now being admonished for churning out too many quickly painted, formulaic works. For this new commission, however, she seems to have heeded Goethe's advice, and painted it in her own time and for her own enjoyment.

The young count is depicted as the archetypal collector, posing next to one of his most recent and cherished acquisitions, Canova's marble sculpture *Theseus Vanquishing the Minotaur*. The sculpture had originally been commissioned by the Venetian ambassador Girolamo Zulian in 1781. By the time of its completion Zulian had left for Constantinople and it was sold directly to Fries instead. When first exhibited in 1783, the work was fervently admired. Widely regarded as certainly meeting, if not surpassing, the ideals of classical sculpture, it established Canova's fame in Rome (see Memes 1825, pp.447–48). Kauffman's inclusion of the sculpture in the portrait was doubtless a personal homage to her friend Canova.

In this well thought-out and intelligent composition Kauffman indulges her skills as a painter by rendering a plethora of different materials and textures, among them silk, stone, skin and feathers. When she had become one of the first two female members of the newly founded Royal Academy of Arts in London in 1768, her gender had prevented her from studying the male nude. Now, the inclusion of Canova's sculpture in her painting gave her the chance to demonstrate her ability to render the idealised male nude.

The spatial arrangement of the portrait gives the impression of a proud owner guarding his sculpture; set back behind a window, the Canova is clearly visible, and identifiable to the knowledgeable viewer, yet it remains unobtainable. Although the count's figure echoes that of the Greek hero, his extravagantly plumed hat and Van Dyck costume make him resemble the much-derided 'macaronies', British dandies who affected Continental fashions; Kauffman was clearly aiming to flatter her sitter by emphasising his dashing looks and princely demeanour. Her decision to depict her patron with a widely known and acclaimed work can, moreover, be regarded as an attempt to prevent speculation about the level of Fries's connoisseurship. Goethe had noted that the count had often been duped into buying fakes, and rumours of his pretensions and gullibility were so widespread that the expression 'E un secondo conte de Fries' had become a commonplace when referring to a person who wasted money on inferior artefacts (Gorani 1793, vol.2, pp.242–48).

The year after the portrait was painted Fries died prematurely of malaria. His Canova was subsequently purchased by the 3rd Marquis of Londonderry who installed it in his London house; it is now in the collection of the Victoria and Albert Museum, London (A.5-1962). Kauffman's admiration for, and friendship with, Canova was mutual: when she died in Rome in 1807, she was honoured with a splendid funeral whose procession, based on the burial of Raphael, was directed by the sculptor himself. AS

## 30
### *Countess Catherine Skavronska*

1789
Oil on canvas, 158 × 122 cm
Germanisches Nationalmuseum, Nuremberg, Gm 1931

PROVENANCE: see Düsseldorf 1998, p.289
EXHIBITED: Flensburg, 1956, no.20; Fort Worth, 1982, no.30; Kassel, 1997, no.333 (illustrated); Düsseldorf, 1998, no.156; Rome, 1998, no.34 (illustrated)
LITERATURE: see Düsseldorf 1998, p.289

When Kauffman painted this portrait, the Russian Countess Catherine Skavronska (*née* Catherine Wasiljewa Engelhardt) (1761–1829), was 28 years old and already looking back on an eventful life. At the age of fifteen she had become the favourite mistress of her famous uncle, the Russian military campaigner and favourite of Catherine the Great, Grigori Alexandrovitch Potemkin (1729–1791). He was clearly attracted by his niece's appearance, calling her 'one of the most beautiful women in the Russian empire'. For her part Catherine initially accepted the relationship 'without passion or depth of feeling' (Fort Worth 1982). Potemkin later saw a convenient match between his niece and the exceedingly rich Count Paul Mattinowitsch Skavronsky (1757–1793), a Livonian aristocrat and great-nephew of Catherine the Great; the two married in 1781.

Skavronsky's appointment as Russian Ambassador at the court of the King of the Two Sicilies at Naples in 1784 depended mainly on Catherine's social networking skills and connections, and was based on a recommendation by Potemkin. When Skavronsky left for Italy, she remained in St Petersburg with her uncle, only joining her husband again when his health deteriorated. Once in Italy, Catherine led an idle existence. Vigée-Lebrun, who painted the countess on at least five occasions, remembered her vividly, commenting in her memoirs that she was 'sweet and pretty as an angel. Her uncle, the famous Potemkin, had showered her with riches, but she made no use of them all. She was happiest lying stretched out on a sofa without her corset and wrapped about with a huge black pelisse … she showed me her jewel case, one of the most splendid imaginable: it contained some enormous diamonds given to her by Potemkin, but I never saw her wear them. I remember her telling me that in order to fall asleep, a slave had to lie under the bed and recite the same story every night. During the day, she was always idle; she had no education, and her conversation was as empty as would be; despite this, her enchanting face and her angelic sweetness lent her an invincible charm' (Vigée-Lebrun 1989, p.101).

A highly regarded and sought-after portraitist, Angelica Kauffman was at this time at the height of her international fame. She first met Skavronska at the court of Naples in 1785, when she painted a more 'sentimental' portrait of the countess with her four-year-old daughter. In this work however, painted in Rome, Kauffman shows the sitter in a very different light. Rather than opting for a fashionable theatrical pose in a pseudo-mythological guise, she depicts the countess in a traditional format, seated, with drapery and a classical column in the background.

As she celebrates Skavronska's beauty and dignity, the artist also captures her bland and non-confrontational nature. This plainness of personality, echoed also in her simple white 'Grecian' dress, is subverted by her flirtatious, almost challenging gaze, and the hint of a smile, which directly engages with the viewer. The countess is seated beside a table on which a sword and belt are placed. She is depicted crowning an antique helmet with a laurel wreath while gently drawing it towards her. The painter thus establishes an intimate connection between the sitter and the military garb. Although the sword and helmet are attributes associated with the goddess Minerva, Vigée-Lebrun's descriptions of the countess's nature and account of her life make an implicit comparison of her character with that of the goddess of wisdom improbable. The symbolic reference to the warrior Potemkin is reinforced by the inscription of his name on the helmet.

Skavronsky's love of music was so extreme that he allegedly spoke mainly in recitative. He was described by the Tsarina as 'a little bit silly and clumsy' but was 'very much in love' with his wife (Vigée-Lebrun 1989). Nevertheless, Potemkin was to remain the most important male figure in the countess's life. He commissioned this portrait, on 26 August (through Signor Gaspare Santini), paid 120 zecchini for it and arranged for the work to be shipped to Russia. The painting can be regarded as a celebration of Potemkin's military success, with the countess represented as a goddess of Victory, symbolically honouring the achievements of her admired uncle. Moreover, in this deliberate ambiguity, Kauffman implies the intimate allegiance between Skavronska and Potemkin and her loyal ties to faraway Russia, to which she immediately returned on the death of her husband, two years after Potemkin had passed away. AS

## Christen Købke
### COPENHAGEN, 1810 – COPENHAGEN, 1848

## 81
### *Frederik Sødring*

1832
Oil on canvas, 42.2 × 37.9 cm
Signed: *C Købke 18 26/5 32*
Inscribed on the reverse in the sitter's hand: *Foræret mig af min Ven Chr. Købke paa min Fødeselsdag den 31 Maj 1832*
Den Hirschsprungske Samling, Copenhagen, 309

PROVENANCE: see Nørregård-Nielsen 1996
EXHIBITED: London, 1984, no.52; Paris, 1984A, no.107; Los Angeles, 1993, no.60
LITERATURE: London 1984, p.196, no.52; Paris 1984A, pp.212, 291, no.107; Schwartz 1992, p.21; Los Angeles 1993, pp.147, 150, 151, 219–20, no.60; Wivel 1993, fig.12; Nørregård-Nielsen 1996, vol.1, pp.194, 196–98, fig.131, and vol.3, p.246, no.37; Wivel 1996, ill. p.145, fig.86

Købke's portrait of his friend, the landscape painter Frederik Sødring (1809–1862), took its inspiration from another image in this exhibition, Wilhelm Bendz's *A Young Artist (Ditlev Blunck) Examining a Sketch in a Mirror* (1826; cat.82) (London 1984, p.196). Købke executed a string of artists' likenesses during his short career (he died of pneumonia in 1848), in addition to the church interiors and architectural landscapes which made him famous. In this early portrait, realised as a gift for Sødring, he shows the landscapist in the studio the two shared in Copenhagen (London 1984, p.196). Købke had been a student of Christoffer Wilhelm Eckersberg, whose stylistic tendencies pervaded his pupils' *œuvre* well after they had left the Royal Academy in Copenhagen. This phenomenon is evident in the crisp line and areas of strong light and shadow in this work. Although these formal investigations are characteristic of Købke's production, this painting stands out among his portraits of artists for its inclusion of objects with symbolic significance (Los Angeles 1993, p.151).

Sødring also attended the Royal Academy in Copenhagen but, unlike Købke, he was never part of Eckersberg's circle, preferring to pursue the more romantic model of painting promulgated by the Norwegian painter Johan Christian Dahl (Los Angeles 1993, p.219). Nor did Sødring make the obligatory pilgrimage to Italy and, specifically, to Rome, like Købke and most of their compatriots. Instead, he eschewed the classical world for the more romantic possibilities afforded him by nature, concentrating his attentions on the landscapes of Norway and Germany.

In this portrait Sødring appears to look directly out at the viewer. In fact, Købke captures him in a moment when he has paused – palette and knife in hand – to evaluate the work done on a canvas, part of which is reflected in the mirror behind his head. Painted in the late spring (Købke inscribed the painting with the date, 26 May 1832), when the sun dominates the skies in Scandinavia, morning light streams in from the right, causing the furniture to cast shadows, and striking the young man's broad, fair forehead, which contrasts with his flushed cheeks. Additional touches of red in the stripes of the chair's upholstery and the little box on the table set off the range of grey tonalities employed in the picture.

The mirror and the arrangement of prints around it, pinned to the double doors, resemble the modest imagery of a *trompe-l'oeil* painting and, in particular, the letter-rack still-life genre, in a visual play which recalls the illusion and mimesis inherent in the art of painting. The reflection itself captures things present in the room beyond the viewer's range, such as a frame corner and easel legs. Bits of paper – from their small, rectangular format they seem to be ticket stubs, visiting cards and small notes – are wedged into the left edge of the oval. The prints tucked behind either side of the mirror, a Dutch landscape with a cow, and four

views of antique Roman columns and ruins, recall the themes of nature and antiquity, and perhaps refer to the different artistic paths chosen respectively by the two artists (Wivel 1993, p.109). The ivy plant, whose delicate tendrils twine their way up and down one side of the doorway, symbolises friendship, an appropriate reference for this portrait. Sødring's profession as a landscape painter is also hinted at by the folding wooden stool, which is just visible, leaning against the wall, in the right corner of the composition. In addition to the symbolism implicit in this portrait, the inscription Sødring added to the verso of the work serves as another reminder that this is a painting made for a close friend and fellow artist: 'Presented to me by my friend Købke on my birthday, 31 May 1832' (London 1984, p.196). VG

# Sir Thomas Lawrence

BRISTOL, 1769 – LONDON, 1830

## 4
### King George III

1792
Oil on canvas, 275.6 × 153.7 cm
The Herbert, Coventry, CH 23

PROVENANCE: commissioned for the City of Coventry by its MPs Lord Eardley and John Wilmot; placed in St Mary's Hall, September 1792; transferred to the Herbert Art Gallery and Museum after 1945
EXHIBITED: Royal Academy, 1792, no.65; for later exhibition history see Garlick 1989, p.192
LITERATURE: Garlick 1962–64, p.85; Garlick 1989, p.192; London 1998, p.135; Levey 2005, pp.114, 118

George III (1738–1820) became King of Great Britain and Ireland and Elector of Hanover in 1763. Thomas Lawrence, a precocious talent who was to become Britain's leading portraitist, arrived in London as a teenager in 1787 and began to exhibit his work regularly. In 1790 the King requested that Lawrence be elected an Associate of the Royal Academy, the first step towards full membership. This was 'a unique intervention by George III, which in fact proved counter-productive': the Academicians refused, but then complied the following year. After Sir Joshua Reynolds's death in 1792, Lawrence was appointed 'Painter-in-Ordinary to His Majesty' (Levey 2005, p.93).

The painter's first brush with royalty came in 1789 when he was summoned to portray Queen Charlotte at Windsor Castle. This picture remained in Lawrence's possession and was shown by him at the Royal Academy in 1790. In the King's portrait, he employed a similar background view – looking down towards the Chapel of Eton College from Windsor Castle – to the one he had used in depicting the Queen. George III apparently sat to Lawrence at Buckingham House (Williams 1831,

vol.1, p.126). Invoking the vista from Windsor, though, tied the later painting to its earlier counterpart, highlighting the artist's record of royal sitters. The location represented also contributed to the portrait's political aspect: not least, the image can be interpreted as a riposte to revolutionary attacks on the monarchy in France, by affirming the sacred aspects of royalty in the person of a British king who stands, with a solemn and elevated gaze, 'on a loggia apparently built in the sky'. While Jacques-Louis David, in his *Oath of the Tennis Court*, an enormous drawing exhibited at the Salon of 1791, 'had shown the Chapel Royal at Versailles struck by revolutionary lightning', Lawrence shows another chapel – that of Eton College, a school founded as an act of piety by an earlier English monarch – which 'glows with transfiguring light'. The King's choice of apparel is highly charged. He is shown wearing the chivalric regalia of the Order of the Garter: with religion behind him, he appears as 'a crusading knight' (London 1998, p.135; my thanks to Desmond Shawe-Taylor for discussing this point).

This was not a royal commission but 'a new, semi-state portrait', requested by the MPs for Coventry, John Wilmot and his brother-in-law Lord Eardley, and presented by them to the city (Levey 2005, p.114). Wilmot gained prominence in 1792 for his fundraising efforts to provide assistance to the large numbers of French Roman Catholic clergy who had fled to England (Polden 2004, p.468). He first wrote to Lawrence in November 1790, hoping that the King might 'condescend to permit Mr Lawrence to take the face in some degree from the life', and that the image would be ready by 4 June 1791 (the King's birthday) (Levey 2005, p.114).

Although this unusual project appears to have met with royal approval, press criticism of the painting's 1792 exhibition suggests that co-operation was somewhat dilatory. The *Morning Herald* declared on 3 May that the image 'will, we doubt not, be entitled to distinguished praise, *when it is finished*. In its present state, it bears evident marks of haste, and has been hurried from the *Easel* to its place in the Academy with a precipitance which might have endangered a reputation less firmly established than that of this promising Artist.' Four days later the *Morning Chronicle* noted: 'We have been told, that HIS MAJESTY did not sit for the face, until a *very, very* short time, before the exhibition opened – and being painted in haste, forms an apology for the Artist.'

On account of its subject Lawrence's portrait 'naturally assumed prime place of honour' within the exhibition space at the Royal Academy's Great Room in Somerset House, hanging at the centre of the north wall (Levey 2005, p.114). For so young an artist this was a remarkable achievement: the other exhibition centrepieces were works by Benjamin West, the Academy's newly elected President. West's most conspicuous images were royal commissions, including two for the Audience Chamber at

Windsor Castle showing scenes from the life of Edward III. Hanging in such company, Lawrence's painting exemplifies the 'renovated and far more assertively nationalistic royal image' which has been seen as an important factor in the revival of the monarchy during George III's reign. The King, particularly, came to be seen as a more sympathetic figure. In the winter of 1788–89 his illness, characterised by mental disturbance, prompted public pity; thereafter, as France radicalised, 'royal celebration throughout Great Britain would increase dramatically in scale and tempo'. Private initiatives – such as the patronage of this portrait – played an important part in this dynamic (Colley 1992, pp.207–16).

That this was Lawrence's first use of an 'oversize' full-length canvas reinforced the work's power to make an impression both as a political statement and an artistic self-advertisement (London 1998, p.135). Later in 1792 the portrait was placed in a more permanent setting in St Mary's Hall, Coventry, crowning a series of earlier images of royalty. Lord Eardley paid Lawrence three hundred guineas for the work, an extraordinary sum at this point in the artist's career and a compliment not only to his painting but also to his royal subject (Williams 1831, vol.1, p.126). SM

### 129
### John Philip Kemble as Coriolanus

1798
Oil on canvas, 287.2 × 179.7 cm
Guildhall Art Gallery, City of London, 844

PROVENANCE: bought from the artist by Sir Richard Worsley, 7th Baronet, of Appuldurcombe, Isle of Wight; bequeathed to his niece, Henrietta Simpson, 1805, who married the Hon. Charles Anderson-Pelham (later the 1th Earl of Yarborough), 1806; by descent to the 4th Earl of Yarborough, who presented it to the Guildhall, 1906
EXHIBITED: Royal Academy, 1798, no.225; for later exhibition history see Garlick 1989, p.216
LITERATURE: see Garlick 1989, p.216

John Philip Kemble (1757–1823) followed his elder sister Sarah Siddons (see cat.130) into the acting profession. Having gained fame in the provinces, he made his début at the Drury Lane Theatre in London in 1783. As actor-manager there from 1788 to 1796, he sought to make Shakespeare central to the theatre's programming. By the time he first played the title role in *Coriolanus* on 20 January 1789 Kemble was the capital's leading tragic actor; the part became closely identified with him (indeed, he gave his valedictory performance in the role in 1817).

Lawrence had a long-standing connection with the Kemble family, and, according to John Taylor, no friendship 'was more sincere and warm than that between the great painter and the great actor' (Baker 1942, p.145). Lawrence reportedly declared in 1810 that 'there had been no other such countenance upon the stage as that of Kemble. If 1,000 men were collected together you wd. be struck with the face of Kemble' (Farington 1978–84,

vol.10, p.3691). It is possible, however, that Lawrence may not even have seen Kemble play this particular role prior to painting this image, for when in 1811 the artist invited his friend Joseph Farington to a performance of Kemble as Coriolanus, he declared that 'I have seen it but once' (Ashton 2006, p.62).

Work was underway on the portrait by 9 January 1798, when Farington noted that Lawrence was painting a 'Colossal figure of Kemble in Coriolanus'; on 22 April, with the work completed, the diarist told Lawrence that it was his masterpiece (Farington 1978–84, vol.3, pp.965, 1001). It was then presented at the Royal Academy exhibition with the title, 'Portrait of Mr. Kemble, as Coriolanus, at the Hearth of Tulius Ausidius'. A sketch version of the image is untraced (Garlick 1989, p.216.)

The version of this play which was performed by Kemble was Thomas Sheridan's reworking of James Thomson's adaptation (Sillars 2006, pp.189–90). As Lawrence's title makes clear, the scene portrayed is that in which Coriolanus, a Roman patrician general, having been banished from his city, presents himself at the house of an enemy general, Tulius Ausidius, and traitorously declares:

> make my misery serve thy turn! so use it
> For I will fight against my canker'd country
> with the spleen
> Of all the under fiends. (Sheridan n.d., p. 33)

The year before Lawrence exhibited his portrait, another artist, Francis Peter Bourgeois, had shown his own version of Kemble as Coriolanus at the Royal Academy (illustrated in West 1991B, p.236). Whereas Bourgeois had offered a literal rendition of the scene, Lawrence's image transcended the text. In particular, Lawrence exploited his subject's past career history, which meant that for contemporaries Kemble's features were imbued with connotations of order and hierarchy: 'the actor's body fuses with the associations of the character to create an icon of patrician dignity and power' (West 1991B, pp.232, 235). In this way, the artist stressed not so much the pride and treachery of Coriolanus as the nobility of his stand against fickle popular opinion: 'Lawrence invested the image of the actor with qualities of aristocracy, loyalty and patriotism while drawing on a fable of rebellion' (West 1991B, pp.235, 239).

The arrangement of Kemble's clothing has the effect of making much of his body below the head resemble a pillar; in this way he is visually allied both to the (almost totally obscured) statue in the left background, and, especially, to the term which can be glimpsed behind him on the right. In being likened to a term, Coriolanus is represented as almost an icon of veneration. The scene as a whole may also echo the formula given in Cesare Ripa's *Iconologia* for symbolising 'Love of One's Country'. In sum, it has been suggested that the artist 'looked beyond this unedifying Shakespearian episode to

the mythical hero of the burgeoning Roman republic, and to the idea of patriotism in general' (Shawe-Taylor 1990, pp.50–52).

Accordingly, it was not without justification that Lawrence described the image as 'a sort of half-history picture' (Williams 1831, vol.1, p.197). Painted as an experiment rather than on commission, for the artist this image was an expression of his ambitions as a painter of elevated themes; as its monumental scale suggests, it was designed to make an impression in the competitive environment of the exhibition room. Press reports suggest that in this it succeeded: one art critic lauded the painting as 'an union of the style of Titian with that of Rembrandt'; another described it as painted 'with a powerful hand … suitable to the elevated character of historical portrait' (*St James's Chronicle*, 24–26 April 1798; *True Briton*, 24 April 1798; London 1979, p.38). The work was also of benefit to the sitter, for having portrayals of himself made by Lawrence and other artists shown at the Royal Academy was valuable publicity (West 1991B, pp.244–45). (Indeed, Lawrence himself had shown a portrait of Kemble at the Royal Academy the previous year.)

By 1805 the artist had sold the painting to Sir Richard Worsley (Williams 1831, vol.1, p.198). Lawrence went on to paint three further large-scale portraits of Kemble, as Rolla in Sheridan's *Pizarro* (1800), as Hamlet (1801) and as Cato in Addison's *Cato* (1812). SM

### 14
### Pope Pius VII

1819
Oil on canvas, 269.4 × 178.3 cm
Not signed or dated
Inscription on the document in the sitter's hand: *Per / Ant* Canova [for Antonio Canova]; inscription on the archway at the left: … *AVIT [P]IUS VII · PONT · MAX*
Lent by Her Majesty The Queen, RCIN 404946

PROVENANCE: commissioned by the Prince Regent (later King George IV) and painted at Rome, 1819
EXHIBITED: see Roberts 2002, p.103
LITERATURE: see Roberts 2002, p.103

This portrait was one of a series of works commissioned from Lawrence by the Prince Regent, later King George IV, of leaders from across Europe who were associated with the defeat of Napoleon. Lawrence arrived in Rome for the first time in May 1819 and was accommodated in the Quirinal Palace. He had nine sittings from the Pope, and the painting was finished by September. During painting, Lawrence wrote (Williams 1831, vol.2, pp.159, 200, 220):

> the Pope being an old man, his countenance has a great deal of detail in it; and a good and cheerful nature, with a clear intellect, gives it variety of expression. In public he appears feeble, from his stooping so much; but in private he seems to be in good health and spirits, speaks with a strong, clear voice, and sustains the sittings with

*undiminished strength. He is a very fine subject, and it is probable that the picture will be one of the best that I have painted.*

Gregorio Chiaramonti (1742–1823) was born into a noble family in Cesena, and became a Benedictine monk; he was elected Pope Pius VII in 1800. Having agreed to the Concordat in 1801, he participated at Napoleon's 1804 coronation as Emperor of the French in Notre Dame. Following France's annexation of the Papal States in 1809, however, he excommunicated Napoleon; he was then himself abducted and held prisoner at Savona and at Fontainebleau until 1814. He emerged from captivity a near-martyr, and a popular hero in Italy (Olson 1986, pp. 83–85). Throughout Europe he had a saintly status; and his features were so widely represented through prints, paintings and sculpture as to make him probably the most recognisable figure, with the exception of Napoleon, for European contemporaries (Levey 1975, p. 197; Levey 2005, p. 228).

Although Lawrence must have been aware of papal portraits of earlier eras, he was particularly alert to the competition of previous portraits of Pius VII by Jacques-Louis David (1805) and Vincenzo Camuccini (1814–15), who were, as he noted, 'the two first painters of Paris and Rome' (Williams 1831, vol. 2, p. 194).

Pius sits on the *sedia gestatoria*, a portable processional papal throne, on which can be seen his coat of arms and his motto 'PAX' (taken from the Benedictine coat of arms) (Olson 1986, p. 90). He wears the Fisherman's Ring, engraved with the seal design of St Peter in a boat (Williams 1831, vol. 2, pp. 187, 195) and is shown looking away from the spectator, 'as if his thoughts went beyond the immediate purpose of his sitting for a portrait' (Garlick 1993, p. 17).

The portrait highlights the Pope's patronage of the arts: the background architecture probably invokes the Braccio Nuovo, a planned but as yet unbuilt wing of the Museo Chiaramonti, a series of additions by Pius to the Vatican museums. The sculptures within – the *Apollo Belvedere*, the *Laocoön* and part of the *Torso Belvedere* – were not in fact housed there, but their presence underlines the importance to Pius of their restoration to the papal collections. As one art historian has observed, these objects, which, like the Pope himself, had been forcibly removed from Rome, represent not only the Pope's 'spiritual curatorial position' but also his 'ultimate triumph over Napoleon' (Ashton 2006, pp. 36, 112). Lawrence himself suggested that if ever Napoleon had come to Rome, then he would have seen that 'In the hands of this old man [Pius VII] had still existed an empire over the soul, that even to himself had shamed his tyranny' (Williams 1831, vol. 2, pp. 148–49). British political intervention had helped to secure the restitution of the majority of the looted papal art works, and the portrait's patron, the Prince Regent, had himself given

200,000 francs towards the cost of shipping them back to Rome (Johns 1998, p. 159). Pius had taken a personal interest in their recovery (O'Dwyer 1985, p. 135).

Pius holds a document with the inscription Per / Antº Canova, making the Pope a link between the great sculpture of the past and 'the great sculptor of the present' (who was also a favourite of the Prince Regent) (Levey 2005, p. 232). The paper may relate to Canova's appointment as Prefect of the Fine Arts at Rome, or perhaps refers to the sculptor's advancement to the rank of Marchese d'Ischia in 1816 following his involvement in negotiations for the return of the papal collections (London 1979, p. 71).

Shown to selected viewers at the Quirinal Palace prior to Lawrence's departure from Rome, the Pope's portrait was international news. Lawrence wrote (Williams 1831, vol. 2, p. 186):

> *No picture that I have painted has been more popular with the friends of its subject, and the public . . . and, according to my scale of ability, I have executed my intention: having given him that expression of unaffected benevolence and worth, which lights up his countenance with a freshness and spirit, entirely free (except in the characteristic paleness of his complexion) from that appearance of illness and decay that he generally has, when enduring the fatigue of his public functions.*

Metternich compared the general opinion of Lawrence's reputation in Rome to that of the Coliseum (Levey 2005, p. 232). *The Times* of 6 January 1820 quoted reports in the French press which described the return homeward of the 'celebrated painter, Sir Thomas Lawrence, whom the amateurs have denominated the English Titian'. Lawrence was paid £525 for the image (Millar 1969, vol. 1, p. 74). SM

## 13
### *George IV*

1822
Oil on canvas, 289.6 × 200.7 cm
Lent by Her Majesty The Queen, RCIN 405918

PROVENANCE: commissioned by George IV
EXHIBITED: probably Royal Academy, 1822, no. 77; for later exhibition history see Garlick 1989, p. 194
LITERATURE: see Garlick 1989, p. 194

George IV (1762–1830) acceded to the throne in January 1820; Lawrence himself was elected President of the Royal Academy later the same year. The coronation took place on 19 July 1821, having been postponed from the previous year because of the return to Britain of the new monarch's estranged wife, Queen Caroline.

The ceremony's total cost was an enormous £238,238 (more than three times as much as Queen Victoria's in 1838). Happily for the British taxpayer, most of the cost was met from the financial indemnity which the French had been obliged to pay following their defeat at Waterloo in 1815

(Cumming 1992, p. 42). George IV's desire, indeed, was not simply to supersede the 1761 coronation of his father, George III, but to eclipse French models, particularly Napoleon's 1804 imperial coronation. Costumes were specially designed for the occasion which harked back to the English Renaissance, thereby stressing the historical legitimacy of the King's title, as against Napoleon's transitory and concocted imperium: 'A tailor was even sent to Paris to inspect and measure the Emperor's robes, to ensure that those being made for George would be finer, and the train longer' (Parissien 2001, p. 304). Lawrence's portrait shows the results: the King was attired in a silver tissue doublet and trunk hose with a crimson velvet surcoat, although they were scarcely discernible under his fur-lined mantle of crimson velvet. The epic train, which required eight bearers, can be seen curling out of the image at the left.

Although the tightly corseted King almost fainted, the coronation was a success. Lawrence, who himself participated in the coronation procession, extolled the celebrations after the crowning as 'a scene of gorgeous triumph and mental heartfelt exultation, as never yet can have been exceeded, or perhaps been equalled' (Williams 1831, vol. 2, p. 254).

The future King had first been painted by Lawrence in 1814 when he was Prince Regent. These sittings provided the basis for a further portrait showing the Regent in Garter robes which was shown at the Royal Academy in 1818; this became his official portrait following his accession. In July 1821 Lawrence saw the King the day after he had been crowned, and his commission to paint him in coronation robes either came then or shortly thereafter. Later that same month, Lawrence noted that the King wished his portrait 'should be instantly finished'. Perhaps on this account – and despite a press report in August which suggested that a more ambitious image was underway – it appears that for the coronation portrait Lawrence simply reworked a version of his 1818 portrait; indeed, *pentimenti* matching the Garter costume can been detected (Millar 1969, vol. 1, pp. xxxiii, 61; Levey 2005, pp. 240–41).

There is little variation in the sitter's surroundings between the two images. Lawrence retained the symbolically important Sèvres 'Table of the Great Generals' at the left of the image: given to the Prince Regent in 1817 by Louis XVIII, the table was one of a pair undertaken for Napoleon in 1806 (Parissien 2001, pp. 278–79; Plumb and Wheldon 1977, p. 226, repr.). The King props his fingers on this symbolic object 'in a gesture which manages to express both his artistic connoisseurship and a disdainful dismissiveness embodying his own imagined contribution to the subjugation of Napoleon' (Parissien 2001, p. 279). The Imperial crown can be seen lying on the table. On top of his robes, the King wears the collars of the Golden Fleece, the Guelphic Order, the Order of the Bath and the Order of the Garter (Millar 1969, vol. 1, p. 61).

Lawrence apparently did revise his sitter's features; although a planned sitting was cancelled shortly after the coronation, a press notice later that year indicated that more than one sitting for the portrait had taken place (Williams 1831, vol. 2, pp. 253–54; Levey 2005, p. 333, note 29). Even so, the final image still 'grossly flatters the appearance of the King, making him look twenty years younger than his real age'; the King's peruke, for instance, takes on the appearance of a real head of hair (Ribeiro 1995, p. 234). Work on the portrait was apparently still ongoing in December 1821; it may have been the 'Portrait of His Majesty' which Lawrence exhibited at the Royal Academy in 1822. The completed image was installed in the throne room at St James's Palace by 1830 (Millar 1969, vol. 1, p. 61).

Lawrence's successor as President of the Royal Academy, Sir Martin Archer Shee, selected this image when he was commissioned by the Academy in 1838 to undertake a copy of 'any' full length portrait of George IV. Completed in 1840, the work cost £315. This commission formed part of a wider initiative by the Academy to update its collection of royal portraits: Shee was also requested to supply a replica of his own full-length portrait of William IV, and, in addition, the Academicians wrote to Queen Victoria seeking a sitting to Shee for her portrait (Essen 1992, p. 249). SM

## 147
### David Lyon

c. 1825
Not signed or dated
Oil on canvas, 219.5 × 134 cm
Museo Thyssen-Bornemisza, Madrid, 217 (1981.55)

PROVENANCE:  Miss E. Carnegy-Arbuthnott OBE, London; sold by her at Christie's, London, 21 November 1980 (lot 114); bought Colnaghi's;  sold to the Baron Thyssen-Bornemisza Collection, Lugano, 1981;  placed in the Thyssen-Bornemisza Museum, Madrid, 1992;  acquired for the Thyssen-Bornemisza Museum, Madrid, 1993
LITERATURE:  Garlick 1989, p. 232

Sir Thomas Lawrence's portrait of David Lyon junior (c. 1794–1872) remained in private ownership until relatively recently, and has received little attention from scholars. Lyon is depicted wearing a black frock-coat trimmed with fur and lined with silk; his gloved right hand rests upon a walking stick, and holds the glove for his bared left hand. He is shown standing in a country setting, perhaps with the suggestion that he owns the land around him. The use of a low viewing point brings the level of the horizon downwards on the canvas space, serving to accentuate Lyon's stature, and this effect is increased by the horizontal banding of the clouds and foliage which form the background. The background light is arranged in such a way that Lyon's coat is palely silhouetted, while his head is set against brooding clouds. One commentator

has suggested that his clothing, pose and hair are typical of the nineteenth-century dandy (Pérez-Jofre 2001, p. 471).

Little is known about the gestation of the work and only the outlines of the sitter's life can be sketched. Of Scottish descent, he was one of the five sons and five daughters of David Lyon senior (c. 1750–1827) and his wife Isabella Read (1766–1836). The sitter's father, a West India merchant partly based in Jamaica, and much of whose trade was in sugar, had amassed a fortune approaching £600,000 by the time of his death. David Lyon junior, after briefly attending Harrow School around 1809, also became a West India merchant, and inherited the major part of his father's wealth. That he was thus favoured, rather than one of his two elder brothers, was possibly because his father anticipated that he would be active in land purchase; indeed, Lyon went on to purchase a small estate, Goring Hall in Sussex, and another in Scotland, Balentore Castle, Forfarshire (Thompson 1990, pp. 54, 60; Thompson 1992, p. 373).

Lyon's portrait comes at the end of the artist's career, when Lawrence was seen as unquestionably England's leading portrait painter. In a letter to his sister in 1825 Lawrence described the exhausting demands of his presidency of the Royal Academy, yet also declared that 'I have never painted better' (Levey 2005, pp. 261, 279). He also painted Lyon's father, and both portraits remained, not yet completed, in the artist's possession at the time of his death in 1830. An initial payment of 250 guineas was made for Lyon's picture in 1828; his father's was paid for in 1818. Regarding the son's portrait, Lawrence's executor wrote that the 'person' was 'finished' and the 'drapery partly' – about three-quarters – complete; the work was eventually delivered later in 1830, when the outstanding balance of 150 guineas was paid (Garlick 1962–64, p. 302). Some of the drapery and landscape were painted by an assistant (Christie's 1980, p. 146). A final coda to Lyon's portrait may also be suggested: at Lawrence's funeral procession, among the carriages of the dignitaries and acquaintances of the artist following the hearse was one belonging to a 'Mr Lyon' (Williams 1831, vol. 2, p. 561).

Although the known information on the painting does not allow for it to be precisely dated, similarities in pose and costume to other works by Lawrence support an approximation that it dates from the mid-1820s. The position of Lyon's left hand, clasping his coat's fur-trimmed edges together, was used in reverse in John Bloomfield (exhibited at the Royal Academy in 1820). Another comparable work is Henry Lascelles, 2nd Earl of Harewood, MP (RA 1823). This too shows a standing figure in a country setting with the accoutrements of walking stick, gloves and a long black coat. It has been observed that the latter portrait exemplifies changing fashions in élite male clothing, which was becoming increasingly restrained; Lyon's

image, by contrast, is comparatively flamboyant (Levey 2005, pp. 246–48).

Lyon served from 1831 to 1832 as MP for Beeralston in Devon, a burgage borough in the influence of the Earl of Beverley, which was disenfranchised by the 1832 Parliamentary Reform Act (to which Lyon was opposed). He employed Sir Francis Chantrey to sculpt a memorial to his mother in 1836; this was placed in the parish church at Goring (which was itself rebuilt to the designs of the architect Decimus Burton, at Lyon's sole expense) (Yarrington et al. 1994, p. 327; Fox-Wilson 1987, pp. 46–53, 139). In 1848 he married Blanche Bury, whose mother was the novelist Lady Charlotte Bury; their London residence was in Mayfair. Benjamin Disraeli, the future Prime Minister, described Lyon in a letter of 1849 as 'the celebrated yachter' and 'very rich' (Disraeli 1982–2004, vol. 3, p. 188). Lyon was made Sheriff of Sussex in 1851, and he died, leaving no issue, in 1872 at Nice. SM

# Jean-Robert Nicolas Lucas de Montigny

ROUEN, 1747 – PARIS, 1810

## 50
### Voltaire

1781
Plaster, 54 × 23 × 37 cm
Inscription on the plinth: *Arouet de Voltaire né à Paris en 1694 mort en 1778. Lucas Montigny fecit*
Institut et Musée Voltaire, Geneva, IC 0045

PROVENANCE:  possibly in the collection of the poet Jean-Antoine Roucher (1745–1794), a friend of the sculptor, probably in 1782;  his widow, who sold the piece in July 1796 (sale advertised in *Affiches, Annonces et Avis divers*, or the *Journal général de France*, no. 3,304, 4 Thermidor, Year IV/22 July 1796, p. 6,323; Mercier 1972, p. 222);  art market in Paris, 1957; gift of Albert Pictet, 1957
EXHIBITED:  Paris, Salon of 1791, no. 495
LITERATURE:  Montagu 1962, p. 228; Mercier 1972, pp. 218–26, 289–90

On 25 June 1782, the following advertisement was printed in the *Journal de Paris*: 'Monsieur Lucas de Montigny ... has just completed the models for full-length statues (measuring twenty inches [54 cm] each) of Molière, Corneille, Racine, Crébillon and Voltaire, to be executed in bronze. He proposes to supply art lovers with these same figures in well-finished plaster, for the sum of 300 *livres*. 150 *livres* will be paid for the subscription and the remaining 150 *livres* on delivery, to be made in the short time it takes to finish the figures, the moulds already having been cast. Those who desire the same statues either in antique bronze or in marble should make individual arrangements' (quoted in Mercier 1972, pp. 218–19).

Jean-Antoine Roucher, the society poet and friend of Voltaire, who was also a friend and patient of the sculptor's brother-in-law (Dr Baignères), undertook to publicise the statuettes, which were executed in a particularly fine material looking much like plaster. In a letter of 30 June inserted in the same newspaper on 3 July 1782, he wrote: 'You have advertised … the full-length statues of Molière, Racine, Corneille, Crébillon and Voltaire, for which the young sculptor, M. Lucas Montigny, has just finished making the models, and which are offered by the artist by subscription. I have seen the images of the fathers of our theatre, and I owe it to a distinguished talent to declare publicly the pleasure he has given me. All those who, like you, Messieurs, are genuinely interested in the honour of the arts, in the success of young artists and the glory of the Nation, which is no more than a compound of all our great men, will not enter the studio of M. Montigny with indifference … If M. Montigny's project is destined to be applauded by a Nation which owes part of its glory to its great dramatic poets, I beg to assure you that the execution is not unworthy of the sublime models. In artistically varied attitudes, he displays the truth of their features and the expression of their individual genius … the sculptor M. Montigny deserves to see his works placed in the display cabinets of art lovers' (quoted in Mercier 1972, pp. 219–20). Roucher acquired four plaster casts himself (*Molière, Racine, Crébillon, Voltaire*), and placed them in his study (Mercier 1972, pp. 220–21). After his execution they were sold by his widow in July 1796. Another of the sculptor's friends, the Comte de Mirabeau, acquired all five of the terracottas. They are described in his posthumous inventory. They adorned a back room adjoining his bedroom on the first floor of his house, 69 rue de la Chaussée d'Antin, Paris, and were placed on wooden columns painted 'turquin' blue (Mercier 1972, p. 221). They were sold at auction on 12 March 1792 (lot 132). Several of the plaster casts have been traced: *Voltaire* (Institut Voltaire, Geneva), *Crébillon* (bearing the inscription 'Lucas Montigny fecit 1780') and *Molière* (the last two were sold in Paris in 1977). Only one terracotta has been traced, on the other hand: *Voltaire*, dated 1781, was sold in Charles Bowyer's sale at Christie's, London, on 15 February 1906, lot 68, where it was acquired by Nathan Wildenstein (Marcel 1909, pp. 107–08, repr.). None of the bronzes has been traced: perhaps the sale of the statuettes disappointed the artist, causing him to give up the idea of paying for a whole series in bronze.

The creation of these five statuettes of illustrious dramatists around 1780–81, with the idea of distributing them publicly, was all part of a trend, characteristic of the period, for celebrating Great Men – although in this case in a minor way. In fact, Lucas de Montigny, even though able to study at the Académie Royal de Peinture as the 'protégé' of Jean-Baptiste Lemoyne from 1774,

never made any headway in the institution: he failed to obtain the first prize and was not therefore eligible for a scholarship to the French Academy in Rome; his application to become an academician in Paris was turned down on 27 September 1788. He could not win royal commissions, nor could he execute his projects in marble, life-size. In order to earn his living as an artist, he had no choice but to devote himself to portrait busts, which he did, and to develop some original ideas: in his case these took the form of statuettes of celebrities, great men of literature and also singers (*Madame de Saint-Huberty as Dido*, plaster, 1784; Louvre, Paris) or fashionable subjects (*Belisarius*, terracotta; acquired by Mirabeau). Another sculptor denied access to the Académie, Robert-Guillaume Dardel, tried to sell small-scale representations of famous men at the same time. He was a pupil of Pajou and a protégé of the Prince de Condé, who acquired several of his works (now in the Musée de Chantilly); he regularly exhibited warriors and kings in action at the Salon de la Correspondance (among them Villars, Vauban, Henri IV, Gustavus-Adolphus, the Grand Condé and Turenne), and also scientific and literary luminaries (such as Copernicus, Descartes, Newton, Corneille, Buffon and Bossuet; see Sanchez 2004, pp. 440–43). Whereas Dardel always attempted to create a historical context around each figure (*Descartes Disentangling Chaos from which He Causes a Ray of Light to Flash*, terracotta, 1782; Wallace Collection, London), Lucas de Montigny had less ambitious aims: his subjects do not stray from fairly straightforward description, with no particular flights of fancy. In this respect, his imagination is less vivid than that of Dardel.

The statuette of François Marie Arouet, known as Voltaire (1694–1778), shows the writer standing in front of an armchair, absorbed in a book. Attired in an unbuttoned dressing gown, with knee breeches over stockings, a carefully buttoned jacket and an unknotted cravat around his neck, he is obviously a member of the social élite. His seat looks comfortable and is of elegant design. The objects strewn around him identify the sitter: the open page of a book bears the titles of Voltaire's tragedies: *Zaïde, Alzire, Mérope* and *Brutus*; various attributes demonstrate the facets of his genius: the globe of Science, the sword of Tragedy, the mask of Comedy, the laurels of History and the lyre of Poetry. The number and evocative power of these objects signal Lucas de Montigny's ambition: to suggest Voltaire's genius in all its aspects, as if the statuette were a commemorative monument.

The sculpture deliberately distances itself from the example by Joseph Rosset, who had been familiar with the philosopher at Ferney and distributed large numbers of small-scale portraits of him (his ivory bust, presented by Voltaire to the Manufacture de Sèvres in 1767, became the model for the edition in biscuit-ware). Rosset's statuette

(a marble version, signed and dated 1773, can be found in the Musée d'Art et d'Histoire in Geneva; see Dôle 2001, no. 1, repr.) was reproduced in several versions; it shows Voltaire standing, dressed as he is in Lucas de Montigny's statuette but with a wig and a fur hat on his head, holding a book, his left hand on his hip and gazing out at the spectator. Compared with Lucas de Montigny's figure, Rosset's character looks anecdotic in his French dress. By choosing to represent the writer almost bald, as in the bust by Pigalle, whose student he claimed to be (this is mentioned in the Salon booklet from 1799), Lucas de Montigny stays closer to the truth. The sitter's concentration on the open pages of the book also conveys an image of the philosopher in action: 'this is the Voltaire of the serious days' (Marcel 1909, p. 108). We are given the impression that reading a certain passage has made him leap out of his armchair. As Chéry noted in his review of the Salon of 1791 (McWilliam 1991, no. 485), the first to be open to all artists, the 'small plaster figure of Voltaire is as large as a giant'.  GS

## 49
### *Jean-Jacques Rousseau*

1790
Terracotta, 44 × 26 × 25 cm
Inscription on the plinth: *J. J. Rousseau né à Genève en 1722; mort à Ermenonville, en 1778. Lucas Montigny, fecit 1790*
Musées Royaux d'Art et d'Histoire, Brussels, 9065

PROVENANCE: collection of the Comte de Mirabeau: the statuette is listed in his posthumous inventory (A. N., Min. Cent., XCIII, 190, I April 1791); his posthumous sale, Hôtel Bullion, Paris, 12 March 1792, no. 132; collection of Charles Bowyer; his sale, Christie's, London, 15–16 February 1906, lot 69; bought by Nathan Wildenstein; acquired from a dealer in Brussels in 1957
EXHIBITED: Brussels, 1975, no. 76
LITERATURE: Marcel 1909, pp. 108–09, repr.; Mercier 1972, pp. 227–30, 300

When the following announcement appeared in the *Journal de Paris* on 25 June 1782: 'Monsieur Lucas de Montigny … has just completed the models for full-length statues (measuring twenty inches [54 cm] each) of Molière, Corneille, Racine, Crébillon and Voltaire (see cat. 50), to be executed in bronze', Jean-Jacques Rousseau was not among those chosen. Naturally, he did not figure in this pantheon of playwrights. However, the lacuna was soon to be filled. Jean-Antoine Roucher, the poet and friend of the sculptor, wrote in the same newspaper on 3 July 1782: 'I desire most sincerely that public demand should encourage him one day to provide us with the élite of our philosophers, by which I mean: Montaigne, Descartes, Montesquieu, J. J. Rousseau and Condillac. These ten statues, placed in a cabinet, would make a nobler and happier decorative scheme than all the small bronzes in furniture that are displayed with such pomp' (Mercier 1972, p. 227). In fact this mixed display of dramatists and philosophers is not without greatness. We do not know why it took Lucas de Montigny so long to realise the project in its entirety.

Were his hopes dashed by the lack of enthusiasm aroused by the first statuettes of writers? It might have been wise, in fact, to have waited until the financial returns began to exceed the cost of making the pieces. The artist was apparently finally satisfied by the formula – we know at least that the terracottas and a series of plaster representations of dramatists were acquired by Mirabeau and Roucher – since at the end of the decade he planned to restart the production of statuettes of illustrious writers. Was he following Roucher's original plan to the letter? We do not know. Only the terracotta statuette of Rousseau is known today. But the recent reappearance of a plaster piece representing Buffon (see cat. 66) gives hope that we may find other figures and complete our knowledge of Lucas de Montigny's project.

The terracotta representing Jean-Jacques Rousseau (1722–1778) is dated 1790. The following year the sculptor exhibited a plaster piece at the Salon (no. 615), probably beside the statue of *Voltaire* (no. 495; see cat. 50). The work is completely different in conception, however: Rousseau is seated on a rock, wearing a dressing gown over an open-necked shirt. In order to mitigate the austerity of the philosopher's attire, Lucas de Montigny decided to adorn the collar of the shirt with embroidery, which lends a curiously dandified air to the figure's appearance. The head is bare, without a wig, and almost bald; the forehead is very broad and the hair cut short. It would be difficult to recognise the figure's identity if the sitter were not identified (as well as by the inscription round the plinth) by his environment: Rousseau sits pensively, holding a manuscript in his left hand and a leaf in his right, a clear allusion to his profession as a writer and his taste for botany. There are books around his feet. At his knee, a child spirit presents him with a spray of laurel. The presence of the child, who is unable to brighten the philosopher's mood, elicited the following ironic comment from a critic at the Salon: 'Rousseau, for heaven's sake look at the child who wants to play with you' (*La Béquille de Voltaire au Salon*, McWilliam 1991, no. 473).

Although the creation of this statuette should be seen in the context of Lucas de Montigny's attempts to market figures of illustrious writers following those made in about 1780 (see cat. 50), it also belongs among the many tributes to Rousseau that burgeoned after the Revolution. On 12 February 1790 a subscription for a statue of Rousseau was launched by the newspaper *Révolutions de Paris*. This led to a decree by the Assemblée Nationale, on 21 December, commanding the elevation of the said statue, and the decision in February 1791 to hold a competition for its design, although this did not happen at once (Gramaccini 1989, p. 894). It seems

Lucas de Montigny wanted to fix a date for his terracotta, as did Jean-Baptiste Stouf with his own, also dated 1790 (Musée des Arts Décoratifs, Paris; see Paris 2003A, no. 57, repr.). Stouf's terracotta was presented at the Salon of 1791, as was Lucas de Montigny's plaster piece and other statuettes of Rousseau by Chaudet and Monot.

If the competition had taken place, and supposing that Lucas had entered the plans for the terracotta under discussion, he would certainly have had no chance of winning. His piece has nothing monumental about it: Rousseau, lost in thought, drowned in his ample dressing gown, looks more like a private image than a piece of public statuary destined for the Assemblée Nationale (as proposed by one deputy). The sculpture by Jean-Guillaume Moitte (another of Pigalle's pupils), adopted almost unanimously in February 1795 by the jury of the competition held in Year II, was more effective in most respects: Rousseau, depicted with his naked upper body draped in a Roman toga, watches a child learning to walk as he meditates upon his *Emile ou De l'éducation* (Musée Carnavalet-Histoire de Paris, Paris; see Paris 2003A, no. 113, repr.). In this monumental context, the limitations of Lucas de Montigny's art are obvious. His sensibility, on the other hand, expresses itself admirably within the restricted register of more amateur work; with this delicate statuette, he has succeeded ably in humanising Rousseau, caught here in a moment of thoughtfulness which equally corresponds to his genius. GS

## 66
### *Buffon*

1791
Plaster, 52 × 21 × 22 cm
Inscription on the plinth, on the reverse: *Montigny 1791*; in front: *Buffon*
Musée Carnavalet-Histoire de Paris, Paris, s 3635

PROVENANCE: bought from a dealer in Paris, 2004
EXHIBITED: Paris, 2004, no. 3

Until very recently, when this plaster piece reappeared in Paris, no one knew that Lucas de Montigny had designed a statuette of Buffon. No mention is made of it in the thesis by the Buffon specialist, Huguette Mercier. Dated 1791, the work was executed after *Voltaire* (cat. 50) and *Jean-Jacques Rousseau* (cat. 49), indicating that the sculptor wished to continue distributing figurines of Great Men ten or more years after the first series. The choice of person is noteworthy: did Lucas want to create a third group consisting of scientists, after his groups of dramatists and philosophers? His enthusiasm may have been curbed by the radicalisation of the Revolution. Further research may allow us to find out more about this matter.

When the artist created this figure of Georges Louis Leclerc, Comte de Buffon (1707–1788), he must have had in mind's eye the most imposing extant image of the scientist: the colossal marble

figure by Augustin Pajou, on public display in the Cabinet d'Histoire naturelle in the Jardin du Roi (fig. 50), now the Muséum National d'Histoire Naturelle, Paris; it also existed as an engraving (see Paris and New York 1997A, no. 112, repr.). From the piece by Pajou, Lucas borrowed most of the elements to be found around Buffon's feet: the lion, the dog, the globe and the crystal (the sponge and the serpent are missing). Even though they are arranged slightly differently – it is the lion, not the dog, that is licking Buffon's foot, the crystal is beside the globe instead of the sponge – the reference to Pajou's masterpiece is obvious. Pajou wanted to illustrate Buffon's attitude to creation. Man is at the centre of the universe, and at the summit of the 'scale of being'. If he places himself 'at the head of all created beings, he will see with astonishment that one can descend by almost imperceptible degrees from the most perfect created being to the most shapeless matter, from the most highly organised animal to the crudest mineral; he will acknowledge that these imperceptible differences are the great work of Nature' (Buffon, *Histoire naturelle*, 1749–78).

To mark the distinction between his work and his sitter, however, Lucas opts to represent the scientist in a far less idealised manner: the marble hero with the naked torso, proudly standing 'in the attire of a philosopher' (Pajou's memoirs) – which means dressed in a classical way – dominating the degrees of creation, is transformed by Lucas de Montigny into a character from modern life, wearing a dressing gown over a shirt with lace edges. The leonine hair of Pajou's Buffon (fig. 50) is transformed into a neatly curled hairstyle. Above all, the scholar is not immortalised holding a chisel, about to etch his thoughts on to a marble panel for eternity: in Lucas's version he is holding a plain sheet of paper. Once again we encounter the sculptor's problem with the figure on an epic scale. In this respect, this collector's statuette suits him perfectly, as does the more restrained, more familiar representation.

The plaster cast in the Musée Carnavalet-Histoire de Paris is, nevertheless, closer to the statue in the museum than the statuette attributed to Pajou or Dardel, possibly reproduced in bronze by Pierre-Philippe Thomire, in which the scientist is depicted sitting in an armchair, also wearing a shirt and a dressing gown (a copy can be found in the Château de Versailles: see Paris 1997A, no. 118, repr.). The impression given is that Lucas wished to present a portrait of Buffon, done with the sitter's blessing, keeping Pajou's idea of the great intellectual dominating nature but softening the external appearance of the character by dressing him in normal clothing. Lucas preferred a more prosaic interpretation of the great man, as he had done ten years earlier with *Voltaire*: the representation of an illustrious person, wearing his everyday clothes but identified by a few carefully chosen accessories. GS

# Pompeo Marchesi

SALTRIO, COMO, 1783 – MILAN, 1858

## 97
### Giulio Mylius

1830
Marble, 75 × 65 × 40 cm
Inscription on lower front: P. MARCHESI F. 1830
Villa Vigoni, Loveno di Menaggio (Como), s. 51

PROVENANCE: the banker Enrico Mylius commissioned this
piece in 1830 after the brutal death of his son Giulio earlier
in the same year. In 1834 the two Marchesi busts, representing
father and son, were placed on either side of a *bas-relief* by the
same sculptor, depicting the death of the young man, in the
memorial temple in Loveno on Lake Como. Around 1850 the
busts were removed to the Salone delle Statue in Villa Vigoni,
before being replaced on the cenotaph around 1927
EXHIBITED: Milan, 1999, no. 28, repr.
LITERATURE: Sassi 2001, pp. 65 and 134, repr.; Musiari,
Di Raddo and Cioccolo 2003, pp. 246 and 253, repr.

Pompeo Marchesi was born into a modest family
of marble masons, studied at the Accademia di
Belle Arte di Brera and finished his training in
Rome before returning to Milan. He was actively
involved in the realisation of sculptures for the
Duomo in Milan between 1810 and 1858 and also
taught at the Accademia di Belle Arti de Brera
from 1826 and 1852. He produced larger numbers
of statues, reliefs, monuments and busts in and
around Milan and developed a sensitive, elegant
neoclassical style.

The eminent position he occupied in artistic
circles in Milan allowed him to meet the wealthy
merchant banker Enrico Mylius, who came
originally from Frankfurt. Mylius was a collector
of contemporary art, patron of the Accademia
di Brera, friend of Goethe and in particular
a great admirer of Bertel Thorvaldsen. The
Danish sculptor gave him a plaster copy of his
statue of Schiller, created for Stuttgart, and also
executed a marble *bas-relief* for him.

As Thomas Besing, author of the entry for
this bust in the catalogue to the exhibition held
in Milan in 1999, suggests, this portrait of Giulio
Mylius (1800–1830) should probably be identified
with the marble bust commissioned by his father
Enrico Mylius, signed by Pompeo Marchesi and
exhibited at the Pinacoteca di Brera in 1830. The
posthumous portrait was commissioned by Enrico
Mylius immediately after the death of his only
son on 26 April 1830. Thomas Besing quotes
another document that suggests that the bust was
completed on 19 November, a little more than six
months after Giulio's death. At this time the bust
was still in Marchesi's studio, and the sculptor was
shortly to receive a commission for a *bas-relief*
representing Giulio's death (Tempietto, Loveno);
the *bas-relief* echoes the one created in 1829 to
commemorate the death of Giovanni Battista
Sommariva (Tremezzo, beside Villa Carlotta,
also on Lake Como).

The artist made the present bust as the exact
pendant to the one representing Enrico, dated 1826
and also now at Villa Vigoni (see Milan 1999,

no. 27, repr.), with a similar column and pedestal.
It was designed to emphasise the strong attachment
between father and son, who was being groomed
by his father as successor to the family business.

Francesco Hayez included Marchesi's bust
in 1832 in one of his finest paintings, the painting
of Giorgio's widow, Luigia Vitali (cat. 98). Hayez
skilfully placed the bust so that it does not face
the spectator – which would have interfered with
the contemplation of the beautiful young widow's
sorrowful face (the marriage took place a few days
before the death) – but turning it slightly so that
the right-hand profile is visible, and placing it
on the left of the composition.

The marble bust is an attractive retrospective
portrait of the young man. He is clothed in flowing
classical drapery with long, inverted pleats; his neck
is left bare. His glorious head, with side whiskers,
is crowned with a mop of curls. His blank eyes
and closed mouth add particular seriousness to
the way he is portrayed. A poignant reminder
of the father's painful memories of his dead
son, this piece also reveals the admiration that
contemporary collectors such as Enrico Mylius
and Giovanni Battista Sommariva felt for the
sculpture of their time. GS

# David Martin

ANSTRUTHER EASTER, 1737 – EDINBURGH, 1797

## 45
### Benjamin Franklin

1767
Oil on canvas, 125.7 × 100.3 cm
Courtesy of the Pennsylvania Academy of the Fine Arts,
Philadelphia, 1943.16.1. Gift of Maria McKean Allen and
Phebe Warren Downes through the bequest of their mother,
Elizabeth Wharton McKean

PROVENANCE: painted for the sitter, by whom sent to America,
c. 1771; bequeathed by the sitter to the Supreme Executive
Council of Pennsylvania; hung in the State House; picture
remained in place when state government left premises, 1799;
painting was incorporated into the display when Charles
Willson Peale's museum moved into the building, 1802; sold
by auction when the gallery closed, 1854; bought Edward
Ingersoll for his brother-in-law, Henry Pratt McKean; by
descent to his son, Thomas McKean; deposited by his children
in the Pennsylvania Academy of the Fine Arts, 1912; given by
Maria McKean Allen and Phebe Warren Downes (the two
surviving daughters of Thomas McKean) through the bequest
of their mother Elizabeth Wharton McKean, 1942
EXHIBITED: original version exhibited at the Society of
Artists, 1767, no. 99
LITERATURE: Sellers 1962, pp. 328–40; Fortune 1999, pp. 26–29

The Scottish painter David Martin is probably
best known for his portrayal of Benjamin Franklin
(1706–1790), undertaken at a period when the
sitter was the leading spokesman in London for
the cause of the American colonies. Franklin
was probably best known to the wider public
of the day, however, on account of his scientific

endeavours (his *Experiments and Observations on
Electricity* had been published in 1751). Attired in a
blue suit braided with gold, and wearing a wig of
the 'physical' type, associated with men of learning,
Martin depicted his sitter as a contemporary
scholar in action (Fortune 1999, pp. 26–27).

Martin's reputation has tended to be
overshadowed by that of his teacher, Allan Ramsay,
to whom he was apprenticed at the age of fifteen
in 1752. Through Ramsay he was able to visit Italy
from 1756 to 1757; and by 1766–67 Martin was
earning over £300 annually for his work as an
assistant to the older artist (Edinburgh 1992, p. 217;
Smart 1992, pp. 131–32). Precisely when Martin
established an independent studio is unknown; the
reminiscences of the artist Joseph Moser suggest
that Martin's painting of Franklin could be seen
in Ramsay's studio (Sellers 1962, pp. 78–79).

There are several ways in which this portrait
shows the influence of Ramsay. Martin had been
involved in producing the many copies that were
needed of Ramsay's official coronation portraits
of George III and Queen Charlotte; although these
were painted in a grand manner, this was tempered
– as in Franklin's image – by a desire to retain
'dignified naturalness' (St Andrews 1997, p. 4).
The actual design of Martin's portrayal of Franklin
is also indebted to works by Ramsay, such as his
*Dr William Hunter* (c. 1764) (Smart 1992, pp. 194, 217,
repr.). It seems likely that in working towards this
commission Martin would have received advice
from Ramsay (Edinburgh 1992, p. 300).

The commission to paint Franklin's portrait
came from Martin's fellow Scot, Robert Alexander,
a merchant, banker and art patron. Franklin seems
to have known Alexander since at least his 1759
visit to Edinburgh, and was apparently attended
by him in early 1765 in London after his return
from America (Sellers 1962, p. 75; Labaree et al.
1959–2003, vol. 8, pp. 443–45, and vol. 12, pp. 70, 156).

That Alexander and Martin were acquainted
at this time is indicated by a mezzotint published
by the artist in 1765 which he dedicated to
Alexander. The print was after a painting by Adrien
Carpentiers showing Louis François Roubiliac
sculpting his bust of Shakespeare, an image owned
by Alexander. It is possible that the inclusion of
Roubiliac's bronze bust of Newton in the portrait
of Franklin was at the suggestion of Alexander
(Sellers 1962, pp. 75, 77). Alternatively, it might have
been selected by Franklin himself; he had praised
Newton in 1748 as 'the prince of astronomers and
philosophers' (Fortune 1999, p. 75). In Franklin's
portrait, the intention was presumably to link the
sitter with an earlier great thinker; the numerous
books and papers on Franklin's desk further attest
to his scholarly interests (Craven 1993, p. 261). With
his fingers touching his chin – possibly in order to
hold his glasses steady – Franklin is 'seen to think'
(St Andrews 1997, p. 4).

The original version of this image (now in the
White House) was probably undertaken in 1766,

and was certainly complete by 22 April 1767 when it was shown at the exhibition of the Society of Artists in London (Sellers 1962, pp.74–76). One exhibition visitor, Horace Walpole, noted that this image was 'a great likeness'. Franklin too must have approved of Martin's portrayal, for he ordered a replica to be made, which is the version shown here. This was undertaken in 1767; on 27 November a payment is recorded in his accounts of £12.12.0 to 'D. Martin Limner'. In Franklin's version of the image, the elaborate carved and gilded chair of the original version was exchanged – presumably at the sitter's request – for a plainer upholstered seat. Thus altered, the chair in the revised image is much less conspicuous; the adjustment also serves to concentrate attention on the sitter (Sellers 1962, pp.77–78, 331).

Commentators have suggested that the papers which Franklin is shown perusing may not have been intended simply to mark his literary and scientific accomplishments, but are possibly also meant to refer to a specific service rendered by Franklin to the painting's patron: the inspection of a 'portfolio containing my papers' which Alexander sent to Franklin on 8 March 1767 (Craven 1993, p.259; Labaree et al. 1959–2003, vol.14, p.75). According to an account of the origins of the image first recorded in 1828, the work was 'designed to perpetuate the circumstances of his [Franklin's] advice, given in consequence of the perusal of certain important papers' belonging to Alexander (Sellers 1962, pp.329–30). These papers were possibly related to legal action taken by Alexander after he had unsuccessfully stood for election as Member of Parliament for Anstruther (incidentally, Martin's birthplace). However, since the first reference to Franklin considering Alexander's papers dates to 8 March 1767, by which time Martin's painting was presumably well underway or already completed, this point unfortunately cannot be firmly substantiated. SM

# Anton Raphael Mengs

AUSSIG, BOHEMIA, 1728 – ROME, 1779

**26**
*Isabel Parreño Arce, Ruiz de Alcarón y Valdés, Marquesa de Llano*

1770
Oil on canvas, 250 × 148 cm
Museo de la Real Academia de Bellas Artes de San Fernando, Madrid, 705

PROVENANCE: in the sitter's family until 1799; mentioned in a document (1802) about the sitter's dowry, when she contracted a second marriage with Don Fernando Queipo de Llano; property of both until 1823; deposited in the Real Academia de Bellas Artes de San Fernando, 1824; bequeathed to the Real Academia by the sitter's husband, 1831, and accepted at an Ordinary Council Meeting, 12 June 1831

EXHIBITED: Madrid, 1902, no.640; Madrid, 1929, no.87; Madrid, 1980, no.24; Madrid, 1988, p.475
LITERATURE: see Roettgen 1999–2003, pp.324–27, no.260

Isabel Parreño Arce, Ruiz de Alcarón y Valdés became Marquesa de Llano on her marriage to José Agustín de Llano y de la Quadra, Muzquez y Llerena, knight of the Order of Santiago and ambassador. She stands elegantly dressed in a complex costume, somewhere between regional Spanish and court dress. In her right hand she carries a mask and in her left a pair of gloves. She stands on a terrace, next to a parrot which perches on decorative metal railings. Behind her is a garden with trees. On the right of the canvas there is a large urn and everything is set against a landscape in which some classical architecture and a sculpture resembling Aesculapius can be seen. She is shown full length, life size, and wears a costume of greyish-white silk with a tight-fitting bodice and a large black apron. Her hair is gathered into a white hairnet and she wears a black velvet hat adorned with a flower.

According to Roettgen (1999), the traditional dating of the work to 1774 – following the opinions of Sánchez Cantón (1927) and Honisch (1965), and also used in the Madrid monographic exhibition catalogue (1980) – should be corrected. Mengs began it in Parma, during his stay in that city in 1770, and finished it the same year, according to information provided by Manuel Salvador Carmona's engraving. In 1770 the sitter's first husband, José Agustín de Llano, was the representative to the court of Parma of Charles III of Spain. Bianconi describes this portrait in a letter to Luigi Crespi in 1771, having seen it in Mengs's house in Rome, among his recent works, in the course of a meeting with the painter shortly after his return from Parma. In florid Italian prose the writer praises both the work and its painter, comparing the quality of his work with that of Van Dyck. He also extols Mengs's success in capturing the lively spirit of his nineteen-year-old sitter, showing her grace and talent for dancing.

When the Marquesa de Llano came to Rome, she entered the exclusive 'Arcadia circle in 1773. A book of poems in praise of her was published, and includes a sonnet (no.41) which expressly refers to this painting. Roettgen mentions this fact, derived from information given by the Roman architect Furio Luccicchenti. The painting was already in Madrid in 1792, the year that it was engraved by Manuel Salvador Carmona (1734–1820). After that the Llanos were in Vienna, where he was Charles IV's ambassador to the Emperor Leopold II, thanks to the support of the influential José Nicolás de Azara. Curiously, a report exists of a copy of the portrait in Amsterdam as early as 1799 (today it is in the Rijksmuseum), as well as another which was the equal of the present painting (Azara 1780, p.XLIX). Various other works are linked to a greater or lesser extent to the portrait under

discussion in other collections and museums (Roettgen 1999, pp.325–26).

In this portrait Mengs reverts to a type that he had used before. However, he had used it only in official portraits of royal personages; now he paints a less exalted sitter in this way. The full-length figure against a landscape appears for the first time in 1750 in the unfinished portrait of Augustus III of Poland, Elector of Saxony (Roettgen 1999, no.150). The same formula can be seen in the 1752 portrait of Arabella Swimmer (Roettgen 1999, no.264), but in that work the figure is three-quarter length.

The choice of a refined form of folk costume instead of court dress is a reflection of changes in Spanish society that had taken place over these years. The fashion known as *costumbrismo* was a rejection of the established ceremonial forms of the court. This costume, which originally came from La Mancha, also contains selected elements of Murcian costume and even of the Madrid *maja*, or working-class girl. The young aristocrat the costume to a ball given in Florence in 1770 by Archduke Peter Leopold of Habsburg-Lorraine, Grand Duke of Tuscany. She also wore it at a gala reception in Vienna in 1792. It not only signifies an ennobling of folk customs, but expresses a new feeling of national pride that arose among the Spanish aristocracy during the reign of Charles III. This can also be seen in the preference for popular scenes in the designs for the Royal Tapestry Works in Madrid, which was also directed by Mengs.

This portrait is key evidence for suggesting that Goya followed Mengs's example in his portrayal of ladies wearing mantillas, such as the portraits of Queen María Luisa, wife of Charles IV (Palacio Real, Madrid), and the Duchess of Alba (Hispanic Society, New York). It is very probable that the vehicle for Mengs's influence on Goya was the engraving by Carmona mentioned earlier. Goya's portraits have the same relationship of figure to landscape, but Goya tends to identify his sitters with the landscape, immersing them into its atmosphere, and this creates a harmony so that the final effect is more lifelike. Mengs's sitters are made to stand in front of their landscape backdrops, and this isolation of the figure from its environment can give a theatrical rather than a natural effect. JJL

# Pierre Mérard

PARIS, 1728 – PARIS, 1800

**20**
*The Prince de Conti*

1776
Terracotta, 71.5 × 57 × 37 cm

Inscription on the pedestal: *PAR MÉRARD EN 8BRE 1776*
Musée des Beaux-Arts, Dijon, D 263

PROVENANCE: bequest of Henriette Dard, 1916
EXHIBITED: Dijon and Orléans, 1992, no.24; L'Isle-Adam, 2000, p.164
LITERATURE: Musée de Dijon 1960, p.48, no.262

Louis-François de Bourbon, Prince de Conti (1717–1776), was a member of the cadet branch of the Bourbon-Condé family – he was the great-grandson of the Grand Condé – cousins of the King. Godson of Louis XV, he married the youngest of the Regent's daughters, thus allying himself with the Orléans family. As 'the most gifted of the princes of the blood' (Antoine 1993, p.354), he was pursuing a brilliant career in the army, but his proud, intractable character often meant that he was in conflict with famous generals (the Maréchal de Saxe), as he also was with important court personalities (Madame de Pompadour). The King liked him, however, and gave him an important part to play in his secret negotiations – until 1756, that is, the date they fell out, mainly because of the alliance with Austria, of which Conti strongly disapproved (Antoine 1993, pp.684–85).

From this moment on, the prince lived away from Versailles – he gave back his apartment to the King – dividing his time between his palace in Paris, in the Enclos du Temple – he was grand prior of the knights of St John of Jerusalem (the Order of Malta) – and his Château de l'Isle-Adam. His life was spent supporting anti-monarchical positions in Parliament, scheming in the shadow of the Duc d'Orléans and protecting Jean-Jacques Rousseau; he was also a libertine, music lover and keen collector of works of art. After a painful year spent suffering from cancer of the pancreas, the prince died on 2 August 1776 without receiving the last sacraments – which caused a scandal and meant that his funeral had to be very discreet. He was interred in the parish church of L'Isle-Adam.

Pierre Mérard worked for him at the end of his life. Mérard collaborated with Augustin Pajou's on the building of the opera house in Versailles, but little is known about him (his date of birth has only recently been discovered: Béziès 2000, p.144, note 28). He was not a member of the Académie Royale de Peinture et Sculpture, but of the rival institution, the Académie de Saint-Luc (in 1763). He exhibited in the Salon of Saint-Luc in 1774, was appointed assistant professor in 1775 and professor the following year. He was certainly in touch with the Prince de Conti in 1774, as the prince settled an annuity of eight hundred *livres* on him on 20 September of that year (Béziès 2000).

Mérard's terracotta bust is dated October 1776: it is therefore a posthumous portrait, unless the sculptor began it before the final phase of the prince's illness; there is no documentary evidence to support this. It seems normal that the prince's son, Louis-François Joseph (1734–1814), should have asked the sculptor (who had known his father) to do his portrait. Mérard used the terracotta bust as a model for a superb marble head, dated May 1777: after the death of the last Conti without any heirs, this head passed to the Orléans family and was included in the sale of the collections of Louis-Philippe (Paris, 28 April 1851, no.329). Since then it has passed from collector to collector; today it belongs to the Duc de Rohan in the Château de Josselin (repr. in Vitry 1908, p.11; Hoog 1993, p.108).

Evidently pleased with the portrait, Conti commissioned Mérard to make a funerary monument for his father; the model for this was visible in the sculptor's studio on 22 December 1777. The marble medallion of the deceased is still located in the church in L'Isle-Adam, next to the fragments of the mausoleum that was partly destroyed during the Revolution (see Béziès 2000, *passim*; repr. p.145).

Comparison of this bust with other portraits of Conti, such as the one painted by Jean-Baptiste Le Tellier (see L'Isle-Adam 2000, p.157), or the miniature by Pierre Adolphe Hall (Jean-Richard 1994, no.283), suggests that Mérard caught the prince's features exceptionally well: the prince's almond-shaped face can be seen, his broad brow, long nose, eyes with drooping eyelids, hollow cheeks and prominent chin. It is so realistic, in fact, that it is difficult to believe that the sculptor worked without any sittings, and without the aid of a funerary mask.

As well as the physical likeness achieved by Mérard in the portrait, the psychological complexity of the prince has been rendered in unforgettable fashion. As we have seen, the prince lived for about twenty years as a voluntary exile from court. The artist has managed to capture the melancholy expression of a disappointed man, a schemer with no proper political purpose: 'Monseigneur le Prince de Conti, the most handsome man imaginable, had much intelligence but lacked any judgement, because he wanted to be the centre of attention. Full of schemes, with a lively imagination, wanting to play his part, exhausting the king, he turned to parliament and hoped with its support to escape from the state of incompetence from which there were so many good reasons for leaving' (Dufort de Cheverny 1990, p.313).

The artist represents him in uniform, laden with honours: his breastplate is worn over an open-necked jacket, from which emerges an embroidered cravat; across his torso he wears the ribbon of the Order of the Holy Spirit with the badge stitched to the coat; round his neck he wears a ribbon from which hangs the cross of the Order of Malta, of which he was Grand Prior. In spite of this array of medals and the opulence of the layout (such as the large drape that concludes the piece and covers the pedestal), the bust gives a sober impression because the composition pales into insignificance compared with the intensity of the face. The disillusionment

expressed in the eyes is striking, their lowered gaze heavy but delicate; to this are added the half-open mouth of a talker, man of letters, music lover and great lover of art. The bags under the eyes, the warts, the limp flesh on the cheeks and under the chin, as well as the implacable accuracy of the psychological analysis, are worthy of the art of Jean-Baptiste Pigalle. Mérard has perfectly represented an eminent member of the old nobility, but he has also managed to catch, in what remains his masterpiece, the true appearance of a fine, wounded man who has aged prematurely. GS

# Franz-Xaver Messerschmidt

WIESENSTEIG, NEAR ULM, 1736 – BRATISLAVA, 1783

## 68
### *Character Head: Self-portrait*

Between 1777 and 1783
Lead, 38.7 × 21 × 21 cm
Incised beneath the right shoulder: *18*
Département des Sculptures, Musée du Louvre, Paris, RF 4724

PROVENANCE: collection of Dr Richard Beer-Hofmann, Vienna; as Dr Hofmann's property, it was confiscated by the Nazis in the Second World War; the piece was exhibited in the Historisches Museum, Vienna, from 1939; returned to Dr Beer-Hofmann's heirs, 2003; sold at Sotheby's, New York, 27 January 2005, no.12; acquired at the sale by the Louvre with the support of the Société des Amis du Louvre and the Fonds du Patrimoine
EXHIBITED: Paris, 1993–94, no.247; Vienna, 2002–03, no.28
LITERATURE: Pötzl-Malikova 1982, no.84, repr.; Scherf 2005B

An exhibition of sixty-nine heads in alabaster and metal (lead and tin), created by an artist who had died ten years earlier, Franz-Xaver Messerschmidt, was held in Vienna in 1793. The sculptor had known a few moments of glory when he was professor at the academy in Vienna, and portraitist, in a totally traditional and pompous style, to the Austrian royal family. Psychological disorders forced him to leave his teaching post in 1774, and to leave Austria in 1777 for isolation in Bratislava, where he remained until his death. It was during the last period of his activity that he developed a series of expressive heads, something that had never been produced before in the history of sculpture. They were called 'character heads' at the exhibition of 1793, and each was given a title, the one in the Louvre, Paris, being designated as 'the bad-tempered man' (*der Mißmutige*); each was given a number, incised in the material, and a label – the traces can be faintly discerned below the neck – and each was engraved before being dispersed and acquired in the course of time by various institutions (particularly in Vienna, Budapest and Germany).

Messerschmidt occasionally received visitors while living as a recluse in Bratislava. Among his visitors was the writer Friedrich Nicolai, who gained the artist's confidence in 1781 and was able to visit him. In 1785 he published a detailed report of their encounter that remains a piece of crucial first-hand evidence. 'Messerschmidt was a man of violent passions, at the same time as being heavily disposed towards solitude. He was incapable of doing anyone wrong, yet felt profoundly conscious of the wrong that was done to him. This feeling embittered his character' (quoted in Wittkower 1991, p.154).

His persecution mania was expressed in a battle with voices, and particularly the spirit of proportion. This caused him suffering, 'and the sculptor, who was aware of the mysterious relationships between certain parts of the body and the face, would pinch himself here and there, and then make the appropriate grimace in front of a mirror to break the power exercised over him by the spirit' (Wittkower 1991, pp.154–55). In order to conquer the spirit that tormented him, the artist decided to reproduce these grimaces. 'All these heads were his portrait … He looked at himself every half minute in the mirror, and made the faces he needed with great precision' (Nicolai, quoted in Bückling 1999, p.109).

In Vienna, Messerschmidt moved in circles that took an interest in magic practices. Those involved included such people as Franz Anton Mesmer, whose portrait he did and in whose house he lived before Mesmer left for France in 1778. Mesmer had invented a theory that was very fashionable at the time: he claimed the existence of a cosmic fluid, known as 'animal magnetism', whose free circulation around the body was the key to good health. He developed a therapeutic technique to capture the fluid, mainly using magnets. It is possible that the object – a kind of strap – closing the lips of the *Character Head* in the Louvre, Paris, has something to do with this treatment (see Vienna 2002): this is the hypothesis that is most commonly supported today, rather than the psychoanalytic explanation of the 1930s when the strap was seen as symbolising a chastity belt, a condition recognised by the artist (see Wittkower 1991, pp.159–60).

In addition to the information they give us about the psychiatric troubles of Messerschmidt, the *Character Heads* should also be seen in the more general context of the studies of the human face developed by Johann Kaspar Lavater, who was also enthusiastic about mesmerism. Lavater 'found the means of distinguishing the difference between characters, passions and minds simply by inspecting the heads of individuals. [He gave] physiognomy a new dimension by developing the idea both of a direct correspondence between the physical and the mental, and also between the external appearance and the moral content of human beings' (Baridon and Guédron 1999, pp.63–64).

This aesthetic of the invisible had an enormous influence following the publication of his *Physiognomische Fragmente zur Beförderung der Menschenkenntnis und Menschenliebe* (1775–78), which was soon translated into several languages. Goethe provided Lavater with drawings for plates illustrating the physiognomy of the cranium, and the English edition was supervised by Johann Heinrich Füssli (Henry Fuseli), a compatriot of the author. Nevertheless, because of their deformities, Messerschmidt's creations do not help to make the face legible and have more to do with the expression of the passions: 'These cathartic busts, by means of which the sculptor hoped to overcome his supernatural persecutors, are shivers, gooseflesh and disturbances of the surface that have more to do with pathognomy than with physiognomy in the strict sense. We know that puckering and wincing were denounced by Lavater and also by supporters of a return to the noble simplicity of classical antiquity because they interfered with the legibility of the face' (Baridon and Guédron, 1999, p.92). The dozens of self-portraits produced by Messerschmidt illustrate intense sessions practising expressions while he was in an acute pathological condition; they are elements of crisis, intercepted by the creative act that nourished and in part helped to save their creator.

These sculptures bear witness to torment of the body and soul, yet they are also works of genius. The *Character Head* in the Louvre, Paris, with its superb silver gloss, represents a bald man, with closed eyes, sealed lips, his whole face distorted by an intense internal combustion: it could not be anything but painful. The artist has painstakingly represented and emphasised on his model all the anatomical elements required to describe this precise moment; the many wrinkles on the face have been analysed from the point of view of a systematic investigation of the deformity of the facial features. No hair or clothing interrupts the perfect geometry of the lines incised in the skin. After being cast, the piece has been carefully chiselled and polished, giving the resulting bust the glow of a superb object, possessed of a strange but magnificent purity. GS

# Martin-Claude Monot

PARIS, 1733 – PARIS, 1803

## 29
*The Comtesse de Ségur*

1783
Marble, 68 × 40 × 25 cm
Musée National des Châteaux de Versailles et de Trianon, MV 5967; RF 1830

PROVENANCE: bequeathed by Comte Louis de Ségur, 1924; entered the museum, 23 April 1924

EXHIBITED: Paris, Salon of 1783, no.261; New York, 1935–36, no.98
LITERATURE: Hoog 1993, p.338, no.1573, pl.p.28

Antoinette Elisabeth Marie d'Aguesseau (1756–1828), granddaughter of the Chancellor, married Comte Louis-Philippe de Ségur (1753–1830) in 1777. Her husband, the count, was the eldest son of Marquis Philippe Henri de Ségur (1724–1801), Secretary of State for War from 1780 to 1787, Minister of State in 1781 and Marshal of France in 1783. The marquis, her father-in-law, was famous for having promulgated, in 1781, an edict prohibiting anyone from rising to the rank of officer who could not prove that they had four quarterings of nobility. The count pursued first a military career, notably in America with the corps of volunteers led by the Comte de Rochambeau, then a diplomatic career (he was appointed ambassador to Russia in 1784).

During the 1780s, the Ségur family was very prominent at Versailles. A close friend of the marquis, the Baron de Besenval was intimate with the marquise to the point of being the father of her second son, Vicomte Joseph Alexandre. Besenval belonged to the inner circle of friends of the Comte d'Artois and the brilliant coterie that was forming around the Queen, Marie-Antoinette. Elisabeth-Louise Vigée-Lebrun, a faithful member of the coterie, painted portraits of the Comtesse de Ségur (1785; Château de Versailles) and the Marquis (1789; replica at Versailles). Her equivalent in these extremely smart circles was the much less celebrated Martin-Claude Monot, the sculptor.

Monot was a student of Louis-Claude Vassé, a member 'agréé' of the Académie Royale from 1769; he was soon noticed by Besenval, who commissioned a marble statue from him for his drawing room, *Love Shooting Its Darts* (the plaster model was exhibited in the Salon of 1769). Two years later, Monot exhibited the marble bust of the Marquise de Ségur, the Baron's beloved, at the Salon. At the exhibition of 1779, the date at which his admission to the Académie was made permanent, he attracted notice with his *Love Trampling Jupiter's Eagle Underfoot*, designed for the vestibule of the Pavillon de Bagatelle, a folly built by the Comte d'Artois. Having become first sculptor to the Comte d'Artois, he showed three marble busts at the Salon of 1783, and this propelled him into the highest circles Versailles had to offer: the bust of the Duc d'Angoulême, eldest son of the Comte d'Artois, and those of the Vicomte and Comtesse de Ségur. In 1785, finally, he exhibited the bust of the Vicomte de Ségur, thus making the family group complete.

The marble busts of the Comte and Comtesse de Ségur by Monot were bequeathed to Versailles in 1924 by one of their descendants, as were the two paintings by Vigée-Lebrun representing the countess and the marquis.

They represent the essence of aristocratic portraiture. The count, who has a haughty air, is represented in military uniform, the prerogative of the old nobility, with his hair curled in ringlets round his head. The austere composition is embellished by a cloak slipped over his shoulders and tied in a bow in front (Hoog 1993, p.338, no.1572, repr.).

The bust of his wife is more pleasing. In fact, it is almost a transcription into marble of a model by Elisabeth-Louise Vigée-Lebrun. A large part of it is given over to the complex hairstyle: the hair, which is probably not powdered but left natural, as in the painting in Versailles (see Bordeaux 2005, no.33, repr.), is curled backwards and rises sharply above the forehead in the style known in French as the *physionomie élevée* (Ruppert 1996, p.173); it is held at the top of the head by a ribbon; large curls embellish the sides of the face, and other curls hang loose on either side of the neck.

The countess wears no jewellery and is dressed in a light dress with a border of lace and a generous décolleté; her waist is emphasised by a belt, which also marks the cut-off point of the bust, above the pedestal. Here the composition brings to mind the paintings of Vigée-Lebrun again, in particular the portrait of the Duchesse de Polignac of 1782, also at Versailles (see Bordeaux 2005, no.32, repr.). The difference is that the sculptor has left out the gauzy veil and bow on the sitter's bare neck. This painterly artifice, playing with a variety of fabrics, could not be employed by the sculptor. Too many effects would have spoiled his work. The artist already had a difficult enough job to evoke, in marble alone, the differences of texture between the hair, the flesh, the lace and the fabric of the dress.

In order to soften the portrait and to add a breath of sensuality, Monot bared the countess's right shoulder and left a large expanse of naked flesh above the bosom, in this way following a convention of court portrait sculpture that originated with Jean-Baptiste II Lemoyne – see, for example, the *Comtesse de Brionne* (marble; 1769: Nationalmuseum Stockholm 1999, p.306, repr.). The absence of any drapery to envelop the composition – Monot differs in this from Lemoyne or Houdon – makes the image, when seen from the front, somewhat intimate and disquieting; is it the broken line round the top of the breasts and the sexy turned-over lace edging? By contrast, the left-hand profile, exposing the majestic, sophisticated curls of the hairstyle and the regular pleats of the dress, presents an altogether ceremonial portrait. It is an astonishing portrait with its two female images: one so close and sensual, the other so distant, and representative of the sitter's social rank. GS

# François-Joseph Navez
CHARLEROI, 1787 – BRUSSELS, 1869

## 144
### *The De Hemptinne Family*

1816
Oil on canvas, 150 × 127 cm
Musées Royaux des Beaux-Arts de Belgique, Brussels

PROVENANCE: acquired from M. Edouard De Hemptinne, May 1896
EXHIBITED: Ixelles, 1985–86, no.425 (S. Valcke)
LITERATURE: Coekelberghs, Jacobs and Loze 1999, pp.20 and 28–29

When he was in exile in Brussels, David met up with various former students, such as Joseph-Denis Odevaere, Joseph Paelinck and François-Joseph Navez, all attempting to perpetuate the lessons of the master – with greater or lesser success. The links seem to have been strongest with Navez, to the point that a number of people have claimed to recognise David's participation in *The De Hemptinne Family*. After studying at the Académie in Brussels, the young Belgian painter was awarded a scholarship by the Société des Beaux-Arts to enable him to continue his training in Paris. Arriving in the French capital in 1813, he immediately entered David's studio, staying there until 1816, the date when the father of the *Oath of the Horatii* was condemned to exile.

Navez followed David to Brussels, then departed for Rome in 1817. The portrait of *The De Hemptinne Family*, regarded as Navez's masterpiece, dates from this period in Brussels. Navez had a very active career as a portrait painter: in 1813 he painted twenty-two portraits, fourteen in 1814 and eight in 1815 (Coekelberghs, Jacobs and Loze, 1999, p.20). As his main aim was to win recognition as a history painter, this situation was bound to be a disappointment to him, but it was the only genre that could provide him with a living. Amongst this production of what were mainly potboilers, the portrait of *The De Hemptinne Family* stands out, partly because of the close ties that existed between the sitters and the painter.

When he arrived in Brussels, Navez took up residence with his friend Auguste-Donat De Hemptinne (1781–1854). A pharmacist by trade, De Hemptinne soon began to encourage his friend's talent by providing him with commissions for pencil and painted portraits and then for history paintings. The artist's *St Veronica of Milan* (Private collection) was painted for him in 1816. Because of his good connections in Brussels society, he turned out to be an excellent agent, obtaining plentiful commissions for Navez. This portrait, which depicts the pharmacist, his wife, Marie-Antoinette De Lathuy (Navez later married her sister) and their daughter, is thus an image of family intimacy in which the artist was a participant. At the same time it is likely that the painting, prominently displayed in the De Hemptinne residence, had a promotional role to play as well, advertising the artist's skill.

This portrait is the first mature work in Navez's career. He had previously painted mainly isolated half-length figures against a blank background; he gradually began to make their poses more natural and their expressions softer, generally with a slight smile; see, for example, *Madame Faber* (1816; Musées Royaux des Beaux-Arts de Belgique). In 1814 he painted a portrait of a *Young Couple* (Musée de l'Art Wallon, Liège), his first attempt at portraying a group, and, although slightly clumsy, it demonstrates a new monumental style, greater attention to accessories and the effects of fabrics, and a direct relationship with the spectator.

The portrait of *The De Hemptinne Family* illustrates these developments, but with an assurance and confidence in the composition that had not been manifested before. Madame De Hemptinne is seen sitting sideways, with her head turned to look at the spectator. Perhaps David remembered this painting, whose composition he must certainly have supervised, when a few years later he painted the daughters of Joseph Bonaparte (1821; J. P. Getty Museum, Los Angeles). Zénaïde Bonaparte is seated in a sideways pose similar to that of Madame De Hemptinne.

In *The De Hemptinne Family*, the mother holds her standing daughter against herself. The movement of the child's head recalls that of the daughter of the Comtesse Vilain XIII, painted by David in the same year (National Gallery, London). Whereas David emphasises the naturalness of the child's pose, contrasting it with the austerity of the Comtesse, Navez uses the more traditional formula of the child standing on the legs of the mother. This recurs in eighteenth-century English portraiture, such as John Singleton Copley's *Sir William Pepperell and His Family* (1778; North Carolina Museum of Art, Raleigh, NC), and contains a distant echo of various virgins and children, the image with which motherhood was most closely associated.

The young De Hemptinne is holding her father's hand, as he gazes tenderly at her mother. The figure of the father is thus integrated into this vision of family intimacy that, in the same spirit as Louis-Edouard Dubufe's *The Artist's Family*, is developed around the child. In this painting, Navez displays his skill at conveying a family portrait in which the relationships between the individuals are not based around the idea of authority and inheritance, but around sentiment and affection. Monsieur De Hemptinne, an attentive father and husband, shows no sign of being a patriarch. Navez's composition therefore allows us to re-evaluate the role of the woman: she is the one who establishes the connection with the spectator, thus gaining in presence. Monsieur De Hemptinne, holding a book in his right hand, is leaning on a piece of furniture in which shells and stones are preserved, an allusion to his collection of minerals. The little girl wears a coral necklace around her neck to protect her; the colour of the coral echoes the colour of her mother's comb, while also, in this context, symbolising her father's passion for natural history.

In this, his most ambitious portrait to date, Navez demonstrates his preoccupation with style. He expresses himself here in a variety of poses united by a broad upward movement, leading from Madame De Hemptinne to her husband. The family, shown against a neutral, dark background, constitutes a cohesive and interdependent group, firmly placed in the middle of the canvas. To the left and right the accessories add a brighter note of colour: the black-and-white shawl placed artlessly on Madame De Hemptinne's chair corresponds to the carpet covering the table. Unlike Ingres, who likes to exploit the graphic details of such objects as shawls and jewellery, Navez concentrates on their colour, using thick paint, sometimes brushed; the drawing is occasionally done in a clumsy way (the end of the shawl on Madame De Hemptinne's legs, the little girl's foot). The red of the daughter's necklace is echoed by the red of the mother's comb, while the white of Monsieur de Hemptinne's cravat matches his wife's lacy collar.

The portrait of *The De Hemptinne Family* depicts family intimacy in the manner favoured by early nineteenth-century bourgeois taste. Yet its formal elegance and the perfectly handled rigour of its composition make it one of the best examples of neoclassical portraiture, enhanced by dense paint applied with visible strokes, in the Flemish manner. Navez was soon to abandon this way of painting in favour of a more realistic and more analytical approach that was also more descriptive. SA

# Joseph Nollekens
LONDON, 1737 – LONDON, 1823

**114**
*Charles James Fox*

1791
Marble, 69 × 54 × 26 cm
Inscription: *Charles James Fox / Aged 43; Nollekens Ft.*
Private collection

PROVENANCE: acquired by Samuel Whitbread II before 1805
EXHIBITED: Washington, 1985, no.476
LITERATURE: Whitbread 1951, p.57; Deuchar 1984, pp.51–52; Whinney 1988; Wilson 2003, p.68

The three different busts by Joseph Nollekens of the statesman Charles James Fox (1749–1806) illustrate the different ways in which a public figure might be represented in sculpture, as well as the political role that such images played. With his flamboyant personality, the radical politician Fox was a favourite subject with engravers of political caricatures, who portrayed him as a dishevelled, unshaven figure. However, supporters of the Whig party, which he led during the 1790s, were keen for

their hero to be represented in a more elevated way in paintings and sculpture. It is, above all, Nollekens's busts that present Fox as his supporters liked to see him. To varying degrees, Nollekens's three busts balance the individuality of Fox's appearance with the exemplary political figure expected by the public.

Nollekens exhibited a marble bust of Fox at the Royal Academy, London, in 1791. It was the portrait commissioned by the Whig magnate, the 4th Earl Fitzwilliam, and discussed with Fox two years earlier. Intended to be placed in the Rockingham Mausoleum at Fitzwilliam's house, Wentworth Woodhouse, alongside busts of other Whig political figures, the first version was in fact sent to Catherine the Great, who placed it between busts of Cicero and Demosthenes. Two other versions were commissioned by Fitzwilliam himself, including one for the Temple and another for Fox's mistress, Mrs Armistead, but others, including one of the brewer Samuel Whitbread, who added verses to the socle of the bust shown here, were acquired by Fox's political supporters. Representing the sitter in a vivid baroque manner, with head boldly turned and wind-swept hair, the bust employs the convention of classicising drapery in a way that allows Fox's distinctive facial features to come to the fore. The impression given is that this bust represents a contemporary man rather than a historical figure. It is interesting to note that the sculptor is shown with a version of this virtuoso bust in Lemuel Francis Abbot's painted portrait. MB

**115**
*Charles James Fox*

c.1802 (but possibly after 1823)
Signed: *J. NOLLEKENS, R.A. Sculp.*
Marble, 72 × 52 × 34 cm
Victoria and Albert Museum, London, A.1-1945

PROVENANCE: given to the museum by Dr W. L. Hildburgh, by whom it was purchased at an unrecorded sale at Christie's
LITERATURE: Whinney 1971, p.122; Whinney 1988, pp.302 and 464, note 20; Bilbey and Trusted 2002, pp.98–99

In contrast to the vivid baroque image made for Fitzwilliam (cat.114), Nollekens produced in 1801 a more classicising bust in which Fox is shown with short hair, thus conforming more closely to a tradition in which public figures were represented in a Roman manner. This was much reproduced by Nollekens's studio – thirty versions existed by 1807 – and was often paired with the same sculptor's bust of William Pitt, Fox's political rival. The pairing of busts in this way was not unusual, and earlier examples range from the linking of the natural philosophers Sir Isaac Newton and Sir Francis Bacon in England, and the military Turenne and the Grand Condé in France. Here, however, the contrast between political rivals illustrates an alternative to the grouping of busts representing political allies (it was in just

such a configuration that Fitzwilliam placed his bust of Fox).

The version of this bust exhibited here was one of the many replicas produced by Nollekens's studio and, as John Kenworthy-Browne has suggested verbally, the unusual format of the sculptor's signature perhaps indicates that it was carved by one of his assistants after his death. MB

**116**
*Charles James Fox*

1805 (but possibly after 1823)
Signed and dated on the reverse: *Nollekens Ft 1805*
Marble, 67 × 42 × 25 cm
National Portrait Gallery, London

PROVENANCE: carved for William Smith MP; given by P. Leigh Smith, 1953
LITERATURE: Saywell and Simon 2004, p.227

This further modification of Fox's image by Nollekens, executed in 1805, represents him bare-chested in a yet more severe classical manner. The version shown here was carved for the Member of Parliament William Smith, and its Latin inscription, on the base, states, 'Charles, alone in our time revived the oratory of Demosthenes'. The association between Fox's rhetorical eloquence and that of classical orators had already been made by Catherine the Great when she set her version of the Fitzwilliam bust between images of Cicero and Demosthenes. The connection with the classical past is, however, made still more apparent in the case of the present bust because of its ostensibly antique format. MB

# Augustin Pajou
PARIS, 1730 – PARIS, 1809

**93**
*Charles de Wailly*

1789
Plaster, 73.5 × 52 × 25 cm
Inscription on the reverse: *DE WAILLY architecte du Roy*; on the reverse of the pedestal: *PAJOU F. 1789*
Palais des Beaux-Arts, Lille, 2001.2.1

PROVENANCE: collection of Baron de Bethmann, Paris, before 1912; his sale, Hôtel Drouot, Paris, 21–22 June 1923, lot 204; acquired at this sale by Raymond Vaxelaire, Brussels; art market, Paris; Karl Lagerfeld Collection; his sale, Christie's Monaco, 29 April 2000, lot 219; acquired at this sale by the museum
LITERATURE: Stein 1912, pp.27–28, repr.; Devigne 1925, pp.5–7, repr.; Paris 1979A, p.22, repr. p.7; Paris 1997A, pp.268–70

**94**
*Madame de Wailly*

1789
Marble, 76.2 × 50.8 cm
Inscription on reverse: *PAJOU, F, 1789*
Lent by The Metropolitan Museum of Art, New York, Fletcher Fund, 1956 (56.105)

PROVENANCE: Madame Camille Lelong; her sale, Paris, 27 April–May 1903, lot 298; collection of the Princesse de Wagram, Paris; collection of David David-Weill, Neuilly-sur-Seine (before 1925); Mrs William Salomon, New York; her sale, New York, 4–7 January 1928, lot 748; collection of J. Horace Harding, New York; his sale, New York, 1 March 1941, lot 68; collection of Baronne Cassel Van Doorn, Englewood; her sale, Paris, 30 May 1956, lot 75; acquired by the museum through the Fletcher Fund
EXHIBITED: Paris, Salon of 1789, no.207; Washington, 1976, no.218; Paris and New York, 1997–98, no.109
LITERATURE: Stein 1912, pp.27–30, repr. pl.II, p.415; Paris 1979A, p.22, repr. p.8

Adélaïde Flore (1765–1838), the daughter of the painter Nicolas Belleville, was sixteen when she married the architect Charles de Wailly (1730–1798), who was fifty-one. De Wailly and Pajou were friends for over 35 years. They met at the French Academy in Rome in 1754, and their friendship endured until the death of the architect (their two houses, built by De Wailly, were next door to one another). They worked together on the construction of the Hôtel de Voyer d'Argenson, one of the most important buildings to be built in Paris in the late 1760s. Later they both took part in the commission, with Hubert Robert, set up to consider the installation of a museum in the Palais du Louvre, and they belonged to the same freemasons' lodge (the Simple Hearts of the Polar Star). De Wailly possessed several works by Pajou, and there is plenty of evidence to testify to their friendship. The bust in the Musée de Lille can therefore be considered a friendship portrait: the architect is represented straightforwardly, his neck almost bare, the two sides of his fur-collared jacket opening onto a shirt with a ruffled edge. The face is impressive, expressing curiosity and good humour. The empathy between an artist and his sitter has seldom been so evident as in this intimate portrait.

The bust of the architect may have been exhibited in the Salon of 1789, but it was too late to appear in the list of works, unlike that of his wife. In the large drawing of the *Project for the Reorganisation of the Salon Carré in the Louvre* executed by De Wailly himself (Wilhelm 1963, repr.) it is can be seen at the lower left, near a window, standing on a quadrangular plinth, as a pendant to the bust of his wife, and below his own drawn plans. Caution is required, however: even though a large number of paintings and sculptures that were shown in the Salon can be recognised, this is an imaginary design in which works of art are placed in ideal positions (De Wailly suggested re-opening the windows so that the sculpture would benefit from lateral natural light). It is thus impossible to confirm that the portrait of De Wailly was present, particularly as it is not mentioned in any review. The introduction of the bust into the drawing might be understood as a friendly gesture made by the architect to the sculptor, or simply a nod in his direction.

The circumstances surrounding the commission given to Pajou for these two busts, dating from 1789, are not known. It seems that De Wailly had suffered a reversal of fortune the previous year which obliged him to sell his art collection. Once he was in funds again, he could afford to purchase the large marble of Adélaïde Flore, whose price was higher than the price of a simple friendship portrait (these tended to be executed in terracotta or plaster): a painting by Marguerite Gérard shows the architect unfolding plans in front of his desk, on top of which stands the bust of his wife (Paris 1997A, fig.176). The marble bust was undoubtedly retained by Madame de Wailly after her husband's death; she remarried two years later. Did Pajou make a marble bust of her husband? In a letter to Alexandre Lenoir written in 1799 Madame de Wailly expresses regret that she does not possess the marble bust – 'if only I had the marble one' (Archives Nationales F17 24 5, piece 39, fol. 144) – and requests Pajou himself to repair a plaster cast that she plans to send to the Musée des Monuments Français (Paris 1997A, p.268; the plaster cast ended up in the Château de Versailles but has since disappeared: Hoog 1993, p.373, no.1748).

Whereas De Wailly's bust is sober and discreet in conception, the bust of his wife is grandiose and showy. Yet it appears that the two busts were designed together: they are the same size and look at one another. Adélaïde Flore, in the full flower of her 24 years, looks magnificent, her leonine locks gorgeously curled; Pajou has achieved a work of pure sculpture in which the marble appears as ductile and malleable as clay. This cascade of locks and curls contrasts with the long regular diagonal pleats of her house coat – a kind of tunic in the classical style. Pajou suggests the sensuality of her breasts beneath the fabric, and produces virtuoso effects of contrast between the hair, the fabric and the naked flesh.

This portrayal of a couple well known to Pajou is extremely subtle. The contrast between the man in contemporary dress and the woman in clothing that harks back to classical antiquity (although there is no archaeological reference) can be found in other examples of the artist's work (for example the two children of 1772, Paris 1997A, figs 144 and 145; or the portrait of Elisabeth-Louise Vigée-Lebrun in the Louvre, Paris 1997A, no.104); Pajou was manifestly uncomfortable with the female fashions of his age (unlike Houdon, for example). The difference between the two busts allows a dynamic comparison between them. The imperious gaze of the young woman – the contour of the iris is only lightly incised and the pupil almost unmarked, according to the usual practice of the sculptor, the head straight above the shoulders – is in some way mitigated by the bust of her architect husband, who looks benevolent under his bushy eyebrows, his head bent forward and his shoulders rounded. GS

# Jean-Baptiste Pigalle
PARIS, 1714 – PARIS, 1785

**76**
*Self-portrait*

c.1776
Plaster, 55 × 27 × 25 cm
Fondation Saint-Thomas, Strasbourg

PROVENANCE: probably presented to the chapter of the Church of St Thomas, c.1776
LITERATURE: Rocheblave 1902, pp.353–59, repr., pp.273 and 275; Rocheblave 1919, pp.272–74, repr. as a frontispiece; Aubert 1950, pp.41–42; Réau 1950, pp.31–32, 169, repr.; Gaborit 1985, pp.81–82, repr.; Beyer and Mugler 1994, pp.76–77, repr.

'Making portraits is so difficult that Pigalle once told me that he had never made one without being tempted to give up. In fact, life, character and physiognomy all reside particularly in the face' (Denis Diderot, *Pensées détachées*, 1776, rev. ed., 1995, p.448). For an artist who loved the truth, as Pigalle did, transcribing the features of a face was a trial. He was 'in love with a kind of excess of expression', for 'he was born a sovereign sculptor, as the ancients were born sovereign poets' (Joseph Joubert, quoted in Rocheblave 1919, p.360). The handful of portraits created by Pigalle, a very small number – compared with his teacher Jean-Baptiste Lemoyne, or his colleagues in Lemoyne's studio, Jean-Jacques Caffieri and Augustin Pajou – succeed in reaching these exacting standards for the faithful representation of the individual. Above all, Pigalle preferred to make portraits of friends, scientists, work colleagues, or intellectuals from the *Encyclopédie* circles – a working, middle-class society such as we find in the work of Jean Siméon Chardin or Jean-Baptiste Greuze. He scrutinised his own face with the same careful attention with which he examined the faces of others.

He probably executed this self-portrait around 1776, the year in which the mausoleum to Maréchal de Saxe was completed in St-Thomas, Strasbourg. The sculptor went there on 18 July 1776. Was it at that time that he left the bust to the members of the chapter to thank them for their welcome? In September of the same year, he was given the title of freeman of the city of Strasbourg. Did he send his portrait to them then? Perhaps the exact date does not matter: the gesture stands for what it is, a reward to the citizens of Strasbourg for their help and appreciation. Victor Hugo saw the sculpture and mentioned it briefly in *Le Rhin*, letter XXX: 'Someone opens a cupboard for you and inside is a bewigged head made of plaster: it is the bust of Pigalle' (quoted in Gaborit 1985, p.81). A sacristan identified it on the premises of the architect Henri Salomon, who discovered it by chance in 1861 in a niche that had been turned into a cupboard. He had it restored by a local sculptor, who applied a coat of terracotta colour to the plaster cast.

Samuel Rocheblave discovered it later, forgotten, in 1902. He looked at the medallion made by Charles-Nicolas Cochin, engraved by Augustin de Saint-Aubin in 1782, compared the two profiles and published the bust definitively. The acquisition by the Louvre in 1949 of a similar version in terracotta caused some confusion: Marcel Aubert and Louis Réau, noticing that the terracotta was slightly smaller than the plaster cast, and sharper in outline, thought that it must be later in date. In fact, it appears that the two pieces are contemporary, and that the plaster cast was moulded on the terracotta piece before firing; the clay contracted in the heat, causing this difference in size. In addition, there are always variations between a clay model, finished by hand, and a plaster cast whose contours have been smoothed by the process of moulding. Pigalle must have kept the clay model and sent a plaster cast to Strasbourg because it was less fragile.

The image Pigalle presents of himself is striking. He is wearing an ordinary workman's shirt, with bare neck, hair curled but not dressed (and without a wig, apologies to Victor Hugo); his mouth is half-open, his wrinkles clearly defined and his eyes tired. This is a man of the people, exhausted by his labours, like the *Citizen* on the pedestal of the royal monument in Rheims – also a self-portrait of the sculptor – and with a frank and loyal gaze. It is a true image, like the image of his friend Diderot made at the same time. The bronze bust of Diderot in the Louvre bears the inscription: 'In 1777, Diderot by Pigalle, his co-sponsor [Pigalle was godfather to the writer's granddaughter], both aged 63 years.'

The difference between this and the pastel portrait by Marie-Suzanne Roslin (cat. 77, a reception piece for the Académie; 1770; Louvre, Paris: Monnier 1972, no. 103, repr.) is impressive. In the pastel, Pigalle is represented as a nobleman, in the clothes of a knight of the Order of St Michael, a sumptuous image equivalent to the self-satisfied portrait of Jean-Jacques Caffieri by Adolf Erik Wertmüller (cat. 77; a reception piece for the Académie, 1784; see Tours 2000, p. 280, R 377) in which the artist, wearing a scarlet suit in the French style, wears the sword of the academician ostentatiously at his side. The aim of these official portraits of professors at the academy was to show off the elevated rank of the eminent sculptors of the institution.

The bust of Pigalle shows nothing of the sort, and bears no resemblance to these conceited status portraits: it is simply the image of an exhausted man, prematurely aged, and very moving. Jean-René Gaborit has pointed out that the artist's gaze 'swivels towards the left, the correct position for a sculptor who is observing himself in a mirror placed on his right'. It is easy to imagine the artist examining his features attentively, like a disillusioned entomologist. 'He had received a knowing eye from nature; in each feature it would discover a thousand features, and in each part an infinity of parts … He seemed to have made it a strict rule just to imitate truth, not only as his eyes saw it but also as his hands could touch it …

He could never express to his own satisfaction all the contours of the human body, as the ancients could never bring them to life to their satisfaction … He was in love with a kind of excess of expression' (Joubert, quoted in Rocheblave 1919, pp. 359 and 360). And Lemoyne wrote to his former pupil, the sculptor Etienne Maurice Falconet: 'All you need do is to be genuine, like Pigalle' (letter from Diderot to Falconet, 29 December 1766; *Correspondance*, rev. ed., 1997, p. 717). GS

## 54
*Voltaire Naked*

1776
Marble, 150 × 89 × 77 cm
Inscription on the plinth: *A MONSIEUR DE VOLTAIRE, PAR LES GENS DE LETTRES, SES COMPATRIOTES ET SES CONTEMPORAINS – 1776*
On the reverse, on the foot of the lyre: *PIGALLE / F. 1776*
Département des Sculptures, Musée du Louvre, Paris (Institut de France deposit), ENT. 1962.1

PROVENANCE: presented to Voltaire by a group of European subscribers; reclaimed after the writer's death, at an unknown date, by his great-nephew Alexandre-François de Dompierre, who installed it in his circular dining room in the Château d'Hornoy (Somme); presented to the Institut de France, 1807; deposited by the Institut in the Louvre, 1962
LITERATURE: Desnoiresterres 1879, pp. 54–65; Réau 1950, pp. 60–67, 158–59, repr.; Colton 1980, repr.; Colton 1981, pp. 533–34; Gaborit 1985, pp. 70–74, repr.; Goodman 1986, repr.; Musée du Louvre 1998, vol. 2, p. 523, repr.

In April 1770 (opinions differ about the exact date) Madame Necker held a dinner party at her home attended by seventeen eminent personalities from the Parisian literary world, including Denis Diderot, Jean le Rond d'Alembert, Guillaume Raynal, Claude Adrien Helvétius, Jean-François de Saint-Lambert, Jean-François Marmontel, André Morellet, Friedrich Melchior Grimm and Jean-Baptiste-Antoine Suard. As a result of the dinner a fund was started with the aim of erecting a statue to Voltaire (1694–1778). Pigalle was entrusted with the task of making the statue.

The sculptor had been alerted in advance and presented a preliminary sketch in terracotta that was immediately described by Grimm in the *Correspondance littéraire*. The essential features of the future statue can be seen in this small figure: the philosopher, wearing a laurel wreath, is represented seated and naked, with a drape covering his left shoulder and arm, and with a sheet of paper on his knee. He holds a pen in his right hand (Musée des Beaux-Arts, Orléans: see Paris 2003A, no. 109, repr.). In the marble version Pigalle set out the accessories at the philosopher's feet – the mask of Thalia (Comedy), the dagger of Melpomene (Tragedy), the lyre and the poet's crown – and removed the laurel wreath.

Once the project had been accepted by the society, Pigalle went to Ferney on 30 May to start making a model of the great man from life. He brought back to Paris a clay head of the writer, and worked on the full-size model from August 1770 to August 1772. Funds continued to be

collected, and, indeed, exceeded expectations: 18,775 *livres* when the account was closed in 1776, whereas the sculptor had requested the sum of 10,000 *livres* (to which should be added the cost of the marble and the cost of the trip to Ferney: Desnoiresterres 1879, pp. 55 and 62).

The decision to make a statue of a live person was an honour usually reserved for the king, his family (sometimes) and the personalities in his entourage – in the last case, an allegorical disguise was a convenient manner of making the celebration less obvious (the Duchesse de Bourgogne as Diana by Coysevox, or Madame de Pompadour as Friendship by Pigalle); some personalities were able to commission their own effigy (for example, Maréchal de Villars by Nicolas Coustou), but this was unusual. This gives some idea of the exceptional significance of the gift made to Voltaire by the 'men of letters' – the inscription on the statue borrows the title of the article written by Voltaire in his *Questions sur l'Encyclopédie*; the 'society of men of letters' was thus described on the title page of the *Encyclopédie* itself.

Diderot, a friend of the sculptor, was behind the operation: Morellet's testimony on this is explicit. Morellet describes the appearance of the statue, directly implicating the philosopher: 'In order to show off his skill in anatomy, Pigalle has created a naked, emaciated old man, a skeleton, a defect that is only half way compensated by the truth and life to be admired in the facial expression and the attitude of the old person. Diderot should be blamed for this blunder, for such it is. It was he who inspired Pigalle to make a classical statue resembling Seneca cutting his veins. Some of us made a fuss when Pigalle brought the model, but in vain. I remember strongly opposing Diderot and Pigalle; but we could neither persuade the philosopher, nor the artist encouraged by the philosopher, to abandon this unwise course of action' (Morellet 1988, p. 175).

The 'Seneca' in the Borghese collection (now in the Louvre: Haskell and Penny 1988, no. 163, repr.) – in fact a fisherman, as Winckelmann has pointed out – was a celebrated classical sculpture: in his *Voyage d'un français en Italie* (published in 1769), Jérôme de Lalande, who was closely connected with Diderot and the *Encyclopédie* circle, describes it as a masterpiece. Diderot, who made the explicit comparison between Voltaire and Seneca in his *Essai sur la vie de Sénèque* (published in 1779; see Colton 1980, p. 1684), advised Pigalle to take his inspiration from the piece, aligning himself with those who viewed heroic nudity as the best way of representing an illustrious man: 'It is because flesh is more beautiful than the most beautiful drapery … By portraying a person naked you distance him from the crowd, you recall a more innocent, simpler age … This is because we are dissatisfied with the present day, and because this return to ancient times does not displease us … *Graeca res est nihil velare* [the custom of the Greeks is to veil nothing

- a quotation from Pliny's *Natural History*]. It was the custom of the Greeks, our masters in all the fine arts' (Diderot, *Essais sur la peinture*, 1766, rev. ed., 1984, p.64).

Pigalle retained the idea of nudity in the classical style, but rather than triumphantly representing a powerful, virile body in the image of the pseudo-Seneca, he decided to represent an emaciated old body, skeletal and flabby, taking an old soldier as his model; the figure is ennobled nevertheless by a magnificent drape that covers part of his back. Pigalle's aim was not to shock: 'He had more feeling for what is true than for what is beautiful' (Suard 1786); but, by not hiding the anatomical truth of a body in old age, he magnified the contrast between the writer's body and his head. Voltaire's face bears an expression of terrific alertness, full of hope: the face of a humanist, of the author of *Traité sur la tolérance* (1763), of the defender of Jean Calas, the Huguenot merchant unjustly executed for supposedly murdering his son, or of the advocate of the people of Lisbon, desperate after the terrible earthquake of 1755.

This intense, complex view of the philosopher is the opposite of that taken by the Comte d'Angiviller, who planned a series of Great Men of France, in modern dress and with historical details, to be begun in the year that Pigalle finished his marble statue (Scherf 1993). It also differs profoundly from the familiar evocation done with the sitter's agreement that was produced later by Houdon in his *Voltaire Seated* (marble; 1781; Comédie-Française, Paris: see Versailles 2004, no.26, repr.). Pigalle's original composition shocked his contemporaries and offended other artists, who could not imagine a nude statue being anything other than idealised and lacking individual characteristics (see examples by Antoine Quatremère de Quincy and Joshua Reynolds), as well as upsetting Voltaire's friends, who were worried about the disastrous consequences of a row.

Voltaire, who tried to quell the sculptor's passionate feelings with some satirical sonnets – written in self-defence, in fact, because large numbers of epigrams were published attacking him about the sculpture – came to accept the work, writing an admirable letter to his friend François Tronchin (see cat.65) on 1 December 1771: 'I can only admire the classical influence in the work of M. Pigalle; naked or clothed, it is of no importance. I shall not inspire disreputable ideas in the ladies, in whatever way I am presented to them. We must leave M. Pigalle to be the absolute master of his statue. It is a crime, in the fine arts, to put obstacles in the way of genius ... I ask you to see M. Pigalle immediately, to tell him what I think, to assure him of my friendship, my gratitude and my admiration. All that I can say to him is that I have never found success in the arts that I have cultivated except when I listened to my own voice' (Voltaire 1962–63, no.16438). GS

# Jean-Marie Pigalle

PARIS, 1792 – PARIS, 1857

## 36
### *The Comtesse du Cayla*

1826
Marble, 77 × 55 × 32 cm
Inscription on the cut surface of the left shoulder: *Pigalle / 1826*
Private collection, Château de Craon, Haroué (Meurthe-et Moselle)

PROVENANCE: in the sitter's collection at the Château de Saint-Ouen (Seine-Saint-Denis); then the collection of her daughter, Ugoline-Louise-Joséphine Valentine de Baschi du Cayla (1806–1885), wife of Edmond-Henri-Etienne Victurnien de Beauvau (1795–1861); remained in the family of Beauvau-Craon
LITERATURE: Lami 1921, p.87; Alcouffe 1991–92, p.7, repr.

The sculptor Jean-Marie Pigalle (no direct relation of Jean-Baptiste Pigalle; see cats 54 and 76) was a student of Antoine-Jean Gros and François-Frédéric Lemot at the Ecole des Beaux-Arts, where his name is mentioned in 1810. He took part regularly in the Salon from 1814, when he exhibited a bust of Louis XVIII. He was a great supporter of the Bourbons, and attracted notice with his portraits and medallions of the aristocrats and nobility of the regime. Pigalle exhibited a bust of the Prince de Condé at the Salon of 1819, and, in 1822, a plaster statue of Louis XVIII made for the Chambre des Pairs, for which he won a second-class medal. His career continued under the July Monarchy from 1830 to 1848 – he executed a bust of Louis-Philippe in 1831 – gaining a certain notoriety with his small bronze statues of celebrated writers.

He remained close to the monarchy under the Restoration, so it is not surprising to learn that he frequently saw the friends of Louis XVIII, the du Cayla family. At the Salon of 1819 he exhibited a bust of the Comte du Cayla, lieutenant general of the kingdom and peer of France, and, in 1824, a bust of Vicomte Sosthène de la Rochefoucauld. He was also the creator of a bronze bust of the Princesse de Craon, a relation of the family. His greatest honour, however, was to make a marble bust of Zoé-Victoire Talon (1785–1852), wife since 1802 of Achille-Pierre-Antoine de Baschi, Comte du Cayla.

The Comtesse du Cayla was the daughter of Antoine-Omer Talon (1760–1811), prosecutor at the Châtelet in Paris, and investigating judge in the case of the Marquis de Favras, who had implicated the Comte de Provence in a conspiracy and had been guillotined in 1790; he was also a royalist agent during the Revolution and the Directoire. The Comtesse du Cayla made the acquaintance of Louis XVIII when she apparently handed over to him some compromising papers from her father (Lamothe-Langon 1987, pp.15–16). Clever and witty, she caught his fancy, becoming his mistress in 1817. In 1822 the King gave her the Château de Saint-Ouen, constructed by Huvé between 1821 and 1822; it was presented to the Comtesse du Cayla fully decorated and furnished.

After her death, her daughter, the Princesse de Beauvau, inherited her property. Having acquired the Château d'Haroué in Lorraine, sold by her nephew Marc de Beauvau-Craon, she moved the entire contents of Saint-Ouen to Haroué: the furniture by Pierre-Antoine Bellangé, the ornamental bronzes by Pierre-Philippe Thomire and the large paintings by François Gérard representing Louis XVIII in his study at the Château des Tuileries (Salon of 1824) and his beloved, the Comtesse du Cayla with her children (signed reductions of these two paintings are now in the Château de Versailles: Constans 1995, vol.1, nos 2141 and 2146 repr.). The portrait of the Comtesse dates from 1826, the same year as Jean-Marie Pigalle's marble bust (we know that he also made a medallion of the Comtesse: Lami 1921, p.87).

'Madame du Cayla has not much intelligence, but the intelligence she has she uses in scheming and calculated behaviour. She has even less education, but what makes her stand out, and also makes her a lot of friends, is her bright, natural sense of humour and extremely equable temperament. She is easily amused by what others say; she laughs at it – in fact she has what might be termed a happy nature. This makes her an excellent companion to everybody' (Duchesse de Maillé in Maillé 1984, p.81).

This bust by Jean-Marie Pigalle is unquestionably one of his best works, strongly influenced by the style of François-Joseph Bosio (1768–1845). Bosio was a member of the Institut (1816) and First Sculptor to Louis XVIII (1822); he was a pivotal member of Restoration society. His bust of the Duchesse de Berry (marble; Musée des Beaux-Arts, Troyes: Hubert 1985, pl.XIII) bears some resemblance to the portrait of the Comtesse du Cayla, even though the latter is presented from the front, whereas the Duchesse de Berry is turning her head to the left. The stunning décolleté, the carefully styled hair with its cascade of ringlets, and the bejewelled diadem holding the hair are comparable, as is the trick of not incising the eyes and presenting a fixed gaze with no pupils.

The Comtesse du Cayla's gown, however, is much more obviously inspired by classical antiquity, with its tunic fastened by a brooch on the right shoulder and the flap of the cloak on the left. Pigalle's dazzling virtuosity with the chisel is particularly evident in the carving of her hair: each curl is chiselled with energy, and the chignon on the back is twisted with refined elegance. The care paid to the details of clothes and makeup, and the choice of extravagant accessories – her jewellery was fabulous – bear witness to the Comtesse's rank and to a certain delight in showing it off, as Marie d'Angoult so maliciously notes, having spotted her at the opera: 'She was, as usual, gorgeously dressed, and plastered in makeup' (quoted in Alcouffe 1991–92, p.15). GS

# Pierre-Paul Prud'hon

CLUNY, 1758 – PARIS, 1823

## 23

*Charles-Maurice de Talleyrand-Périgord in the Robes of the Grand Chamberlain*

1807
Oil on canvas, 212 × 138 cm
Signed and dated at lower left: *P. Prud'hon f. 1807*
Musée Carnavalet-Histoire de Paris, Paris

PROVENANCE: commissioned for the Palais de Fontainebleau, 1806; displayed in the Galerie de Diane, Palais des Tuileries, August 1807, then in the Salon des Grands Officiers, Palais de Campiègne, May 1808; offered to the sitter, 1815; returned to the artist, 1817; Charles-Pompée Le Boulanger de Boisfremont (1773–1838); his daughter, Madame Power; purchased from her by Laurent Laperlier (1805–1878); his sale, 11–13 April 1867, no.44; purchased by the city of Paris; office of the Prefect; exhibited at the Pavilion de Flore, Palais de Louvre, Paris; damaged by the fire of 1871; entered the Musée Carnavalet, Paris, 1911 (for fuller provenance see Laveissière 1998)
EXHIBITED: Paris, 1874, no.34; Paris, 1885, no.223; Paris, 1889, no.545; Paris, 1891, no.408; Versailles, 1963, no.288; Tokyo, Hiroshima, Fukuoka and Shizuoka, 1987–88, no.67; Paris and New York, 1997–98
LITERATURE: Burty 1867, p.vii; Clément 1872, pp.304–05, note 1; Goncourt 1876, p.38; Burty 1879, p.149; Jouin 1886; Marmottan 1890; Escholier 1922, p.114, note 4; Guiffrey 1924, p.239, no.628; Lacour-Gayet 1946–47, vol.2, p.222, pl.IV facing p.192; Baruteau 1958, pp.51–52, 55–56; Zieseniss 1969, pp.135, 138, 140, 141, 145, 146, 150, 155, 157, fig.7, facing p.144; Metropolitan Bulletin 1994, p.40; Laveissière 1998, p.193, no.134

This full-length portrait of Charles-Maurice de Talleyrand-Périgord, the most celebrated diplomat of his age, was painted at the height of Prud'hon's creative power and professional success. The artist was in great favour at the Imperial court, and was to exhibit his allegorical masterpiece, *Justice and Divine Vengeance Pursuing Crime* (1808; Louvre, Paris), at the Salon the following year.

The portrait was a state commission issued by the Director-General of Museums, Vivant Denon, as part of a suite of paintings depicting Napoleon's most prominent ministers. In deference to Talleyrand's dual role in the administration, Prud'hon was requested to produce another portrait showing him as Foreign Minister as well as this one depicting him in the official robes of the Grand Chamberlain. Both works were originally intended for the Palais de Fontainebleau, but ended up making their début at the Tuileries in August 1807, before being transferred to the Palais de Campiègne.

Talleyrand must have approved of his likeness, as when the portraits were returned to him after the fall of Napoleon in 1815, he asked the artist to update this version by repainting the figure in town dress. Prud'hon was unhappy at the thought of recycling the existing portrait, and instead insisted on producing an entirely new canvas (1817; Metropolitan Museum of Art, New York) in which the figure is replicated almost exactly but the costume, interior and – most importantly – the bust of the fallen Emperor are completely reworked.

Talleyrand was himself an old hand at reworking his image to accord with a transformed political climate; by the end of his career he had earned the staggering distinction of having held high office under no fewer than five successive regimes. Revered for his unrivalled mastery of statecraft and his brilliant wit, he was loathed in equal measure as a venal hypocrite, famously earning from Napoleon the soubriquet, 'a shit in a silk stocking'. This portrait finds an amusing counterpart in the collection of the Musée Carnavalet-Histoire de Paris in the form of a caricature from 1815 showing Talleyrand with six heads on one body, each proclaiming loyalty to a different master. Prud'hon received his commission in the midst of one of these notorious shifts in allegiance. Talleyrand had served Napoleon energetically since helping to bring him to power in the coup of Brumaire, but in recent years their relationship had begun to deteriorate as their views on foreign policy became increasingly divergent. Talleyrand, who consistently advocated the creation of a stable balance of European powers that would allow France to consolidate her recent territorial gains, had become increasingly frustrated by his failure to rein in the Emperor's expansionist ambitions. In the aftermath of the Treaty of Tilsit, in which Napoleon had acted in disregard of all his counsel, Talleyrand resigned from his position as Foreign Minister. Although he retained his title of Grand Chamberlain until 1809, and was periodically asked to perform diplomatic duties, from this point on he began a covert campaign to undermine the leader whom he had once sworn to serve until the end of his days.

Despite this backdrop of political discord, Prud'hon's portrait exudes a heroic confidence that exemplifies the grandest tradition of the portrait as social signifier. Talleyrand, who was renowned for his extravagant lifestyle and impeccable taste, is depicted in a refined neoclassical interior, dressed in sumptuous scarlet and gold ceremonial attire. The artist deploys his characteristic tenebrist style, interspersing the modulated golden tones with exquisitely painted highlights on the brocade and mouldings. The strongest shaft of light hits Talleyrand's face and illuminates his forehead – a trope commonly used to denote masculine genius. The air of erudition is heightened in the preparatory drawing for the portrait (Musée Carnavalet-Histoire de Paris, Paris) by the inclusion of a bust of Minerva rather than Napoleon, but perhaps Prud'hon thought it judicious to emphasise the current loyalty of a subject who was so prone to changing sides. The minister is posed in an attitude of stiff formality, making the painting an atypical addition to the *œuvre* of an artist celebrated primarily for the delicate grace and charm of his figures. If Madame de Staël and Fanny Burney can be trusted, Talleyrand possessed plenty of charm, but grace was never his strong suit; he walked with a pronounced limp throughout his life – a disability that Prud'hon tactfully disguises here with a pose that puts the weight on his sitter's healthy left foot. The portrait certainly evokes none of the tender sympathy that the artist was able to communicate for his female sitters – most famously in his pensive Joséphine – but that is unsurprising given Talleyrand's famous ability to maintain a veneer of urbane self-control at all times. It is this demeanour of ironic detachment that Prud'hon emphasises. Talleyrand assesses the viewer with an astute glance, conveying some of the incisive intelligence, tinged with world-weary cynicism, that made him the quintessential political survivor. KB

# Sir Henry Raeburn

STOCKBRIDGE, 1756 – EDINBURGH, 1823

## 55

*James Hutton*

*c.*1789–90
Oil on canvas, 125.1 × 104.8 cm
Scottish National Portrait Gallery, Edinburgh, PG 2686

PROVENANCE: John Davidson of Stewartfield and Haltree, WS; by whom bequeathed to Hugh Warrender, WS; his nephew, Sir George Warrender, 4th baronet of Lochend; by descent to Sir Victor Warrender, 8th baronet, later Lord Bruntsfield of Boroughmuir; Christie's, London, 18 April 1986, lot 129B; bought Scottish National Portrait Gallery
EXHIBITED: see Edinburgh 1997, p.66
LITERATURE: see Edinburgh 1997, p.66

Henry Raeburn was brought up near Edinburgh; a goldsmith's apprentice in 1772, he had established himself as a portrait painter by 1784. As one art historian has noted, Raeburn 'worked in a context that rated certain kinds of intellectual achievement extremely highly – the polite, humane and civilising knowledge embodied in the leading lights of Scottish, especially, Edinburgh, culture'. Science was 'central to this ethos' (Jordanova 2000, p.134). This portrait is an early example of Raeburn's engagement with intellectual culture; the life of his sitter, the polymath James Hutton (1726–1797), 'spanned the greatest years of the Scottish Enlightenment and, of its number, only Joseph Black made a greater contribution to science' (Jones 2004, p.60). It is not known when the painting was undertaken. The artist travelled to Italy between 1784 and 1786, and some authorities suggest that Hutton's picture dates from before this journey (NACF 1987, p.141). The fullest and most recent account of the image, however, argues that 'a date of 1789 or 1790 seems most likely' (Edinburgh 1997, p.66).

Hutton was the son of a prosperous Edinburgh merchant, William Hutton, and his wife Sarah Balfour, who was also from a merchant family. Educated at the Royal High School and then at Edinburgh University, Hutton moved in late 1747 to Paris to continue his studies in medicine and eventually graduated as a doctor in 1749 in Leiden. Returning home, he did not practise medicine but went into a business partnership in the manufacture of ammonium chloride, an enterprise which made him rich; he then studied agricultural innovations and began farming near Duns, Berwickshire, before moving back to Edinburgh in 1767.

Following the foundation of the Royal Edinburgh Society in 1783, Hutton began in earnest to present his work on a wide range of scientific subjects. He won abiding renown for a lecture he gave in 1785 entitled *Theory of the earth, or, An investigation of the laws observable in the composition, dissolution, and restoration of land upon the globe*. This was first published in full in 1788, shortly before the putative date of Raeburn's portrait. Hutton's pioneering theory held that eroded material from rocks on the earth's surface was deposited on the seabed, and then reconstituted over millions of years to form land; this process, he argued, was driven by subterranean heat and ensured that the planet's crust would be perpetually renewed, indicating that the earth was much older than had hitherto been believed. As he famously put it, 'we find no vestige of a beginning – no prospect of an end' (Jones 2004, pp.60–61). One scholar has commented: 'Hutton ventured a true secularisation of Nature' (Porter 2000, p.140).

Raeburn's portrayal refers closely to Hutton's scientific pursuits. Hutton's publications are suggested by the papers and quill pen which lie on the table at his side. Alongside are geological specimens which have been identified as 'a chalk fossil (shell), two examples of mineral veins, a druse, a septarian nodule and a breccia'. These objects constitute 'a still-life of a modernity that is difficult to see equalled anywhere at this time'. Moreover, they each refer expressly to Hutton's theories: 'the fossil shell as evidence that the land has been raised from the sea floor; the nodule as evidence of the power of heat and fusion on rocks; and the veined rocks as evidence of the intrusive power of molten rock' (Edinburgh 1997, pp.66, 68).

Raeburn's approach to painting has been characterised as 'empirical'; largely self-taught, he drew 'with a brush directly on the canvas' (Thomson 2004, p.782). Although this gave him the benefit of spontaneity, lack of preliminary planning could cause problems. In this image, the chair has been noted for its 'summary treatment', the imperfect perspective of the chair back making Hutton's left shoulder seem as though it is 'impaled by the upright rather than positioned in front of it' (Edinburgh 1997, p.66). His unplanned approach may also have led to the large empty space to the right of the sitter, 'where there are indications that he originally intended to include a swag of "baroque" drapery'; this he began and then painted out. The solution left a 'flat, almost neo-classically severe area that seems entirely appropriate to the man portrayed' (Thomson 1994, p.7).

Hutton's portrait is imbued throughout by a restrained palette of green and reddish brown hues (Edinburgh 1997, p.66). Against this background, Hutton's face shines out, 'lit up by an intense sensibility to intellectual pleasure' (Buchan 2003, p.298). Raeburn achieves here 'that sense of engagement with a real, breathing individual which was to be so characteristic' of his best work (Thomson 1994, p.7).

Although Hutton's *Theory of the Earth* initially found few proponents, half a century later it was 'universally accepted in all its essentials' (Jones 2004, p.62). As one historian of science has noted, one difficulty was that 'within a year of the publication of Hutton's *Theory*, the French Revolution broke out. Conservative hysteria in Britain against the Revolution was quickly to blackball all speculative natural philosophy, all science derived from Enlightenment naturalism, all views of Earth history which seemed to assail Christianity', and 'Hutton's *Theory* was guilty on all scores' (Porter 1977, p.198). If the dating of Raeburn's portrait to this period is correct, then from the sitter's point of view it may have offered not just the chance to commemorate his works, but also another means of asserting their validity. SM

### 40
*Major William Clunes*

After 1809
Oil on canvas, 236 × 150 cm
National Gallery of Scotland, Edinburgh, NG 903

PROVENANCE: bequeathed by Lady Siemens to the Royal Scottish Academy, 1902; transferred to the National Gallery of Scotland, 1910
EXHIBITED: *Portraits by the late Sir Henry Raeburn*, 32 York Place, Edinburgh, 1824, no.55; *Raeburn*, National Gallery of Scotland, Edinburgh, 1956, no.35; *Raeburn*, Scottish National Portrait Gallery, Edinburgh, 1997–98, no.42
LITERATURE: Edinburgh 1997, p.142

This image shows a British army officer, Major William Clunes (died 1831), standing alongside his horse, a bay charger, with man and mount dividing the canvas space between them. The two are, indeed, given a certain parity thanks to the foreshortening of the animal and the positioning of its head so that it is on the same level as Clunes's. As well as being physically connected – Clunes holds the horse's reins with his left hand – the pair are also brought together by the continuous passages of roughly defined paint which describe the background space between their heads (Edinburgh 1997, p.142).

Raeburn's sitter was a son of Colonel Gordon Clunes (1736/7–1814) of Crakaig, Sutherland (*Gentleman's Magazine*, 84, April 1814, p.416). William Clunes's own military career had commenced by 1790, when he joined the 50th Regiment. He became a lieutenant in 1794 and then a captain in 1797. Having served in the initial campaign in the Peninsula, which culminated in a long fighting retreat during the winter of 1808–09,

Clunes transferred in July 1809 to the 54th Regiment and was promoted to major. It is in this uniform in which he appears in Raeburn's portrait; he left the army at some point around 1811–12 (Edinburgh 1997, p.142). He died on 24 November 1831 at Crakaig (*Blackwood's Edinburgh Magazine*, 29, January–June 1831, p.575).

While serving as a captain with the 50th Regiment, Clunes performed valorously at the battle of Corunna on 16 January 1809, and this may be the context behind Raeburn's portrait. Clunes's regiment was at the centre of the action, in the 'portion of the British army' which 'suffered most severely' in terms of casualties (Milburne 1809, p.58). A French advance having begun, the 50th Regiment's commander, Major Charles Napier, sought approval to counter-attack from his general, Sir John Moore. Permission was obtained and, as Napier wrote the year after the battle: 'Turning round, I saw Capt Clunes … and said to him, Clunes, take your grenadiers and open the ball. He stalked forward alone, like Goliath before the Philistines, for six foot five he was in height, and of proportionate bulk and strength: his grenadiers followed, and thus the battle began on our side' (Napier 1857, vol.1, p.96).

It was presumably at this stage that Clunes attacked a group of six French sharpshooters, and struck down, or took prisoner, all of them, using only a heavy blackthorn stick which he bore in preference to a sword (Haythornthwaite 2001, p.75).

Though successful, the regiment's attack could not be consolidated, as in rapid succession Napier and his deputy were respectively severely injured and killed (meanwhile Sir John Moore himself was mortally wounded). Thus, when the regiment was ordered to withdraw, it was Clunes who gathered its remnants (Holloway 1973, pp.22–23). He was lightly wounded (MacCarthy 1836, p.96). Having avoided defeat, the British army was evacuated from Spain, and eventually returned to achieve victory under Wellington.

Raeburn undertook other portraits of officers and mounts depicting Scots who had served with distinction at Corunna (Sir David Baird and John Hope, 4th Earl of Hopetoun, both more senior than Clunes). It is possible that Raeburn's commissions from these various veterans may have been interrelated. In any case, Clunes was himself well connected in Edinburgh – where the artist practised – through his sister Anne and her husband Joseph Gordon, a writer to the signet. (Clunes's portrait eventually passed to their daughter, also named Anne, who married the celebrated engineer William Siemens.)

By depicting Clunes in a dismounted equestrian portrait, Raeburn invoked a type of picture long-established in depictions of military and royal leadership, horsemanship being a symbol of command. *Major William Clunes* especially recalls a number of paintings by Sir Joshua Reynolds, notably his portrait of George, Prince of Wales, exhibited at the Royal Academy in 1784, in which the heir to the throne was shown in military dress standing by his horse under a dramatic sky; this in turn was closely related to an earlier and highly successful image exhibited in 1766 by the same artist depicting the celebrated general John Manners, Marquis of Granby (Ferrara 2005, pp. 25, 105, repr.). Both works were available as engravings. The pose in which Raeburn has set Clunes's horse, above all, seems a direct visual quotation from the foremost British portraitist of the previous generation.

This borrowing from Reynolds was perhaps not only a compliment to the late master, but reflected a desire to realise the potential financial rewards of Reynoldsian portraiture. For Raeburn was in great need of money during the later part of his career. In addition to his painting, he had embarked on a series of sideline businesses; they seem to have foundered, for in January 1808 he was declared a bankrupt. By the end of that year Raeburn reached an agreement with his creditors – whose total claims came to more than £36,000 – to reimburse them, pledging to 'task the remaining years of his life', until 'the trembling hand of age' overtook him. This burden, together with demand for his work, brought about an increased output of paintings from Raeburn; although consequently haste was to compromise the quality of many of his post-1808 works, the painting depicting William Clunes is an exception to this trend (Thomson 2004, pp. 783–84). SM

# Allan Ramsay

EDINBURGH, 1713 – DOVER, 1784

## 48
*David Hume*

1766
Oil on canvas, 76.2 × 63.5 cm
Inscription on the lower of the two books at bottom right:
*TACITI / OPERA*
Scottish National Portrait Gallery, Edinburgh. PG 1057

PROVENANCE: painted for the sitter; by descent to Mrs Macdonald Hume, who presented it to the National Gallery of Scotland, 1858; subsequently transferred to the Scottish National Portrait Gallery
EXHIBITED: see Smart 1999, p. 139
LITERATURE: Smart 1999, p. 139; Fordham 2006

This portrait shows one of the key figures of what is now known as the Scottish Enlightenment, the philosopher and historian David Hume (1711–1776); its painter, Allan Ramsay, was himself an important contributor to Scotland's cultural distinction at the time.

The connection between artist and sitter was one of long standing. Ramsay had previously painted Hume's portrait in 1754. That same year Ramsay, together with Hume and Adam Smith, launched the Select Society, an Edinburgh debating club. Around the same period Hume had consulted Ramsay on sections of the initial volume of his *History of England*. The success of this work, rather than his philosophical writings, had allowed Hume to become (in his words) 'not only independent, but opulent' (Hume 1985, p. xxxviii). Ramsay's own literary works, notably his *Dialogue on Taste* (1755), were profoundly influenced by Hume (Edinburgh 1992, p. 145). Another aspect of their friendship, as Ramsay acknowledged in 1760, was 'much drinking' (Smart 1952, p. 117).

Ramsay's travels brought him to Paris in the autumn of 1765, where he renewed his friendship with Hume, who was at that time chargé d'affaires at the British embassy. When Hume returned to London the following year, Jean-Jacques Rousseau came with him, seeking refuge in England. The two writers had their portraits undertaken, as a pair, by Ramsay. A mezzotint after the portrait of Hume by Ramsay's assistant David Martin was exhibited at the Society of Artists in 1767. The inscription to this print stated that Ramsay's painting was undertaken in London in 1766; Hume was in the city between January and October.

The focus of light upon Hume's face in the portrait, perhaps indebted to Ramsay's study of Rembrandt, may suggest 'the light of intellect illuminating the surrounding darkness' (Edinburgh 1992, p. 145). The book of Tacitus' works visible at bottom right highlights Hume's eminence as a historian. Hume's description of Tacitus – as a writer 'noted for candour and veracity, and withal, the greatest and most penetrating genius, perhaps of all antiquity; and so free from any imputation to credulity, that he even lies under the contrary imputation, of atheism and profaneness' – might well be taken to apply to himself (Hume 1748, p. 192).

Hume's gaudy tunic has been identified with one which he had worn when assisting the special envoy General James St Clair on his military embassy to Vienna and Turin in 1748 (Edinburgh 1992, p. 145). Lord Charlemont, a student in Turin at the time of Hume's visit, recorded that given the martial nature of St Clair's embassy it was 'thought necessary that his Secretary should appear to be an Officer, and poor Hume was accordingly disguised in Scarlet, while his broad Face was rendered still broader by a smart Wig à la militaire' (Mossner 1980, pp. 208–09, 213).

An anecdote has it that Ramsay showed the image to George III, who 'thought the picture very like, but thought the dress rather too fine', to which the artist replied that he wished 'posterity should see that one philosopher during your Majesty's reign had a good coat upon his back' (Rogers 1874, p. 255). This episode, it has been suggested, may obliquely indicate 'the easy relationship that existed between the King and his favourite painter' (Smart 1992, p. 210). It may also be read from Ramsay's comment that he intended to depict Hume in his capacity as a philosopher (Edinburgh 1992, p. 145). Indeed, Ramsay's remark may have alluded to Rousseau as well as to Hume. His portrait of Rousseau, completed by mid-March 1766, showed the sitter in exotic 'Armenian' garb; it may have been to counterpoint this that Hume was portrayed wearing his spurious 'uniform'. Moreover, the artist had been very much aware of (and was possibly an intermediary in) efforts by Hume to solicit a royal pension for Rousseau. When this was offered to Rousseau in the summer of 1766, he did not accept it, but instead prevaricated. One would-be recipient of a royal pension was Hume – he eventually received £200 in 1768 – and so a possible implication of Ramsay's depiction of him wearing a 'fine scarlet suit' was that 'some philosophers, at least, knew how to appreciate a king's beneficence' (Fordham 2006, pp. 513–14, 517).

Hume and Rousseau had proceeded to fall out in spectacular fashion following the completion of the latter's portrait; disagreements about the image itself, indeed, formed an important aspect in the deterioration of their relationship, with the sitter coming to dislike his representation by Ramsay and to be suspicious of Hume's role in its instigation. The date when Hume's portrait was undertaken during the development of the two men's dispute, and hence its precise polemical terms of reference, remains uncertain. Nevertheless, Ramsay was clearly 'an active participant in the Rousseau–Hume affair', and one possible motivation behind Hume's portrait was 'the desire to salvage Hume's reputation at court following the royal pension debacle'; that Hume later displayed both portraits in his Edinburgh home may suggest that the comparison they offered was one designed to flatter him (Fordham 2006, pp. 508–14). SM

# Christian Daniel Rauch

AROLSEN, 1777 – DRESDEN, 1857

## 127
*Queen Luise of Prussia as the Ludovisi Juno*

1805–06
Marble, 77 × 42 × 40 cm
Skulpturensammlung, Stiftung Preussische Schlösser und Gärten Berlin-Brandenburg, 1015, GK III 4821

PROVENANCE: acquired from the artist
LITERATURE: Sydow 1909, pp. 464ff., p. 467; Grundmann 1950, pp. 86, 91ff., p. 97f., ill. 9; Balty 1989, *passim*; Simson 1990, p. 276f., ill. 4; Simson 1996, pp. 51–53, ill. 52

The colossal head of the *Ludovisi Juno* used to be considered to be one of the greatest works of classical antiquity. After 1622 it was the property of Cardinal Ludovico Ludovisi, hence its name.

Authors such as Johann Joachim Winckelmann wrote extravagant eulogies of this head, describing it as the ideal embodiment of Juno's beauty. Juno was the supreme goddess of the Romans and of the Greeks (who called her Hera), and was held to be the incarnation of majesty and dignity, but also of femininity and motherhood. Friedrich Schiller – following in Winckelmann's wake – describes this head in his fifteenth letter *On the Aesthetic Education of Man in a Series of Letters* (1794), adding his reflections on the grace and dignity of the 'feminine god or the divine woman' (Grundmann 1950, p.96).

Goethe possessed a plaster cast of the celebrated marble head, for which he developed an almost idolatrous passion during his travels in Italy. With the art treasures of Rome in mind, he writes: 'The first place was occupied for us by the *Ludovisi Juno*, specially venerated and appreciated because the original could seldom be seen and then only by chance, and we could only think what good fortune it was to have the head ever before our eyes; of our contemporaries who stood before the head for the first time, no single one of them could claim to have been equal to the experience' (Goethe, *Italian Journey*, second stay in Rome, April 1788). Elsewhere, the writer plays on the ambivalence of the goddess; this colossal head was 'his first love in Rome', he writes, anthropomorphising the piece, and at the same time emphasising and extolling its divine aspects: 'No words can give any idea of it. It is like a lyric from Homer' (Goethe, *Italian Journey*, 6 January 1787).

Thus eulogised, the classical sculpture, widely known through plaster casts and publications, inevitably took on enormous importance in the eyes of other artists and of Goethe's friends, for example Wilhelm von Humboldt. As luck would have it, Humboldt was staying in Rome when the young Christian Daniel Rauch arrived there. Rauch had for years been in the service of Queen Luise, before leaving his position in 1804 to make a journey to Italy, financed by a bursary from the King; in Italy, nearing thirty, he could at last devote himself to the career of sculptor of which he had dreamed for so long. Before then he had been responsible for supporting his family, including his mother and brothers and sisters, who lived in the modest village of Arolsen.

We may suppose that it was his closest mentors, Wilhelm von Humboldt, and his wife Caroline, who drew Rauch's attention to the *Ludovisi Juno*, and pointed out the head's exemplary virtues. By executing the portrait of the Queen whom he had served for so many years, and by imitating the colossal sculpture, the young artist was likening his subject to this mother goddess, and also comparing his own creation to one of the pinnacles of classical sculpture, and himself to the greatest sculptors of antiquity. This ambition, or rather this presumption, may seem astonishing or excessive, particularly as this bust of Queen Luise was one of the first pieces by a relatively

inexperienced artist. Nevertheless, the ambitious sculptor, encouraged by a mentor who was no less ambitious, had good reasons for representing the Queen of Prussia with such very unusual features. There were already numerous portraits at this time of the Queen, who was venerated and loved by her subjects, in particular different busts by Johann Gottfried Schadow, Carl Friedrich Hagemann and Heinrich Sigismund Bettkober. They were all life-size, sometimes smaller; and all were designed on the principle that the Queen had to be represented with realism and nobility, in accordance with her rank, of course, but always as a terrestrial being.

Rauch's portrait is the opposite: it is a transposition rather than a reproduction. The portrait is erased by the message. In an earlier bust of Queen Luise, now lost, Rauch had put the emphasis on the subject's youthful femininity. This time he emphasises her divinity and feminine maturity. The way this herm is portrayed from the front indicates a strong desire to express her grandeur. The fine tunic with little gathers, slightly mechanically modelled perhaps, and the ornamental treatment of the hair do no disservice to the concentrated dignity and noble gravity of the subject. Even if the hair falling over her forehead could seem a little overworked, with sheer imagination, the effect is no more than a game with internal forms dominated by symmetry. The undulations of the hair, divided into two by a centre parting, and the locks falling on the nape of the neck and shoulders are all borrowed from the *Ludovisi Juno*. The diadem perched above the elaborately curled hair is the main concrete reference to the *Ludovisi Juno*, as well as being an element in the Queen's apotheosis. This attribute had certainly been used on earlier busts of the Queen, after 1797, but here the quotation leaves us in no doubt: the *Ludovisi Juno* was Rauch's inspiration for the ornamentation of the diadem, with the alternating five- and seven-branched palmettes.

The forms of the classical sculpture make a relatively coherent, calm impression, while Rauch's piece seems more profoundly tormented, and the details are much more intensively worked over. The artist could not have achieved this result without exceptional effort: he clearly wanted to outdo the classical model's fine carving, hoping to demonstrate a technique that was superior to that of any other sculptor before him. It is not surprising, therefore, that Caroline von Humboldt was moved to assert that the bust was 'beautiful, and very, very painstakingly carved'. However, she added (with a wink?): 'About the resemblance, I am less well equipped to judge' (Sydow 1909, p.465), implying that she had her doubts about the accuracy of the likeness. Whether consciously or intuitively, Caroline von Humboldt stated that Rauch had in this case created an ideal vision of classical inspiration, but had not made an individual portrait.

Although King Friedrich-Wilhelm III did not find the portrait a very convincing likeness, after the unexpected death of the Queen in 1810, the bust was temporarily installed on her tomb in Charlottenburg. Rauch had not yet produced the marble version: he carved it down to the last detail in Rome and sent it to Berlin. Soon afterwards he received a commission for the recumbent statue of the Queen for her tomb. This time he obviously did not represent Luise as Juno, but delved into the traditions of devotional art, using Marian iconography. This was in tune with the spirit of the age all over Europe; from its classical roots, art was gradually moving towards the Christian traditions of the romantic period. BM

## 58
*Johann Wolfgang von Goethe*

1823
Plaster, 42 × 34 × 14 cm
Inscription, below the seat on the right: *1823./ 26 Ocb*
Inscription, lower back: *D. 26. OCTOBER 23*
Staatliche Museen zu Berlin, Nationalgalerie, RM 14

## 59
*Johann Wolfgang von Goethe*

1824
Plaster, 46 × 34 × 14 cm
Inscription, below seat on the left: *4.JUNI 1824*
Staatliche Museen zu Berlin, Nationalgalerie, RM 15

PROVENANCE: artist's studio; in the Christian Daniel Rauch Museum, Bad Arolsen, since 1865
EXHIBITED: Berlin, 1979, no.333, with illustrations
LITERATURE: Eggers 1877, p.6, nos 12–13; Eggers 1889, *passim*; Eggers 1892, p.7, nos 14–15; Otten 1976, pp.73, 134–36, ill. 185–96; Fritze 1980; Simson 1996, pp.206–10, with illustrations; Maaz 2006, pp.489–90, with illustrations

Monuments of important personalities used often to be erected posthumously. Friedrich II, for example, refused to be 'immortalised' during his lifetime. Johann Gottfried Schadow recommended that portrait busts should be executed from a live model, as this made it possible to obtain an authentic likeness. He was probably thinking that a portrait bust could be the basis of a later monument. This is certainly what happened in 1820, when Christian Daniel Rauch modelled the portrait of Goethe (1749–1832): the bust was completed in the space of a few days and was known as a bust *a tempo*. It portrays the sitter with a grave expression and a bare chest. Executed as it was from life, this slightly heroic portrait became immediately celebrated and was reproduced in many different versions, in plaster, marble, bronze, alabaster and porcelain. It could be used as a base when the plan for a monument to Goethe's memory was conceived.

The project dated back to 1819: Goethe was approaching his seventieth birthday. A group of admirers hatched a plan to erect a monument to him during his lifetime, in his birthplace, Frankfurt-am-Main. As public space was reserved for full-length portraits of rulers and military leaders, the committee decided to erect a monument in the shape of a temple. At the outset, a bust was planned, to be decorated with a frieze on the theme of Goethe's epic poem, *Hermann and Dorothea* of 1798. The committee responsible for planning and executing the project included various art connoisseurs, Sulpiz Boisserée and the banker and politician Simon Moritz von Bethmann among them.

In 1822 Rauch was commissioned to make a marble statue, although it was not specified whether it should portray the poet standing or seated. The committee was no longer thinking of the temple by this stage, another plan had been proposed: the erection of the statue in the open air. Rauch had not been briefed about the costume the poet should be wearing either. He first submitted a model for a full-length statue, which can still be seen in a small version in Weimar: it shows Goethe holding a large wreath in his left hand (he had already been awarded the crown of laurels), his body wrapped in a tunic and toga. His right hand is supported on an elaborately carved tripod, vital for stabilising the projected marble statue. After this first statue, the plan changed course again: Rauch delivered three versions of a seated statue, all three of them rough sketches.

Over fifty years later, when the contents of Rauch's studio, which had been divided amongst museums, were inventoried by Friedrich Eggers in a printed catalogue, Eggers described the three maquettes of the portrait (which were still in Berlin) clearly and concisely: 'Rough model of the statue of Goethe seated. Project of 1823. Goethe on a seat, wearing a toga, also covering his right hand, which is placed on his knees; left shoulder and arm naked, the arm resting on the armrest, the hand on his heart; the right leg behind, the left in front, the head turned towards the right' (Eggers 1877, p.6). Eggers mentions all the limbs, and all the elements of the costume, because he has to convey, through his comparative descriptions, to the visitor to the museum and the reader of the catalogue the aspects that distinguish the three preliminary maquettes from one another: 'Second model of the statue of Goethe seated. Project of 1824. Same pose as in the previous number. A tunic has been added under the toga; the toga covers the left arm, the left hand holds a book, whereas the right hand holds a pencil' (Eggers 1877, no.13).

Although a year had passed between their design, the two projects are extremely similar. Rauch did not reproduce everything in the second version, however. He used an existing composition that he thought suitable, reworking only the details. The details are extremely important, in fact, and are more than just iconographic attributes. As so often in classical sculpture, Rauch takes his inspiration from antiquity in this seated portrait. Friedrich Tieck, who worked in the same studio as Rauch, in 1822 prepared a seated portrait of August Wilhelm Iffland for the Schauspielhaus in Berlin (destroyed during the Second World War). Tieck's seated portrait became a model for sculpture in Berlin: it was inspired by antiquity, heroic in style with a semi-naked chest, the arm enveloped in drapery, one leg forward with a sandaled foot, the other leg folded backwards on the plinth and the head turned to one side.

It is hardly surprising that Rauch wanted to try the same composition, because the reference implicit in archaeological sources was just as suitable for the planned monument to the glory of Goethe as it was for the seated portrait of *Wilhelm Iffland*: the tradition goes back to the classical seated portraits of Chrysippus, Menander (today identified as a consul) and Pindar, in other words, to representations of great philosophers and poets. It was not primarily the seated French portraits of the eighteenth and nineteenth centuries then – Jean-Antoine Houdon's *Voltaire*, Louis-Simon Boizot's *Racine*, Jean-Jacques Caffieri's *Molière*, or, at a later date, the *Talma* by David d'Angers – that perpetuated this pose in German classicism, but rather the classical tradition.

The statuette was cast in bronze in 1824, probably by the Castner foundry. Rauch's main concern must have been that such an important subject should be executed in a durable material as soon as possible.

Rauch executed a third and final plaster maquette for the seated portrait of Goethe. It is now in the Nationalgalerie, Berlin, in fragmentary form. The design is a sort of amalgamation of the two previous projects. Rauch modelled it in a smaller format than the two earlier versions; this final model was nevertheless also cast in bronze. The artist chose classical dress again: it was considered to be the ideal antithesis, both to the various modern outfits with their fussy, realistic details, and to uniforms with their narrative message – which he had had to use in his full-length portraits of military leaders in Berlin, but for which he in fact had a certain disdain.

Only this third and final version obtained the full approval of both Goethe and his artistic adviser in Weimar. None of Rauch's projects was ever realised, for various reasons: public opinion – or rather the participation of the romantic poet Bettina von Arnim in the design of the monument (she had a very different and somewhat eccentric design in mind, with an allegorical display) – and also the fact that Rauch's studio was already overwhelmed with large orders. The death of Bethmann in 1826 robbed the project of one of its most energetic supporters. This explains why it never came to fruition.

It was not until five years after Goethe's death that the idea was revived in Frankfurt, and that a committee was formed for the erection of a monument. Bertel Thorvaldsen was one of the first people to be consulted, but his design, which he submitted somewhat late, did not meet with the approval of the committee. The bronze monument by Ludwig Michael Schwanthaler was executed between 1841 and 1844 and is still *in situ* today. It consists of a silhouette of the poet, ludicrously elongated in height, wearing contemporary dress and standing on a plinth on which are engraved romantic reliefs illustrating his works. This is very far from the classical vision inspired by antiquity proposed by Rauch. The narrative reliefs carved on the plinth of Schwanthaler's monument, with their genre figures, belong firmly to the romantic spirit of the age; only a few details, such as the roll of paper and the laurel wreath held in the hands of the standing figure, are borrowed from Rauch's repertoire.

After his statue of Goethe, planned for Frankfurt but never erected, Rauch displayed his continuing interest in the personality of the poet, and his belief in the importance of this prince among poets from Weimar, executing in 1828 the famous statue of Goethe 'in his dressing gown', soon to become one of the bestsellers of the nineteenth-century industry of copying art. It shows the poet standing with his hands crossed behind his back, as he would have been at home, pacing up and down the study from which he dictated thousands of letters and even whole novels: this is Goethe as a living person and not a representation, speaking rather than lost in thought, a contemporary physical being rather than a timeless antiquity. The type of statuette chosen by Rauch this time was thoroughly in tune with the realist spirit of the times.

On inspecting the first version of this statuette Goethe found himself too fat (a problem that had not arisen with the seated portrait). Rauch's pupil Ernst Rietschel had to travel to Weimar to reduce the poet's girth, in accordance with his wishes. The choice of this type of representation was not questioned by the poet of Weimar, who was by this time very old. In order to give the statuette a more solemn aspect, and as a kind of profession of faith, Rauch added some details that were most unusual for the period: the plinth was adorned on all four sides and on the corners with masks and little scenes from the works of Goethe. Thus the representation gained a literary and narrative component, just as might be seen on the plinth of an official monument. The idea of the seated portrait was certainly very classical and conventional by comparison. The juxtaposition of all the different designs proposed by Rauch suggests that by about 1830 purely classical forms were already out of date. BM

# Jean-Baptiste Régnault

PARIS, 1754 – PARIS, 1829

## 121
### The Physical Man, the Moral Man and the Intellectual Man

*c.*1810
Oil on canvas, 159 × 131 cm
Musée des Beaux-Arts, Brest, 72.5-1

PROVENANCE: retained by the artist until his death; bequeathed to his children; estate sale of his son Antoine-Louis Régnault, Paris, 24 January 1857 (no.32); bought back by the family; acquired by the Musée des Beaux-Arts, Brest, 1972
EXHIBITED: Paris, 1974A, no.151 (J.-P. Cuzin); Besançon, 2005

Jean-Baptiste Régnault was fond of allegory as a genre throughout his career; his celebrated *Liberty or Death*, exhibited at the Salon of 1795 and now in the Kunsthalle, Hamburg, bears witness to this. This painting, which belongs to a hybrid genre, is a further example. The artist has depicted himself in the foreground – comparing this work with his self-portraits leaves us in no doubt about this. Probably aged about fifty, he figures in the centre of a complex composition in which the portrait genre is transcended by the use of allegory.

In his will, the artist, who seems to have held this work in particular esteem, insists that it should remain in the family 'until such time as circumstances permit it to be made known, and turned to good account'. The portrait is obviously a profession of faith, linked to the idea of the imminent advent of a society in which it might be understood; Régnault's gesture gives some idea of the didactic intention of the image, whose meaning is supplied by the title given in the will: 'The physical man, the moral man and the intellectual man.'

In the catalogue to the exhibition entitled 'De David à Delacroix', Jean-Pierre Cuzin decodes the complex iconography of the painting and arrives at a Masonic interpretation. The main figure represents the initiate surrounded by the instruments of scientific enquiry (the retort, the globe, the astronomical telescope) and of the liberal arts (the musical instrument, the laurel wreath), all essential for the freemason. In the centre, the peacock symbolises immortality (as it has done since classical times). The group on the right consists of two women protecting two children, an allusion to mutual help, one of masonry's basic virtues. Behind this group a man wearing a mitre (a priest?) holds out a threatening dagger, while beside him two grimacing figures brandish a broken mirror and a mask: these three constitute an allegory of obscurantism and the moral blindness of religion. The upper part of the painting is occupied by a group dominated by the figure of the Supreme Being, crowned with nine stars. He is accompanied by two female figures, one veiled (associated with Isis) and the other armed with a hammer (an allusion to freemasonry).

The use of allegory in a portrait is often a means of elevating this inferior genre and conferring new dignity on the sitter, thus transcending the basic idea of imitation; such use of allegory was a particularly effective way to give a historical twist to female portraits, since women by their nature lacked the male attributes of political or social action. In this case, as in James Barry's painting *Burke and Barry in the Characters of Ulysses and a Companion Fleeing from the Cave of Polyphemus* (cat.122), this usage, particularly associated with the self-portrait, has a completely different significance: it is a profession of faith with, in this particular work, an anticipated didactic message. AA

# Sir Joshua Reynolds

PLYMPTON, 1723 – LONDON, 1792

## 38
### Sir Jeffrey Amherst

1765
Oil on canvas, 125.7 × 100.3 cm
Numerous inscriptions on the map at the bottom of the image entitled 'Plan *of the Island of* Montreal *& its* Environs'
Mead Art Museum, Amherst College, Amherst 1967.85

PROVENANCE: by descent to Lord Amherst 1956; acquired by Amherst College, 1967
EXHIBITED: Society of Artists, 1766, no.138; for later exhibition history see Mannings and Postle 2000, vol.1, p.60
LITERATURE: Trapp 1986, pp.4–5, 11; New York 1988, pp.21–22; Mannings and Postle 2000, vol.1, p.60

Sir Joshua Reynolds's portrait commemorates the greatest success of his sitter, the general Sir Jeffrey Amherst (1717–1797): the conquest of Canada. Amherst, appointed commander-in-chief of the British army in North America in September 1758, won a string of victories culminating in his carefully planned invasion of Canada in 1760. Amherst's forces converged on Montreal, where the French governor-general, the Marquis de Vaudreuil, attempted to play for time by proposing a truce. Amherst refused, declaring: 'I have come to take Canada, and I will take nothing less' (Long 1933, p.133). Vaudreuil surrendered New France on 8 September 1760.

The landscape beyond Amherst, it has been suggested, 'reflects the actual terrain that had to be traversed, as Amherst's forces were transported down the rapids of the St Lawrence towards Montreal' in canoes. One of Amherst's officers, Thomas Davies, made a wash drawing illustrating this operation. This survives, and bears Reynolds's own collector's stamp, indicating that it may be directly associated with the completed portrait (Trapp 1986, pp.11, 13, repr.; New York 1988, p.22).

The map at the bottom of the image, entitled 'Plan *of the Island of* Montreal *& its* Environs', also refers to the campaign. On this map rest both Amherst's helmet and his baton of command, whose upward line is continued in his right forearm

and hand, visually linking his head to his successful military plans. His ungloved right hand may suggest that he has laid down the gauntlet of challenge, or perhaps alludes to the readiness to 'shake the hand of his defeated opponent' which has been detected in another portrait of a military hero, *John Manners, Marquis of Granby*, displayed by Reynolds at the same 1766 exhibition at which *Sir Jeffrey Amherst* was shown (Postle, in Ferrara 2005, p.104).

Conspicuous endorsement of Amherst's leadership is given by the diagonal line of coloured ribbon which runs across his costume and the badge on his breastplate: these are the insignia of a Knight of the Order of the Bath, to which order Amherst was elevated in 1761 in recognition of his military achievements. This chivalric honour – which gives a degree of narrative warrant to Amherst's armour-clad depiction by Reynolds – was in fact one which Amherst had not wished for, considering it an inadequate distinction (Long 1933, pp.150–51). Amherst returned from America in late 1763, and his later career proved something of an anticlimax. As well as sitting to Reynolds in May and June 1765, he also commemorated his most famous victory by having his family seat at Riverhead, Kent, demolished and replaced with a new house named 'Montreal'.

By exhibiting Amherst's portrait, Reynolds was able to strengthen his self-presentation strategy. As one scholar has noted, the artist profited from 'exploiting the public's jingoistic interest in military heroes' (Postle, in Ferrara 2005, p.39). When it was shown in 1766, the qualities of Reynolds's image were extolled in newspaper reports. One reviewer exulted: 'I know not from whose Genius I shall steal Applause equal to the Merit of this Piece', and acclaimed that 'this Picture is every Thing a Portrait should be' (*Public Advertiser*, 28 April 1766). SM

## 56
### Joseph Banks

1771–73
Not signed or dated
Inscription on the paper beneath the sitter's left hand: *Cras Ingens Iterabimus aequor* ('tomorrow we will sail the high seas again'; Horace, *Odes*, I, vii, 32)
Oil on canvas, 127 × 101.5 cm
National Portrait Gallery, London, NPG 5868

PROVENANCE: the sitter's wife, Dorothea, Lady Banks; passed to the family of her brother-in-law, Sir Edward Knatchbull, 8th baronet; by descent to Sir Wyndham Knatchbull, 12th baronet; his cousin, Cecil Marcus, 4th Baron Brabourne of Mersham-le-Hatch, from whom bought, 1918, by Weetman Pearson, 1st Viscount Cowdray; his son, Clive Pearson of Parham Park; by descent to Clive Gibson, from whom purchased by private treaty sale through Agnew's in 1986 by the National Portrait Gallery with the aid of the National Heritage Memorial Fund, the National Art Collections Fund and The Pilgrim Trust
EXHIBITED: Royal Academy, 1773, no.239; for later exhibition history see Ingamells 2004, p.26
LITERATURE: see Ingamells 2004, p.26

Reynolds began this portrait of Joseph Banks (1743–1820) in late 1771, at a time when the sitter was celebrated for his participation in Captain Cook's *Endeavour* voyage to the Pacific from 1768 to 1771.

Having inherited a fortune on his father's death in 1761, Banks had dedicated himself to the pursuit of natural history. First intrigued by the subject as a schoolboy at Eton College (1756–60), he went on to Oxford University. On finding that the professor of botany, Dr Humphrey Sidthorp, was unwilling to teach, Banks himself sponsored a substitute series of lectures by the Cambridge botanist Israel Lyons. Having further consolidated his studies in London, Banks put his skills to use for the first time on a voyage to Labrador and Newfoundland from 1766 to 1767; during his absence he was elected a fellow of the Royal Society.

Banks later remarked that, while other young men were touring France and Italy, he was touring the globe (Tobin 1999, p.87). He joined the *Endeavour* expedition at his own expense, bought its scientific equipment, and hired the services of the Linnaean botanist Daniel Solander and specialist draughtsmen. The main aim of the journey was to observe the transit of Venus at Tahiti; the expedition then turned south to circumnavigate New Zealand before continuing to the east coast of Australia. Around 1,400 plant species new to science were classified, and examples of over 1,000 animal species were collected (Carter 1988, p.95). As one biographer notes, this journey of discovery 'lifted Banks from the ranks of gentlemen naturalists to become a figure of international scientific significance'; on his return, he received 'a rapturous welcome which overshadowed that of Cook himself' (Gascoigne 2004, p.692). Banks became a subject of society gossip (not least owing to stories of his liaisons with Tahitian women and of the unrequited love of a Miss Harriet Blosset); he was presented to the King at court; and he received an honorary doctorate from Oxford University.

Reynolds's portrait, and another undertaken by Benjamin West at around the same time showing Banks with exotic artefacts, may have been undertaken for Banks's uncle (and one-time guardian) Robert Banks-Hodgkinson (1722–1792) (Carter 1988, p.99; Ingamells 2004, p.26). Both images were exhibited at the Royal Academy in 1773 and engraved for the print market. In Reynolds's representation, Banks is 'epitomised as the restless traveller' (Joppien 1994, p.89). His role in intrepid exploration is highlighted by the conspicuous globe: if the topography displayed is unclear, this may reflect the artist's intention to suggest his sitter's engagement with the world's 'dimly apprehended, uttermost parts' (Cameron 1952, p.60). The globe also visually links Banks to the seascape vista through the window – a prospect made all the more immediate by the window's apparent lack of glazing. Reynolds drew on a tradition of representations of scholarly contemplation (Fortune 1999, p.24). But

Banks's pose is an active one: leaning forward towards the viewer, he appears about to push himself up from his chair with his right hand in a stance that may derive from Rembrandt's *The Syndics* (1662) (Shawe-Taylor 1990, p.94). His left hand draws the audience's attention to papers on his desk, one bearing the inscription '*cras ingens iterabimus aequor*' (tomorrow we will sail the high seas again). Mistakenly identified by Banks, in a letter to his sister Sarah Sophia Banks, as 'taken from a part of Virgil's Eneid' – the correct source for the quotation is Horace's *Odes* – this motto refers both to Bank's recent enterprise with Cook and perhaps also to the invitation he received to join Cook's second Pacific voyage in 1772 (Ingamells 2004, p.26).

Banks in fact withdrew from this fresh venture, organising a shorter scientific expedition to Iceland instead. His final sittings to Reynolds for this image came in 1773, following a further brief trip to Holland. This was his last foray abroad; by the time of this portrait's completion Banks was turning his energies homewards, establishing himself in a leading position in science. From 1773, under the King's patronage, he transformed the Royal Botanic Gardens at Kew from royal pleasure grounds into a major scientific centre. Banks later became the longest-serving President of the Royal Society (1778–1820), and was created a baronet in 1781. SM

## 125
### *The Montgomery Sisters:* 'Three Ladies Adorning a Term of Hymen'

1773
Not signed or dated
Oil on canvas, 233.7 × 290.8 cm
Tate, London, N00079. Bequeathed by the Earl of Blessington, 1837

PROVENANCE: Luke Gardiner; by descent to Charles John Gardiner, 1st Earl of Blessington (died 1829), who bequeathed it to the National Gallery, London (received 1837); transferred to the Tate Gallery, 1968
EXHIBITED: Royal Academy, 1774, no.216; for later exhibition history see Mannings and Postle 2000, vol.1, p.340
LITERATURE: see Mannings and Postle 2000, vol.1, p.340

Reynolds's painting shows the three daughters of William Montgomery (who was created a baronet in 1775) and Hannah Tomkyns; from left to right they are Barbara (*c*.1757–1788), Elizabeth (1751–1783), and Anne (*c*.1752–1819). Barbara kneels by a flower basket and holds the end of a garland of flowers. Elizabeth, with one knee on a gilt stool, raises the garland to Anne, who stands holding it aloft in order to decorate the statue of Hymen, Greek god of marriage, that looms above them.

The painting was made for a wealthy Irishman, Luke Gardiner (1745–1798), who married Elizabeth Montgomery. By the time Gardiner purchased this 450 guinea work he had already shown himself to be a significant art patron. When in Rome during his Grand Tour of 1770–72, he had commissioned a history painting from Gawen Hamilton. In 1773

he was elected to the Society of Dilettanti, an exclusive group of connoisseurs of which Reynolds was a leading light; also that year, he became an Irish MP (Coleman 1999, pp.163–64).

Gardiner had recently had his own portrait undertaken by Reynolds when, on 27 May 1773, a week before his marriage, he wrote to the artist from Dublin explaining that his future wife and her two sisters would be coming to sit for their portrait. He explained that he wanted an image 'representing some emblematical or historical subject; the idea of which, and the attitudes which will best suit their forms, cannot be so well imagined as by one who has so eminently distinguished himself by his genius and poetic invention'.

A few months later Reynolds replied with thanks 'for the agreeable employment in which you have engaged me', and described the picture (Northcote 1813, pp.185–87), which was by then well underway, sittings having begun in June:

> You have already been informed, I have no doubt, of the subject which we have chosen; the adorning of a Term of Hymen with festoons of flowers. This affords sufficient employment to the figures, and gives an opportunity of introducing a variety of graceful historical attitudes. I have every inducement to exert myself on this occasion … I flatter myself that, however inferior the picture may be to what I wish it, or what it ought, it will be the best picture I ever painted.

Making the immediate subject of the picture the worship of the god of marriage was wholly fitting given the occasion for Gardiner's commission, and the fact that his new wife's sisters were also of marriageable age (eight days before Gardiner wrote to Reynolds with his commission, Anne Montgomery had married, becoming Viscountess Townshend). Within the image, indeed, the sisters are positioned in relation to Hymen in accordance with their proximity to marriage. Critics at the time noted as much when the painting was exhibited at the Royal Academy in 1774: 'the married Lady has the principal employment; the second (who was then going to be married, and is since Mrs. Gardner [*sic*]) is assisting her at a distance, and the other supplying them with flowers' (*Morning Chronicle*, 28 April 1774). Barbara Montgomery married later that year.

Reynolds's thematic conception for the picture served the purposes of portrait narrative while also operating at the level of a broader statement. As he had declared in his fourth Discourse (1771), 'if a portrait painter is desirous to raise and improve his subject, he has no other means than by approaching it to a general idea' (Reynolds 1997, p.72; Pointon 1997A, p.60). The women's pseudo-classical clothing, too, is deliberately generalised. Flowing clothing also drew attention to the 'natural' female body; and that the women are here placed in a natural setting intimates a symbolic correlation between woman and nature (Perry 1994, p.29). As one newspaper account of Reynolds's 1774 portrait exhibits asserted: 'while some Artists paint only to this age and this nation, he paints to all ages and all nations; and he may justly say with the Artist of old, *In aeternitatem pingo*' (*London Chronicle*, 7–10 May 1774). This commentary was itself a paraphrase of Reynolds's prescription for the ideal artist in his third Discourse in 1770 (Postle 1995, pp. 51–52).

Invoking an allegorical context also placed the painting in a tradition of representations. Reynolds himself had previously essayed the garlanding of a term of Hymen in a single female portrait, *Elizabeth Keppel* (1761–62); in devising his much more ambitious undertaking for Gardiner, another important stimulus was probably Joseph-Marie Vien's *Proserpine Garlanding a Statue of Her Mother Ceres*, which was shown at the Salon of 1757, and re-exhibited (possibly in a variant form) at the Salon of 1763 (Paris 1985, pp. 49–50, repr.). The most direct visual cross-reference, however, is to an image illustrating an unrelated theme: the poses of Barbara Montgomery and Elizabeth Gardiner are taken from an engraving of a *Sleeping Silenus* by Michael Natalis after Francesco Romanelli; this visual quotation was identified (and criticised for its directness) by Reynolds's contemporary Nathaniel Hone in 1775 (Paris 1985, pp. 262, 350–52, repr.). Among the various sources adduced for Lady Townshend's pose, Poussin's *The Triumph of Pan* (National Gallery, London), which also includes the festooning of a term, has found much favour (Gombrich 1942; Mannings and Postle 2000, vol. 1, pp. 340–41).

A pair of sketches relating to the painting survive; since from Reynolds's letter to Gardiner it seems the latter was not involved in the choice of design, these works were probably prepared either to canvass the sitters' approval for the composition, or to assist the artist (Paris 1985, pp. 328–29, repr.). SM

## 25
## Mary, Countess of Bute

c. 1777–79
Not signed or dated
Inscribed at bottom left: *MARY WORTLEY MONTAGU, COUNTESS OF BUTE*; and at the bottom right: *REYNOLDS*
Oil on canvas, 236 × 145 cm
Private collection, Mount Stuart

PROVENANCE: by descent
EXHIBITED: see Mannings and Postle 2000, vol. 1, p. 438
LITERATURE: see Mannings and Postle 2000, vol. 1, p. 438

The subject of this portrait, Mary, Countess of Bute (1718–1794), was born in Turkey during the embassy to Constantinople of her father, Edward Wortley Montagu. Her mother, Lady Mary Wortley Montagu, was famed as a proponent of inoculation against smallpox, and especially as a writer (the recipient of many of her celebrated *Letters* was her daughter). Mary the younger married John Stuart, 3rd Earl of Bute, in 1736, although he was not her father's favoured choice; indeed, he withheld her

expected dowry. Despite this Bute was reported by one contemporary, Eleanor Verney, to have 'shewed himself a man of Honour' by saying that 'he liked the young Lady and if she would be content to live in Scotland he would marry her, she said, any where rather than stay with her Mother' (Grundy 1999, p. 327). The two spent the opening years of their marriage at Bute's home, Mount Stuart, on the Isle of Bute. Horace Walpole was not a fan of Lady Mary Wortley Montagu, but in 1761 he described her daughter as 'one of the best and most sensible women in the world, and who educated by such a mother, or rather with no education, has never made a false step' (Walpole 1937–82, vol. 21, p. 472). The Butes' marriage was a successful one, and they had five sons and six daughters.

On her father's death in 1761, an immense fortune amounting to around £50,000 per year came to Lady Bute for her life interest (it subsequently passed to her second son, James), and thereafter she effectively bankrolled much of the family's expenditure. This included, it would seem, the 1762 purchase (and subsequent renovation) of Luton Park, Bedfordshire, the mansion which came to house her portrait by Reynolds. While her husband assembled a library and an art collection of rare distinction, Lady Bute herself eventually collected 'above 6 thousand Capital' shells (Russell 2004, pp. 44, 62, 121). The political fortunes of the family, meanwhile, were rapidly advanced following the accession to the throne of George III, who had been tutored by Bute. Lady Bute was created Baroness Mount Stuart of Wortley in the peerage of Great Britain in 1761 (her husband, a Scottish peer, was not automatically entitled to sit in the House of Lords, and Lady's Bute's new title ensured that their descendants would do so). Ultimately, from 1762 to 1763, Lord Bute served as Prime Minister. Criticised for being the King's favourite, Bute proved extremely unpopular, and eventually insisted on retiring from office.

Even after his resignation, Bute remained a powerful figure in art patronage. Reynolds had apparently been a friend of Lady Bute's mother (their connection is suggested by the survival of a ring inscribed from her to him dated 1762, the year of her death) (Grundy 1999, pp. 620–21). Bute, however, had long lent his influential support to the established Scottish artist Allan Ramsay rather than his younger rival Reynolds. Indeed, it seems that Reynolds himself took steps to cultivate his acquaintance with Bute in 1763. When Lord Eglinton requested Bute to sit to Reynolds for his portrait that year, it was reported that Reynolds himself had orchestrated the request. The painting which resulted, a double portrait of Bute and his secretary, Charles Jenkinson, was apparently completed in late 1763 (after Bute had ceased to be Prime Minister). When the monarch was shown this impressive image of his favourite, he insisted on buying it himself. Aside from furthering his profile at court, Reynolds's first brush with Bute seems to

have helped make the artist an obvious choice for later Bute commissions. Ramsay's career effectively drew to a close in 1773; that same year, Reynolds painted Bute again, and it was presumably to serve as a pendant to this image that Lady Bute's portrait was later commissioned. The images are of the same size and both cost the standard 150 guineas which Reynolds charged for whole-lengths at this period (the fee for Lady Bute's picture was paid from her account at Coutts bank & Co. in 1786). By 1799, and probably well before then, the two works were hung above chimneypieces at either end of the Saloon in the centre of their Luton Park residence. Reynolds also undertook a pair of portraits of the Butes' eldest son, John, Lord Mountstuart, around 1775 (Whitley 1928, vol. 1, pp. 252–54; Mannings and Postle 2000, vol. 1, pp. 437–38; Russell 2004, pp. 53–55, 77, 103, 194–95).

Reynolds's 1773 portrait of Lord Bute had showed him in his Garter robes. No mere formulaic counterpart to her husband's image, the contrastingly informal portrait of Lady Bute shows her walking outdoors. She wears an open silk robe and train with a ruched trimming, a fashionably wide skirt with hip pads, and a black silk hooded cloak edged with black spotted net. She also carries a parasol (used throughout the eighteenth century by women to protect the complexion from the elements, but only rarely shown in portraits) (Paris 1985, p. 292). The attendant dog may be a symbol of fidelity, drawing attention to the absence of her husband (Lady Bute had, in fact, long exercised an unusual degree of independent responsibility over her family's affairs). Three sittings to Reynolds are recorded in 1777, two more in 1779, and another in 1780; the artist's records contain gaps during the years 1774–76, 1778 and 1783–85, thus the dating of the image to 1777–79 may be incomplete. Certainly, the portrait was partially reworked at some stage, for a large urn and pedestal initially painted in the background at the upper left were painted over with trees, presumably because either the artist or his patrons found them unsatisfactory; deterioration in the pigment has since revealed these details once more. SM

## 2
## George III

1779
Oil on canvas, 277.4 × 185.5 cm
Royal Academy of Arts, London, 03/1303

PROVENANCE: presented to the Royal Academy of Arts by George III
EXHIBITED: see Mannings and Postle 2000, vol. 1, p. 214
LITERATURE: see Mannings and Postle 2000, vol. 1, p. 214

## 3
## Queen Charlotte

1779–80
Oil on canvas, 278.2 × 185.7 cm
Royal Academy of Arts, London, 03/1304

PROVENANCE: presented to the Royal Academy of
Arts by George III
EXHIBITED: see Mannings and Postle 2000, vol. 1, p. 214
LITERATURE: see Mannings and Postle 2000, vol. 1, p. 214

Reynolds undertook this pair of portraits of
George III (1738–1820) and Queen Charlotte
(1744–1818) so as to adorn the Royal Academy's
new apartments at Somerset House, a former royal
palace. Given the sovereign's role in establishing the
institution in 1768, and then in providing it with
its splendid new base, it was a prerequisite that
his portrait and that of his consort should occupy
pride of place in the Academicians' Council Room.
The public were able to see the royal portraits
when the Academy opened for the inaugural
annual exhibition at its new building in 1780. In
such circumstances, as one quasi-official guidebook
to the Academy that year trumpeted, the institution
could but attract 'the attention of the world; and
while they stand astonished at the excellence to
which it has arisen, they remember, with gratitude
and rapture, that they are indebted to your Majesty
for its foundation' (Candid Review 1780, pp. i–ii;
Hallett 2001, p. 72).

This guide also gave particulars of
Reynolds's portraits, describing how the King
was shown 'in the Coronation Chair in *Westminster
Hall*, with all the insignia of Royalty'. (He wears
robes of state, and bears the sceptre in his right
hand; St Edward's Crown is on a cushion at the
left of the image.) The Queen, it was noted, was
'also drawn sitting in the Chair of State, and drest
in her royal robes'. (Her sceptre lies on a cushion
in front of her.) While claiming that the portrayal
of the King was 'the most agreeable impression
of his Majesty of any portrait which has yet been
done', when judging the Queen's portrait this
account allowed that the 'likeness' was 'strong'
but suggested that 'there wants that graceful ease
which generally characterises the portraits of
*Sir Joshua*' (Candid Review 1780, p. 10; Millar 1969,
vol. 1, p. 107).

When even a generally obsequious account
such as this was prepared to hint at criticism, it
is not surprising that some other commentators
on Reynolds's images proved more scathing.
One newspaper declared: 'whether it be owing
to that profusion of ornament, and that glare of
magnificence which are seen in the royal robes, we
will not attempt to decide, but certain it is, that
these paintings have not captivated us in an equal
degree with some others in a more plain and simple
style' (*London Courant*, 4 May 1780). Another press
review punned that it would quite openly criticise
Reynolds's portraits of the King and Queen 'were
it not likely to be deemed high treason against the
*Prince of Painters*' (*Morning Post*, 2 May 1780; Ferrara
2005, p. 33, note 47).

One particular difficulty that Reynolds's pair
faced when first put on show in 1780 was that they
were upstaged by another pair of royal portraits,
by Benjamin West, which formed part of the

Academy's annual exhibition that year (Hoock
2003, pp. 152–54).

More generally, that the paintings were
deemed deficient may also relate to difficulties
in Reynolds's relationship with the court. Horace
Walpole annotated his copy of *A Candid Review*
with the observation that: 'This was the first time
the King had sat to Sir Joshua, tho' numberless
times to other painters' (Whitley 1928, vol. 1,
pp. 254–55). (As Prince of Wales, however, he
had sat to Reynolds in 1759.) Reynolds had four
appointments with the King which have been
identified as likely sittings between late April
and late May 1779; and with the Queen he had
four appointments in December 1779 and another
in April 1780 (Mannings and Postle 2000, vol. 1,
p. 214). According to later remarks attributed to
Reynolds's pupil James Northcote, the upshot
of the sitting for these portraits was that 'The King
and Queen could not endure the presence of him;
he was poison to their sight' (Whitley 1928, vol. 1,
pp. 255–56). The royal couple never sat to
Reynolds again.

Reynolds's poor relations with the court were
of long standing. Samuel Johnson's remarks on
the matter were recorded in 1764: 'It has ever been
more profitable to be popular among the people
than favoured by the King: it is no reflection on
Mr. Reynolds not to be employed by them; but
it will be a reflection on the Court not to have
employed him.' Benjamin West later reported that
the King 'entertained a prejudice against Reynolds'
as a result of the artist's having at first hesitated
when he was offered the post of President of the
Royal Academy, taking advice from Johnson and
Edmund Burke before accepting. In the course of
the 1770s, moreover, Reynolds came increasingly
to be identified with the King's Whig political
opponents (Postle 2001, pp. 108–19). It has been
remarked that George III's attitude to Reynolds
was characterised by 'personal, political and
artistic aversion' (Hoock 2003, pp. 167–68).

Reynolds's paintings of the royal pair were
first mentioned in catalogues for the Academy's
annual exhibitions in 1811, when they were described
as having been 'presented to the Royal Academy by
its most Gracious Founder'; a note in Reynolds's
ledgers records a payment of 400 guineas for 'His
Majesty and the Queen' which probably refers to
the payment for the images. The paired portraits
became the official images of the King and
Queen when Reynolds succeeded Allan Ramsay
as Principal Painter to the King in 1784, with
numerous replicas produced in the artist's studio
(a procedure which was continued after Reynolds's
death in the studio of his successor in the post,
Sir Thomas Lawrence).

Recent technical evaluation of paint samples
from the pair has noted that both images have an
unusual number of paint layers. This is especially
true of the King's portrait, where the layering of
paint may indicate several attempts to resolve the

space. In the Queen's portrait, paint is particularly
built up in the costume and in the architectural
components at the left. Examination using X-ray
images has revealed that alterations were made to
the position of the Queen's crown, and the canvas
used for her portrait was painted on the unprimed
side, as possibly was that of the King. SM

## 73
## *Self-portrait*

c.1779–80
Oil on panel, 127 × 101 cm
Royal Academy of Arts, London, 03/1394

PROVENANCE: painted for the Royal Academy of Arts
EXHIBITED: see Plymouth 1992, p. 30
LITERATURE: Paris 1985, pp. 287–88; London 1991A, pp. 25–26;
Plymouth 1992, pp. 5, 30; Mannings and Postle 2000, vol. 1, p. 51;
Ferrara 2005, p. 82

Sir Joshua Reynolds came to dominate the British
art world during the second half of the eighteenth
century. The 'most innovative portrait painter of
his generation', he became the first President of
the Royal Academy on its foundation in 1768,
and in this role he set out his authoritative views
on art theory and practice in a series of discourses
to students (Postle 2004B, pp. 563–64). Reynolds
portrayed himself in around thirty paintings and
drawings over half a century. Taken together, these
indicate the extent to which he 'promoted his own
image in order to shape his reputation, thus
ensuring that his face, which expressed confidence,
authority and intelligence, was closely allied to his
fortune'. This image, painted in 1780 or slightly
earlier, forms one aspect of a vigorous campaign
of self-advertisement (Ferrara 2005, p. 73).

In 1780 the Royal Academy moved to new
apartments at Somerset House, and Reynolds's
self-portrait was painted to hang in the Assembly
Room there. For the same space Reynolds supplied
likenesses of the King and Queen (cats 2 and 3),
as well as a portrait of Sir William Chambers
(the Academy's Treasurer, and the architect of
the building). Chambers's portrait appears to
have been intended as a counterpart to Reynolds's
self-portrait from an early stage, with both
images envisaged as hanging on either side of
a chimneypiece (Paris 1985, pp. 284–85). In the end,
however, it seems that the two works were placed
side by side on the room's south wall; they were
thus installed by 1781 (Ear-Wig 1781, p. 22).

Fittingly for a self-portrait destined for an
institutional display space, Reynolds presented
himself not dressed as an artist, but wearing
academic robes. Indeed, the doctorate of civil law
awarded him by the University of Oxford in 1773
was the honour which Reynolds prized most
(Postle 2004B, p. 558). Under his robes, Reynolds
wears a fur-edged red silk suit (Paris 1985, p. 287).
With its emphasis on erudition, his self-portrait
was designed to bring to mind the way that writers
and philosophers had traditionally been represented

(Plymouth 1992, p.5). The most conspicuous association, though, is that Reynolds divides the composition with a sculpted bust of Michelangelo. This version or cast of a work by Daniele da Volterra had previously been featured in a 1767 portrait of Reynolds by Angelica Kauffman, and was probably the 'bust in Plaister, of M. Angelo' sold in 1821 after the death of Reynolds's niece and heiress (Paris 1985, p.287). In Reynolds's estimation, Michelangelo was the most admirable of all artists (Mannings and Postle 2000, vol.1, p.51). He had lauded Michelangelo in his fifth discourse on art at the Royal Academy in 1772, declaring that 'his ideas are vast and sublime; his people are a superior order of beings; there is nothing about them, nothing in the air of their actions or their attitudes, or the style and cast of their limbs or features, that reminds us of their belonging to our own species' (Reynolds 1997, p.83). Painted as it was when the artist 'was at the peak of his powers and the undisputed leader of the country's artistic community', it has been suggested that the assertive panache of this self-portrait is such that, whether or not Reynolds intended it, 'even the shadowy bust of Michelangelo appears to nod in deference towards him' (Ferrara 2005, p.82).

It appears that the painting's final composition was achieved only after a lengthy development process. Initially, Reynolds appears to have produced another image entirely, in which a piece of drapery partially concealed the bust and Reynolds showed himself holding a paper inscribed 'The President and Council of the Royal Academy'; this version remained in the artist's possession and is now known only through a nineteenth-century engraving. Once this first arrangement was completed, Reynolds appears to have concluded that it was insufficiently vivid: although dignified, 'it would not serve to promote the sort of public image he wanted' (Plymouth 1992, pp.5, 28). He found the key to improving his self-presentation in a baroque print showing the artist Adam de Coster, available in the *Iconography*, a seventeenth-century collection of prints compiled by Anthony van Dyck. Reynolds used the angle of the figure of de Coster for his revised self-portrait. He first painted a study version to ensure that he wished to pursue the borrowing from this source, before incorporating this adjusted pose into the earlier layout, with one further change: the removal of the drapery, so as to allow the bust more fully to dominate the right side of the picture space.

A self-portrait of 1691 by Michael Dahl is one precedent for an artist's picturing himself with a bust. Furthermore, there is a possibility that Reynolds may have been acquainted with Rembrandt's *Aristotle Contemplating a Bust of Homer* (1653), a work which bears a marked affinity to this self-portrait (Plymouth 1992, p.5). The connection remains unproven: although the Rembrandt belonged by 1815 to a friend of Reynolds, Sir

Abraham Hume, its whereabouts at the time the artist was painting his self-portrait are unknown (Rousseau 1962, p.155). In any case, Rembrandt's works had been a formative influence on Reynolds. The latter's velvet cap, indeed, may offer a nod to those worn by Rembrandt in his self-portraits (Ribeiro 1995, p.23). In his eighth Discourse (1778), Reynolds characterised Rembrandt's manner as one which often 'exhibits little more than one spot of light in the midst of a large quantity of shadow', and it has been suggested that comparable lighting effects can be observed in this work (London 1991A, p.26; Reynolds 1997, p.147). SM

## 90
### Georgiana, Duchess of Devonshire and Her Daughter, Lady Georgiana Cavendish

1784–86
Oil on canvas, 112.5 × 142.7 cm
Chatsworth Settlement Trustees, 528

PROVENANCE: painted for the 5th Duke of Devonshire; by descent
EXHIBITED: Royal Academy 1786, no.166; for later exhibition history see Mannings and Postle 2000, vol.1, p.124
LITERATURE: see Mannings and Postle 2000, vol.1, p.124

In 1774 Georgiana Cavendish (1757–1806), *née* Spencer, married William Cavendish, 5th Duke of Devonshire. Her husband was the head of one of the nation's most powerful families, and she rapidly became one of the most prominent women of her era; by the time of Reynolds's portrait she was an acknowledged arbiter of fashion, and there was a great market for likenesses of her (Foreman 1998, pp.93, 176).

Although earlier images of the sitter shown at the Royal Academy had celebrated her as an icon of glamour, this example instead shows her in the role of mother (Ferrara 2005, p.134). In part this departure was an obvious consequence of the birth in July 1783 of the Devonshires' first child, Lady Georgiana Cavendish (1783–1858), with the commission of Reynolds's image of mother and daughter marking an event long wished for. Although the painting points to the future, it also had its counterpart in the past, for Reynolds had previously painted the duchess as a two-year-old with her own mother from 1759 to 1761. Further indication of the duchess's devotion to her family duties is the black dress she wears in mourning for her father who had died in October 1783. The painting stresses aristocratic status – the grand setting includes a swag of drapery, a classical urn and the hint of a landscape beyond – and aristocratic succession, but the intimacy of the scene would also have recalled to contemporaries the ways in which the sitter's maternal character went beyond the merely conventional. Her daughter's birth had been a subject of public interest, with the duchess lauded in the press for exercising 'the duty of a mother' in deciding to breastfeed her infant (the custom for women of her

class was to employ a wet nurse) (Foreman 1998, p.122). By stylistically evoking such seventeenth-century painters as Van Dyck and Rubens, Reynolds created 'at once a portrait of a mother and a Baroque drama' (Steward 1995, pp.115–16).

The nature of the representation was probably also motivated by vitriolic criticisms in the press to which the duchess had been exposed shortly before the painting was begun, when she participated in the spring 1784 election campaign for the leading Whig politician Charles James Fox. Not least, she had been lambasted in a succession of satirical prints which maligned her as unbecomingly involved in public life; scurrilous and often pornographic, these satires variously suggested that she had abandoned her proper functions as a wife and mother, indicated that she traded sexual favours for political influence, or insinuated an affair with Fox.

A particularly powerful print which united a number of these traits was Thomas Rowlandson's *Political Affection*. This shows the duchess suckling a fox cub – caricature shorthand for Fox – in disregard of the claims of maternal affection, for which her baby cries out in the corner of the image. Affinities have long been observed between this print and Reynolds's painting (Paris 1985, p.391 repr.; McCreery 2002, p.190). Both works show Lady Georgiana in a distinctive pose with her arms extended. In the painting this contributes to the sense of interaction between mother and child, whereas in Rowlandson's image the pose is used to show maternal neglect. This correspondence may, indeed, be a deliberate act of visual quotation, recasting in positive form a motif which Rowlandson had used as a critique – a remarkable cross-pollination, given how uncommon it was for painters to allude to satirists' works. Reynolds's image may thus form part of 'an attempt to reassert the duchess's moral status, to present her as an exemplary mother' (Retford 2006, p.200). The Duke of Devonshire had certainly been mortified by caricatures showing him as a cuckold, and the duchess herself had resorted to having the most offensive images bought up as they appeared in the print shops (Foreman 1998, pp.151, 161). Commissioning a painterly retort from Reynolds also brought the artist's own cultural capital into operation (and one of his specialisms was paintings of mothers and children).

Sittings for the painting began in July 1784 and concluded in April 1786, shortly before it was put on exhibition the following month at the Royal Academy (the birth of the Devonshires' second child, Henrietta, during 1785 may have delayed completion of the portrait, and renewed the topicality of its theme). The prospect of Reynolds's forthcoming exhibition piece was a source of great expectation, and was much touted in the press. An additional attraction was possibly a sighting of the duchess herself: it was reported of the exhibition rooms that 'curiosity has been divided between the portraits and the originals', and that in her case this comparison – 'the hardest trial' that 'a portrait can have' – was a vindication of Reynolds's image (*Morning Chronicle*, 4 May 1786). Poetasters penned panegyrics to the personal qualities the image proved both in the artist ('Majesty and grace so rarely giv'n / To mortal man, not taught by art but Heaven') and in the sitters ('In smiling DEVON and her infant Dove, / We view fair *Virtue* and the Cherub *Love!*') (*Daily Universal Register*, 22 May 1786; *Morning Herald*, 2 May 1786).

There were some subversive voices amid the general adulation. One account acknowledged that Reynolds had arranged his image so that 'Her Grace is described playing with her infant', but added that 'the action of the Dutchess's arm is censured by many, as not expressing the design: and that instead of her Grace tickling her child, and suddenly withdrawing her hand, it rather imports that she is in the act of giving a slap' (*Morning Herald*, 3 May 1786). It seems that any direct allusion to Rowlandson's print in which Reynolds's composition may have been conceived in 1784 was lost on its 1786 viewers. SM

## 85
### *The Braddyll Family*

1789
Oil on canvas, 238.1 × 147.3 cm
Not signed or dated
Lent by the Syndics of the Fitzwilliam Museum, Cambridge, PD.10-1955. Given by the National Art Collections Fund, 1955

PROVENANCE: Lt.-Col. Thomas Richmond-Gale-Braddyll (Master Braddyll in the picture); his sale, Christie's, 23 May 1846, lot 44; bought Bishop; according to W. Cotton, *Sir Joshua Reynolds and His Works* (London 1856), p.171, footnote, it belonged 'lately' to W. J. Isbell of Stonehouse; lent by T. Pooly Smyth of Plymouth to the Manchester 'Art Treasures' exhibition in 1857, although it may still have belonged to Mr Bishop of Plymouth who lent it to the exhibition at Truro, 1861; bought in by Bishop at Christie's, 13 June 1859, lot 213; Revd W. C. Randolph by 1890; Lionel, 2nd Lord Rothschild, at Tring Park, by 1899; his nephew, Nathaniel, 3rd Lord Rothschild, who sold it (Lord Baldwin Fund for Refugees) at Christie's, 25 May 1939, lot 256; bought Gooden & Fox, who sold it to Ernest E. Cook; bequeathed to the National Art Collections Fund; presented to the Fitzwilliam Museum in 1955
EXHIBITED: see Mannings and Postle 2000, vol.1, p.103
LITERATURE: see Mannings and Postle 2000, vol.1, p.103

This group portrait was the last of several images by Sir Joshua Reynolds to show members of the family of Wilson Gale-Braddyll (1756–1818), the figure dressed in a red coat at the centre of the composition. An associate of the Prince of Wales, Braddyll had been MP for Lancaster from 1780 to 1784, supporting Charles James Fox; he joined the Whig Club in 1785. Reynolds's painting dates to 1789; the previous year Braddyll had began serving as an officer in the militia, and he returned to parliament in 1790. Born Wilson Gale, he had assumed the additional surname Braddyll when he succeeded to a cousin's estate, Conishead Priory, Lancashire, in 1776. That same year he married his heiress cousin Jane Gale (died 1819), who is shown seated on a bench. Alongside stands their only son,

Thomas (1776–1862), then at Eton College and later an officer in the Coldstream Guards and an MP; they also had four daughters (Thorne 1986, vol.3, pp.240–41).

Sittings mostly took place over the spring of 1789. The portrait proved to be one of Reynolds's final works: his eyesight rapidly deteriorated in July, which led him effectively to retire from painting. Indeed, as one critic wrote in September 1789, regarding this portrait, 'about Mrs. B.'s hands and drapery there are some parts not finished' (Graves and Cronin 1899–1901, vol.1, p.111). Thus, it is not entirely clear whether the spaniel which Mrs Braddyll pets sits on her lap or on part of the bench. One important visual function of the dog, though, seems to be to occupy the centre of the composition, linking the family members together and completing a diamond shape of heads.

Thomas Braddyll leans against a plinth which supports a copy of the Medici Vase (identified by Robert Lloyd Parry of the Fitzwilliam Museum). From the mid-seventeenth until the mid-nineteenth centuries, this first-century neo-Attic work (now in the Uffizi, Florence) was one of the most admired of antique marble vases. Copies of the Medici Vase were popular as garden ornaments throughout the eighteenth and nineteenth centuries (Haskell and Penny 1981, pp.315–16). It is not known whether the Braddylls owned such a copy, although it is certain that Reynolds had made a drawing of the Vase at the Villa Medici in Rome in 1750; he had also incorporated a part of the Vase's relief into his 1764 portrait of Anne Dashwood (Gourlay 1983, p.223). Furthermore, his use of the Vase was possibly a visual reference to a 1656 etching by Stefano della Bella showing a young man, thought to be Cosimo III de' Medici, with the Vase (illustrated in Haskell and Penny 1981, p.56). Portraying a sitter in easy familiarity with symbols of the classical past was often a way of making claims about their status as members of the cultural and social élite; the Medici Vase had, for instance, recently been used as a prop in Grand Tour portraits of young Britons by the Italian artist Pompeo Batoni (Clark 1985, pp.330, 361).

Moreover, Thomas Braddyll's pose bears close comparison to an earlier portrait of him exhibited by Reynolds at the Royal Academy in 1784, in which he was also placed alongside an antique urn (Goodison 1977, p.205). (His pose can be further traced to Reynolds's 1782 portrait of Colonel George Coussmaker.) Similarly, Mrs Braddyll's costume resembles that which she wore in a 1788 portrait by Reynolds (and that same year the artist also exhibited an untraced image of Mr Braddyll at the Royal Academy). Thus, the final group painting of the family may have served to evoke a sense of continuity with these earlier works by the same artist, in whose company it may have been hung. Payment of £420 was made by Mr Braddyll in May 1792, after Reynolds's death (Mannings and Postle 2000, vol.1, p.103).

It seems that such lavish expenditure was unsustainable for the family. The diarist Joseph Farington noted in 1796 that Thomas Braddyll's likely inheritance had been rapidly depleted because: 'so much has been wasted by his Father. – It is not supposed that Bradyll consumed his Fortunes by gaming but by inattention to his expenses, & by various profuseness of living. – Though he had very expensive establishments to support he lived much at Taverns as a profuse Bachelor … His connexion with Mrs. Billington [a *cantatrice*] was supposed to be attended with vast expense' (Farington 1978–84, vol.3, p.677).

Also costly was socialising with the Prince of Wales (who gave a portrait of himself to Braddyll, also by Reynolds) (Ferrara 2005, p.136). Braddyll's largesse also extended to artists other than Reynolds. John Hoppner, for example, painted a full-length portrait of Mrs Braddyll, exhibited at the Royal Academy in 1788 and now lost. The previous year Hoppner had undertaken a picture of the prize-fighter Richard Humphries for Braddyll, a boxing enthusiast (Baetjer 1999, pp.51–52). Indeed, managing and promoting Humphries was probably Braddyll's chief distinction at the time of Reynolds's family portrait. SM

# Sir Joshua Reynolds and Studio

## 130
### *Mrs Siddons as the Tragic Muse*

1789
Oil on canvas, 239.7 × 147.6 cm
Signed and dated
Inscribed on hem of skirt: *JOSHUA REYNOLDS PINXIT* 1789
By permission of the Trustees of Dulwich Picture Gallery, London, DPG 318

PROVENANCE: Noël Desenfans by 1804; bequeathed to Sir Francis Bourgeois, 1807; Bourgeois bequest to Dulwich College, 1811
EXHIBITED: original version, Royal Academy 1784, no.190; for exhibition history of the present version, see Mannings and Postle 2000, vol.1, p.415
LITERATURE: see Ferrara 2005, p.222

Sarah Siddons (1755–1831), an actress who specialised in tragic roles, rapidly became an iconic figure on the London stage from 1782. She recorded that Reynolds 'often honourd me by his presence at The Theatre' (Siddons 1942, p.19). Indeed, contemporary art and theatre were two forms of spectacle which 'enjoyed a symbiotic relationship, both fuelling and fuelled by the culture of celebrity' (Perry 2001, p.111). Theatrical portraits operated both as works of art and commercial commodities that 'mutually benefited the artist and the subject' (McPherson 2000, p.405). The number of known portraits of Siddons, across a range of media, including prints, sculpture and porcelain, vastly exceeds that of any British actress before her. It has been observed that she 'clearly possessed a superior understanding, command of, and commitment to the fine arts as a means of advancing her career and public stature' (Asleson 2003, p.4).

Reynolds's original portrait of *Mrs Siddons as the Tragic Muse* was exhibited at the Royal Academy in 1784, at a time when a desire among the public to see likenesses of Siddons was pronounced (Los Angeles 1999, p.69). The portrait was painted speculatively, and one press eulogy declared that it 'should be in the King's Collection' (*Public Advertiser*, 29 April 1784). The work did not in fact find a buyer until 1790, when it was purchased, via the French art dealer and collector Noël Joseph Desenfans, by Charles-Alexandre de Calonne, previously Louis XVI's Minister of Finance, for 700 guineas (it is now in the Huntington Art Gallery, San Marino); the present image is a replica, dated 1789, and seems to have been acquired by Desenfans himself in exchange for a painting by Rubens. Although it is signed by the artist, it seems probable that the work was largely painted by studio assistants; Mrs Siddons described it in 1811 as 'but a poor imitation' of the original (Los Angeles 1999, pp.129–40; McPherson 2000, p.408; Ferrara 2005, p.222).

When the original version was exhibited in 1784, the press reaction was mostly rapturous. As one newspaper punned, the picture was 'a most sublime and capital Performance!' and a work for which 'it is not possible for Praise to be sufficiently lavish' (*Public Advertiser*, 27 April 1784). Before long, it was being heralded as 'one of the best, if not the best work of this great master' (*Morning Chronicle*, 17 May 1784). For another writer it was the 'most distinguished of all modern works. The more we attempt to praise, the more we feel our inability to do it any degree of justice; we therefore leave it to the admiring spectator, to feel from the view what we are unable to write' (*Morning Post*, 5 May 1784).

Reynolds's association of the actress with Melpomene, the Tragic Muse, was not in itself novel. George Romney had previously portrayed the actress Mary Ann Yates as the Tragic Muse in 1771, and in early 1783 he began a portrait of Mrs Siddons in the same guise (Los Angeles 1999, pp.64–70, repr.). Among literary precursors was a poem by William Russell, published in March 1783: *The Tragic Muse. Addressed to Mrs. Siddons*, which described 'that new Queen … sublimely seated on the Tragic Throne'. When Reynolds began his painting of Mrs Siddons in around the spring of that year, his challenge was 'to create the definitive representation of the greatest tragédienne to grace the British stage' (McPherson 2000, pp.408, 411).

In her reminiscences, drafted during the last years of her life, Siddons gave her own highly theatrical account of the production of Reynolds's image. In this, she declared: 'When I attended him

for the first sitting, after many more gratifying encomiums than I dare repeat, he took me by the hand, saying, "Ascend your undisputed throne, and graciously bestow upon me some grand Idea of The Tragick Muse." I walkd up the steps & seated myself instantly in the attitude in which She now appears. This idea satisfyd him so well that he, without one moment's hesitation, determined not to alter it' (Siddons 1942, p.17).

This and other accounts of how the pose was settled upon have to be borne against the visual evidence that 'the whole composition was most carefully contrived' (Paris 1985, p.325). Possibly the most direct source for Siddons's pose may be Domenichino's *St John the Evangelist* (Glyndebourne, East Sussex) (Merz 1995, p.517, repr.). Further visual references to Michelangelo's Sistine *Sibyls* and *Prophets* (particularly the portrayal of Isaiah) may be noted. By such visual quotation, Reynolds 'elevated' his sitter's portrait to the level of history painting and equated 'her tragic acting style with the grand style of painting' (West 1991A, p.114).

To Siddons's right and left loom a pair of figures (the first holds a dagger and the other a cup, both attributes associated with Melpomene); following Aristotle's definition of tragedy, these represent 'Pity' and 'Terror'. Reynolds seems to have modelled the pose of 'Terror' on an illustration of 'Fright' in John William's 1734 translation of Charles Le Brun's *Conférence sur l'expression*. He also seems to have given 'Terror' his own likeness (a self-portrait drawing appears to be a preliminary study) (San Marino 1971, pp.49–51). In addition, the work also incorporates Reynolds's signature. According to Siddons, when she was invited to see the completed 1784 image, Reynolds declared: 'here is my name, for I have resolved to go down to posterity upon the hem of *your* Garment' (Siddons 1942, p.18). SM

# Jean-Baptiste Louis Roman
PARIS, 1792 – PARIS, 1835

## 155
### *Girodet*

1827
Marble, 78 × 67 × 44 cm
Département des Sculptures, Musée du Louvre, Paris, CC 182

PROVENANCE: commissioned by the Minister for the King's Household for the painting galleries in the Louvre, 6 November 1826; entered the Louvre, 1828
EXHIBITED: Paris, Salon of 1827, no.1181. Duisburg, Karlsruhe, Gotha and Paris, 1989–90, no.69; Paris, 2005C, p.182, ill. 109
LITERATURE: Vitry 1930, pp.138 and 140; Musée du Louvre 1998, vol.2, p.572, repr.

During the reign of Louis XVI, there was a project to adorn the Grande Galerie of the Louvre, Paris, the backbone of the royal museum planned by the

Comte d'Angiviller, with marble statues of the Great Men of France, commissioned in series from the King's sculptors (Scherf 1993). The statues were far too heavy, however, to be installed upstairs and feasibility studies, mainly looking into reinforcing the floor, came to nothing. The statues remained in the Salle des Antiques, the repository for the royal collections, on the ground floor of the west wing of the Cour Carré, where they formed a backdrop to meetings of the Institut from 1795.

Nevertheless, the idea of adorning the painting galleries of the museum with sculptures was retained. The museum had recovered (from the Garde-meuble royal) marble busts of Raphael and Annibale Carracci, executed in the early seventeenth century by Alessandro Rondoni; they were the inspiration for the marble sculptures made by Pietro Paolo Naldini for the tombs of the two painters in the Pantheon in Rome (Martinelli and Pietrangeli 1955, nos 17 and 68). This relationship with the Pantheon, Rome's shrine to memory and to the cult of the artist (see Pasquali 2004) was thus the symbolic point of departure for the new plan to decorate the gallery: busts of illustrious painters presented alongside masterpieces of painting.

Seven busts were commissioned by the administration in 1802 (see Bresc-Bautier 1999, pp.136–37), mainly of Frenchmen, including Nicolas Poussin, the only artist celebrated by the Comte d'Angiviller and the sole link with the earlier project. Other commissions followed, and parity with Italian art was re-established, in particular with a copy by Guillaume Boichot of the bust of Michelangelo on his funerary monument in the church of Santa Croce, another celebrated pantheon, this time in Florence. All the artists selected lived in the sixteenth and seventeenth centuries, with one exception: Claude-Joseph Vernet (1714–1789), the first (almost) contemporary painter to be admitted into this glorious company. His bust, carved from marble by Louis-Simon Boizot (1802–06; Musée Calvet, Avignon: see Versailles 2001, no.47, repr.), was sent to the Luxembourg in 1807 to stand beside his series of *Ports of France*.

After the Restoration, the museum's acquisitions began to move more in the direction of the modern French school. The bust of the sculptor Denis-Antoine Chaudet (1763–1810) by Achille Valois, exhibited at the Salon of 1817, was bought in 1820 (Musée des Beaux-Arts, Angers: see Angers 1994, no.28, repr.). In 1826 busts were commissioned of Pierre-Paul Prud'hon (1758–1823) by Célestin Nanteuil (1826–28: Musée du Louvre 1998, vol.2, p.503, repr.) and of Girodet by Roman. In 1835, the July Monarchy under Louis-Philippe commemorated Pierre Narcisse Guérin (1774–1833; replica by Jean Marie Bonnassieux of a bust by Augustin Dumont, 1829) and Antoine-Jean Gros (1771–1835; replica by Jean-Baptiste Debay *père* of a bust in the Salon of 1827), reacting rapidly to their deaths. The government included in their celebrations a memorial to Jacques-Louis David, who died in exile in Brussels in 1825 and whose crime of regicide was absolved through a process of reconciliation, led by Louis-Philippe. The gallery of memorial busts to great artists of the past, established in the early days of the century in an encyclopaedic spirit of idealised 'pantheonisation', was thus completed after the 1820s with celebrations of the contemporary French school.

The bust of Anne-Louis Girodet de Roucy, known as Girodet-Trioson (1767–1824), by Roman, commissioned on 6 November 1826, was completed in record time. The block of marble was delivered to the sculptor on 10 March 1827 and the work was finished in time to be exhibited at the Salon in the same year. The marble bust of the painter by Debay *père*, intended for the Institut, was exhibited at the same Salon (*in situ*: Paris 2005E, p.167, no.169, repr.). The short interval between the painter's death and the commissioning of the memorial busts shows clearly how great a reputation he enjoyed – his funeral was a dazzling occasion – and the place he was considered to occupy in French art at the time of David's death.

It seems evident that Roman knew Girodet and was aware of his self-portraits in particular. The drawing Girodet made of himself at the end of his life, seated at a table, his shoulder draped with a cloak, was engraved after his death and became 'the official portrait for posterity' (Champion 2005, p.104, ill. 58, p.106). The painter is shown with tousled curly hair, dense side whiskers covering his cheeks, mouth closed, square jaw and a serious, determined expression. The cloak thrown boldly over his shoulder completes the image of a slightly fierce character. A wax painting by Paul-Claude-Michel Carpentier, now in the Musée de Montargis (Champion 2005, ill. 57, p.106) uses the same image but restores Girodet's baldness – his broad brow is revealed.

The same elements can all be found in Roman's bust: large head with receding hairline, thick curls at the side of his head and generous side whiskers, plus an ample cloak draped over an open shirt. The sculptor has given special emphasis to the subject's hair and tousled locks, bare neck (a sine qua non of the bust of the artist), and to the wide pleats of the garment, which give intense effects of light and shade. The sculptor's decision not to incise his sitter's eyes produces a singularly vital look, as if the absence of pupils imparted objective strength, a kind of inner energy. François Rude, who was a friend of Roman, remembered his portrait of Girodet when he created his bust of David (after 1835; Musée du Louvre 1998, vol.2, p.575, repr.): although he reused the model of the head he had made in Brussels in 1826 (see cat.152), he transformed the torso by using a half figure, as in *Girodet*, and draping the painter in a voluminous cloak. This was also the essential attribute of the

two busts by Debay in the Salon of 1827 (*Girodet* for the Institut, and *Gros* known through a replica in the Louvre). Debay's portraits do not, however, achieve the same epic impact as the masterpieces by Roman and Rude. GS

# George Romney
DALTON-IN-FURNESS, 1734 – KENDAL, 1802

**124**
*The Leveson-Gower Children*

*c.*1776–77
Oil on canvas, 202 × 232 cm
Abbot Hall Art Gallery, Kendal, AH 1185/74

PROVENANCE: painted for Granville, 2nd Earl Gower, and Susanna, Countess Gower; by descent to Elizabeth, Countess of Sutherland; Christie's, London, 23 June 1972, lot 109; bought by Leger; from whom it was purchased by Abbot Hall Art Gallery, 1973
EXHIBITED: see Liverpool, 2002, p.115
LITERATURE: see Liverpool 2002, p.115

This painting, produced at a turning-point in Romney's career, has been characterised as the apogee of the artist's mature style (Liverpool 2002, p.115). His presentation of the children depicted has few parallels in British art of the period (Cross 2000, p.119). The subjects are the five youngest of the eight children of Granville Leveson-Gower, 2nd Earl Gower. They are, from left to right, Lady Georgina (1769–1806), Lady Susanna (1772–1838), Lord Granville (1773–1846), Lady Charlotte Sophia (1771–1854), and Lady Anne (1761–1832). Anne was the last child of Gower's second marriage to Lady Louisa Egerton; the four younger siblings were the offspring of his third marriage to Lady Susanna Stewart. It has been noted that, in a society in which 'a person's destiny and importance were largely established at birth', children's portraiture recorded the future élite (Tscherny 2002, p.35). This was certainly true for *The Leveson-Gower Children*: Anne went on to marry a future Archbishop of York; the other girls eventually became respectively Countess of St Germans, Countess of Harrowby and Duchess of Beaufort; Granville was later created Earl Granville, and served as British ambassador to Paris. The image can also be seen to embody the very process of social development: Georgina and Susanna look up 'reverently' towards Anne, 'as if to an ideal, a perfection of beauty and womanhood, to which they aspire' (Shawe-Taylor 1990, p.215).

In several ways, this work stems from the artist's journey to Italy from 1773 to 1775. Romney's main aim in his Continental tour, it has been suggested, was 'to enhance his credibility in the eyes of influential patrons'. Returning to London, he took an expensive lease on a house and studio in fashionable Cavendish Square,

'a calculated gamble' to win new aristocratic business. This portrait vindicated his strategy, with the commission coming from a new client, Lord Gower, who was to become Romney's 'most important patron of all' during this transformative stage of his career. Indeed, the painting itself was a catalyst for the artist's further success: because 'the sittings for this ambitious work were necessarily protracted, it stood for many months in Romney's painting room, a timely and magnificent advertisement of his power' (Kidson 2004, pp.673–74). Sittings are recorded between March and June 1777 but may in fact have begun in December 1776; Romney was paid 200 guineas for the work (Liverpool 2002, p.115).

Romney's travels also provided direct inspiration. He recorded the striking visual charm of seeing women dancing hand in hand in a ring around maypoles in the streets of Nice: 'The air of antiquity it carried along with it had the most enchanting effect; I thought I was removed a thousand years back, & a spectator of the scenes in Arcadia.' In the countryside near the city he later saw another maypole ring: young men and women dancing 'hand in hand, with that glee which arises from innocence, simplicity, & liveliness' (Romney 1773). When in Rome, he studied classical sculptural reliefs showing dancing figures and may also have seen Poussin's *A Dance to the Music of Time* (*c.*1639; Wallace Collection, London), an image which also features the juxtaposition of a ring of dancers alongside a musician, and whose focus on the transient and fragile human condition could readily be translated to Romney's representation of childhood (Liverpool 2002, p.117).

Anne's tambourine-playing pose had been used previously by Romney in *Mirth* (1770); his original source may have been a maenad tambourinist in Sebastiano Ricci's *Triumph of Bacchus* at Burlington House (Wilson 1988, pp.764–75, repr.). Although the instrument is one associated with bacchantes, it has been observed that in Romney's classicised rendition of Anne its use appears chastened, and that it may invoke 'the Christian idea of music as harmony between body and soul'. The tambourine also has a structural role as 'a visual device to capture and then lead the spectator's eye down and along the linked hands' of the children (Wallis 1999, p.4). This 'sweeping semi-circle', an incomplete 'u'-curve, underpins the design (Liverpool 2002, pp.115–17).

The balance between Anne and her younger half-siblings is central to the composition's arrangement. In terms of the scene's action, it is Anne's graceful music-making which provides the animating direction for the others' dancing. Formally, if the classical structure with its tall pilaster in the background perhaps parallels Anne, the children have a natural counterpart in the vegetation behind them. The relatively few sketches for the portrait indicate, it has been suggested, that Romney began with a solid sense of what his fundamental design was to be. His early preliminary drawings do not, however, include Granville: he was 'put into the portrait only belatedly' – perhaps he was initially deemed too young by his parents – and the image seems to have been well advanced by the time of his inclusion (Liverpool 2002, p.115). The girls on either side of Granville mark the image's golden sections, so embodying the scene's 'perfect balance' between playfulness and order (Rump 2002, p.6). Yet despite the 'strong sense of centrifugality', there is 'no one crossing-point of all the various lines': the actual midpoint of the canvas is 'an anonymous spot on the pilaster to the right of Granville's head' (Liverpool 2002, p.117). This architectural feature emphasises the 'practically empty' space at 'the visual middle of the painting': at this point Romney separates the ring of dancing bodies, leaving only the outstretched arms of the children, which form a diamond shape in the negative space. By this 'ingenious conceit' the gesture of their connecting hands is reinforced by being isolated at centre-stage (Rump 2002, p.8). SM

# François Rude

DIJON, 1794 – PARIS, 1855

## 152
### Jacques-Louis David

1831 (after a model of 1826)
Marble, 57.5 × 26 × 21 cm
Département des Sculptures, Musée du Louvre, Paris, RF 419

PROVENANCE: probably the marble bust retained by Rude; then his wife, mentioned as 'in the drawing room' by Madame Rude in her estate inventory following her death in 1868; apparently given to Jean-Baptiste Paul Cabet (1815–1876), pupil and husband of the sculptor's niece; then his daughter Françoise Cabet, wife of René-Louis Faber; bequeathed to the Louvre by René-Louis Faber in his will, 12 November 1876; entered the Louvre after his death, 1881
EXHIBITED: Paris, Salon of 1831 (not in catalogue); Dijon, 1955, no.12; Los Angeles and Williamstown, 2005, no.57
LITERATURE: Fourcaud 1904, pp.449–50, 456–57; Holderbaum 1980, p.42, fig.27; Ixelles 1985, p.425, no.422; Musée du Louvre 1998, vol.2, p.575, repr.

When François Rude went to Brussels in 1815, following his friend and protector Louis Frémiet, a fervent Bonapartist, he paid a visit to the most famous French artist living there, the painter Jacques-Louis David (1748–1825). After many years of friendship (Rude's wife, Sophie Frémiet, painted and collaborated with David), the two men fell out. 'I had not mentioned our quarrel with M. David because there are some details which could not be written down' wrote the sculptor's wife in a letter of 4 February 1823 (quoted in Fourcaud 1904, p.449). After the painter's death, Rude made peace with his family (he was a pallbearer at the funeral). 'Rude has just finished the bust of M. David, commissioned

by the artist's family. The children told him that it was the best portrait anyone had made of their father. I think he will produce it in marble for the David family' (letter from Madame Rude, 8 May 1826, quoted in Fourcaud 1904, p.449). The sculptor apparently took a cast of the painter's right hand. Did he also take a cast of the face?

A plaster bust, bearing the inscription 'F. Rude Brux. 1826' (Private collection: see Ixelles 1985, no. 422, repr. p.441), represents David wearing classical clothing. Another version of this type of bust, cut a little higher under the shoulders, was recently acquired by the Musée des Beaux-Arts, Dijon (repr. *Revue du Louvre*, April 2002, p.97). In the same year, Rude produced a bronze bust for the David family in which the painter is portrayed without classical clothing (signed 'Rude Bruxelles 1826'; this version remained with David's grandson until 1880 and was acquired in 1971 by the Musée de Dijon).

When the sculptor returned to Paris in 1827, with (it appears) all the plaster models for both versions, he used the unclothed version to make a marble bust of the same type as the bronze, but cut it shorter: this was exhibited at Salon of 1831 and reached the Louvre through Rude's pupil, Paul Cabet. Finally, the portrait of David appeared in its last incarnation as a marble bust, executed by Rude for the painting galleries in the Louvre at the request of the royal household: half life-size, it was commissioned in 1835 and finished in 1838 (Musée du Louvre 1998, vol.2, p.575, repr.). The face is the same as on the other compositions, although turned slightly more towards the front. However, the painter is clothed in an overcoat with a large collar, generously draped in front, which gives him the aspect of a romantic hero – in the same vein as Jean-Baptiste Louis Roman's *Girodet* (cat.155).

Rude's desire to become David's sculptor, as Jean-Antoine Houdon was sculptor to Voltaire and Jean-Jacques Rousseau, by multiplying the versions – dressed in the classical style, unclothed, wrapped in a mantle – and the dimensions, is evident. He knew the painter well at the end of his life and could be regarded as a reliable witness. It is probable that David's son Eugène was thinking of him when he wrote, in his will, on 14 April 1830: 'I desire that the body of my father should be transported as soon as possible from Brussels to the cemetery to the east of Paris, and that a marble bust of him should be made for his tomb' (see Paris 1989E, p.636). His desire to see his father's body transported to Paris was refused. By exhibiting the bust of the regicide painter in Paris at the first Salon after the Bourbon debacle under the new regime of Louis-Philippe, whose father, the Duc d'Orléans, had voted for the death of Louis XVI, like the painter, Rude was acting provocatively. He was linking the commemoration to a personal connection (his friendship with David's family) with a confirmed opinion: the present reality of David to a political and artistic landscape that had changed.

One problem that Rude had in representing David was how to reproduce his deformed left cheek when depicting his facial features; his cheek was disfigured by an enormous cyst, probably caused by a tumour of the parotid gland (see Paris 1989E, p.238). Portraits of him made by his pupils carefully show him from the right side (for example Antoine-Jean Gros: see Los Angeles 2005, p.336), or by hook or by crook avoid reproducing his disfigurement when he poses face on (see the paintings by François-Joseph Navez in Ixelles 1985, p.427). Very few painted the unsightly excrescence as it was, as did Jérôme-Martin Langlois (painting of 1825 in the Louvre). Rude has none of this fastidiousness: he reproduces David's deformity as it is, as his duty as a faithful portraitist demands; but he encloses it in a broader vision, modifying its impact by the magical use of polished marble all over the surface of the sculpture.

This ensures that the bust of 1831 has three different aspects: the realistic reproduction of a face; the global idealisation of the composition (unclothed cut and blank eyes with no pupils in the classical style); and the evocation of the genius of the painter by the wild curls rising above his forehead, the latter a 'romantic cliché', as Philippe Bordes points out. Similar curls are to be found, for example on the bust of the French poet Alphonse de Lamartine by David d'Angers (marble; 1830: Musée du Louvre 1998, vol.1, p.204, repr.). GS

# Philipp Otto Runge

WOLGAST, 1777 – HAMBURG, 1810

## 91
### The Artist's Parents

1806
Oil on canvas, 196 × 131 cm
Inscription on the reverse: *Daniel Nicolaus Runge. Geb. in Wollgast 30ten Dezember 1737 – und Magdalena Dorothea Runge – geborene Müller. Geb. in Wolgast den 7ten Junius 1737. Diese meine Eltern habe ich meinen Geschwistern und mir zum Angedenken gemalt und zur Lust mein Söhnlein Otto Sigismund alt 1 Jahr, und meines Bruders Jacobs Söhnlein Friedrich alt 3 Jahr. Wollgast im Sommer 1806.*
Kunsthalle, Hamburg, 1001

PROVENANCE: remained with the artist's descendants until its acquisition by the Kunsthalle, Hamburg, 1904
EXHIBITED: Hamburg 1977–78, no.236
LITERATURE: Traeger 1975, no.355; Jensen 1977, pp.217–21; Hoffmann 1995, p.477

Philipp Otto Runge's portrait of his parents is his most imposing painting – the artist usually worked in more modest formats. Here Runge provides an interpretation of his family portrait, which, behind the apparent clarity of the representation, contains the same complex symbolism that runs through all his work. This painting, a testimony to filial piety, was designed to keep the memory of their grandparents alive in the minds of the Runge children. The artist's long-term intention was to revive art along humanist and Christian lines; he wanted to convey the essence of family relationships without including any manifest social implications (see *We Three*; 1805; destroyed); with this in mind, he does not try to stage an artificially intimate or reconstructed scene, but to translate the moral value (in the true sense) of these relationships. In this painting he is led by the spiritual intensity of his aims to emphasise the contrast between the intimate destination of the work and the monumentality of its conception; echoes can be found of the conventions of full-length portraits of couples that were so much in vogue in England at the time.

In addition, the layout with the opening on to a landscape obviously goes back to the Venetian tradition, which, reinterpreted by Van Dyck, was one of the conventional commonplaces of the aristocratic portrait. However, the manner in which Runge organises this glimpse of landscape is highly original, recalling, as it obviously does, the open windows so much favoured by Caspar David Friedrich. In this composition the artist does away with any middle ground. The wall of the house has no depth, and the spectator's gaze passes abruptly from the space where the parents are standing to the landscape, which is handled on a much smaller scale. Our notions of interior and exterior space are disturbed because the parents are supposed to be outside the house.

Far from being composed in a realistic manner, the two spaces separated by the wall without thickness and the fence are symbols of the world of the family and the big world outside. The same idea of a family enclosure can be found in the famous portrait of *The Hülsenbeck Children*, painted the same year (Kunsthalle, Hamburg). The landscape shows the River Peene, beside which stood the family house at Wolgast, on the shores of the Baltic. A Swedish flag can be clearly seen on one of the boats, interpreted by some critics as a point scored over Napoleon (Traeger). A sketch in the Kunsthalle, Hamburg (inv. 1029), probably a first draft of the composition, shows a much less detailed landscape.

According to the sketch, it appears that the artist was not originally thinking of including in the painting the portraits of his son Otto Sigismund and his nephew Friedrich. The inclusion of the children makes the meaning of the painting more complex; from being a simple portrait it becomes an allegory of life and moral values that, in the context of Protestant Germany, make the family 'the sacred kernel of social life' (Hoffmann 1995). This outlook on life was a reaction to the lighter morals preached by French society. Such a way of representing two adults and two children seems to owe a lot to two engravings made by Daniel Niklaus Chodowiecki to illustrate the book by the scientist Georg Christoph Lichtenberg, *Natürliche und Affektierte Handlungendes Lebens*; one of

them depicts a couple with a dog forgetting their duties as parents, the other a couple preceded by their children, for whom they serve as guides and models.

Bourgeois morality is tinged here with a genuine, more philosophical reflection on the passage of time, since the adults are not parents but grandparents. Runge's parents are made monumental by the solid assurance of their principles; their features are rendered with almost expressionist realism as they look towards the spectator. Runge's mother holds firmly on to her husband's arm and grips a rosebud, probably as a symbol of the enduring quality of the couple. Traeger relates the astonishing green of the outside wall of the house to the artist's theory of colour. Runge associated yellow with men, blue with women and green, the result of mixing the first two colours, with reality.

On a more pragmatic note, it is worth remembering that green backgrounds were often used in sixteenth-century German portraits. Albrecht Dürer organised the colour scheme of some of his works by using intense green and brown, heightened with a touch of red or orange: the *Portrait of Emperor Maximilian I* (1519; Kunsthistorisches Museum, Vienna) or, on a more intimate scale, the *Portrait of Michael Wolgemut* (1516; Germanisches National Museum, Nuremberg). Everything about the figure of Runge's father – the pose, the very graphic way in which the wig is depicted around the forehead, the uneven drawing of the cheek, the pinching of the lips, the emphasis on the wrinkle that leads from the nose to the corner of the lips – all these details bring to mind the *Portrait of Michael Wolgemut*. Whether Runge was aware of it or not, these comparisons underscore his intention of working in a tradition that was specifically German. The commemorative text on the back of the canvas could also be interpreted as a revival of the inscriptions that used to figure on the front of portraits during the German Renaissance.

As in the portrait of *The Hülsenbeck Children*, Otto Sigismund and Friedrich are associated with a flower, here a lily. The larger of the two children grabs his cousin's left arm very firmly as if he wanted to stop him doing what he was. This adds subtle drama to a static painting, and the boy's upward glance creates a dramatic tension between the principal actors in the painting. The plants in the foreground are painted with descriptive realism that is also reminiscent of Dürer. Planted very artificially, they underline the moral significance of the work. According to Traeger, the lily is a symbol of the soul's aspiration to a more elevated life; the thistle symbolises the dangers that lie ahead for the grandparents and the children.

Like Vincent's contemporary painting, this family portrait goes deeper than the representation of family intimacy, despite its apparent realism. However, whereas Vincent was demonstrating the social value of the family unit in post-revolutionary,

secular France, Runge was emphasising the spiritual value of the family – as was appropriate for a German Protestant painter. By making a contrast between painstaking attention to reality in the details and the subjectivity of the representation (abandonment of planes, unreal colours, anatomical distortion), Runge exalts the sublime content of his portrait, just as Caspar David Friedrich was breathing his own sublime subjectivity into his portraits. SA

# Henri-Joseph Rutxiehl
LIERNEUX, PAYS DE LIÈGE, 1775 – PARIS 1837

106
*Elfride Clarke de Feltre*

1813?
Marble, 50 × 27 × 20 cm
Musée des Beaux-Arts, Nantes, 1844

PROVENANCE: Edgard Clarke de Feltre Bequest, 1852
LITERATURE: Musée de Nantes, 1854. no.82; Musée de Nantes, 1859, no.1027; Musée de Nantes, 1876, no.62; Nicolle 1913, no. 1844

This portrait represents the daughter of the eminent Henri Jacques Guillaume Clarke (1765–1818), created Duke of Feltre in 1809. Clarke was the only son of an Irish officer who lived in France, but was born into an old British aristocratic family. He fought during the Revolution and was made a general in 1793. Having been one of Napoleon's accomplices at the time of the coup d'état of 18 Brumaire in 1799, he pursued a fine career under the Consulate and the Empire: ambassador in Tuscany (1801–04), Conseiller d'Etat (1804), then private secretary to Napoleon, whom he accompanied on all his campaigns. He was made governor of Vienna (1805) and Berlin (1806), then Minister of War (1807–14). He rallied to the Bourbons under the first Restoration (he was created a peer of France in 1814), accompanying Louis XVIII to Ghent during the Hundred Days of Napoleon's rule between 20 March and 8 July 1815, then returning to his ministerial post until 1817 (he was created Marshal of France in 1816).

He had one daughter from his first marriage (which ended in divorce in 1795), Henriette, who married Aimery de Montesquiou-Fezensac in 1808. He and his second wife, Françoise Zaepffel, from a reputable bourgeois family in Alsace, were married in 1799. She bore him four children (Valynseele 1962, pp.65 and 79): Edgard (1799–1852), second Duke of Feltre; Arthur (1802–29); Alphonse (1806–51), a lieutenant in the cuirassiers and a composer; and Elfride (1808–13). Unlike Henriette, these four children produced no heirs.

François-Xavier Fabre, whom Clarke had known since his posting in Florence, painted a large portrait of the family, *The Duchess of Feltre and Her Children* (exhibited in the Salon of 1810; Musée Marmottan, Paris). The youngest child, Elfride, is standing near her mother embracing her tenderly. She died shortly afterwards, on 6 August 1813. Madame de Souza wrote to the Countess of Albany, on 24 September 1813: 'I am certain that M. Fabre is missing that pretty little daughter of the Duke of Feltre, who died after intolerable suffering. I cannot possibly imagine the heartbreak one must feel on losing a child. I dare not even think about it' (Pélissier 1902, p.66).

It is not known at what date Rutxiehl executed the small marble bust of her. The memory of Elfride lingered for a long time in the family, as the only image of childhood for the three brothers, who remained unmarried. It is the only piece of sculpture (among seventy-seven paintings and four drawings) in Edgard Clarke's large bequest made to the city of Nantes in 1852. Clarke stipulated, via his executors, the Marquis de Cubières and M. Aubry, on 28 July 1852, that the bust of Elfride was to be exhibited on a column 'in fine French marble, marbled and decorated with flowers' beside the busts of her two brothers (made by Jean-Louis-Nicolas Jaley in 1854 at the city's expense) in a room specially designed to accommodate the collection.

The bust is not signed, and it is thanks to the earliest museum catalogues that we have been able to identify its author, whose name was apparently provided by the heir (Rutxiehl exhibited a plaster bust of the Duke of Feltre at the Salon of 1819). Rutxiehl originated from the countryside around Liège and studied in Paris, first in Jean-Antoine Houdon's studio, then with Jacques-Louis David in Paris. In 1808 he received the first prize for sculpture at the Ecole des Beaux-Arts, which allowed him to continue his studies at the French Academy in Rome. He stayed in Rome during 1809, then went to Tuscany and in 1810 moved to Carrara.

When he returned to Paris, he devoted himself to portraiture, producing a statue of Napoleon for the Banque de France (marble, installed in 1813; now in Versailles), and another of the King of Rome (plaster; signed and dated 1811); Musée des Beaux-Arts et de la Céramique, Verviers), plus a number of busts. His success brought him the title of 'sculptor to the prince imperial' in 1812. During this period under the Empire his career reached its peak, as illustrated by the enormous success of his group *Zephyr and Psyche* (marble, exhibited at the Salons of 1812 and 1814; Louvre, Paris), begun in Italy and carved with great flair. His success continued under the Restoration: the Duke and Duchess Clarke de Feltre commissioned this famous sculptor whose qualities as a portraitist (particularly of children) were renowned, as was his dexterity with marble.

The bust of Elfride Clarke de Feltre is one of the artist's masterpieces. The cut of the bust, with no clothes, is borrowed from Houdon, in particular from the bust of Sabine Houdon aged four years (plaster original in the Louvre: Scherf 2006, no. 32,

repr.), which includes her chest, shoulders and the top of her arms. However, her hair is quite different: smooth and carefully combed on the top of the head, it divides into ringlets all round the head, with charming kiss-curls on either side of the face. Such mildly affected details, which are a pretext for dazzling carved effects, are unknown in Houdon's art.

Another basic difference is the choice of presenting blank eyes in the classical style, with no demarcation of the pupil or the iris. This detail can be found on other marble works by Rutxiehl (*Zephyr and Psyche*), and also, notably, on various busts of children made under the Restoration – *Mademoiselle d'Artois* (marble, Salon of 1827, Château de Versailles: Hoog 1993, no.1394) or the *Duc de Bordeaux* (marble, Salon of 1827, Château de Versailles: Hoog 1993, no.194, repr.). These two examples are brought to life and, to an extent, softened by being dressed in contemporary clothing.

In the case of Elfride's bust, what should we think of the choice of representing her naked, with blank eyes? Was the sculptor's decision an aesthetic preference for the classical manner, in the style of Roman portraits, or the portraits of Lorenzo Bartolini, whom he had just left in Carrara? Or did his clients dictate the choice? In the absence of any documentation concerning the date when the bust was made, we do not have an answer. Was the portrait executed while Elfride was alive, or was it created posthumously, soon after the death of the small girl? It should be noted that she is not portrayed in a cheerful way. Her face, with its closed mouth and empty eyes, seems vacant, as if fixed for all eternity. It would be easier to understand if it were a posthumous portrait. We know that the child died 'after intolerable suffering'. It must certainly have been hard for the whole family to bear her painful death. The marble portrait of her after her death may have helped to lessen the pain, providing a peaceful and timeless image of a body that had suffered so acutely. It would also explain the attachment of the three brothers to this precious and distressing memorial. GS

# Jean-Pierre Saint-Ours

GENEVA, 1752 – GENEVA, 1809

## 65
*François Tronchin*

1796
Oil on canvas, 112.5 × 85 cm
Signed and dated on the shaft behind the sitter's head:
TRONCHIN / AMATEUR / ES / UX ARTS / NE A / GENEVE / 1704 / PEINT PAR / ST OURS / 1796 / DELICES
Société des Arts, Geneva

PROVENANCE: commissioned by François Tronchin, 1796
EXHIBITED: Geneva, 1974, pp.186–88

François Tronchin (1704–1798) was one of the most brilliant collectors in eighteenth-century Geneva. Having become involved in various risky banking schemes in Paris at the end of the 1730s, he returned to his native Switzerland, where he played an active part in the civic and cultural life of Geneva. He was a friend of Voltaire, whose money was managed by the Tronchin bank, and took over his property, Les Délices, when the philosopher moved to the Château Ferney; here he assembled a large collection of seventeenth-century Flemish and Dutch paintings, including the famous *Woman in a Bed* by Rembrandt (National Gallery of Scotland, Edinburgh). He had many connections in the commercial art world and expected to make money from his collection. In 1770 he sold almost all of it to Catherine II, making a substantial profit. Hardly had he let this first collection go than, with the help of the Parisian dealer Jean-Baptiste Lebrun, husband of Elisabeth-Louise Vigée-Lebrun, he built up a second in the same genre; in 1780 he drew up a catalogue which contained no fewer than 123 entries. The catalogue may have been published in order to attract buyers, in particular the Comte d'Angiviller, Director of Buildings to King Louis XVI. Tronchin continued his dealing into the 1790s, by which time he was already an old man. The present portrait, painted in 1796, is the last representation of the illustrious citizen of Geneva.

Although Tronchin had contacts with some of the most important personalities in the art world, such as Baron Grimm, Diderot, Lebrun the dealer and the painter Joseph Vernet, he seems to have shown little interest in contemporary art. Nevertheless, he encouraged the two most important portrait painters in Geneva: Jean-Etienne Liotard and Jean-Pierre Saint-Ours. In 1757 Liotard produced a celebrated pastel portrait of Tronchin seated at a table (Private collection, Geneva), in which the sitter points at Rembrandt's *Woman in a Bed*, the masterpiece of his first collection. Forty years later, Saint-Ours, by then one of the most prominent artists in Geneva, took up the general scheme of his predecessor's portrait. Tronchin is seated at a table on which are placed, as in the pastel, a compass and a musical score, to illustrate the sitter's interest in architecture and music. Tronchin points to a painting in a superb Louis XVI frame from his second collection: Gérard Dou's *A Hermit Reading the Bible* (whereabouts unknown). This time, however, the portrait's subject is not dressed in street clothes: he wears a dressing gown and a night cap. The portrait is of value for the social and intimate information it contains. In this final portrait, painted a few years before his death, Tronchin constructs his image for posterity, as he did with his catalogues, the last of which appeared posthumously in 1798. The background to the picture, with its *trompe-l'oeil bas-relief*, music, painting and drawing, stands as his monument. AA

# Johann Gottfried Schadow

BERLIN, 1764 – BERLIN, 1850

## 138
*Princesses Luise and Frederika of Prussia*

*c.*1796–97 (from a model of 1796)
Porcelain, 55 × 30 × 19.5 cm
Marked with a blue sceptre; engraved: *1246*
Museum für Kunst und Gewerbe, Hamburg, 1906.272

PROVENANCE: acquired in 1906
LITERATURE (all versions): Friedländer 1890, pp.6off.; Mackowsky 1951, pp.99–102, ills. 72, 73; Eckardt 1987, pp.38–40; Eckardt 1990, pp.64–69; Graefrath and Maaz 1993, pp.72–82; Lindemann 1997, *passim*; Mirsch 1998, *passim*; Maaz 1998, *passim*; Lessmann 2006, p.123; Maaz 2006, pp.664–66

This statue, representing the Crown Princess of Prussia Luise (1776–1810) and her younger sister Frederika (1778–1841) illustrates the extent to which bourgois ideas had penetrated official art by 1800; the divisions between the classes were beginning to collapse and the naturalness promoted since the days of Rousseau was beginning to be valued more highly than court etiquette. It is true that Luise, born in the Mecklemburg region (as was her sister), stands a little straighter than Frederika, and the carriage of her head suggests that she is already conscious of her role as the future queen; Frederika has her head winsomely lowered, indicating perhaps that she has managed to escape the rules of conduct at court. Each sister is captured in a natural pose. The emotionally charged device of their encircling arms – one placed on the sister's hip, the other on the other sister's shoulder – and the studied (and appealing) gesture of their hands meeting on the younger sister's shoulder demonstrates above all their strong affection for one another. In the spirit of the Enlightenment, their sibling closeness is valued more highly than consciousness of rank and its official representation.

An original plaster model of this sculpture and another life-size marble version can be found in the Alte Nationalgalerie in Berlin. The likeness of the two figures was apparently so good that spectators from the period were aware that the ambitious marble group immortalised two princesses in the then unusual guise of two sisters, with nothing inaccessible about them. Yet the portrait, in fact, depicted two representatives of the highest nobility. Only those who could read the Latin inscriptions on the socle of the marble version or on the plinth of the smaller version would realise that the work was based on the court. The inscription indicates that the piece dates from the eleventh year of the reign of Friedrich-Wilhelm II. The idea behind the inscription is to identify the Hohenzollerns as patrons of the arts in general, and this King in particular. This ambition may have persuaded the monarch to commission the marble version of the group, which stood for a long time in the palace in Berlin and is now in the Nationalgalerie.

Schadow seems to have undertaken the life-size model in plaster on his own initiative in 1795. As it was well received at the exhibition held by the Berlin Academy that year, various intermediaries managed to encourage the King to commission a version in marble. The story that Schadow created the life-size model with the sole intention of making a smaller version in biscuit was discredited years ago. If that had been his aim, he would not have made a model that was at least twice as large.

Biscuit versions of this ravishing group are still available today. The first copies were certainly made for the royal family. They do not bear the inscriptions that figure in the marble and on the plinth. The version now in Hamburg is one of the earliest to have been produced in porcelain biscuit. The model from which it was cast can be dated to 1796; the engraved number 1246 has not yet been interpreted, but it could be the number of the cast.

Schadow depicts two young women of the era known as the 'period of sensibility'. He presents them as the young beauties they were, thus producing a valid image of ideal humanity. The classicising treatment of the clothing and shoes transcends the contemporary image, created by the individual handling of each figure and by the scarf worn by Luise around her neck. In his choice of two sisters, Schadow is making a reference to the classical group known as *Castor and Pollux* (Prado, Madrid), and the reference extends also to the equilibrium of their two forms leaning one against the other. As usual, however, he does not quote literally from antiquity, appropriating the classics by adapting them in an original manner.

The critics, who wielded enormous power over artists at this period, persuaded Schadow to get rid of the small basket of flowers that Luise was originally holding in her hand, because they considered it to have no classical legitimacy. Schadow probably carried out this alteration at the end of 1795 or in 1796. The reference to nature made by this small basket – and possibly also to the flowering youth of the two princesses – was an echo of English portraiture, and of the close links established in English painting between landscape and human beings. In the eyes of the critics, however, Schadow was making too obvious a reference to idealised country life, and thus offending against notions of decorum and propriety at the time. The artist solved the problem by making the princess hold a piece of fabric drawn forward from behind, producing a stylishly classical effect: drapery superimposed over regular pleats. The model in the Nationalgalerie makes it possible to see clearly the way Schadow modified the figure using the simplest possible methods: a piece of fabric was plunged into liquid plaster and, when hardened, was fixed to the back at waist level. Comparison of this model with the marble version – which is essentially by Claude Goussaut, Schadow having worked only on the face and the arms – reveals that the carved piece differs in a number of details. The eyes, which in the model were pierced and looked livelier, are here blank, creating a more abstract appearance. BM

# Gottlieb Schick

STUTTGART, 1776 – STUTTGART, 1812

## 139
*Wilhelmine von Cotta*

1802
Oil on canvas, 132 × 140 cm
Signed and dated on the balustrade: *Schick faciebat 1802*
Staatsgalerie, Stuttgart, GVL 87

PROVENANCE: in the possession of the sitter's descendants; acquired by the Staatsgalerie, Stuttgart, 1951
EXHIBITED: Tübingen, 1959, no.70; Stuttgart, 1976, no.39; London, 2002A
LITERATURE: Hoffmann 1960, no.64

The portrait of *Wilhelmine von Cotta* by Gottlieb Schick is a typical example of the fact that French models moved in German circles and were reinterpreted in a very German way – graphically and sculpturally. Gottlieb Schick, who trained in Stuttgart in the studio of the sculptor Heinrich Dannecker, spent the years from 1798 to 1802 improving his skills in Paris. He entered David's studio and seems to have been heavily influenced by the '*barbus*', a group of David's students who reacted against his painting of the Sabines when it was shown in 1799 and decided to be more primitive than the master: in 1800 he exhibited an *Eve* in the Salon (1800; Wallraf-Richartz Museum, Cologne), a female version of the androgynous narcissi so popular with the devotees of primitivism. Purity of outline, a sculptural feeling for line and the allegorical eccentricity of the figure demonstrate his affinity with the movement – in which Ingres himself showed an interest. Indeed, Schick seems to have had contact with the master from Montauban. The painting he submitted for the Grand Prix de Rome competition, *Agamemnon's Envoys in the Tent of Achilles* (destroyed), is very close in composition to his colleague's painting on the same subject (Ecole Nationale des Beaux-Arts, Paris); some of the figures, probably studio models, are identical.

Encouraged by this experience, Schick returned to Stuttgart in March 1802, leaving for Rome in November in order to complete his training, which involved studying the works of classical antiquity and Raphael. During these few months, his first mature period, he painted his two masterpieces, two portraits, one of the wife of his teacher, Heinrich Dannecker (Nationalgalerie, Berlin) and the other of the wife of Swabia's most influential publisher, Wilhelmine von Cotta (1771–1821). The portrait of *Wilhelmine von Cotta* was begun straight after the portrait of Dannecker's wife, as can be gathered from the series of studies in a sketchbook.

Both owe something to David's instruction, although they are very different in spirit, as if the artist were experimenting (brilliantly) with the techniques he had learned. The portrait of Heinrich Dannecker is more primitive in feeling; the profile is an exploration of the perfection of a geometric line, tenderly curved. The pose was one never used by David but it must have been popular in France, as it can be found in a preparatory drawing by Prud'hon for his portrait of *The Empress Joséphine in the Park at Malmaison*. In addition, the elegant position of her left hand is reminiscent of the graceful gestures to be found in painting, in Prud'hon's *The Empress Joséphine*, and also in sculpture, in Joseph Chinard's bust of *Juliette Récamier* (fig.67) or the statue of *Pauline Borghese as Venus* by Antonio Canova (Villa Borghese, Rome).

The portrait of Wilhelmine von Cotta belongs to another school. Less formally abstract, it is 'realistic' in the sense that the sitter's features are more clearly rendered. The difference may be attributed to the history of the painting. The portrait of Heinrich Dannecker, a close friend of Schick, seems to have been used by the artist as an opportunity for formal experimentation. In the case of Wilhelmine von Cotta, however, as the portrait was a genuine commission, there was greater pressure to produce a good likeness. The artist delivered an image that adapted to the Swabian capital the latest innovations in fashionable female portraiture, as practised in Paris by David, Gérard or Prud'hon.

Wilhelmine von Cotta, portrayed full length, is seated on a bench with her elbow on a balustrade. The pose is directly inspired by David's portrait of Madame Récamier (fig.68). Schick made a sketch of this portrait in one of his notebooks; David was painting it during his apprenticeship in his studio. From it, we gain some idea of the diversity of German portrait painting around 1800, and the strong regional variations that existed. To the expressionist and symbolic realism of Runge in Hamburg (cat.91), to the poetic primitivism of the Nazarenes in Rome and Vienna, Schick brings the more European elegance of the female portrait.

In this painting the sitter was keen to present herself as a fashionable woman: her full, fluid white dress looks like the last word in fashionable elegance, as does the simple but valuable coral necklace, whose colour is picked up by the large red cashmere shawl and the fabulous striped shoes. Wilhelmine von Cotta is holding the handle of a handbag in her right hand, a new accessory made necessary by the appearance of dresses with no pockets. Remaining faithful to his training with

a sculptor, and to the descriptive realism that was part of the German tradition, Schick gives a painstaking, detailed description of all the accessories, such as the hairstyle of carefully dressed curls, rejecting the French habit of simplifying details by idealising them. He manages to merge the ideal pose, which is both Davidian and neoclassical, and the realism of the detail and the sitter's features. With her slightly tilted eyes and her high cheekbones, Wilhelmine should be immediately recognisable; the elegant simplicity of the composition compensates for the slight coarseness of her ears and nose, which are depicted with an unsparing eye.

Although French portraiture of the period had a decisive influence on the work of Schick, the English portrait also seems to have engaged his interest, if the landscape in the background of this work is anything to go by. Wilhelmine von Cotta is seated in a garden, with an elegant parasol beside her. This costly accessory could be found (in the shape of an umbrella) in numerous English portraits, such as Joshua Reynolds's *Lady Mary Wortley Montagu, the Countess of Bute* (cat.25 ).

The park disappearing into the distance in the background, consisting of a lawn and large cypress trees, is evocative of the landscape gardens that came to be called 'English gardens'; they came into fashion at the end of the eighteenth century, particularly in Germany. The foliage, treated in an extremely graphic way, creates a large patch of green against which the white dress stands out clearly, with the red shawl acting as contrast. With the mixture of influences in this portrait, and without departing from the analytical spirit that was so much a part of German art, Gottlieb Schick was participating in an individual and sensitive manner in the beginnings of European Neoclassicism, giving the genre unprecedented monumentality and grace. SA

# Sir Martin Archer Shee

DUBLIN, 1769 – BRIGHTON, 1850

## 13A
### After Sir Thomas Lawrence
*George IV*

c.1838–40
Oil on canvas, 275 × 183.7 cm
Royal Academy of Arts, London, 03/1307

PROVENANCE: painted at the request of the General Assembly of the Royal Academy, 1838
EXHIBITED: *London: World City, 1800–1840*, Villa Hügel, Essen, 1992, no.35
LITERATURE: Essen 1992, p.249

See the catalogue entry for the original portrait by Sir Thomas Lawrence (cat.13).

# Fedot Ivanovich Shubin

POMOR, NEAR KHOLMOGORY, 1740 – ST PETERSBURG, 1805

## 6
### *Catherine II, Empress of Russia*

1771
Marble, 80.5 × 33.5 × 30 cm
Inscription: on the reverse, in Cyrillic characters: *Exécuté à Rome 1771. F. I. Choubine*
Victoria and Albert Museum, London, A. 32-1964

PROVENANCE: commissioned in Rome by Count Ivan Ivanovich Shuvalov, founder of the Academy of the Three Noblest Arts (later the Imperial Academy of Arts) in St Petersburg; then owned by his nephew, Prince F. N. Golitsin, in his palace in Petrovskoye, near Moscow, where the bust was still in place in 1910 (visible in an old photograph); bought by Voldemar Wehrlin, legal councillor to the Swiss legation to the USSR between 1918 and 1920 (and also the representative of the Swiss Red Cross in Moscow), c.1920; put up for sale by him at Sotheby's, London, 29 June 1964 (no.134); it remained unsold and was bought by the Victoria and Albert Museum, London, with a generous contribution from the friends of Syrie Maugham, in her memory, 1964
EXHIBITED: Norwich and Kenwood, 1996–97, no.71
LITERATURE: Wehrlin and Schlumberger 1964, p.43, repr.; Tarasova 2000, pp.54–55, repr.; Toronto 2005, p.160

This bust of Catherine II (1729–1796), Empress of Russia (1762–96), is one of Shubin's earliest known works. Shubin studied at the Imperial Academy of Arts in St Petersburg (1761–67) under the Frenchman Nicolas-François Gillet, obtaining a gold medal; this award allowed him to go abroad to complete his training. He travelled to Paris, where the ambassador, Dimitri Alexeyevich Golitsin, a friend of Diderot, introduced him into Jean-Baptiste Pigalle's studio (September 1767–69). He left for Italy in 1770. His career took off there (he was admitted into the Accademia Clementina in Bologna in 1773): while there, he produced portraits of Count Ivan Ivanovich Shuvalov and his nephew, Prince F. N. Golitsin (the State Tretyakov Gallery, Moscow: Moscow 1994, nos 2 and 4, repr.), and also the Counts Orlov, brothers of Catherine's favourite (St Petersburg, National Museum of Russia: Moscow 1994, no.3, repr.).

Shubin was in close contact with Shuvalov, founder of the Academy of the Three Noblest Arts (later the Imperial Academy of Arts) in St Petersburg and former favourite of the Empress Elizabeth; he was dismissed by Catherine and lived thereafter between Rome and Paris until his return to Russia in 1777. Shuvalov played the part of protector to his compatriots in Rome. He bought works of art for the Empress, including antiques, and was familiar with the antique dealers and the art enthusiasts doing the Grand Tour (Androssov 2000, pp.42–43). The bust of Catherine was probably taken back to Russia by her nephew, Golitsin. It remained with his descendants until the 1920s; the family had to get rid of it then because the Soviet government had forbidden private citizens to keep images of the former Russian rulers. Thanks mainly to this piece, Shubin was accepted by the Imperial Academy of Arts in St Petersburg in 1774. He rapidly became a well-known portrait artist, particularly to Catherine II.

Shubin was far from his native soil when he produced this portrait. He must have found inspiration in illustrations (perhaps a bust-sized engraving of Eriksen's portrait: see Toronto 2005, p.273) in order to achieve a likeness, as did Jean-Antoine Houdon at almost the same moment at the request of Count Alexander Stroganov (1773; Hermitage Museum, St Petersburg) (Arnason 1976, p.15). The Russian sculptor depicted a smiling face, although in later portraits he portrayed her in a more severe way. He avoided a ceremonial representation, possibly because he was anxious about reproducing the costume accurately – or he may not have had a sufficiently large block of marble at his disposal.

Shubin chose a short torso, cut in a curve just below the shoulders, with no clothes. This way of depicting his sitter had the advantage of being restrained, and of evoking Roman statuary, understandable in a young artist living in Italy, even if it would have been inconceivable to the Romans to apply it to a woman. The reference to classical antiquity is emphasised by the laurel wreath, carved with great skill and admirably fastened with a ribbon at the nape of the neck. Catherine's hair is pushed back, revealing her forehead as fashion demanded, and a few heavy locks fall over her neck. The chignon, held up by a bow, is a successful adaptation of an Italian hairstyle, inspired by the elegant ladies of classical antiquity and of more modern times (for example Bernini's *Costanza Bonarelli*, 1636–38, in the Museo Nazionale del Bargello, Florence). A tiara on her head tells us that Catherine is queen.

The bust also displays a subtle wish to link the Empress of Russia – who had been on the throne since 1762 – with a distinguished and enlightened past. At that period the Semiramis of the North, as Voltaire put it, enjoyed intense relations with the heralds of the Enlightenment – Voltaire, d'Alembert and Diderot: Shubin's image avoids showing the Empress as a despot, bearing the attributes of her position; he depicts her as a smiling sovereign, anxious for the well-being of her people, for whom she had established a new code of laws governed by reason. The laurel wreath is not so much that of the conqueror of the Turks (the Russian naval victory in the Battle of Cesme, 1770) as that of the shrewd legislator; it is 'the reward for Valour and Virtue' (Lacombe de Prezel, vol.2, 1779, p.39).

In 1783, twelve years later, the sculptor repeated the pose, with the same curved cut and similar proportions, the laurel wreath, the tiara and the locks of hair on the shoulder; but the heroism lent by the expanse of naked flesh is replaced by a gown adorned with the necklace of the Order of St Andrew, lending authority to the sovereign's body the State Russian Museum, St Petersburg; the model of the bust, or an earlier version, was painted in 1782 by Levitsky beside the portrait of Alexander Lanskoy in the same museum, a sign of the symbolic value acquired by Shubin's composition (see New York 2005, pp.126–27, nos 62 and 63, repr.). In 1783, the image of the autocrat is made public, whereas in 1771 it was only implicit.

The marble bust in the Victoria and Albert Museum, London, carved with enormous skill and sensitivity, is a precious jewel among the numerous depictions of Catherine: distance allowed the sculptor to produce an objective view of the Empress, a much more subtle portrayal than the pompous ceremonial portrait produced by Houdon. It is possible that Shubin chose to portray Catherine with naked shoulders in the ancient style because he came into contact with the art of Joseph Nollekens in Rome: Shubin may have met him before he left for England in 1770 through Shuvalov, who had business dealings with him over copies of antiquities (Androssov 2000, p.43). Nollekens's male portraits use this formula for contemporary portraits in the antique manner (*Laurence Sterne*, c.1766, National Portrait Gallery, London) (Whinney 1988, fig.203).

The Russian artist may also have been influenced by the Englishman's treatment of eyes, with the iris lightly hollowed out and the pupil standing out in relief; but he could also have observed this feature in the work of Italian baroque sculptors. The portrait of F. N. Golitsin of 1777 (see Moscow 1994, no.2, repr.) is cut short in the antique manner; the upper part of the torso is draped, the pupils are incised, and the figure has a contemplative air and distinguished pout in the style of Christopher Hewetson, the fashionable Irish sculptor whom Shubin may have also met in Rome. After his return to Russia, Shubin abandoned the naked classical style in his many portraits of dignitaries; this one is unique in his *oeuvre*, tinged with Italian idealism.  GS

# Henry Singleton
LONDON, 1766 – LONDON, 1839

## 72
### *The Royal Academicians in General Assembly*

1795 (with portions reworked until 1798)
Inscribed at bottom left: *H. Singleton 1795*
Oil on canvas, 198.1 × 259 cm
Royal Academy of Arts, London, 03/1310

PROVENANCE: commissioned by Cantelowe Bestland for the purpose of making an engraving; still in the artist's possession, 1822; given to the Royal Academy by Philip Hardwick RA, 1861
EXHIBITED: put on show at the artist's house, 4 Haymarket, June 1795; British Institution, 1822, no.291; for later exhibition history, see Washington 1982, p.33
LITERATURE: London 1991, pp.63–64

The painter of this group portrait of the Royal Academicians, Henry Singleton, was a precocious artistic talent who trained at the Academy's Schools but never became an Academician. Although his image depended on informal support from the artists depicted, it was apparently not directly sponsored by the Academy. According to the landscape artist Joseph Farington, Singleton had been engaged 'at large expence' to paint 'portraits of all the Academicians' by the engraver Cantelowe Bestland, whose engraving after Singleton's painting was 'nearly *etched*' in May 1796 and finally published in 1802 (Farington 1978–84, vol.1, pp.248, 251, vol.2, pp.557, 571).

Bestland may have spotted potential profit in revisiting the tableau of Royal Academicians painted a generation earlier by Johann Zoffany (cat.70). Thirteen Academicians who had featured in that earlier image are among the forty shown by Singleton; Zoffany himself can be seen in profile in the top row of figures, at almost the exact centre of the canvas.

The painting appears to have remained in Singleton's possession, for he exhibited it in 1822 at the British Institution under the title *The President and Royal Academicians, assembled in their Council Chamber to adjudge the Medals to the successful students in Painting, Sculpture, Architecture and Drawing*. As this suggests, the artist gave his image a narrative thread by making its ostensible subject the allocation of prizes at a General Assembly of the Academicians (a theme which may have owed something to James Barry's 1777–84 mural, *The Distribution of Premiums by the Society of Artists*).

Singleton's scene is set in the Royal Academy's apartments at Somerset House, which had been rebuilt according to the designs of Sir William Chambers, the Academy's first treasurer. The picture shows the southeast corner of the Council and Assembly Room. Benjamin West sits on the presidential chair, wearing the hat which it was his habit to don on formal occasions; on the table before him can be seen papers and medals to be awarded. Seated at the table with a quill pen to hand is John Richards, secretary of the Academy. To his left, Edward Burch (standing) and Thomas Sandby (seated) inspect an unframed image: this, together with the architectural design visible on the table, and the other works propped up around the room, are presumably students' productions awaiting judging. In fact, the gathering depicted never actually occurred; Singleton includes Chambers (seated to the right of the table), who died in 1796, while he evidently continued to adjust the image until 1798, for he includes William Beechey (the sixth head from the left), who was elected an Academician that year.

Unlike in Zoffany's painting, the two female Academicians, Angelica Kauffman and Mary Lloyd (*née* Moser), are present in person, and in a prominent position behind West's chair. They are also represented by their works: on the wall immediately behind them hang a pair of oval flower paintings by Moser, while on the ceiling above can be seen two roundels, *Design* and *Composition*, by Kauffman.

Singleton's image seems to give an accurate rendition of the Council Room's usual contents, and indeed it was a showcase of the Academy's collection, illustrating its members' talents, its corporate history and ambitions, and fulfilling the hope expressed at the time of the institution's installation in its new premises in 1780 that 'an out-line may be formed for the *English* School' by the Council Room's accumulation of paintings (Candid Review 1780, p.11). Above Moser's images hangs West's *Christ Blessing Little Children* (1781), on either side of which can be seen Reynolds's portraits of George III and Queen Charlotte (cats 2 and 3). In front of this ensemble stands Carlini's equestrian statue of George III (cat.1). On the wall to the right can be seen Reynolds's self-portrait (cat.73) and, to the right of that, Copley's diploma work, *The Tribute Money* (1782). Plaster casts had also been in place in the room from 1780; the major items shown are, from left to right, the *Belvedere Torso*, the *Borghese Gladiator*, the *Laocoön*, the *Medici Venus*, *Alcibiades' Dog* and the *Apollo Belvedere*.

Technical examination has indicated that nearly all of the composition was altered during painting, which Farington's diaries show to have been a drawn-out and acrimonious process. Preparatory work at least was underway by 5 May 1794, when the diarist first sat to Singleton for 'his Academy picture'; he recorded three more sittings, his last in January 1796 (in the final image he is sixth from the right, facing Copley, who stands alongside him).

George Dance (fifth from the left in the final image) initially refused to sit to Singleton, 'as He does not think the Architects are placed in situations such as that class of Artist should have had': they 'were to be placed only in the back ground'. This 'derangement' was apparently caused by Burch, 'who vehemently insisted upon being placed in a front situation, as He was an officer of the Academy (librarian) besides his other pretensions'. Joseph Nollekens (shown to the left of Kauffman) was reported to be 'also disatisfied [*sic*] with his situation' – and Mrs Nollekens had 'expressed herself warmly' on the 'disrespect' shown her husband. The painting was initially put on display at the artist's house in 1795; when Barry saw the image, he 'consented to set for his Portrait which He had before refused thinking the distribution of situations not sufficiently equal' (Farington 1978–84, vol.1, pp.186, 195, 266, 277–78, vol.2, pp.287–88, 352).

The British Museum holds a related drawing by Singleton showing the same scene but with a different arrangement of sitters, sculptures and paintings in the room. Singleton exhibited a portrait of Sir William Chambers at the Royal Academy in 1795, following this in 1797 with portraits of Northcote, Thomas Sandby, Cosway, Zoffany and Humphry; presumably these were related to the group image. SM

# Johann Valentin Sonnenschein

STUTTGART, 1749 – BERNE, 1828

## 145
### *Charlotte Wyttenbach*

1807
Terracotta, 35 × 32.5 × 28 cm
Formerly annotated in paint on the base: *CHARLOTTE WYTTENBACH GEB. VON GREUERS, GEB. DEN 10. JUNI 1785. VERMÄHLT DEN 9. OCTOB. 1805. GEST. DEN 14 MAY 1807*
Bernisches Historisches Museum, Berne, 18473

PROVENANCE: collection of Dr A. von Ins in Berne, 1911; presented to the museum by the Association de Soutien du Musée d'Histoire de Berne, 1927
LITERATURE: Breitbart 1912, p.291, fig.3; Bucher 1989, vol.1, p.178, vol.2, W 117, p.258

This statuette is typical of the work of Johann Valentin Sonnenschein. The son of a tailor, Sonnenschein was trained in Stuttgart between 1763 and 1766, in the workshop of Lodovico Bossi, official stuccoist to the court of Duke Charles Eugène of Württemberg. He succeeded Bossi in 1771. Badly paid, and physically affected by the harshness of his trade, Sonnenschein left for Switzerland in 1775. Having sought asylum in Zurich, he soon became successful, producing delicate stucco decorations and working as a modeller for the porcelain factory at Kilchberg. In 1779 he decided to move to Berne, where he was offered a position as drawing teacher at the Ecole des Beaux-Arts (from 1779 to 1815). His career took off in a new direction in this city: he produced numerous terracotta busts of the aristocracy of Berne, also having considerable success with his commemorative statuettes and groups in terracotta, works commissioned in memory of a deceased person.

The statuette depicting Charlotte Wyttenbach (1785–1807), née von Greyerz, is absolutely typical of Sonnenschein's fairly abundant output in this vein. The young woman, elegantly dressed and coiffed, is seated on a stool and leans her right elbow on a heavily draped table. She looks thoughtful, and has been interrupted while reading the book that she is holding in her left hand and that rests on her right leg. As a member of the professional ruling class of the city, Charlotte could afford to read for pleasure. With this skilful composition, the sculptor sets the exquisitely modelled sculpture securely in its general context. The pensive air of his model and the sense of an interrupted activity can be found in nearly all the artist's commemorative terracottas, signalling their funerary nature. In addition, the cut flower beside the bowl on the table reminds us of the model's youth – she died at the age of twenty-two.

Charlotte Wyttenbach is thus the sister (so to speak) of Julia Risolt (Kunstmuseum, Berne: Berne, 1986, p.27, no.37, repr.) plaiting a garland of flowers, or of Maria Kirchberger (Private collection: Bucher 1986, p.45, fig.31), captured in a melancholy pose with her head on her elbow. The young

women died in 1807 and 1809 respectively. These discreet, sensitive pieces, in which the main figure is accompanied by accessories depicting the lifestyle of a wealthy member of the bourgeoisie, give us a foretaste of the elegant, anecdotic compositions of Biedermeier society. GS

# Gilbert Stuart

KINGSTON, 1755 – BOSTON, 1828

## 5
### *George Washington*

(Also known as the Munro-Lenox portrait)
*c*.1800
Oil on canvas, 241.3 × 162.6 cm
Inscription on table brace: *G. St*
Judy and Michael Steinhardt, New York. Courtesy Richard L. Feigen & Co.

PROVENANCE: Peter Jay Munro, New York, *c*.1800–33; by descent in the family; purchased by James Lenox, 1845; gift to the Lenox Library (which became the New York Public Library in 1895), 1870
EXHIBITED: Washington, 2002, pp.96–99; Sotheby's, 2005, no.5, p.32
LITERATURE: see Sotheby's 2005, no.5, pp.32–33

Gilbert Stuart, undoubtedly America's premier portrait painter of the Federal era, produced a large number of portraits of George Washington in a variety of formats: full length and half length, in formal dress and in military guise. The image by which we know Washington today, in fact, relies primarily upon the painting in which Stuart immortalised him well over 200 years ago.

After living in the British Isles, where he had gone in 1775 (first to London and then to Dublin), Stuart returned to the United States in 1793, partly in order to achieve his aim of painting a portrait of Washington (New York 2004, p.79). Having lived in New York for a short time, he moved to Philadelphia in 1794, the largest centre of the United States at the time and the country's temporary capital (New York 2004, p.129). When he had established his home and studio there, he painted his first image of Washington in 1795, a work that is now probably lost (New York 2004, p.130, and Evans 1999, p.60).

Stuart had always planned to make many versions of his Washington portraits, an undertaking he knew would prove lucrative. Indeed, these works were highly popular, with commissions following each other in rapid succession, among the notables of the new nation. However, few of the portraits were done from life. There is little documentation regarding the dates and number of sittings for Stuart's portraits of Washington. We do know that Stuart completed three portraits from life – the Vaughan (1795; Andrew W. Mellon Collection), the Athenaeum

(1796; National Portrait Gallery, Smithsonian Institution, Washington DC), and the Lansdowne (1796; National Portrait Gallery, Smithsonian Institution, Washington DC) – and that the President sat for the iconic Lansdowne portrait in 1796 (New York 2004, p.133, and Evans 1999, p.63). The artist then used his own paintings and, in particular, the unfinished Athenaeum image, which he kept until his death, as the source for the replicas and variations he produced of the nation's first president. In the end there were about 100 of them New York 2004, p.133).

The Lansdowne portrait, the most significant portrait Stuart painted of Washington, was made for the English Marquis of Lansdowne (New York 2004, p.166). It was a gift from the prosperous American businessman, William Bingham, and his wife, as a gesture of friendship and a symbol of the economic relationship forged between men of the two countries (New York 2004, p.171). Stuart then made the replicas of this work now found in the collections of the Pennsylvania Academy of the Fine Arts and the Brooklyn Museum.

While the details and early history surrounding the Munro-Lenox commission are unclear, we know that this was the first in a series of four versions after the Lansdowne. The others were the canvases painted for the state governments of Rhode Island (two were done) and Connecticut. These four works vary in significant ways from the Lansdowne (New York 2004, p.186). Washington's hand now rests upon the table, instead of being raised as though he were giving an oratory, and the floor, which had been covered with an oriental carpet, now has a more austere tile pattern (Evans 1999, p.69). More importantly, the President gazes out at the viewer rather than to the side. There is a theory that the Athenaeum served as the model for Washington's face in this work, rather than the Lansdowne (New York 2004, p.188).

Stuart painted this full-length image in the grand style associated with royalty and the nobility. A dramatic swath of drapery in the background is drawn back to reveal a baroque view of sky between classical columns and rich red velvet cascades over a gilt, neoclassical table with an elaborate leg that has a fasces motif topped by a four-sided eagle capital. In this work the artist not only showcases what he had learned as a portrait painter abroad, but also visually communicates the elevated position of power held by Washington by the use of this accepted iconography. However, Stuart has used the pictorial language appropriate for kings for a different kind of leader: the man who had been the commander-in-chief of the constitutional army in the Revolution and overturned the rule of the English king, George III, in favour of a democracy. The inclusion of the red, white and blue stars and stripes in the medallion of the chair and the books on and under the table – among them *American Revolution* and *Constitution and Laws of the United States* – emphasise that Washington is not a king, but the

president of an independent country. Moreover, while this picture is full of the accoutrements and setting befitting European royalty, Washington himself appears as a legislator, in a sombre black suit (albeit velvet, with lace collar and cuffs), which he wore for formal occasions, and a sheathed dress sword (New York 2004, p.169). In these respects, Stuart's painting looks forward to the painterly interpretations another commoner-turned-ruler would receive, the portraits of Napoleon in his study by David, Ingres and others. VG

# Bertel Thorvaldsen
COPENHAGEN, 1770 – COPENHAGEN, 1844

## 110
*Princess Maria Feodorovna Bariatinskaya*

1818
Plaster, 180 × 57 × 60 cm
Thorvaldsens Museum, Copenhagen, A 172

PROVENANCE: commissioned and executed in Rome, 1818; presented by the sculptor, with the rest of his works and all his collection, to the city of Copenhagen in 1837; transported from Rome to Copenhagen, 1838, for the Thorvaldsens Museum, which opened in 1848
LITERATURE: Plon 1874, p.465; Sass 1963–65, vol.1, pp.472–68; Musée Thorvaldsen 1966, p.61; Jornaes 1997, p.106; Floryan 2004, p.172

Thorvaldsen was acquainted with Maria Wilhelmine Luise von Keller (1793–1858) in Rome; following her marriage to Prince Ivanovich Bariatinski in 1813, she became Princess Maria Feodorovna Bariatinskaya. German by birth, she was the daughter of the Prussian diplomat Count Dorothe Ludwig Christopher von Keller. Her husband, born into a large Russian family under the protection of Catherine II, was also a diplomat (he was ambassador to Munich), and she visited Rome with him in 1818.

Thorvaldsen first made a portrait bust of her. The plaster model is now in the Thorvaldsens Museum, Copenhagen (Sass 1963–65, vol.1, repr. pp.463, 465), and the bust was probably never executed in marble. He later made a full-length statue. The contract between the sculptor and the prince, written in French, is dated Rome, 4 August 1818 (Floryan 2004, pp.171–72): '1) The Chevalier Thorvaldsen is pleased to make a statue of Madame la princesse Bariatinsky. 2) It will be made in white Carrara marble, life-size, dressed in the fashion of classical antiquity, as has been agreed between the contracting parties. 3) The Chevalier Thorvaldsen undertakes to complete the said statue in the space of three years from the date this contract is signed. 4) The price agreed for the said statue is 3,000 Roman *scudi*, and since His Excellency Monsieur le prince Bariatinsky has given the requisite orders to Torlonia and Co. that a third

of the said sum should be paid beforehand in advance, viz. 1,000 Roman *scudi*, and the rest when the statue is finished, Chevalier Thorwaldsen declares forthwith that he is satisfied with the said mode of payment.' In 1819, Thorvaldsen returned to his own country: the plaster model was finished and his Roman studio assistants could work on the marble version in his absence (Jornaes 1997, p.106). The sculptor returned in 1820 and supervised the completion of the work, putting in some finishing touches, as was his habit. We do not know why the marble statue, which had already been partly paid for, was not delivered to the prince (it was returned to Copenhagen with the rest of the contents of the Roman studio and is today preserved in the Thorvaldsens Museum). It was arranged that the statue would be transported to Odessa and then on to the Bariatinski Palace in Kursk. Following claims made by the princess's son in 1846 a marble version was prepared by H. W. Bissen, Thorvaldsen's ablest Danish student, and this was finally sent to Russia (it is now in the Pushkin Museum in Moscow).

Thorvaldsen made very few full-length portraits of contemporary women: in fact, only three. On the other hand, he made 178 busts (Sass 1963–65, vol.3, p.7), and complained endlessly that this activity prevented him from devoting his time to his essential task: the creation of statues and *bas-reliefs*. In his busts, the artist made an effort to reproduce the facial features of his sitters with some care; however, in the case of the statues the head is united with the rest of the figure and is largely idealised. Thus, the bust of Princess Bariatinskaya modelled in 1818 bears some resemblance to the facial features of the sitter, whereas the face on the statue, so idealised as to be no longer recognisable, has lost this likeness. As with Canova, the execution of a life-size statue required the creation of a work according to a canon of idealised beauty, the matter of physical resemblance being forgotten.

The princess is represented in classical dress, dressed in a tunic (the *chiton*) and a cloak (the *hymation*) with long, soft pleats. Sandals adorn her feet. Her hairstyle is highly sophisticated: a chignon tightly bound with ribbons produces a flourish of small, chiselled locks at the top of her head, reminding one of the elegant curls worn by the patrician ladies of Imperial Rome, and also by contemporary beauties. It was by such details, assimilated from classical models, that Thorvaldsen was able to conform to his clients' desire to be depicted in fashion. The eyes are almost un-incised – the contours of the iris and the pupil only lightly engraved – and this veils their gaze, giving them a diffident, inward-looking aspect. The beauty of the composition is derived from features borrowed directly from classical art.

The gesture of the elbow of the right arm leaning on the hand of the folded left arm comes from the statue of *Modesty* in the Vatican (which came from the Villa Mattei to the Museo Pio

Clementino in 1774; Haskell and Penny 1988, no.157). In the mid-eighteenth century, *Modesty* was considered to be one of the most beautiful classical pieces in Italy: Winckelmann thought it a portrait representing Melpomene, the Muse of Tragedy, because of its solemn gaze; Visconti saw it as either Melpomene or Pudicitia (Modesty). The motif is recurrent in classical art, both in statuary (there are examples in the Musei Capitolini) as well as in mural painting (Pompeii), and it found favour with neoclassical artists such as Ingres. The gesture of the index finger under the chin is probably borrowed from a funerary relief in the Galleria Borghese, showing a Roman matron between two men in togas (Hartmann 1979, pl.31, fig.4), of which Thorvaldsen made a drawing (Hartmann 1989, p.70).

The artist's other statues of women are also derived from famous classical works: Princess Caroline Amalia, with her right hand above her right shoulder, reproduces the gesture of *Diane de Gabies* (Borghese collection; Haskell and Penny 1988, no.101); the Countess Osterman-Tolstoy echoes the pose of the *Seated Agrippina* in the Musei Capitolini (Haskell and Penny 1988, no.69), as does Canova's *Madame Mère*. These idealised sculpted portraits of great ladies imitating the poses of classical marble statues also reflect the contemporary taste for *tableaux vivants* and the striking of 'attitudes', enjoyed by fashionable society ladies. Elisabeth-Louise Vigée-Lebrun, the Comtesse de Genlis, Emma Hamilton and Ida Brun were all famed for having composed, mimed and sung playlets from classical literature. Was Princess Bariatinskaya inspired as they were, on a day of social recreation? We should also admire this masterpiece for the exceptional empathy shown by the sculptor in the way he contrasts the sensibility of the young woman with the evanescence of an ideal, dreamlike world. GS

## 120
### Apotheosis of Napoleon I

*c.*1830
Marble, 105 × 67 × 46 cm
Thorvaldsens Museum, Copenhagen, A 867

PROVENANCE: commissioned by Alexander Murray (before 1801–45) of Broughton, *c.*1829; displayed in his house (Cally House) in Kirkcudbrightshire, Scotland; his estate sale, 1846; acquired by the 10th Duke of Hamilton and moved to Hamilton Palace, South Lanarkshire; his sale, 1882, no.542; acquired by J.B. Greenshields of Kerse, Lanarkshire; sold at Sotheby's, London, 1916; acquired by the Parisian antique dealer Martin Bacri, who sold it to M. Thionville, Paris; acquired in Paris by the Danish consul-general, Valdemar Glückstadt, 1918; his sale, Copenhagen, 1923; acquired by M. Bruun; sold by his daughter, Mrs Eleanor Vestergaad, to the Thorvaldsens Museum, Copenhagen, 1929
EXHIBITED: Rome, 1989B, no.65
LITERATURE: Plon 1874, pp.165–66, 469; Sass 1963–65, vol.2, pp.230–38, repr.; Sass 1963–65, vol.3, p.97, no.151; Hubert 1964A, p.450, fig.225; Musée Thorvaldsen 1966, p.33, no.252; Hartmann 1979, pp.84–88, pl.32, fig.5

This astonishing work was commissioned by the Francophile Scotsman Alexander Murray, a Whig

parliamentarian who was connected to the Earls of Galloway, an eminent family allied to the Stuarts. It was acquired after Murray's death by another Whig parliamentarian, the Duke of Hamilton, who exhibited it in the place of honour in the gallery of his castle. The original plaster model was not part of the foundation collection of the Thorvaldsens Museum, Copenhagen; it was acquired in 1974 (inv. A 909; Sass 1963–65, vol.2, repr. p.231).

Other marble versions of similar size are known. One copy, probably made in Thorvaldsen's Roman studio, was exhibited during the Second Empire in the throne room of the Château des Tuileries (photographs in the Musée Carnavalet-Histoire de Paris, Paris, and in the Château de Malmaison: Rondot 1994). It was saved in 1871 from the fire that partly destroyed the palace, and transferred to the Louvre, Paris, on 3 May (Plon 1874, p.469). This may have been the version returned to the Empress Eugénie (Granger 2005, p.764), sold at Farnborough Hall on 18 July 1927 and given in the same year by Moss Davis to the Art Gallery of Auckland, New Zealand (Auckland Quarterly 1976, repr.). A plaster cast, deposited by the Louvre at the Château de Fontainebleau in 1907, is now in the Musée National du Château de Bois-Préau. Another marble version, unfinished at the time of Thorvaldsen's death, was finished by Bissen for the Thorvaldsens Museum (inv. A 732: see Cologne 1977, no.34). Also worth mentioning is a free copy executed in the form of a herm by another pupil of Thorvaldsen, Luigi Bienaimé, for the Protomoteca Capitolina. The piece was also distributed in reduced-scale copies, in Copenhagen biscuit-ware, as well as in marble.

Because Thorvaldsen had never made a portrait of Napoleon during his lifetime, he took his inspiration from the funerary mask, of which he owned a copy in plaster (Sass 1963–65, vol.2, p.233, repr.). This mask was moulded in St Helena by Antonmarchi, the Emperor's doctor, two days after the Emperor's demise, and was very widely circulated (see Paris 1969, no.578). The sculptor mingled features of the mask with other references, in particular the canonical image of Napoleon's face provided by Chaudet's 1804 bust, marble versions of which were produced in large numbers by the workshops in Carrara during the Empire (production topped over 1,000 copies); copies were also produced in biscuit-ware by the Sèvres Porcelain Factory, and in bronze (Hubert and Ledoux-Lebard 1999, pp.78–87).

Thorvaldsen composed a portrait that was a good likeness as well as being idealised: he repeated the square chin, straight nose, the battered forehead with the small locks of hair (the most recognisable feature of all), and conveyed the Emperor's energy and strong will via his tightly closed lips and blank eyes without pupils. He emphasised the heroic character of the sitter with a laurel wreath, tied at the back by a ribbon whose two ends dangle on

either side of the neck, as in the bust by Lorenzo Bartolini – which was also widely circulated by the Banca Elisiana of Carrara (Hubert and Ledoux-Lebard 1999, pp.100–01). The horizontal cut below the shoulders and the absence of clothing echo the presentation of the bust as a herm by Chaudet and Bartolini. In this respect, Thorvaldsen deliberately makes his work different from the creation by his rival Canova, whose bust, lively and impetuous as it is, is made to a different set of criteria.

The Danish sculptor chose a grandiose setting for his bust, one that recalls the apotheoses of classical antiquity. On the right shoulder of his hero he has placed the aegis (the shield of the gods, in particular of Jupiter and, above all, Minerva), adorned with the head of Medusa entwined with snakes; here his inspiration came from Roman models such as the cameo portrait of the first Roman Emperor, Augustus, now in the British Museum, London (Hartmann 1989, p.71). Napoleon is perched on the terrestrial globe, an indication of the universal scope of his power. The ensemble is supported at the front by an eagle with spread wings, the insignia of imperial glory, and, on the reverse, by a palm tree with spreading branches; the palm frond was as an accessory to the victorious hero.

Thorvaldsen must have taken his inspiration from a work in his collection that presented a similar arrangement, a bust of Hadrian that he assumed to be classical (in fact it was an eighteenth-century fake: Sass 1963–65, vol.2, p.235, repr.). The most obvious source, however, is the colossal group of the *Apotheosis of the Emperor Claudius* in the Colonna collection, restored by Orfeo Boselli and presented to Philip IV of Spain (now partly destroyed), of which there were engravings (Hartmann 1979, pl.32, fig.3). The apotheosis on an eagle was a common theme in antiquity: there is a celebrated apotheosis of Titus on the vault of his arch in Rome (Kleiner 1992, p.189, fig.157); there are examples on jewellery (the *Apotheosis of Faustina*, engraved by Levesque de Gravelle in 1737) and on objects in gold and silver (the *Apotheosis of Homer*, a silver dish from Herculanium drawn by Pajou).

If we are to believe a sketch on a fragment of a letter (Thorvaldsens Museum, inv. C 349: see Cologne 1977, no.B 53), Thorvaldsen originally planned to place his composition on a pedestal adorned with a bas-relief depicting Victory writing on a tablet. This stereotype of Roman art is represented on Trajan's Column, and the artist possessed a plaster cast of the detail (Hartmann 1989, p.71). He also had in his collection plaster casts of classical eagles, and lamps with the image of Jupiter in the back of the eagle (Hartmann 1979, pl.32, fig.2), all objects that may have stimulated his imagination.

Thorvaldsen's creation, a sublime evocation of the Napoleonic myth, deriving its immortality from the splendour of Imperial Rome, was followed almost immediately by the *Apotheosis* of *Napoleon I* designed by James Pradier in 1834 to crown the Arc de Triomphe in the Place de l'Etoile in Paris (plaster cast in the Louvre: see Musée du Louvre 1998, vol. 2, p. 543), in which the Emperor, portrayed to the waist, is carried off by an eagle. The piece was never executed to monumental scale, depriving those suffering nostalgia for the Napoleonic myth of a spectacular image. GS

## 79
*Horace Vernet*

1832–33
Marble, 50 × 27 × 19.7 cm
Inscription, front: *HORACE VERNET*;
back: *A. THORVALDSEN fecit*
Musée Calvet, Avignon

PROVENANCE: presented to the museum by Horace Vernet, 1835
EXHIBITED: Nuremberg and Schleswig, 1991–92, no. 4.12
LITERATURE: Sass 1963–65, vol. 2, pp. 283–84, repr.; Sass 1963–65, vol. 3, p. 100; Hubert 1964A, p. 451; Rome 2003, p. 214, fig. 45a and p. 558

Bertel Thorvaldsen's portrait of the painter Horace Vernet (1789–1863) provides strong evidence of the esteem in which the two artists, who were both at the time very well known, held one another. The sculptor in fact considered Vernet to be the 'the painter of the century' (letter of 9 June 1838: Sass 1963–65, vol. 2, p. 284), and owned a painting by him (the portrait of an Armenian priest, now in the Thorvaldsens Museum, Copenhagen). The painter had the same admiration for the sculptor and painted some portraits of him.

The two men got to know each other when Vernet was Director of the French Academy in Rome (from 1829 to 1835); we know that Thorvaldsen was a frequent visitor at the Villa Medici. Vernet painted a portrait of the sculptor in 1831 in which he is posed beside a sketch of the Lucerne *Lion* (painting now lost). Thorvaldsen began work on the bust of the painter in August 1832. It was finished during the first few months of the following year (payments made on 25 August 1832 and 4 February 1833: Sass 1963–65, vol. 2, p. 284). The clay model is depicted by Vernet in another portrait of the sculptor, signed and dated 1833 (see cat. 80): Thorvaldsen, dressed for work, holding a modelling tool in his hand, leans his elbows on a turntable on which stands the bust of Vernet on which he is working. His attitude before the piece of his own work is more self-satisfied than that of Denis-Antoine Chaudet, as portrayed by Jean-Baptiste Desmarais (cat. 78).

The clay model has not survived: unfired, it would immediately have been cast in plaster, the usual practice in Thorvaldsen's workshop. For practical reasons, Thorvaldsen (like Jean-Antoine Houdon) preferred to store plaster casts and not clay models, which are so much more fragile. The plaster cast, still visible in the Thorvaldsens Museum (see Rome 2003, p. 558, no. 46), served as a model for the marble version in the Musée Calvet,

Avignon, which is a very accurate transcription of the sober herm designed by the sculptor. A colossal version of the portrait, also in marble, was begun in Rome in 1834 and finished in 1856 in Copenhagen, after Thorvaldsen's death, under the supervision of his pupil Herman Wilhelm Bissen: although the head is a copy of the plaster cast (and thus of the Avignon marble), the circular cut at the base of the bust and its presentation on a pedestal are different (Sass 1963–65, vol. 2, p. 285).

A drawing by Bissen from a Roman sketchbook (c. 1832–32; Ny Carlsberg Glyptotek, Copenhagen: Sass 1963–65, vol. 3, p. 101, repr.) shows Vernet sitting for Thorvaldsen. We can recognise the painter's broad forehead and moustache. During his career as a portrait sculptor, Thorvaldsen used the herm composition several times; its geometrical clarity allows the face, emerging above a pure shape, to be shown to best advantage. Vernet's fine inspired head, with its mop of curls apparently prolonged by the thick side whiskers and moustache, and its lively gaze (thanks to discreet hollowing of the eyes), rises convincingly above the block of marble, mitigating the severity of the rectangular cuts and the absence of clothing. GS

# Unknown Artist

## 92
*A Man and His Children* (formerly known as *Michel Gérard, Deputy at the Assemblée Nationale, and His Children*)

c. 1810
Oil on canvas, 160 × 127 cm
Musée de Tessé, Le Mans, 10.288

PROVENANCE: collection of Abel Vautier, 1861; sold at his estate sale, 9 December 1863; collection of the Comte de Saint-Albin; bequeathed to the town of Le Mans, 1879
EXHIBITED: Le Mans, 1999, p. 118
LITERATURE: Le Feuvre and Alexandre 1932, no. 113

This large family portrait, one of the best of its kind, has still not revealed the name of its author, nor the name of the main sitter, previously identified as Michel Gérard (1737–1815), a member of the National Convention. The realism in the rendering of the facial features, the rigour of the composition and the uncompromising character of the layout caused it to be ascribed by some art historians to Jacques-Louis David; however, this flattering attribution is no longer upheld. In fact, although the painting possesses exceptional qualities, its tenderness and a tendency towards the simplification of facial features, particularly those of the boys, mean that it could not be a part of David's *oeuvre*. In addition, the taste for detail that emerged at the end of David's life (in the portrait

of *Juliette de Villeneuve*; cat. 143) is not compatible with the probable date of this portrait.

Other critics have compared this painting to *The De Hemptinne Family* by Navez (cat. 144). Although both paintings depict bourgeois family intimacy, the colour scheme of this family portrait and the lightness of touch with which it is painted bear no relation to the thicker paint, warmer colours and hastier drawing of the Belgian artist. All the evidence suggests that the painting belongs within David's circle; it bears a resemblance to Gérard's early style, but does not have his taste for effects of light and shade.

The father of the family sits squarely on a chair with his youngest son between his knees; the boy seems to have interrupted what he was doing to listen to his sister playing the piano. The older brothers are depicted standing behind the main group. The portrait wavers between the artificiality of the pose – expressed in the rigorous way the father and eldest son are depicted from the front and the little girl's gaze – and the more informal arrangement of the conversation piece (the youngest and middle sons). The sitters occupy almost all the space, identified as a bourgeois interior by the side table and fireplace. The artist seems to be familiar with northern painting – as is shown by the *trompe l'oeil* effect of the letter tucked into the mirror frame and the reflection of the cup.

Behind its straightforward appearance, the painting conceals a strict separation of roles: the citizen-father is glorified as the head of the family and a role model in post-revolutionary society. His function here is as the person responsible for his children's education. The small boy holds a book in his hands, probably a reading book; the artist wants us to believe that the father was busy hearing the boy's homework when they were interrupted to have their portraits painted. He might also have been paying attention to the musical education of his daughter. It is worth noting the strict divide between the masculine virtues (connected with study) and the more feminine skills (connected with the development of artistic talents intended to produce an accomplished young woman and, in time, a good wife). The same dichotomy can be found in Vincent's painting, *M. de la Forest, His Wife and Daughter*.

The contrast between the slightly untidy dress of the father, his craggy looks and forthright gaze and the boy's elegant clothing and fine manners could possibly contain the seeds of the idea of social advancement, made easier by a democratic society. At any rate, his protective gesture towards his brother – the least prominent figure in this painting – leaves no room for doubt about his ability to assert himself as his father's successor. The composition and colour scheme of the painting confirm this interpretation of the family portrait as symbolic of the new bourgeois society and its values. In fact, although the white mass of the shirt, echoed by the small girl's dress and the collars or cravats of the boys, dominates the whole group, drawing the spectator's eye towards the father, the pyramidal composition has the face of the son and heir at its apex.

It is surprising to note that the mother is missing. The number of children and the presence of the little girl make it unlikely that this large painting was meant to be accompanied by a 'female' pendant, just as the portraits executed by Louis-Léopold Boilly for the Oberkampf family (Private collection) were. Perhaps the mother is dead, or is she behind the easel, painting her own family? AA

# Horace Vernet

PARIS, 1789 – PARIS, 1863

## 80
### Bertel Thorvaldsen

1833
Oil on canvas, 99.8 × 75.2cm
Signed and dated: *Horace Vernet à Son illustre ami Torwaldsen Rome 1833*
Thorvaldsens Museum, Copenhagen, B 95

PROVENANCE: commenced February 1833, in exchange for Vernet's portrait bust by Thorvaldsen (cat. 79); given to Thorvaldsen in Rome before Vernet's departure, 1835; taken to Copenhagen by Thorvaldsen on his return in 1837; entered the museum's collection, 1848
EXHIBITED: Rome, 1835; Charlottenburg, 1845, no. 376; Rome and Paris, 1980, no. 64, p. 89; Rome, 1989B, fig. 4, p. 30; Nuremberg and Schleswig, 1991–92
LITERATURE: Beulé 1863; Thiele 1852–54, vol.3, pp.532–33; *Gazette des Beaux-Arts*, 1868, pp.546–61, 553; Hammerich 1870, pp.86–87; Plon 1874, frontispiece; Trier 1903, pp.166–67; Jensen and Marcus 1926; Thorvaldsens Museum 1931, no.95; Rostrup 1945, vol.2, p.26, no. 152; Sass 1963–65, vol.2, p.281; Hartmann 1971; Talbot 1980; Rome 1980, no.64, p.89; Rome 1989B, fig.4, p.30; Friborg 2000, pp.36–38

When praised by the composer Felix Mendelssohn as an artist who 'produces with incredible facility and freshness' (letter, 1 March 1831), the French painter Horace Vernet had just embarked upon this portrait of the Danish sculptor Bertel Thorvaldsen (1770–1844). Thorvaldsen and Vernet had met while living in the thriving expatriate artistic community in Rome in the 1830s. They became great friends and, a sign of their mutual esteem, decided in 1832 to execute portraits of each other. Vernet's double portrait, representing Thorvaldsen with the bust he has carved of Vernet (cat.79), highlights the poles of artistic expression at the time, ranging from Thorvaldsen's classical ethos to Vernet's contemporary naturalism.

Horace Vernet came from an august family of painters. He was born in the Louvre, where his parents had apartments during the year of the Revolution. His father was Carle Vernet, with

whom he trained, and his grandfather was the celebrated marine painter Joseph Vernet. Coming of age in the 1820s, Horace Vernet joined Géricault, Delacroix and Scheffer as the leading proponents of Romanticism. An ardent Bonapartist, he followed Napoleon on his early campaign trails, gaining renown for the speed and facility with which he transcribed his observations onto canvas. He is remembered for his large-scale scenes of military battle, such as *Clichy Gate: The Defence of Paris, 30 March 1814* (1820; Louvre, Paris), where he was actually engaged in combat. Vernet was part of the school that was less interested in traditional history painting than focusing on scenes from contemporary history, depicting men and animals in dramatic action, with a concentration on naturalistic, faithful detail. Later on, he became enthralled with the Orient, a fascination crystallised by his 1833 visit to Algeria on the heels of the French army. He then travelled extensively in Egypt, Syria and Turkey. Although his large-scale *tableaux* seldom attained the tragic, eloquent dimensions of his friend Géricault's work, Vernet's military and battle scenes are engaging commemorations of contemporary events. Despite turbulent changes of regime and shifts in the political and ideological backdrop which occasionally threatened his security, the artist was fêted, received honours in his lifetime and, ultimately, was well represented at the 1855 Exposition Universelle.

In 1820, after the Restoration, when his years of favour under Bonaparte had long since ended, Vernet departed for Rome with his father. In 1828, he was elected Director of the French Academy in that city (he was to be succeeded by Ingres in 1835). Vernet's natural ebullience and forceful character made his private atelier a lively social scene and revitalised the institution's vitality, which had faded under his predecessor Pierre Guérin. During Vernet's directorship, the Villa Medici was, as Stendhal remarked, 'Paris in Rome' (Talbot 1980, p.144), and became the epicentre for cultivated, fashionable gatherings, which included Mendelssohn, Léopold Robert, and Vernet's septuagenarian father.

Thorvaldsen had long been a resident of Rome, having arrived there on a scholarship from the Royal Danish Academy of Fine Arts in 1797. He returned only intermittently to his homeland until near the end of his life. The visual, aesthetic and physical experience of living day-to-day among the antiquities of Rome brought about an artistic epiphany in the young sculptor. In 1802, a financially timely commission from the British connoisseur Thomas Hope, *Jason with the Golden Fleece* (1803; Thorvaldsens Museum, Copenhagen), made his reputation overnight, due to the formidable bearing of the statue, at which 'everyone was struck with astonishment. The people believed they were looking at Apollo, Bacchus or Mars' (Plon 1874, p.179). Through his astonishingly rapid rise to fame, Thorvaldsen was appointed Professor of

the Royal Danish Academy of Fine Arts in Copenhagen *in absentia* in 1805. He later became the Director of the Accademia di San Luca in Rome, of which he had been a member since 1808, a rare honour for a Protestant foreigner. Throughout, he ran a prolific studio and his forceful, graceful work was in enormous demand throughout Europe, Russia, and in his adopted country. He executed many portraits of political and cultural luminaries, heads of state, friends, and Scandinavian, Italian and French artists. He was also commissioned to produce ideologically significant monuments in many nations, such as Warsaw's equestrian statue of Prince Jozef Poniatowski (1826–27).

By the time this portrait was begun, Thorvaldsen was one of the most celebrated artists alive and the leading exponent of neoclassical sculpture (his position was uncontested after the death of Canova in 1822). He was an avid art collector, from antiquities to works by the contemporary Nazarenes. Vernet shows him at the moment at which he has completed his portrait bust: a classically idealised head, with brushed-forward curls, *à l'Antique*, and sideburns accentuating angular cheekbones. Vernet's likeness is truthful, and Thorvaldsen's age and weariness are evident. His skin is loose, his face lined, his eyes red-rimmed and underlined by bags. Yet the sculptor's expression is sharp and decisive. As if contemplating his long efforts, with an air of finality, he brings his arm down in repose upon the sturdy wooden pedestal which supports the bust of Vernet, the veins slightly visible in his hands suggesting his exertions. With no semblance of the artisan, Thorvaldsen cuts an elegant figure, attired in a pristine white shirt, with only his one up-turned cuff as reference to his labours. The position of his head, turned slightly to the left, his forehead and face bathed in light, is similar to that of his portrait by the 'father of Danish painting', C. W. Eckersberg (1819–20; Landesmuseum, Schleswig-Holstein). Eckersberg, whose *plein-air* techniques engendered the Golden Age of Danish painting during the Biedermeier period, had painted Thorvaldsen in Rome previously (1814; Royal Danish Academy of Fine Arts, Copenhagen), to celebrate the pre-eminence of his countryman. But, unlike Eckersberg's more formalised, but youthful portrayal of 1814, in which Thorvaldsen is attired in the black robes of the Accademia di San Luca, Vernet's friendship portrait emphasises the rapport that existed between two important artists in Rome, the dialectic of the neoclassical and the romantic, and the significant exchange between portraiture in painting and sculpture in what is, finally, a testament to the creative relationship between two individuals. CC

# Antoine Vestier

AVALLON, 1740 – PARIS, 1824

## 19
## A Knight of Malta Holding the Portrait of Commander Texier d'Hautefeuille

1788
Oil on canvas, oval, 102 × 83 cm
Signed and dated at the lower right: *Vestier Pictor Regis 1788*
Musée des Beaux-Arts, Dijon, 3496

PROVENANCE: Général Comte d'Armandy, 1930; presented by the Comtesse d'Armandy to the Musée des Beaux-Arts, Dijon, 1936
EXHIBITED: Dijon, 1969, no.25; Valetta, 1970, no.211
LITERATURE: Georgel and Lecoq 1987, p.235; Passez 1989, no.69

When he executed this painting in 1788, Antoine Vestier was at the pinnacle of his career. Because of his attachment to the type of portrait suited to the *ancien régime* and to clients belonging to the aristocracy, he fell out of favour during the French Revolution. He entered the Académie Royale de Peinture et de Sculpture in 1785, and was much helped by Joseph-Siffred Duplessis, who had painted a portrait of Louis XVI and whose taste for the effects of fabrics and other materials he shared. His mentor may have wished, in the heart of this prestigious institution, to assert the importance of artists working exclusively in this inferior but lucrative genre, and demand for portraits grew considerably during the 1780s.

The signature '*Vestier Pictor Regis*' betrays pride in this official recognition, at a time when professional portrait painters were rare in the Académie. Vestier used it from 1787 for his official portraits of prominent people, as in the portrait of the *Baron de Doué* (1788; Private collection, France), and, in two areas that often go together, in the paintings he presented at the Salon, such as *Jean Theurel* (Salon of 1789; Musée des Beaux-Arts, Tours). The reference to the King thus served the painter, giving him unrivalled prestige, but also suited the person commissioning the painting, who was able to employ an academician rather than just a straightforward portrait painter. This tells us something about the game of social signs that was inherent in the genre.

It is not known how this painting came to be commissioned, but it appears to be a portrait designed for private use. The portrait in a medallion, much in fashion during the 1770s, is often found in aristocratic interiors and apartments. After the portrait of his daughter *Marie-Nicole Vestier* (1785; Private collection, Buenos Aires), which opened the doors of the Académie to Vestier, he sometimes chose to paint portraits within portraits, such as *Madame Vestier* (Salon of 1787; Louvre, Paris). This was an old tradition that enjoyed its hour of glory during the seventeenth century, permitting the artist to demonstrate his pictorial skills by emphasising the illusionism of the genre. In this particular case, the artifice, which dates back many centuries, is used with great

originality; the skill of the painter at rejuvenating conventional models with great naturalness is clearly demonstrated. Perhaps his journey to England in 1776 made him aware that a pose could be more spontaneous and less formal. In this portrait the main figure, seated in an armchair, takes the spectator to one side and shows him another medallion, set in a beautiful Louis XVI frame with beaded edge.

Although the identity of the sitter is not known, the person portrayed in the medallion can clearly be identified as Marie-Gabriel-Louis Texier d'Hautefeuille, Commander of the Order of Malta since 1776, whom Vestier had painted in 1784 (whereabouts unknown; Passez 1989, no.40). The main figure also ostentatiously wears the Cross of the Order of Malta, suspended from a black ribbon. If this is not a family portrait, it is very probable, as A.-M. Passez suggests, that its motive is commemorative, the main figure paying tribute to Commander Texier d'Hautefeuille, whose patronage may have allowed him to join the order. Vestier's skill lies in using only the language of the image, with artful contrivance, instead of an inscription that would normally have celebrated the event.

Although the relatively new nature of the pose may demonstrate English influence, everything else in Vestier's technique reveals the lessons of French portraiture, as practised during the 1780s. The accurate, smooth touch, which harks back to the miniature painter that Vestier once was, shows to advantage his rendering of fabrics and surfaces, and their contrasts: the iridescence of the satin, the brightness of the shirt, the reflective surface of the gold frame. The harmony of the subtle yet bold colours (the green of Texier d'Hautefeuille's jacket, the amaranth green of the sitter's jacket standing out against a green background) give this medallion a sophistication that was typical of the final years of the *ancien régime*. SA

# Elisabeth-Louise Vigée-Lebrun

PARIS, 1755 – PARIS, 1842

## 22
## Charles-Alexandre de Calonne

1784
Oil on canvas, 149 × 128 cm
Signed and dated at lower right: *Le Brun fe 1784*
Lent by Her Majesty The Queen

PROVENANCE: collection of Charles-Alexandre de Calonne; collection of George IV after 1806, hung in Carlton House
EXHIBITED: Paris, Salon of 1785, no.87; London, 1954–55, no.339; London, 1966, no.6
LITERATURE: Vigée-Lebrun 1835–37, vol.I, pp.105–06, 111–12, 153; Nolhac 1908, pp.57–62; Hautecoeur 1917, pp.68–69; Fort Worth 1982, p.55; Fort 1999, p.290

The Salon of 1785 represented one of the peaks of Vigée-Lebrun's career. She presented more than ten paintings, including the famous *Seated Bacchante* (Musée Nissim de Camondo, Paris), the *Children of France* (Musée National du Château, Versailles), the *Grétry* (also Musée National du Château, Versailles) and the *Baroness of Crussol* (Musée des Augustins, Toulouse). At the height of her powers, the artist intended to demonstrate the scope of her talent and to make her name as a history painter rather than just a portrait painter. *The Bacchante*, in fact, with its innovatory realism, helped to revive the moribund genre that had ensured the success of a painter such as Charles-Joseph Natoire. The imposing and ambitious portrait of *Charles-Alexandre de Calonne* was an essential factor in this strategy.

The Comte de Calonne (1735–1802), then Minister of Finance, was one of the most powerful men in the kingdom; with this portrait, Vigée-Lebrun confirmed her status as a painter of great statesmen, not without a fierce debate, however. At the time of the exhibition there was a rumour that she was the minister's mistress, something that she denies categorically in her *Memoirs*. Leaving aside the anecdote, the gossip illustrates the privileged relationship that she, like a new Titian, enjoyed with her sitters, particularly the most prominent ones, and the way she could take advantage of her position for 'publicity'. The debate also posed a more general question about the status of the artist and his or her relationship with power, emphasising the position of the female painter Vigée-Lebrun worked so hard to be recognised: 'Here is a sorry letter, written to make one feel disgusted by celebrity, particularly when one has the misfortune to be a woman,' she wrote, referring to the scandal surrounding the portrait of Calonne. For the first time, a woman, a member of the Académie, had managed to win recognition as an official painter. Her strategy bore fruit: at the end of the Salon she received a commission to paint the immense portrait of *Marie-Antoinette and Her Children* (Salon of 1787; Musée National du Château, Versailles), designed to improve the Queen's public image – a strategy already tried in England (see cat.90).

With the portrait of *Charles-Alexandre de Calonne*, Vigée-Lebrun revived the formula of the ceremonial portrait that the most celebrated portrait painters of the period, such as Joseph-Siffred Duplessis, were striving to diversify. She depicts the minister in a relatively conventional manner, seated on a Louis XV chair at his desk. In the background, a large pilaster supports the composition on the left, giving a sense of space. On the right a sumptuous red drape indicates the official nature of the image. The composition, which is broader than usual (see *Comte de Vaudreuil*, 1784; Virginia Museum of Fine Arts), lends the figure an unusually monumental quality; the pose was noticed, as Sophie Arnould's ironic remark demonstrates: 'Madame Lebrun has cut off his legs so that he stays put.' Calonne is in fact represented almost full length. The composition increases the distance separating the sitter from the spectator, while also ensuring that the sitter's presence is enhanced.

The originality of the portrait resides in the way the artist transcends the conventions inherent in the genre with a naturalness rejected by most portrait painters. The pose is not fixed. Calonne seems to have been interrupted by the spectator. He is not ostensibly showing a paper lying on the table but, in a procedure inherited from Van Dyck (see *Portrait of Agostino Pallavicini*, Getty Center, Los Angeles), is holding a letter that he is preparing to send to the King. The inscription 'To the King' is evidently designed to emphasise the importance of the minister and, in return, the quality of his portraitist. The writer of the *Mémoires secrets* understood this desire to give life to the composition and described the painting as a 'skilful historical portrait'.

Although she was granted few sittings – to the extent (according to her memoirs) that she had not had time to paint the hands from life – Vigée-Lebrun succeeded in reproducing the minister's features in a very realistic way. This focus on resemblance rather than the symbolism of the sitter's function, in a court portrait, upset her contemporaries: 'The resemblance to the personality is such that everyone can name him at first glance … it is he, in a word, it is M. de Calonne exactly, but it is not the Comptroller General; he looks more distracted than busy' (Fort 1999, p.299). The rules of propriety, in this case, as defined by G. P. Lomazzo in the sixteenth century, encouraged painters to give more importance to the position, the gestures and the accessories appropriate to the sitter's social function than to the sitter's physical appearance. This process of generalisation brought the portrait closer to the history portrait, by bypassing the description of the features and transforming an individual sitter into someone more generalised. Vigée-Lebrun overturned these principles, in particular the strict division between the private and public spheres, between the man and his function, between the part played by realism and the ideal. Calonne is not wearing fancy costume; his clothes are as black as they are sumptuous. In her concern for the verisimilitude of her portrait, Vigée-Lebrun has pursued realism to the extent of painting traces of powder from the wig on the shoulders of the *Receveur Général*. In so doing, she draws attention to Calonne's taste for this accessory: 'M. de Calonne always seemed rather unattractive to me; because he wore a fiscal wig. Imagine how I, with my love of the picturesque, could have dealt with a wig!' (Vigée-Lebrun 1835–37, p.106).

In this portrait of *Charles-Alexandre de Calonne*, Vigée-Lebrun displays her talent as a painter. The black clothing gives her the opportunity to capture, with stunning virtuosity, the reflections and the iridescence of satin. The richness of the colour, the perfect mastery of the lighting effects, as in the *Bacchante*, the realistic flesh and the vivacity of the pose betray the skill of a true history painter. SA

## 27
### The Comtesse de la Châtre

1789
Oil on canvas, 114.3 × 87.6 cm
Lent by The Metropolitan Museum of Art, New York. Gift of Jessie Woolworth Donahue, 1954 (54.182)

PROVENANCE: in the collection of the sitter and her heirs; Stillman Collection; collection of Mrs Jessie Woolworth Donahue, who presented it to the Metropolitan Museum, 1954
EXHIBITED: Los Angeles, 1976–77, no.59; Fort Worth, 1982 (J. Baillio)
LITERATURE: Vigée-Lebrun 1986, vol.1, p.337; Nolhac 1908, p.140; Hautecoeur 1917, p.65

In the list of paintings and portraits executed before she left France, tacked on by Vigée-Lebrun to her memoirs as an appendix, this handsome portrait figures under the year 1789 and is entitled *Comtesse de la Châtre*. Marie-Charlotte de la Châtre (1762–1848), the daughter of Bontemps, First Valet to Louis XV, was married at the time to the Comte de la Châtre, a descendant of one of the oldest aristocratic families in France. The countess felt no fondness for the ultra-conservative husband who was seventeen years her senior. She had an affair with the Comte de Jaucourt, whom she finally married once she had divorced her first husband. This painting is therefore sometimes known as the *Marquise de Jaucourt*. The countess belonged to the upper echelons of the aristocracy, familiars at court, who were Vigée-Lebrun's clientele on the eve of the Revolution.

*The Comtesse de la Châtre*, painted two years after her self-portraits with her daughter (Louvre, Paris), shows greater restraint in the artist's style. Seated on a sofa, wearing an elegant, full dress in white muslin and a straw hat adorned with a spectacular bow, the countess looks out at (and slightly down on) the spectator. The comparison with David's contemporary portrait of *Anne-Marie-Louise Thélusson, Comtesse de Sorcy* (1790; Neue Pinakothek, Munich) immediately springs to mind. In her memoirs, Vigée-Lebrun tells us that the master of the *Oath of the Horatii* had in his studio a book about Calonne, kept open at the page in which the slanderous comments connected with the portrait of the minister occur (cat.22). Whether the anecdote is true or not, it symbolises the genuine spirit of competition that existed between the two painters. Each in their respective portraits plays with a large blank figure standing out against a bare, subtly shaded background and warmed by a single touch of colour (the belt in one case, the belt and the bow on the hat in the other). Through this apparent simplicity we can measure the impact of fashion on the development of the genre.

Nevertheless, the spirit expressed in the portrait of the *Comtesse de la Châtre* is different from the spirit of *Anne-Marie-Louise Thélusson*. David in fact increased the artificiality of the pose, relying on a monumental format to magnify the young woman and transform her into a hieratic icon. She is at once close and distant, and, with her sophistication, commands respect from the spectator; arrogant David, rejecting any sign of the picturesque, is asserting with authority his dignity as a history painter.

Vigée-Lebrun has more empathy with her sitter and lends her a more feminine tenderness; she handles the *topoi* of the court portrait with subtlety, moving as she does in the upper reaches of society, and showing herself to be more experienced in court circles than her colleague. In this comparison the tension that afflicted the genre at the end of the eighteenth century can be felt – the tension between the imperative of social representation and the assertion of the sitter's own individuality. As in many of her portraits, Vigée-Lebrun depicts the countess interrupted in an activity – in this case, reading – which is simply a pretext to 'historicise' the portrait. The book that the Comtesse de la Châtre is holding is probably a novel, and is not there to identify her as a woman of letters, as the book does in François Boucher's famous portrait of Madame de Pompadour (1756; Alte Pinakotek, Munich). Nevertheless it holds a social message: it identifies the sitter as a woman of the upper class, engaged in a non-lucrative activity.

By avoiding the classic front view, used so powerfully by David, Vigée-Lebrun introduces a feeling of movement and time, in the tradition of Van Dyck. The figure of the Comtesse de la Châtre, arranged in a perfect triangle, is softened by a series of serpentine lines organised around the twist of her bust and suggested by the folds of fabric. The great hat, an accessory with a real touch of bravura, shows the subtly shaded face to best advantage, in stark contrast to the crudeness of the lighting in David's portrait of Madame Thélusson. In this portrait of the Comtesse de la Châtre, Vigée-Lebrun succeeds in bringing naturalness and immediacy to the flattering conventions inherent in the court portrait. However, unlike David, psychological analysis goes no further than the appearance; this is a portrait that still belongs to the *ancien régime*. SA

## 131
### Madame de Staël as Corinne

1809
Oil on canvas, 140 × 118 cm
Collection des Musées d'Art et d'Histoire de la Ville de Genève, Geneva

PROVENANCE: commissioned by Madame de Staël; bequeathed to Madame Albertine-Andrienne Necker-de Sassure, 1816; gift to the Musée Rath, Geneva, 1841; then Musée d'Art et d'Histoire, Geneva, 1910; on deposit to the Bibliothèque Publique et Universitaire, Salle Lullin, Geneva, 1966
EXHIBITED: see Loche, 1996, p.302
LITERATURE: see Loche 1996, p.304, no.78, ill. p.303; Pitt-Rivers 2001, pp.214–21, fig.30; May 2005, pp.182–84, pl.16

'She wore a white tunic with a blue drapery fastened beneath her breast … Her arms ravishingly beautiful; her tall full figure, reminiscent of Greek statuary, vigorously conveyed youth and happiness. In her expression there was something inspired.' (Madame de Staël, *Corinne, or Italy*, 1807, p.21.)

Germaine Necker de Staël (1766–1817) was a cultural luminary of pre- and post-revolutionary France. A Paris-born Swiss-Frenchwoman, she married the Swedish Baron de Staël-Holstein – then ambassador to France – in 1786 (Bredin 1999, p.167). She soon turned to intellectual pursuits, publishing a work on Rousseau in 1788, as well as presiding over one of the most important literary and political salons in Paris. De Staël was later forced into exile by Napoleon and went to live at her family home in Coppet, where she continued to write prolifically and re-established her acclaimed Salon. Among her regular visitors were Swiss writer and politician, Benjamin Constant, German Romantic poet and author, August Schlegel, and a Frenchwoman famous for her beauty and, like de Staël, known for her salon, Madame Juliette Récamier.

Published in 1807, the novel *Corinne, or Italy* was one of de Staël's main achievements. A hyperbolic tale of the Grand Tour experience, overwrought emotion and ill-fated love, this work made her name. The novel addressed the theme of national temperament and captured the northern European's idealised vision of Italy as an idyllic place overflowing with classical antiquities. The title character, Corinne, named after the ancient Greek poet Corinna, was the embodiment of Italy. Despite *Corinne*'s overwhelming popularity in its day, it is de Staël's 1810 study, *On Germany*, which remains her best-known work. This study of German culture was instrumental in introducing German Romantic thought to French readers. Published in France, it also proved to be de Staël's most notorious work, for Napoleon banned the book for its anti-French stance and all but a few copies were destroyed.

Elisabeth-Louise Vigée-Lebrun was another of France's major female cultural figures and the Queen's artist of choice in pre-revolutionary times. In 1807, while on a trip in Switzerland, she travelled to Coppet and visited de Staël (Loche 1996, p.304). There they agreed that Vigée-Lebrun would make a portrait of the noted author as the personification of her fictional heroine, who was a semi-autobiographical figure and, like de Staël, a creative, intellectual woman of independent means.

Vigée-Lebrun sought to evoke the sentiments intrinsic to *Corinne* in her image of de Staël. She portrayed a moment in the episode when Corinne and the book's male protagonist, Scottish peer Oswald, Lord Nelvil, were touring the countryside and ruins around Vesuvius. When at the Cape Miseno, Corinne improvised a performance in verse

with her lyre ('her favourite instrument', de Staël 1991, p.26). Vigée-Lebrun, taking her cues from the novel, shows de Staël in a white Grecian tunic and red drapery, holding a lyre as she gazes up for inspiration. Ironically, while the romantic setting is meant to evoke Campania, it was, in fact, a mixture of places. De Staël posed outside her home in Coppet, but the landscape is embellished with a *tempietto* at the top of the mountain behind her. This fanciful addition replicates the Temple of the Sibyl at Tivoli, which was visible from Corinne's villa in the novel, and reinforces the literary references in the painting (Sheriff 1996, p.247).

When she had finished the portrait in 1809, Vigée-Lebrun sent it to Coppet. Despite her high aspirations for the painting, de Staël was said to have been unhappy with her portrayal as Corinne. Noted for her mind, de Staël was not a beautiful woman and had a heavy stature. (Vigée-Lebrun described her in this way, 'not beautiful, but her lively face can lend her an air of beauty'. Vigée-Lebrun 1984, p.182.) Notwithstanding her literary guise, de Staël may have resented the perhaps too accurate depiction of her plain face and her plump figure, which appears large and dominates the composition. Nevertheless, she sent Vigée-Lebrun an appreciative note: 'I have finally received your marvellous painting, Madame, and, without thinking about my portrait, I admire your work. Your talent is evident in it, and I would very much like to think that mine could be encouraged by your example' (Vigée-Lebrun 1984, p.181). VG

# Il Volpato (Giovanni Trevisan)

BASSANO DEL GRAPPA, 1735 – ROME, 1803

## 113
### *José Nicolas de Azara and Anton Raphael Mengs*

*c.*1785
Porcelain, 28.1 × 17 × 14 cm
Inscription: *G. Volpato – Roma*
Accademia Carrara, Bergamo, sc. 167

PROVENANCE: Rome, Munoz collection; collection of Federico Zeri (before 1972); bequeathed by Zeri, 1998
EXHIBITED: London, 1972, no.1474; Milan and Bergamo, 1989, no.24; Padua and Dresden, 2001, no.11
LITERATURE: Jordan de Urries 2000, p.72, fig.7; Santuccio 2000, p.44

The hard-paste porcelain manufacture established in 1785 by Volpato in Via Pudenziana in Rome was one of the most ambitious enterprises of the neoclassical period in Italy. The objects made there in biscuit-ware, mainly reduced versions of the most celebrated antiquities in Rome

(a catalogue printed in 1795 exists in the Victoria and Albert Museum, London), were contemporary with the small bronzes produced by Francesco Righetti and Giovanni Zoffoli, or the porcelain objects produced by Filippo Tagliolini in Naples (Honour 1967; Haskell and Penny 1988, pp.113–14). The Volpato manufacture thus participated in the tremendous dissemination of masterpieces of classical antiquity throughout Italy during the last quarter of the eighteenth century. The antiquities were considerably reduced in size to make distribution easier.

Giovanni Trevisan, better known as Volpato – the name probably came from an ancestor of his mother's – arrived in Rome in 1771; he was an engraver of repute and a friend of Gavin Hamilton, Angelica Kauffman and Canova. He lived in a world of artists, collectors and dealers whose passion for archaeology was nurtured by the wealth of the tourists engaged in the Grand Tour. In 1786 he wrote to Pope Pius VI that 'he had done something useful to the public and to himself in creating a factory for the manufacture of white porcelain commonly known as biscuit-ware, to be used in the supply of herms, small statues, *bas-reliefs*, vases, all of them modelled on the antique' (quoted in Santuccio 2000, p.39). His factory, active between 1785 and 1831, produced a very fine biscuit which, although not attaining the translucence of Sèvres, was suited to very intricate detail. The paste could be used to simulate the patina of archaeological objects, with a colour that varied from ivory to pale grey – or greenish. Although the choice of sitters to be reproduced can be ascribed to Volpato, he did not carry out the work; the names of the sculptors who worked for him have not survived.

In this output devoted to the reproduction of antique sculpture, this 'herm' bust bearing the faces of Anton Raphael Mengs (1728–1779) and José Nicolas de Azara (1730–1804) is a most remarkable exception. In fact very few contemporary portraits made in biscuit-ware in the Volpato factory are known (a *Pius VI* exists in the Museo Civico, Turin). It is quite likely that the double portrait was commissioned by Azara, the Spanish ambassador, who was deeply affected by the death of Mengs.

Azara and Mengs were great friends. Azara wrote a biography of Mengs in 1780, a year after the painter's death. Christopher Hewetson, an Irish sculptor working in Rome, made busts in bronze of the two men (Bibliothèque Mazarine, Paris), as a pair, one turning towards the other, represented in dignified fashion, broadly cut below the shoulders in the antique style, the eyes not incised, and unclothed (*Azara* is signed and dated 1778, *Mengs* is not; both busts bear an inscription on the front with their respective names and the date, 1779: see the catalogue to the exhibition in Paris, 1994, nos 60 and 61, repr.). After Mengs's death, the sculptor made a marble bust from the same model in 1781;

the following year, Azara presented this to the Pantheon (it was transferred in 1820 to the Protomoteca of the Capitol; Martinelli and Pietrangeli 1955, no. 46, pl. VIII, exhibited in Milan, 2002, no. VII.21). It was the major ornament of a memorial monument. The date of the double portrait made by the Volpato factory must lie between the establishment of the factory (1785) and Azara's departure from Rome (1796); we can guess that the bust was modelled closely on the memorial to Mengs in the Pantheon, which would give due credit to the fidelity of his friend. The small size of the piece makes it a precious, intimate object, which would surely have occupied a place of honour in the ambassador's display cabinet (a copy is listed in his posthumous inventory; see Padua 2001, p. 119).

The composition of the piece derives from a type that was familiar in Roman antiquity: a double portrait of two thinkers, in the form of a herm. The twin-bust formula, uniting two people back to back, was used to depict a Greek and a Roman (*Aristophanes and Terence*, Museo Archeologico Nazionale, Naples), or a master and his disciple (*Epicurus and Metrodorus*, Musei Capitolini, Rome), or two rival writers in the same genre (*Herodotus and Thucydides*, Musei Capitolini, Rome). This type of portrait is rich in connotations, the personality of one man being affected and enriched by the other, both as competitive as they are complementary. The richness of this cultural context certainly stimulated Azara's imagination: his collection included herm portraits from classical antiquity (Jordan de Urries 2000, p. 72) and he counted among his friends such learned men as Ennio Quirino Visconti. It was probably Azara himself who guided Volpato in the creation of the piece made to commemorate his friendship with Mengs and their shared passion for antiquity.

Volpato's transcription of the features of the two men was inspired by different models. Azara, as we have seen, had been portrayed in a bust by Hewetson. Mengs executed a portrait of his friend a few years earlier, in 1774, painting him in less heroic style, in an overcoat with an open-necked shirt, carrying a book, his face smiling and benevolent, in perfect empathy with the artist (Private collection; Jordan de Urries 2000, fig. 1). The iconography of Mengs is abundant. In addition to the sculpture by Hewetson – the Irish sculptor knew Mengs during the last year of his life – his face was widely known through his own self-portraits, which were engraved and copied (see Padua 2001, nos 5–9). GS

# Ferdinand Georg Waldmüller

HINTERBRÜHL, MÖDLING, 1793 – VIENNA, 1865

## 146
### *The Eltz Family*

1835
Oil on canvas, 124 × 110 cm
Signed and dated on the right: *Waldmüller, 1835*
Österreichische Galerie Belvedere, Vienna, 2567

PROVENANCE: collection of Dr Josef August Eltz, Vienna; Dr Ludwig Friedrich Eltz, Vienna; Ida Sassi, Vienna; Dr Moriz Sassi, Vienna, until 1926
EXHIBITED: exhibited at the Académie, Vienna, 1836; Bad Ischl, 1966, no. 60; Vienna, 1990, no. 39
LITERATURE: Feuchtmüller 1996, pp. 97–101 and no. 449

Ferdinand Georg Waldmüller was one of the leading figures in Austrian Biedermeier. He was renowned mainly for his genre scenes, depicting peasants in the Vienna Woods or in the Salzkammergut. However, he was also a great portrait painter and an admirable landscape painter, two skills that he combines in his portrait of *The Eltz Family*. Every summer Waldmüller would go to Bad Ischl, about 30 kilometres east of Salzburg. During the 1820s, the small town, which, during Franz-Josef's reign (1848–1916), became the most celebrated summer resort for the court, had already begun to develop thanks to its popularity with the imperial family. Viennese high society would go there to take the waters. It was there, in 1835, that Waldmüller painted this monumental portrait; it marked a significant development in his art.

The Viennese notary Josef August Eltz, who owned a property in Ischl, is portrayed coming back from a hike in the mountains with two of his sons. He is greeted by a third son, while his wife, seen sitting on a garden chair, is surrounded by her daughters and her youngest son. In the background, the sumptuous panorama of the Salzkammergut unfolds. This way of adding a narrative thread to a portrait via the welcoming home of one of the figures creates a dynamic in the genre that helps avoid the rigour of the pose, lending it an informal character in the spirit of Biedermeier. Some examples of this can be found in British portraiture, such as Singleton Copley's *Portrait of the Sitwell Children* (Private collection, Great Britain). In *The Eltz Family* this artifice, which directs the eyes to the figure of the father, engineers a natural note (to suit the landscape) into a composition that is in reality posed in a stiff way. Waldmüller combines in one painting a subject that is often divided between a pair: the portrait of the father standing to one side with the boys, and the mother seated to the other side with the girls. The pyramidal composition of the group of women gives the painting an imposing structure, but this is subtly modified by the delicacy of the colours of the costumes, which mingle dark red, green, blue and pink with large expanses of white. By contrast, the group of men is handled in plain browns and whites that stand out against the black of Herr

Eltz's coat. The urban elegance of the father's clothing and his patent leather shoes betray the artificiality of the rest of the scene.

Waldmüller's major innovation lies in the manner in which he places his sitters in a grandiose (though real) landscape without dwarfing them, thereby managing to convey the worldly sophistication of this mountain retreat. It is possible that this new slant could have been requested by Eltz, who commissioned the portrait, to show off the elegance of the resort patronised by his family. During the same year, the artist painted a full-length picture of *Councillor Mathias Kerzmann and His Wife* (Österreichische Galerie Belvedere, Vienna), which used the formula of the aristocratic family portrait, inspired by English painting, in an impressive way: the figures are placed on a small terrace in front of a balustrade, in a park leading to some mountains, themselves painted in a summary manner.

In fact, this innovatory scheme corresponded to the artist's own personal development. His frequent visits to Ischl had awoken him to the beauty of the mountains in the region. His work as a landscape artist progressed by leaps and bounds. He has left numerous views, particularly of the Dachstein, some painted from life; whether painted in small or large format, they convey the feeling of grandeur inspired by landscape; the artist pays particular attention to contrasts of light and shade. As the art historian Rupert Feuchtmüller notes, the view of the Dachstein is realistically painted, but despite this it does not correspond to the panorama the visitor would have been able to admire from the villa occupied by the Eltz family. The artist has recomposed the scene. Just as the narrative arrangement of the figures masks the artist's respect for the social conventions of the family portrait, the view of the natural world composed via the artist's imagination introduces a heroic dimension into the portrait by emphasising the ideal. In this painting, Waldmüller succeeds in renewing the classical tradition in the spirit of Biedermeier. SA

# Henry Walton

BAPTISED DICKLEBURGH, NORFOLK, 1746 – LONDON, 1813

## 88
### *Sir Robert and Lady Buxton with Their Daughter Anne*

*c.*1786
Oil on canvas, 73.6 × 92.5 cm
Norwich Castle Museum and Art Gallery, 1963.268.9

PROVENANCE: by descent to Mrs Maud Buxton; bequeathed to the museum by her, 1963
EXHIBITED: see Bell 1998–99, p. 53
LITERATURE: see Bell 1998–99, p. 53

This conversation piece by Henry Walton shows Robert John Buxton of Shadwell (1753–1839), a Norfolk squire and magistrate, with his family. Buxton had married Juliana Mary Beevor (c.1759–1843) in 1777 at St George's, Hanover Square, London. Their wedding took place without the approval of Buxton's father, from whom he was at the time estranged (Buxton Papers, 109/8–9). He was eventually reconciled to his father, and succeeded him in 1782. That same year, the couple's first child Anne Elizabeth (died 1848) was born. It seems the familial felicity artfully displayed by Walton was no illusion. As Juliana Buxton declared in a poem addressed to her husband written shortly before the painting was undertaken (Buxton Papers, 113/20, lines 1–2, 5–6):

*Oh Robert my Dearest could you but know*
*The disquiet my heart feels when you are away*
. . . . . . . . . . . . . . . . . .
*. . . tho' I was eight years ago made your bride*
*Love's alarms beat as high in my breast as they did.*

The image has been noted for its tonal restraint and for the artist's use of a relatively plain setting so as to concentrate the viewer's gaze on the sitters. Thanks to the arrangement of their arms, the visual effect is of a literal family circle. The child is the visual centre of the image and the fulcrum of its action, bringing her parents together. Mrs Buxton seems to hold the book in her hands open for her daughter's viewing, so making this a scene of education as well as of domestic cohesion (Steward 1995, p.107). Given Anne's youth, the object of her gaze seems likely to be a book illustration, unless the text is being read to her. Her father has apparently interrupted his own reading to turn his attention to his daughter's activity. Further books and booklets on the table and sofa create a horizontal line with Anne in the middle; another volume lies on the floor, near to her child-sized chair. The tambour frame with material fixed to it lying on the table offers evidence of female domestic accomplishments. That Mrs Buxton constitutes a model which Anne is being brought up to mirror is perhaps further hinted at by the correlation between the mother's workbasket and the child's miniature basket.

As this image shows, the depiction of an ostensibly 'natural' moment required careful planning. The sitters' poses suggest they are not on public view. Even the furniture is in a state of relaxation: the Buxtons' sofa is under wraps, suggesting, as contemporary viewers would have realised, that the family were not receiving visitors (Emmerson 1992, p.19). Accordingly, among the thrills the image offers its viewers is access to a private spectacle, around which they may imagine narratives (Pointon 1993, p.159). At one remove, they participate in the 'conversation'. It has been remarked that Walton here presents his audience with a vision which embraces more than just one family, for the scene occurs in so unadorned

a domestic space as to give it a universal currency (Moore and Crawley 1992, p.115). The Buxtons exemplify a model of family relations. Indeed, informality in visual representation, a generic convention of conversation pieces, was itself something of a patriotic gesture (Leppert 1988, p.8).

When he undertook this painting Walton lived not far from Shadwell, at Burgate, where he had a farm. He made a number of conversation pieces around this period; they have been likened to earlier images by Johann Zoffany, who had taught Walton around 1770. Walton was also noted for his portraits and genre paintings, a number of which he exhibited during the 1770s. He appears to have spent more time at Burgate after having been turned down for membership of the Royal Academy in 1778, perhaps because of his earlier association with the rival Society of Arts (Bell 1998–99, p.43).

Buxton, who had travelled to France and Italy from 1775 to 1776, had a long-standing interest in the visual arts; correspondence survives from 1781 regarding the purchase for him at Christie's of a *Pool of Bethesda* (Buxton Papers, 109/3, 112/2, 34/197–8). Buxton's account books of 31 October 1785 apparently refer to Walton's painting: 'To Mr Walton for painting a family piece of three figures at 10G [guineas] a figure. £31. 10s. od.' (Moore and Crawley 1992, p.122). A small oval portrait of around the same date has been identified as being a depiction by Walton of Mr Buxton. His accounts also contain an entry in 1794 recording paying 'Mr Walton for painting my picture and two others 13. 13. o.' – the former may be the oval. Walton also served Buxton as an art dealer, selling him a number of paintings and drawings, including a Poussin and a Claude, in 1790 and 1805 (Bell 1998–99, p.53).

A political career beckoned for Buxton at the time that Walton's depiction of his family was made. Receiving some encouragement at the Norwich by-election of 1786, which was contested by his father-in-law, Buxton eventually became an MP in 1790. He proved to be a relatively vocal parliamentarian, and consistently voted for the abolition of the slave trade, which he described as 'a disgrace to England'. A supporter of William Pitt, he was created a baronet in 1800 (Thorne 1986, vol.3, p.350). SM

# Adolph-Ulrich Wertmüller

STOCKHOLM, 1751 – CHESTER, DELAWARE, 1811

## 77
*Jean-Jacques Caffieri*

1784
Oil on canvas, 129 × 96 cm
Signed and dated lower left: *A. Wertmüller / Paris 1784*
Museum of Fine Arts, Boston. Ernest Wadsworth Longfellow Fund

PROVENANCE: Académie Royale de Peinture, 1785; Comte Jean de la Riboisière, Paris, 1910–36; Hôtel Drouot, Paris, 27 March 1936, no.9 (as David); Mrs Meyer Sassoon; by descent to her daughter, Mrs Derek Fitzgerald, Heathfield Park, Sussex; Fitzgerald sale, Sotheby's, London, 3 July 1963, no.1; Kleinberger and Co., New York, 1963; sold to the MFA (accession date 18 September 1963)
EXHIBITED: Paris, Salon of 1785, no.123; for later exhibition history see Zafran 1998, no.71
LITERATURE: see Zafran 1998, no.71

This accomplished portrait, one of two paintings submitted by the Swedish artist Adolph-Ulrich Wertmüller for his reception into the Académie Royale, depicts the sculptor Jean-Jacques Caffieri (1725–1792) in front of his statue of Pierre Corneille.

Although he had himself trained as a sculptor in his native Stockholm, Wertmüller switched to the more lucrative art of painting in 1771, perhaps influenced by his uncle Alexander Roslin, who had become one of the most sought-after portraitists in Europe. Seeking to emulate his uncle's dazzling success, Wertmüller set out for Paris the following year, where, at Roslin's request, he was accepted as a student of Joseph-Marie Vien, one of the pioneers of the neoclassical style. A prolonged stay in Italy between 1775 and 1779, during Vien's directorship of the Académie Française in Rome, permitted the young Swede to absorb at first hand the lessons of antique art, and exposed him to the developing aesthetic of his master's most brilliant student: Jacques-Louis David. Wertmüller returned to France determined to make an impression on the highest ranks of society, and by the time he painted Caffieri's portrait, he appeared to be on the brink of achieving this ambition. His work had caught the eye of King Gustav III of Sweden, who appointed him First Painter to his court, and assigned to him the task of producing a large portrait of Marie-Antoinette strolling in the gardens of the Petit Trianon (Musée National du Château, Versailles).

Flushed with the honour of such a prestigious royal commission, Wertmüller raced to finish the painting in time for the Salon of 1785, only to be met with disapproval from the critics, who censured the portrait's indecorous informality, and dismay from the Queen, who found the likeness unflattering. This public-relations disaster permanently damaged the artist's prospects in Paris.

In contrast, the other works that Wertmüller presented at the same Salon were warmly praised for 'the great truth, beautiful poses, and faces, which reflect the character of the sitters, which is the difficult but divine task of art' (Zafran 1998, no.71), and their author was unanimously accepted into the Académie. Caffieri's portrait was hung alongside a pendant portrait of the painter Jean-Jacques Bachelier, who is shown beside his own *morceau de reception* – a version of the Roman Charity myth. These reception pieces were intended to function as an official definition of Wertmüller's artistic identity and a forum to demonstrate his talent to his fellow artists and to the public, so it is appropriate that he chose to depict two eminently successful academicians. Caffieri, who hailed from a well-established family of sculptors and metalworkers, was one of the most prominent sculptors of the day. His skilful carving and graceful rococo style, demonstrated in his lively busts of Mme du Barry (State Hermitage Museum, St Petersburg) and Canon Pingré (Louvre, Paris), had made him a favourite at the court of Louis XV. He was especially renowned for his ability to capture a faithful likeness of his sitters, a reputation which presented Wertmüller with a piquant challenge when he came to create his own image of Caffieri. Here the sculptor is shown standing before a reduced version of one of his most celebrated works: a life-size statue of Pierre Corneille, the founding father of French classical tragedy. Portraits of literary celebrities were something of a speciality for Caffieri. An avid theatre fan, he had struck a deal with the Comédie Française under whose terms he was to produce a series of portrait busts of great writers and actors for the foyer of the playhouse in return for admission for life. However, the statue depicted here by Wertmüller was the product of a rather more conventional commission issued by the Comte d'Angivillier, Director of Buildings to the King, for contributions to a series of sculptures of the 'Great Men of France'. The statue (Louvre, Paris), exhibited in 1779, captures the great playwright in a dishevelled moment of intense concentration, as he pauses, quill in hand, to compose a verse. This tribute to the genius of Corneille provides an echo to Wertmüller's own homage to the achievement of Caffieri, placing artistic endeavour at the thematic heart of the portrait.

The compositional clarity and meticulous brushwork of the portrait demonstrate Wertmüller's thorough grounding in the neoclassical idiom; indeed, the work is executed with such assured flair that it was attributed to David himself until 1936. The artist's technical virtuosity is particularly evident in the fabrics of Caffieri's costume; the luxuriant red velvet of the frock-coat and breeches, and the shimmering cream satin and gold embroidery of the waistcoat, are rendered with a breathtaking verisimilitude. In emphasising the costly attire and debonair elegance of his artist-sitter, Wertmüller may have recalled some advice he had received from Roslin in a letter of 1779: 'If you wish to have any success … you must not look like a beggar, you must have assurance in yourself and try to overcome your too great timidity and put yourself at ease. If not, it will be impossible to become a Portrait Painter, for talent is not always sufficient, you must know how to get along with everybody' (Scott 1963, p.3). Caffieri's self-assured stance and amiable

countenance exemplify this approach to life. While highlighting his sitter's artistic achievement, Wertmüller chooses to portray him as a gentleman with a sword at his belt, dressed as his aristocratic clients, rather than as an artist at work in the studio. There is no hint of either the burst of creative energy celebrated in the sculpture of Corneille, or the introverted individualism that was to characterise the romantic artistic persona; instead, Wertmüller presents a vision of worldly sophistication and professional success that he no doubt hoped to secure in his own career as a result of the portrait. He could hardly have foreseen at the time the work was painted that the downturn in his reputation following the Marie-Antoinette debacle, coupled with the turmoil of the revolutionary years, would lead him to America, where he was eventually to settle and live out his days as a farmer in rural Delaware. KB

# Benjamin West

SPRINGFIELD, PENN., 1738 – LONDON, 1820

## 71
*Self-portrait*

1792 or 1793
Oil on panel, 101.5 × 132 cm
Signed and dated bottom left: *B. West / 1793* (or possibly: *1792*); on the spines of the top three books piled at the right of the image can be read, respectively, *ROME; HISTORY OF GREECE* and *HISTORY OF ENGLAND*
Royal Academy of Arts, London, 03/285

PROVENANCE: sold by West's sons, Robins, London, 20–22 June 1829, lot 88; presented to the Royal Academy by Joseph Neeld MP, April 1830
EXHIBITED: perhaps Royal Academy, 1804, no.37: for later exhibition history see Erffa and Staley 1986, p.452
LITERATURE: see Erffa and Staley 1986, p.452

The American-born artist Benjamin West was the natural choice to become President of the Royal Academy following the death in 1792 of Sir Joshua Reynolds, who had held the office from the institution's foundation in 1768. This image, the largest known self-portrait by West, commemorated his election to the position on 17 March 1792. It was painted either in 1792 or 1793 (the date painted on the image is unclear) and was perhaps the 'Portrait of himself' which the artist exhibited at the Academy in 1802 (Erffa and Staley 1986, p.452).

The prospect behind West shows the southern block of Somerset House, the view from the rooms of the Royal Academy, then housed in the northern block. The defining importance of this vista to West's self-portrayal is such that, as one scholar observes, 'the composition seems to have been stretched horizontally to make room for it' (Staley, in Baltimore 1989, p.25). Among the objects lying

on his desk are a portfolio, a magnifying glass, papers and a quill pen, which suggest that West is occupied with Academic affairs, highlighting the authority with which he is invested. Indeed, West had to spend much of his working day on official business; he told his fellow artist Joseph Farington that interruptions were so frequent that he had begun to do most of his painting at night (Alberts 1978, p.198).

His elegant attire is completed by his tricorn hat (on the right of the table), symbolically resonant because on being elected President he took to sporting it during Academy meetings 'so as to bring dignity to the office' (Whitley 1928, vol. 2, p.161). Grasping the presidential chair upon which he sits with his right hand, the painter holds in his left the lowermost of a stack of books that includes works entitled *History of Greece* and *History of England*; on the visible part of the spine of the topmost book the word *Rome* can be read. Thus, West's body links his current eminent seat with his background as an artist, taking his sources from historical subjects. This serves both to affirm the Academy's elevated purposes as a learned body and to proclaim West in particular as 'the ideal representative of the standards the Academy existed to uphold' (Baltimore 1989, pp.23–25). The final component to the still-life at the right of the image is a cast of the *Belvedere Torso*. This antique sculpture, housed in the Vatican and acclaimed by Michelangelo and by Reynolds, was considered a touchstone of excellence for high art; the Royal Academy's collection possessed a cast.

In this self-presentation, West avoided making reference to painting as a practical occupation. Instead, he staked his cultural and institutional authority – and the consequence of his art – on the more far-reaching basis offered up so insistently by the attributes of distinction he depicted around himself. This form of painterly manifesto was indebted to an earlier self-portrait by Reynolds (cat.73), in which he presented himself as a learned figure rather than a practising artist; and in constructing his own image, West apparently sought to vindicate his claims to be the former President's worthy successor (Baltimore 1989, p.25). Reynolds had presented his self-portrait to the Royal Academy. West, by contrast, did not make his a gift to the institution; presumably he anticipated that it would be bought by or for the Academy. In fact, it remained in his possession until his death. The painting thus testifies, it has been suggested, to 'the ambiguities that surrounded the relationship of portraiture to ideas of worth, whether financial or artistic' (Pointon 2001, p.97).

Indeed, reading against the grain of West's intensely grandiose self-presentation, it has been argued that he appears to be a 'simple provincial' placed in an 'imposing setting' where he is 'dwarfed' (Abrams 1985, p.22). As the leading authority on West has concluded: 'His self-portraits have been criticised as images of vanity and pomposity; more

charitably it could be said that pride and self
satisfaction radiate from West's likenesses of
himself because he believed in his own genius and
in the quality and significance of the works he
produced. His view of himself was affectionately
encapsulated by his great-nephew Leigh Hunt in
an account of boyhood visits to West's painting
room, where he generally found "the mild and quiet
artist at his work; happy, for he thought himself
immortal'" (Staley, in Baltimore 1989, p.25). SM

# Joseph Wright of Derby
DERBY, 1734 – DERBY, 1797

## 62
*Mrs Sarah Clayton*

c.1769
Oil on canvas, 127 × 101.6 cm
Fitchburg Art Museum, Fitchburg, Mass., 1953.1

PROVENANCE: painted for the sitter, then passed to the Parker
family, Cuerdon Hall, Preston, Lancashire, and from Robert
Towneley Parker by descent; sale, property of the Trustees of
the late R. A. Tatton of Cuerdon Hall, Christie's, London, 28
February 1947, lot 102; bought in; anon. sale (property of Capt.
T. A. Tatton), Christie's, London, 18 April 1947, lot 74; bought
Roland; anon. sale (property of Roland Browse & Delbanco),
Christie's, London, 25 June 1948, lot 135; bought Koetzer (art
dealer); John Nicholson Gallery, New York, 1952; Charles
Childes, Boston, 1953; Miss Louise I. Doyle, by whom presented
to Fitchburg Art Museum, 1953
EXHIBITED: see London 1990, p.67
LITERATURE: Nicolson 1968, vol.1, pp.34, 99, 189; Detroit
1968, p.67; London 1990, pp.67–68; Shelton 2001, pp.125–39

Sarah Clayton (1712–1779) inherited substantial
wealth and property, and was one of Liverpool's
leading business magnates. Wright painted her
portrait during his career-transforming stay in the
city from 1768 to 1771. He was able to profit from
the port's rapidly developing fortunes; numerous
potential clients were enriching themselves. Another
artist in Liverpool seeking work, Peter Romney
(a younger brother of George Romney), lamented
in a letter of 1769: 'Mr. Wright, a famous painter
from Derby, is here, who swallows up the business.
He is indeed a true copier of nature; he is of a
studious disposition, has a fine taste, and is, in
short qualified for a portrait painter of the first
class' (Romney 1830, p.300).

The sitter's affluence was founded in the
business success of her father, William; he died in
1715 having been Liverpool's mayor in 1689 and an
MP for the city from 1698 to 1708 and from 1713
to 1715. Until her mother Elizabeth's death in 1745,
Sarah Clayton 'lived the life of a wealthy young
woman' (Langton 2004, p.995). Thereafter, having
inherited an interest in the coal-rich Parr Hall
estate, the development of the Sankey canal allowed
her to capitalise upon colliery development. For
a time, Mrs Clayton – who, although unmarried,

insisted on being called 'Mistress Clayton'
(Barker and Harris 1950, p.26) – was 'probably
the most important' merchant in the city
(Langton 1979, p.221). Around mid-century,
she had Liverpool's 'first private carriage'
(Nonagenarian 1863, p.132).

It has been suggested that the relative
inexperience of both artist and sitter in 'staging
large, ambitious portraits' may have contributed to
their somewhat 'effortful and strained engagement'
(Shelton 2001, p.125). Thus, while Clayton's rich,
substantial costume – its satin and lacework
surfaces emphasised by strong lighting – speaks
of her material prosperity, the 'hyper-clarity of
detail in the treatment' of the clothing, especially
her skirt which dominates the foreground and
hides the floor, 'threatens to overtake the image'
with 'insistent materiality' (Shelton 2001, p.128).

The key to fathoming what Clayton's portrait
was intended to convey lies in the drawing at the
centre of the image, to which she points. An
architectural plan, it spills over the edge of an
unfolding table, and one reason why this small,
functional piece of furniture stands in a scene
whose other, grander features are an elegant
column and billowing drapery is perhaps because
its slight dimensions allow the drawing to curl
out for the viewer's inspection.

In broad terms, this drawing invokes
Clayton's longstanding involvement in matters
of design. Herself the commissioner of a memorial
monument to her mother (now destroyed, repr.
Shelton 2001, p.132), her architectural interests were
stimulated by a visit in 1749 to Bath, a city reshaped
by the developer John Wood, whose appointment
to a range of Liverpudlian civic projects, notably
the New Exchange, she advanced (Harris 1949,
pp.55–62). In the 1750s she began the expensive
process of laying out Clayton Square, and lived
in the largest of its finished houses at the time
of Wright's portrait (Harris 1949, p.56). Another
facet to this patron's tastes may be her picture's
highly decorated, and possibly original, late
rococo frame (Mitchell 1990, p.277).

The architectural plan shown also has
specific significance. What it depicts has
been identified as the ancient Propylaeum, the
gatehouse of the Acropolis in Athens; it reproduces
an illustration published in Julien-David Le Roy's
book *Ruin des plus beaux monuments de la Grèce* (Paris,
1758) (repr. Shelton 2001, p.135). As the scholar
who has identified this detail affirms, its inclusion
in any British portrait of this period would have
been 'startlingly precocious': Clayton hints at
no mere conventional interest in architecture,
she claims a 'brand of rarefied, elitist, genteel
knowledge' not readily available to a provincial,
non-aristocratic woman. The most abstract of
the visual arts, architecture was generally considered
a male preserve. Clayton's gesture subverts this
prejudice, 'asserting her ability to translate the
purely abstract pattern of lines and circles on the

sheet before her into an imaginative re-creation
of three-dimensional reality' (Shelton 2001,
pp.135–36).

Wright's image registers a contention that
the sitter was unusually well informed aesthetically;
and for her to have solicited such a complex
portrait was a crowning illustration of her
investment in the arts. If this ambitious pictorial
statement ultimately fails to convince, this may
reflect 'the tenuous relationship of Wright's sitter
with the cultural and intellectual discourses upon
which a more confident cosmopolitanism was
founded' (Shelton 2001, p.139).

The wealth that underpinned Clayton's
claimed place as an art connoisseur and patron
proved precarious too: around the time of Wright's
portrait, her colliery was in difficulties on account
of increasingly bitter competition and managerial
embezzlement (Barker 1949, p.151; Langton 2004,
p.996). A year before she died, she was declared
a bankrupt, and her assets and personal effects –
smart clothes and foreign books presumably
included – were seized. The portrait, now sadly
hubristic, came to her brother-in-law's family. SM

## 136
*The Reverend d'Ewes Coke with His Wife
Hannah and Daniel Parker Coke MP*

c.1780–82
Oil on canvas, 152.4 × 177.8 cm
Derby Museums and Art Gallery, 676-1965

PROVENANCE: by descent to R. G. S. Coke;
purchased by Derby Art Gallery, 1965
EXHIBITED: see London 1990, p.217
LITERATURE: see London 1990, p.217

In this outdoor conversation piece, the Revd d'Ewes
Coke (1747–1811) stands with his arm around his
wife Hannah (died 1818). Their seated companion
is Daniel Parker Coke MP (1745–1825), a distant
cousin. Embowered by trees, the group form a
triangle based on the table and centred upon
d'Ewes Coke. The image was probably begun after
he inherited Brookhill Hall, Derbyshire, from his
guardian's family in 1780; he paid Wright's £75.12s
fee in January 1783. At around this time, Daniel
Parker Coke acquired a pair of landscape paintings
from Wright (Nicolson 1968, vol.1, pp.72, 265;
Nicolson 1988, p.756).

D'Ewes Coke, orphaned at the age of eleven,
was educated at Repton and St John's College,
Cambridge, and took holy orders. He served as
rector of Pinxton and South Normanton, both
near Brookhill, from 1771 until his death. Some
time after 1783 he became a member of the Derby
Philosophical Society, and in 1789 he helped to
catalogue Derbyshire's plants (Sturges 1978, p.228;
Pilkington 1789, vol.1, p.vi). He married Hannah,
the heiress daughter of George Heywood of
Birmingham Hall, around 1772. Their sons were
the heirs of Daniel Parker Coke, when he died
childless (Coke 1880, p.36).

Daniel Parker Coke studied at Queen's College and All Souls, Oxford, and at Lincoln's Inn; he became a barrister practising on the Midland circuit. From 1780 he was MP for Nottingham, having previously represented Derby (1776–80). Coke was described around 1780 in the *English Chronicle* as 'a gentleman of small fortune' but 'as independent in his parliamentary conduct as any man in the House'. His first known vote was against the war in America in 1778; but two years later he declared in Parliament that – although 'he had been one of those who lamented the commencement of the American war, and disapproved many of the measures adopted in its prosecution' – as America had since become 'the confederate of the House of Bourbon', he saw 'no medium between unconditional submission to the enemy and the most spirited exertions'. He became a commissioner for settling American loyalist claims (1782–85) (Namier and Brooke 1964, p.233; Pottle 2004, p.450).

The artist had managed to re-establish himself in Derby when he had returned to his home town in 1777, having spent much of the previous decade elsewhere. This image exemplifies how Wright created 'a sense of psychological unity in his figure groups by focusing their attention on some sort of narrative incident' (Fraser 1979, p.15). Daniel Parker Coke's comparison of a piece of paper to the landscape constitutes the key 'action' of the painting (Nicolson 1968, p.39).

Two explanations for this have been proposed. One interpretation is that the paper in his hand, which occupies the group's attention, is a plan for landscaping the scene which they survey (NACF 1966, p.17). The other reading – which has found most favour – posits the group's activity as a sketching excursion, in which a representation is compared to a real view surveyed by the subjects (Hayes 1991, p.120). The design may be by d'Ewes Coke, who holds a pencil holder or an engraving tool (it seems that 'he was an extremely clever artist' in copper etching [Coke 1880, p.93]). It could also be the work of Hannah Coke: she looks at the landscape while pointing to the drawing with her right hand; and her left hand holds a portfolio, one sheet from which slips partly into our view and appears to be a sketch. This portfolio and d'Ewes Coke's drawing implement are complemented by a third luxury item on the table: a sun-shade or umbrella – the latter would still have been something of an exotic article in provincial England in 1780. Wright reused this trio of accoutrements several years later in another painting, *The Revd Thomas Gisborne and His Wife Mary* (1786; Yale Center for British Art, New Haven).

The harmony of the sitters finds an echo in their natural setting. In some measure, indeed, it is unimportant who created the design they analyse: rather, its value comes from its employment by the group in fruitful discussion. The same is true of Wright's image as a whole: the conversation piece itself offers an act of representation, and contemporary observers would have compared the likenesses of those depicted to reality, just as, in the image, the sitters are shown assessing the verisimilitude of a depiction of nature. In broader terms, the sitters' enjoyment of, and engagement with, the countryside amounts to a celebration of land ownership and a sense of divine sanction for the scene is imparted by the distant church spire visible below the Revd Coke's outstretched hand.

Yet, for all the harmonious companionability on show, the scene's authority remains firmly founded with the men. The Revd Coke 'commands the picture', pointing out 'some relation between what they see and what has been drawn' (Daniels 1999, pp.46–47). Mrs Coke appears to lack her husband's sense of wider horizons, which he seeks to impress upon her by directing her gaze: and if it is her drawing being examined, his gesture may be a corrective one. Her 'green dress turns to yellow as the sun catches it' (Nicolson 1968, vol.1, p.72). Thus naturalised, she is perhaps cast as a fertility symbol. Scholars observe that she both embodies the guiding figure of Muse or Sybil, and serves as 'the source and object of tender feelings' (Shawe-Taylor 1990, p.127). Because the hue of her clothing and hair interleaves her with their environment, she can be identified as 'a Muse of Nature to accompany and inspire the men' (Daniels 1999, p.47). Such a role, though, was narrow: a muse represents only 'an abstract potential that may only be brought into consciousness and into culture through the work of another, the artistry of a real artist' (Bermingham 2000, p.186). SM

## 134
### Sir Brooke Boothby

1781
Signed and dated on tree trunk at lower right: *I. Wright pin'. /1781*; the book in Boothby's left hand is labelled *Rousseau*
Oil on canvas, 149 × 207 cm
Tate, London, N04132. Bequeathed by Miss Agnes Ann Best, 1925

PROVENANCE: Sir William Boothby Bt sale, Ashbourne Hall: paintings in supplementary catalogue 11–12 November 1847 (no.5); bequeathed by Miss Agnes Ann Best to the National Gallery, 1925; transferred to the Tate Gallery, 1961
EXHIBITED: Royal Academy, London, 1781 (no.245); for later exhibition history see London 1990, p.116
LITERATURE: see London 1990, p.116

Brooke Boothby (1744–1824) was the heir to a baronetcy who described his youth as that of 'a man of fashion and the *bon ton*'. Indeed, he is portrayed by Wright in a costume that has been termed 'a definite statement of high fashion': a double-breasted waistcoat cut short, and frock-coat sleeves 'so modishly tight that they have to be unbuttoned at the wrist' to aid arm movement (Ribeiro 1995, p.48).

Yet his pose is unconventional: portraits usually showed male sitters upright. One close precedent for Boothby's posture was a Jacobean miniature by Isaac Oliver, *Edward Herbert*; this was engraved in 1764 and was perhaps known to Wright or Boothby. As the scholar who identified this precedent argues, not only the miniature's form but the melancholic meaning intended by the form both operate in *Boothby*. The arm supporting the head was a traditional motif of melancholy reflection – in tomb sculpture for example – and Boothby's portrait 'self-consciously illustrates his erudition' and 'intellectual predilections' (Cummings 1968, pp.660–63).

Links with earlier Wright works have also been mooted: a sketch of 1774 has a comparable male pose (Graciano 2002B, pp.88–89). Most horizontally posed portraits, however, were of women – for instance Sir Godfrey Kneller's *Lady Howard* (now lost, but known through a mezzotint), an image with which Wright may have been familiar (Stewart 1976, p.410). Wright emphasises the curve of Boothby's body in a way which is somewhat sexually ambiguous (West 2004, pp.160–61).

Literary sources too have been adduced for *Boothby*'s setting, from Robert Burton's *The Anatomy of Melancholy* (1638) – 'most pleasant it is … to such as are melancholy given … to walk alone in some solitary Grove, betwixt Wood and Water, by a Brook side, to meditate' – to Henry Mackenzie's Rousseauvian novel *The Man of Feeling* (1771), in which the hero 'lay himself down to sleep … on the banks of a rivulet … stretched on the ground his head resting on his arm'.

The book Boothby holds, labelled 'Rousseau', is the key to the image. Boothby was 'one of the few Englishmen that Jean-Jacques Rousseau could abide' (Mitchell 2004, p.328). The two met in 1766 when Rousseau, exiled in Britain, moved to Wootton Hall, Derbyshire, neighbouring Boothby's family seat. Boothby spent much of 1774–78 touring the Continent, visiting Rousseau in Paris several times (Zonneveld 2003, pp.54–80). Rousseau died in 1778, and Wright's painting in part commemorates Boothby's grief at an event which, he wrote, 'afflicts me out of measure. To a person whose passions are awake to few objects the loss of one is heavily felt … I believe that all that remained in me of enthusiasm was directed to this one point' (Leigh 1965–98, vol.41, pp.67–68).

At Paris in 1776, Rousseau had entrusted a manuscript to Boothby: the first dialogue of his *Rousseau juge de Jean-Jacques*. He told Boothby he wanted it published. Boothby arranged this, at his own expense, in April 1780. In September he commissioned Wright's painting (which cost £50 8s.). When the finished painting was displayed at the Royal Academy, the press identified Boothby as 'lately a little known as the Editor of the Posthumous Work of J. J. Rousseau' (*Public Advertiser*, 2 May 1781). The painting is 'not just a portrait but an advertisement' of Boothby's involvement with Rousseau, especially the publication of his text, avowed a 'sacred duty' by Boothby (Schama 2002, p.21).

The discussion in Rousseau's text reflects upon his own works, describing him as 'the portrayer of nature and the historian of the human heart', and as teaching his readers to find within themselves 'the enjoyment and happiness that others seek so far from themselves'. This mirrors Boothby's engagement with Rousseau's works in Wright's image (Graciano 2002B, p.100). Scholars note that Boothby's waistcoat is 'left unbuttoned the better to expose the transparent sincerity of his heart' (Schama 2002, p.21); similarly, by a contrived accident, 'the index finger of one of Boothby's hands points to the name, while that of the other points to his temple, to underline the fact that he is contemplating his mentor's ideas' (Shawe-Taylor 1990, p.77).

In what may be a double pun linking the two men with the natural setting, Brooke Boothby is reading Rousseau by a brook, in French, a 'ruisseau' (Rosenthal 1999, p.244). One hobby that Rousseau pursued during his English sojourn and shared with Boothby was botany – in later years aged yokels recalled 'owd Ross Hall' coming and going 'gethering his yarbs' (Howitt 1840, p.512). In Rousseau's formulation, botany was a pleasurable activity concerned with nature appreciation – an interest suited to the sensitive man of leisure – rather than the study of plants for medicinal use. Thus, arguably, Wright's depiction of Boothby in modish clothes and an unusual pose is designed to 'highlight the aristocrat as the corporeal embodiment of botany as leisured activity'. But meanwhile, a visual joke places Boothby near plants which have been identified as sweet violet and pilewort, both of known pharmacological value. That the painting should depict flora which represent 'a medical foil to botanical pleasure' suggests that the connection drawn between Rousseau and Boothby is also wittily subverted by Wright. The visual humour goes further: these plants were associated with purgative use, a treatment for melancholy (Graciano 2002B, pp.101–09).

Boothby wrote in his preface to Rousseau's manuscript that therein 'sensitive and virtuous people, *the inhabitants of the ideal world*, will at once recognise their compatriot'. Wright's image, while humorously acknowledging the tensions between the man of fashion and the man of nature, registers Boothby's claims to be a fellow citizen of Rousseau's ideal world. SM

## 103
### *Three Children of Richard Arkwright with a Goat*

1791
Oil on canvas, 190.5 × 149.9 cm
Private collection

PROVENANCE: Arkwright family
EXHIBITED: Corporation Art Gallery, Derby, 1883, no.74; Royal Academy, London, 1886, no.16; Henry Graves and Co. Ltd, London, 1910, no.15; Corporation Art Gallery, Derby, 1934, no.136; *Joseph Wright of Derby 1734–1797*, Tate Gallery, London,

and Walker Art Gallery, Liverpool, 1958, no.31
LITERATURE: Nicolson 1968, vol.1, pp.176–77

This image shows three of the grandchildren of Sir Richard Arkwright, an industrialist who made a fortune by the development of cotton-spinning machinery. From left to right, the subjects are Elizabeth (1780–1838), Charles (1786–1850) and John (1785–1858), with a goat. This painting and its pair – showing their three eldest brothers, Robert, Richard and Peter, with a kite – completed a sequence representing three generations of the Arkwright family undertaken by Joseph Wright from 1789 to 1791. The two other pictures commissioned were one of Sir Richard Arkwright himself, and another showing the children's parents, Richard Arkwright, junior, and his wife Mary, with another child.

By the time he painted the Arkwrights' pictures, Wright was firmly established as a portraitist for prominent Derbyshire families. He may have come to the notice of the Arkwrights through the Hurt family, for whom he undertook a number of portraits, the first of which date from around 1780 (a year which saw the marriage of Charles Hurt to Susanna Arkwright, the aunt of the children shown here) (London 1990, pp.203–04, 208–09). Wright's first-known direct contact with the Arkwrights was an appointment in 1783 to paint for Richard Arkwright, senior, yet it seems that nothing came of this; apparently the artist's chief patron for the eventual group of family portraits was Richard Arkwright, junior. Correspondence between him and the artist reveals that the paired images of the six eldest Arkwright children had been commissioned by December 1790 and were begun the following year; by late June 1791 they were almost complete. Wright visited the children at their home in Bakewell to take their likenesses; the finished works cost £94 10s. each (Nicolson 1968, vol.1, pp.164–69, 175–77).

Paintings of young children were one of Wright's several specialisms. It has been observed that in such works the artist often posed his young sitters in close proximity, suggesting an affectionate family; here, John supports his younger brother Charles on top of the goat's back, while Elizabeth, the eldest child, controls the animal by its horns. Wright's images of children differed markedly from 'the stiffly posed, buttoned-up embryonic adults of earlier child portraiture': he offered instead 'physically real, full-cheeked, sturdy-limbed children dressed in loose-fitting clothes which encourage them to range freely' (Daniels 1999, pp.45–46). The relatively casual clothing shown by Wright in such paintings was, it has been noted, 'de rigueur for a child of any Briton familiar with the writings of Jean-Jacques Rousseau. It allowed children a freedom of movement necessary for their unfettered exploration of the world around them'. The artist raised his own children along such Rousseauvian lines (Graciano 2002A, p.70).

Wright's series of representations of the Arkwright family provides evidence for the contrast between generations in a family rapidly establishing itself among the gentry (Nicolson 1968, vol.1, pp.168–69). The depiction of children at play was itself an oblique advertisement of the wealth which could provide such leisure. Yet Wright also gave a narrative thread to this representation of the Arkwright siblings by showing them playing outdoors with a goat. They are thus, as it has been remarked of another portrait of children by Wright, 'present in the landscape for a purpose, no longer there for the mere sake of the land but for their recreation and health' (Steward 1995, p.134). That the young Arkwrights are accompanied only by an animal may suggest that the scene summons up an innocent realm of childhood. Although Charles wields a whip, its serious use appears unlikely; kind treatment of animals, indeed, had been identified as a marker of children's goodness in a popular moral tale for the young, *The History of Sandford and Merton* (1783–89), written by Wright's Rousseauphile friend Thomas Day (Steward 1995, pp.21, 94).

All the Arkwright children received generous financial support from their father. He gave Elizabeth £15,000 upon her marriage to Francis Edward Hurt, of Alerwasley, in 1802. At around that time John and Charles, then at school at Eton College, were causing parental concern, illicitly contracting debts at a local inn and amusing themselves with guns in a manner described by their headmaster as 'unwarrantable & dangerous'. They both went on to Trinity College, Cambridge, and were later set up as landowners by their father, John at Hampton Court in Herefordshire, and Charles at Dunstall Hall, Staffordshire; each later became Justice of the Peace and High Sheriff of their adopted counties (Fitton 1989, pp.264–65, 270–71, 296). SM

## Johann Zoffany
FRANKFURT AM MAIN, 1733 – LONDON, 1810

### 87
*Queen Charlotte with Her Two Eldest Sons*

c.1764–65
Oil on canvas, 112 × 130 cm
Lent by Her Majesty the Queen, RCIN 400146

PROVENANCE: first recorded in the possession of the Prince of Wales, 1794
EXHIBITED: see London 1976, p.34
LITERATURE: see London 2004, p.26

Princess Charlotte of Mecklenburg-Strelitz, a small Protestant state north of Berlin, came to England aged seventeen in 1761. On the afternoon of her arrival in London she met her husband-to-be,

George III, for the first time; they married that evening. Johann Zoffany – also of Germanic origin – had arrived the year before. His ability 'to speak in her own language to a young woman who, on her arrival, knew no English whatsoever' may have been one reason why he was selected to paint the Queen and her two infant sons in 1764 (Pointon 1993, p.162). Joseph Farington recorded in the early nineteenth century that it was Zoffany's early patron the Prime Minister Lord Bute who had 'introduced Him to the notice of the Royal Family' (Farington Notebooks, typescript p.111; reproduced by kind permission of the Royal Collection).

The setting shown is Buckingham House, bought by George in 1762 as a gift for his bride and known as 'The Queen's House'. Theirs proved a morally exemplary marriage: George was 'the first English king to be completely free from sexual scandal since Charles I' (Blanning 2002, p.344). It was fruitful too, producing fifteen children in twenty-two years. Shown with the Queen are the two-year-old Prince of Wales (later George IV) and his one-year-old brother Frederick, both in fancy dress. The heir holds a spear and leads a boar-hound by the collar, the dog's size highlighting the boys' youth. A drum and flag lying on the chair at the left are also part of his accoutrements; the three feathers worn at the front of his helmet are the heraldic device of the Prince of Wales.

Although in reality the Queen's dressing room was located on the first floor, Zoffany's scene is apparently set on the ground floor, perhaps to emphasise the garden view (London 2004, p.26). The clock by the doorway seems to show the time as two o'clock, a time 'when members of the royal family received visitors, including their own children' (Steward 1995, p.23). The woman whose face can be seen reflected in a mirror in the adjoining room is almost certainly the royal governess, Lady Charlotte Finch (London 2004, p.26). She recorded an order for boys' costumes in her diary on 6 September 1764: 'a Telemachus dress for the Prince of Wales and a Turk's for Prince Frederick' (Hedley 1975, p.93).

The eldest son's apparel thus invokes a classical comparison flattering to himself and to his parents, likening him to the worthy heir of the heroic warrior-king Ulysses through his faithful marriage to Penelope. The point of reference may be not solely Homer's *Odyssey* but also Fénélon's *Télémaque* (1699), written for the instruction of an heir to the French throne (London 1977, p.11). The conspicuous overdoor painting within the image may portray an episode from the *Odyssey* (Pointon 1993, p.166).

Zoffany's picture has been noted for its boldness in moving away from traditional court portraiture towards 'making the imagery of royal home life acceptable' (Schama 1988, p.171). It is one of the first examples of the informal royal conversation piece as a genre (Webster 2004, p.1001). At other social levels, conversation pieces

were well established, and it has been argued that an analysis of this image sheds much light on the nature of the wider genre, demonstrating 'precisely the unnaturalness of an art form that has often been construed as part of a move away from "formal" and "public" portraiture in the eighteenth century to a celebration of the intimacy of family relations' (Pointon 1993, p.160).

Not least, conversation pieces offered the 'possibility of publicly enumerating material possession'. The princes' attire, it has been noted, is only the most spectacular of the scene's exotic dressings: 'The sumptuous stuff that masks the toilet-table is "Superfine Flanders point", the carpet is Turkish, the clock with its figure of Father Time is French, the gilt toilet service is probably of German origin, lacquered Chinese mandarins flank ornate mirror behind the queen' – and the window offers the vista of a flamingo on the lawn. 'The visual geography extends in time and place from ancient Rome to the English court and from the Far East to the defeated ever-threatening neighbour, France' (Pointon 1993, pp.162–63).

All this richly varied property amounts to a form of 'cultural annexation': 'otherness is identified only to be assimilated'. The British monarchy is presented as both 'a proper parent to its children' and as ruler of the world. This double vision implies that the 'greatness bestowed on the queen by the absent king' bears with it 'the gifts of all nations; it also carries the responsibility of taming and containing children and animals, as well as (if by default) Chinese and Turks'. Within this 'discourse of military and cultural supremacy', the Queen has 'a crucial role as mother of sons', perpetuating family – and national – inheritance (Pointon 1993, pp.162–66). Her own adornments too are a showcase of wealth: indeed, Charlotte was 'the first English queen since the early seventeenth century to possess jewels rivalling the Continental royalty' (Pointon 1997B, p.495; Campbell Orr 2005).

It has been argued that the missing figure of the King is in some ways the key to the whole picture. The open door may suggest his imminent presence; just as Telemachus 'stood in for his missing father', so too here 'the prince represents the absent king' (Pointon 1993, pp.166–68). The image's mirrorings, both figurative and actual – particularly the Queen's mirrored face – offer didactic models worth reflecting on and imitating. This educative function, ostensibly showing the cultural reproduction of royalty, serves also to impress the image's potential wider audience. Simultaneously, the motif of appearances and reappearances draws the viewer's consideration to the elaborate painterly artifice underway. As this image indicates, for all the apparent privacy of the conversation-piece genre, its dual concern with documenting progeny and property gave it a public dimension. If its political face was less obvious than that of other genres such as courtly

portraiture, this was part of its power (Pointon 1993, pp.159, 164). SM

70
*The Academicians of the Royal Academy*

1771–72
Oil on canvas, 101.1 × 147.5 cm
Lent by Her Majesty The Queen, RCIN 400747

PROVENANCE: presumably painted for George III
EXHIBITED: Royal Academy, 1772, no.290; for later exhibition history see London 1976, p.57
LITERATURE: see London 2004, p.184

The foundation of the Royal Academy was approved by George III in 1768. Zoffany's canvas celebrated the personnel and the practices of the young institution. The action around which the image is constructed is a life class, but one without students, who are replaced by a gathering of Academicians. The President, Sir Joshua Reynolds, stands near the centre of the image (identifiable by the ear trumpet he holds, a reference to his deafness); immediately to his left is Sir William Chambers, the Academy's Treasurer. Benjamin West, Reynolds's eventual successor as President, is the fourth figure from the left of the image.

The focus of attention is an adjustment being made to a life model's pose by George Moser, Keeper of the Academy Schools; he is apparently guided by Francesco Zuccarelli (standing to the left of the model), exercising his responsibility as one of the Visitors to the Schools. Another model is at rest, with an hourglass (at the bottom right of the image) marking the lapse of time. A student at the Academy wrote of the life modelling there in around 1777 that 'two men sit two hours each night by turns every week' (Whitley 1928, vol.1, p.276). The younger model, depicted dressing or undressing, sits in an attitude which recalls the *Spinario*, a well-known antique statue (Cardiff 1990, p.132).

There was no direct injunction against the study of the nude model by the two female Academicians, Mary Moser and Angelica Kauffman; the fact that both are shown in portraits on the wall, however, suggests that their presence in the scene would have been considered improper (Nottingham 1991, p.42). Indeed, it would seem deliberate that the women's portraits are placed *behind* the model (Mellor 1995, p.136). Their exclusion is also, by extension, an exclusion from the idea of the artist (Pollock 1988, p.45).

Twenty-nine of the original thirty-four members of the Royal Academy are shown in Zoffany's painting. Two founding members had since died; the others missing are George Dance and his brother Nathaniel Dance, and Thomas Gainsborough. The last two had 'quarrelled with Sir Joshua' according to Horace Walpole, writing in 1773, which may account for the absences (Paris 1985, p.341). Zoffany and William Hoare were nominated by the King in 1769 to join the Academy on an equal footing with its initial members; Zoffany pictures himself holding his palette at the bottom left of the image, Hoare is the final figure at the right of the scene. Also included are the three most recently elected Academicians: Edward Burch and Richard Cosway, both elected in 1771, and Joseph Nollekens, an Academician since February 1772. The latter's inclusion suggests that the image was only finalised shortly before the opening of the Royal Academy's 1772 exhibition, at which it was displayed, in late April. Zoffany appears to have begun working towards this image in 1770 (Ingamells 2004, p.507).

As well as the life models, two further non-Academicians are included in the image. One is Tan Chitqua, a Chinese artist, who can be seen among the standing figures at the far left. He spent a number of years in England, winning a fashionable following and receiving several commissions from the King. A contemporary account describes a visit made by him to the Academy Schools in 1771, when his portrait was 'introduced by Mr. Zoffany into a capital picture of the members of that noble institution, which that eminent artist is executing for a great personage' (presumably the King) (Whitley 1928, vol.1, p.271; Millar 1969, vol.1, p.152).

The final non-Academician, Dr William Hunter, the Academy's Professor of Anatomy, stands at the centre of the image to the right of Reynolds. His presence, and the plaster écorché figure below the lamp, invoke the study of anatomy. The room also contains casts of antique sculptures. Anatomy, the antique and the living model were the three principal strands of an artist's training (Nottingham 1991, p.8). So, as well as a group portrait of the Academicians, Zoffany also offers a visual manifesto of the central aspects of the Academy's artistic instruction. Teaching was one of the body's two main functions, the other being the holding of annual exhibitions. Itself shown at the Academy's 1772 show, Zoffany's painting accordingly exemplified the institution's purposes, and in the process contributed to its public consolidation. When on show, it seems to have been 'the canvas which drew the densest crowd about it' (Leslie and Taylor 1865, vol.1, p.446).

Walpole wrote that Zoffany 'made no design for it, but clapped in the artists as they came to him, and yet all the attitudes are easy and natural, most of the likenesses strong' (Graves 1905–06, vol.8, p.412). During painting Zoffany had enlarged the canvas on the right by around 19.7 cm (Millar 1969, vol.1, pp.153–54). This might in some measure bear out Walpole's declaration that Zoffany undertook the image on an ad hoc basis. Nevertheless, Zoffany's arrangement of the figures was not arbitrary: in the canvas's initial dimensions, the picture may have broken off at the right after the two models, and in this form the loose symmetrical correspondence between their poses and those of Zoffany and West at the other side of the canvas would have been more pronounced. Equally, despite the apparent informality of the final configuration, it has been noted that the composition is 'carefully crafted to underline the hierarchy of the newly formed institution' (Ferrara 2005, p.258).

The location of Zoffany's scene has long been assumed to be a room in that part of the royal palace at Old Somerset House which was opened for use by the Royal Academy in 1771. Yet it has recently been observed that the painting's setting may in fact be at the Academy's initial Pall Mall base (at which premises its 1772 exhibition was held) (Ingamells 2004, p.507). SM

# Endnotes

## I  Portraiture: Facts versus Fiction
ROBERT ROSENBLUM

1   For a full account of this portrait, see Smith McCrea 2005.

2   For the essential study of this change in the image of royalty, see Schama 1988.

3   For an informed medical account of his ailment, see Jelinek 1979.

## II  Sculpted Portraits, 1770–1830: 'Real Presences'
GUILHEM SCHERF

1   Borrowed from an expression used by Louis Marin about the portrait of the king (Marin 1981, pp.12–13).

2   Unlike painting, sculpture did not flourish in the United States of America during the period under consideration; large projects were systematically entrusted to such European artists as Houdon, Canova, Lazzarini and Chantrey. The only American sculptor worthy of note, William Rush, pursued a fairly marginal career.

3   A number of these had very short lives, including Ceracchi and Chaudet; others enjoyed an extended creative lifespan, for example Nollekens and Pajou.

4   Apart from Jean-Baptiste Pigalle (1714–1785), the doyen of our selection, and Messerschmidt (1736–1783), who lived only a short time, the artists of this first group died in about 1800: Banks, Caffieri, Ceracchi, Shubin, Mérard, Monot, Trippel. Claude-André Deseine was no longer active after this date.

5   The following artists died before the early 1820s: Adán, Boizot, Canova, Chaudet, Chinard, Louis-Pierre Deseine, Lucas de Montigny, Nollekens, Pajou. To this should be added those who no longer worked after 1820 (Houdon), or whose activity slowed (Dannecker, Schadow).

6   Artists born in the 1770s: Bartolini, Rauch, Rutxiehl, Thorvaldsen; the 1780s: Chantrey, David d'Angers; and the 1790s: Mahlknecht, Moine, Jean-Marie Pigalle, Roman, Rude. All died after 1830. Espercieux (1757–1840) is a special case: he was still active under the July Monarchy.

7   See its catalogue (London 1972).

8   Brilliant 2002, p.11.

9   Pommier 1998B, p.11.

10   Falconet [1761], 1808, pp.2, 3.

11   Pommier 1998B, p.11.

12   Agulhon 1978.

13   Martinelli and Pietrangeli 1955. Pasquali 2004. The commemoration of illustrious Florentines in the basilica of Santa Croce in Florence (their pantheon) was achieved only through funerary monuments.

14   Bonnet 1998.

15   The marble statues remained in store until studies had been made for the consolidation of the gallery. See Scherf 1993.

16   Bonnet 1998, p.103.

17   Poisson 1987.

18   Ozouf 1984. Deming 1989.

19   McClellan 1994, p.179.

20   Voltaire, *Lettres philosophiques*, [1734], Mille et une nuits, Paris, 1999, p.127.

21   Hoock 2003, p.73. Potts 1981A.

22   London 2003B, pp.45–46, no.3.

23   Craske 2004. Hoock 2004.

24   Traeger 1987.

25   Baker 1995.

26   Guiffrey 1877. Quarré 1940.

27   Kenworthy-Browne 1989. Wilson 2003.

28   Mercier 1994, chapter CDXLIX, p.1233.

29   Scherf 2004A.

30   For more on the Trippel see Schaffhausen 1993, pp.64–66, no.8.

31   Smith 1986, p.35. For his bust of the politician Spencer Perceval, Nollekens took a mould of the shoulders of a Chelsea Pensioner (Smith 1986, p.258).

32   Pliny 1997, p.7. 'Our ancestors exhibited in their *atria* … masks moulded from wax, each in its own niche: that way the portraits could take part in family gatherings.'

33   Maaz 1995, p.307, no.100, fig.82.

34   Kenworthy-Browne 1995, pp.65–66.

35   Kenworthy-Browne 1972, pp.322–23.

36   The terracotta bust, by Chinard, is now in the Frick Collection, New York; the painting is in a private collection. See Bailey 2005.

37   Pliny 1997, p.9. 'The custom is to erect effigies in libraries … in honour of those whose immortal souls speak to us in just such places as these.'

38   See Lundberg 1957, p.189, a portrait by Roslin (1776) in a private collection in Sweden.

39   See Martin Archer Shee's portrait of William Roscoe (1815–17) in the Walker Art Gallery, Liverpool.

40   Whinney 1988, p.329, fig.238, and p.403, fig.295.

41   Flaxman, *Monument to Lady Fitzharris*, 1815; Christchurch Priory, Hampshire (Penny 1977, p.159, fig.118). Chantrey, *Monument to David Pike Watts*, 1827; Ilam, Staffordshire (Penny 1977, p.84, fig.61).

42   Gorgone 2004, p.27.

43   The group was executed between 1830 and 1834. The attendant scandal was so great that the work could not be placed in Westminster Abbey. It was recovered in 1837 by the Earl of Munster, the king's illegitimate son, and returned to the royal collection. See London 1981, p.32.

44   Penny 1975, pp.124–25, fig.8.

45   Simson 1996, p.437, no.298.

46 Scherf 2001, pp.20–21.

47 Whinney 1988, p.464, note 16.

48 Scherf 2004, pp.20–21.

49 See Stuttgart 1987, nos 58, 69, 102 and 116.

50 Hubert and Ledoux-Lebard 1999, p.81.

51 Henri-François-Alphonse Esquiros in 1844, on the subject of David d'Angers (quoted in Barbillon 2004, p.237).

52 He is dressed in the style of classical antiquity for the Corps Législatif (Chaudet; Hermitage Museum, St Petersburg); in coronation robes for the School of Law (Cartellier; Château de Versailles), the Institute (Roland; *in situ*) and the Senate (Ramey; Musée du Louvre); and in court undress for the Banque de France (Rutxiehl; Château de Versailles). See Hubert and Ledoux-Lebard 1999, figs 110, 119, 125, 126 and 127.

53 Honour 1973.

54 Hubert and Pillepich 1995, p.58.

55 Diderot, *Essais sur la peinture* [1766], 1984, p.64.

56 Voltaire faced with Pigalle's project, Washington faced with Houdon's project, and Napoleon faced with Canova's statue.

57 Quatremère de Quincy 1834, p.207.

58 Herrmann Fiore 1997, p.211.

59 *Trajan*: see Kleiner 1992, p.210, fig.172. *Bernadotte, c.* 1800, terracotta; Waldemarsudde Castle, Sweden: see Rome 1989A, p.70. *Ludwig I*, 1821, marble; Glyptotek, Munich: see Rome 1989B, p.177.

60 *Eschine*: Haskell and Penny 1988, pp.179–80. Angelini, *Monument to Piranesi*: see Lilli 1991, fig.19. Chinard, *Self-portrait*: see Paris 2003A, ill. p.42. The concealed hand corresponds in rhetoric to self-control (Fleckner 2000, p.30 and fig.6)

61 Honour 1973, p.180.

62 Maaz 2004, p.35, fig.10.

63 Bruel 1958, vol.1, p.99.

64 Moscow 1994, p.87.

65 Hüneke 2000, p.261, no.30.

66 Diderot, *Pensées détachées sur la peinture*, [1776], 1995, p.445.

67 Penny 1977, p.50, fig.35.

68 For Bartolini's marble of Madame Eynard, before 1823 (Private collection; plaster cast in the Galleria dell'Accademia, Florence) see Prato 1978, no.6.

69 His first attempt in this genre was the portrayal of a young boy, Henryk Lubomirski, whom he represented as Cupid. The marble statue is at Lancut Castle in Poland; see Honour 1994, pp.131–33.

70 For the Pajou see Paris 1997A, fig.178; the Schadow see Mirsch 1998, p.68, fig.44; and the Rauch see Simson 1996, p.61, cat.23.

71 Diderot, *Pensées détachées sur la peinture*, [1776], 1995, p.448.

72 Pliny 1997, pp.7 and 135.

73 Pope-Hennessy 1966, p.77.

74 Among them Houdon, Nollekens and Tieck.

75 Smith 1986, p.292.

76 Bruel 1958, vol.1, p.99.

77 Silvestre de Sacy 1953, p.145. Morris 2002, p.69.

78 Anonymous critic published in *Sans Quartier au Salon*, 1783 (McWilliam 1991, p.369).

79 The plaster cast of Hewetson's *Clement XIV* can still be seen at Canova's studio in Possagno. See Honour 1959, p.226.

80 He used the *camera lucida* for the bust of Coke at Holkham Hall (Potts 1981B, p.54). See Whinney 1988, p.416.

81 Pliny 1997, p.133.

82 Hobson 2002, p.217.

83 Ferrara 2005, no.88.

84 Gage 2000, p.37.

85 Boudon-Machuel 2004, pp.66–69.

86 See the account of the Salon of 1763 (*Louis XV* by Lemoyne), quoted in Réau 1927, p.85.

87 Courtine and Haroche 1994. Baridon and Guédron 1999.

88 David d'Angers, quoted in Jouin 1878, vol.2, p.234.

89 Canova's statue, executed between 1805 and 1808, was transferred to Turin in 1809 and made a triumphal return to Rome in 1814. In 1820, worried by this *succès de scandale*, Pauline and the papal authorities requested that Prince Borghese conceal the statue. As a result it was put away until 1838, when it was exhibited at the Villa Borghese on the Pincio. See Herrmann Fiore 1997.

## III Between the Novel and History: French Portraiture towards 1835

SÉBASTIEN ALLARD

1 Jal 1833, p.82.

2 Louis Peisse, 'Salon de 1841', *Revue des Deux-Mondes*, 1 April 1841.

3 Jal 1833, note 1, p.103.

4 Which was not really the case under the July monarchy, if we remember the great commissions for Versailles, or for churches and public buildings.

5 Girardin 1986, p.116.

6 Karr 1858, vol.1, p.188.

7 Jal 1833, note 1, p.83.

8 See Martin-Fuigier 1990, p.393.

9 Lenormant 1833, p.57.

10 Planche 1831, p.63.

11 Planche 1831, p.63.

12 Letter from Ingres to Gilibert, 2 October 1841.

13 Allard and Chaudonneret 2006, p.80.

14 Jal 1833, note 1, p.84.

15 Heinrich Heine, *Salon de 1833*, quoted in Ternois 2001, p.211.

16 Laviron and Galbaccio 1833, p.152.

17 Laviron 1834, p.193.

18 On this article and the relationship between Delacroix and Lawrence, see Hannoosh 2005.

19 Delacroix 1923, p.161.

20 Laviron and Galbaccio 1833, p.148.

21 Planche 1831, note 10, p.265.

22 Planche 1831, p.192.

23 Gautier 1996, p.364.

24 Gautier 1996, p.367.

25 *Journal des artistes*, 22 February 1846, p.62.

## IV The Role of Prints and Printmakers in the Diffusion of Portraiture

TIM CLAYTON

1 *Morning Chronicle*, 26 May 1772.

2 Gougenot 1749, pp.136–37.

3 *The Literary Gazette and Journal*, 1822, pp.85–86; Whitley 1928, vol.2, pp.6–10; Antony Griffiths in London 1978, pp.38–39.

4 Jean Rouquet, *L'Etat des arts en Angleterre*, Paris, 1755: 'Les Peintres de quelque réputation, et ceux qui n'en ont point, cherchent également à se célébrer par son [sic] moyen; ils font graver un ou plusieurs de leurs portraits dans ce genre, sous toutes sortes de prétextes, mais le dessein de s'afficher est leur véritable motif.'

5 See Clayton 1997, pp.275–77.

6 Sayer and Bennett's enlarged *Catalogue of New and Valuable Prints...*, London, 1775, pp.16–19 (facsimile: London, 1970).

7 See Hill 1965, p.140.

8 Page 361. On the *Neue Bibliothek* see Tim Clayton, 'Reviews of English Prints in German Journals 1750–1800', *Print Quarterly*, 10, 1993, pp.123–37; 'The Reviews of English Art in the *Neue Bibliothek*' in Anneliese Klingenberg, Katharina Middell, Matthias Middell and Ludwig Stockinger (eds), *Sächsische Aufklärung*, Leipziger Universitatsverlag, 2001.

9 *Magazin des Buch- und Kunsthandels*, neuntes Stück, 1780.

10 *Serie di Stampe Inglesi intagliate da' più rinomati incisori che si trovano vendibili in Merceria al negozio di Teodoro Viero incisore, e negoziante di ogni sorte di stampe*, Venice, 1787, p.v.

11 Griffiths 1978, p.37.

12 David Alexander, 'A Reluctant Communicator: George Romney and the Print Market', in Kidson 2002, pp.251–88.

13 My own translation from Roger de Piles, *L'Abrégé de la vie des peintres*, Paris, 1699, p.86: 'Prémiérement [sic] les Portraits des Souverains qui ont gouverné un Païs, les Princes & Princesses qui en sont descendus, ceux qui ont tenu quelque rang considérable dans l'Etat, dans l'Eglise, dans les Armes, dans la Robe: ceux qui se sont rendus recommandables dans les différentes Professions, & les Particuliers qui ont quelque part dans les Evénemens [sic] historiques.'

14 J. van der Waals, 'The Print Collection of Samuel Pepys', *Print Quarterly*, 1, 1984, pp.236–57; Tim Clayton, 'The Print Collection of George Clarke at Worcester College, Oxford', *Print Quarterly*, 9, 1992, pp.123–41.

15 See Pointon 1993, pp.53–78.

16 Quoted in Pointon 1993, p.59.

17 Georg Meusel (ed.), *Museum für Künstler und für Kunstliebhaber*, 10, 1790, pp.375–77.

18 Quoted in Pointon 1993, p.62.

## 2 The Status Portrait

SÉBASTIEN ALLARD

1 Diderot, *Entretiens sur le fils naturel*, 'Troisième entretien'.

2 Solkin 1986.

3 On this, see the text by MaryAnne Stevens on pp.246–52.

4 On the allegorical portrait, see my text with Guilhem Scherf on pp.228–31.

5 On this, see the text by Robert Rosenblum on pp.14–24 and my text on pp.37–49.

## 3 The History Portrait

GUILHEM SCHERF

1 Mercier, vol.IV, 1783, chapter CCCLIII, 1994 edition, vol.1, pp.975–76.

2 Mercier, vol.VI, 1783, chapter DXXIX, 1994 edition, vol.1, p.1466.

3 Petrarch, quoted in Pommier 1998B, p.35.

4 Plutarch, 'Alexandre the Great', French edition, Paris, 1967, vol.2, p.383.

5 Letter from Voltaire to Thiriot, 1735 (quoted in Saint-Girons 1998, pp.142–43).

6 1739. Quoted in Bonnet 1998, p.34.

7 See Versailles 2004, p.110, fig.1.

8 Quatremère de Quincy 1834, p.302. Canova's marble statue, completed in 1821, was destroyed in Raleigh ten years later. The plaster cast is in Possagno: Pavanello 1976, no.306, repr.

9 Lieberman 1989, fig.1. Yarrington 2000, p.145.

10 Diderot, *Salon of 1781*, 1995 edition, p.357: on the subject of Houdon's *Tourville*, one of the 'Great Men' chosen by d'Angiviller to adorn the Louvre; see Dowley 1957.

11 Antoine Schnapper in Paris 1989E, p.386.

12  Equestrian statues of Louis XIV by Bernini (marble, Château de Versailles, placed in the eighteenth century at the far end of the Pièce d'Eau des Suisses) and of Peter I by Falconet (bronze, St Petersburg, known mainly through engravings). See David's sketch in Paris 1989E, p.386, no.162, repr.

13  The painter Rigo in the *Moniteur universel*, 18 June 1801, quoted by Philippe Bordes in Los Angeles 2005, p.90.

14  Lavin 1987, pp.447–51.

15  Quoted by Jacques Vilain in Paris 1974A, p.476.

16  The head of the statue was reproduced in bronze (a copy exists in the Musée de Saumur, bequeathed by the sculptor's son).

17  Only the boot is a concession to modern dress.

18  Caso 1988, pp.76–84.

19  1826–27. Stone statue in the square in Pin-en-Mauges (plaster: see Angers 1994, no.37, repr.).

20  David d'Angers, Carnet 2 (1828) and Carnet 16 (October–December 1831, January–April 1832); Bruel 1958, vol.1, pp.19, 172.


## 4  The Cultural Portrait

GUILHEM SCHERF

1  Pommier 1998B, p.362, following a commentary on Tischbein's portrait of Goethe.

2  The word 'culture' can be used in the figurative sense: it means to 'work on the culture of the mind' (*Dictionnaire de l'Académie*, 1762).

3  Brilliant 2002, p.122.

4  Letter dated Rome, 30 August 1787, to the German *Merkur*, quoted in Pommier 1998B, p.360.

5  Watelet 2004, pp.10, 28 and 42.

6  Ligne 1997, p.70.

7  Quoted in Todorov 1996, pp.49–50.

8  Lenoir 1797, p.209, no.401.

9  Martinelli and Pietrangeli 1955, no.89, pl. X. Pommier 2003, fig.9.

10  Pommier 2003, fig.12. Mengs's painting is in the Metropolitan Museum of Art, New York.

11  Letter to the Duc de Richelieu, 17 October 1754, quoted in Hébert de la Rousselière 1959, p.74.

12  Letter from Madame Necker to Voltaire, about 9 April 1770: Voltaire 1962–63, letter no.15282.

13  Letter from Voltaire to Dorat, 1 October 1770: Voltaire 1962–63, letter no.15660.

14  Quoted from the report, decree of 9 May 1780: Furcy-Raynaud 1927, p.239.

15  Buffon, *Histoire naturelle*, vol.2, p.518: quoted by James David Draper in Paris 1997A, p.287.

16  1774. Ferrara 2005, no.76.

17  Fernando Mazzocca, quoted by Sylvain Laveissière in Paris 1997B, p.278.

18  David d'Angers, notebook 16, October–December 1831, January–April 1832: Bruel 1958, vol.1, p.171.

19  David d'Angers, quoted in Jouin 1878, vol.1, p.203.


## 5  The Place for Experimentation: Artists' Portraits and Self-portraits

VIVIEN GREENE

*I would like to thank Anne Archenoul for her patient assistance with certain details of this text. I am also grateful to Jonah Siegel and Nancy Yousef for their interesting observations on philosophical developments during the period.*

1  Jean-Jacques Rousseau, *The Confessions*, J. M. Cohen (trans.), New York, 1953, p.17.

2  See Kant's section in the *Critique of Judgement* entitled 'Beautiful Art Is the Art of Genius'. He states: '*Genius* is the talent (or natural gift) which gives the rule to art. Since talent, as the innate productive faculty of the artist, belongs itself to nature, we may express the matter thus: Genius is the innate mental disposition (*ingenium*) through which nature gives the rule to art.' Immanuel Kant, *Critique of Judgement*, J. H. Bernard (trans.), New York, 1951, p.150.

3  A key reference on artists' self-portraits is Liverpool 1994.

4  A recent exploration of this is Ferrara 2005.

5  See Tomlinson 1992.

6  Canova's exceptional position is explored at length in Johns 1998.

7  David's self-portraiture is examined in Clark 1994.

8  For the relationship between sovereigns, artists and academies see, for example, the discussion of the situation in Britain in Hoock 2003. The annual exhibition became a widely attended event in France and England and made artistic production available to a wider audience. For a look at this phenomenon in France see, for example, Crow 1985, and, in Britain, London 2001. Denis Diderot publicised the French Salons in his writings, which in themselves constituted the beginnings of art criticism, and served to enhance the importance of art and its makers in the eyes of the art-going public. See Fried 1980.

9  Reynolds delivered this speech on 2 January 1769. Reynolds 1992, p.80.

10  Peale and his position in Federalist America are treated in Ward 2004.

11  For women's self-portraiture see Borzello 1998.

12  Hume 2000. See in particular 'Of Personal Identity', I.4.6., pp.164–71.


## 7  The Portrait after the Antique

MALCOLM BAKER

1  For a discussion of the classicising bust in a wider context see Keller 1970.

2  Janson 1998.

3  Lavin 1998.

4  For a discussion of the Brutus portrait and the *all'antica* bust in the sixteenth century see Martin 1993.

5  Honour 1958.

6  For the British example see Solkin 1982, and the French, Crow 1985.

7  Peach 2000; Baker forthcoming.

8  Hubert 1964A, pp.342–58; Hubert and Ledoux-Lebard 1999, pp.78–101.

9  Avery 1985.

10  Baker 2007.

11  Potts 2000; Haskell and Penny 1981.

12  Bann 1994.


## 8  The Allegorical Portrait

SÉBASTIEN ALLARD
AND GUILHEM SCHERF

1  Examples from the first half of the eighteenth century include, in sculpture, *Louis XV as Jupiter*, by Coustou (marble, 1731; Musée du Louvre, Paris) and, in painting, the innumerable portraits by Nattier.

2  See, for example, Chinard's marble portrait of Juliette Récamier (fig. 67), Gérard's portrait of Thérésia Cabarrus (cat. 140) and Prud'hon's portrait of the Empress Joséphine in the park at Malmaison (1805–09; Musée du Louvre, Paris).

3  See Johns 1998, Chapter 4.

4  Ford 1974A.

5  The marble group is now at Spencer House, London. See Robinson 1993, p.15.

6  Caricature in sculpture only developed after the July Monarchy, with the small plaster busts made and distributed by Jean-Pierre Dantan. Daumier's character portraits in clay were not supposed to be on public display. In any case, they are not allegorical portraits: what a pity it is that Daumier never made a pear-shaped head of Louis-Philippe. See Paris 2005B.

7  On this, see Sébastien Allard's 'Between the Novel and History: French Portraiture towards 1835' on pp.37–49.


## 9  Nature and Grace: The Landscape and the Figure

MARYANNE STEVENS

1  Porter 2000, p.295.

2  Thomson, *The Seasons*, London, 1730 (revised 1744): 'Summer', lines 1138–41.

3  Oliver Goldsmith, *A History of the Earth and Animated Nature*, London, 1774, vol.8, p.400.

4  Anon., *The Rise and Progress of the Present Taste in Planting Parks, Pleasure Grounds, Gardens, Etc.*, 1767; reprinted in Dixon Hunt and Willis 1975, p.299.

5  Himmelfarb 2000, p.33.


## Grace and Naturalness: Some Definitions

GUILHEM SCHERF

1  Pommier 1991.

2  Voltaire in *L'Encyclopédie*, vol. VII, Paris, 1757, pp.805–06.

3  Watelet, *ibid.*

4  Marmontel, in the *Supplément* to the *Encyclopédie* published by Panckoucke (1776–77).

5  Sulzer, *ibid.*

6  Pommier 1991, p.45.

7  Pommier 1991, pp.62–63.


## 10  Portraiture from 1815 to 1830: Ideal Families and Tormented Geniuses

ROBERT ROSENBLUM

1  The similarity was first observed in Jenkins 1945.

# Bibliography

ABRAMS 1985
A. U. Abrams, *The Valiant Hero*, Washington DC, 1985

AGULHON 1978
Maurice Agulhon, 'La "Statuomanie" et l'histoire', *Ethnologie Française*, 1978, pp.145–72

AIX-EN-PROVENCE 1986
Xavier Lavagne, *Méjanes 1786–1986*, exh. cat., Hôtel de Ville, Aix-en-Provence, 1986

AJACCIO 2001
Jean-Marc Olivesi (ed.), *Napoléon, les Bonaparte et l'Italie*, exh. cat., Musée Fesch, Ajaccio, 2001

ALAZARD 1950
Jean Alazard, *Ingres et l'ingrisme*, Paris, 1950

ALBERTS 1978
R. C. Alberts, *Benjamin West: A Biography*, Boston, 1978

ALCOUFFE 1991–92
Daniel Alcouffe, 'Le Goût de la comtesse du Cayla', *Dossier de l'Art*, 5, December 1991 – January 1992, pp.6–15

ALEXANDER 2002
John K. Alexander, *Samuel Adams: America's Revolutionary Politician*, Lanham, Maryland, 2002

ALLARD 2005
Sébastien Allard (ed.), *Paris 1820: L'Affirmation de la génération romantique*, Berne, 2005

ALLARD AND CHAUDONNERET 2006
Sébastien Allard and Marie-Claude Chaudonneret, *Ingres: La Réforme des principes (1806–1834)*, Lyons, 2006

ALVAREZ N.D.
Antonio Alvarez y Ximénez, *Memoria*, in Barriga 1941–48, vol. 3 (1946)

AMAURY-DUVAL 1993
Eugène Emmanuel Amaury-Duval, *L'Atelier d'Ingres, édition critique de l'ouvrage publié en 1878*, Daniel Ternois (ed.), Paris, 1993

AMMF 1883–97
*Inventaire général des richesses d'art de la France. Archives du musée des monuments français*, vol.1, Paris, 1883; vol.2, Paris, 1886; vol.3, Paris, 1897

AMSTERDAM 1957
*Van Gotiek tot Empire*, exh. cat., Rijksmuseum, Amsterdam, 1957

ANDERSEN 1965
Troels Andersen, 'Vigilius Eriksen in Russia', *Artes: Periodical of the Fine Arts*, 1, October 1965

ANDERSEN 1970
Troels Andersen, 'Vigilius Erichsen, List of Paintings, 1757–72', *Artes: Periodical of the Fine Arts*, 1970

ANDERSON 2000
Fred Anderson, *Crucible of War: The Seven Years' War and the Fate of the Empire in British North America, 1754–1766*, London, 2000

ANDROSSOV 2000
Sergei Androssov, 'Artisti romani e mecenati russi nel Settecento', in Massa 2000, pp.25–48

ANGELIS 1976
Rita de Angelis, *Tout l'oeuvre peint de Goya*, with an introduction by Paul Guinard, Paris, 1976

ANGERS 1994
Patrick Le Nouëne, *Autour de David d'Angers. Sculptures du XVIIIe siècle et du début du XIXe dans les collections des musées d'Angers*, exh. cat., Musée des Beaux-Arts, Angers, 1994–95

ANNAND 1961
A. McK. Annand, 'Hugh Montgomerie, 12th Earl of Eglinton, K.T.', *Journal of the Society for Army Historical Research*, 39, 1961, pp.37–40

ANNET AND TRIANON 1833
Alfred Annet and Henry Trianon, *Examen critique du Salon de 1833*, Paris, 1833

ANNUAL REGISTER 1780
*The Annual Register, or a View of the History, Politics, and Literature for the Year 1779*, London, 1780

ANTOINE 1993
Michel Antoine, *Louis XV*, Paris [1989], 1993

ARNASON 1976
H. Harvard Arnason, *Jean-Antoine Houdon, le plus grand sculpteur français du XVIIIe siècle*, Lausanne, 1976

ASFOUR AND WILLIAMSON 1999
Amal Asfour and Paul Williamson, *Gainsborough's Vision*, Liverpool, 1999

ASHTON 2006
Geoffrey Ashton, *Thomas Lawrence*, London, 2006

ASLESON 2003
Robyn Asleson (ed.), *Notorious Muse: The Actress in British Art and Culture, 1776–1812*, New Haven and London, 2003

ASPDEN 2004
Suzanne Aspden, 'Linley, Elizabeth Ann (1754–1792)', in H. C. G. Matthew and Brian Harrison (eds), *Oxford Dictionary of National Biography*, Oxford, 2004, vol.33, pp.923–25

ATHANASSOGLOU-KALLMYER 2005
Nina Athanassoglou-Kallmyer, 'Ambiguïtés britanniques: le peintre, le critique et monsieur le baron', in Mollier, Reid and Yon 2005, pp.159–68

AUBERT 1950
Marcel Aubert, 'Au département des Sculptures: un buste de Pigalle, par lui-même', *Bulletin des Musées de France*, March 1950, pp.41–42

AUCKLAND QUARTERLY 1976
'T. G.', 'Bertel Thorvaldsen: Napoléon I', *Auckland City Art Gallery Quarterly*, 62–63, December 1976, pp.31–33

AUDE 1912
Edward Aude, *Le Musée d'Aix-en-Provence*, Paris, 1912

AUDE 1933
Edward Aude, 'Le Marquis de Méjanes', *Les Trésors des bibliothèques de France*, 4, 1933, pp.35–44

AUGÉ 1996
Jean-Louis Augé, 'Le Portrait de Manuel Osorio à l'âge de trois ans', in *Goya: Les Dossiers de l'art*, 1996, pp.44–45

AVERY 1985
Charles Avery, 'Neo-Classical Portraits by Pistrucci and Rauch', in his *Studies in European Sculpture*, London, 1985, pp.253–60

AZARA 1780
José Nicolás de Azara, *Obras de D. Antón Rafael Mengs*, Madrid, 1780

AZCUE BREA 1994
Leticia Azcue Brea, *La Escultura en la Real Academia de Bellas Artes de San Fernando (Catalogo y Estudio)*, Madrid, 1994

BADET 1989
Claude Badet, *Marseille en Révolution Française*, Paris, 1989

BADINTER 1990
Elisabeth and Robert Badinter, *Condorcet*, Paris, 1990

BAD ISCHL 1966
*Vom Biedermeier zur Jahrhundertwende*, exh. cat., Kurhaus, Bad Ischl, 1966

BAETJER 1999
Katharine Baetjer, 'British Portraits in the Metropolitan Museum of Art', *The Metropolitan Museum of Art Bulletin*, 57.1, summer 1999, pp.5–72

BAILEY 2002
Colin B. Bailey, *Patriotic Taste: Collecting Modern Art in Pre-Revolutionary Paris*, New Haven and London, 2002

BAILEY 2005
Colin B. Bailey, 'The Frick Purchases Joseph Chinard's Portrait of Etienne Vincent-Marniola', *The Frick Collection Members' Magazine*, winter 2005, p.8611

BAILLIO 1981
Joseph Baillio, 'Le Dossier d'une oeuvre d'actualité politique: Marie-Antoinette et ses enfants par Mme Vigée Le Brun. Première partie', *L'Oeil*, 38, March 1981, pp.34–42, 74–75

BAKER 1942
H. Baker, *John Philip Kemble: The Actor in His Theatre*, Cambridge, Mass., 1942

BAKER 1995
Malcolm Baker, 'The Portrait Sculpture', in David McKitterick (ed.), *The Making of the Wren Library, Trinity College, Cambridge*, Cambridge, 1995, pp.110–37

BAKER 2007
Malcolm Baker, '"For Pembroke, Statues, Dirty Gods and Coins": The Collecting, Display and Uses of Sculpture at Wilton House', in Eike Schmidt (ed.), *Collecting Sculpture in Early Modern Europe*, Studies in the History of Art, National Gallery of Art, Washington DC, forthcoming (2007)

BAKER FORTHCOMING
Malcolm Baker, 'Making the Portrait Bust Modern: Tradition and Innovation in British Eighteenth-century Sculptural Portraiture', in Jeanette Kohl and Rebecca Müller (eds), *Integrität und Fragment. Kopf und Büste vom Mittelalter bis zum 18. Jahrhundert*, forthcoming

BALTIMORE 1989
Allen Staley, *Benjamin West: American Painter at the English Court*, exh. cat., Baltimore Museum of Art, 1989

BALTY 1989
Jean-Charles Balty, 'Christian Daniel Rauch, Friedrich Tieck et l'antique. A propos de deux marbres de la Villa Ludovisi', *Beiträge zur Ikonographie und Hermeneutik. Festschrift für Nikolaus Himmelmann*, 1989, pp.521–26

BANN 1994
Stephen Bann, *Frankenstein: Creation and Monstrosity*, London, 1994

BARBILLON 2004
Claire Barbillon, 'Que disent les descriptions des portraits sculptés au XIXe siècle?', in *La Description de l'oeuvre d'art. Du modèle classique aux variations contemporaines*, papers published after a conference organised by Olivier Bonfait at the Villa Medici, Rome (13–15 June 2001), Paris, 2004, pp.229–48

BARCELONA 1977
*Goya*, exh. cat., Palacio de Pedralbes, Barcelona, 1977

BARIDON AND GUÉDRON 1999
Laurent Baridon and Martial Guédron, *Corps et arts. Physionomies et physiologies dans les arts visuels*, Paris, 1999

BARKER 1949
T. C. Barker, 'The Sankey Navigation', *Transactions of the Historic Society of Lancashire and Cheshire*, 100, 1949, pp.121–55

BARKER 2005
Emma Barker, *Greuze and the Painting of Sentiment*, Cambridge, 2005

BARKER AND HARRIS 1954
T. C. Barker and J. R. Harris, *A Merseyside Town in the Industrial Revolution: St Helens, 1750–1900*, Liverpool, 1954

BARRELL 1992
John Barrell, *The Birth of Pandora and the Division of Knowledge*, London, 1992

BARRIGA 1937
Víctor M. Barriga, *Mapa topográfico de Arequipa y sus provincias*, in *El Deber*, Arequipa, 9 November 1937

BARRIGA 1941–48
Víctor M. Barriga, *Memorias para la historia de Arequipa*, Arequipa, 1941–48, 3 vols

BARRY 1783
James Barry, *An Account of a Series of Pictures in the Great Room of the Society of Arts, Manufactures, and Commerce, at the Adelphi*, London, 1783

BARUTEAU 1958
Claude Baruteau, 'Prud'hon: Portraitiste de Talleyrand et de la duchesse de Dino', *Annales de Bourgogne*, 30, January–March 1958, pp.48–57

BASILY-CALLIMINSKI 1909
J. B. Basily-Calliminski, *Isabey: sa vie, son temps, 1767–1855*, Paris, 1909

BASSANO DEL GRAPPA 2003
Sergei Androssov, Mario Guderzo and Giuseppe Pavanello, *Canova*, exh. cat., Museo Civico, Bassano del Grappa, and Gipsoteca, Possagno, 2003

BATH 2001
Hugh Belsey et al., *Love's Prospect: Gainsborough's 'Byam Family' and the Eighteenth-Century Marriage Portrait*, exh. cat., Holburne Museum of Art, Bath, 2001

BATH 2002
*Pickpocketing the Rich: Portrait Painting in Bath, 1720–1800*, exh. cat., Holburne Museum of Art, Bath, 2002

BATÎCLE 1992
Jeannine Batîcle, *Goya*, Paris, 1992

BATÎCLE 1995
Jeannine Batîcle, *Goya*, Paris, 1995

BATÎCLE 1998
Jeannine Batîcle, 'La pintura de Goya en París y Burdeos: 1824–28', in Bilbao 1998

BAUMGÄRTEL 1998
Bettina Baumgärtel, *Angelika Kauffmann (1741–1807): 'Eine Dichterin mit dem Pinsel'*, Ostfildern-Ruit, 1998

BAUMGÄRTEL FORTHCOMING
Bettina Baumgärtel, *Kritisches Werkverzeichnis der Gemälde, Zeichnungen und Druckgraphik von Angelika Kauffmann (1741–1807)*, forthcoming

BAZIN 1987
Germain Bazin, *Théodore Géricault: Etude critique, documents, et catalogue raisonné*, Paris, 1987, 7 vols

BAZIN 1992
Germain Bazin, *Théodore Géricault: étude critique, documents et catalogue raisonné*, Paris, 1992

BELFAST 1999
*James Stewart of Killymoon: An Irishman on the Grand Tour, 1766–68*, exh. cat., Ulster Museum, Belfast, 1999

BELL 1998–99
Evelyne Bell, 'The Life and Work of Henry Walton', *Gainsborough's House Review*, 1998–99, pp.40–102

BELLA BARSALI 1985
Isa Bella Barsali, second enlarged edition of *Mostra di Pompeo Batoni*, exh. cat., Amministrazione provinciale di Lucca [1967], Lucca, 1985

BENISOVICH 1956
M. N. Benisovich, 'Wertmüller et son livre de raison intitulé la Notte', *Gazette des Beaux-Arts*, 48, 1956, p.51

BENOIST 1928
Luc Benoist, *La Sculpture romantique*, Paris, 1st edition 1928; revised edition by Isabelle Leroy-Jay Lemaistre, Paris, 1994

BERGERET 1848
Pierre Nolasque Bergeret, *Lettre d'un artiste sur l'état des arts en France, considérés sous les rapports politiques, artistiques, commerciaux et industriels*, Paris, 1848

BERGOT 1973
F. Bergot, 'Musée des Beaux-Arts de Rennes: Récents Enrichissements', *Revue du Louvre*, 1973, 1, p.56

BERLIN 1979
*Berlin und die Antike. Architektur, Kunstgewerbe, Malerei, Skulptur, Theater und Wissenschaft vom 16. Jahrhundert bis heute*, exh. cat., Schloss Charlottenburg, Berlin, 1979

BERLIN 2005
*Goya. Prophet des Moderne*, exh. cat., Nationalgalerie, Berlin, and *Francisco de Goya, 1746–1828*, Kunsthistorisches Museum, Vienna, 2005–06

BERMINGHAM 2000
Ann Bermingham, *Learning to Draw: Studies in the Cultural History of a Polite and Useful Art*, New Haven and London, 2000

BERNE 1986
*Kunstmuseum Bern. Skulpturen und Objekte*, Berne, 1986

BERUETE Y MORET 1916
A. de Beruete y Moret, *Goya pintor de retratos*, Madrid, 1916, 2 vols

BESANÇON 2005
*Une Fraternité dans l'histoire. Les artistes et la franc-maçonnerie aux XVIIIe et XIXe siècles*, exh. cat., Musée des Beaux-Arts et d'Archéologie, Besançon, 2005

BESSIS 1969
Henriette Bessis, 'Ingres et le portrait de l'Empereur', *Archives de l'art français*, 24, Paris, 1969

BEULÉ 1863
M. Beulé, *Notice sur la vie et les ouvrages de M. Horace Vernet*, Paris, 1863

BEYER AND MUGLER 1994
Victor Beyer and Yves Mugler, *Le Mausolée du maréchal de Saxe*, Strasbourg, 1994

BÉZIÈS 2000
Caroline Béziès, 'Le Mausolée du prince de Bourbon-Conti par Mérard', in L'Isle-Adam 2000, pp.139–46

BILBAO 1998
*Goya y Moratín en Burdeos: 1824–1828*, exh. cat., Museo de Bellas Artes, Bilbao, and Musée des Beaux-Arts, Bordeaux, 1998

BILBEY AND TRUSTED 2002
Diane Bilbey and Marjorie Trusted, *British Sculpture, 1470 to 2000: A Concise Catalogue of the Collection at the Victoria and Albert Museum*, London, 2002

BLANNING 2002
Timothy C. W. Blanning, *The Culture of Power and the Power of Culture: Old Regime Europe 1660–1789*, Oxford, 2002

BONNET 1998
Jean-Claude Bonnet, *Naissance du Panthéon. Essai sur le culte des Grands Hommes*, Paris, 1998

BOOTHBY 1796
Brooke Boothby, *Sorrows: Sacred to the Memory of Penelope*, London, 1796

BORDEAUX 1951
*Francisco de Goya 1746–1828*, exh. cat., Musée des Beaux-Arts, Bordeaux, 1951

BORDEAUX 1979
*El arte europeo en la corte de España durante el siglo XVIII*, exh. cat., Musée des Beaux-Arts, Bordeaux, Museo Nacional del Prado, Madrid, and Grand Palais, Paris, 1979

BORDEAUX 2005
Bernadette de Boysson and Xavier Salmon (eds), *Marie-Antoinette à Versailles. Le goût d'une reine*, exh. cat., Musée des Arts Décoratifs, Bordeaux, 2005

BORDES 1976
Philippe Bordes, 'Le "Mirabeau" de Claude-André Deseine', *Revue du Louvre*, 2, 1976, pp.61–66

BORDES 1988
Philippe Bordes, *David*, Paris, 1988

BORDES AND MICHEL 1988
Philippe Bordes and Régis Michel, *Aux Armes et aux arts! Les Arts de la Révolution 1789–1799*, Paris, 1988

BORDES AND POUGETOUX 1983
Philippe Bordes and Alain Pougetoux, 'Les Portraits de Napoléon en habits impériaux par Jacques-Louis David', *Gazette des Beaux-Arts*, 102, July–August 1983, pp.21–34

BÖRSCH-SUPAN 1977
Helmut Börsch-Supan, *Die Werke Christian Daniel Rauchs im Schlossbezirk von Charlottenburg*, Berlin, 1977

BORZELLO 1998
Frances Borzello, *Seeing Ourselves: Women's Self-portraits*, London and New York, 1998

BOSSÉNO 2003
Christian-Marc Bosséno, 'Le Député noir Belley par Girodet: l'impossible portrait de la Révolution?', *Les Portraits du pouvoir*, papers published after a conference organised by Olivier Bonfait and Brigitte Marin at the Villa Medici, Rome (24–26 April 2001), Paris, 2003, pp.135–55

BOSTON 1983
Theodore E. Stebbins, *A New World: Masterpieces of American Painting 1760–1910*, exh. cat., Museum of Fine Arts, Boston, 1983

BOSTON 1995
Carrie Rebora et al., *John Singleton Copley in America*, exh. cat., Museum of Fine Arts, Boston, The Metropolitan Museum of Art, New York, Museum of Fine Arts, Houston, and The Art Museum, Milwaukee, 1995–96

BOSWELL 1970
James Boswell, *Life of Johnson*, R. W. Chapman (ed.), corrected J. D. Fleeman, Oxford, 1970

BOTTINEAU 1975
Josette Bottineau, 'Les Portraits des généraux vendéens, commande et critique, diffusion et destin', *Gazette des Beaux-Arts*, May–June 1875, pp.175–92

BOTTINEAU 1986
Yves Bottineau, *L'Art de cour dans l'Espagne des Lumières 1746–1808*, Paris, 1986

BOUDON-MACHUEL 2004
Marion Boudon-Machuel, 'La "Ressemblance vivante" et le buste funéraire à Rome dans les années 1620', *Bernini dai Borghese ai Barberini. La cultura a Roma intorno agli anni venti*, papers published after a conference organised by Olivier Bonfait and Anna Colina at the Villa Medici, Rome (17–19 February 1999), Paris, 2004, pp.64–75

BRAVO 1993
Carlo del Bravo, 'Bartolini interpretato con Jean-Jacques', *Artibus et historiae: An Art Anthology*, 27, 14, 1993, pp.141–52

BREDIN 1999
Jean-Denis Bredin, *Une Singulière Famille: Jacques Necker, Suzanne Necker et Germaine de Staël*, Paris, 1999

BREITBART 1912
Owsei Breitbart, 'Johann Valentin Sonnenschein, 1749–1828', in *Anzeiger für Schweizerische Altertumskunde*, n.s., 13, 1911, 4, Zürich, 1912, pp.272–99

BRÉON 1984
Emmanuel Bréon, 'Une Revanche pour les Dubufe: à propos d'une donation', *Revue du Louvre*, 1984, 2, pp.117–27

BRESC-BAUTIER 1999
Geneviève Bresc-Bautier, 'Dominique-Vivant Denon, premier directeur du Louvre', in *Paris 1999*, pp.130–45

BRIÈRE 1924
Gaston Brière, *Ecole français*, Paris, 1924

BRIÈRE 1931
Gaston Brière, 'L'Exposition des chefs-d'oeuvre des musées de province (1931). Observations et remarques…', in *Bulletin de la Société d'Histoire de l'Art français*, 1931, p.189

BRILLIANT 2002
Richard Brilliant, *Portraiture*, London, [1991], 2002

BRØNS 2002
Marianne Brøns (ed.), *Aeldre dansk malerkunst: Kunstnere født før 1876*, Copenhagen, 2002

BROOKNER 1972
Anita Brookner, *Greuze: The Rise and Fall of an Eighteenth-Century Phenomenon*, London, 1972

BROOKNER 1980
Anita Brookner, *Jacques-Louis David*, London, 1980

BROOKNER 2000
Anita Brookner, *Romanticism and Its Discontents*, London, 2000

BRUEL 1958
André Bruel (ed.), *Les Carnets de David d'Angers, publiés pour la première fois intégralement avec une introduction par André Bruel*, Paris, 1958, 2 vols

BRUSSELS 1975
*L'Art français aux Musées Royaux d'Art et d'Histoire*, exh. cat., Musées Royaux d'Art et d'Histoire, Brussels, 1975

BUCHAN 2003
James Buchan, *Capital of the Mind: How Edinburgh Changed the World*, London, 2003

BUCHER 1986
Werner Bucher, 'Plastiken von Valentin Sonnenschein', in *Bernisches Mobiliar des Klassizismus von Christoph Hopfengärtner, 1758–1843 und Zeitgenossen. Plastiken von Valentin Sonnenschein, 1749–1828*, exh. cat., Schloss Jegenstorf, Berne, 1986, pp.30–47

BUCHER 1989
Werner Bucher, *Valentin Sonnenschein 1749–1828. Ein frühklassizistischer Bildhauer und Stukkateur*, PhD thesis, University of Basel, unpublished typescript, 1989, 2 vols

BÜCKLING 1999
Maraike Bückling, 'Der Bildhauer Franz Xaver Messerschmidt. Ein exemplarisches Künstleroeuvre der Umbruchzeit', in *Mehr Licht. Europa um 1770. Die bildenden Kunst der Aufklärung*, exh. cat., Städelsches Kunstinstitut und Städtische Galerie, Frankfurt, 1999, pp.100–19

BURNEY 1988–2003
*The Early Journals and Letters of Fanny Burney*, Lars E. Troide, Stewart J. Cooke and Betty Rizzo (eds), Oxford, 1988–2003, 4 vols

BURTY 1867
Philippe Burty, 'Le Collection Laperlier', in *Collection de M. Laperlier: Tableaux & Dessins de l'école française du XVIII siècle et de l'école moderne. Miniatures, terres cuites par Clodion et Marin, objets divers*, sales catalogue, Hôtel Drouot, Paris, 11–13 April 1867, pp.i–x

BURTY 1879
Philippe Burty, 'Profils d'amateurs. I. Laurent Laperlier', *L'Art*, 16, 1879, pp.147–51 (the same text appears in the preface to the catalogue of the Laperlier sale at the Hôtel Drouot, Paris, 17–18 February 1879)

BUXTON PAPERS
Buxton Papers, Cambridge University Library, 34/197–8, 109/3, 109/8–9, 112/2, 113/20

CAMERON 1952
Hector Charles Cameron, *Sir Joseph Banks*, London, 1952

CAMPAN 1988
*Mémoires de Madame Campan, première femme de chambre de Marie-Antoinette*, with an introduction by Jean Chalon and notes by Carlos de Angulo, Paris, 1988

CAMPBELL ORR 2005
Clarissa Campbell Orr, 'Queen Charlotte's Jewellery: Reconstructing a Lost Collection', in Jonathan Marsden (ed.), *The Wisdom of George III*, London, 2005

CANDID REVIEW 1780
'An Artist', *A Candid Review of the Exhibition (Being the Twelfth) of the Royal Academy, M DCC LXXX. Dedicated to His Majesty*, London, 1780 (2nd edition)

CANELLAS 1981
Angel Canellas, *Diplomatario. Francisco de Goya*, Saragossa, 1981

CANTINELLI 1905
Richard Cantinelli, 'L'Exposition rétrospective des artistes lyonnais peintres et sculpteurs (deuxième et dernier article)', *Gazette des Beaux-Arts*, February 1905, pp.141–52

CARDIFF 1990
M. Evans, *The Royal Collection: Paintings from Windsor Castle*, exh. cat., National Museum of Wales, Cardiff, 1990

CARTER 1988
Harold Burnell Carter, *Sir Joseph Banks, 1743–1820*, London, 1988

CASO 1988
Jacques de Caso, *David d'Angers. L'avenir de la mémoire. Etude sur l'art signalétique à l'époque romantique*, Paris, 1988

CASO 1996
Jacques de Caso, 'Géricault, David d'Angers, le Monument à l'Emancipation et autres objets ou figures du racisme romantique', *Géricault*, papers of a conference organised by Régis Michel at the Musée du Louvre, Paris, and the Musée des Beaux-Arts, Rouen (14–17 November 1991), Paris, 1996, 2 vols, pp.533–60

CASTRES 1973
*Les Femmes peintres au XVIIIe siècle*, exh. cat., Musée Goya, Castres, 1973

CAYLUS 1752
Comte de Caylus, *Recueil d'antiquités égyptiennes, étrusques, grecques et romaines*, Paris, 1752

CHAMPION 2005
Jean-Loup Champion, 'Un Théâtre de miroirs. Les autoportraits de Girodet', in *Paris 2005c*, pp.96–107

CHATEAUBRIAND 1998
François-René de Chateaubriand, *Mémoires d'outre-tombe*, Jean-Claude Berchet (ed.), Paris, 1998

CHAUDONNERET 1999
Marie-Claude Chaudonneret, *L'Etat et les artistes, de la Restauration à la monarchie de Juillet (1815–1833)*, Paris, 1999

CHAUSSARD 1808
Jean-Baptiste Chaussard, *Le Pausanias français ou description du Salon de 1806*, Paris, 1808

CHESNEAU AND METZGER 1934
Georges Chesneau and Charles Metzger, *Ville d'Angers. Musée des Beaux-Arts: Les Œuvres de David d'Angers*, Angers, 1934

CHEVALIER 1994
Alain Chevalier, 'Le Portrait de Paul-François des Hours de Calviac (1771–1835) au Musée des Beaux-Arts de Rennes', *Revue du Louvre*, 1994, 3, pp.54–57

CHRISTIE'S 1980
Christie's auctioneers, *Important English Pictures*, sale catalogue, London, 21 November 1980

CLARK 1985
Anthony Morris Clark, *Pompeo Batoni: A Complete Catalogue of His Works with an Introductory Text*, Edgar Peters Bowron (ed.), Oxford, 1985

CLARK 1994
T. J. Clark, 'Gross David with the Swoln Cheek: An Essay on Self-portraiture', in Michael S. Roth (ed.), *Rediscovering History: Culture, Politics and the Psyche*, Stanford, 1994, pp.243–307

CLARKE 1989
Michael Clarke, 'Madame Mère by Gérard', *National Art Collections Fund Review*, 1989, pp.139–41

CLAYTON 1997
Tim Clayton, *The English Print 1688–1802*, New Haven and London, 1997

CLÉMENT 1872
Charles Clément, *Prud'hon: sa vie, ses oeuvres et sa correspondance*, Paris, 1872

CLERMONT-FERRAND 1983
Gérard Tisserand (ed.), *Louis Charles Antoine Desaix général*, exh. cat., Musées d'Art, Clermont-Ferrand, 1983

COEKELBERGHS, JACOBS AND LOZE 1999
Denis Coekelberghs, Alain Jacobs and Pierre Loze, *François-Joseph Navez (Charleroi 1787 – Bruxelles 1869). La nostalgie de l'Italie*, Ghent, 1999

COKE 1880
John Talbot Coke, *Coke of Trusley*, London, 1880

COLDING 1970
Torben Holck Colding, 'Om Vigilius Eriksen og hans vaerksted I Rusland' in *C. L. Davids Samling: Fjerde del Jubilaeumsskrift 1945–70*, Copenhagen, 1970, pp.1–19

COLEMAN 1999
John Coleman, 'Luke Gardiner (1745–1798): An Irish Dilettante', *Irish Arts Review Yearbook*, 15, 1999, pp.161–68

COLLÉ 1868
Charles Collé, *Journal et mémoires de Charles Collé sur les hommes de lettres, les ouvrages dramatiques et les événements les plus mémorables du règne de Louis XV...*, with an introduction and notes by Honoré Bonhomme, Paris, 1868

COLLEY 1992
Linda Colley, *Britons: Forging the Nation 1707–1837*, New Haven and London, 1992

COLOGNE 1977
*Bertel Thorvaldsen. Skulpturen, Modelle, Bozzetti, Handzeichnungen. Gemälde aus Thorvaldsens Sammlungen*, exh. cat., Kunsthalle, Cologne, 1977

COLTON 1980
Judith Colton, 'Pigalle's *Voltaire*: Realist Manifesto or Tribute *all'antica*?', in *Transactions of the Fifth International Congress of Enlightenment* (*Studies on Voltaire and the Eighteenth Century*), 193, 1980, pp.1680–87

COLTON 1981
Judith Colton, 'From Voltaire to Buffon: Further Observations on Nudity, Heroic and Otherwise', *Art, the Ape of Nature: Studies in Honor of H. W. Janson*, New York, 1981, pp.531–48

COMPIÈGNE 2004
Françoise Maison (ed.), *La Pourpre et l'exil: L'Aiglon (1811–1832) et le Prince impérial*, exh. cat., Musée National du Château, Compiègne, 2004

CONNOLLY 1980
John L. Connolly, 'Napoleon and the Age of Gold', in *Consortium on Revolutionary Europe, 1750–1850*, Tallahassee, Florida, 1980, pp.52–68

CONSTANS 1995
Claire Constans, *Musée national du château de Versailles. Les peintures*, Paris, 1995, 3 vols

COOPER 1932
Duff Cooper, *Talleyrand*, London, 1932

COPENHAGEN 1983
Hanne Jönsson (ed.), *C. W. Eckersberg og hans elever*, exh. cat., Statens Museum for Kunst, Copenhagen, 1983

COPENHAGEN 1991
Bjarne Jørnaes and Stig Miss (eds), *Constantin Hansen, 1804–1880*, exh. cat., Thorvaldsens Museum, Copenhagen, and Aarhus Kunstmuseum, 1991; especially Stig Miss, 'Constantin Hansens portrætter', pp.35–45

COPENHAGEN 1996A
Hans Edvard Nørregård-Nielsen and Kasper Monrad (eds), *Christen Købke, 1810–1848*, translated by Glyn W. Jones, exh. cat., Statens Museum for Kunst, Copenhagen, 1996

COPENHAGEN 1996B
Marianne Saabye et al., *Wilhelm Bendz, 1804–1832: A Young Painter of the Danish Golden Age*, exh. cat., Hirschsprung Collection, Copenhagen, 1996

COPENHAGEN 2001
Lene Bøgh Rønberg, Kasper Monrad and Ragni Linnet, *Two Golden Ages: Masterpieces of Dutch and Danish Painting*, exh. cat., Statens Museum for Kunst, Copenhagen, and Rijksmuseum, Amsterdam, 2001

COPENHAGEN 2002
Marianne Brøns (ed.), *Ældre Dansk Malerkunst: Kunst født før 1876*, exh. cat., Statens Museum for Kunst, Copenhagen, 2002

CORK 2005
Tom Dunne (ed.), *James Barry: The 'Great Historical Painter'*, exh. cat., Crawford Art Gallery, Cork, 2005

COURTINE AND HAROCHE 1994
Jean-Jacques Courtine and Claudine Haroche, *Histoire du visage. Exprimer et taire ses émotions (XVIe–début XIXe siècle)*, Paris, 1994

CRASKE 1997
Matthew Craske, *Art in Europe, 1700–1830*, Oxford, 1997

CRASKE 2004
Matthew Craske, 'Westminster Abbey 1720–70: A Public Pantheon Built upon Private Interest', in *Pantheons: Transformations of a Monumental Idea*, Richard Wrigley and Matthew Craske (eds), Aldershot, 2004, pp.57–79

CRAVEN 1993
Wayne Craven, 'The American and British Portraits of Benjamin Franklin', in J. A. Leo Lemay (ed.), *Reappraising Benjamin Franklin: A Bicentennial Perspective*, Newark, Delaware, 1993, pp.247–89

CRÓNICA 1994
*Crónica de España*, Barcelona, 1994, 2 vols

CROOKSHANK AND GLIN 2002
Anne Crookshank and the Knight of Glin, *Ireland's Painters, 1600–1940*, New Haven and London, 2002

CROSS 2000
David A. Cross, *A Striking Likeness: The Life of George Romney*, Aldershot, 2000

CROSS 2002
David A. Cross, 'The "Admiral of the Blues": Romney, Depression and Creativity', in Liverpool 2002, pp.10–32

CROW 1985
Thomas E. Crow, *Painters and Public Life in Eighteenth-century Paris*, New Haven and London, 1985

CROW 1995
Thomas Crow, *Emulation: Making Artists for Revolutionary France*, New Haven and London, 1995

CULLEN 1983
Fintan Cullen, 'Hugh Douglas Hamilton: "Painter of the Heart"', *Burlington Magazine*, 125: 964, July 1983, pp.417–19, 421

CULLEN 1984
Fintan Cullen, 'The Oil Paintings of Hugh Douglas Hamilton', *Journal of the Walpole Society*, 50, 1984, pp.165–208

CULLEN 1997
Fintan Cullen, *Visual Politics: The Representation of Ireland, 1750–1930*, Cork, 1997

CULLEN 2000
Fintan Cullen, *Sources in Irish Art: A Reader*, Cork, 2000

CUMMING 1992
Valerie Cumming, 'Pantomime and Pageantry: The Coronation of George IV', in Essen 1992, pp.39–50

CUMMINGS 1968
Frederick Cummings, 'Boothby, Rousseau and the Romantic Malady', *Burlington Magazine*, 110: 789, December 1968, pp.659–67

CUZIN 1997
Jean-Pierre Cuzin, 'Le Centenaire de la Société des Amis du Louvre et le don au musée d'un chef-d'oeuvre de David, le portrait de Juliette de Villeneuve', *Revue du Louvre*, 1997, 2, pp.13–15

CUZIN AND ALLARD 2002
Jean-Pierre Cuzin and Sébastien Allard, *Nouvelles Acquisitions du département des peintures (1996–2001)*, Paris, 2002

DANIELS 1999
Stephen Daniels, *Joseph Wright*, London, 1999

DAVID 1867
Jacques-Louis-Jules David, *Notice sur le Marat de Louis David suivie de la liste de ses tableaux dressée par lui-même*, Paris, 1867

DAVID 1880
Jacques-Louis-Jules David, *Le Peintre Louis David. Souvenirs et documents inédits*, Paris, 1880

DAWSON 1958
Warren Royal Dawson (ed.), *The Banks Letters*, London, 1958

DAWSON 2004
Ruth Dawson, 'Perilous Royal Biography: Representations of Catherine II Immediately after Her Seizure of the Throne', *Biography*, 27, 3, summer 2004

DELACROIX 1923
Eugène Delacroix, *Oeuvres littéraires*, Paris, 1923

DELÉCLUZE 1983
*Louis David, son école et son temps. Souvenirs par E. J. Delécluze*, preface and notes by Jean-Pierre Mouilleseaux, Paris, 1983 (1st edition, Paris, 1855)

DELESTRE 1845
Jean-Baptiste Delestre, *Gros et ses ouvrages*, Paris, 1845

DELESTRE 1867
Jean-Baptiste Delestre, *Gros, sa vie et ses ouvrages*, Paris, 1867

DEMING 1989
Mark K. Deming, 'Le Panthéon révolutionnaire', in Paris 1989D, pp.97–150

DESNOIRESTERRES 1879
Gustave Desnoiresterres, *Essai d'iconographie voltairienne*, Paris, 1879; reprinted Geneva, 1970

DESPARMET FITZ-GERALD 1928–50
Xavière Desparmet Fitz-Gerald, *L'Oeuvre peint de Goya*, Paris, 1928–50

DESPORTES 1963
Ulysse Desportes, 'Giuseppe Ceracchi in America and His Busts of George Washington', *Art Quarterly*, summer 1963, pp.141–78

DE STAËL 1991
Germaine de Staël, *Corinne, or Italy*, Avriel H. Goldberger (trans. and ed.), New Brunswick and London, 1991

DESVERNAY 1915
Félix Desvernay, *Le Vieux Lyon à l'exposition interurbaine de 1914*, chapter 24, 'Le Sculpteur lyonnais Joseph Chinard', Lyons, 1915, pp.122–47

DETROIT 1968
Frederick J. Cummings, Allen Staley and Robert Rosenblum, *Romantic Art in Britain: Paintings and Drawings, 1760–1860*, exh. cat., Detroit Institute of Arts and Philadelphia Museum of Art, 1968

DEUCHAR 1984
Stephen Deuchar, *Paintings, Politics and Porter: Samuel Whitbread II (1764–1815) and British Art*, London, 1984

DEVIGNE 1925
Marguerite Devigne, 'Quelques oeuvres de sculpture française du XVIIIe siècle à Bruxelles', *Le Flambeau*, Brussels, 1925, pp.3–8

DIDEROT 1984
Denis Diderot, *Essais sur la peinture*, Gita May (ed.); *Salons de 1759, 1761, 1763*, Jacques Chouillet (ed.), Paris, 1984

DIDEROT 1995
Denis Diderot, *Héros et martyrs. Salons de 1769, 1771, 1775, 1781. Pensées détachées sur la peinture, la sculpture, l'architecture et la poésie*, Else Marie Bukdahl, Michel Delon, Didier Kahn, Annette Lorenceau and Gita May (eds), Paris, 1995

DIDEROT 1997
Denis Diderot, *Correspondance*, Laurent Versini (ed.), Paris, 1997

DIJON 1955
*François Rude 1784–1855. Commémoration du centenaire*, exh. cat., Musée des Beaux-Arts, Dijon, 1955

DIJON 1969
*Trois Peintres bourguignons du XVIIIe siècle: Colson, Vestier, Trinquesse*, exh. cat., Musée des Beaux-Arts, Dijon, 1969

DIJON 1992
*Portraits sculptés XVe–XVIIIe siècle. Collections du musée du Louvre et des musées des Beaux-Arts de Dijon et d'Orléans*, exh. cat., Musée des Beaux-Arts, Dijon, and Musée des Beaux-Arts, Orléans, 1992

DIMIER 1914
Louis Dimier, *Histoire de la peinture française au XIX siècle (1793–1903)*, Paris, 1914

DISRAELI 1982–2004
Benjamin Disraeli, *Letters*, M. G. Wiebe et al. (eds), Toronto and London, 1982–2004, 7 vols

DIXON HUNT AND WILLIS 1975
John Dixon Hunt and Peter Willis (ed.), *The Genius of the Place: The English Landscape Garden 1620–1820*, London, 1975

DOLE 2001
*Les Rosset. Un atelier jurassien au temps des Lumières*, exh. cat., Musée des Beaux-Arts, Dole, 2001–02

DOWLEY 1957
Francis H. Dowley, 'D'Angiviller's *Grands Hommes* and the Significant Moment', *Art Bulletin*, 39, December 1957, pp.259–77

DUFORT DE CHEVERNY 1990
Jean Nicolas Dufort, Comte de Cheverny, *Mémoires*, Jean-Pierre Guicciardi (ed.), Paris, 1990

DUISBURG 1989
Isabelle Leroy-Jay Lemaistre and Guilhem Scherf, *Skulptur aus dem Louvre. 89 Werke des französischen Klassizismus 1770–1830*, exh. cat., Wilhelm Lehmbruck Museum, Duisburg, Prins-Max-Palais, Karlsruhe, Schlossmuseum, Gotha, and Musée du Louvre, Paris, 1989–90

DUPUY-BAYLET 1998
Marie-France Dupuy-Baylet, 'Les Pendules des lendemains de la Révolution, une multitude de modèles', *L'Estampille: L'Objet d'art*, May 1998, pp.54–64

DÜSSELDORF 1998
Bettina Baumgärtel (ed.), *Angelika Kauffmann, Retrospektive*, exh. cat., Kunstmuseum, Düsseldorf, Haus der Kunst, Munich, and Bündner Kunstmuseum, Chur, 1998

DWYER 2002
Philip G. Dwyer, *Talleyrand*, London and New York, 2002

EAR-WIG 1781
*The Ear-Wig; or An Old Woman's Remarks on the Present Exhibition of Pictures of the Royal Academy*, London, 1781

ECKARDT 1987
Götz Eckardt (ed.), *Johann Gottfried Schadow. Kunstwerke und Kunstansichten*, Berlin, 1987

ECKARDT 1990
Götz Eckardt, *Johann Gottfried Schadow. Der Bildhauer*, Leipzig, 1990

EDINBURGH 1824
*Portraits by the late Sir Henry Raeburn*, exh. cat., 32 York Place, Edinburgh, 1824

EDINBURGH 1956
*Raeburn*, exh. cat., National Gallery of Scotland, Edinburgh, 1956

EDINBURGH 1985
*French Connections: Scotland and the Art of France*, exh. cat., Royal Scottish Museum, Edinburgh, 1985

EDINBURGH 1992
Alastair Smart, *Allan Ramsay 1713–1784*, exh. cat., Scottish National Portrait Gallery, Edinburgh, 1992

EDINBURGH 1995
Timothy Clifford, Hugh Honour, John Kenworthy-Browne et al., *The Three Graces: Antonio Canova*, exh. cat., National Gallery of Scotland, Edinburgh, 1995

EDINBURGH 1997
Duncan Thomson et al., *Raeburn: The Art of Sir Henry Raeburn, 1756–1823*, exh. cat., Scottish National Portrait Gallery, Edinburgh, 1997

EGERTON 1998
Judy Egerton, *National Gallery Catalogue: The British School*, London, 1998

EGGERS 1877
Karl Eggers, *Das Rauch-Museum zu Berlin. Verzeichnis seiner Sammlungen*, Berlin, 1877

EGGERS 1889
Karl Eggers (ed.), *Rauch und Goethe. Urkundliche Mitheilungen*, Berlin, 1889

EGGERS 1892
Karl Eggers, *Das Rauch-Museum zu Berlin. Verzeichnis seiner Sammlungen*, Berlin, 1892

EISEN 1932
Gustavus A. Eisen, *Portraits of Washington*, New York, 1932, 3 vols

EISENSTADT 1982
*Joseph Haydn und seiner Zeit*, exh. cat., Haydn Museum, Eisenstadt, 1982

EISLER 1977
Colin T. Eisler, *Paintings from the Samuel H. Kress Collection, vol. 4: European Schools, excluding Italian*, London, 1977

EITNER 1959
Lorenz Eitner, 'The Sale of Géricault's Studio in 1824', in *Gazette des Beaux-Arts*, February 1959

EITNER 1960
Lorenz Eitner, *Géricault*, Chicago, 1960

EITNER 2000
Lorenz Eitner, *French Paintings of the Nineteenth Century, vol.1: Before Impressionism (The Collection of the National Gallery of Art)*, Washington DC, 2000

ELLING 1935
Christian Elling, *Rokokoens Portraetmaleri I Danmark*, Copenhagen, 1935

EMMERSON 1992
Robin Emmerson, 'Lively Images', in Moore and Crawley 1992, pp.13–19

ENGERAND 1901
Fernand Engerand, *Inventaire des tableaux commandés et achetés par la direction des Bâtiments du roi (1709–1792)*, Paris, 1901

ERFFA AND STALEY 1986
Helmut von Erffa and Allen Staley, *The Paintings of Benjamin West*, New Haven and London, 1986

ESCHOLIER 1922
Raymond Escholier, 'Pierre-Paul Prud'hon. A propos de l'exposition du Petit-Palais', *La Revue de l'art ancien et moderne*, 42, June–December 1922, pp.109–19

ESCHOLIER 1936
Raymond Escholier, *Gros: ses amis, ses élèves*, Paris, 1936

ESCHOLIER 1941–43
Raymond Escholier, *La Peinture française, XIXe siècles*, Paris, vol. 1, 'De David à Géricault', 1941; vol. 2, 'Ingres, Delacroix, Daumier, Corot', 1943

EGERTON 1998
Celina Fox (ed.), *London: World City, 1800–1840*, exh. cat., Villa Hügel, Essen, 1992

EVANS 1999
Dorinda Evans, *The Genius of Gilbert Stuart*, Princeton, 1999

FALCONET 1808
Étienne-Maurice Falconet, *Réflexions sur la sculpture*, 1761; *Oeuvres complètes*, vol.3, Paris, 1808, pp.1–46

FARINGTON 1978–84
*The Diary of Joseph Farington*, Kenneth Garlick and Angus Macintyre (eds), New Haven and London, 1978–84, 16 vols

FARINGTON NOTEBOOKS
James Farington, 'Notebooks on Artists': original manuscript in the Royal Library, Windsor Castle; edited typescript copy at the Department of Prints and Drawings, British Museum, London

FAUQUÉ VILLANUEVA ETCHEVERRÍA 1982
Jacques Fauqué-Ramón Villanueva Etcheverría, *Goya y Burdeos 1824–1828*, Saragossa, 1982

FEHL 1968
Philipp Fehl, 'Thomas Appleton of Livorno and Canova's statue of George Washington', *Festschrift Ulrich Middeldorf*, Antje Kosegarten and Peter Tigler (eds), Berlin, 1968, pp.523–52

FERGUSON 1999
Patricia F. Ferguson, 'Indoor Gardening in the Eighteenth Century', *The Magazine Antiques*, 155, 1, January 1999

FERRARA 2005
Martin Postle (ed.), *Joshua Reynolds: The Creation of Celebrity*, exh. cat., Palazzo dei Diamanti, Ferrara, and Tate Britain, London, 2005

FEUCHTMÜLLER 1996
Rupert Feuchtmüller, *Ferdinand Georg Waldmüller 1793–1865. Leben, Schriften, Werke*, Vienna and Munich, 1996

FEUGÈRE 1922
Anatole Feugère, *Bibliographie critique de l'abbé Raynal, section III: Notes d'iconographie*, Angoulême, 1922, pp.92–95

FIELDING 1923
Mantle Fielding, *Gilbert Stuart's Portraits of George Washington*, Philadelphia, 1923

FIGGIS AND ROONEY 2001
Nicola Figgis and Brendan Rooney, *Irish Paintings in the National Gallery of Ireland, Dublin*, Dublin, 2001

FITTON 1989
R. S. Fitton, *The Arkwrights*, Manchester, 1989

FLAMENT 1921
Albert Flament, 'Un Peintre sportsman et dandy: Alfred de Dreux', in *La Renaisssance de'art français*, April 1921

FLECKNER 2000
Uwe Fleckner, 'La Rhétorique de la main cachée. De l'Antiquité au Napoléon, Premier Consul de Jean-Auguste Dominique Ingres', *Revue de l'Art*, 130, 2000, pp.27–35

**FLENSBURG 1956**
*BK Adelkultur des 18. Jahrhunderts in Schleswig-Holstein*, exh. cat., Städtisches Museum, Flensburg, 1956

**FLORYAN 2004**
Margrethe Floryan, 'Thorvaldsen und Rauch in Rom und in russischen Diensten', in *Kolloquium zur Skulptur des Klassizismus*, papers of a conference organised by Birgit Kümmel and Bernhard Maaz at the Christian Daniel Rauch-Museum, Bad Arolsen, 2004, pp.165–74

**FONTAINEBLEAU 2005**
Vincent Droguet and Marc-Henri Jordan (eds), *Théâtre de Cour. Les Spectacles à Fontainebleau au XVIIIe siècle*, exh. cat., Musée National du Château, Fontainebleau, 2005

**FORD 1974A**
Brinsley Ford, 'The Earl-Bishop. An Eccentric and Capricious Patron of the Arts', *Apollo*, June 1974, pp.426–34

**FORD 1974B**
Brinsley Ford, 'James Byres: Principal Antiquarian for English Visitors to Rome', *Apollo*, June 1974, pp.446–61

**FORDHAM 2006**
Douglas Fordham, 'Allan Ramsay's Enlightenment: Or, Hume and the Patronising Portrait', *Art Bulletin*, 88: 3, September 2006, pp.508–24

**FOREMAN 1998**
Amanda Foreman, *Georgiana, Duchess of Devonshire*, London, 1998

**FORT 1999**
Bernadette Fort (ed.), *Les Salons des 'Mémoires secrets' 1767–1787*, Paris, 1999

**FORTUNE 1999**
Brandon Brame Fortune with Deborah J. Warner, *Franklin and His Friends: Portraying the Man of Science in Eighteenth-Century America*, Philadelphia, 1999

**FORT WORTH 1982**
Joseph Baillio, *Elisabeth Louise Vigée-Le Brun (1755–1842)*, exh. cat., Kimbell Art Museum, Fort Worth, 1982

**FOURCAUD 1904**
Louis de Fourcaud, *François Rude, sculpteur: ses oeuvres et son temps (1784–1855)*, Paris, 1904

**FOX-WILSON 1987**
F. Fox-Wilson, *The Story of Goring and Highdown*, Goring, 1987

**FRASER 1979**
David Fraser, *Joseph Wright of Derby*, Derby, 1979

**FRIBORG 2000**
Flemming Friborg, *Det Gode Selskab: Kunstforeningens historier 1825–2000*, Gyldendal, 2000

**FRIED 1980**
Michael Fried, *Absorption and Theatricality: Painting and the Beholder in the Age of Diderot*, Chicago, 1980

**FRIEDLÄNDER 1890**
Julius Friedländer (ed.), *Gottfried Schadow. Aufsätze und Briefe, nebst einem Verzeichnis seiner Werke*, Stuttgart, 1890

**FRIES 1903**
August von Fries, *Die Grafen von Fries. Eine genealogische Studie*, Dresden, 1903 (second edition)

**FRITZE 1980**
Marie-Elisabeth Fritze, 'Christian Daniel Rauch und Johann Wolfgang von Goethe', in Max Kunze (ed.), *Christian Daniel Rauch. Beiträge zum Werk und Wirken*, Stendal, 1980, pp.23–52

**FROISSART 1999**
Albéric Froissart, 'Denis-Antoine Chaudet et *L'Amitié enchaînant l'Amour*: une oeuvre de jeunesse retrouvée', *Bulletin de la Société de l'Historie de l'Art français* [1998], 1999, pp.175–86

**FURCY-RAYNAUD 1927**
Marc Furcy-Raynaud, 'Inventaire des sculptures exécutées au XVIIIe siècle pour la direction des Bâtiments du Roi', *Archives de l'art français*, 14, 1927

**GABORIT 1985**
Jean-René Gaborit, *Jean-Baptiste Pigalle. Sculptures du musée du Louvre*, Paris, 1985

**GAGE 2000**
John Gage, 'Busts and Identity', in Leeds 2000, pp.36–48

**GALASSI 2006**
Susan Grace Galassi, 'Joaquín María Ferrer', in New York 2006

**GARLICK 1962–64**
Kenneth Garlick, 'A Catalogue of the Paintings, Drawings and Pastels of Sir Thomas Lawrence', *Journal of the Walpole Society*, 39, 1962–64

**GARLICK 1989**
Kenneth Garlick, *Sir Thomas Lawrence: A Complete Catalogue of the Oil Paintings*, Oxford, 1989

**GARLICK 1993**
Kenneth Garlick, *Sir Thomas Lawrence: Portraits of an Age, 1790–1830*, Alexandria, Virginia, 1993

**GASCOIGNE 2004**
John Gascoigne, 'Banks, Sir Joseph, baronet (1743–1820)', in H. C. G. Matthew and Brian Harrison (eds) *Oxford Dictionary of National Biography*, Oxford, 2004, vol.3, pp.691–95

**GASSIER AND WILSON 1970**
Pierre Gassier and Juliet Wilson, *Vie et oeuvre de Francisco de Goya*, Freiburg, 1970 (English edition, London and New York, 1971)

**GAUTIER 1996**
Théophile Gautier, *Paris et les Parisiens*, Paris, 1996

**GENEVA 1939**
*Les Chefs-d'oeuvre du Musée du Prado*, exh. cat., Musée d'Art et d'Histoire, Geneva, 1939

**GENEVA 1974**
*De Genève à l'Ermitage. Les collections de François Tronchin*, exh. cat., Musée Rath, Geneva, 1974

**GENTLEMAN'S MAGAZINE 1798**
'H. O.', 'Historical Memoirs of the Late Colonel St George', *Gentleman's Magazine*, 68, February 1798, pp.97–99

**GEORGEL AND LECOQ 1987**
Pierre Georgel and Anne-Marie Lecoq, *La Peinture dans la peinture*, Dijon, 1987

**GÉRARD 1852–57**
Henri Alexandre Gérard (ed.), *Oeuvre du Baron Gérard, 1789–1836*, Paris, 1852–57, 3 vols

**GÉRARD 1867**
Henri Alexandre Gérard (ed.), *Correspondance de François Gérard, peintre d'histoire, avec les artistes et les personnages célèbres de son temps, précédée d'une notice sur la vie et les oeuvres de Gérard, par Adolphe Viollet-le-Duc*, Paris, 1867; second edition, Paris, 1886

**GÉRARD LETTERS 1880**
*Lettres addressées au baron François Gérard*, Paris, 1880

**GÉRARD 1886**
H. Gérard (ed.), *Correspondance de François Gérard, peintre d'histoire, avec les artistes et les personnages célèbres de son temps, precedée d'une notice sur la vie et les oeuvres de Gérard, par Adolphe Viollet-le-Duc*, Paris, 1867; second edition, Paris, 1886

**GERARD POWELL AND RESSORT 2002**
Véronique Gerard Powell and Claudie Ressort, *Musée du Louvre: département des peintures. Ecoles espagnole et portugaise*, Paris, 2002

**GIRARDIN 1986**
Delphine de Girardin, *Lettres parisiennes du vicomte de Launay par Madame de Girardin*, Paris, 1986

**GLENDINNING AND MEDRANO 2005**
Nigel Glendinning and José Miguel Medrano, *Goya y el Banco Nacional de San Carlos*, Madrid, 2005

**GOETZ 2005**
Adrien Goetz, *Ingres collages: dessins d'Ingres du musée de Montauban*, Montauban, 2005

**GOMBRICH 1942**
E. H. Gombrich, 'Reynolds's Theory and Practice of Imitation', *Burlington Magazine*, 80: 467, February 1942, pp.40–45

**GONCOURT 1876**
Edmond de Goncourt, *Catalogue raisonné de l'oeuvre peint, dessiné et gravé de P. P. Prud'hon*, Paris, 1876

**GONCOURT 1880**
Edmond and Jules de Goncourt, *L'Art du dix-huitième siècle*, Paris, 1880

**GOODDEN 2006**
Angelica Goodden, *Miss Angel: The Art and World of Angelica Kauffman*, London, 2006

**GOODISON 1977**
J. W. Goodison, *Fitzwilliam Museum, Cambridge. Catalogue of Paintings III: British School*, Cambridge, 1977

**GOODMAN 1986**
Dena Goodman, 'Pigalle's "Voltaire nu": The Republic of Letters Represents Itself to the World', *Representations*, 16, 1986, pp.86–109

**GORANI 1793**
J. Gorani, *Mémoires secrets et critiques des cours, des gouvernements, et des moeurs des principaux états de l'Italie*, Paris, 1793, 3 vols

**GORGONE 2004**
Giulia Gorgone, 'Je suis la petite Napoléon: l'infanza della principessa Napoleona Elisa Baciocchi', in Rome 2004, pp.24–35

**GOTHA 1999**
Bärbel Kovalevski (ed.), *Zwischen Ideal und Wirklichkeit. Künstlerinnen der Goethe-Zeit zwischen 1750 und 1850*, exh. cat., Schloßmuseum, Gotha, 1999

**GOUGENOT 1749**
Louis Gougenot, *Lettre sur la peinture, la sculpture, et l'architecture*, second edition, Amsterdam, 1749

**GOURLAY 1983**
Alexander S. Gourlay, 'Iphigenia in England: A Postscript to "The Melancholy Shepherdess"', *Bulletin of Research in the Humanities*, 86, summer 1983, pp.223–26

**GRACIANO 2002A**
Andrew Sean Graciano, 'Property as Wealth: Joseph Wright's Portraits of Industrial Power', in his *Art, Science and Enlightenment Ideology: Joseph Wright and the Derby Philosophical Society* (PhD thesis, University of Virginia, 2002), Ann Arbor, 2002, pp.49–82

**GRACIANO 2002B**
Andrew Sean Graciano, '"Garlands for Shepherdesses Among Herbs for Enemas": Botanical Pleasure and Utility in Wright's Portrait of Brooke Boothby', in his *Art, Science and Enlightenment Ideology: Joseph Wright and the Derby Philosophical Society* (PhD thesis, University of Virginia, 2002), Ann Arbor, 2002, pp.83–110

**GRAEFRATH AND MAAZ 1993**
Robert Graefrath and Bernhard Maaz, *Die Friedrichswerdersche Kirche in Berlin. Baudenkmal und Museum*, Berlin, 1993

**GRAMACCINI 1989**
Gisela Gramaccini, 'Sur le projet d'élever un monument en l'honneur de Rousseau', in Paris 1989A, vol.3, pp.893–97

**GRANGER 2005**
Catherine Granger, *L'Empereur et les arts. La liste civile de Napoléon III*, Paris, 2005

**GRAVES 1905–06**
Algernon Graves, *The Royal Academy of Arts: A Complete Dictionary of Contributors and Their Work from Its Foundation in 1769 to 1904*, London, 1905–06, 8 vols

**GRAVES AND CRONIN 1899–1901**
Algernon Graves and William Vine Cronin, *A History of the Works of Sir Joshua Reynolds*, London, 1899–1901, 4 vols

**GREEN 1988**
Richard Green, '"The Hon. Lady Stanhope and the Countess of Effingham as Diana and Her Companion" by Francis Cotes', *National Art Collections Fund Review*, 1988, pp.106–09

**GRIFFITHS 1978**
Antony Griffiths, 'Prints after Reynolds and Gainsborough', in London 1978, pp.29–59

GRIMM 1880
Melchior Grimm, *Correspondance littéraire, philosophique et critique par Grimm, Diderot, Raynal, Meister, etc.*, Maurice Tourneux (ed.), Paris, 1880, 12 vols

GRÖSCHEL 1994
Sepp-Gustav Gröschel, 'Heros Winckelmann', *Antike Welt*, 25, 1994, pp.11–25

GROSS 1997
Jonathan David Gross, *Byron's Corbeau Blanc: The Life and Letters of Lady Melbourne*, Houston, 1997

GRUNCHEC 1978
Philippe Grunchec, *L'opera completa di Géricault (Tout l'oeuvre peint de Géricault)*, Milan and Paris, 1978 (1995)

GRUNDMANN 1950
Günther Grundmann, 'Die Büste der Königin Luise von Preußen in Schloß Eckersdorf in Schlesien. Ein Frühwerk Christian Daniel Rauchs', *Zeitschrift für Kunstwissenschaft*, 4, 1950, pp.81–103

GRUNDY 1999
Isobel Grundy, *Lady Mary Montagu Wortley*, Oxford, 1999

GUIFFREY 1877
Jules Guiffrey, *Les Caffiéri, sculpteurs et fondeurs ciseleurs*, Paris, 1877

GUIFFREY 1924
Jean Guiffrey, *L'Oeuvre de Pierre-Paul Prud'hon*, Paris, 1924

THE HAGUE 1970
Jeannine Batîcle, *Goya*, exh. cat., Mauritshuis, The Hague, and Orangerie des Tuileries, Paris, 1970

THE HAGUE 1997
*Peintures de l'Age d'or du Danemark*, Het Palais, The Hague, and Musée National d'Histoire et d'Art, Luxembourg, 1997

HALLETT 2001
Mark Hallett, '"The Business of Criticism": The Press and the Royal Academy Exhibition in Eighteenth-Century London', in London 2001, pp.65–75

HALLIDAY 1998
Tony Halliday, 'Academic Outsiders at the Paris Salons of the Revolution: The Case of Drawings à la manière noire', *Oxford Art Journal*, 21, 1, 1998, pp.69–86

HALLIDAY 2000
Tony Halliday, *Facing the Public. Portraiture in the Aftermath of the French Revolution*, Manchester and New York, 2000

HAMBURG 1977
Werner Hoffmann (ed.), *Runge in seiner Zeit. Die Kunst um 1800*, Hamburger Kunsthalle, Hamburg, 1977–78

HAMBURG 1995
Joist Grolle, *Kant in Hamburg. Der Philosoph und sein Bildnis*, exh. cat., Hamburger Kunsthalle, Hamburg, 1995

HAMMERICH 1870
Martin Hammerich, *Thorvaldsen og hans kunst*, Copenhagen, 1870

HAMWOOD PAPERS 1930
*The Hamwood Papers of the Ladies of Llangollen and Caroline Hamilton*, G. H. Bell (ed.), London, 1930

HANNOOSH 2005
Michele Hannoosh, 'Les premiers peintres romantiques: Delacroix et l'école anglaise', in Allard 2005, pp.113–15

HANNOVER 1901
Emil Hannover, *Maleren Constantin Hansen: en studie i dansk kunsthistorie*, Copenhagen, 1901

HARRIS 1949
Stanley A. Harris, 'Sarah Clayton's Letter and John Wood of Bath', *Transactions of the Historic Society of Lancashire and Cheshire*, 100, 1949, pp.55–72

HARTFORD 1976
*Jean-Baptise Greuze 1725–1805*, exh. cat., Wadsworth Atheneum, Hartford, The California Palace of the Legion of Honor, San Francisco, and Musée des Beaux-Arts, Dijon, 1976–77

HARTMANN 1971
Jorgen Birkedal Hartmann, *Bertel Thorvaldsen, scultore danese, romano d'adozione*, Rome, 1971

HARTMANN 1979
Jorgen Birkedal Hartmann, *Antike Motive bei Thorvaldsen. Studien zur Antikenrezeption des Klassizismus*, Tübingen, 1979

HARTMANN 1989
Jorgen Birkedal Hartmann, 'Motivi antichi nell'arte di Thorvaldsen', in Rome 1989B, pp.62–74

HASKELL 1975
Francis Haskell, 'Un monument et ses mystères. L'art français et l'opinion anglaise dans la première moitié du XIXe siècle', *Revue de l'Art*, 30, 1975, pp.61–76

HASKELL AND PENNY 1981
Francis Haskell and Nicholas Penny, *Taste and the Antique: The Lure of Classical Sculpture, 1500–1900*, New Haven and London, 1981

HASKELL AND PENNY 1988
Francis Haskell and Nicholas Penny, *Pour l'amour de l'antique. La statuaire grécoromaine et le goût européen 1500–1900*, trans. François Lissarrague, Paris, 1988

HAUTECOEUR 1913
Louis Hautecoeur, *Greuze*, Paris, 1913

HAUTECOEUR 1917
Louis Hautecoeur, *Mme Vigée-Lebrun*, Paris, n.d.[1917]

HAYES 1982
John T. Hayes, *The Landscape Paintings of Thomas Gainsborough: A Critical Text and Catalogue Raisonné*, London, 1982, 2 vols

HAYES 1991
John T. Hayes, *The Portrait in British Art*, London, 1991

HAYES 1992
John T. Hayes, *The National Gallery of Art, Washington DC: British Paintings of the Sixteenth through Nineteenth Centuries*, Washington and Cambridge, 1992

HAYES 2001
John T. Hayes (ed.), *The Letters of Thomas Gainsborough*, New Haven and London, 2001

HAYLEY 1809
William Hayley, *The Life of George Romney*, Chichester, 1809

HAYTHORNTHWAITE 2001
Philip Haythornthwaite, *Corunna 1809*, Oxford, 2001

HÉBERT DE LA ROUSSELIÈRE 1959
Hébert de la Rousselière, 'Histoire d'une statue de Voltaire', *Mémoires de l'Académie des Sciences, Belles Lettres et Arts d'Angers*, 8th series, 3, 1959, pp.60–74

HECHT 1997
Johanna Hecht, 'A Philosophe's Odyssey: How Houdon's Bust of Condorcet Made Its Way to Philadelphia', in *Franklin and Condorcet. Two Portraits from the American Philosophical Society*, Philadelphia, 1997, pp.5–21

HEDLEY 1975
Olwen Hedley, *Queen Charlotte*, London, 1975

HEIM, BÉRAUD AND HEIM 1989
Jean-François Heim, Claire Béraud and Philippe Heim, *Les Salons de peinture de la Révolution française (1789–99)*, Paris, 1989

HENRY 2002
Christophe Henry, 'Bonaparte franchissant les Alpes au Grand-Saint-Bernard. Matériaux et principes d'une icône politique', in Roche 2002, pp.347–65

HERRMANN FIORE 1997
Kristina Herrmann Fiore, 'Unpublished Letters on the Statue of Pauline Borghese', *Venere Vincitrice. La Sala di Paolina Bonaparte alla Galleria Borghese*, Rome, 1997, pp.201–14

HEWITT 1981
David Hewitt (ed.), *Scott on Himself: A Selection of the Autobiographical Writings of Sir Walter Scott*, Edinburgh, 1981

HIGHFILL ET AL. 1991
Philip H. Highfill Jr, Kalman A. Burnim and Edward A. Langhan, *A Biographical Dictionary of Actors, Actresses, Musicians, Dancers, Managers and Other Stage Personnel in London, 1660–1800*, Carbondale and Edwardsville, Illinois, 1991: 'Sheridan, Mrs', vol.13, pp.326–36

HILAIRE 2000
Michel Hilaire, 'Fabre et le paysage', *L'Estampille: L'Objet d'art*, special edition: *François-Xavier Fabre, peintre et collectionneur*, 2000, pp.52–71

HILL 1965
Draper Hill, *Mr Gillray the Caricaturist*, London, 1965

HIMMELFARB 2000
Gertrude Himmelfarb, *The Roads to Modernity: The British, French and American Englightenments*, New York, 2000

HOBSON 2002
Marian Hobson, 'La Physionomie: le portrait d'un exemple', in *Le Metamorfosi del ritratto*, Renzo Zorzi (ed.), Venice, 2002, pp.203–19

HOFFMANN 1960
Werner Hoffmann, *Das irdische Paradies*, Munich, 1960

HOFFMANN 1995
Werner Hoffmann, *Une Epoque en rupture, 1750–1830*, Paris, 1995

HOLDERBAUM 1980
James Holderbaum, 'Portrait Sculpture', in Los Angeles 1980, pp.36–51

HOLLAND 1851
John Holland, *Memorials of Sir Francis Chantrey RA, Sculptor*, Sheffield, 1851

HOLLOWAY 1973
Roger Holloway, *The Queen's Own Royal West Kent Regiment*, London, 1973

HONISCH 1965
Dieter Honisch, *Antón Raphael Mengs Und Die Bildform des Fruhklassizismus*, Recklinghausen, 1965

HONOUR 1958
Hugh Honour, 'English Patrons and Italian Sculptors in the First Half of the Eighteenth Century', *The Connoisseur*, 141, 1958, p.220

HONOUR 1959
Hugh Honour, 'Antonio Canova and the Anglo-Romans. Part I: The First Visit to Rome', *The Connoisseur*, June 1959, pp.241–321

HONOUR 1967
Hugh Honour, 'Statuettes after the Antique. Volpato's Roman Porcelain Factory', *Apollo*, 85, May 1967, pp.371–73

HONOUR 1968
Hugh Honour, 'English Patrons and Italian Sculptors in the First Half of the Eighteenth Century', *The Connoisseur*, 141, 1968, pp.220

HONOUR 1972
Hugh Honour, 'Canova and David', *Apollo*, October 1972, pp.312–17

HONOUR 1973
Hugh Honour, 'Canova's Napoleon', *Apollo*, September 1973, pp.180–85

HONOUR 1994
Hugh Honour, 'Canova's "Amorini" for John Campbell and John David La Touche', *La Scultura. Studi in onore di Andrew S. Ciechanowiecki, Antologia di Belle Arti*, new series, 48–51, 1994, pp.129–39

HONOUR 1995
Hugh Honour, 'Luciano Bonaparte e Canova', in *Luciano Bonaparte, le sue collezioni d'arte, le sue residenze a Roma, nel Lazio, in Italia (1804–1840)*, Marina Natoli (ed.), Rome, 1995, pp.249–61

HOOCK 2003
Holger Hoock, *The King's Artists: The Royal Academy of Arts and the Politics of British Culture 1760–1840*, Oxford and New York, 2003

HOOCK 2004
Holger Hoock, 'The British Military Pantheon in St Paul's Cathedral: The State, Cultural Patriotism, and the Politics of National Monuments, c.1790–1820', in *Pantheons: Transformations of a Monumental Idea*, Richard Wrigley and Matthew Craske (eds), Aldershot, 2004, pp.81–105

HOOG 1993
Simone Hoog, *Musée national du château de Versailles. Les sculptures. 1: Le musée*, Paris, 1993

HOUSTON 1986
*A Magic Mirror: The Portrait in France, 1700–1900*, exh. cat., Museum of Fine Arts, Houston, 1986

HOUSTON 1995
Emily Ballew Neff et al., *John Singleton Copley in England*, exh. cat., Museum of Fine Arts, Houston, 1995

HOWITT 1840
William Howitt, *Visits to Remarkable Places: Old Halls, Battle Fields, and Scenes Illustrative of Striking Passages in English History and Poetry*, London, 1840 (second edition)

HUBERT 1964A
Gérard Hubert, *La Sculpture dans l'Italie napoléonienne*, Paris, 1964

HUBERT 1964B
Gérard Hubert, *Les Sculpteurs italiens en France sous la Révolution, l'Empire et la Restauration 1790–1830*, Paris, 1964

HUBERT 1976
Gérard Hubert, 'Sculptures and Bronzes of the First Empire', *Apollo*, 103, 172, June 1976, pp.464–71

HUBERT 1978
Gérard Hubert, 'Bartolini et la France. Problèmes de sculpture (formation, commandes, style)', *Prato. Storia e Arte*, 51, April 1978, pp.5–32

HUBERT 1985
Gérard Hubert, 'François-Joseph Bosio, sculpteur monégasque', *Annales monégasques*, 9, 1985, pp.27–76

HUBERT AND LEDOUX-LEBARD 1999
Gérard Hubert and Guy Ledoux-Lebard, *Napoléon, portraits contemporains, bustes et statues*, Paris, 1999

HUBERT AND PILLEPICH 1995
Gérard Hubert and Alain Pillepich, 'Napoléon et Canova. Leurs entretiens en 1810', *Le Souvenir napoléonien*, 400, March–April 1995, pp.57–65

HUBERT AND POUGETOUX 1989
Gérard Hubert and Alain Pougetoux, *Châteaux de Malmaison et de Bois-Préau, musées napoléoniens de l'île d'Aix et de la maison Bonaparte à Ajaccio*, Paris, 1989

HUCHARD 1984
Viviane Huchard, *Galerie David d'Angers*, Angers, 1984 (new edition, 2001)

HUME 1748
David Hume, *Philosophical Essays Concerning Human Understanding*, London, 1748

HUME 1766
[David Hume], *Concise and Genuine Account of the Dispute between Mr Hume and Mr Rousseau: with the Letters that passed between them during their Controversy . . . Translated from the French*, London, 1766

HUME 1985
David Hume, *Essays Moral, Political and Literary*, E. F. Miller (ed.), Indianapolis, 1985

HUME 2000
David Hume, *A Treatise of Human Nature*, Oxford and New York, 2000; French edition: *Traité de la nature humaine*, Philippe Baranger and Philippe Saltel (trans.), Paris, 1995

HÜNEKE 2000
Saskia Hüneke, *Bauten und Bildwerken im Park Sanssouci*, Berlin, 2000

HUNTER 1894
*The Journal of General Sir Martin Hunter G.C.M.G., C.H., and Some Letters of His Wife, Lady Hunter . . .*, Anne Hunter and Elizabeth Bell (eds), Edinburgh, 1894

INGAMELLS 1997
John Ingamells, *Dictionary of British and Irish Travellers in Italy: 1701–1800*, New Haven and London, 1997

INGAMELLS 2004
John Ingamells, *National Portrait Gallery: Mid-Georgian Portraits 1760–1790*, London, 2004

INGERSOLL-SMOUSE 1913
Florence Ingersoll-Smouse, 'Lettres inédites de J.-J. Caffieri', *Bulletin de la Société de l'Histoire de l'Art français*, 1913, pp.202–22

IRWIN 1973
Francina Irwin, 'Early Raeburn Reconsidered', *Burlington Magazine*, 115: 841, April 1973, pp.239–44

L'ISLE-ADAM 2000
*Les Trésors des princes de Bourbon-Conti*, exh. cat., Musée d'Art et d'Histoire Louis-Senlecq, L'Isle-Adam, 2000

IXELLES 1985
Denis Coekelberghs and Pierre Loze, *1770–1830. Autour du néoclassicisme en Belgique*, exh. cat., Musée Communal des Beaux-Arts, Ixelles, 1985

JAL 1833
Auguste Jal, *Causeries du Louvre*, Paris, 1833

JANSON 1998
Horst W. Janson, 'The Revival of Antiquity in Early Renaissance Sculpture', in Sarah Blake McHam, *Looking at Italian Renaissance Sculpture*, Cambridge, 1998, pp.40–59

JEAN-RICHARD 1994
Pierrette Jean-Richard, *Inventaire des miniatures sur ivoire conservées au Cabinet des Dessins, musée du Louvre et musée d'Orsay*, Paris, 1994

JELINEK 1979
Josef E. Jelinek, 'Jean-Paul Marat; The Differential Diagnosis of His Skin Disease', *American Journal of Dermatopathology*, 1, 3, autumn 1979, pp.251–52

JENKINS 1945
Marianna Duncan Jenkins, *The State Portrait: Its Origin and Evolution*, New York, 1945

JENSEN 1977
Jens Christian Jensen, *Philipp Otto Runge. Leben und Werk*, Cologne, 1977

JENSEN AND MARCUS 1926
Johannes Jensen and Aage Marcus, *Thorvaldsens Portrætbuster*, Copenhagen, 1926

JOBERT 1998
Barthélémy Jobert, *Delacroix*, Paris, 1998

JOHANSSON 1996
Ejner Johansson, 'The Painter Wilhelm Bendz, 1804–1832', in Copenhagen 1996B, pp.9–19

JOHNS 1998
Christopher M. S. Johns, *Antonio Canova and the Politics of Patronage in Revolutionary and Napoleonic Europe*, Berkeley, Los Angeles and London, 1998

JOHNS 2004
Christopher M. S. Johns, 'Portraiture and the Making of Cultural Identity: Pompeo Batoni's *The Honourable Colonel William Gordon* (1765–66) in Italy and North Britain', *Art History*, 27, 3, June 2004

JOHNSON 1976
Edward Mead Johnson, *Francis Cotes*, Oxford, 1976

JOHNSON 1981
Lee Johnson, *The Paintings of Eugène Delacroix. A Critical Catalogue, vol.1: 1816–1831*, Oxford, 1981

JOHNSTON-LIIK 2002
Edith Mary Johnston-Liik (ed.), *History of the Irish Parliament, 1692–1800*, Belfast, 2002, 6 vols

JONES 2004
Jean Jones, 'Hutton, James (1726–1797)', in H. C. G. Matthew and Brian Harrison (eds), *Oxford Dictionary of National Biography*, Oxford, 2004, vol.29, pp.60–63

JOPPIEN 1994
Rüdiger Joppien, 'Sir Joseph Banks and the World of Art in Great Britain', in R. E. R. Banks et al. (eds), *Sir Joseph Banks: A Global Perspective*, Kew, 1994

JORDAN DE URRIES 2000
Javier Jordan de Urries y de la Colina, 'El diplomatico José Nicolas de Azara, protector de las bellas artes y las letras', *Boletin del Museo e Instituto 'Camon Aznar'*, 81, 2000, pp.61–87

JORDANOVA 2000
Ludmilla Jordanova, *Defining Features: Scientific and Medical Portraits 1600–2000*, London, 2000

JØRNAES 1997
Bjarne Jørnaes, *Bertel Thorvaldsen, la vita et l'opera del scultore*, Rome, 1997

JOUIN 1878
Henry Jouin, *David d'Angers. Sa vie, son oeuvre, ses écrits et ses contemporains*, Paris, 1878, 2 vols

JOUIN 1886
Henry Jouin, 'Prud'hon et le portrait du prince de Benevent (1807). Document communiqué par M. Edmond-Frédéric Le Blunt, membre de l'Institut', *Nouvelles Archives de l'art français*, 3rd series, 2, 1886, pp.239–40

KARLSRUHE 2005
*Zu Gast aus dem Louvre: Rigaud, Duplessis, Fragonard*, exh. cat., Staatliche Kunsthalle, Karlsruhe, 2005

KARR 1858
Alphonse Karr, *Les Guêpes*, [1840], Paris, 1858

KASSEL 1997
*Katharina die Grosse*, exh. cat., Staatliche Museen Kassel, Museum Fridericanum Kassel, 1997

KELLER 1970
Harald Keller, *Das Nachleben des antiken Bildnisses von der Karolingerzeit bis zur Gegenwart*, Fribourg, 1970

KENWORTHY-BROWNE 1972
John Kenworthy-Browne, 'A Ducal Patron of Sculptors', *Apollo*, October 1972, pp.322–31

KENWORTHY-BROWNE 1978
John Kenworthy-Browne, Review of the Bartolini Exhibition at Prato, *Burlington Magazine*, 120, 1978, pp.338–41

KENWORTHY-BROWNE 1989
John Kenworthy-Browne, 'The Temple of Liberty at Woburn Abbey', *Apollo*, July 1989, pp.27–69

KENWORTHY-BROWNE 1995
John Kenworthy-Browne, 'The Sculpture Gallery at Woburn Abbey and the Architecture of the Temple of the Graces', in Edinburgh 1995, pp.60–71

KERHOAS 2005
Marie-José Kerhoas, 'Louis-René Boquet et les dessins de costumes', in Fontainebleau 2005, pp.98–104

KIDSON 2002
Alex Kidson (ed.), *Those Delightful Regions of Imagination: Essays on George Romney*, New Haven and London, 2002

KIDSON 2004
Alex Kidson, 'Romney, George (1734–1802)', in H. C. G. Matthew and Brian Harrison (eds), *Oxford Dictionary of National Biography*, Oxford, 2004, vol.47, pp.671–77

KLEINER 1992
Diana E. E. Kleiner, *Roman Sculpture*, New Haven and London, 1992

KONSTANZ 1992
'. . . und hat als Weib unglaubliches Talent' (Goethe). *Angelika Kauffmann (1741–1807), Marie Ellenrieder (1791–1863)*, exh. cat., Städtische Museen Konstanz, 1992

KÜMMEL AND MAAZ 2002
Birgit Kümmel and Bernhard Maaz (eds), *Christian Daniel Rauch-Museum, Bad Arolsen*, Munich and Berlin, 2002

LABAREE ET AL. 1959–2003
Leonard W. Labaree et al. (eds), *The Papers of Benjamin Franklin*, New Haven and London, 1959–2003

LA CHAPELLE 1896–97
Simon de La Chapelle, 'Joseph Chinard sculpteur. Sa vie et son oeuvre', *Revue du Lyonnais*, August 1896, pp.77–98; February 1897, pp.141–57

LACOMBE DE PREZEL 1779
Honore Lacombe de Prezel, *Dictionnaire iconologique*, [first edition, 1756], Paris, 1779, 2 vols

LACOUR-GAYET 1946–47
Georges Lacour-Gayet, *Talleyrand 1754–1838*, Paris, 1946–47 (1st edition, 1931–33), 3 vols

LAFENESTRE 1888
Georges Lafenestre, *Le Livre d'Or du Salon de Peinture et de Sculpture*, Paris, 1888

LAFONT 2003
Anne Lafont, 'Les Rencontres hypothétiques du peintre et de son modèle: clefs sociales dans l'interprétation du tableau', in *Les Portraits du pouvoir*, papers published after a conference organised at the Villa Medici, Rome, by Olivier Bonfait and Brigitte Marin (24–26 April 2001), Rome and Paris, 2003, pp.115–25

LAJER-BURCHARTH 1997
Ewa Lajer-Burcharth, 'The Exceptional Woman: Elisabeth Vigée-Lebrun and the Cultural Politics of Art; The Art of Louis-Leopold Boilly: Modern Life in Napoleonic France; The Rococo Interior: Decoration and Social Spaces in Early Eighteenth-Century Paris' (book review), *Art Bulletin*, 79: 4, December 1997, pp.726–31

LAMI 1921
Stanislas Lami, *Dictionnaire des sculpteurs de l'école française au dix-neuvième siècle*, Paris, 1921

LAMOTHE-LANGON 1987
Etienne-Léon de Lamothe-Langon, *Mémoires et souvenirs d'une femme de qualité sur le Consulat et l'Empire*, Ghislain de Diesbach (ed.), Paris, 1987

LANG, STOLL AND BECKER 1997
Paul Lang, Anna Stoll and Thomas Becker, *Joseph Bonaparte et le château de Prangins. Deux acquisitions du Musée national suisse*, Zurich, 1997

LANGTON 1979
John Langton, *Geographical Change and Industrial Revolution: Coalmining in South West Lancashire, 1500–1799*, Cambridge, 1979

LANGTON 2004
John Langton, 'Clayton, Sarah (1712–1779)', in H. C. G. Matthew and Brian Harrison (eds), *Oxford Dictionary of National Biography*, Oxford, 2004, vol.11, pp.995–96

LAPAUZE 1911
Henry Lapauze, *Ingres, sa vie et son oeuvre d'après des documents inédits*, Paris, 1911

LA ROCHELLE 1989
Véronique Wiesinger, *Les Américains et la Révolution française*, exh. cat., Musée du Nouveau Monde, La Rochelle, and Musée de la Coopération franco-américaine, Blérancourt, 1989

LARSEN 1997
Peter Nørgaard Larsen, 'Lieu de travail et lieu de culte. Le peintre de l'Age d'Or dans son atelier', in The Hague 1997, pp.85–101

LATREILLE 1973
Alain Latreille, *François Gérard (1770–1837): catalogue raisonné des portraits peints par le baron François Gérard*, thesis, Ecole du Louvre, Paris, 1973

LAVAGNE 1988
Xavier Lavagne, 'Le Marquis de Méjanes et ses livres', in Claude Jolly (ed.), *Histoire des bibliothèques françaises. Les bibliothèques sous l'Ancien Régime 1530–1789*, Paris, 1988, pp.257–59

LAVEISSIÈRE 1980
Sylvain Laveissière, 'Jean-Baptiste Greuze', in *Dictionnaire des artistes et ouvriers d'art de Bourgogne*, Paris, 1980, pp. 249–50

LAVEISSIÈRE 1998
Sylvain Laveissière, *Pierre-Paul Prud'hon*, New York, 1998

LAVEISSIÈRE 2001
Sylvain Laveissière (ed.), *Pierre-Paul Prud'hon*, papers published after a conference organised by the Service Culturel du Louvre (17 November 1997), Paris, 2001

LAVEISSIÈRE 2004
Sylvain Laveissière (ed.), *Napoléon et le Louvre*, Paris, 2004

LAVIN 1987
Irving Lavin, 'Le Bernin et son image du Roi-Soleil', *'Il se rendit en Italie'. Etudes offertes à André Chastel*, Rome, 1987, pp.441–78

LAVIN 1998
Irving Lavin, 'On the Sources and Meaning of the Renaissance Portrait Bust', in Sarah Blake McHam, *Looking at Italian Renaissance Sculpture*, Cambridge, 1998, pp.60–78

LAVIRON 1834
Joseph-Gabriel-Hippolyte Laviron, *Salon de 1834*, Paris, 1834

LAVIRON AND GALBACIO 1833
Joseph-Gabriel-Hippolyte Laviron and Bruno Galbacio, *Le Salon de 1833*, Paris, 1833

LE CHATELIER 1903
Georges Le Chatelier, *Deseine le sourdmuet. Claude-André Deseine (1740–1823). Notice biographique*, Paris, 1903

LE CHATELIER 1906
Georges Le Chatelier, *L.-P. Deseine, statuaire, 1749–1822*, Paris, n.d. [1906]

LEDOUX-LEBARD 1949
R., G. and C. Ledoux-Lebard, 'Chinard et ses rapports avec les Récamier. A propos d'une oeuvre identifiée du sculpteur ayant figuré dans la chambre de Mme Récamier', *Bulletin de la Société de l'Histoire de l'Art français* [1947–48], 1949, pp.72–77

LEEDS 2000
*Return to Life: A New Look at the Portrait Bust*, exh. cat., Henry Moore Institute, Leeds, National Portrait Gallery, London, and Scottish National Portrait Gallery, Edinburgh, 2000–01

LE FEUVRE AND ALEXANDRE 1932
Arsène Le Feuvre and Arsène Alexandre, *Musée du Mans. Catalogue du musée des Arts*, Le Mans, 1932

LEIGH 1965–98
R. A. Leigh (ed.), *Correspondance complète de Jean-Jacques Rousseau*, Institut et Musée Voltaire, Geneva, and Taylorian Institute, Thorpe Mandeville and Oxford, 1965–98, 52 vols

LELOIR 1951
Maurice Leloir, *Dictionnaire du costume et de ses accessoires, des armes et des étoffes, des origines à nos jours*, Paris, 1951

LEM 1963
F.-H. Lem, 'Géricault portraitiste', *L'Arte*, June–July 1963

LE MANS 1999
Françoise Chaserant (ed.), *Les Musées ont 200 ans*, exh. cat., Musée de Tessé, Le Mans, 1999

LEMOINE 1989
Yves Lemoine, *La Diplomatie française pendant la Révolution*, Paris, 1989

LENOIR 1797, 1802
Alexandre Lenoir, *Description historique et chronologique des monumens de sculpture, réunis au musée des monumens français...*, Paris, year V (1797); year X (1802)

LENOIR 1815
Alexandre Lenoir, *Musée royal des monumens français, ou Mémorial de l'histoire de France et de ses monumens*, Paris, 1815

LENORMANT 1833
Charles Lenormant, *Les Artistes contemporains. Salon de 1831*, Paris, 1833

LENORMANT 1846–87
Charles Lenormant, *François Gérard: Peintre d'Histoire*, Paris, 1846–47, 2 vols

LEPPERT 1988
Richard Leppert, *Music and Image: Domesticity, Ideology and Socio-Cultural Formation in Eighteenth-Century England*, Cambridge, 1988

LEROY-JAY LEMAISTRE 1986
Isabelle Leroy-Jay Lemaistre, 'La Statuette romantique' and 'Romantisme', in Paris 1986, pp.254–61 and 310–26

LEROY-JAY LEMAISTRE 1989
Isabelle Leroy-Jay Lemaistre, 'Joseph Chinard', in Lyons 1989, pp.73–89

LEROY-JAY LEMAISTRE 1998
Isabelle Leroy-Jay Lemaistre, 'Chaudet, Denis-Antoine', *Saur Allgemeines Künstler-Lexicon. Die Bildenden Künstler aller Zeiten und Völker*, vol.18, Munich and Leipzig, 1998, pp.330–32

LESLIE AND TAYLOR 1865
Charles Robert Leslie and Tom Taylor, *The Life and Times of Sir Joshua Reynolds, with Notices of Some of His Contemporaries*, London, 1865, 2 vols

LESSMANN 2006
Johanna Lessmann, *Porzelan. Glanzstücke der Sammlung des Museums für Kunst und Gewerbe Hamburg*, Hamburg, 2006

LEVEY 1975
Michael Levey, 'Lawrence's Portrait of Pope Pius VII', *Burlington Magazine*, 117: 865, April 1975, pp.194–204

LEVEY 2004
Michael Levey, 'Lawrence, Sir Thomas (1769–1830)', in H. C. G. Matthew and Brian Harrison (eds), *Oxford Dictionary of National Biography*, Oxford, 2004, vol.32, pp.859–65

LEVEY 2005
Michael Levey, *Sir Thomas Lawrence*, New Haven and London, 2005

LIEBERMAN 1989
Ilene D. Lieberman, 'Sir Francis Chantrey's Monument to George Washington: Sculpture and Patronage in Post-Revolutionary America', *Art Bulletin*, 71, 2, June 1989, pp.254–68

LIGNE 1997
Prince Charles-Joseph de Ligne, *Coup d'oeil sur Beloeil* [3rd edition expanded, Vienna, 1795], Frédéric Chaleil (ed.), Paris, 1997

LILLE 1988
*Boilly, 1761–1845. Un Grand Peintre Français de la Révolution à la Restauration*, exh. cat., Musée des Beaux-Arts, Lille, 1988

LILLE 1998
*Goya. Un regard libre*, exh. cat., Palais des Beaux-Arts, Lille, and The Philadelphia Museum of Art, 1998–99

LILLI 1991
Maria Sofia Lilli, *Aspetti dell'arte neoclassica. Sculture nelle chiese romane 1780–1845*, Rome, 1991

LINDEMANN 1997
Bernd W. Lindemann, 'Zwei Schwestern und ein verschwundenes Blumenkörbchen. Zu Johann Gottfried Schadows Prinzessinnengruppe', *Zeitschrift des Deutschen Vereins für Kunstwissenschaft*, 51, 1997, pp.151–78

LIVERPOOL 1994
Xanthe Brooke, *Face to Face: Three Centuries of Artists' Self-portraiture*, exh. cat., Walker Art Gallery, Liverpool, 1994

LIVERPOOL 2002
Alex Kidson, *George Romney 1734–1802*, exh. cat., Walker Art Gallery, Liverpool, National Portrait Gallery, London, and The Huntington Library, Art Collections and Botanical Gardens, San Marino, 2002

LOCHE 1996
Renée Loche, *Catalogue raisonné des peintures de l'école française XVIe, XVIIe et XVIIIe siècles*, Geneva, 1996, pp.302–07, cat. 78

LONDON 1932
*Exhibition of French Art 1200–1900*, exh. cat., Royal Academy of Arts, London, 1932

LONDON 1948–49
*David: Exhibition of Paintings and Drawings*, The Arts Council of Great Britain, Tate Gallery, London, and City Art Gallery, Manchester, 1948–49

LONDON 1954
*European Masters of the Eighteenth Century*, exh. cat., Royal Academy of Arts, London, 1954

LONDON 1958
*Joseph Wright of Derby 1734–1797*, exh. cat., Tate Gallery, London, and Walker Art Gallery, Liverpool, 1958

LONDON 1966
*George IV and the Arts of France*, exh. cat., The Queen's Gallery, Buckingham Palace, London, 1966

LONDON 1967
*Great Britain, USSR*, exh. cat., Victoria and Albert Museum, London, in association with the Arts Council, 1967

LONDON 1972
*The Age of Neoclassicism* (with texts on sculpture by Hugh Honour, Gérard Hubert, John Kenworthy-Browne et al.), exh. cat., Royal Academy of Arts, London, and Victoria and Albert Museum, London, 1972

LONDON 1976
Mary Webster, *Johan Zoffany*, exh. cat., National Portrait Gallery, London, 1976

LONDON 1977
Michael Levey, *A Royal Subject: Portraits of Queen Charlotte*, exh. cat., National Gallery, London, 1977

LONDON 1978
Timothy Clifford, Antony Griffiths and Martin Royalton-Kisch, *Gainsborough and Reynolds in the British Museum*, exh. cat., British Museum, London, 1978

LONDON 1979
Michael Levey, *Sir Thomas Lawrence, 1769–1830*, exh. cat., National Portrait Gallery, London, 1979

LONDON 1981
Alex Potts, *Sir Francis Chantrey 1781–1841, Sculptor of the Great*, exh. cat., National Portrait Gallery, London, and Mappin Art Gallery, Sheffield, 1981

LONDON 1983
William L. Pressly, *James Barry: The Artist as Hero*, exh. cat., Tate Gallery, London, 1983

LONDON 1984
Kasper Monrad (ed.), *Danish Painting: The Golden Age*, exh. cat., National Gallery, London, 1984; French edition: *L'Age d'Or de la peinture danoise, 1800–1850*, exh. cat., Galeries Nationales du Grand Palais, Paris, 1984

LONDON 1988
*A Nest of Nightingales*, exh. cat., Dulwich Picture Gallery, London, 1988

LONDON 1990
Judy Egerton (ed.), *Joseph Wright of Derby 1734–1979*, exh. cat., Tate Gallery, London, Galeries Nationales du Grand Palais, Paris, and Metropolitan Museum of Art, New York, 1990–91

LONDON 1991A
Helen Valentine, Becky McGinnis and MaryAnne Stevens, *From Reynolds to Lawrence: The First Sixty Years of the Royal Academy of Arts and Its Collections*, exh. cat., Royal Academy of Arts, London, 1991

LONDON 1991B
John T. Hayes, *The Portrait in British Art*, exh. cat., National Portrait Gallery, London, 1991

LONDON 1998
*Art Treasures of England: The Regional Collections*, exh.cat. Royal Academy of Arts, London, 1998

LONDON 1999A
Stephen Daniels, *Joseph Wright*, exh. cat., Tate Gallery, London, 1999

LONDON 1999B
Gary Tinterow and Philip Conisbee (eds), *Portraits by Ingres: Image of an Epoch*, The National Gallery, London, The Metropolitan Museum of Art, New York, and The National Gallery of Art, Washington DC, 1999–2000

LONDON 2001
David H. Solkin (ed.), *Art on the Line: The Royal Academy Exhibitions at Somerset House 1780–1836*, exh. cat., Courtauld Institute of Art, London, 2001

LONDON 2002A
Anne Hollander, *Fabric of Vision: Dress and Drapery in Painting*, exh. cat., National Gallery, London, 2002

LONDON 2002B
Michael Rosenthal, Martin Myrone et al., *Gainsborough*, Tate Britain, London, The National Gallery of Art, Washington DC, and the Museum of Fine Arts, Boston, 2002–03

LONDON 2003A
Patrick Noon, *Constable to Delacroix: British Art and the French Romantics*, exh. cat., Tate Gallery, London, Minneapolis Institute of Arts and The Metropolitan Museum of Art, New York, 2003–04

LONDON 2003B
David Bindman, *Flaxman 1755–1826: Master of the Purest Line*, exh. cat., Sir John Soane's Museum and University College, London, 2003

LONDON 2004
Jane Roberts (ed.), *George III and Queen Charlotte: Patronage, Collecting and Court Taste*, exh. cat., The Queen's Gallery, Buckingham Palace, London, 2004

LONDON 2005
Julius Bryant (ed.), *Thomas Banks (1735–1805): Britain's First Modern Sculptor*, exh. cat., Sir John Soane's Museum, London, 2005

LONG 1933
J. C. Long, *Lord Jeffery Amherst: A Soldier of the King*, New York, 1933

LOS ANGELES 1971
*Géricault*, exh. cat., Los Angeles County Museum of Art, Detroit Institute of Arts, and Philadelphia Museum of Art, 1971–72

LOS ANGELES 1976
Anne Sutherland Harris and Linda Nochlin, *Women Artists, 1550–1950*, exh. cat., Los Angeles County Museum of Art, 1976–77

LOS ANGELES 1980
Peter Fusco and Horst W. Janson (eds), *The Romantics to Rodin. French Nineteenth-century Sculpture from North American Collections*, exh. cat., Los Angeles County Museum of Art, 1980

LOS ANGELES 1993
Kasper Monrad (ed.), *The Golden Age of Danish Painting*, exh. cat., Los Angeles County Museum of Art, and The Metropolitan Museum of Art, New York, 1993

LOS ANGELES 1999
Robyn Asleson (ed.), *A Passion for Performance: Sarah Siddons and Her Portraitists*, exh. cat., J. Paul Getty Museum, Los Angeles, 1999

LOS ANGELES 2005
Philippe Bordes (ed.), *Jacques-Louis David: Empire to Exile*, exh. cat., The J. Paul Getty Museum, Los Angeles, and the Sterling and Francine Clarke Institute, Williamstown, 2005

LUNDBERG 1957
Gunnar W. Lundberg, *Roslin*, Stockholm, 1957, 2 vols

LUNDBERG 1970
Gunnar W. Lundberg, *Le Peintre suédois de Marie-Antoinette: Adolf Ulrik Wertmüller à Bordeaux, 1788–90*, Bordeaux, 1970

LYONS 1989
*Les Muses de Messidor. Peintres et sculpteurs lyonnais de la Révolution à l'Empire*, exh. cat., Musée des Beaux-Arts, Lyons, 1989–90

LYONS 2006
Bruno Chenique (ed.), *Géricault. La Folie d'un Monde*, exh. cat., Musée des Beaux-Arts, Lyons, 2006

MAAZ 1995
Bernhard Maaz, *Christian Friedrich Tieck. Leben und Werk*, Berlin, 1995

MAAZ 1998
Bernhard Maaz, 'Edle Natürlichkeit und aufrechte Offenheit. Gottfried Schadows Standbild der Prinzessinnen Luise und Friederike von Preussen', *Belvedere. Zeitschrift für bildende Kunst*, 4, 2, 1998, pp.48–63

MAAZ 2004
Bernhard Maaz, *Vom Kult des Genies. David d'Angers' Bildnisse von Goethe bis Caspar David Friedrich*, Munich and Berlin, 2004

MAAZ 2006
Bernhard Maaz (ed.), *Nationalgalerie Berlin. Das XIX. Jahrhundert. Bestandskatalog der Skulpturen*, Leipzig, 2006

MACCARTHY 1836
J. E. C. MacCarthy, *Recollections of the Storming of the Castle of Badajos*, London, 1836

MCCLELLAN 1994
Andrew McClellan, *Inventing the Louvre: Art, Politics and the Origins of the Modern Museum in Eighteenth-Century Paris*, Cambridge, 1994

MCCREERY 2002
Cindy McCreery, *The Satirical Gaze: Prints of Women in Late Eighteenth-Century England*, Oxford, 2002

MCCULLOCK 2006
Ian Macpherson McCullock, *Sons of the Mountains: The Highland Regiments in North America during the French and Indian War 1756–67*, New York and Toronto, 2006, 2 vols

MCINTYRE 2003
Ian McIntyre, *Joshua Reynolds: The Life and Times of the First President of the Royal Academy*, London, 2003

MACKENZIE 1927
Henry Mackenzie, *The Anecdotes and Egotisms of Henry Mackenzie*, Harold William Thompson (ed.), London, 1927

MACKOWSKY 1951
Hans Mackowsky, *Die Bildwerke Gottfried Schadows*, Berlin, 1951

MCPHERSON 2000
Heather McPherson, 'Picturing Tragedy: Mrs Siddons as The Tragic Muse Revisited', *Eighteenth-Century Studies*, 33, 3, spring 2000, pp.401–30

MCWILLIAM 1991
Neil McWilliam (ed.), Vera Schuster and Richard Wrigley, *A Bibliography of Salon Criticism in Paris: From the Ancien Régime to the Restoration 1699–1827*, Cambridge, 1991

MADRID 1900
*Catálogo de las obras de Goya*, exh. cat., Ministero de Instrucción Pública, Madrid, 1900 (edition by Nigel Glendinning and Jesusa Vega, Madrid, 2002)

MADRID 1980
*Antonio Rafael Mengs 1728–1779*, exh. cat., Museo del Prado, Madrid, 1980

MADRID 1988
*Goya and the Spirit of the Enlightenment*, exh. cat., Museo Nacional del Prado, Madrid, The Metropolitan Museum of Art, New York, and the Museum of Fine Arts, Boston, 1988–89

MADRID 1992
Nigel Glendinning (ed.), *Goya. La Década de los Caprichos. Retratos 1792–1804*, exh. cat., Real Academia de Bellas Artes de San Fernando, Madrid

MADRID 1996
Juan Luna and Margarita Moreno de la Heras (eds), *Goya 250 aniversario*, exh. cat., Museo Nacional del Prado, Madrid, 1996

**MADRID 2001**
Anna Reuter and Janis A. Tomlinson, *Goya. Imagen de la mujer* (*Goya: Images of Women*), exh. cat., Museo Nacional del Prado, Madrid, and the National Gallery of Art, Washington DC, 2001–02

**MAILLÉ 1984**
Duchess of Maillé, *Souvenirs des deux Restaurations. Journal inédit*, Xavier de La Fournière (ed.), Paris, 1984

**MALTESE 1965**
Corrado Maltese, *Delacroix*, place of publication unknown, 1965

**MALVANO 1989–90**
Laura Malvano, 'Note sulla fortuna critica del "Marat" di David', *Prospettiva*, 57–60, 1989–90, pp.369–76

**MANNERS AND WILLIAMSON 1924**
Lady Victoria Manners and C. G. Williamson, *Angelica Kauffmann RA: Her Life and Her Works*, London, 1924

**MANNINGS AND POSTLE 2000**
David Mannings and Martin Postle, *Sir Joshua Reynolds: A Complete Catalogue of His Paintings*, New Haven and London, 2000, 2 vols

**MANTE 1772**
Thomas Mante, *The History of the Late War in North-America, and the Islands of the West-Indies, including the Campaigns of MDCCLXIII and MDCCLXIV against His Majesty's Indian Enemies*, London, 1772

**MARCEL 1901**
Henry Marcel, 'Essai sur l'iconographie de Mirabeau', *Revue de l'art ancien et moderne*, 49, April 1901, pp.269–80

**MARCEL 1909**
Henry Marcel, 'Sur quelques ouvrages peu connus de Lucas de Montigny', *Revue de l'art ancien et moderne*, 25, January–June 1909, pp.105–11

**MARIE-ANTOINETTE 2005**
*Marie-Antoinette: Correspondance (1770–1793)*, Evelyne Lever (ed.), Paris, 2005

**MARIN 1981**
Louis Marin, *Le Portrait du roi*, Paris, 1981

**MARMOTTAN 1890**
Paul Marmottan, 'Deux Portraits du prince de Talleyrand par Prud'hon (1815)', *Nouvelles Archives de l'art français*, 3rd series, 6, 1890, pp.231–32

**MARTIGUES 2004**
Gérard Fabre et al., *Joseph Boze, 1745–1826: Portraitiste de l'ancien régime à la restauration*, exh. cat., Musée Ziem, Martigues, 2004

**MARTIN 1993**
Thomas Martin, 'Michelangelo's Brutus and the Classicising Portrait Bust in Sixteenth-century Italy', *Artibus et Historiae*, 27, 1993, pp.67–83

**MARTIN-FUGIER 1990**
Anne Martin-Fugier, *La Vie élégante ou la formation du Tout-Paris 1815–1848*, Paris, 1990

**MARTIN AND MASSON 1908**
J. Martin and C. Masson, *Catalogue raisonné de l'oeuvre peint et dessiné de J.-B. Greuze*, Paris, 1908

**MARTINELLI AND PIETRANGELI 1955**
Valentino Martinelli and Carlo Pietrangeli, *La Protomoteca Capitolina*, Rome, 1955

**MASSA 2000**
Sergei Androssov, Massimo Bertozzi, Lina Tarasova et al., *Sotto il cielo di Roma. Scultori europei dal barocco al verismo nelle collezioni dell'Ermitage*, exh.cat., Palazzo Ducale, Massa, 2000

**MATHERON 1857**
Laurent Matheron, *Goya*, Bordeaux, 1857; Spanish edition: Madrid, 1890

**MAY 2005**
Gita May, *Elisabeth Vigée Le Brun: The Odyssey of an Artist in an Age of Revolution*, New Haven and London, 2005

**MAZZOCCA 1994**
Fernando Mazzocca, *Francesco Hayez. Catalogo ragionato*, Milan, 1994

**MELLINI 1999**
Gian Lorenzo Mellini, *Canova. Saggi di filologia e di ermeneutica*, Milan, 1999

**MELLOR 1995**
A. K. Mellor, 'British Romanticism, Gender, and Three Women Artists', in Ann Bermingham and John Brewer (eds), *The Consumption of Culture 1600–1800: Image, Object, Text*, London and New York, 1995, pp.121–42

**MEMES 1825**
John Smythe Memes, *Memoirs of Antonio Canova, with a Critical Analysis of His Works*, Edinburgh, 1825

**MENA MARQUÉS 2000**
Manuela B. Mena Marqués, *Goya y la Pintura Española del Siglo XVIII*, Madrid, 2000

**MENA MARQUÉS 2006**
Manuela B. Mena Marqués, 'Goya en la vida de la duquesa de Alba', in Manuela B. Mena Marqués and Gudrun Mühle-Maurer, *Goya y la duquesa de Alba*, Madrid, 2006, pp. 75–107

**MERCIER 1972**
Huguette Mercier, *Jean-Robert-Nicolas Lucas de Montigny (1747–1810) sculpteur*, records of research undertaken at the Ecole du Louvre (unedited typescript), 1972

**MERCIER 1994**
Louis-Sébastien Mercier, *Tableau de Paris* [1782–1788], Jean-Claude Bonnet (ed.), Paris, 1994, 2 vols

**MERZ 1995**
Jorg Martin Merz, 'Reynolds's Borrowings', *Burlington Magazine*, 137: 1109, August 1995, pp.516–17

**METROPOLITAN BULLETIN 1994**
'Recent Acquisitions: A Selection 1993–94', *The Metropolitan Museum of Art Bulletin*, new series, 52, 2, autumn 1994, p.40

**MEYER 1995**
Arline Meyer, 'Re-Dressing Classical Statuary: The Eighteenth-Century "Hand-in-Waistcoat" Portrait', *Art Bulletin*, 77: 1, March 1995, pp.45–63

**MFA 1999**
*MFA: A Guide to the Collection of the Museum of Fine Arts, Boston*, with notes by Gilian Shallcross Wohlauer, Boston, 1999

**MICHEL 1996**
Régis Michel (ed.), *Géricault*, Paris, 1996

**MILAN 1989**
Andrea Bacchi, *Il conoscitore d'arte. Sculture dal XV al XIX secolo della collezione di Federico Zeri*, exh. cat., Museo Poldi-Pezzoli, Milan, and Accademia Carrara, Bergamo, 1989

**MILAN 1999**
'...respettabilissimo Goethe...caro Hayez...adorato Thorvaldsen...': Gusto e cultura europea nelle raccolte di Enrico Mylius*, Rosanna Pavoni (ed.), exh. cat., Museo Bagatti-Valsecchi, Milan, 1999, especially Christiane Liermann, 'Alle radici dell'agire', pp.21–27

**MILAN 2002**
*Il Neoclassicismo in Italia: Da Tiepolo a Canova*, exh.cat., Palazzo Reale, Milan, 2002

**MILBURNE 1809**
Henry Milburne, *A Narrative of the Circumstances Attending the Retreat of the British Army under the Command of Lieut. Gen. Sir John Moore*, London, 1809

**MILLAR 1969**
Oliver Millar, *The Later Georgian Pictures in the Collection of Her Majesty The Queen*, London, 1969, 2 vols

**MIRSCH 1998**
Beate Christine Mirsch, *Anmut und Schönheit. Schadows Prinzessinnengruppe und ihre Stellung in der Skulptur des Klassizismus*, Berlin, 1998

**MITCHELL 1990**
Paul Mitchell, 'Wright's Picture Frames', in London 1990, pp.273–88

**MITCHELL 2004**
L. G. Mitchell, 'Sir Brooke Boothby, Rousseau's Roving Baronet Friend', *Notes and Queries*, 51: 3, September 2004, pp.327–28

**MOLLIER, REID AND YON 2005**
Jean-Yves Mollier, Martine Reid and Jean-Claude Yon (eds), *Repenser la Restauration*, place of publication unknown, 2005

**MONNIER 1972**
Geneviève Monnier, *Musée du Louvre-Cabinet des Dessins. Pastels XVIIe et XVIIIe siècles*, Paris, 1972

**MONRAD 1989**
Kasper Monrad, *Hverdagsbilleder: dansk guldalder, kunstnerne og deres vilkår*, Copenhagen, 1989

**MONRAD 1994**
Kasper Monrad, *Dansk Guldalder, Hovedvaerker på Statens Museum for Kunst*, Copenhagen, 1994

**MONTAGU 1962**
Jennifer Montagu, 'Inventaire des tableaux, sculptures, estampes, etc. de l'Institut et musée Voltaire', *Studies on Voltaire and the Eighteenth Century*, 20, 1962, pp.223–47

**MONTARGIS 2005**
*Au delà du maître*, exh. cat., Musée Girodet, Montargis, 2005–06

**MONTAUBAN 1967**
*Ingres et son temps. Exposition organisée pour le centenaire de la mort d'Ingres*, exh. cat., Musée Ingres, Montauban, 1967

**MONTAUBAN 1980**
*Ingres et sa postérité jusqu'à Matisse et Picasso*, exh. cat., Musée Ingres, Montauban, 1980

**MONTHLY REGISTER 1792–93**
*The Monthly Register of Literature*, London, 1792–93, 2 vols

**MONTPELLIER 1979**
*Le Portrait à travers les collections du musée Fabre*, exh. cat., Musée Fabre, Montpellier, 1979

**MONTREAL 2006**
Nathalie Bondil (ed.), *Catherine the Great: Art for Empire. Masterpieces from the State Hermitage Museum, Russia*, exh. cat., Montreal Museum of Fine Arts, 2006

**MONVAL 1897**
Georges Monval, *Les Collections de la Comédie-Française. Catalogue historique et raisonné*, Paris, 1897

**MOORE AND CRAWLEY 1992**
Andrew Moore and Charlotte Crawley, *Family and Friends: A Regional Survey of British Portraiture*, London, 1992

**MORALES Y MARÍN 1994**
José Luis Morales y Marín, *Goya: catálogo de la pintura*, Saragossa, 1994

**MORALES Y MARÍN 1997**
José Luis Morales y Marín, *Goya: A Catalogue of His Paintings*, Saragossa, 1997

**MOREAU-NÉLATON 1909**
Etienne Moreau-Nélaton, 'Chinard de Lyon et son ami Gauldrée-Boilleau', *Bulletin de la Société de l'Historie de l'Art français*, 1909, pp.224–31

**MORELLET 1988**
*Mémoires de l'abbé Morellet de l'Académie française sur le dix-huitième siècle et sur la Révolution*, introduction and notes by Jean-Pierre Guicciardi, Paris, 1988

**MORRIS 2002**
*Journal de Gouverneur Morris (1789–1792), ministre plénipotentiaire des Etats-Unis en France*, Antoine de Baecque (ed.), Paris, 2002

**MORTENSEN 2000**
Klaus Peter Mortensen, *Spejlinger: litteratur og reflexion*, Hellerup, spring 2000, pp.114–52

**MORTENSEN 2001**
Klaus Peter Mortensen, *Wilhelm Bendz*, Copenhagen, 2001

**MOSCOW 1994**
*Fedot Choubine 1740–1805*, exh. cat., Tretyakov Gallery, Moscow, and State Russian Museum, St Petersburg, 1994

OSSNER 1980
rnest C. Mossner, *The Life of David Hume*,
xford, 1980 (2nd edition)

ÜHLE-MAURER 2005
udrun Mühle-Maurer, 'María Tomasa
alafox y Portocarrero, Marquesa de
illafranca', in Berlin 2005, p.220

UNICH 1964
anzösische Malerei des 19. Jahrhunderts von David
s Cézanne, exh. cat., Haus der Kunst,
unich, 1964–65

USÉE CARNAVALET 1903
uide explicatif du musée Carnavalet, Charles
llier, Prosper Dorbec and Georges Cain
ds), Paris, 1903

USÉE DE DIJON 1960
usée des Beaux-Arts de Dijon. Catalogue des
ulptures, Pierre Quarré (ed.), Dijon, 1960

USÉE DE NANTES 1854
atalogue des tableaux et statues du musée de Nantes,
antes, 1854

USÉE DE NANTES 1859
atalogue des tableaux et statues du musée de Nantes,
antes, 1859

USÉE DE NANTES 1876
atalogue des objets composant le musée municipal des
eaux-Arts, Nantes, 1876

USÉE DU LOUVRE 1998
usée du Louvre, département des Sculptures du Moyen
ge, de la Renaissance et des Temps modernes. Sculpture
ançaise II: Renaissance et Temps modernes, Jean-
ené Gaborit (ed.), Paris, 1998, 2 vols

USÉE THORVALDSEN 1966
usée Thorvaldsen, Copenhagen, 1966

USIARI, DI RADDO AND CIOCCOLO 2003
ntonio Musiari, Elena Di Raddo and
ottardo Cioccolo, *Pompeo Marchesi. Ricerche
lla personalità e sull'opera*, Gavirate, 2003

YERS 1964
ernard Myers, *Goya*, London, 1964

YRONE 2005
artin Myrone, *Bodybuilding: Reforming
asculinities in British Art, 1750–1810*,
ew Haven and London, 2005

ACF 1966
ational Art Collections Fund: Sixty-second Annual
eport, 1965, London, 1966

ACF 1987
ational Art Collections Fund Review, London, 1987

AMIER AND BROOKE 1964
ir Lewis Namier and John Brooke, *The House
f Commons 1754–1790*, London, 1964

ANCY 2006
an-Baptiste Isabey, exh. cat., Musée des Beaux-
rts, Nancy, and Musée National des
hâteaux de Malmaison et Bois-Préau, 2006

NANTES 1995
*Les Années romantiques. La peinture française de 1815
à 1850*, exh. cat., Musée des Beaux-Arts,
Nantes, Galeries Nationales du Grand Palais,
Paris, and Palazzo Gotico, Piacenza, 1995–96

NAPIER 1857
William S. Napier (ed.), *The Life and Opinions
of General Sir Charles James Napier*, London,
1857, 4 vols

NATIONALMUSEUM STOCKHOLM 1999
*Nationalmuseum Stockholm. Illustrated Catalogue of
Swedish and European Sculpture*, introduction by
Görel Cavalli-Björkman, Stockholm, 1999

NEFF 1995
Emily Ballew Neff, *John Singleton Copley
in England*, London, 1995

NEW ORLEANS 2003
*Jefferson's America and Napoleon's France*, exh. cat.,
New Orleans Museum of Art, 2003

NEW YORK 1935
*French Painting and Sculpture of the XVIIIth Century*,
exh. cat., The Metropolitan Museum of Art,
New York, 1935–36

NEW YORK 1988
F. A. Trapp, *The Grand Tradition: British Art from
Amherst College*, exh. cat., The American
Federation of Arts, New York, 1988

NEW YORK 1992
Jill Newhouse, *Baron François Gérard
(1770–1837): Exhibition and Sale of Paintings and
Drawings, April 1992*, exh. cat., Galerie Arnoldi-
Livie, New York, 1992

NEW YORK 1995
Colta Feller Ives and Susan Alyson Stein (eds),
*Goya in the Metropolitan Museum of Art*, exh. cat.,
The Metropolitan Museum of Art, New
York, 1995

NEW YORK 1997
Ann Dumas, Colta Feller Ives, Susan Alyson
Stein and Gary Tinterow, *The Private Collection of
Edgar Degas*, exh. cat., The Metropolitan
Museum of Art, New York, 1997–98

NEW YORK 2004
Carrie Rebora Barratt and Ellen G. Miles,
*Gilbert Stuart*, exh. cat., Metropolitan Museum
of Art, New York, 2004

NEW YORK 2005
*Russia! Nine Hundred Years of Masterpieces
and Master Collections*, exh. cat., Solomon
R. Guggenheim Museum, New York, 2005

NEW YORK 2006
*Goya's Last Works*, exh. cat., The Frick
Collection, New York, 2006

NICOLLE 1913
Marcel Nicolle, *Ville de Nantes. Musée municipal des
Beaux-Arts. Catalogue*, Nantes, 1913

NICOLLE 1931
Marcel Nicolle, 'Chefs-d'Oeuvres des musées
de province. Ecole française, XVIIe et XVIIIe
siècles', in *Gazette des Beaux-Arts*, 6 August 1931,
p.127

NICOLSON 1968
Benedict Nicolson, *Wright of Derby: Painter
of Light*, London, 1968, 2 vols

NICOLSON 1988
Benedict Nicolson, 'Wright of Derby:
Addenda and Corrigenda', *Burlington Magazine*,
130: 1027, October 1988, pp.745–58

NOCHLIN 1976
Linda Nochlin, 'A.-C.-H. Haudebourg-
Lescot', in Los Angeles 1976, pp.218–19

NOCHLIN 1996
Linda Nochlin, 'Géricault and the Absence
of Women', in Michel 1996, pp.403–21

NOLHAC 1908
Pierre de Nolhac, *Mme Vigée-Lebrun peintre de la
reine Marie-Antoinette*, Paris, 1908

NONAGENARIAN 1863
[John Stonehouse], *Recollections of Old Liverpool
by a Nonagenarian*, Liverpool, 1863

NØRREGÅRD-NIELSEN 1996
Hans Edvard Nørregård-Nielsen, *Christen
Købke, Omkring Kastellet*, Copenhagen, 1996

NØRREGÅRD-NIELSEN AND MONRAD 1996
Hans Edvard Nørregård-Nielsen and Kasper
Monrad (eds), *Christen Købke, 1810–1848*,
trans. Glyn W. Jones, Copenhagen, 1996

NORTHCOTE 1813
James Northcote, *Memoirs of Sir Joshua Reynolds*,
London, 1813

NORTHCOTE 1815
James Northcote, *Supplement to the Memoirs
of the Life, Writings, Discourses, and Professional Works
of Sir Joshua Reynolds*, London, 1815

NORWICH 1996
Andrew W. Moore, *Norfolk and the Grand Tour:
Eighteenth-century Travellers Abroad and Their
Souvenirs*, exh. cat., Norwich Castle Museum,
and The Iveagh Bequest, Kenwood, 1996–97

NOTTINGHAM 1991
Ilaria Bignamini and Martin Postle, *The Artist's
Model: Its Role in British Art from Lely to Etty*, exh.
cat., Nottingham University Art Gallery, 1991

NÚÑEZ ARENAS 1950
M. Núñez Arenas, 'Manojo de noticias:
La suerte de Goya en Francia', *Bulletin
Hispanique*, 52, 3, 1950, p.239–73

NUREMBERG 1991
*Künstlerleben in Rom: Bertel Thorvaldsen
(1770–1844). Der dänische Bildhauer und seine
deutschen Freunde*, exh. cat., Germanisches
Nationalmuseum, Nuremberg, and Schleswig-
Holsteinisches Landesmuseum Schloß
Gottorf, Schleswig, 1991–92

OCKMANN 1995
Carole Ockmann, *Ingres's Eroticised Body: Retracing
the Serpentine Line*, New Haven and London,
1995

O'DWYER 1985
Margaret M. O'Dwyer, *The Papacy in the Age of
Napoleon and the Restoration: Pius VII, 1800–1823*,
Lanham, Maryland, 1985

OLSON 1986
Roberta J. M. Olson, 'Representations of
Pope Pius VII: The First Risorgimento Hero',
*The Art Bulletin*, 68, 1, March 1986, pp.77–93

O'NEILL 1977
Mary O'Neill, *Musée des Beaux-Arts d'Orléans.
Peintres de l'école française des XVIIe et XVIIIe siècles:
catalogue critique*, Nantes, 1977, 2 vols

ORLÉANS 1953
*Dessins français des XVIe et XVIIe siècles*, exh. cat.,
Musée des Beaux-Arts, Orléans, 1953

OSMOND 1947
Marion W. Osmond, *Jean-Baptiste Isabey:
The Fortunate Painter*, London, 1947

O'TOOLE 1997
Fintan O'Toole, *A Traitor's Kiss: The Life of
Richard Brinsley Sheridan*, London, 1997

OTTEN 1976
Frank Michael Otten, *Ludwig Michael
Schwanthaler*, Munich, 1976

OXFORD 1997
K. A. T. Eustace (ed.), *Canova's Ideal Heads*,
exh. cat., Ashmolean Museum, Oxford, 1997

OZOUF 1984
Mona Ozouf, 'Le Panthéon, l'école normale
des morts', in *Les Lieux de mémoire. I: La
République*, Pierre Nora (ed.), Paris, 1984,
pp.139–66

PADUA 2001
Steffi Roettgen, *Mengs. La scoperta del Neoclassico*,
exh. cat., Palazzo Zabarella, Padua, and
Schloss, Dresden, 2001

PARDO CANALÍS 1958
Enrique Pardo Canalís, *Escultura Neoclásica
Española*, Madrid, 1958

PARDO CANALÍS 1960
Enrique Pardo Canalís, 'Dos retratos inéditos
de Carlos IV y Maria Luisa de Parma',
*Goya*, 35, 1960, pp.335–36

PARDO CANALÍS 1979
Enrique Pardo Canalís, 'Una visita a la Galeria
del Principe de La Paz', *Goya*, 148–50,
January–June 1979, pp.300–11

PARIS 1878
Frédéric Villot and Both de Tauzia, *Notice des
tableaux exposés dans les galeries du Musée impérial du
Louvre*, exh. cat., Musée du Louvre, Paris, 1878

PARIS 1883
*Portraits du siècle (1783–1883)*, exh. cat., Ecole
des Beaux-Arts, Paris, 1883

PARIS 1895
*Exposition Historique et Militaire de La Révolution et
l'Empire*, exh. cat., Galerie des Champs-Elysées,
Paris, 1895

PARIS 1900
*Centennale de l'art français*, exh. cat., Grand Palais,
Paris, 1900

PARIS 1909
Paul Vitry, *Exposition d'oeuvres du sculpteur Chinard
de Lyon (1756–1813)*, exh. cat., Musée des Arts
décoratifs, Paris, 1909–10

PARIS 1913
Exposition David et ses élèves, exh. cat., Palais des Beaux-Arts de la Ville de Paris, 1913

PARIS 1923
L'Art et la vie romantique, exh. cat., Galerie Charpentier, Paris, 1923

PARIS 1924
Géricault, exh. cat., Galerie Charpentier, Paris, 1924

PARIS 1931
Les Chefs d'Oeuvre des Musées de Provence, exh. cat., Musée de l'Orangerie, Paris, 1931

PARIS 1936
Gros, ses amis et ses élèves, exh. cat., Petit Palais, Paris, 1936

PARIS 1945
Portraits Français, exh. cat., Galerie Charpentier, Paris, 1945

PARIS 1954
Gros, Géricault, Delacroix, exh. cat., Galerie Bernheim-Jeune, Paris, 1954

PARIS 1955
De David à Toulouse-Lautrec. Chefs-d'oeuvre des collections américaines, exh. cat., Musée de l'Orangerie, Paris, 1955

PARIS 1963
Maurice Sérullaz, Exposition Eugène Delacroix organisée au musée du Louvre à l'occasion du centenaire de la mort de l'artiste, exh. cat., Musée du Louvre, Paris, 1963

PARIS 1967
Ingres, exh. cat., Petit Palais, Paris, 1967

PARIS 1969
Gérard Hubert, Napoléon, exh. cat., Galeries Nationales du Grand Palais, Paris, 1969

PARIS 1974A
Pierre Rosenberg, Robert Rosenblum and Antoine Schnapper (eds), French Painting, 1774–1830: The Age of Revolution, exh. cat., Galeries Nationales du Grand Palais, Paris, Detroit Institute of Art, and The Metropolitan Museum of Art, New York, 1974–75

PARIS 1974B
Louis-Philippe, l'homme et le roi 1773–1850, exh. cat., Archives nationales, Hôtel de Rohan, Paris, 1974

PARIS 1974C
Portraits français XIX et XX siècles, exh. cat., Galerie Schmit, Paris, 1974

PARIS 1979A
Monique Mosser and Daniel Rabreau, Charles De Wailly, peintre, architecte dans l'Europe des Lumières, exh. cat., Hôtel de Sully, Paris, 1979

PARIS 1979B
L'Enfant dans les collections de la ville de Paris, exh. cat., Hôtel de Ville, Paris, 1979

PARIS 1981
John T. Hayes, Gainsborough 1727–1788, exh. cat., Galeries Nationales du Grand Palais, Paris, 1981

PARIS 1983
Jacques Foucart, Nouvelles Acquisitions du département des Peintures (1980–1982), exh. cat., Musée du Louvre, Paris, 1983

PARIS 1984A
Kasper Monrad (ed.), L'Age d'Or de la peinture danoise, 1800–1850, exh. cat., Association Française d'Action Artistique, Galeries Nationales du Grand Palais, Paris, 1984

PARIS 1984B
Diderot et l'art, de Boucher à David: Les Salons 1759–1781, exh.cat., Hôtel de la Monnaie, Paris, 1984–85

PARIS 1985
Nicholas Penny (ed.), Reynolds, exh. cat., Galeries Nationales du Grand Palais, Paris, and Royal Academy of Arts, London, 1985–86

PARIS 1986
Anne Pingeot, La Sculpture française au XIXe siècle, exh. cat., Galeries Nationales du Grand Palais, Paris, 1986

PARIS 1989A
Jean-René Gaborit, La Révolution française et l'Europe, exh. cat., Galeries Nationales du Grand Palais, Paris, 1989–90

PARIS 1989B
Les Donateurs du Louvre, exh. cat., Musée du Louvre, Paris, 1989

PARIS 1989C
Modes et Révolutions 1780–1804, exh. cat., Musée de la Mode et du Costume, Paris, 1989

PARIS 1989D
Daniel Rabreau, Mark K. Deming et al., Le Panthéon, Symbole des révolutions, Hôtel de Sully, Paris, and Centre canadien d'Architecture, Montreal, 1989

PARIS 1989E
Antoine Schnapper and Arlette Sérullaz, Jacques-Louis David 1748–1825, exh. cat., with a chronology by Elisabeth Agius-d'Yvoire, Musée du Louvre, Paris, and Musée National du Château, Versailles, 1989–90

PARIS 1991
Sylvain Laveissière, Régis Michel and Bruno Chenique (eds), Géricault, Galeries Nationales du Grand Palais, Paris, 1991–92

PARIS 1993
Jean Clair, L'Ame au corps, exh. cat., Galeries Nationales du Grand Palais, Paris, 1993

PARIS 1994
Olivier Meslay, Arlette Sérullaz and Barthélémy Jobert, D'outre-Manche. L'art britannique dans les collections publiques françaises, exh.cat., Musée du Louvre, Paris, 1994

PARIS 1997A
James David Draper and Guilhem Scherf, Pajou, Sculpteur du roi 1730–1809, exh. cat., Musée du Louvre, Paris, and The Metropolitan Museum of Art, New York, 1997

PARIS 1997B
Sylvain Laveissière , Prud'hon ou le rêve du bonheur, exh. cat., Galeries Nationales du Grand Palais, Paris, and The Metropolitan Museum of Art, New York, 1997

PARIS 1997C
Des Mécènes par milliers: un siècle de dons par les Amis du Louvre, exh. cat., Musée du Louvre, Paris, 1997

PARIS 1999
Pierre Rosenberg and Marie-Anne Dupuy (eds), Dominique-Vivant Denon, L'oeil de Napoléon, exh. cat., Musée du Louvre, Paris, 1999–2000

PARIS 2000
Bijoux et parures romantiques, exh. cat., Musée de la Vie Romantique, Paris, 2000

PARIS 2002A
Emmanuelle Héran, Le Dernier Portrait, exh. cat., Musée d'Orsay, Paris, 2002

PARIS 2002B
Frédéric Dassas, Dominique de Font-Réaulx and Barthélémy Jobert (eds), L'Invention du sentiment aux sources du romantisme, exh. cat., Musée de la Musique, Paris, 2002

PARIS 2003A
James David Draper and Guilhem Scherf, L'Esprit créateur de Pigalle à Canova. Terres cuites européennes 1740–1840, Musée du Louvre, Paris, The Metropolitan Museum of Art, New York, and Nationalmuseum, Stockholm, 2003–04

PARIS 2003B
Geneviève Lacambre and Gary Tinterow (eds), Manet–Velázquez. La manière espagnole au XIXe siècle, Galeries Nationales du Grand Palais, Paris, and The Metropolitan Museum of Art, New York, 2003

PARIS 2004
André Lemaire and Albéric Froissart, Choix de sculptures XVIIIe–XXe siècle, exh. cat., Galerie André Lemaire, Paris, 2004

PARIS 2005A
Au temps des merveilleuses. La société parisienne sous le Directoire et le Consulat, exh. cat., Musée Carnavalet, Paris, 2005

PARIS 2005B
Edouard Papet, Daumier. Les Célébrités du Juste milieu (1832–1835). Etude et restauration, exh. cat., Musée d'Orsay, Paris, 2005

PARIS 2005C
Sylvain Bellenger, Girodet 1767–1824, Musée du Louvre, Paris, The Art Institute of Chicago, The Metropolitan Museum of Art, New York, and Musée des Beaux-Arts, Montreal, 2005–07

PARIS 2005D
Sylvain Laveissière, Le Sacre de Napoléon par David, exh. cat., Musée du Louvre, Paris, 2005

PARIS 2005E
Christiane Dotal and Nicole Garnier-Pelle (eds), Gloires de marbre. Trois siècles de portraits sculptés à l'Institut de France, exh. cat., Paris, 2005

PARIS 2006
Vincent Pomarède, Stéphane Guégan, Louis-Antoine Prat and Eric Bertin, Ingres 1780–186[?] exh. cat., Musée du Louvre, Paris, 2006

PARISSIEN 2001
Steven Parissien, George IV: The Grand Entertainment, London, 2001

PARKER AND WHEELER 1938
Barbara Neville Parker and Anne Bolling Wheeler, John Singleton Copley, Cambridge, Mass., 1938

PASQUALI 2004
Susanna Pasquali, 'From the Pantheon of Artists to the Pantheon of Illustrious Men: Raphael's Tomb and Its Legacy', in Pantheons: Transformations of a Monumental Idea, Richard Wrigley and Matthew Craske (eds), Aldershot, 2004, pp.35–56

PASSEZ 1989
Anne-Marie Passez, Antoine Vestier (1740–1824), Paris, 1989

PAULSON 1989
Ronald Paulson, Breaking and Remaking, New Brunswick, 1989

PAVANELLO 1976
Giuseppe Pavanello, L'opera completa del Canova, Milan, 1976

PEACH 2000
Annette Peach, 'Portraits of Byron', in Journal of the Walpole Society, 92, 2000

PÉLISSIER 1902
Léon-G. Pélissier, Le Portefeuille de la comtesse d'Albany (1806–1824). Lettres mises en ordre et publiées [...], Paris, 1902

PELLICER 2000
Laure Pellicer, 'Sublime Miroir qui dit la vérité...', L'Estampille: L'Objet d'art, special edition: François-Xavier Fabre, peintre et collectionneur, 2000, pp.24–39

PENNY 1975
Nicholas Penny, 'The Sculpture of Sir Richard Westmacott', Apollo, August 1975, pp.120–27

PENNY 1977
Nicholas Penny, Church Monuments in Romantic England, New Haven and London, 1977

PÉREZ-JOFRE 2001
Teresa Pérez-Jofre, Highlights of Art: Thyssen-Bornemisza Museum, Madrid, Cologne and London, 2001

PÉREZ SÁNCHEZ 1988
A. E. Pérez Sanchez, Colección de Pintura del Banco de España, Madrid, 1988

PERRY 1994
Gillian Perry, 'Women in Disguise: Likeness, the Grand Style and the Conventions of "Feminine" Portraiture in the Work of Sir Joshua Reynolds', in Gillian Perry and Michael Rossington (eds), Femininity and Masculinity in Eighteenth-Century Art and Culture, Manchester, 1994, pp.18–40

ERRY 2001
Gillian Perry, 'The Spectacle of the Muse: Exhibiting the Actress at the Royal Academy', in London 2001

PHILADELPHIA 1987
Joseph J. Rishel, *The Henry P. McIlhenny Collection: An Illustrated History*, exh. cat., Philadelphia Museum of Art, 1987

PHILADELPHIA 2000
Edgar Peters Bowron and Joseph J. Rishel (eds), *Art in Rome in the Eighteenth Century*, exh. cat., Philadelphia Museum of Art and Museum of Fine Arts, Houston, 2000

PHILLIPSON 1997
Nicholas Phillipson, 'Manners, Morals and Characters: Henry Raeburn and the Scottish Enlightenment', in Edinburgh 1997, pp.29–38

PICQUENARD 1996
Thérèse Picquenard, 'Louis-Simon Boizot. Marie-Antoinette d'Autriche, reine de France', in *Musée du Louvre. Nouvelles acquisitions du département des Sculptures 1992–95*, Paris, 1996, pp.92–100, repr.

PIETRANGELI 1971
Carlo Pietrangeli, *Il Museo di Roma: documenti iconografia*, Bologna, 1971

PILKINGTON 1789
James Pilkington, *A View of the Present State of Derbyshire*, Derby, 1789, 2 vols

PINELLI 2001
Antonio Pinelli, 'Prud'hon et Canova', in Laveissière 2001

PIOTROVSKI 2000
Mikhail Piotrovski (ed.), *Treasures of Catherine the Great*, London and New York, 2000

PITT-RIVERS 2001
Françoise Pitt-Rivers, *Madame Vigée Le Brun*, Paris, 2001

PLANCHE 1831
Gustave Planche, *Salon de 1831*, Paris, 1831

PLINY 1997
Pliny the Elder, *Histoire naturelle. Livre XXXV. La Peinture*, translation by Jean-Michel Croisille, Paris, 1997

PLON 1874
Eugène Plon, *Thorvaldsen. Sa vie et son oeuvre*, Paris, 1874; English edition, 1874

PLUMB AND WHELDON 1977
J. H. Plumb and Huw Wheldon, *Royal Heritage: The Treasures of the British Crown*, New York and London, 1977

PLUTARCH 1967
Plutarch, *Vies parallèles des hommes illustres*, translation by Jean Amyot, introduction and notes by Jean Massin, Paris, 1967, 2 vols

PLYMOUTH 1992
David Mannings, *Sir Joshua Reynolds PRA 1723–1792: The Self-portraits*, exh. cat., Plymouth City Museums and Art Gallery, 1992

POINTON 1993
Marcia Pointon, *Hanging the Head: Portraiture and Social Formation in Eighteenth-Century England*, New Haven and London, 1993

POINTON 1997A
Marcia Pointon, 'Marriage and Its Boundaries: The Montgomery Sisters Adorning a Term of Hymen', in her *Strategies for Showing: Women, Possession and Representation in English Visual Culture, 1665–1800*, Oxford, 1997

POINTON 1997B
Marcia Pointon, 'Intriguing Jewellery: Royal Bodies and Luxurious Consumption', *Textual Practice*, 11: 3, 1997, pp.493–516

POINTON 2001
Marcia Pointon, '"Portrait! Portrait!! Portrait!!!"', in London 2001

POISSON 1985
Georges Poisson, 'Les Statues du pont de la Concorde', *Bulletin de la Société d'histoire de Paris et d'Ile-de-France* (1985), 1987, pp.173–93

POLDEN 2004
Patrick Polden, 'Wilmot, John Eardley Eardley- (bap. 1749, d. 1815)', in H. C. G. Matthew and Brian Harrison (eds), *Oxford Dictionary of National Biography*, Oxford, 2004, vol.59, p.468

POLLOCK 1988
Griselda Pollock, *Vision and Difference: Femininity, Feminism, and Histories of Art*, New York and London, 1988

POMMIER 1989
Edouard Pommier, 'Winckelmann et la vision de l'Antiquité classique dans la France des Lumières et de la Révolution', *Revue de l'Art*, 83, 1989, pp. 9–20

POMMIER 1991
Edouard Pommier, 'La Notion de la grâce chez Winckelmann', *Winckelmann: la naissance de l'histoire de l'art à l'époque des Lumières*, papers of a series of conferences organised by Edouard Pommier at the Musée du Louvre (11 December 1989 – 12 February 1990), Paris, 1991, pp.39–81

POMMIER 1998A
Edouard Pommier, 'L'Invention du monument aux grands hommes (XVIIIe siècle)', in *Le Culte des Grands Hommes au XVIIIe siècle*, papers of a conference in the series 'Entretiens de la Garenne-Lemot', organised by Jackie Pigeaud and Jean-Paul Barbe (3–5 October 1996), Paris and Nantes, 1998, pp.7–23

POMMIER 1998B
Edouard Pommier, *Théories du portrait. De la Renaissance aux Lumières*, Paris, 1998

POMMIER 2003
Edouard Pommier, *Winckelmann, inventeur de l'histoire de l'art*, Paris, 2003

POPE-HENNESSY 1966
John Pope-Hennessy, *The Portrait in the Renaissance*, Washington DC, 1966

PORTER 1977
Roy Porter, *The Making of Geology: Earth Science in Britain 1660–1815*, Cambridge, 1977

PORTER 2000
Roy Porter, *Enlightenment: Britain and the Creation of the Modern World*, London and New York, 2000

POSTLE 1995
Martin Postle, *Sir Joshua Reynolds: The Subject Pictures*, Cambridge, 1995

POSTLE 2001
Martin Postle, 'Sir Joshua Reynolds, Edmund Burke, and the *Grand Whiggery*', in Elise Goodman (ed.), *Art and Culture in the Eighteenth Century: New Dimensions and Multiple Perspectives*, Newark, NJ, 2001

POSTLE 2003
Martin Postle, '"Painted Women": Reynolds and the Cult of the Courtesan', in Asleson 2003, pp.104–27

POSTLE 2004A
Martin Postle, 'Cotes, Francis (1726–1770)', in H. C. G. Matthew and Brian Harrison (eds) *Oxford Dictionary of National Biography*, Oxford, 2004, vol.13, pp.566–68

POSTLE 2004B
Martin Postle, 'Reynolds, Sir Joshua (1723–1792)', in H. C. G. Matthew and Brian Harrison (eds), *Oxford Dictionary of National Biography*, Oxford, 2004, vol.46, pp.551–65

POTTLE 2004
Mark Pottle, 'Coke, Daniel Parker (1745–1825)', in H. C. G. Matthew and Brian Harrison (eds), *Oxford Dictionary of National Biography*, Oxford, 2004, vol.12, pp.450–51

POTTS 1981A
Alex Potts, 'Chantrey as the National Sculptor of Early Nineteenth-century England', *The Oxford Art Journal*, 4, 2, November 1981, pp.17–27

POTTS 1981B
Alex Potts, 'Sculptor to an Age: The Public and the Private Image in Chantrey's Portrait Busts', *Sir Francis Chantrey. Sculptor to an Age, 1781–1841*, Clyde Binfield (ed.), Sheffield, 1981, pp.51–82

POTTS 2000
Alex Potts, 'The Classical Ideal on Display', *Ricerche di Storia dell'Arte*, 72, 2000, pp.29–36

PÖTZL-MALIKOVA 1982
Maria Pötzl-Malikova, *Franz-Xaver Messerschmidt*, Vienna and Munich, 1982

PRAT AND ROSENBERG 2002
Louis-Antoine Prat and Pierre Rosenberg, *Jacques-Louis David, catalogue raisonné des dessins*, Milan, 2002

PRATO 1978
Sandra Pinto and Ettore Spaletti, *Lorenzo Bartolini*, exh. cat., Palazzo Pretorio, Prato, 1978

PRESSLY 1981
William L. Pressly, *The Life and Art of James Barry*, New Haven and London, 1981

PRESSLY 1983
William L. Pressly, *James Barry: The Artist as Hero*, London, 1983

PRESSLY 1995
William L. Pressly, 'The Challenge of New Horizons', in Neff 1995, pp.23–59

PRESSLY 2004
William L. Pressly, 'Barry, James (1741–1806)', in Colin Matthew and Brian Harrison (eds), *Oxford Dictionary of National Biography*, Oxford, 2004, vol.4, pp.134–39

PRESSLY 2005
William L. Pressly, 'Barry's Self-portraits: Who's Afraid of the Ancients?', in Cork 2005, pp.60–77

PRESTON 1983
*Polite Society by Arthur Devis, 1712–1787: Portraits of the English Country Gentleman and His Family*, exh. cat., Harris Museum and Art Gallery, Preston, and National Portrait Gallery, London, 1983

PROBSZT 1927
Günther Probszt, *Friedrich von Amerling. Der Altmeister der Wiener Porträtmalerei*, Zurich, Leipzig and Vienna, 1927

PROWN 1966
Jules David Prown, *John Singleton Copley*, Cambridge, Mass., 1966, 2 vols

QUARRÉ 1940
Pierre Quarré, 'Les Bustes de Caffieri offerts à l'Académie de Dijon', *Mémoires de l'Académie des Sciences, Arts et Belles-Lettres de Dijon* (1939), 1940, pp.323–28

QUATREMÈRE DE QUINCY 1834
Antoine-Chrysostome Quatremère de Quincy, *Canova et ses ouvrages ou Mémoires historiques sur la vie et les travaux de ce célèbre artiste*, Paris, 1834

RADCLIFFE 1969
Anthony Radcliffe, 'Acquisitions of Sculpture by the Royal Academy During Its First Century', *Apollo*, 89, 1969, pp.44–51

RÉAU 1927
Louis Réau, *Les Lemoyne*, Paris, 1927

RÉAU 1950
Louis Réau, *Jean-Baptiste Pigalle*, Paris, 1950

RÉAU 1964
Louis Réau, *Houdon. Sa vie et son oeuvre*, Paris, 1964, 2 vols

REBORA 1999
Sergio Rebora, 'La formazione del collezionismo impreditoriale in Lombardia (1829–1881)' in Giovanna Ginex and Sergio Rebora (eds), *Imprenditori e cultura. Raccolte d'arte in Lombardia 1829–1926*, Milan, 1999, pp.33–105

RETFORD 2006
Kate Retford, *The Art of Domestic Life: Family Portraiture in Eighteenth-century England*, New Haven and London, 2006

REUTER 2001
Anna Reuter, 'La Marquesa de Villafranca pintando a su marido', in Madrid 2001, p.258

REYNOLDS 1992
Sir Joshua Reynolds, *Discourses*, introduction by Pat Rogers, London and New York, 1992

REYNOLDS 1997
Sir Joshua Reynolds, *Discourses on Art*, Robert R. Wark (ed.), New Haven and London, 1997

RIBEIRO 1995
Aileen Ribeiro, *The Art of Dress: Fashion in England and France, 1750–1820*, New Haven and London, 1995

RIBEIRO 1999
Aileen Ribeiro, *Ingres in Fashion. Representation of Dress and Appearance in Ingres's Images of Women*, New Haven and London, 1999

RIBEIRO 2003
Aileen Ribeiro, 'Costuming the Part: A Discourse of Fashion and Fiction in the Image of the Actress in England, 1776–1812', in Asleson 2003, pp.104–27

ROBAUT 1885
Alfred Robaut, with commentaries by Ernest Chesneau, *L'Oeuvre complet d'Eugène Delacroix. Peintures, dessins, gravures, lithographies*, Paris, 1885

ROBERTS 1989
Warren Roberts, *Jacques-Louis David, Revolutionary Artist: Politics and the French Revolution*, Chapel Hill and London, 1989

ROBERTS 2002
Jane Roberts, *Royal Treasures: A Golden Jubilee Celebration*, London, 2002

ROBERTSON AND JULIA 1974
Sarah Robertson and Isabelle Julia, 'A.C.H. Haudebourg-Lescot', in Paris 1974A, pp.486–87

ROBINSON 1993
John Martin Robinson, *Spencer House*, London, 1993

ROCHEBLAVE 1902
Samuel Rocheblave, 'Jean-Baptiste Pigalle et son art', *Revue de l'art ancien et moderne*, 12, 1902, pp.267–80, 353–69

ROCHEBLAVE 1919
Samuel Rocheblave, *Jean-Baptiste Pigalle*, Paris, 1919

ROCHE 2002
Daniel Roche, *Le Cheval et la guerre*, Paris, 2002

ROCHER-JAUNEAU 1957
Madeleine Rocher-Jauneau, 'Le Buste de Madame Récamier par Canova au Musée des Beaux-Arts de Lyon', *Bulletin des Musées lyonnais*, 2, 1957, 3, pp.53–56

ROCHER-JAUNEAU 1978A
Madeleine Rocher-Jauneau, 'Joseph Chinard et les bustes de Mme Récamier', *Bulletin des Musées et Monuments lyonnais*, 6 (1977–1981), 1978, 2, pp.133–45

ROCHER-JAUNEAU 1978B
Madeleine Rocher-Jauneau, *L'Oeuvre de Joseph Chinard (1755–1813) au musée des Beaux-Arts de Lyon*, Lyons, 1978

RODEZ 1996
*Guillaume-Thomas Raynal, philosophe des Lumières*, exh. cat., Archives départementales de l'Aveyron, Rodez, 1996

ROETTGEN 1999–2003
Steffi Roettgen, *Anton Raphael Mengs 1728–1779*, Munich, 1999–2003, 2 vols

ROGERS 1874
The Revd Charles Rogers (ed.), *Boswelliana: The Commonplace Book of James Boswell*, London, 1874

ROME 1979
*Géricault*, exh. cat., Villa Medici, Rome, 1979–80

ROME 1980
*Horace Vernet (1789–1863)*, exh. cat., Académie de France, Rome, and Ecole Nationale Supérieure des Beaux-Arts, Paris, 1980

ROME 1989A
Patrizia Masini et al., *Giuseppe Ceracchi (1751–1801), scultore giacobino*, exh. cat., Palazzo dei Conservatori, Rome, 1989

ROME 1989B
Elena Di Majo, Bjarne Jørnaes and Stefano Susinno (eds), *Bertel Thorvaldsen 1770–1844, scultore danese a Roma*, exh. cat., Galleria Nazionale d'Arte Moderna, Rome, 1989–90

ROME 1998
Oscar Sandner, *Angelika Kauffmann e Roma*, exh.cat., Accademia Nazionale di San Luca, Rome, 1998

ROME 2000
*Goya*, exh. cat., Galleria Nazionale d'Arte, Palazzo Barberini, Rome, 2000

ROME 2003
Olivier Bonfait (ed.), *Maestà di Roma. Da Napoleone all'Unità d'Italia. D'Ingres à Degas. Les artistes français à Rome*, exh. cat., Académie Française, Rome 2003

ROME 2004
Giulia Gorgone (ed.), *Elisa Bonaparte. Ritratti di famiglia*, exh. cat., Museo Napoleonico, Rome, 2004

ROME 2005
Anna Lo Bianco and Angela Negro (eds), *Il Settecento a Roma*, exh. cat., Palazzo Venezia, Rome, 2005–06

ROMNEY 1773
George Romney's journal of his tour in France and Italy, 1773, Fitzwilliam Museum, Cambridge, Ms 1-1917

ROMNEY 1830
The Revd John Romney, *Memoirs of the Life and Works of George Romney*, London, 1830

RØNBERG 2001
Lene Bøgh Rønberg, 'Bourgeois Home Life in the Two Golden Ages. Influences and Correspondences', in Copenhagen 2001 pp.72–141

RONDOT 1994
Bertrand Rondot, 'La Salle du Trône des Tuileries sous le Second Empire', *Société des Amis de Malmaison. Bulletin*, 1994, pp.56–57

ROSENBLUM 1968
Robert Rosenblum, *Ingres*, Paris, 1968

ROSENBLUM 1989
Robert Rosenblum, *The Romantic Child: From Runge to Sendak*, London and New York, 1989

ROSENTHAL 1996
Angela Rosenthal, *Angelika Kauffmann: Bildnismalerei im 18. Jahrhundert*, Berlin, 1996

ROSENTHAL 1999
Michael Rosenthal, *The Art of Thomas Gainsborough: 'A Little Business for the Eye'*, New Haven and London, 1999

ROSENTHAL 2006
Angela Rosenthal, *Angelika Kauffman: Art and Sensibility*, New Haven and London, 2006

ROSTRUP 1945
Haavard Rostrup, *H. W. Bissen*, Copenhagen, 1945, 2 vols

ROTH 1994
Michael S. Roth (ed.), *Rediscovering History: Culture, Politics and the Psyche*, Stanford, 1994

ROUSSEAU 1947
Jean-Jacques Rousseau, *Les Confessions*, Paris, 1947

ROUSSEAU 1962
Theodore Rousseau, 'Aristotle Contemplating the Bust of Homer', *Bulletin of the Metropolitan Museum*, 20: 5, January 1962, pp.149–56

ROUSSEAU 1969
Jean-Jacques Rousseau, *Emile ou De l'Education*, Paris [1762], 1969

RUBIN 1979
James Henry Rubin, 'Gros and Girodet', *Burlington Magazine*, 121, November 1979, pp.708–21

RULL SABATER 1991
Alberto Rull Sabater, *Diccionario sucinto de Ministros de Hacienda*, Madrid, 1991

RUMP 2002
Gerhard Charles Rump, '"How to Be Formal without Really Trying": George Romney and Pictorial Form', *Transactions of the Romney Society*, 7, 2002, pp.4–12

RUPPERT 1996
Jacques Ruppert et al., *Le Costume français*, Paris, 1996

RUSSELL 2004
Francis Russell, *John, 3rd Earl of Bute: Patron and Collector*, London, 2004

ST ANDREWS 1997
Lucy Dixon, *David Martin (1737–1797)*, exh. cat., Crawford Arts Centre, St Andrews, 1997

SAINT-GIRONS 1998
Baldine Saint-Girons, 'Grand homme, Génie sublime', in *Le Culte des Grands Hommes au XVIIIe siècle*, papers of a conference in the series 'Entretiens de la Garenne-Lemot', organised by Jackie Pigeaud and Jean-Paul Barbe (3–5 October 1996), Paris and Nantes, 1998, pp.139–51

SAMOYAULT-VERLET AND SAMOYAULT 198
Colombe Samoyault-Verlet and Jean-Pierre Samoyault, *Château de Fontainebleau. Musée Napoléon Ier. Napoléon et la famille impériale 1804–1815*, Paris, 1986

SANCHEZ 2004
Pierre Sanchez, *Dictionnaire des artistes exposant dans les Salons des XVIIe et XVIIIe siècles à Paris et en province 1673–1800*, Dijon, 2004, 3 vols

SÁNCHEZ CANTÓN 1927
F. J. Sánchez Cantón, *Mengs en España*, Madrid, 1927

SAN MARINO 1971
Robert R. Wark, *Ten British Pictures, 1740–1840*, exh. cat., The Huntington Library, San Marino, 1971

SANTUCCIO 2000
Giuliana Santuccio, 'Le catalogue "Tatham" de la fabrique de Giovanni Volpato à Rome', *Sèvres. Revue de la Société des Amis du musée national de Céramique*, 9, 2000, pp.38–44

SAPORI 2003
Michelle Sapori, *Rose Bertin, ministre des modes de Marie-Antoinette*, Paris, 2003

SARAGOSSA 1996
*Realidad e imagen. Goya, 1746–1828*, exh. cat., Museo de Zaragoza, Saragossa, 1996

SASS 1963–65
Af Else Kai Sass, *Thorvaldsens Portraetbuster*, Copenhagen, 1963–65, 3 vols

SASSI 2001
Amerigo Sassi, *Pompeo Marchesi Scultore*, Gavirate, 2001

SAUERLÄNDER 2005
Willibald Sauerländer, *Essai sur les visages des bustes de Houdon*, first edition, Munich, 2002; French edition: Paris, 2005

SAYWELL AND SIMON 2004
David Saywell and Jacob Simon, *Complete Illustrated Catalogue of the National Portrait Gallery, London*, London, 2004

SCHAFFHAUSEN 1993
Dieter Ulrich and Daisy Sigerist, *Alexander Trippel (1744–1793), Skulpturen und Zeichnungen*, exh. cat., Museum zu Allerheiligen, Schaffhausen, 1993

SCHAMA 1988
Simon Schama, 'The Domestication of Royal Family Portraiture, 1500–1850', in Robert I. Rotberg and Theodore K. Rabb (eds), *Art and History: Images and Their Meaning*, Cambridge, 1988, pp.155–83

SCHAMA 1989
Simon Schama, *Citizens: A Chronicle of the French Revolution*, New York, 1989

SCHAMA 2002
Simon Schama, *A History of Britain: The Fate of Empire, 1776–2000*, London, 2002

SCHERF 1988
Guilhem Scherf, 'Un buste de l'abbé Raynal à l'Académie de Lyon', *Bulletin des Musées et Monuments lyonnais*, 1, 1988, pp.10–19

SCHERF 1993
Guilhem Scherf, 'La Galerie des "Grands Hommes" au coeur des nouvelles salles consacrées à la sculpture française du XVIIIe siècle', Revue du Louvre, 5–6, 1993, pp.58–67

SCHERF 2001
Guilhem Scherf, 'Jean-Baptiste Nini et le portrait sculpté en médaillon', in Urbino 2001, pp.85–91

SCHERF 2004
Guilhem Scherf, 'Houdon au-dessus de tous les artistes modernes', in Versailles 2004, pp.14–25

SCHERF 2005A
Guilhem Scherf, 'Le Portrait sculpté d'enfant: un genre nouveau en France au XVIIIe siècle', Péristyles, 26, 2005, pp.89–98

SCHERF 2005B
Guilhem Scherf, 'Une Tête de caractère de Messerschmidt au Louvre', Revue du Louvre, 2, April 2005, pp.15–16

SCHERF 2006
Guilhem Scherf, Houdon 1741–1828. Statues, portraits sculptés…Collections du musée du Louvre, Paris, 2006

SCHNAPPER 1980
Antoine Schnapper, David, témoin de son temps, Paris, 1980

SCHNEIDER 1912
René Schneider, 'Le Mythe de Psyché dans l'art français depuis la Révolution', Revue de l'art ancien et moderne, 32, 1912, pp.241–54

SCHOMMER 1968
Pierre Schommer, 'Le Général comte de Lasalle (1775–1809), son portrait par Antoine-Jean Gros', Revue de la Société des Amis du musée de l'Armée, 72, 1968, pp.37–39

SCHULZ 1953
Arthur Schulz, Die Bildnisse Johann Joachim Winckelmanns, Berlin, 1953

SCHWARTZ 1992
Sanford Schwartz, Christen Købke, New York, 1992

SCOTT 1963
Franklin Daniel Scott, Wertmüller, Artist and Immigrant Farmer, Chicago, 1963

SELLERS 1962
Charles Coleman Sellers, Benjamin Franklin in Portraiture, New Haven and London, 1962

SEWARD 1810
The Poetical Works of Anna Seward, Walter Scott (ed.), Edinburgh, 1810, 3 vols

SEWARD 1811
Letters of Anna Seward, Archibald Constable (ed.), Edinburgh, 1811, 6 vols

SHAWE-TAYLOR 1990
Desmond Shawe-Taylor, The Georgians: Eighteenth-century Portraiture and Society, London, 1990

SHELTON 2001
Andrew Carrington Shelton, 'Storming the Acropolis: Gender, Class and Classicism in Eighteenth-Century England', in Elise Goodman (ed.), Art and Culture in the Eighteenth Century: New Dimensions and Multiple Perspectives, Newark, NJ, 2001, pp.125–41

SHELTON 2005
Andrew Carrington Shelton, Ingres and His Critics, Cambridge and New York, 2005

SHERIDAN 1960
Betsy Sheridan's Journal, William LeFanu (ed.), London, 1960

SHERIDAN 1966
The Letters of Richard Brinsley Sheridan, C. J. L. Price (ed.), Oxford, 1966, 3 vols

SHERIDAN N.D.
Thomas Sheridan, Coriolanus; or, the Roman Matron. A Tragedy. Altered from Shakespeare, by Mr. T. Sheridan, London, undated

SHERIFF 1996
Mary D. Sheriff, The Exceptional Woman, Elisabeth Vigée-Lebrun and the Cultural Politics of Art, Chicago, 1996

SIDDONS 1942
The Reminiscences of Sarah Kemble Siddons, 1773–1785, William Van Lennep (ed.), Cambridge, Mass., 1942

SIEGFRIED 1980
Susan Siegfried, 'Napoleon Enthroned', in Consortium on Revolutionary Europe, 1750–1850, Tallahassee, Florida, 1980, pp.69–81

SIEGFRIED 1995
Susan L. Siegfried, The Art of Louis-Léopold Boilly: Modern Life in Napoleonic France, New Haven and London, 1995

SILLARS 2006
Stuart Sillars, Painting Shakespeare: The Artist as Critic, 1720–1820, Cambridge, 2006

SILVESTRE 1926
Théophile Silvestre, in Les Artistes vivants, Paris, 1926, 2 vols

SILVESTRE DE SACY 1953
Jacques Silvestre de Sacy, Le Comte d'Angiviller, dernier directeur général des Bâtiments du roi, Paris, 1953

SIMSON 1990
Jutta von Simson, 'Die Büsten der Königin Luise von Christian Daniel Rauch', in Hartmut Krohm and Christian Theuerkauff (eds), Festschrift für Peter Bloch zum 11. July 1990, Mainz, 1990, pp.271–82

SIMSON 1996
Jutta von Simson, Christian Daniel Rauch. Oeuvre-Katalog, Berlin, 1996

SLOMAN 2002
Susan Sloman, Gainsborough in Bath, New Haven and London, 2002

SMART 1952
Alastair Smart, The Life and Art of Allan Ramsay, London, 1952

SMART 1992
Alastair Smart, Allan Ramsay: Painter, Essayist and Man of the Enlightenment, New Haven and London, 1992

SMART 1999
Alastair Smart, Allan Ramsay: A Complete Catalogue of His Paintings, John Ingamells (ed.), New Haven and London, 1999

SMITH 1986
John Thomas Smith, Nollekens and His Times, London [1828], 1986

SMITH MCCREA 2005
Rosalie Smith McCrea, 'Portrait Mythology? Representing the "Black Jacobin"; Henri Christophe in the British Grand Manner', The British Art Journal, 6, 2, autumn 2005, pp.66–70

SOLKIN 1982
David H. Solkin, Richard Wilson: The Landscape of Reaction, London, 1982

SOLKIN 1986
David H. Solkin, 'Great Pictures or Great Men? Reynolds' Male Portraiture, and the Power of Art', The Oxford Art Journal, 1986, 9, 2, pp.36–49

SORIA 1957
Martín S. Soria, Agustín Esteve y Goya, Valencia, 1957

SOTHEBY'S 2005
Sotheby's auctioneers, American Paintings, Drawings and Sculpture, sale catalogue, New York, 30 November 2005

STAFFORD 2004
Fiona Stafford, 'Striking Resemblances: National Identity and the Eighteenth-Century Portrait', Eighteenth-Century Ireland, 19, 2004, pp.138–62

STAITI 1995
Paul Staiti, 'Accounting for Copley', in Boston 1995, pp.25–51

STANHOPE 1932
The Letters of Philip Dormer Stanhope, 4th Earl of Chesterfield, Bonamy Dobrée (ed.), London, 1932, 6 vols

STEEB 1999
Christian Steeb, Die Grafen von Fries: eine Schweizer Familie und ihre wirtschaftspolitische und kulturhistorische Bedeutung für Oesterreich zwischen 1750 und 1830, Bad Voeslau, 1999

STEEGMAN 1946
John Steegman, 'Some English Portraits by Pompeo Batoni', Burlington Magazine, March 1946, 88: 516, pp.54–63

STEFANI 1999
Ottorino Stefani, Antonio Canova. La statuaria, Milan, 1999

STEIN 1912
Henri Stein, Augustin Pajou, Paris, 1912

STEPHENS 2004
H. M. Stephens, 'Conolly, Thomas (1738–1803)', revised A. T. Q. Stewart, in H.C.G. Matthew and Brian Harrison (eds), Oxford Dictionary of National Biography, Oxford, 2004, vol.12, pp.985–86

STERLING AND ADHÉMAR 1958–61
Charles Sterling and Hélène Adhémar, La Peinture au Musée du Louvre: Ecole Française XIXe Siècle, Paris, 4 vols (A–C, 1958; D–G, 1959; H–O, 1960; P–Z, 1961)

STEWARD 1995
James Christen Steward, The New Child: British Art and the Origins of Modern Childhood, 1730–1830, Berkeley and Washington DC, 1995

STEWART 1976
J. D. Stewart, 'Kneller's Long Shadow: John Smith's Mezzotints and Joseph Wright of Derby', Burlington Magazine, 118: 879, June 1976, pp.410–13

STOCKHOLM 1994
Le Soleil et l'étoile du nord: La France et la Suède au XVIIIe siècle, exh. cat., Nationalmuseum, Stockholm, and Galeries Nationales du Grand Palais, Paris, 1994

STOCKHOLM 1999
Magnus Olausson, Catherine the Great and Gustav III, exh. cat., Nationalmuseum, Stockholm, 1999

STURGES 1978
R. P. Sturges, 'The Membership of the Derby Philosophical Society, 1783–1802', Midland History, 4: 3 and 4, 1978, pp.212–29

STUTTGART 1976
Ulrike Gauss and Christian von Holst, Gottlieb Schick. Ein Maler des Kassizismus, exh. cat., Staatsgalerie, Stuttgart, 1976

STUTTGART 1987
Christian von Holst, Johann Heinrich Dannecker. Der Bildhauer, exh. cat., Staatsgalerie, Stuttgart, 1987

SUARD 1786
Jean-Baptiste Suard, 'Eloge de Pigalle', Journal de Paris, 12–24 September 1786

SWOZILEK 1999
Helmut Swozilek (ed.), Memorie istoriche di Maria Angelica Kauffmann Zucchi riguardanti l'arte della pittura da lei professata scritte da Giuseppe Carlo Zucchi, Venezia MDCCLXXXVIII, Bregenz, 1999

SYDOW 1909
Anna von Sydow (ed.), Wilhelm und Caroline von Humboldt in ihren Briefen, Berlin, 1909, 3 vols

TAIGNY 1859
E. Taigny, J.-B. Isabey, sa vie et ses oeuvres. Extrait de la Revue européenne, Paris, 1859

TALBOT 1980
William S. Talbot, 'Cogniet and Vernet at the Villa Medici', Bulletin of The Cleveland Museum of Art, January 1980, pp.135–48, fig.15

TARASOVA 2000
Lina Tarasova, 'Scultori russi pensionnaires dell'Accademia pietroburghese di belle arti a Roma', in Massa 2000, pp.49–78

TEN EYCK GARDNER 1948
Albert Ten Eyck Gardner, 'Fragment of a Lost Monument', *The Metropolitan Museum of Art Bulletin*, March 1948, pp.189–97

TERNOIS 1980
Daniel Ternois, *Ingres*, Paris, 1980

TERNOIS 1998
Daniel Ternois, *Monsieur Bertin*, Paris, 1998

TERNOIS 2001
Daniel Ternois, *Lettres d'Ingres à Marcotte d'Argenteuil. Dictionnaire*, Archives de l'Art français, n.s., vol.36, Nogent-le-Roi, 2001

TERNOIS AND CAMESASCA 1968
Daniel Ternois and Ettore Camesasca, *Tout l'oeuvre peint d'Ingres*, Paris, 1968

THIELE 1852–54
T. M. Thiele, *Thorvaldsen Biographi*, Copenhagen, 1852–54, 3 vols

THOMPSON 1990
F. M. L. Thompson, 'Life after Death: How Successful Nineteenth-Century Businessmen Disposed of Their Fortunes', *Economic History Review*, n.s. 43: 1, February 1990, pp.40–61

THOMPSON 1992
F. M. L. Thompson, 'Stitching It Together Again', *Economic History Review*, n.s. 45: 2, May 1992, pp.362–75

THOMSON 1994
Duncan Thomson, *Sir Henry Raeburn, 1756–1823*, Edinburgh, 1994

THOMSON 2004
Duncan Thomson, 'Raeburn, Sir Henry (1756–1823)', in H. C. G. Matthew and Brian Harrison (eds), *Oxford Dictionary of National Biography*, Oxford, 2004, vol.45, pp.780–86

THORNE 1986
Roland G. Thorne, *The House of Commons 1780–1820*, London, 1986, 5 vols

THORVALDSENS MUSEUM 1931
*Catalogue illustré*, Thorvaldsens Museum, Copenhagen, 1931

TINTI 1936
Mario Tinti, *Lorenzo Bartolini*, Rome, 1936, 2 vols

TOBIN 1999
Beth Fowkes Tobin, *Picturing Imperial Power: Colonial Subjects in Eighteenth-Century British Painting*, Durham, NC, and London, 1999

TODOROV 1996
Tzvetan Todorov, 'Goethe sur l'art', in *Goethe. Ecrits sur l'art*, Jean-Marie Schaeffer (ed.), Paris, 1996

TOKYO 1987
Juan J. Luna, *Spanish Paintings of the Eighteenth and Nineteenth Centuries: Goya and His Time*, exh.cat., Tokyo, Amagasaki, and Iwaki, 1987

TOKYO 1991
Michel Laclotte (ed.), *Portraits du Louvre*, exh.cat., Tokyo Metropolitan Art Museum, 1991

TOKYO 1993
*Masterpieces from the National Galleries of Scotland*, exh. cat., The Isetan Museum of Art, Tokyo, The Museum and Cultural Institutions of Miyazaki Prefecture, Miyazaki, and The Sogo Museum of Art, Yokohama, 1993–94

TOKYO 1997
*Les Peintures françaises du XVIIIe siècle dans les collections du Louvre*, exh. cat., Tokyo Metropolitan Art Museum, and Municipal Museum of Art, Kyoto, 1997

TOKYO 2006
*De Tiziano a Goya. Obras maestras del Museo del Prado*, exh. cat., Metropolitan Museum of Art, Tokyo, and Municipal Museum of Art, Osaka, 2006

TOMLINSON 1989
Janis A. Tomlinson, *Francisco Goya: The Tapestry Cartoons and Early Career at the Court of Madrid*, Cambridge, 1989

TOMLINSON 1992
Janis A. Tomlinson, *Goya in the Twilight of Enlightenment*, New Haven and London, 1992

TOMLINSON 1994
Janis A. Tomlinson, *Francisco Goya y Lucientes*, London, 1994

TORMO 1916
Elías Tormo, *Pintores Españoles del 800. Los todavía setecentistas*, Madrid, 1916

TORONTO 2005
Nathalie Bondil (ed.), *Catherine la Grande, un art pour l'Empire. Chefs-d'oeuvre du musée de l'Ermitage de Saint-Pétersbourg*, exh. cat., Musée des Beaux-Arts, Toronto, and Musée des Beaux-Arts, Montréal, 2005–06

TOULOUSE 2002
Alain Daguerre de Hureaux and Charlotte Riou (eds), *Cent ans de sculpture (1750–1850). La collection du musée des Augustins*, exh. cat., Musée des Augustins, Toulouse, 2002

TOURNEUX 1912
Maurice Tourneux, 'Lettre de Mme Vandeul, née Diderot, sur le salon de l'an X', *Bulletin de la Société de l'Histoire de l'Art français*, 1912, pp.124–40

TOURNEUX 1913
Maurice Tourneux, 'Hommages rendus à Diderot par ses compatriotes (1780–81)', *Bulletin de la Société de l'Histoire de l'Art français*, 1913, pp.184–91

TOURS 1873
*Exposition rétrospective des Beaux-Arts*, exh. cat., Musée des Beaux-Arts, Tours, 1873

TOURS 2000
*Les Peintres du roi 1648–1793*, exh. cat., Musée des Beaux-Arts, Tours, and Musée des Augustins, Toulouse, 2000

TOUSSAINT 1985
Hélène Toussaint, *Les Portraits d'Ingres*, Paris, 1985

TOUSSAINT 2002
Jacques Toussaint (ed.), *Portrait en Namurois*, Namur, 2002

TRAEGER 1975
Jorg Traeger, *Philipp Otto Runge und sein Werk. Monographie und kritischer Katalog*, Munich, 1975

TRAEGER 1987
Jorg Traeger, *Der Weg nach Walhalla. Denkmallandschaft und Bildungsreise im 19. Jahrhundert*, Regensburg, 1987

TRAPP 1986
F. A. Trapp (ed.), *British Art*, Amherst, Mass.,1986

TRIER 1903
Sigurd Trier, *Thorvaldsen*, Copenhagen, 1903

TRIPIER-LEFRANC 1880
J. Tripier-Lefranc, *Histoire de la vie et de la mort du baron Gros, le grand peintre, rédigée sur de nouveaux documents d'après des souvenirs inédits*, Paris, 1880

TROYEN 1995
Carol Troyen, 'Samuel Adams', in Boston 1995, pp.275–78

TRUSTED 1992–93
Majorie Trusted, '"A Man of Talent": Agostino Carlini (c. 1718–1790)', *Burlington Magazine*, 134, 1992, pp.776–84, and 135, 1993, pp.190–201

TSCHERNY 2002
Nadia Tscherny, '"Persons and Property": Romney's Society Portraiture', in Liverpool 2002, pp.33–61

TÜBINGEN 1959
Liselotte Lohrer (ed.), *Cotta in Tübingen: Dokumente, Handschriften, Bücher*, exh. cat., Tübingen, 1959

URBINO 2001
Anna Cerboni Baiardi and Barbara Sibille (eds), *Jean-Baptiste Nini 1717–1786. D'Urbino aux rives de la Loire. Paysages et visages européens*, exh. cat., Palazzo Ducale, Urbino, and Château, Blois, 2001–02

VALLETTA 1970
*The Order of St John in Malta*. exh. cat., St John's Museum, Valletta, 1970

VALYNSEELE 1962
Joseph Valynseele, *Les Maréchaux de la Restauration et de la monarchie de Juillet, leur famille et leur descendance*, Paris, 1962

VANDEUL 1830
Angélique de Vandeul, 'Mémoires pour servir à l'histoire de la vie et des ouvrages de Diderot, par Madame de Vandeul, sa fille', *Mémoires, correspondance et ouvrages inédits de Diderot...*, Paris, 1830, vol.1, pp.1–69

VATTIER 1890
Gustave Adolphe Vattier, *Une Famille d'artistes: les Dumont (1660–1884)*, Paris, 1890

VENICE 1978
Giuseppe Pavanello et al., *Venezia nell'età di Canova 1780–1830*, exh. cat., Museo Correr, Venice, 1978

VENICE 1992
Giuseppe Pavanello, Fernando Mazzocca et al., *Antonio Canova*, exh. cat., Museo Correr, Venice, 1992

VERSAILLES 1962
*La Comédie-Française 1680–1962*, exh. cat., Musée National du Château, Versailles, 1962

VERSAILLES 2001
Thérèse Picquenard, Anne Billon, Guilhem Scherf et al., *Louis-Simon Boizot 1743–1809. Sculpteur du roi et directeur de l'atelier de sculpture à la Manufacture de Sèvres*, Musée Lambinet, Versailles, 2001–02

VERSAILLES 2004
Anne L. Poulet, Guilhem Scherf, Ulrike Mathies, Christoph Frank et al., *Houdon, sculpteur des Lumières*, exh. cat., Musée National du Château, Versailles, 2004

VIENNA 1990
*Ferdinand Georg Waldmüller*, exh. cat., Kunstforum Länderbank, Vienna, 1990

VIENNA 2002
Michael Krapf, *Franz Xaver Messerschmidt*, exh.cat., Osterreichische Galerie Belvedere, Vienna, 2002–03

VIENNA 2003
Sabine Grabner, *Friedrich von Amerling, 1803–1887*, exh. cat., Osterreichische Galerie Belvedere, Vienna, 2003

VIGÉE-LEBRUN 1835–37
Elisabeth-Louise Vigée-Lebrun, *Souvenirs de Mme Vigée-Lebrun*, Paris, 1835–37

VIGÉE-LEBRUN 1984, 1986
Elisabeth-Louise Vigée-Lebrun, *Souvenirs*, Paris, 1984, 2 vols; second edition, 1986

VIGÉE-LEBRUN 1989
Elisabeth-Louise Vigée-Lebrun, *The Memoirs of Elisabeth Vigée-Le Brun*, translated by Sîan Evans, London, 1989

VIGNE 1995
Georges Vigne, *Ingres*, Paris, 1995

VITRY 1908
Paul Vitry, 'Exposition de cent pastels et de bustes du XVIIIe siècle... I: Les sculptures', *Les Arts*, 82, October 1908, pp.1–12

VITRY 1922
Paul Vitry, *Le Musée d'Orléans (Collections Publiques de France)*, Paris, 1922

VITRY 1930
Paul Vitry, 'Liste des bustes d'artistes commandés pour la Grande Galerie et les salles de peinture du Louvre', *Bulletin de la Société de l'Histoire de l'Art français*, 1930, pp.137–41

VITRY 1931
Paul Vitry, 'Le Première Exposition de
Chefs-d'Oeuvres des Musées de Province,
à l'Orangerie des Tuileries', *Bulletin des Musées
de France*, April 1931

VOLTAIRE 1962–63
Voltaire, *Correspondance*, Theodor Besterman
(ed.), vol. 75, Geneva, 1962; vol. 80, Geneva,
1963

VOLTAIRE 1999
Voltaire, *Lettres philosophiques* [1734], Paris, 1999

WALLIS 1999
Jean Wallis, 'The Mind and Soul of Romney's
Art and the Poussin Connection', *Transactions
of the Romney Society*, 4, 1999, pp. 4–11

WALPOLE 1937–82
*Horace Walpole's Correspondence*, Wilmarth
S. Lewis (ed.), New Haven, 1937–82, 48 vols

WARD 2004
David C. Ward, *Charles Willson Peale: Art and
Selfhood in the Early Republic*, Berkeley, 2004

WARK 1954
Robert R. Wark, 'The Iconography and
Date of James Barry's Self-portrait in Dublin',
*Burlington Magazine*, 96: 614, May 1954,
pp. 153–54

WARREN–ADAMS LETTERS 1917
*Warren–Adams Letters*, The Massachusetts
Historical Society, Boston, 1917

WASHINGTON 1976
William Howard Adams (ed.), *The Eye of
Jefferson*, exh. cat., National Gallery of Art,
Washington DC, 1976

WASHINGTON 1982
Ellis Waterhouse, Sidney C. Hutchison et al.,
*Paintings from the Royal Academy: Two Centuries of
British Art*, exh. cat., International Exhibitions
Foundation, Washington DC, 1982

WASHINGTON 1985
Gervase Jackson-Stops (ed.), *The Treasures
Houses of Britain. Five Hundred Years of Private
Patronage and Art Collecting*, exh. cat., National
Gallery of Art, Washington DC, 1985

WASHINGTON 2002
Richard Brookhiser, Margaret C. S. Christman
and Ellen G. Miles (eds), *George Washington:
A National Treasure*, exh. cat., National Portrait
Gallery, Washington DC, 2002

WASHINGTON 2003
Anne L. Poulet, Guilhem Scherf, Ulrike
Mathies, Christoph Frank et al., *Jean-Antoine
Houdon, Sculptor of the Enlightenment*, exh. cat.,
National Gallery of Art, Washington DC,
and The J. Paul Getty Museum, Los Angeles,
2003–04

WATELET 1786
Claude Henri Watelet, *Dictionnaire des Arts
de Peinture, Sculpture et Gravure*, Paris, 1786

WATELET 2004
Claude Henri Watelet, *Essai sur les jardins*,
1st edition, Paris, 1774; Paris, 2004

WEBSTER 2004
Mary Webster, 'Zoffany, Johan Joseph
(1733–1810)', in H. C. G. Matthew and Brian
Harrison (eds), *Oxford Dictionary of National
Biography*, Oxford, 2004, vol. 60, pp. 999–1003

WEHRLIN AND SCHLUMBERGER 1964
Woldemar Wehrlin interviewed by Eveline
Schlumberger, 'Mon musée russe',
*Connaissance des Arts*, August 1964, pp. 40–45

WEST 1991A
Shearer West, *The Image of the Actor: Verbal and
Visual Representation in the Age of Garrick and Kemble*,
London, 1991

WEST 1991B
Shearer West, 'Thomas Lawrence's "Half-
History" Portraits and the Politics of Theatre',
*Art History*, 14: 2, June 1991, pp. 225–49

WEST 2004
Shearer West, *Portraiture*, Oxford, 2004

WESTON 1994
Helen D. Weston, 'Representing the Right
to Represent: The Portrait of Citizen Belley,
Ex-Representative of the Colonies by A.-L.
Girodet', *RES. Anthropology and Aesthetics*, 26,
autumn 1994, pp. 84–99

WHINNEY 1971
Margaret Whinney, *Victoria and Albert Museum:
English Sculpture, 1720–1830*, London, 1971

WHINNEY 1988
Margaret Whinney, *Sculpture in Britain 1530
to 1830*, revised edition by John Physick,
London, 1988

WHITBREAD 1951
S. Whitbread, *Southill: A Regency House*,
London, 1951

WHITLEY 1915
William T. Whitley, *Gainsborough*, London, 1915

WHITLEY 1928
William T. Whitley, *Artists and Their Friends in
England, 1700–1799*, Boston and London, 1928

WILDENSTEIN [1954–56]
Georges Wildenstein, *Ingres: Catalogue complet
des peintures*, London and Paris, n.d. [1954–56]

WILHELM 1963
Jacques Wilhelm, 'Un projet de Charles De
Wailly pour l'aménagement du Salon du
Louvre', *Bulletin du musée Carnavalet*, June 1963,
pp. 5–10

WILLIAMS 1831
D. E. Williams, *The Life and Correspondence
of Sir Thomas Lawrence*, London, 1831, 2 vols

WILSON 1988
John Wilson, 'Hoppner's "Tambourine Girl"
Identified', *Burlington Magazine*, 130: 1027,
October 1988, pp. 763–67

WILSON 2003
David Wilson, 'Nollekens and Fox in the
Temple. The "Armistead" Bust', *The British Art
Journal*, 4, 3, autumn 2003, pp. 65–79

WIND 1986
Edgar Wind, *Hume and the Heroic Portrait: Studies
in Eighteenth-Century Imagery*, Jaynie Anderson
(ed.), Oxford, 1986

WITTKOWER 1991
Rudolf and Margot Wittkower, *Les Enfants
de Saturne. Psychologie et comportement des artistes,
de l'Antiquité à la Révolution française*, Paris, 1991

WIVEL 1993
Mikael Wivel, *Christen Købke*, translated
by Reginald Spink, Hellerup, 1993

WIVEL 1996
Mikael Wivel, 'Købke: A Closer Look',
in Copenhagen 1996A, pp. 108–343

WORCESTER 1964
H. Harvard Arnason, *Sculpture by Houdon*, exh.
cat., Art Museum, Worcester, Mass., 1964

YARRINGTON ET AL. 1994
Alison Yarrington, Ilene D. Lieberman, Alex
Potts and Malcolm Baker, 'An Edition of the
Ledger of Sir Francis Chantrey, R.A., at the
Royal Academy, 1809–41', *Journal of the Walpole
Society*, 56 (1991–92), 1994

YARRINGTON 2000
Alison Yarrington, 'Anglo-Italian Attitudes.
Chantrey and Canova', in Cinzia Sicca and
Alison Yarrington (eds), *The Lustrous Trade.
Material Culture and the History of Sculpture in
England and Italy, c. 1700 – c. 1860*, London and
New York, 2000, pp. 132–55

YOKOHAMA 2005
Sébastien Allard and Vincent Pomarède, *Chefs-
d'oeuvre de la peinture française du XIXe siècle dans
les collections du Louvre*, exh. cat., Yokohama
Museum of Art, and Municipal Museum
of Art, Kyoto, 2005

YRIARTE 1867
Charles Yriarte, *Goya, sa biografie, les fresques,
les toiles, les tapisseries, les eau-fortes et le catalogue
de l'oeuvre*, Paris, 1867

ZAFRAN 1998
Eric M. Zafran, *French Paintings in the Museum
of Fine Arts, Boston*, Boston, 1998

ZERNER 1996
Henri Zerner, 'Le Portrait, ni plus, ni moins',
in Michel 1996, pp. 321–36

ZIESENISS 1969
Charles Otto Zieseniss, 'Les Portraits des
ministres et des grands officiers de la
couronne', *Archives de l'art français*, n.s., 24, 1969,
pp. 133–58

ZONNEVELD 2003
Jacques Zonneveld, *Sir Brooke Boothby: Rousseau's
Roving Baronet Friend*, Voorburg, 2003

# Lenders to the Exhibition

Her Majesty The Queen

AIX-EN-PROVENCE
Bibliothèque Méjanes
Musée Granet

AMHERST
Mead Art Museum, Amherst College

ANGERS
Musées d'Angers

AVIGNON
Musée Calvet

BERGAMO
Accademia Carrara

BERLIN
Skulpturensammlung, Stiftung
Preussische Schlösser und Gärten
Berlin-Brandenburg
Staatliche Museen zu Berlin,
Nationalgalerie

BERNE
Bernisches Historisches Museum

BIRMINGHAM
Birmingham Museum
and Art Gallery

BOSTON
Museum of Fine Arts

BREST
Musée des Beaux-Arts
The Andrew Brownsword Arts
Foundation. On long-term loan to the
Holburne Museum of Art, Bath

BRUSSELS
Musées Royaux d'Art et d'Histoire
Musées Royaux des Beaux-Arts
de Belgique

CAMBRIDGE
The Syndics of the
Fitzwilliam Museum

CHATSWORTH
Chatsworth Settlement Trustees

CLERMONT-FERRAND
Musée d'Art Roger-Quilliot

COMO
Villa Vigoni, Loveno di Menaggio

COPENHAGEN
Den Hirschsprungske Samling
Statens Museum for Kunst
Thorvaldsens Museum

CORK
Crawford Art Gallery

COVENTRY
The Herbert

DERBY
Derby Museums and Art Gallery

DIJON
Musée des Beaux-Arts

DUBLIN
National Gallery of Ireland

EDINBURGH
National Gallery of Scotland
Scottish National Portrait Gallery

FITCHBURG
Fitchburg Art Museum

GENEVA
Collection des Musées d'Art et
d'Histoire de la Ville de Genève
Institut et Musée Voltaire
Société des Arts

HAMBURG
Kunsthalle
Museum für Kunst und Gewerbe

ICKWORTH
The Bristol Collection
(The National Trust)

KENDAL
Abbot Hall Art Gallery

LANGRES
Musée d'Art et d'Histoire de Langres

LE MANS
Musée de Tessé

LILLE
Palais des Beaux-Arts

LONDON
The Trustees of
Dulwich Picture Gallery
Guildhall Art Gallery
The National Gallery
National Portrait Gallery
Royal Academy of Arts
Tate
Victoria and Albert Museum

LYONS
Musée des Beaux-Arts

MADRID
Banco de España
Museo Nacional del Prado
Museo de la Real Academia de Bellas
Artes de San Fernando
Museo Thyssen-Bornemisza
Palacio Real de Madrid

NANTES
Musée des Beaux-Arts

NEW YORK
The Metropolitan Museum of Art

NORWICH
Norwich Castle Museum
and Art Gallery

NUREMBERG
Germanisches Nationalmuseum

ORLÉANS
Musée des Beaux-Arts

PARIS
Musée de l'Armée
Musée des Arts Décoratifs
Musée Carnavalet-Histoire de Paris
Musée du Louvre

PHILADELPHIA
American Philosophical Society
Philadelphia Museum of Art

Private collection, Château de Craon,
Haroué (Meurthe-et-Moselle)

Private collection, Mount Stuart

Private collection, Switzerland

RENNES
Musée des Beaux-Arts

ROME
Museo di Roma, Palazzo Braschi
Promoteca Capitolina, Musei
Capitolini

SAINT-GENIEZ-D'OLT
Mairie

Yves Saint-Laurent and Pierre Bergé

Judy and Michael Steinhardt

STRASBOURG
Fondation Saint-Thomas

STUTTGART
Staatsgalerie

VERSAILLES
Musée National des Châteaux
de Versailles et de Trianon

VIENNA
Historisches Museum der Stadt Wien
Osterreichische Galerie Belvedere

WASHINGTON
National Gallery of Art

YORK
York Museums Trust
(York Art Gallery)

*and others who wish to remain anonymous*

# Photographic Acknowledgements

All works of art are reproduced by kind permission of the owners. Specific acknowledgements are as follows:

Aix-en-Provence: Bibliothèque Méjanes, cat.67

Aix-en-Provence: Musée Granet/ Bernard Terlay, cat.46

Angers: © Musées d'Angers/ David, cat.153

Aranjuez: Palacio Real, fig.2

Bath: © The Andrew Brownsword Arts Foundation, cat.86

Bergamo: Accademia Carrara, cat.113

Berlin: © BPK, distr. RMN/ Mai & Kilger, cats 58 and 59; BPK, distr. RMN/Saczewski, fig.8

Birmingham: Museum and Art Gallery, cat.151

Boston: © 2007 Museum of Fine Arts, cats 42, 77 and 132

Brussels: Musées royaux d'Art et d'Histoire, cat.49

Brussels: Musées royaux des Beaux-Arts de Belgique, cat.144

Cambridge: © Fitzwilliam Museum, University of Cambridge, cats 85 and 133

Chatsworth: © The Devonshire Collection, Chatsworth. Reproduced by permission of the Chatsworth Settlement Trustees, cat.90

Clermont-Ferrand: Musée Roger-Quilliot, cats 8 and 123

Copenhagen: Hirschsprungske Samling/Petersen, cat.81

Copenhagen: Statens Museum for Kunst, cats 82 and 108

Copenhagen: © Thorvaldsens Museum/Ole Woldbye, cat.80; Klemp, cat.110; Larsen cat.120

Cork: Crawford Art Gallery, cat.122

Coventry: The Herbert Art Gallery and Museum, cat.4

Derby: Derby Museums and Art Gallery, cat.136

Dijon: Musée des Beaux-Arts, cat.20; Jay, cat.19

Dublin: National Gallery of Ireland, cats 74 and 95, fig.66

Edinburgh: © The National Gallery of Scotland, cats 31 and 40

Edinburgh: © Scottish National Portrait Gallery, cats 41 and 48; Antonia Reeve, cat.55

Florence: Galleria dell'Accademia/ Battaglini, fig.69

Florence: © Photo Scala, figs 52 and 59

Fox, Roy, cat.103

Geneva: © Musée d'Art et Histoire, Ville de Genève/Yves Siza, cat.131

Geneva: © Société des Arts de Genève/Maurice Aeschimann, cat.65

Geneva: Bibliothèque Universitaire de Genève/Meylan, cat.50

Hamburg: Kunsthalle, cat.111

Hamburg: Museum für Kunst und gewerbe, cat.138

Ickworth: The National Trust, cat.35

Karlsruhe: Staatliche Kunsthalle, fig.28

Kendal: Abbot Hall Art Gallery, cat.124

Langres: Musée d'Art et d'Histoire/ Jay, cat.53

Le Mans: Musée de Tessé, cat.92

London: Apsley House, English Heritage, fig.45

London: © The British Museum, figs 37, 39 and 61

London: Courtauld Institute of Art, Conway Library, fig.12

London: Dulwich Picture Gallery, cat.130

London: The National Gallery, cat.148

London: © National Portrait Gallery, cats 18, 56 and 116, figs 7, 35, 38 and 58

London: © Royal Academy of Arts, London/Paul Highnam, cat.1; John Hammond, cats 2, 3, 71 and 72; cat.73, fig.34

London: The Royal Collection © 2006 Her Majesty Queen Elizabeth II, cats 13, 14, 22, 70 and 87/ A.C.Cooper Ltd, cat.7, fig.15

London: Sir John Soane's Museum, fig.9

London: © Tate 2007, cats 125 and 134, figs 44 and 56

London: V&A Images/Victoria and Albert Museum, cats 6, 83, 115 and 118

Lyons: Musée des Beaux-Arts, fig.62; Basset, cat.100, fig.67

Madrid: All rights reserved © Museo Nacional del Prado, cats 11, 32, 63 and 101

Madrid: © Museo Thyssen-Bornemisza, cat.147

Madrid: Patrimonio National, cat.10

Milan: Pinacoteca di Brera, Sovrintendenza per i Beni Artistici e Storici, fig.51

The Minneapolis Institute of Arts, fig.63

Nantes: Musée des Beaux-Arts, cat.106

New Haven: Yale Center for British Art (Paul Mellon Collection), figs 43 and 53

New York: © 2007 The Metropolitan Museum of Art, cats 27, 94, 102, 107 112 and 142

New York: The New York Public Library, cat.5

Norwich: © Norwich Castle Museum and Art Gallery, cat.88

Paris: AKG, figs 49 and 55

Paris: Bridgeman Art Library, figs 4, 17, 19, 20, 27, 41, 54 and 70

Paris: Collection de la Comédie-Française, fig.46

Paris: © Musée de l'Armée, Distr. RMN/Josse, cat 39; Segrette, cat.12; cat.39

Paris: Musée des Arts décoratifs/ Tholance, cat.96

Paris: Musée du Louvre, Paris/ Philibert, cats 54 and 68

Paris: Photothèque des musées de la ville de Paris/Degraces/Pierrain, cat.23; Pierrain, cat.66; Joffre, cat.140

Paris: © Rennes, Distr. RMN/ © Patrick Merret, cat.104

Paris: RMN, figs 33 and 40; RMN/ Arnaudet, figs 23 and 57; RMN/ Bellot, fig.32; RMN/Lewandowski, figs 3 and 30; RMN/Frank Raux, fig.22

Paris: © RMN/© droits réservés, cats 69 and 152; © RMN, cats 52, 121, 128 and 141; © RMN/ © Berizzi, cat.84; © RMN/Berizzi, cats 143 and 155; © RMN/Bernard, cat.93, figs 64 and 65; © RMN/ Blot, cats 28, 29, 34, 99 and 156, figs 29, 47 and 68; © RMN/ © Blot, cats 89 and 137; RMN/ Blot and Jean, cat.37; © RMN/ Ojéda, cats 9, 16, 44 and 51; © RMN/© Ojéda, cat.105

Philadelphia: American Philosophical Society, cat.43 and fig.36

Philadelphia Museum of Art/ Joseph Mikuliak, cat.33

Rebsamen, Stefan cat.145

Rennes: © Rennes, distr. RMN/ Deschamps, cat.47

Rome: Archivio Fotografico dei Musei Capitolini, cats 15 and 119

Rome: © Antonio Idini, cat.61

Saint-Geniez-d'Olt, Mairie, cat.117

Schaffhausen: Museum zu Allerheiligen, fig.13

Sevestre, cat.78

Stockholm: Nationalmuseum, fig.5

Strasbourg: Fondation Saint-Thomas, cat.76

Stuttgart: Staatsgalerie, cats 75 and 139; © Volker Naumann: fig.16

Tribes, Y., fig.72

Vienna: © Museum der Stadt, Vienna/Fotostudio Otto, cat.60

Vienna: Osterreichische Galerie Belvedere, cats 146 and 154

Washington: © 2007 Board of Trustees, National Gallery of Art, cats 24 and 135

Washington: The Phillips Collection, fig.31

Winterthur: Museum Oskar Reinhart am Stadtgarten, fig.6

York Museums Trust (York Art Gallery) cat.126

All references are to page numbers;
those in red type indicate catalogue plates,
and those in **bold** type indicate
essay illustrations

## A

Ab., Madame 304
Abbot, Lemuel Francis 360
Abington, Mrs **84**, 85
Abrantès, Duchesse d' 341
Académie Française 28
Académie des Inscriptions 28
Académie Royale des Beaux-Arts 157
Acton, Mrs Penelope Lee 247
Adams, Samuel 23, 24, 113, 122, 305
Adán Morlán, Juan
    *Charles IV, King of Spain* 63, 74, 290
Addington, Dr Thomas 222, 291
Addison, Joseph 350
Agoult, Marie d' 41, 363
Alba, Duchess of 329, 356
Alba, Don José Alvarez de Toledo y Gonzaga,
    Duque de 103–05, 149, 327
Albany, Duchess of 320
Albrizzi, Isabella Teotochi 300
albums, prints 55, 56
*Alcibiades' Dog* 383
Alembert, Jean le Rond d' 27, 340, 362, 382
Alexander, Robert 355
Alexander the Great 115
Alfieri, Vittorio 320
Algardi, Alessandro 304
allegorical portraits 226–43
Alston, Lady 85
Altamira, Don Vicente Joaquín Osorio
    de Moscoso y Guzmán, Conde de
    92, 326–7
Alvarez y Ximénez, Antonio 331
American Philosophical Society 341
American Revolution 15, 23, 266, 305
Amerling, Friedrich von
    *Amalie Klein, née von Henikstein* **285**,
        290–1
    *Bertha von Neuhaus* 290
    *Franz I in the Uniform of a Prussian General*
        290
    *Kaiser Franz I of Austria in Imperial Robes*
        290
Ames, Joseph 55
Amherst, Sir Jeffrey 52, **52**, 53, 113, 118, 369
Amsterdam 54
Amyot, Jacques 112
Andries, Lise 312
Angelo, Henry 55
Angiviller, Comte d' 27, 34, 316, 363, 375,
    379
Angoulême, Duc d' 358
antique portraits 210–25
Antonmarchi, Dr 385
Apelles 114
*Apollo Belvedere* 44, 114, 306, 351, 383
*Apotheosis of Homer* 385
*Apotheosis of the Emperor Claudius* 385
Argyll, Duke of 293
Ariosto, Ludovico 292
*Aristophanes and Terence* 391
Aristotle 375
Arkwright family 204, 396
Arkwright, Richard 83, **83**, 396
Armistead, Mrs 360
Arnao, Vicente González 330
Arnim, Bettina von 368
Arnould, Sophie 31, 239, 339, 388
Arrieta, Dr **158**, 159–60
artists' portraits 154–79
Artois, Comte d' 358
Athanassoglou-Kallmyer, Nina 314
Aubert, Marcel 362
Aucourt de Saint-Just, Madame d' 246, **247**
Aucourt de Saint-Just, Monsieur d' 185, **248**,
    249, 250
Audéoud, Anne 343
Augé, Jean-Louis 327
Augsburg 54
Augustus, Emperor 385
Augustus III of Poland, Elector of Saxony
    356

Aurelius, Marcus 21, 62, 212
Austen, Jane 250
Azara, José Nicolas de 219, 300, 356, 390–1

## B

Bacelli, Giovanna 85, **85**
Bachelier, Jean-Jacques 392
Baciocchi, Elisa 30, 214
Bacon, Sir Francis 63, 360
Baird, Sir David 365
Ballanche, Pierre-Simon 300
Banks, Joseph 133, 141, 369–70
Banks, Thomas 34, 342
    *Dr Thomas Addington* 222, 291
    *Penelope Boothby* 30
Banks-Hodgkinson, Robert 370
Bann, Stephen 216
Barante, Prosper de 334
Barbier, Baron Raoul 15
Bardou, Emmanuel 335
Bardua, Caroline
    *Caspar David Friedrich* 21, **22**
Bariatinskaya, Princess Maria Feodorovna
    217, 384–5
Bariatinski, Prince Ivanovich 384
Barras, Paul 324
Barry, James 383
    *Burke and Barry in the Characters of Ulysses
        and a Companion Fleeing from the Cave
        of Polyphemus* 21, 231, 233, 291–2, 369
    *Crowning the Victors at Olympia* 292
    *The Distribution of Premiums by the Society
        of Artists* 382
    *Self-portrait as Timanthes* 22, 169, 267,
        292–3
Bartolini, Lorenzo 30, 31, 33, 214, 228,
    380, 386
    *Elizabeth Albana Upton, Marchioness of Bristol*
        108, 293
    *Emma and Julia Campbell Dancing* 30, 252,
        **253**, 254
Bartolozzi, Francesco 301
Bathurst, Benjamin 321
Bathurst, Peter 321
Batoni, Pompeo 130, 133, 320, 374
    *Colonel William Gordon* 334
    *John Chetwynd Talbot* 294
    *John Staples* 147, 294
    *Thomas Dundas* 294
    *Wills Hill, Earl of Hillsborough,
        later 1st Marquis of Downshire*
        142, 144–5, 293–4
Baudelaire, Charles 44, 47
Baverstock, Jean 315
Beauharnais, Hortense de 184, 323
Beaumont family 182, **183**
Beauvau, Princesse de 363
Bedford, Duke of 28, 29
Beechey, William 60, 382
Belgiojoso, Princesse de 41
Bellangé, Pierre-Antoine 363
Bellay, F. 326
Belley, Jean-Baptiste 319
Belot, Michel 150, 316–17
*Belvedere Torso* 383, 393
Bendz, Wilhelm 316
    *A Young Artist (Ditlev Blunck)
        Examining a Sketch in a Mirror* 159, 177,
        294–5, 349
Bergeret, P. N. 347
Berlioz, Hector 312
Bernadotte, Jean-Baptiste 32
Bernini, Gianlorenzo 35, 62
    *Costanza Bonarelli* 382
Bernis, Cardinal de 323

Berry, Duc de 323
Berry, Duchesse de 313, 363
Berry, Mary 293
Berthaud, Marie 303
Berthier, General 297
Bertin, Louis-François 24, 41, 48, 49, **49**, 83, 86, 287, 346–7
Bertin, Rose 297
Besenval, Baron de 358
Besing, Thomas 355
Bessborough, Earl of 305
Bestland, Cantelowe 382
Bethmann, Simon Moritz von 368
Bettkober, Heinrich 367
Biedermeier period 271, 303, 383, 387
Bienaimé, Luigi 385
Billington, Mrs 228
Bingham, William 384
Bissen, Herman Wilhelm 384, 385, 386
Black, Joseph 364
Bleschamp, Alexandrine de **132**, 228
Blondel, Merry-Joseph 317
Blunck, Ditlev 159, 177, 294–5
Boichot, Guillaume 375
Boilly, Louis-Léopold 316, 387
  *Isabey and His Family* 295
  *Madame d'Aucourt de Saint-Just* 246, **247**
  *Monsieur d'Aucourt de Saint-Just* 185, **248**, 249, 250
  *A Reunion of Artists in Isabey's Studio* 162–3, 295–6, 316, 323
Boisgelin, Mgr de 342
Boisserée, Sulpiz 368
Boizot, Louis-Simon 323, 375
  *Marie-Antoinette, Queen of France* 63, 73, 296–7
  *Racine* 368
Bonaparte, Charlotte 310
Bonaparte, Joseph 310, 359
Bonaparte, Louis 184
Bonaparte, Maria Laetitia Ramolino (Madame Mère) 30, 102, 323–4, 385
Bonaparte, Zénaïde 310, 359
Bonchamps, Marquis de **115**, 116, 334
Bonington, Richard Parkes 330
Bonnassieux, Jean Marie 375
Bonnemaison, Ferréol 309
Boothby, Sir Brooke 185, 250, 256–7, 336, 395–6
Boothby, Penelope 30
Boquet, Louis-René 339
Borbón, Don Luis de 331
Bordes, Philippe 377
Borghese, Prince 32
Borghese, Princess Pauline 32, 36, **36**, 228
*Borghese Gladiator* 383
Boselli, Orfeo 385
Bosio, François-Joseph 363
Bossi, Lodovico 383
Boston Tea Party 304
Bouchardon, Edmé 213, 302
Boucher, François 22, 332, 389
Boulanger, Louis
  *Achille Dévéria* 45, **46**
Bourbon-Condé family 357
Bourge, Auguste-Romain de 343
Bourgeois, Francis Peter 350
Bourgogne, Duchesse de 362
Boutard, Jean-Baptiste 347
Boydell 55
Boze, Joseph 315
  *Honoré-Gabriel Riqueti, Comte de Mirabeau* 16, **126**, 297–8
Braddyll family 182, 186, 374–5
Brandes, Georg Friedrich 56
Brant, Joseph 250
Breda, Carl Fredrik von
  *The Swedish Crown Prince, Gustav IV Adolf* 19, **19**
Bréa 315
Bremer, C. 55
Bridan, Charles-Antoine 319

Bristol, Elizabeth Albana Upton, Marchioness of 108, 293
Bristol, Frederick Hervey, 4th Earl of 229–30
Broche, Ignace 303
Bromley, H. 55
Brongniart, Louise and Alexandre 343
Brooke, Jonas 336
Brown, Henry Kirke 302
Brown, Lancelot 'Capability' 249
Browne, George and Mary 248
Brummel, Beau 314
Brun, Ida 254, 385
Bryant, Julius 291
Buffon, Georges Louis Leclerc, Comte de **131**, 132, 152, 340, 353, 354
Buhner, Madame 337
Buller, Francis 305
Burch, Edward 382, 398
Burke, Edmund 21, 233, 291–2, 293, 372
Burney, Frances (Fanny) 322, 364
Burns, Robert 306
Burton, Decimus 352
Burton, Robert 395
busts 26, 28–34, 63, 82, 212–16
Bute, John Stuart, 3rd Earl of 84–5, 371, 397
Bute, Mary, Countess of 84–5, 96, 247, 371, 381
Buxton family 184, 189, 392
Byam family 187, 321
Byres, James 294
Byron, Lord 213–14

# C

Cabarrús, Conde Francisco de 326
Cabet, Paul 377
Cacault, François 301
Caffieri, Jean-Jacques 28, 35, 172, 340, 361, 392–3
  *Jean de Rotrou* 112, **113**
  *Molière* 368
  *Monument to Madame Favart* 303
Callet, Antoine-François 60
  *Louis XVI* 16, 72, 298
Calonne, Comte Charles-Alexandre de 82, 93, 328, 375, 388–9
Calviac, Paul-François Des Hours de 205, 333
Cambridge, Trinity College 28
Campbell, Emma and Julia 30, 252, **253**, 254
Camuccini, Vincenzo 62, 351
Candido, Francesco Saverio 299
Canova, Antonio 22, 27, 30, 32, 33, 34, 35, 63, 113, 157, 228, 293, 302, 336, 347, 348, 351, 381, 384, 385, 387, 390
  *Alexandrine de Bleschamp as Terpsichore* **132**, 133, 228
  *Apollo* 299
  *Cicognara* 300
  *Domenico Cimarosa* 21, 213, 223, 299–300
  *First Consul* 33
  *Ideal Head: Helen* 300
  *Ideal Head: Juliette Récamier as Beatrice* 243, 254, 300
  *Madame Mère* 385
  *Napoleon* 299
  *Napoleon as Mars the Peacemaker* **214**, 215
  *Palamedes* 133
  *Pauline Borghese as Venus Victrix* 36, **36**, 228, 381
  *Perseus* 299
  *Pope Pius VII* 62, 79, 298–9, 300
  *Sartori* 300
  *Theseus Vanquishing the Minotaur* 347
Caraman, Thérésia Cabarrus, Comtesse de (Madame Tallien) 251, 263, 324

Caravaggio
  *Deposition from the Cross* 312
Carlini, Agostino 301
  Model for an equestrian statue of George III 63, 65, 301, 383
Carmona, Manuel Salvador 356
Caroline, Queen 351
Caroline Amalia, Princess 385
Carpentier, Paul-Claude-Michel 376
Carpentiers, Adrien 355
Carracci, Annibale 27, 299, 375
Carradori, Francesco 299
Castiglione, Baldassare 39, 49, 253, 254
Castner foundry 368
*Castor and Pollux* 380
Cathelineau 115–16, 334
Catherine II the Great, Empress of Russia 16, 18, 30, 33, 60, 63, 70, 71, 214, 318–19, 348, 360, 379, 381–2, 384
Caulfield, James 55
Cavendish, Lady Georgiana 191, 373–4
Caylus, Comte de 296, 344
Ceracchi, Giuseppe 21, 32, 299
  *Anne Seymour Damer as the Muse of Sculpture* 21, **229**
  *George Washington* 218, 301–2
  *Reynolds* 35
Cézanne, Paul 14, 15
Chalier, Joseph 314
Chambers, Sir William 372, 382, 383, 397
Champmartin
  *Gustave Wasa* 39
Chantrey, Sir Francis 27, 29, 31, 34, 63, 212, 213, 301, 352
  *Arthur Wellesley, 1st Duke of Wellington* **112**, 112–13
  *Dorothy Jordan and Her Children* 30, **31**
  *Edward Johnstone* 213, 282, 302
  *John Raphael Smith* 178, 302
  *The Robinson Sisters* 30
Chardin, Jean Baptiste Siméon 15, 318, 332, 361
Charlemagne, Emperor 344
Charlemont, Lord 366
Charles I, King of England 83, 301, 397
Charles III, King of Spain 61, 325, 326, 327, 356
Charles IV, King of Spain 17, 61, 63, 74, 290, 320, 326, 327, 328, 330, 356
Charles X, King of France 337, 346
Charles Eugène, Duke of Württemberg 383
Charlotte, Queen 17–18, 60, 61, 67, 183–4, 188, 349, 355, 371–2, 396–7
Chassériau, Théodore
  *Father Dominique Lacordaire* 40, 41
Chateaubriand, François-René de 251, 300, 313, 322, 323
Chatham, William Pitt, Earl of 82, 305
Châtre, Comte de la 389
Châtre, Comtesse de la 98, 389
Chatsworth, Derbyshire 28
Chaudet, Denis-Antoine 31, 173, 213, 214, 295, 309, 316, 354, 375, 385, 386
  *Belisarius* 303
  *Cyparissus Weeping for His Stag* 303
  *Friendship Enchaining Love* 303
  *Napoleon the Legislator* 316
  *Patriotic Duty* 316
  *Paul and Virginie in the Cradle* 303
  *A Woman Holding a Portrait of Her Husband in Her Arms* 197, 302–3
Chaussard, J. B. 344
Cherubini, Luigi 47
Chesterfield, Lord 307
Chezal-Benôit, Abbé de 332
children, family portraits 182–5
Chinard, Joseph 31
  *Fanny Perrin, with the Attributes of Psyche, Playing with a Wreath of Flowers* 185, 234, 304
  *Juliette Récamier* 251, 252, 304, 381
  *Madame Chinard* 201, 303–4
  *Perseus Rescuing Andromeda* 303
  *Self-portrait* 33

Chinard, Madame (Antoinette Perret) 201, 303–4
Chinchón, Condesa de 332
Chodowiecki, Daniel Niklaus 378
Chopin, Frédéric 312
Chrysippus 369
Cicero 214, 316, 340, 360
Cicognara, Leopoldo 300
Cimarosa, Domenico 21, 213, 223, 299–300
Clarke, Edgard 379
Clarke, George 55
Clarke, Sir Simon 302
Clarke, Susanna Farnham 305
Claude Lorrain 246, 392
Claudot, Jean-Baptiste Charles 323
Clayton, Mrs Sarah 23, 148, 394
Clement XIV, Pope 34, 299
Clemente, Francesco 14
Clerk, Sir John and Lady 248, **249**, 254
Close, Chuck 14
Clunes, Major William 84, 120, 365–6
Cobham, Lord 213
Cochin, Charles-Nicolas 361
Coke, Daniel Parker 131, 249–50, 259, 394–5
Coke, Reverend d'Ewes 130–1, 249–50, 259, 394–5
Coke, Hannah 130–1, 249–50, 259, 394–5
collections, portrait prints 55–6
Collin d'Harleville 342
Collot, Marie-Anne 340
Comédie Française 112
Condé, Prince de 353, 360, 363
Condorcet, Marie Jean Antoine Nicolas Caritat, Marquis de 30, 123, 319, 332, 341
Conolly, Thomas 294
Consalvi, Cardinal Ercole 299
Constable, John
  *The Hay Wain* 313
  *View of the Stour* 313
Constant, Benjamin 390
Conti, Louis-François de, Prince de 82, 91, 356–7
Conti, Louis-François Joseph de 356–7
Cook, Captain James 133, 370
Copia, Jacques-Louis 131, 312, 316
Copley, John Singleton
  *The Death of the Earl of Chatham* 82, 305
  *Major Hugh Montgomerie* 114, 121, 306
  *Portrait of the Sitwell Children* 391
  *Samuel Adams* 23, 24, 113, 122, 304–5
  *Sir William Pepperell and His Family* 359
  *The Tribute Money* 383
  *William Murray, 1st Earl of Mansfield* 82, 89, 305
copyright, prints 52–3
Corday, Charlotte 311
Cordier, Charles 344
Corelli, Arcangelo 299
Corneille, Pierre 352, 353, 392–3
Cornelius, Peter von 317
Cornwallis, Marquis 28
Coster, Adam de 373
Cosway, Richard 383, 398
Cotes, Francis
  *The Hon. Lady Stanhope and the Countess of Effingham as Diana and Her Companion* 21, 237, 306–7
Cotta, Wilhelmine von 252, 254, 262, 380–1
Coussmaker, Colonel George 374
Coustou, Nicolas 362
Coysevox, Antoine 362
Craon, Princesse de 363
Crébillon, Prosper Jolyot de 352, 353
Créqui, Marquise de 342
Crespi, Luigi 356
Cubism 15
cultural portraits 128–33
Cunningham, Allan 291
Cuzin, Jean-Pierre 369

# D

Daguerre, Louis 24
Dahl, Michael 373
Damer, Anne Seymour 21, 228, **229**
Dance, George 383, 397
Dance, Nathaniel 397
Daniele da Volterra 373
Dannecker, Johann Heinrich 31, 380
  *Friedrich von Schiller* 31, **32**
  *Self-portrait* 170, 307–8
Dannery 300
Dante Alighieri 300
Danton, Georges Jacques 314
Dardel, Robert-Guillaume 353, 354
  *Descartes Disentangling Chaos...* 353
Dashwood, Anne 374
David, Jacques-Louis 22, 23, 43, 62–4, 113,
  157, 212, 214, 268, 283, 293, 296, 299, 316,
  317, 320, 323, 324, 332, 333, 334, 337, 345,
  346, 351, 359, 360, 376, 376–8, 377, 379,
  380, 381, 384, 386, 392, 393
  *Alexandre Lenoir* 311
  *Ange-Pauline-Charlotte Ramel de Nogaret,*
    *née Pancoucke* 24, **24**
  *Anger of Achilles* 311
  *Anne-Marie-Louise Thélusson, Comtesse de Sorcy*
    308, 389
  *Antoine-Laurent Lavoisier and His Wife* 311
  *Comte de Turenne* 310
  *Comtesse Daru* 345
  *The Comtesse Vilain XIIII and Her Daughter*
    310, 345
  *Cupid and Psyche* 310
  *The Death of Marat* 20, 113, 117, 267, 311–12
  *The Death of Socrates* 312
  *The Emperor Napoleon in His Study at the*
    *Tuileries* 17, 56, 95, 309–10, 310, 311
  *General Etienne-Maurice Gérard, Marshal*
    *of France* 266, 273, 310
  *Juliette de Villeneuve* 24, 266, 274, 310–11,
    380
  *Le Pelletier de Saint-Fargeau on His Deathbed*
    311
  *Madame Charles-Pierre Pécoul* 308
  *Madame Raymond de Verninac* 308
  *Madame Récamier* 252, **252**, 381
  *Napoleon Crossing the Alps* 114, **114**, 309,
    334–5
  *Oath of the Horatii* 359, 389
  *Oath of the Tennis Court* 349
  *Robertine Tourteau, Marquise de Orvilliers*
    99, 308
David, Jules 312
David d'Angers, Pierre-Jean 31, 34, 36,
  48, 116, 378
  *Funerary Monument to the Marquis*
    *de Bonchamps* 115, **115**
  *Grand Condé* 335
  *Johann Wolfgang von Goethe* 33, **33**, 313
  *Lamartine* 313
  *Niccolò Paganini* 46–7, 268–9, 284,
    312–13
  *Talma* 368
Davies, Thomas 369
Day, Thomas 396
De Fabris, Giuseppe 299
De Hemptinne family 271, 275, 359–60, 386
De Lathuy, Marie-Antoinette 359
De Rossi, Angelo 299
De Wailly, Charles 194, 360–1
  *Reorganisation of the Salon Carré in the Louvre*
    361
De Wailly, Madame 195, 361
Debay, Jean-Baptiste *père*
  *Girodet* 375, 376
  *Gros* 376
Debucourt, P. L. 316
Decaisne, Henri
  *La Malibran as Desdemona* 44
Dedreux, Alfred and Elisabeth 209, 325
Degas, Edgar 331
Delacroix, Charles 328

Delacroix, Eugène 44–5, 48, 290, 328, 387
  *General Charles Delacroix at Louroux* 313
  *Louis-Auguste Schwiter* 44, 45, 252–3,
    279, 313–14
  *Madame Simon* 44–5, **45**
  *The Massacre at Chios* 41, 330
  *Paganini* 46, **47**
  *Self-portrait as Ravenswood* 231
Delaroche, Paul 41
  *Comte de Pourtalès-Gorgier* 41, **41**
Delaval 335
Delécluze, Jean-Etienne 346
Delestre, J. B. 333
Della Bella, Stefano 374
Della Gatta, Xavier 336
Della Porta 35
Demidoff, Anatole 324
Demidoff, Princess Mathilde **38**, 39
Demosthenes 214, 360
Denon, Dominique Vivant 27–8, 335, 364
Desaix de Veygoux, Louis-Jean 304
Deseine, Claude-André
  *Mirabeau* 113, 127, 314–15
Deseine, Louis-Pierre 315
  *Johann Joachim Winckelmann* 131, 138,
    315–16
Desmarais, Jean-Baptiste
  *Denis-Antoine Chaudet* 173, 303, 316, 386
Desportes, Ulysse 301
Dévéria, Achille 45, **46**
Devillers, Hippolyte 344
Devis, Arthur 293
Devonshire, Georgiana, Duchess of
  84, 183, 191, 373–4
Devonshire, William Cavendish, 5th Duke of
  373
Devonshire, William Cavendish, 6th Duke of
  29–30
*Diane de Gabies* 385
Diderot, Denis 18, 21, 32, 33, 37, 82, 84, 131,
  138, 182, 296, 319, 332, 340, 341, 361, 363,
  379, 381, 382
Disraeli, Benjamin 352
Doell, Friedrich W. 131, 315
Domenichino
  *St John the Evangelist* 375
dotted plates, prints 53
Dou, Gérard
  *A Hermit Reading the Bible* 379
Douglas, Marquis of 309
Drolling, Martin
  *Michel Belot* 150, 316–17
  *Portrait of the Artist's Son* 316
Drolling, Michel-Martin 316
Dryden, John 229
Du Barry, Madame 296, 297, 393
du Cayla, Comte 363
du Cayla, Comtesse (Zoë-Victoire Talon)
  85, 109, 310, 363
Du Louvre, Augustin 303
Dublin, Trinity College 28
Dubufe, Claude-Marie 40, 43
  *Apollo and Cyparissa* 317
  *The Artist's Family* 182, 200, 317, 359
  *Reading* 317
  *Young Woman in Pain* 317
Dubufe, Joséphine-Anne 317
Ducreux, Rose
  *Self-portrait with Harp* 311
Dudley, Henry Bate 321
Dudley and Ward, Viscount 305
Duménillet, Mademoiselle 317
Dumont, Augustin 375
Dumont, Jacques-Edmé
  *Madame Dumont, the Artist's Mother* 206,
    317–18
Dumont, Jacques-Philippe 314
Dumont, Madame (Marie-Françoise
  Bertault) 206, 317–18
Dumont, Marie-Nicole
  *The Artist at Her Occupations* 159
Dundas, Thomas 294
Dupaty, President 342

Duplessis, Joseph-Siffred 60, 388
Dürer, Albrecht
  *Portrait of Emperor Maximilian I* 378
  *Portrait of Michael Wolgemut* 378

# E

Eardley, Lord 349
Eckersberg, Christoffer Wilhelm 337, 349, 387
Edinburgh 212
Edward Augustus, Duke of York 293
Effingham, Countess of 21, 237, 306–7
Effingham, 3rd Earl of 307
Eggers, Friedrich 368
Eglinton, Lord 371
Elizabeth Petrovna, Empress of Russia 318
Eltz family 253, 271, 277, 391
engravings 53
Enlightenment 86, 132, 156, 182, 246, 310, 319,
  322, 326, 328, 340, 341, 342, 364, 366, 380,
  382
Enville, Duchesse d' 30, 341–2
*Epicurus and Metrodorus* 391
equestrian monuments 62–3, 114–15, 212
Eriksen, Vigilius 382
  *Catherine II, Empress of Russia* 60, 71,
    318–19
  *Portrait of Catherine II in Front of a Mirror*
    319
Espagnac, Abbé de 314
Espercieux, Jean-Joseph
  *The Abbé Raynal* 222, 319
Esquirol, J.-E.-D. 326
Esteve y Marqués, Agustín 329
  *Don Mariano San Juan y Pinedo, Conde*
    *Consorte de La Cimera* 202, 319–20
Eugénie, Empress 385
Evans, Richard
  *Henri-Christophe, King of Haiti* **16**, 17
Eyck, Jan van 344

# F

Fabre, François-Xavier 157
  *Allen Smith Before a View of Florence* 130,
    255, 320–1
  *The Duchess of Feltre and Her Children* 379
Fabre d'Eglantine 332
Falconet, Etienne Maurice 63, 340, 362
family portraits 180–209, 270
Farel, François 333
Farington, Joseph 291, 350, 374, 382, 383, 393,
  397
Feltre, Elfride Clarke de 207, 378–9
Feltre, Henri Jacques Guillaume, Duke of
  378, 379
Fénelon, François de Salignac de la Mothe
  397
Feoli, Vincenzo
  *Galleria dei Busti, Museo Pio-Clementino*
    **215**, 216
Ferdinand IV, King of Spain 299, 327
Ferdinand VII, King of Spain 16, 60, 75,
  320, 329–30
Fernán-Núñez, Condesa de 329
Ferrer, Manuela Alvarez Coíñas Thomas de
  281, 331–2
Ferrer y Cafranga, Francisco Javier 331
Ferrer y Cafranga, Joaquín María 280, 330–1

Ferrer y Cafranga, José Joaquín 331
Feuchtmüller, Rupert 391
Feugères, Baron de 26
Fielding, Anthony Copley 330
Fielding brothers 314
Fisher, Kitty 53, 229
Fitzgerald, Lord Edward 322
Fitzgerald, Lady Margaretta 293–4
Fitzwilliam, 4th Earl 360
Flandrin, Hippolyte
  *Napoleon III* 310
Flaxman, John 133, **133**, 291, 303
  *Monument to the Earl of Mansfield* 28, **28**
Florence 34, 130
Floridablanca, Conde de 88, 325–6
Fontaine, Pierre 344
Forbin, Comte de 345, 346
Fourier, Charles 44, **44**
Fourment, Suzanne 44
Fournaise, Alphonsine 15
Fournier-Sarlovèze, General 334
Fox, Charles James 28, 30, 31, 214, 220, 221,
  230, 322, 360, 373
Foy, General 116
Franklin, Benjamin 52, **52**, 82, 124, 125, 332,
  339–40, 341, 355
Franz I, Emperor of Austria 291
Frederick, Duke of York 18, 396–7
Frederika, Princess of Prussia 30, 252, 254,
  261, 380
Frémiet, Louis 377
Frémiet, Sophie 377
French Revolution 16, 42, 86, 132, 156,
  266, 295, 296, 297, 298, 314, 320, 326,
  365, 388
Freud, Lucian 14
Friedrich II, King of Prussia 301, 341, 367
Friedrich, Caspar David 21, **22**, 317, 378
Friedrich-Wilhelm II, King of Prussia 380
Friedrich-Wilhelm III, King of Prussia
  335, 367
Fries, Joseph Johann, Graf von 146, 347–8
Fuseli, Henry 291, 336, 358

# G

Gaborit, Jean-René 361
Gabriel, Infante Don 328
Gaignières, François-Roger de 55
Gainsborough, Thomas 15, 60, 247, 314, 333,
  336, 397
  *Mr and Mrs Andrews* 247
  *George Byam with His Wife Louisa and*
    *Their Daughter Selina* 187, 321
  *Giovanna Bacelli* 85, **85**
  *Lady Alston* 85
  *Mrs Sheridan* 247, 258, 321–2
Galbaccio 42–3, 45–6, 47
Gale-Braddyll, Wilson 374
Gall, Franz Joseph 36, 313
Gardiner, Luke 370
Garrick, David 229, 293
Gauffier, Louis 320
Gauldrée-Boilleau, Madame 304
Gautier, Théophile 48, 347
Genlis, Comtesse de 385
Genod, Michel Philibert 30
George III, King of England 16, 18, 51, 60,
  61, 63, 65, 66, 68, 183, 291, 293, 301, 305,
  318, 349–50, 351, 355, 366, 371–2, 383,
  384, 397
George IV, King of England 16, 18, 60,
  61, **62**, 62, 63, 77, 212, 302, 351–2,
  381–2, 397
Gérard, General Etienne-Maurice 266, 273,
  310

Gérard, François 183–4, 295, 309, 310, 334, 346, 363, 381, 386
  *Belisarius* 323
  *Corinne at Cape Misenum* 228, **230**
  *Entry of Henri IV into Paris* 310
  *Jean-Baptiste Isabey and His Daughter Alexandrine* 185, 190, 322–3
  *Madame Barbier-Walbonne* 324
  *Madame Récamier* 251–2, 324
  *Maria Laetitia Ramolino Bonaparte, 'Madame Mère'* 30, 102, 323–4
  *Napoleon I in Coronation Robes* 309
  *Queen Hortense and Her Son, the Prince Royal* 324
  *Thérésia Cabarrus, Comtesse de Caraman* 251, 263, 324
Gérard, Marguerite 361
Gérard, Michel 193, 387
Géricault, Théodore 45, 334, 387
  *Alfred and Elisabeth Dedreux* 209, 325
  *Alfred Dedreux Seated in a Landscape* 325
  *D'Alfred et Elise Dedreux* 325
  *Elisabeth Dedreux Seated in a Landscape* 325
  *The Raft of the Medusa* 326
  *The Woman with Gambling Mania* 45, **46**
Gibbs, Samuel 31
Gigoux, Jean
  *Charles Fourier* 44, **44**
Gilbert and George 14
Gillet, Nicolas-François 381
Gillray, James
  *Metallic Tractors* 53, **53**
Gilly, Friedrich 21, 307
Gilpin, Revd William 250
Giorgione 43, 47
Girardet, Jean 323
Girardin, Delphine de 38, 48
Girardon, François 387
Girodet, Anne-Louis 251, 269–70, 286, 296, 319, 333, 334, 335, 375–6
  *Mademoiselle Lange as Danaë* 230–1, **231**
Giroust, Jean Antoine Theodore
  *Mademoiselle d'Orléans Taking a Harp Lesson* 311
Gisburne, Revd Thomas 248
Glorious Revolution (1688) 246
Gluck, Christoph Willibald von 339–40
Gobelins factory 312
Godoy, Manuel de 290, 320, 326, 327
Goethe, Johann Wolfgang von 20–2, 31–3, **33**, 130, 131, 143, 213, 303, 308, 313, 320, 338, 347, 348, 355, 358, 367–8
Gois, Etienne Pierre Adrien 303, 316
Goldsmith, Oliver 248–9
Golitsin, Dimitri Alexeyevich 381
Golitsin, Prince F. N. 381, 382
Gonon, Honoré 46, 313
Gordon, Colonel William 334
Gougenot, Abbé Louis 50
Goussaut, Claude 381
Gower, Granville Leveson-Gower, 2nd Earl 376
Goya y Lucientes, Francisco de 17, 23, 61, 85, 156–7, 290, 320, 356
  *Caprices* 328
  *Don José Alvarez de Toledo y Gonzaga, XIII Duque de Alba and XI Marqués de Villafranca* 103, 104–5, 149, 327–8
  *Don José Moñino y Redondo I, Conde de Floridablanca* 88, 325–6
  *Don Manuel Osorio Manrique de Zuñiga* 184, 203, 327
  *Don Vicente Joaquín Osorio de Moscoso y Guzmán, XI Conde de Altamira* 92, 326–7
  *Ferdinand VII in Royal Robes* 16, 60, 75, 329–30
  *Ferdinand Guillemardet* 23–4, 82, 87, 328–9
  *Joaquín María Ferrer y Cafranga* 280, 330–1
  *Manuela Alvarez Coiñas Thomas de Ferrer* 281, 331–2

  *The Marquesa de Villafranca Painting Her Husband* 103, 329–30
  *Self-portrait with Dr Arrieta* **158**, 160
Graff, Anton 307
  *The Artist's Family in Front of a Portrait of Johann Georg Sulzer* 19–20, **20**
Granby, John Manners, Marquis of 83–4, 366, 369
Grand Tour 130, 133, 293, 294, 320, 370, 374, 381, 390
Granet, François-Marius 251
Granger, James 55
Green, Valentine 50–1, **51**, 52, 55
Greuze, Jean-Baptiste 18, 317, 362
  *Claude Henri Watelet* 137, 332
  *The Emperor Severus Reprimanding His Son Caracalla* 332
  *Etienne Jeaurat* 346
  *A Girl Weeping over Her Dead Bird* 332
  *The Marriage Contract* 332
Griffith, Elizabeth 20
Grimm, Friedrich Melchior, Baron von 26, 332, 362, 379
Gros, Antoine-Jean 39, 60, 63, 309, 329, 364, 375, 376, 377
  *Battle of Aboukir* 333
  *Bonaparte at the Ponte d'Arcole* 334, 335
  *General Lasalle at the Siege of Stettin* 113, 119, 333–4
  *Joachim Murat, King of Naples* 334, 335
  *Napoleon Bonaparte Visiting the Plague-Stricken in Jaffa* 333
  *Napoleon Distributing Swords of Honour ...* 334
  *Napoleon on the Battlefield of Eylau* 334
  *Paul-François Des Hours de Calviac* 205, 333
  *Portrait of Second Lieutenant Charles Legrand* 334
  *Wounded Cavalryman Leaving the Firing Line* 334
Guérin, Paulin 334
Guérin, Pierre-Narcisse 316, 325, 375, 387
  *Henri de La Rochejacquelin* 115, 267–8, 272, 334–5
Guillemardet, Ferdinand 23–4, 82, 87, 328–9
Guillon, Guillaume 337
Gustav III, King of Sweden 392
Gustav IV Adolf, Crown Prince of Sweden 19, **19**


## H

Hackert, Jacob Philippe 320
Hadrian, Emperor 26, 386
Hagemann, Carl Friedrich 367
  *Immanuel Kant* 21, 218, 335–6
  *Naiad* 335
Hale, Mrs 228
Hall, Pierre Adolphe 357
Hamilton, Duke of 385
Hamilton, Lady Emma 229, 254, 385
Hamilton, Gavin 390
Hamilton, Hugh Douglas
  *Lieutenant Richard Mansergh St George* 22, 185, 196, 336–7
Hamilton, William 293
Hancock, John 304
Hansen, Constantin
  *The Artist's Sisters Signe and Henriette Reading a Book* 208, 271, 337
Harewood House, Yorkshire 228
Haudebourt-Lescot, Hortense
  *Le Choix d'un chapeau* 338
  *Self-portrait* 179, 337–8
Haward, Francis 51, **51**
Haydn, Joseph 328

Hayez, Francesco
  *Count Colonel Francesco Teodoro Arese Lucini in Jail* 338
  *Cristina di Belgioioso* 338
  *Luigia Vitali, Mylius's Widow* 199, 338–9, 355
Hayley, William 133, **133**
Hecht, Johanna 341
Heine, Heinrich 42
Heinrich, Prince of Prussia 341
Helius, Julius 299
Helvétius, Claude Adrien 362
Helvétius, Madame 341
Henikstein, Josef Ritter von 290
Henri-Christophe, King of Haiti 16, 17
Henry IV, King of Spain 326
Herbert, Edward 250
Herculaneum 23
herms 213–14
*Herodotus and Thucydides* 391
Hess, Jonas Ludwig von 336
Hewetson, Christopher 34, 299, 382, 390, 391
Hillsborough, Wills Hill, Earl of 142, 144–5, 293–4
history portraits 110–16
Hoare, William 397
Hogarth, William 302
Hohenzollern family 380
Holbein, Hans 347
Holland, Lady Elisabeth 327, 329
Holland, John 302
Holland, Lord 327
Homer 292, 397
Hone, Nathaniel 371
Hope, Thomas 387
Hopetoun, John Hope, 4th Earl of 365
Hoppner, John 374
Horace 292, 370
Houdon, Anne-Ange 343
Houdon, Claudine 343
Houdon, Jean-Antoine 31, 34, 35, 63, 296, 297, 301, 314, 334, 359, 363, 368, 380, 382, 386
  *Benjamin Franklin* 82, 124, 339–40
  *Condorcet* 30, 123, 341
  *Denis Diderot* 29, 128, 340
  *George Washington* 31, 34, **35**
  *John Paul Jones* 31
  *Madame Houdon* 260, 341–2
  *The Marquis de Méjanes (Jean-Baptiste Marie de Piquet)* 132, 153, 342
  *Molière* 112
  *Princesse de Mecklembourg-Schwerin* 296
  *Sabine Houdon Aged Ten Months* 184–5, 207, 342–3
  *Sophie Arnould in the Title Role of Gluck's 'Iphigenia in Aulis'* 31, 239, 339
  *Voltaire Seated* 31, 363
Houdon, Madame (Marie-Ange-Cécile Langlois) 260, 342
Houdon, Sabine 184–5, 207, 342–3, 379
Howe, Countess 247
Huet, Paul 314
Hugo, Victor 46, 361
Humboldt, Adelaïde von **34**
Humboldt, Alexander von 323
Humboldt, Caroline von 367
Humboldt, Wilhelm von 367
Hume, Sir Abraham 373
Hume, David 134, 159, 250, 366
Humphries, Richard 374
Humphry, Ozias 321, 383
Hunt, Leigh 394
Hunter, Anne 328
Hunter, Dr William 398
Hurt family 396
Hutcheson, Francis 250
Hutchinson, Governor Thomas 304
Hutchison, Thomas 23
Hutton, James 140, 364–5

## I

Iffland, August Wilhelm 368
*Ilissos* 115
Impressionism 14, 15
Ingres, Jean-Auguste-Dominique 40–2, 44, 47–9, 63, 64, 85, 251, 293, 311, 314, 330, 331, 337, 360, 380, 384, 385, 387
  *Cherubini Accompanied by the Muse* 47
  *Comte de Pastoret* 345
  *Comte Molé* 40, 49, 346
  *The Comtesse de Tournon* 106, 344–5
  *Louis-François Bertin (Monsieur Bertin)* 24, 41, 48, 49, **49**, 83, 287, 346–7
  *Madame Devauçay* 346
  *Madame Marcotte de Sainte-Marie* 48, 107, 290, 291, 345–6
  *Madame de Sennones* 345
  *The Martyrdom of St Symphorien* 346
  *Monsieur de Norvins* 345
  *Napoleon I on the Imperial Throne* 16, 76, 290, 343–4, 346
  *Paganini* 46–7, **47**
  *Sabine Rivière* 345
  *The Vow of Louis XIII* 330
Inguimbert, Mgr de 342
Iriarte, Bernardo de 329
Isabey, Alexandrine 190, 322–3
Isabey, Jean-Baptiste 162–3, 185, 190, 295–6, 322–3

## J

Jal, Auguste 37, 38, 39, 41, 49, 317, 338
Jaley, Jean-Louis-Nicolas 379
Jaucourt, Comte de 389
Jaucourt, Madame de 85
Jaudenes y Nebot, Josef de 301
Jefferson, Thomas 301, 341
Jenkinson, Charles 371
Johnson, Samuel 29, 322, 372
Johnstone, Edward 213, 282, 302
Jones, John Paul 31
Jordan, Dorothy 30, **31**
Joseph II, Emperor 301
Joséphine, Empress 252–3, 254, 303, 324, 364
Joubert, Madame Louise-Adéone 316
Joubert, Monsieur 312
Jovellanos, Gaspar Melchor de 327, 328, 329

## K

Kant, Immanuel 21, 156, 218, 335–6
Karr, Alphonse 38, 40
Katz, Alex 14
Kauffman, Angelica 20, 83, 159, 315, 329, 373, 383
  *Composition* 383
  *Countess Catherine Skavronska* 101, 348
  *Design* 383
  *Joseph Johann, Graf von Fries* 146, 347–8
Kemble, John Philip 240, 350
Kenworthy-Browne, John 360
Keppel, Commodore 83
Khovanskaia, Princess Katerina 18–19, **19**
Khrouchtchova, Katerina 18–19, **19**
Kirchberger, Maria 383
Klein, Amalie 285, 290–1

Klein, Carl Ferdinand 200
Kneller, Sir Godfrey
    Lady Howard 395
Købke, Christen
    Frederik Sødring 176, 270, 348–9
Koch, Joseph Anton 307

# L

La Fayette, Marquis de 43–4, **43**, 341
La Rochefoucauld, Duc Louis Alexandre de 341
La Rochefoucauld, Vicomte Sosthène de 363
La Rochejacquelein, Henri de 115, 267–8, 272, 334–5
La Rochejacquelein, Louis de 335
La Tour, Maurice-Quentin de 297
Labille-Guiard, Adélaïde
    Self-portrait with Two Pupils,
    Mademoiselle Marie Gabrielle Capet and
    Mademoiselle Carreaux de Rosemond 159
Laborde, Comte Alexandre de **42**, 43
Laborde, Marquis de 18
Laborde, Nathalie de 33
Lacordaire, Father Dominique **40**, 41
Lalande, Jérôme de 342, 362
Lamartine, Alphonse de 377
Lampi, Giovanni Battista 157
Landon, Charles Paul 316
landscape, portraits in 244–63
Lanfranco, Giovanni
    Orco, Norandino e Lucina 292
Lange, Mademoiselle 230–1, **231**
Langlois, Jérôme-Martin 377
Lansdowne, Marquis of 384
Lanskoy, Alexander 382
Laocoön 351, 383
Lapauze, Henry 346
Larrumbe, Francisco Javier de 326
Lasalle, General Antoine-Louis-Charles 113, 119, 333–4
Lavater, Johann Kaspar 35, 36, 159, 313, 358
Laviron, Joseph-Gabriel-Hippolyte 42–3, 45–6, 47
Lawrence, Sir Thomas 17, 41, 43, 44, 60, 157, 212, 290, 314, 322, 372
    David Lyon 253, 278, 314, 352
    The Duke of Wellington 313
    George IV 60, 61, **62**, 77, 351–2, 381–2
    Henry Lascelles, 2nd Earl of Harewood, MP 352
    John Bloomfield 352
    John Philip Kemble as Coriolanus 240, 350
    King George III 61, 68, 349–50
    Lady Peel 313
    Lord Lambton 313
    Pope Pius VII 44, 62, 78, 300, 313, 350–1
    Sir Walter Scott **42**
Le Brun, Charles 35, 375
Le Pelletier de Saint-Fargeau, Michel 311, 312
Le Roy, Julien-David 394
Le Sueur, Hubert 301
Le Tellier, Jean-Baptiste 357
Lebrun, Jean-Baptiste 379
Lefevre, Robert 316, 334, 344
    Honoré-Gabriel Riqueti, Comte de Mirabeau 126, 297–8
Lehmann, Henri 41
Lelong, P. 56
Lemot, François-Frédéric 363
Lemoyne, Jean-Baptiste 31, 35, 296, 340, 353, 359, 361
    Comtesse de Brionne 359
    Madame Adélaïde 296
Lenoir, Alexandre 27, 131, 309, 311, 315–16, 361
Lenormant, Charles 39

Leopold II, Emperor 356
Lespinasse, Julie de 341
Lessing, Gotthold Ephraim 19
Levasseur, Rosalie 339
Leveson-Gower family 228, 235, 376–7
Levesque de Gravelle 385
Levitski, Dmitri
    Katerina Khrouchtchova and the Princess
    Katerina Khovanskaia 18–19, **19**
Lichtenberg, Georg Christoph 378
Liotard, Jean-Etienne 379
Liszt, Franz 312
lithography 53
Litta, Cardinal 32
Llano, Isabel Parreño Arce, Ruiz de Alcarón y Valdés, Marquesa de 97, 356
Llano, José Agustín de 356
Locke, John 184
Lomazzo, G. P. 389
London 54
    Apsley House 214–15
    St Paul's Cathedral 28
    Westminster Abbey 27–8, 30
Londonderry, Marquis of 348
López Portaña, Vicente 157
Louis XIV, King of France 26, 61, 63, 114, 267, 298, 301, 344
Louis XV, King of France 26, 63, 296, 297, 357, 389, 393
Louis XVI, King of France 16, 72, 297, 298, 310, 311, 323, 339, 377, 388
Louis XVIII, King of France 115, 266, 310, 334, 363, 378
Louis-Joseph-Xavier-François de France 333
Louis-Philippe, King of France 266, 346, 357, 363, 375
Lucas de Montigny, Jean-Robert Nicolas 315
    Belisarius 353
    Buffon 132, 152, 353, 354
    Crébillon 352, 353
    Jean-Jacques Rousseau 132, 135, 314, 353–4
    Madame de Saint-Huberty as Dido 353
    Molière 352, 353
    Racine 352, 353
    Voltaire 132, 136, 352–3, 354
Luccicchenti, Furio 356
Ludovisi Juno **238**, 366
Ludwig I, King of Bavaria 28, 32
Luise, Princess of Prussia 30, 252, 254, 261, 380
Luise, Queen of Prussia 238, 366–7
Lyon, David 253, 278, 314, 352
Lyon, Pat 266–7, **267**

# M

Macaulay, Catherine 20
Mackenzie, Henry 395
MacLeod, Norman 83
Madrazo, José de
    King Charles IV in Rome 17, **17**
Mahlknecht 115–16
Maillé, Duchesse de 363
Maintenon, Madame de 18
Malaspina, Alejandro 327
Maldá, Baron 328
Malibran, Marie 44
A Man and His Children 193, 386–7
Manet, Edouard 324, 331
    Eva Gonzalés in Her Studio 329
    Repose 329
Mann, Sir Horace 293
Mannerism 314
Mansergh St George, Lieutenant Richard 22, 185, 196, 336–7

Mansfield, William Murray, 1st Earl of 28, **28**, 82, 89, 305
Manzoni, Alessandro 338
Marat, Jean-Paul 20, 113, 117, 267, 311–12, 314
Maratta, Carlo 300
Marbeuf, Comte de 323
Marchesi, Pompeo 338
    Giulio Mylius 198, 355–6
Marcotte, Charles 39, 344
Marcotte de Sainte-Marie, Madame 48, 107, 290, 291, 345–6
Marcus Aurelius 63, 212
María Luisa, Queen of Spain 326, 329, 356
Maria Theresa, Empress of Austria 296
Marie-Amélie, Queen of France **270**, 271
Marie-Antoinette, Queen of France 61, 63, 73, 84, 159, 271, 296–7, 298, 323, 339, 358, 359, 388, 392, 393
Marie-Thérèse Charlotte de France 333
Marigny, Marquis de 18, **18**
Marmontel, Jean-François 362
Marniola, Marquise de 30
Martin, David 366
    Benjamin Franklin 52, **52**, 125, 355–6
Mary II, Queen of England 246
Matheron, Laurent 329
Mathon de la Cour 35
Matisse, Henri 14, 15
Mauzaisse 334
Mazzini, Giuseppe 339
Meade, Richard 301
Mecklembourg-Schwerin, Princesse de 296
Medici, Cosimo III de' 374
Medici Vase 374
Medici Venus 332, 383
Méjanes, Jean-Baptiste Marie de Piquet, Marquis de 132, 153, 342
Mélon, Abbé 330
Menander 340, 368
Mendelssohn, Felix 387
Mendelssohn, Moses 19
Mengs, Anton Raphael 27, 131, 219, 299, 300, 316, 326, 390–1
    Isabel Parreño Arce, Ruiz de Alcarón y Valdés, Marquesa de Llano 97, 356
Mérard, Pierre
    The Prince de Conti 82, 91, 356–7
Mercier, Huguette 352, 354
Mercy-Argenteau, Comte de 339
Mérimée, Léonor 343
Mesmer, Franz Anton 358
Messerschmidt, Franz-Xaver 36
    Character Head: Self-portrait 159, 161, 357–8
Metastasio, Pietro 300
Métra, François 340
Metternich 271, 352
mezzotints 53
Michallon, Claude 315
Michelangelo 158, 212, 325, 373, 375, 393
    Prophets 229, 375
    Sibyls 375
Mickiewicz, Adam 268, **269**
Miel 115, 335
Mignard, Nicolas 112
Mirabeau, Honoré-Gabriel Riqueti, Comte de 16, 113, 126, 127, 132, 297–8, 314–15, 317, 342, 353, 354
Missirini, Melchior 300
Modesty 384
Moine, Antonin
    Queen Marie-Amélie **270**, 271
Moitessier, Madame 40, 42, 48, 49
Moitte, Jean-Guillaume 354
Mola, Pier Francesco 325
Molé, Comte Mathieu 40, 49
Molière 112, 352, 353
Mondrian, Piet 14
Monet, Claude 15
Monot, Martin-Claude 354
    Child Playing with His Feet 343
    The Comtesse de Ségur 85, 100, 358–9
    Love Shooting Its Darts 358
    Love Trampling Jupiter's Eagle Underfoot 358

Montagu, Lady Mary Wortley 371
Montesquieu, Charles de Secondat, Baron de 342
Montgomerie, Archibald 306
Montgomerie, Major Hugh 114, 121, 306
Montgomery sisters 85–6, 236, 370–1
Montijo, Condesa de 329
Montmartel, Pâris de 343
Moore, Sir John 365
Mopinot, Antoine 26
Moratín, Leandro Fernández de 330
Morellet, André 340, 341, 362
Morimura, Yasumasa 14
Morisot, Berthe 329
Morris, Governor 34
Morse, Samuel 43–4
Moser, George 397
Moser, Joseph 355
Moser, Mary 382, 397
Mountstuart, Lord 371
Muller 316
Murray, Alexander 385
Muster, Mrs 228
Mylius, Enrico 338–9, 355
Mylius, Giulio 198, 338, 355

# N

Naldini, Pietro Paolo 375
Nanteuil, Célestin 375
Napier, Major Charles 365
Napoleon I, Emperor 16, 17, 20, 29–32, 39, 53, 56, 62–4, 76, 95, 113, 114, **114**, 157, 213–15, **214**, 224–5, 266, 290, 297, 298, 299, 300, 309–10, 310, 311, 316, 322–4, 334–5, 343–4, 346, 351, 364, 378, 385, 387, 391
Napoleon II, King of Rome 30, **184**, 185, 379
Napoleon III, Emperor 266, 310
Natalis, Michael 371
Natoire, Charles-Joseph 388
Navez, François-Joseph 375
    The De Hemptinne Family 275, 359–60, 386
    Madame Faber 359
    St Véronica of Milan 359
    Young Couple 359
Nazarenes 381, 387
Neagle, John
    Pat Lyon at the Forge 266–7, **267**
Necker, Jacques 29, **30**, 228
Necker, Madame 131–2, 362
Nelson, Admiral Lord 28, 53
Neoclassicism 381
Neue Bibliothek der schönen Wissenschaften und der freyen Künste 54–5
Newton, Sir Isaac 27, 246, 353, 355, 360
Nicolai, Friedrich 358
Nini 31
Noel 316
Nogaret, Ange-Pauline-Charlotte Ramel de 24, **24**
Nollekens, Joseph 29, 33, 34, 63, 214, 342, 383, 398
    Charles James Fox 31, 220, 221, 360
    Laurence Sterne 382
    Pitt 31
Nollekens, Mrs 382
North, Lord 230
Northcote, James 372, 383
Norvins, M. de 344, 345

# O

Oberkampf family 387
Odevaere, Joseph-Denis 359
Oliver, Isaac 251
   *Edward Herbert* 395
Omai 83, 250
Orléans, Duc d' 314, 315, 357, 377
Orléans family 357
Orlov, Counts 381
Orme, Robert 84
Orme de l'Isle, Jeanne de l' 304
Orvilliers, Robertine Tourteau, Marquise d'
   99, 308
Osterman-Tolstoy, Countess 385
Osuna, Dukes of 320
Osuna family 327
Ottoboni, Cardinal 300
Ouvrard, Gabriel 324
Oxford, All Souls College 28

# P

Pacetti brothers 39
Packenham, Major General 31
Paelinck, Joseph 359
Paganini, Niccolò 46–7, 47, 269, 284, 312–13
Paisiello, Giovanni 300
Pajou, Augustin 35, 296, 314, 318, 333, 343,
   353, 354, 357, 360, 361, 385
   *Buffon* 131, 132
   *Charles de Wailly* 194, 360–1
   *Madame de Wailly* 195, 360–1
   *Madame du Barry* 296
   *Nathalie de Laborde as Filial Piety* 33
Palagi, Pelagio 338
Palomino 326
Panzer, Georg Wolfgang 55–6
papal portraits 62
Paris 54
   Château des Tuileries 29
   Comédie-Française 28
   Louvre 376
   Musée des Monuments Français 27,
      131, 315
   Opéra 28
   Panthéon 314
   Sainte-Geneviève 28
Passez, A.-M. 388
Pastoret, Comte de 41
Pastoret, Madame Louise de 308, 312
Patte, Pierre 26
Paul I, Tsar 26
Peale, Charles Willson
   *Self-portrait with Angelica and
      Portrait of Rachel* 157, 159
Peisse, Louis 37
Pelham, Mrs 33
Pellico, Silvio 339
Pembroke, Earl of 215
Penny, Nicholas 33
Penrose, Revd John 321
Pepys, Samuel 55
Perantoni, Pietro 230, 300
Percier, Charles 344
Pérez Cuervo, Tiburcio 331
Pericles 115
Périn-Salbreux, Louis Lié 341
Perkins, Benjamin 53
Perkins, Elisha 53
Permont, Albert de 304
Perrin, Fanny 185, 234, 304
Pestalozzi, Johann Heinrich 20
Peter the Great, Tsar 63, 115, 318
Peter Leopold, Archduke 356
Pevsne, Antoine 33
Phidias 115, 133

Philadelphia 55
Philip IV, King of Spain 385
Picasso, Pablo 14, 15
Piccini, Niccolò 339
'Picturesque' 250
Pierret, Jean-Baptiste 313
Pigalle, Jean-Baptiste 33, 228, 353, 355, 357, 381
   *Child with a Cage* 343
   *Self-portrait* 171, 361–2
   *Voltaire Naked* 131–2, 139, 362–3
Pigalle, Jean-Marie 85
   *The Comtesse du Cayla* 85, 109, 363
Piles, Roger de 55
Pincepré, Arnoux-Philibert de 317
Pindar 368
Pingré, Canon 393
Piranesi, Giambattista 32–3
Pitt, William 31, 212, 230, 291, 360, 392
Pius VI, Pope 299, 301, 390
Pius VII, Pope 27, 44, 62, 78, 79, 298–9, 300,
   313, 350–1
Planche, Gustave 40, 46, 313
Plato 27
Pliny 34–5, 56, 292, 363
Plutarch 29, 112, 309
Plutarchism 27
Polignac, Duchesse de 359
Pollock, Jackson 15
Pommier, Edouard 133
Pompadour, Madame de 22, 228, 297, 323,
   357, 362, 389
Pompeii 23
Poniatowski, Prince Josef 387
Pontejos, Marqués de 330
Ponz, Antonio 328
Pope, Alexander 305
Porter, Roy 246
Posier, Jeremiah 318
Potemkin, Grigori Alexandrovitch 348
Pott, Emily 229
Pourtalès-Gorgier, Comte de 41, 41
Poussin, Nicolas 27, 246, 299, 300, 375, 392
   *A Dance to the Music of Time* 376
   *The Triumph of Pan* 371
Pradel, Comte de 334
Pradier, James
   *Apotheosis of Napoleon I* 386
Praxiteles
   *Apollo Sauroctonos* 294
prints 50–6
Prud'hon, Pierre-Paul 63, 252–3, 295, 303,
   324, 333, 375
   *Charles-Maurice de Talleyrand-Périgord
      in the Robes of the Grand Chamberlain*
      94, 364
   *The Empress Joséphine in the Park at Malmaison*
      381
   *Giovanni Battista Sommariva* 132, 133
   *Justice and Divine Vengeance Pursuing Crime*
      364
   *The King of Rome* 184, 185
Prussian Academy of Arts 157
Purcell, Richard 52

# Q

Quatremère de Quincy, Antoine 27, 32,
   299, 363
Quellin, Artus I 304
Quin, Henry 336
Quintilian 32

# R

Racine, Jean 352, 353
Radet, Jean-Baptiste 296
Raeburn, Sir Henry 251
   *James Hutton* 140, 364–5
   *Major William Clunes* 84, 120, 365–66
   *Sir John and Lady Clerk of Penicuik* 248, 249,
      254
Rameau, Jean-Philippe 339
Ramirez 290
Ramsay, Allan 60, 83, 333, 355, 371, 372
   *David Hume* 134, 366
   *Dr William Hunter* 355
   *Queen Charlotte with Her Two Eldest Children*
      60
Räntz, Elias 33
Raphael 27, 62, 159, 299, 300, 348, 375, 380
   *Baldassare Castiglione* 39, 49, 49, 347
   *Maddalena Doni* 346
   *Pope Leo X and His Nephews* 346
   *Tommaso Inghirami* 346
Rauch, Christian Daniel 33, 215, 335
   *Adelaïde von Humboldt as Psyche* 34
   *Alexandrine of Prussia* 35
   *Goethe and Schiller* 31
   *Johann Wolfgang von Goethe* 20, 131, 143,
      367–8
   *Queen Luise of Prussia as the Ludovisi Juno*
      238, 366–7
Raynal, Abbé Guillaume 222, 319, 362
Real Academia de Bellas Artes San Fernando
   157
Real Accademia di Belle Arti di Brera 158
Réau, Louis 362
Récamier, Juliette 243, 251–2, 251, 252, 254,
   300, 304, 322, 323, 324, 381, 390
*Regisole* 62
Régnault, Jean-Baptiste
   *Liberty or Death* 369
   *The Physical Man, the Moral Man and the
      Intellectual Man* 231, 232, 369
Reiffenstein, Johann Friedrich 300
Rembrandt 158, 159, 325, 338, 350, 366
   *Aristotle Contemplating a Bust of Homer* 373
   *The Syndics* 370
   *Woman in a Bed* 379
Renaissance 35, 60, 82, 212, 246, 253
Renoir, Pierre Auguste
   *Luncheon of the Boating Party* 15
Reynolds, Sir Joshua 24, 35, 52, 53, 55, 60, 83,
   158, 228, 247, 250, 266, 271, 291, 292, 294,
   301, 307, 314, 322, 325, 333, 349, 363, 365–6,
   393, 397
   *The Braddyll Family* 182, 186, 374
   *Elizabeth Keppel* 371
   *Garrick between Tragedy and Comedy* 229
   *George III* 16, 60, 66, 371–2
   *Georgiana, Duchess of Devonshire and
      Her Daughter, Lady Georgiana Cavendish*
      84, 191, 373–4
   *The Infant Academy* 51
   *John Manners, Marquis of Granby* 83–4, 366,
      369
   *Joseph Banks* 133, 141, 369–70
   *Lady Sarah Bunbury Sacrificing to the Graces* 307
   *The Ladies Waldegrave* 86
   *Mary, Countess of Bute* 84–5, 96, 247, 371,
      381
   *Miss Bowles* 333
   *Mrs Abington* 84, 85
   *Mrs Billington* 228
   *Mrs Hale as Euphrosyne* 228
   *Mrs Muster* 228
   *Mrs Siddons as the Tragic Muse* 21, 50–1, 51,
      229, 241, 374–5
   *The Montgomery Sisters: 'Three Ladies Adorning a
      Term of Hymen'* 85–6, 236, 370–1
   *Portrait of Master Hare* 333
   *Queen Charlotte* 60, 67, 371–2, 383
   *Robert Orme* 84
   *Self-portrait* 51, 51, 55, 158, 168, 373–4, 383
   *Sir Jeffrey Amherst* 52, 52, 113, 118, 369

Ricci, Sebastiano
   *Triumph of Bacchus* 376
Richards, John 382
Richardson, Samuel 303
Richelieu, Duc de 313
Rietschel, Ernst 368
Rigaud, Hyacinthe 60
   *Louis XIV* 61, 267, 298, 344
Righetti, Francesco 390
Rilliet, Jacques 308
Riminaldi, Cardinal 300
Ripa, Cesare 329, 339, 350
Riquet, François-Joseph-Philippe, Comte de
   Caraman 324
Risolt, Julia 383
Rivière, Caroline 343
Rivière, Sabine 345
Robert, Hubert 332, 343, 361
Robert, Léopold 337, 387
Robespierre, Maximilien de 157, 314, 324,
   332
Robinson family 30
Rochambeau, Comte de 358
Rocheblave, Samuel 361
Rockingham, Marquis of 28
Rococo style 332
Rodríguez, Ventura 327
Roettgen, Steffi 356
Roman, Jean-Baptiste Louis
   *Girodet* 269–70, 286, 375–6, 377
Romanelli, Francesco
   *Sleeping Silenus* 371
Romanticism 21, 22, 25, 156, 159, 269, 270,
   333, 338, 387, 390
Rome 54
   Museo Pio-Clementino 215, 216
   Palazzo Borghese 36
   Pantheon 26–7, 299, 375
   Villa Albani 33
Romney, George 247, 250, 375
   *The Beaumont Family* 182, 183
   *The Children of Earl Gower* 54, 55
   *The Hon. William Courtenay* 336
   *John Flaxman Modelling His Bust of
      William Hayley* 133, 133
   *The Leveson-Gower Children* 228, 235,
      376–7
   *Mirth* 376
Romney, Peter 394
Rondoni, Alessandro 375
Roquet, Jean 52
Rosa, Salvator 325
Roscoe, William 30
Roslin, Alexander 393, 394
Roslin, Marie-Suzanne 362
Rosset, Joseph 353
Rothko, Mark 14
Rotrou, Jean de III, 112
Roubiliac, Louis-François 291, 302, 355
Roucher, Jean-Antoine 353, 354
Rouillard, Sébastien
   *Comte Alexandre de Laborde* 42, 43
Rousseau, Jean-Jacques 20, 27, 132, 135,
   156, 159, 182, 185, 250–2, 314, 332, 333,
   336, 340, 342, 353–4, 357, 366, 377, 390,
   395–6
Rowlandson, Thomas 230
   *Political Affection* 373
Royal Academy of Arts 60, 158, 164–5, 167,
   291, 301, 349, 350, 372, 373, 382–3, 397–8
royal conversation pieces 61–2
Royal Danish Academy of Fine Arts 158, 337,
   387
Rubens, Peter Paul 60, 159, 266, 325, 334, 375
   *Suzanne Fourment* 44
Rude, François
   *Jacques-Louis David* 157, 268, 283, 377
Ruff, Thomas 14
Runge, Philipp Otto 159
   *The Artist's Parents* 192, 377–8
   *The Hülsenbeck Children* 378
Russell, William 375
Russian Academy of Arts 158

Rutxiehl, Henri-Joseph
  Duc de Bordeaux 379
  Elfride Clarke de Feltre 207, 378–79
  Mademoiselle d'Artois 379
  Zephyr and Psyche 379
Ryland, William Wynne 52
Rysbrack, John Michael 291, 301

## S

Saavedra, Don Francisco de 328
Sabatini, Francesco 326
Sacchini, Antonio 299
Saint-Aubin, Augustin de 341, 361
St Clair, General James 366
Saint-Lambert, Jean-François de 362
Saint-Ours, Jean-Pierre
  François Tronchin 151, 379–80
Saint-Pierre, Abbé de 112
Salomon, Henri 361
Salon, Paris 37, 38, 39, 41, 82, 231, 269, 295,
  296, 332, 333, 337, 338
Saly 343
Samuel, Richard
  The Nine Living Muses of Great Britain 20, 21
San Carlos, Duque de 330
San Juan y Pinedo, Mariano 202, 319–20
Sánchez Bort, Julián 326
Sánchez Cantón 356
Sandby, Thomas 382, 383
Santa Cruz, Marquesa de 329
Santini, Gaspare 348
Sargent, John Singer 15
Sarto, Andrea del 347
Sartori, Giambattista 300
Sauerländer, Willibald 339
Savage, Edward 52, 52, 53
Saxe, Maréchal de 357, 361
Sayer, Robert 52
Sayers, James
  The Patriot Exhalted 213
Schadow, Friedrich Wilhelm 317
Schadow, Johann Gottfried 34, 335, 342, 367
  Friederike Unger as Hope 33
  Friedrich Gilly 21, 307
  Princesses Luise and Frederika of Prussia
    30, 252, 254, 261, 380
Scheemakers, Peter 213, 291, 301
Scheffer, Ary 387
  Marquis de La Fayette 43, 43
  Princess Mathilde 38, 39
Schick, Gottlieb
  Agamemnon's Envoys in the Tent of Achilles 380
  Eve 380
  Wilhelmine von Cotta 252, 254, 262, 380–1
Schiller, Friedrich von 19, 31, 32, 308, 355, 367
Schinkel, Karl Friedrich 130
Schlegel, August 390
Schnauss, Friederike 338
Schnetz, J.-V. 337
Schumann, Robert 312
Schwanthaler, Ludwig Michael 368
Schwarzenberg, Prince of 290
Schwiter, Louis-Auguste 44, 45, 252–3, 279,
  313–14
Scott, Sir Walter 42, 251, 302
Scottish Enlightenment 364–5
sculpture 25–36
  death masks 34
  eyes 35
  funerary art 30–1
  monuments 26–8, 32–3
  portrait busts 26, 28–34, 63, 82, 212–16
  portraits from the antique 212–25
  state portraits 62–3
  statues of women 33

Seated Agrippina 308, 323, 385
Séguin, Armand 296
Ségur, Comtesse de 85, 100, 358–9
Ségur, Louis-Philippe, Comte de 358
Ségur, Philippe Henri, Marquis de 358
self-portraits 154–79
Seneca 362
Sennones, Madame de 345
Serangeli, G. G. 312
Sergel 34, 342
Sermézy, Sophie de
  To the Memory of the Best of Fathers 303
Séroux d'Agincourt, Jean-Baptiste-
  Louis-George 300
Seven Years' War 306
Sèvres porcelain factory 296, 353, 385, 390
Seward, Anna 336
Shaftesbury, Lord 250
Shakespeare, William 350, 355
Shee, Sir Martin Archer
  George IV 352, 381
Sheridan, Elizabeth 20, 247, 258, 321–22
Sheridan, Richard Brinsley 51, 322, 350
Sheridan, Thomas 350
Sherman, Cindy 14
Short, William 341
Shubin, Fedot Ivanovich 33
  Catherine II, Empress of Russia 63, 70, 381–2
  Paul I 26
Shuvalov, Count Ivan Ivanovich 381, 382
Siddons, Sarah 21, 50–1, 51, 229, 241, 350,
  374–75
Silvestre, Théophile 347
Simon, Madame 44–5, 45
Singleton, Henry
  The Royal Academicians in General Assembly
    167, 382–83
Skavronska, Countess Catherine 101, 348
Skavronsky, Count Paul Mattinowitsch 348
Smith, Adam 250, 366
Smith, Allen 130, 255, 320–1
Smith, John Raphael 178, 302
  The Children of Earl Gower 54, 55
Smith, William 360
Smolny Institute 18
Soane, Sir John 22
Société des Amis des Noirs 319, 341
Society of Artists of Great Britain 50
Society of Arts, London 292, 392
Society of Jesus 326
Socrates 21
Sødring, Frederik 176, 270, 348–9
Solana, Marquesa de la 329
Solander, Daniel 370
Solkin, David 83
Sommariva, Giovanni Battista 132, 133, 355
Sonne, Carl Edvard 295
Sonnenschein, Johann Valentin
  Charlotte Wyttenbach 276, 383
Sophocles 27
Soria, Martín 320
Souza, Madame de 379
Staël, Madame de 228, 242, 268, 300, 322,
  364, 389–90
Stahlin, Jakob von 318
Stanhope, Lady 21, 237, 306–7
Stanhope, Sir William 307
Stapleaux, Michel 311
Staples, John 147, 294
state portraits 60–1
status portraits 81–6
steel engravings 53
Stendhal 299, 387
Stepney, Anne 336
Steuben 334
Stosch, Philipp von 213
Stouf, Jean-Baptiste 303, 316, 354
Stowe, Buckinghamshire 213
Stroganov, Count Alexander 382
Stuart, Gilbert 266
  George Washington (Munro-Lenox portrait)
    16, 60, 69, 383–4
Sturm und Drang movement 328

Suard, Jean-Baptiste-Antoine 362
subscriptions, prints 54
Sully, Thomas 266
Sulzer, Johann Georg 19, 20, 254
Surrealism 15
Swimmer, Arabella 354

## T

Tacitus 366
Tagliolini, Filippo 390
Talbot, John Chetwynd 294
Talleyrand-Périgord, Charles-Maurice de
  94, 299, 323, 328, 364
Tallien, Jean-Lambert 324
Tallien, Thérésia 251–2
Talon, Antoine-Omer 363
Tan Chitqua 398
Tassaert, Jean Pierre Antoine 319
Taylor, John 350
Teba, Conde de 329
Tessier 314
Texier d'Hautefeuille, Commander 90, 388
Thélusson, Anne-Marie-Louise, Comtesse
  de Sorcy 308, 389
Therbouche, Madame 340
Thévenin, Charles 345
Thew, R. 333
Thomas, Antoine-Léonard 27
Thomas y Ramzé, Doña Isabel 331
Thomire, Pierre-Philippe 354, 363
Thomson, James 248, 350
Thorvaldsen, Bertel 29, 32, 33, 34, 35, 175,
  228, 299, 355, 368, 387
  Apotheosis of Napoleon I 20, 113, 224, 225,
    385–6
  Horace Vernet 174, 386
  Jason with the Golden Fleece 387
  Nemesi 338
  Nido degli amori 338
  Princess Maria Feodorovna Bariatinskaya
    217, 384–5
Tiberius in a Toga 83
Tieck, Friedrich 335
  August Wilhelm Iffland 368
  Jacques Necker 29, 30
Timanthes 22, 169, 292–3
'La Tirana' 329
Tischbein, Wilhelm
  Goethe in the Roman Campagna 22, 130,
    130, 320
Titian 43, 62, 159, 325, 350
  Man with a Glove 346
  Pietro Aretino 346
  Self-portrait 346
Titus, Emperor 385
Tjernysjev, Zacharias 30
Tocqué, Louis 318
Tolosa, Marqués de 326
Tolstoy, Count Leo 271
Tormo, Elías 320
Toro y Zambrano, José de 326
Tournon, Camille de 344
Tournon, Comtesse de 106, 344–5
Traeger, Jorg 312, 378
Trajan, Emperor 32
Trippel, Alexander 308
  The Artist's Aunt 29, 29, 318
  Goethe 32, 213
Tronchin, François 151, 363, 379–80
Trudaine, Madame Louise 308, 312
Turenne, Comte Henri Amédée de 310,
  353, 360
Turgot, Anne Robert Jacques 34, 341
Tussaud, Madame 312

## U

Unger, Friederike 33
United States of America 54
Urquiijo, Mariano de 328

## V

Valdés, Meléndez 329
Vallabriga, Doña María Teresa de 331
Valois, Achille 375
Van Dyck, Anthony 60, 83, 228, 246, 266,
  310, 323, 324, 325, 356, 373, 378, 389
  Charles I 83
  Portrait of Agostino Pallavicini 389
Van Loo, Louis-Michel 340
  The Marquis de Marigny and His Wife
    18, 18
Vargas Ponce, José de 329
Vassé, Louis-Claude 303, 343, 358
Vaudreuil, Marquis de 369
Velázquez, Diego de Silva y 60, 62, 326
  Las Meninas 18, 329
Vélez Rodríguez, Francisco 331
Venice 43
Vergennes, Comte de 296
Vernet, Carle 295, 297, 325, 387
Vernet, Claude-Joseph 375, 379, 387
Vernet, Horace 174, 325, 333, 386
  Bertel Thorvaldsen 175, 387
  Clichy Gate: The Defence of Paris, 30 March
    1814 387
Verney, Eleanor 371
Verninac, Madame de 304
Veronese 43
Verrocchio 304
Vestier, Antoine 298
  Baron de Doué 388
  Jean Theurel 388
  A Knight of Malta Holding the Portrait
    of Commander Texier d'Hautefeuille
    90, 388
  Madame Vestier 388
  Marie-Nicole Vestier 388
Victoria, Queen of England 351
Vien, Joseph-Marie 392
  Proserpine Garlanding a Statue of Her
    Mother Ceres 371
Vigée-Lebrun, Elisabeth-Louise 40, 85,
  159, 229, 254, 296, 297, 298, 308, 316,
  328, 329, 330, 333, 339, 340, 343, 346,
  348, 358, 359, 361, 379, 385
  Baroness of Crussol 388
  Charles-Alexandre de Calonne 82, 93, 328,
    388–9
  Children of France 388
  The Comtesse de la Châtre (Marquise
    de Jaucourt) 98, 389
  Grétry 388
  Hubert Robert 316
  Madame de Jaucourt 85
  Madame de Staël as Corinne 228, 242, 268,
    389–90
  Marie-Antoinette and Her Children 61, 84,
    298, 388
  Seated Bacchante 388
Vilain XIII, Comtesse 310, 346, 359
Villafranca, Francisco de Borja Alvarez
  de Toledo, Marqués de 329
Villafranca, María Tomasa, Marquesa de
  327–8
Villahermosa family 328
Villars, Maréchal de 362
Villegagnon, Comtesse de 342
Villeneuve, Jérôme Pétion de 314

Villeneuve, Juliette de 24, 266, 274, 310–11, 386
Vincent 378
    *M. de la Forest, His Wife and Daughter* 386
Virgil 294
Visconti, Ennio Quirino 391
Vitali, Luigia 199, 338–9, 355
Il Volpato (Giovanni Trevisan)
    *José Nicolas de Azara and Anton Raphael Mengs* 219, 390–1
Voltaire 27, 31, 32, 112, 131–2, 136, 139, 253, 336, 340, 341, 342, 352–3, 354, 362–3, 377, 379, 382
Voyer d'Argenson, Comte de 343

Wright of Derby, Joseph 247, 248
    *Dorothy Gell of Hopton* 336
    *Mrs Sarah Clayton* 23, 148, 394
    *The Revd d'Ewes Coke with His Wife Hannah and Daniel Parker Coke MP* 130–1, 249–50, 259, 394–5
    *The Revd Thomas Gisborne and His Wife Mary* 395
    *Richard Arkwright* 83, **83**
    *Sir Brooke Boothby* 185, 250, 256–7, 395–6
    *Three Children of Richard Arkwright with a Goat* 204, 396
Wyttenbach, Charlotte 276, 383

# W

Wahl, Johann Salomon 318
Waldegrave family 86
Waldmüller, Ferdinand Georg
    *Councillor Mathias Kerzmann and His Wife* 391
    *The Eltz Family* 253, 271, 277, 391
Walpole, Horace 292, 305, 307, 322, 356, 371, 372, 397, 398
Walpole, Thomas 342
Walton, Henry
    *Sir Robert and Lady Buxton with Their Daughter Anne* 184, 189, 391–2
Wankowicz, Walenty
    *Adam Mickiewicz on the Cliff of Judah* 268, **269**
Ward, James 22, **23**
    *Portrait of Fanny, a Favourite Dog* **23**
Warhol, Andy 14
Washington, George 16, 31, 32, 34, **35**, 52, 53, 60, 69, 113, 218, 301–2, 340, 342, 383–4
Watelet, Claude-Henri 137, 253, 332
Watson, James 52
Weiss, Rosarito 331
Wellesley, Richard Colley, Marquis 302
Wellington, Arthur Wellesley, 1st Duke of **112**, 112–13, 214–15, 302
Wentworth Woodhouse, Yorkshire 28
Wertmüller, Adolph-Ulrich
    *Jean-Jacques Caffieri* 172, 362, 392
West, Benjamin 60, 350, 370, 373, 382, 395, 397, 398
    *Christ Blessing Little Children* 383
    *Self-portrait* 166, 393–4
Westmacott, Sir Richard 63
    *Major General Packenham and Samuel Gibbs* 31
Wheatley 248
Whig party 28
Whitbread, Samuel 360
Wichmann brothers 335
Wickstead, Philip 294
Wilhelmine, Margravine of Bayreuth 33
Wille, Jean Georges 332
William III, King of England 246, 301
William IV, King of England 30
Williams, John 375
Wilmot, John 349
Wilson, Richard 212, 248
Wilton House, Wiltshire 216
Winckelmann, Johann Joachim 27, 131, 138, 215, 253, 254, 294, 299, 300, 315–16, 362, 367, 385
Woburn Abbey, Bedfordshire 28, 29
Wolfe, James 53
Wood, John 394
Wordsworth, William 213
Worsley, Sir Richard 350

# Y

Yates, Mary Ann 375
Young, Edward 247
Youssoupov family 332
Yriarte, Charles 328

# Z

Zaepffel, Françoise 378
Zoffany, Johann 382, 383, 392
    *The Academicians of the Royal Academy* 158, 164–5, 296, 397–8
    *Queen Charlotte with Her Two Eldest Sons* 17–18, 19, 61, 183–4, 188, 396–7
Zoffoli, Giovanni 390
Zuccarelli, Francesco 397
Zucchi, Antonio 347
Zulian, Girolamo 348
Zuñiga, Don Manuel Osorio Manrique de 184, 203, 327

Carole Turner Record
Mr and Mrs Philip Renaud
Mr and Mrs Justus Roele
Sylvia Scheuer
Mr and Mrs Thomas Schoch
Ms Tara Stack
Carl Stewart
John and Sheila Stoller
Mrs Betty Thayer
Mr and Mrs Julian Treger
Michael and Yvonne Uva
Mary Wolridge
Sir Robert Worcester
*and others who wish to remain anonymous*

## SCHOOLS PATRONS GROUP

*Chairman*
John Entwistle OBE DL

Gold Patrons
The Brown Foundation, Inc, Houston
The Ernest Cook Trust
D'Oyly Carte Charitable Trust
The Gilbert & Eileen Edgar Foundation
The Eranda Foundation
Mr and Mrs Jack Goldhill
The David Lean Foundation
The Leverhulme Trust
Paul and Alison Myners
Newby Trust Limited
Edith and Ferdinand Porjes Charitable Trust
Paul Smith and Pauline Denyer-Smith
Oliver Stanley Charitable Trust
The Starr Foundation
Sir Siegmund Warburg's Voluntary Settlement
The Harold Hyam Wingate Foundation

Silver Patrons
Lord and Lady Aldington
The Celia Walker Art Foundation
Mr and Mrs Ian Ferguson
Philip Marsden Family Trust
The Radcliffe Trust
The Stanley Picker Trust

Bronze Patrons
Mrs Elizabeth Alston
Lee Bakirgian Family Trust
Mark and Lucy Blair
The Charlotte Bonham-Carter Charitable Trust
The Selina Chenevière Foundation
May Cristea Award
The Delfont Foundation
John Entwistle OBE DL
Mr and Mrs John A Gardiner
Professor and Mrs Ken Howard RA
The Lark Trust
Mr Colin Lees-Millais FRICS
Mrs Diana Morgenthau
Pickett
Peter Rice Esq
Anthony and Sally Salz
Mr and Mrs Robert Lee Sterling, Jr
Roger Taylor
Mr and Mrs Denis Tinsley
The Worshipful Company of Painter-Stainers
*and others who wish to remain anonymous*

## CONTEMPORARY PATRONS GROUP

*Chairman*
Susie Allen

Mrs Alan Artus
Susan and John Burns
Dr Elaine C Buck
Debbie Carslaw
Mr S A Church and Dr D Schulman
Dania Debs-Sakka
Chris Drake
Mr John Eldridge
Lawton Wehle Fitt
Ruth Finch
Melanie C Gerlis
Mrs Robin Hambro
Marion and Guy Naggar
Angela Nikolakopoulou
Libby Paskin and Daniel Goldring
Maria N Peacock
Ramzy and Maya Rasamny
Mr Andres Recoder and Mrs Isabelle Schiavi
John Tackaberry and Kate Jones
Britt Tidelius
Mr and Mrs John D Winter
Mary Wolridge
*and others who wish to remain anonymous*

## AMERICAN ASSOCIATES OF THE ROYAL ACADEMY TRUST

**Burlington House Trust**
Mr and Mrs Donald P Kahn
Mrs Nancy B Negley
Mr and Mrs James C Slaughter

Benjamin West Society
Mrs Walter H Annenberg
Mr Francis Finlay

Benefactors
Ms Susan Baker and Mr Michael Lynch
Mrs Deborah Loeb Brice
Mrs Edmond J Safra
The Honorable John C Whitehead
Mr and Mrs Frederick B Whittemore

Sponsors
Mrs Herbert S Adler
Ms Britt Allcroft
Mrs Katherine D Findlay
Mrs Henry J Heinz II
Mr David Hockney RA
Mr Arthur L Loeb
Mr Hamish Maxwell
Mrs Lucy F McGrath
Mr Achim Moeller
Mr Arthur O Sulzberger and Ms Allison S Cowles
Mr and Mrs Vernon Taylor Jr

Patrons
Ms Helen H Abell
Mrs Russell B Aitken
Mr and Mrs Steven Ausnit
Mr and Mrs E William Aylward
Mr Donald A Best
Mrs Edgar H Brenner
Mr and Mrs Henry W Breyer III
Mrs Mildred C Brinn
Mrs Benjamin Coates
Mrs Catherine G Curran
Anne S Davidson
Ms Zita Davisson
Mrs Frances Dulaney
Mrs June Dyson
Mr Jonathan Farkas
Mrs A Barlow Ferguson
Mr and Mrs John Fiorilla
Mr Richard E Ford
Ms Barbara Fox-Bordiga
Mr and Mrs Lawrence S Friedland
Mr John Gleiber
Mr and Mrs Eugene Goldberg
Mr O Delton Harrison, Jr
Mr and Mrs Benjamin D Holt
Dr Bruce C Horten
Ms Betty Wold Johnson and Mr Douglas F Bushnell
The Honorable and Mrs W Eugene Johnston
Mr William W Karatz
Mr and Mrs Gary Kraut
The Honorable and Mrs Philip Lader
Mrs Katherine K Lawrence
Dr Jean McCusker
Ms Marcia V Mayo
Ms Barbara T Missett
The Honorable and Mrs Willliam A Nitze
Ms Diane A Nixon
Mr and Mrs Wilson Nolen
Mr and Mrs William O'Boyle
Mrs Evelyn Peterson
Mr and Mrs Jeffrey Pettit
Ms Barbara Pine
Lady Annie Renwick
Mr and Mrs Peter Sacerdote
Ms Louisa Stude Sarofim
Mrs Frances G Scaife
Dr and Mrs Myron Scholes
Mr and Mrs Stanley De Forest Scott
Mr and Mrs Morton I Sosland
Mrs Frederick M Stafford
Mr and Mrs Stephen Stamas
Ms Joan Stern
Ms Brenda Neubauer Straus
Ms Elizabeth F Stribling and Mr Guy Robinson
Mr Martin J Sullivan
Ms Britt Tidelius
Mr and Mrs Lewis Townsend
Mr and Mrs Stanford Warshawsky
Mr and Mrs George White
Dr and Mrs Robert D Wickham
Mr Robert W Wilson

Corporate and Foundation Support
AIG
American Express
The Brown Foundation
General Atlantic
General Motors
GlaxoSmithKline
The Horace W Goldsmith Foundation
Henry Luce Foundation
Sony

## CORPORATE MEMBERS OF THE ROYAL ACADEMY OF ARTS

Launched in 1988, the Royal Academy's Corporate Membership Scheme has proved highly successful. Corporate Membership offers benefits for staff, clients and community partners and access to the Academy's facilities and resources. The outstanding support we receive from companies via the scheme is vital to the continuing success of the Academy and we thank all Members for their valuable support and continued enthusiasm.

Premier Level Members
CB Richard Ellis
Deutsche Bank AG
Ernst & Young LLP
GlaxoSmithKline plc
Goldman Sachs International
Hay Group
HSBC plc
Intercontinental London Park Lane
ITV plc
Jacksons of Piccadilly
King Sturge
Rio Tinto plc
Smith and Williamson
Standard Chartered

Corporate Members
3i Group plc
All Nippon Airways
Aon
Arcadia Group plc
A. T. Kearney
Bear, Stearns International Ltd
Bibendum Wine Limited
BNP Paribas
The Boston Consulting Group
Bovis Lend Lease Limited
Bridgewell Securities
British American Business Inc.
The British Land Company PLC
Calyon
Cantor Fitzgerald
Capital International Limited
Christie's
Citigroup
Clifford Chance
Concordia Advisors
De Beers
Diageo plc
EADS Space
Epson (UK) Ltd
F & C Management plc
Gallery 88
GAM
Heidrick & Struggles
Insight Investment
Ivy Production Ltd
John Lewis Partnership
KPMG
Lazard
LECG
Lehman Brothers
Linklaters
London College of Fashion
L'Oréal UK
Man Group plc
Mizuho International
Momart Limited
Morgan Stanley
The National Magazine Company Ltd
Nedrailways
Norton Rose
Novo Nordisk
Pentland Group plc
The Royal Bank of Scotland
The Royal Society of Chemistry
Schroders & Co
SG
Slaughter & May
Thinc Destini
Timothy Sammons
Troika
Trowers & Hamlins
UBS Wealth Management
Unilever UK Limited
Veredus Executive Resourcing
Weil, Gotschal & Manges

## SPONSORS OF PAST EXHIBITIONS

The President and Council of the Royal Academy would like to thank the following sponsors and benefactors for their generous support of major exhibitions during the last ten years:

2006
*238th Summer Exhibition*
Insight Investment
*Chola: Sacred Bronzes of Southern India*
Travel Partner: Cox & Kings
*Premiums* and *RA Schools Show*
Mizuho International plc
*RA Outreach Programme*
Deutsche Bank AG
*Rodin*
Ernst & Young

2005
*China: The Three Emperors, 1662–1795*
Goldman Sachs International
*Impressionism Abroad: Boston and French Painting*
Fidelity Foundation
*Matisse, His Art and His Textiles: The Fabric of Dreams*
Farrow & Ball
*Premiums* and *RA Schools Show*
The Guardian
Mizuho International plc
*Turks: A Journey of a Thousand Years, 600–1600*
Akkök Group of Companies
Aygaz
Corus
Garanti Bank
Lassa Tyres

2004
*236th Summer Exhibition*
A. T. Kearney
*Ancient Art to Post-Impressionism: Masterpieces from the Ny Carlsberg Glyptotek, Copenhagen*
Carlsberg UK Ltd
Danske Bank
Novo Nordisk
*The Art of Philip Guston (1913–1980)*
American Associates of the Royal Academy Trust
*The Art of William Nicholson*
RA Exhibition Patrons Group
*Vuillard: From Post-Impressionist to Modern Master*
RA Exhibition Patrons Group

2003
*235th Summer Exhibition*
A. T. Kearney
*Ernst Ludwig Kirchner: The Dresden and Berlin Years*
RA Exhibition Patrons Group
*Giorgio Armani: A Retrospective*
American Express
Mercedes-Benz
*Illuminating the Renaissance: The Triumph of Flemish Manuscript Painting in Europe*
American Associates of the Royal Academy Trust
Virginia and Simon Robertson
*Masterpieces from Dresden*
ABN AMRO
Classic FM
*Premiums* and *RA Schools Show*
Walker Morris
*Pre-Raphaelite and Other Masters: The Andrew Lloyd Webber Collection*
Christie's
Classic FM
UBS Wealth Management

2002
*234th Summer Exhibition*
A. T. Kearney
*Aztecs*
British American Tobacco
Mexico Tourism Board
Pemex
Virginia and Simon Robertson
*Masters of Colour: Derain to Kandinsky. Masterpieces from The Merzbacher Collection*
Classic FM
*Premiums* and *RA Schools Show*
Debenhams Retail plc
*RA Outreach Programme**
Yakult UK Ltd
*Return of the Buddha: The Qingzhou Discoveries*
RA Exhibition Patrons Group

2001
*233rd Summer Exhibition*
A. T. Kearney
*Botticelli's Dante: The Drawings for Dante's Divine Comedy*
RA Exhibition Patrons Group
*The Dawn of the Floating World (1650–1765). Early Ukiyo-e Treasures from the Museum of Fine Arts, Boston*
Fidelity Foundation
*Forty Years in Print: The Curwen Studio and Royal Academicians*
Game International Limited
*Frank Auerbach, Paintings and Drawings 1954–2001*
International Asset Management
*Ingres to Matisse: Masterpieces of French Painting*
Barclays
*Paris: Capital of the Arts 1900–1968*
BBC Radio 3
Merrill Lynch
*Premiums* and *RA Schools Show*
Debenhams Retail plc
*RA Outreach Programme**
Yakult UK Ltd
*Rembrandt's Women*
Reed Elsevier plc

2000
*1900: Art at the Crossroads*
Cantor Fitzgerald
The Daily Telegraph
*232nd Summer Exhibition*
A. T. Kearney
*Apocalypse: Beauty and Horror in Contemporary Art*
Eyestorm
The Independent
Time Out
*Chardin 1699–1779*
RA Exhibition Patrons Group
*The Genius of Rome 1592–1623*
Credit Suisse First Boston
*Premiums* and *RA Schools Show*
Debenhams Retail plc
*RA Outreach Programme**
Yakult UK Ltd
*The Scottish Colourists 1900–1930*
Chase Fleming Asset Management

1999
*231st Summer Exhibition*
A. T. Kearney
*John Hoyland*
Donald and Jeanne Kahn
*John Soane, Architect: Master of Space and Light*
Country Life
Ibstock Building Products Ltd
*Kandinsky*
RA Exhibition Patrons Group
*LIFE? or THEATRE? The Work of Charlotte Salomon*
The Jacqueline and Michael Gee Charitable Trust
*Monet in the Twentieth Century*
Ernst & Young
*Premiums*
Debenhams Retail plc
The Royal Bank of Scotland
*RA Schools Show*
Debenhams Retail plc
*RA Outreach Programme**
Yakult UK Ltd
*Van Dyck 1599–1641*
Reed Elsevier plc

1998
*230th Summer Exhibition*
Diageo plc
*Chagall: Love and the Stage*
RA Exhibition Patrons Group
*Picasso: Painter and Sculptor in Clay*
Goldman Sachs International
*Premiums* and *RA Schools Show*
The Royal Bank of Scotland
*RA Outreach Programme**
Yakult UK Ltd
*Tadao Ando: Master of Minimalism*
The Drue Heinz Trust

1997
*229th Summer Exhibition*
Guinness PLC
*Art Treasures of England: The Regional Collections*
Peterborough United FootballClub
*Braque: The Late Works**
The Royal Bank of Scotland
*Denys Lasdun*
The Drue Heinz Trust
The Headley Trust
Land Securities PLC
*Hiroshige: Images of Mist, Rain, Moon and Snow*
The Nippon Foundation
*Premiums* and *RA Schools Show*
The Royal Bank of Scotland
*RA Outreach Programme**
Yakult UK Ltd
*Sensation: Young British Artists from The Saatchi Collection*
Christie's
Time Out
*Victorian Fairy Painting*
Friends of the Royal Academy

* Recipients of a Pairing Scheme Award, managed by Arts + Business. Arts + Business is funded by the Arts Council of England and the Department for Culture, Media and Sport

## OTHER SPONSORS

Sponsors of events, publications and other items in the past five years:
Carlisle Group plc
Country Life
Derwent Valley Holdings plc
Dresdner Kleinwort Wasserstein
Foster and Partners
Goldman Sachs International
Gome International
Gucci Group
Rob van Helden
IBJ International plc
John Doyle Construction
Martin Krajewski
Marks & Spencer
Michael Hopkins & Partners
Morgan Stanley Dean Witter
Prada
Radisson Edwardian Hotels
Richard and Ruth Rogers
Strutt & Parker